# XNA 3.0 Game Programming Recipes

## A Problem-Solution Approach

Riemer Grootjans

Apress®

**XNA 3.0 Game Programming Recipes: A Problem-Solution Approach**

**Copyright © 2009 by Riemer Grootjans**

ISBN-13 (pbk): 978-1-4302-1855-5

ISBN-13 (electronic): 978-1-4302-1856-2

Printed and bound in the United States of America 9 8 7 6 5 4 3 2 1

Lead Editor: Ewan Buckingham
Development Editor: Joohn Choe
Technical Reviewer: Fabio Claudio Ferracchiati
Editorial Board: Clay Andres, Steve Anglin, Mark Beckner, Ewan Buckingham, Tony Campbell,
    Gary Cornell, Jonathan Gennick, Michelle Lowman, Matthew Moodie, Jeffrey Pepper,
    Frank Pohlmann, Ben Renow-Clarke, Dominic Shakeshaft, Matt Wade, Tom Welsh
Project Manager: Richard Dal Porto
Copy Editors: Heather Lang, Kim Wimpsett
Associate Production Director: Kari Brooks-Copony
Production Editor: Elizabeth Berry
Compositor: Linda Weidemann, Wolf Creek Publishing Services
Proofreader: April Eddy
Indexer: Broccoli Information Management
Artist: April Milne
Cover Designer: Kurt Krames
Manufacturing Director: Tom Debolski

Distributed to the book trade worldwide by Springer-Verlag New York, Inc., 233 Spring Street, 6th Floor, New York, NY 10013. Phone 1-800-SPRINGER, fax 201-348-4505, e-mail orders-ny@springer-sbm.com, or visit http://www.springeronline.com.

For information on translations, please contact Apress directly at 2855 Telegraph Avenue, Suite 600, Berkeley, CA 94705. Phone 510-549-5930, fax 510-549-5939, e-mail info@apress.com, or visit http://www.apress.com.

Apress and friends of ED books may be purchased in bulk for academic, corporate, or promotional use. eBook versions and licenses are also available for most titles. For more information, reference our Special Bulk Sales–eBook Licensing web page at http://www.apress.com/info/bulksales.

The source code for this book is available to readers at http://www.apress.com. You may need to answer questions pertaining to this book in order to successfully download the code.

*To Elisa, the most lovely woman I know.*
*Without your love and support, this would not have been possible.*

*To my parents and brothers, for giving me each and every opportunity.*

*To my friends and coworkers, for their support and laughs.*

# Contents at a Glance

# Contents

# About the Author

**RIEMER GROOTJANS** received a degree in electronic engineering with a specialization in informatics at the Vrije Universiteit Brussel in Brussels, Belgium. He is currently working toward a Ph.D. degree as a member of a research team. The goal of the team is to develop a real-time, 3D, depth-sensing camera, and he is responsible for (among other things) the analysis and visualization of the 3D data. For a few years, Riemer has been maintaining a website with tutorials for DirectX. Since the launch of XNA in December 2006, he has ported all his content to XNA and is helping more than 1,500 people on their paths to XNA success every day. In July 2007 and July 2008, he received the Microsoft MVP Award for his contributions to the XNA community.

# About the Technical Reviewer

A prolific writer on cutting-edge technologies, **FABIO CLAUDIO FERRACCHIATI** has contributed to over a dozen books on .NET, C#, Visual Basic, and ASP.NET. He is a .NET MCSD and lives in Milan, Italy.

# Acknowledgments

I would like to express my appreciation and thankfulness to the skillful group of professionals at Apress who helped me complete this book.

Thanks to Regis Le Roy for the 3D models he provided me to play around with and test the code on. Furthermore, I would like to thank Danc from `http://lostgarden.com` for the 2D artwork used in my book and code. There are some real gems to be found on your site!

And last but definitely not least, I thank Xan Tium from `http://x-scene.com` for providing me with the necessary hardware on which to test my code.

# Introduction

When Microsoft released XNA in December 2006, it immediately became clear that this new technology would have a major impact on the possibilities for game developers. XNA was designed from the ground up with ease of use in mind, while not sacrificing performance or capabilities to achieve this goal. As a bonus, any game you create in XNA for the PC also runs on the Xbox 360 console! With the coming of XNA 3.0, you can even run your 2D game on the Zune handheld device.

In the span of two years, a large user community has grown around XNA. You can find code examples on a vast number of sites, ask your questions in one of the lively forums, or even meet local people who share the same passion in one of the XNA user groups. Whether you want to get up to speed with XNA quickly or you have tried some of the tutorial sites and are looking for the next step, this book is for you. With almost 100 recipes dealing with various challenges you may encounter during your journey with XNA, this book covers each corner of the XNA Framework.

The first recipes of the chapters in this book explain some stand-alone concepts and have been kept as clear as possible. As an example, a recipe explaining how to load a 3D `Model` from a file and render it to the screen will not render any trees in the background to make the final result look nicer, because this would clutter the code and make it more complex than it should be.

On the other hand, each chapter ends with some recipes that combine all you've learned thus far into something new and powerful. As such, you can step through the recipes, building up your experience in XNA as you move to the next recipe.

This book explains the functionality of the XNA 3.0 Framework. If any updates are made to the XNA Framework in the future, I will update the code for this book and make it available for download from my website at `www.riemers.net/`. If you have any questions regarding the text or code examples found in this book, I kindly invite you to post them on the forum on my site so you can get an answer as soon as possible.

The XNA Framework is roughly divisible into three parts. The main part contains your XNA project and its code. Next in line is the content pipeline, a flexible component allowing you to preprocess any art assets you want to load into your XNA project. Last, but definitely not least, are the High-Level Shading Language (HLSL) effects, which are used mainly to improve the visual quality of the final image you render to the screen.

Each chapter starts with some recipes that cover the XNA functionality related to the chapter. However, this book can also be used as a detailed guide to the content pipeline and to HLSL effects. Whether you're brand new to XNA or looking to take the step from 2D to 3D, this book will help you on your way.

# If You're New to XNA and Starting Your First 2D Game

If you're completely new to XNA, you might be interested in going through the following recipes to get you up and running as fast as possible:

- 1-1. Install XNA Game Studio 3.0
- 1-2. Start Your First XNA 2.0 Project
- 1-6. Customize Game Loop Timings
- 3-1. Display 2D Images: Load and Render Images Using the SpriteBatch Class
- 3-2. Rotate, Scale, and Mirror an Image
- 3-3. Render Transparent Images Using Layers
- 3-4. Consider Performance When Using the SpriteBatch Class
- 3-5. Display Text

# If You're Going from 2D to 3D

The step from 2D to 3D often seems much steeper than it actually is. If you go through the following recipes in the listed order, you'll learn all about what's needed to define your own 3D worlds:

- 2-1. Set Up the Camera: Position, Target, and View Frustum
- 2-2. Specify the Target of Your Camera
- 2-3. Create a First-Person Shooter Camera: A Quake-Style Camera
- 4-1. Load and Render a Model Using the BasicEffect Class
- 4-2. Set Different World Matrices for Different Objects, Combining World Matrices
- 5-1. Render Triangles, Lines, and Points in a 3D World
- 5-2. Apply a Texture to Your Triangles

# Start Using the Content Pipeline

If you're interested in getting into the XNA content pipeline, I advise you to read the following recipes in this order:

- 3-9. Extend the Image Content Processor
- 3-10. Extend the Image Content Processor: Grayscale Conversion and Processor Parameters
- 4-13. Gain Direct Access to Vertex Position Data by Extending the Model Processor

## Enhance the Final Image with HLSL Shaders

This book also contains a lot of HLSL samples. You can follow these recipes in this order:

## Prerequisites

The software you need to develop your own games in XNA 3.0 is completely free. As I'll explain in recipe 1-1, you'll need both the Visual C# 2008 Express Edition and XNA 3.0 Game Studio, which you can download for free from Microsoft's website.

The only cost incurred will be if you want to upload your finished game to your Xbox 360 console, when an annual subscription is payable to Microsoft. If you're just targeting the PC development environment, you won't have to pay anything.

## Downloading the Code

The accompanying code for this book can be downloaded for free from this book's page on the Apress website (`www.apress.com/view/book/143021855x`) and `www.riemers.net`.

## Contacting the Author

You can ask any question and share all comments on my forum at `www.riemers.net/Forum`, which I visit as frequently as I can.

# CHAPTER 1

■ ■ ■

# Getting Started with XNA 3.0

The first part of this chapter will get you up and running with XNA 3.0 by guiding you through the installation process and helping you get your code running on a PC and on the Xbox 360 console. The second part of this chapter contains some more advanced topics for those interested in the inner workings of the XNA Framework.

Specifically, the recipes in this chapter cover the following:

- Installing XNA Game Studio 3.0 and starting your first XNA 3.0 project (recipes 1-1 and 1-2)

- Running your code on the PC, Zune, and the Xbox 360 console (recipes 1-3, 1-4, and 1-5)

- Learning more about the timing followed by the XNA Framework (recipe 1-6)

- Making your code plug-and-play using GameComponent classes and GameServices (recipes 1-7 and 1-8)

- Allowing users to save and load their games using XNA's storage capabilities (recipe 1-9)

## 1-1. Install XNA Game Studio 3.0

### The Problem

You want to start coding your own games.

### The Solution

Before you can start coding your own games, you should install your development environment. XNA Game Studio 3.0 allows you to create your whole game project using a single environment. Best of all, it's completely free to install.

First, you need a version of Visual Studio 2008 that allows you to develop C# programs. This is required because XNA uses C#.

On top of Visual Studio 2008, you will install XNA Game Studio 3.0.

## How It Works

### Installing Visual Studio 2008

XNA Game Studio 3.0 requires Visual Studio 2008 to be installed on your PC. If this is not yet the case, you can download the Visual C# 2008 Express Edition for free.

To do this, go to www.microsoft.com/express/download/ and find the Visual C# 2008 Express Edition box (make sure you select the C# edition, indicated by the green color). Select the language of your choice, and hit the Download button. This will download a very small file, which you should run afterward.

During setup, use the default selections and hit Next until the program starts downloading and installing.

---

**■Note**  You can find updated links to these packages on the Download section of my site (www.riemers. net).

---

### Installing XNA Game Studio 3.0

Go to http://creators.xna.com/en-US/downloads, and click the Download XNA Game Studio 3.0 link at the bottom-right corner of the top box. On the page that opens, click the Download button (just above the Quick Details section) to download XNA Game Studio 3.0.

Once you've downloaded and run the file, the installer will check whether you have installed Visual C# Express Edition 2008. If you have followed the instructions in the previous section, you shouldn't be getting any error messages.

During setup, you will be presented with the Firewall Setup page. Make sure you select the first option, and allow both suboptions. If you don't, you will run into trouble when connecting to your Xbox 360 or when testing multiplayer games between multiple PCs. Keep in mind that when you experience trouble when connecting your game over other PCs or consoles, the problem might be caused by incorrect or third-party firewall settings.

Finally, hit the Install button to install XNA Game Studio 3.0.

# 1-2. Start Your First XNA 3.0 Project

## The Problem

You want to start coding a new XNA 3.0 game. In addition, the default startup code already contains a few methods, so you want to know what these are for and how they help make your life easier.

## The Solution

Opening a new project is the same in most Windows programs. In XNA Game Studio 3.0, go to the File menu, and select New ➤ Project.

# How It Works

## Starting XNA Game Studio 3.0

Start XNA Game Studio 3.0 by clicking the Start button and selecting Programs. Find Microsoft XNA Game Studio 3.0, click it, and select Microsoft Visual Studio 2008 (or Microsoft Visual C# 2008 Express Edition if you installed the free version).

## Starting a New XNA 3.0 Project

In XNA Game Studio 3.0, open the File menu, and select New ➤ Project. In the list on the left, XNA Game Studio 3.0 under Visual C# should be highlighted by default, as shown in Figure 1-1. On the right, highlight Windows Game (3.0). Give your new project a fancy name, and hit the OK button.

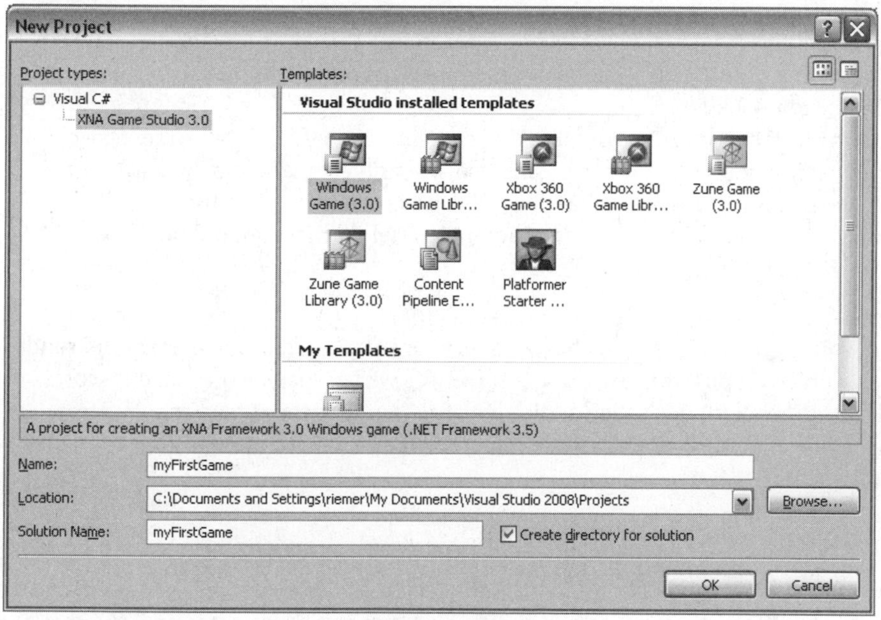

**Figure 1-1.** *Starting a new XNA 3.0 project (Visual Studio 2008 Express Edition)*

## Examining the Predefined Methods

When you start a new XNA 3.0 project, you will get a code file already containing some code. Comments (shown in green) make up more than 50 percent of the code to help you get started.

In a few moments, you will find that the methods you're presented with really are quite useful, because they greatly reduce the time you would otherwise spend doing basic stuff. For example, when you run your project at this moment, you will already be presented with an empty window, meaning you don't have to waste your time coding a window or processing the window's message queue.

The predefined methods are discussed in the following sections.

### Game1 Constructor

The Game1 method is called once, at the very moment your project is run. This means none of the internal clockwork has been initialized the moment this method (the constructor) is called. The only code you should add here consists of the instantiations of GameComponent classes (see recipe 1-7), because you cannot access any resources (such as the GraphicsDevice class) since they haven't been initialized at this point.

### Initialize Method

The Initialize method is also called once, after all the internal initialization has been done. This method is the ideal place to set the initial values of the objects in your game, such as the starting positions and starting speeds of the objects of your game. You have full access to all resources of your Game object.

### Update Method

When running your game, XNA will make its best effort to call the Update method exactly 60 times per second (once every 0.0167 seconds). For more information on this timing, including how to change it, read recipe 1-6.

This makes the Update method an excellent place to put code that updates the logic of your game. This can include updating the positions of your objects, checking whether some objects collide, starting an explosion at that position, and increasing the score.

Also, processing user input and updating camera/model matrices should be done here.

### Draw Method

In this method, you should put the code that renders your scene to the screen. It should render all 2D images, 3D objects, and explosions to the screen, as well as display the current score.

By default, the Draw method is called at the same frequency as the screen refresh rate, which depends on the screen or on the Zune device. See recipe 1-6 for more information on the Draw method.

### LoadContent Method

Whenever you start a game, you will want to load art (such as images, models, and audio) from disk. To speed things up and allow a lot of flexibility, XNA manages this art through the content pipeline.

All art loading should be done in the LoadContent method. This method is called only once at the beginning of your project.

A detailed example on how to load a 2D image into your XNA project is given in recipe 2-1. The same approach can be used to load any kind of art.

### UnloadContent Method

If some of the objects used in your game require specific disposing or unloading, the UnloadContent method is the ideal spot to do this. It is called once, before the game exits.

### Adding an .fx HLSL File

If you want to go one step further and add an HLSL file to your project, simply find the Content entry in your Solution Explorer at the top-right of your screen. Right-click it, and select Add ➤ New Item. Select "Effect file," and give it a name of your choice.

You'll get some default code, which you'll want to extend or replace with code you find elsewhere in this book. After that, you need to import it like any other content object: by creating a suitable variable and linking this file to that variable.

Add this variable to the top of your main Game class:

```
Effect myEffect;
```

Then link it to your code file in the LoadContent method:

```
protected override void LoadContent()
{
    myEffect = Content.Load<Effect>("effectFile");
}
```

---

■**Note**  You'll have to change the name of the asset, effectFile in this case, to the name of your HLSL file.

---

# 1-3. Deploy Your XNA 3.0 Game on Xbox 360

## The Problem

Once you have created and tested your code on the PC, you want to upload your game to and run it on your Xbox 360 console.

## The Solution

One of the nicest features of XNA is that you can make your code run on both PCs and on Xbox 360, without having to change anything. There are a few prerequisites before you can upload your working code to Xbox 360 though.

First, you need to have an Xbox Live account, which can be created for free through the http://creators.xna.com site or on Xbox 360.

Next, you need a Creators Club license, which is free for most students or can be bought through the Xbox Live Marketplace. This license costs $49 USD for four months or $99 USD for one year. If you are a student, you might have access to a free license.

Next, you need to download and install XNA Game Studio Connect, the front-end program that listens for a connection from your PC.

Last but definitely not least, you need a LAN connection between your PC and Xbox 360, and the Xbox 360 should be connected to the Internet. The PC and Xbox 360 should also be paired, because you would otherwise run into trouble when you have multiple Xbox 360 consoles in your network.

Once you have fulfilled these four prerequisites, you can upload and run your code on Xbox 360 from within XNA Game Studio 3.0 on your PC very easily.

## How It Works

### Setting Up the Xbox Live Account

Signing up for a Silver Xbox Live account is free and required if you want to run your own code on your Xbox 360 console. If you have already used your Xbox 360 console, you'll probably already have a Live account. If you haven't, start your Xbox 360 console, insert a game disc, and follow the instructions on your screen.

### Obtaining the Creators Club License

If you are a student, chances are you can obtain a free license from the Microsoft DreamSpark program. You can access this from `http://downloads.channel8.msdn.com`. Log in with your student credentials to obtain a code, which you can enter by going to the Marketplace tab in your Xbox 360 dashboard and choosing "Redeem code."

Otherwise, you can simply log your Xbox 360 console on to the Xbox Live Marketplace and then navigate to Games ➤ All Game Downloads. In the list, find XNA Creators Club, and select it.

Then select Memberships, and you can buy a license for four months or for one year. Alternatively, you can also enter a code that you can find on a Creators Club voucher card.

### Installing XNA Game Studio Connect on Your Xbox 360

This program makes your Xbox 360 listen for any incoming connections from your PC.

You can download this for free by going to the Xbox Live Marketplace and browsing to Game Store ➤ More ➤ Genres ➤ Other. Start the program after you've finished installing it.

### Connecting Your Xbox 360 and PC

Before your PC can stream data to the Xbox 360, the two devices need to be connected by a LAN and to the Internet. If both your Xbox 360 and PC are attached to a router, switch, or hub, this should be OK.

Nowadays, more and more home networks are relying on a wireless network. This might be a problem, because the Xbox 360 doesn't ship with a wireless adapter by default. One solution is to have a PC with both a wireless and a wired (Ethernet) network, which is common for most new laptops. Connect the PC to your wireless network at home, and add a $5 patch cable between your Xbox 360 and PC. Finally, on your PC, click the Start button, and navigate to Settings ➤ Network Connections. Highlight both your wireless and Ethernet adapters, right-click one, and select Bridge Connections, as shown in Figure 1-2. Wait for a few minutes, and both machines should be connected to the Internet and to each other!

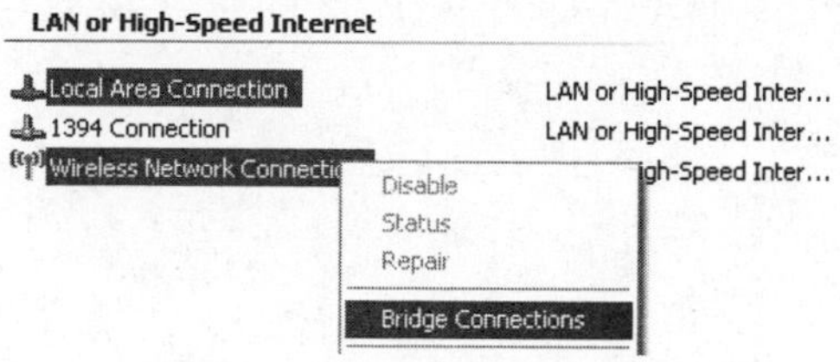
LAN or High-Speed Internet
Local Area Connection
1394 Connection
Wireless Network Connecti
LAN or High-Speed Inter...
LAN or High-Speed Inter...
gh-Speed Inter...
Disable
Status
Repair
Bridge Connections

**Figure 1-2.** *Bridging two network adapters on one PC*

## Pairing Your PC and Xbox 360

In case you have multiple Xbox 360 consoles in your network, you should specify which Xbox 360 you want to upload your code to. If you haven't done already, start XNA Game Studio Connect on your Xbox 360 by going to the Game tab and selecting Games Library ➤ My Games ➤ XNA Game Studio Connect. If this is the first time you've launched Connect, you will be presented with your Xbox 360's serial number, a series of five five-character strings.

On your PC, click the Start button, and navigate to Programs ➤ Microsoft XNA Game Studio 3.0 ➤ XNA Game Studio Device Center. Click the Add Device button, click the Xbox 360 icon, and give your Xbox 360 console a name of your choosing. Next, you are invited to enter the serial number shown by your Xbox 360. If both your Xbox 360 and PC are connected by the network, the pairing should succeed, and your console should appear in the device list. The green sign indicates your currently active Xbox 360, in case you have paired your PC to multiple Xbox 360 consoles.

## Generating an Xbox 360 Project from an Existing XNA 3.0 Project

In XNA Game Studio 3.0, it's easy to convert your PC game to an Xbox 360 project. Simply open your project, and find the Solution Explorer at the top-right of your screen. Right-click your project's name, and select Create Copy of Project for Xbox 360, as shown in Figure 1-3.

This will result in a second project being created and added to your solution. All files of your original project will be referenced by the new project, not copied, so that any changes you make in a file in one project will be visible in the other project as well.

In some cases, you might need to add some references that the wizard has forgotten to copy, but all in all, the wizard will save you quite a bit of time.

From now on, you can select on which target you want to run your project at the top of your screen. If this is the first time you've run a project on Xbox 360, you need to add the Xbox 360 profile by selecting "Configuration Manager" at the top of your screen, as shown in Figure 1-4.

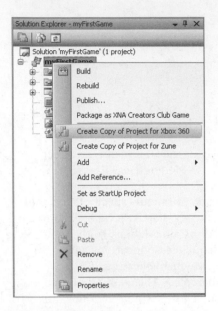

**Figure 1-3.** *Generating an Xbox 360 project*

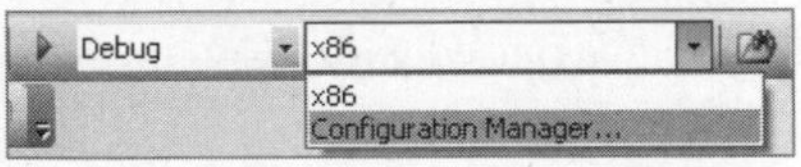

**Figure 1-4.** *Selecting the Configuration Manager*

In the dialog that appears, click the "Active solution platform" list and select <New...>. Next, select Xbox360, and close all dialogs.

From now on, the list shown in Figure 1-4 should contain an Xbox360 entry, which you should select whenever you want to deploy to your Xbox360 console. Make sure your Xbox is running XNA Game Studio Connect and is waiting for a connection. When you hit F5, your files will be uploaded to and executed on your Xbox 360 console!

# 1-4. Deploy Your XNA 3.0 Game on the Zune

## The Problem

Once you have created and tested your 2D game on the PC, you want to upload your game to your Zune and run it.

## The Solution

One of the main new features of XNA 3.0 is Zune support for 2D games. Since the Zune obviously can't compare to the power of the graphics card inside your computer, you cannot execute any XNA 3D application on the Zune. However, the complete SpriteBatch API is available on the Zune, allowing you to create mobile 2D games.

# How It Works

As with the Xbox360 console, you don't have to make any adjustments to your code to make it run on the Zune. Just connect the Zune to your PC, set it as the active target, and deploy your game.

## Connecting the Zune to Your PC

Connect the Zune to your PC using the USB cable that shipped with the Zune, and power it on. Next, open the XNA Game Studio Device Center by clicking the Start menu and selecting Programs ➤ Microsoft XNA Game Studio 3.0 ➤ XNA Game Studio Device Center. Click the Add Device button, and select the Zune. If you haven't done so yet, you might be asked to download an up-to-date version of the Zune software by following the provided link.

  If you have installed the software, make sure the firmware on your Zune is up to date. You can do so by connecting your Zune and opening up the Zune software on your PC. If your PC is connected to the Internet and a newer version of the firmware is found, the Zune software will show the Device Update screen, allowing you to update your firmware by clicking the Install button (make sure you never power off any device while you are reprogramming its firmware).

  When you have installed the Zune software, updated the Zune firmware, and connected the Zune, your Zune should be listed on your screen when you click the Zune button in the XNA Game Studio Device Center. Select your Zune, and click Next. After the connection has been verified, your Zune should be listed in the XNA Game Studio Device Center main screen.

## Setting the Zune As a Target Platform in XNA 3.0 Game Studio

With the Zune connected, go to XNA 3.0 Game Studio to deploy your 2D game to the Zune. As with the Xbox360 console, the first time you deploy to the Zune, you need to set it as a deployment target. This can be done by clicking the Solution Platforms box in the top-center of the screen and selecting Configuration Manager, as shown in Figure 1-4.

  In the upcoming dialog, select <New…> from the Active solution configuration list at the top-left of the screen, and select your Zune from the top list in the following screen. After clicking the OK button a couple of times, you should see your Zune as the target platform at the top-center of your window.

## Deploying Your XNA 3.0 Game to the Zune

Finally, you need to duplicate your XNA PC project to an XNA Zune project. This is done very easily, by right-clicking your project in the Solution Explorer and selecting Create Copy of Project for Zune. This option is also shown in the list of Figure 1-3. XNA will add this project to your Solution Explorer and will sync both projects whenever you change either of them.

  To upload your game to the Zune, make sure the Zune is selected as the active target platform at the top-center of your screen and that the Zune software is not running on your PC, and hit F5 to initiate the deployment.

  Once your Zune screen indicates the deployment has been completed, restart your Zune, select Games in your Zune's main menu, and start your game!

# 1-5. Deploy Your XNA 3.0 Game on Another PC

## The Problem

You have finished the first version of your game and want to show it off on a friend's PC. However, when you double-click the .exe file, you get some errors.

## The Solution

Distributing XNA games to different PCs has become easier than it was in version 2.0. At the time of this writing, you still need to make sure two other packages are already installed on the other PC before you can feel safe running your game's executable.

The two packages that need to be installed first:

- The XNA Framework Redistributable 3.0
- The .NET 3.5 Framework

The good news is that XNA is now compatible with Visual Studio's ClickOnce technology, allowing you to create a single .exe file that first checks whether these packages are there and to install the packages before installing your game if they're absent. Nevertheless, if you want to use the networking functionality in XNA 3.0 (see Chapter 8), you still have to install the complete XNA Game Studio 3.0 package on the destination PC.

## How It Works

### Installing the XNA 3.0 Framework Files

The first solution is downloading and installing the two packages on the PC, together with your game's binary files. You can solve this by downloading and installing the XNA Framework Redistributable 3.0, which you can find by searching for it on the Microsoft site at www.microsoft.com. The package is very small and contains all the basic XNA 3.0 Framework files.

### Installing the .NET 3.5 Framework Files

XNA is the new managed wrapper around DirectX. Because it uses a managed .NET language (C#), you'll also need to make sure the .NET Framework 3.5 files are present on the system. You can download this package from the Microsoft site by searching for *.NET 3.5*.

### Copying Binary Files

After you've compiled and tested your game, go to the executable directory, which can be any combination between bin\x86\Debug and bin\x64\Release. Make sure you copy all files and sub-maps you find that map to the destination PC. If you installed both packages, you shouldn't receive any error messages when you double-click the .exe file to start your game.

## Creating a Single ClickOnce Installation Package Containing All Prerequisites

New to XNA 3.0, ClickOnce installation lets you create an .exe install file that installs both prerequisite packages. To create the install file, follow these steps:

1. In the Solution Explorer, right-click your project, and select Properties.

2. In the window that opens, select Publish at the bottom-left.

3. Click the Prerequisites button on the next screen.

4. You'll see a list of all Microsoft packages that can be packed with your game. Make sure you select .NET Framework 3.5 (SP1) and Microsoft XNA Framework Redistributable 3.0.

5. Most importantly, select "Download prerequisites from the same location as my application." This will cause the packages to be copied to the map where your project is published.

6. Hit OK, and close the Properties window of your project.

With all of this done, whenever you feel the need to publish your project, just right-click your project, select Publish, and hit Finish in the dialog that appears.

---

■**Note**  Unfortunately, there currently is a bug in Visual Studio that causes problems when publishing your project this way, which will hopefully be fixed by a next update or service pack. Therefore, for now, you should deselect the .NET Framework 3.5 (SP1) prerequisite in step 4, and include this as an additional installation file.

---

## Creating a Setup Project for Your Game

Using this slightly more advanced approach, you can create a more customizable setup application that automatically detects the presence of both prerequisite packages and, if necessary, installs them.

---

■**Note**  This approach doesn't suffer from the bug mentioned in the ClickOnce approach.

---

To create a setup project, follow these steps:

1. Open XNA Game Studio 3.0.

2. Open the File menu, and select New ➤ Project.

3. In the tree view on the left, select Other Project Types ➤ Setup and Deployment.

4. On the right side, make sure Setup Project is selected.

5. Give a name to this project, such as **[name]**. During setup execution, this will be used as in "Welcome to the [name] Setup Wizard."

6. Click OK to start the new setup project.

7. Find the Applications Folder entry on the left side of the screen.

8. In Windows Explorer, browse to the output directory of your XNA game, which contains the .exe file of your game. Select all of the files and submaps (such as Content), and drag them onto the Applications Folder of step 7.

9. Back in XNA Game Studio 3.0, open the Project menu, and select "[name] properties."

10. Click the Prerequisites button.

11. Make sure Windows Installer 3.1, .NET Framework 3.5, and Microsoft XNA Framework Redistributable 3.0 are selected.

12. At the bottom of the dialog, select "Download prerequisites" from the same location as "my application."

13. Click OK twice to return to the setup project.

14. Click Application Folders.

15. In the Properties box at the bottom-right of the screen, remove [Manufacturer] from the target directory.

16. Now, press F6 to build the setup project solution.

This procedure will generate a map containing all the prerequisites and a simple setup.exe, which installs whatever necessary to run your XNA game on another PC.

# 1-6. Customize Game Loop Timing

## The Problem

You want to change the default timing intervals at which the Update and Draw methods are called.

## The Solution

By default, the Update method is called exactly 60 times each second, while the Draw method is called as often as possible, with the refresh rate of your screen at maximum.

By changing the values of the TargetElapsedTime and IsFixedTimeStep static properties of the Game class and the SynchronizeWithVerticalRetrace property of the GraphicsDevice class, you can change this default behavior.

# How It Works

## Changing the Update Frequency

By default, the Update method of your Game is called exactly 60 times each second, or once every 16.667 milliseconds. You can change this by adjusting the value of the TargetElapsedTime variable:

```
this.TargetElapsedTime = TimeSpan.FromSeconds(1.0f / 100.0f);
```

When you call this line of code, XNA will make sure the Update method will be called 100 times per second.

You can also instruct XNA to call the Update method not at regular intervals but instead each time before the Draw method is called. You do this by setting the IsFixedTimeStep variable to false:

```
this.IsFixedTimeStep = false;
```

## Using IsRunningSlowly

You can specify an Update frequency of your choice. However, when the number you specified is too high, XNA will not be able to call your Update method at that frequency. If this is the case, the gameTime.IsRunningSlowly variable will be set to true by XNA:

```
Window.Title = gameTime.IsRunningSlowly.ToString();
```

---

■**Note**  You should check the gameTime argument passed to the Update method, and not the gameTime argument passed to the Draw method, to verify this.

---

## Changing the Draw Frequency

While running the game, XNA will call the Draw method as frequently as possible, limited by these two rules:

- There's no use in calling the Draw method more frequently than the screen refresh rate. If a screen refreshes only 100 times per second, rendering 110 frames per second won't be helpful. On the PC and Xbox 360 console, screen refresh rates are determined by the PC screen and its settings. The Zune 30 refreshes 60 times per second; the other Zune devices show only 30 frames per second.

- The Update method should be called 60 times per second. If your game is too calculation intensive, the Draw method will be called less frequently to ensure XNA can call the Update method 60 times per second.

In some cases, it can be useful to call your Draw method at maximum frequency, for example, to determine the maximum frame rate of your Game. You can do this by setting the graphics.SynchronizeWithVerticalRetrace variable to false:

```
graphics.SynchronizeWithVerticalRetrace = false;
```

■**Note**  You must put this line in the Game1 constructor at the top of your code, because XNA needs to be aware of this before it creates GraphicsDevice.

### Understanding the Importance of the Update and Draw Frequencies

Since you'll put your update login in the Update method, a (temporal) decrease of the Update frequency would make all objects in your game move more slowly, which is very annoying.

When the Draw frequency is called less than the screen refresh rate, only the visual appearance of your game will suffer for a moment. It's less annoying that your game temporally only renders 80 instead of 100 frames per second to the screen.

Therefore, and as mentioned previously, if required, XNA will decrease the Draw frequency to ensure the Update method is called exactly 60 times each second.

# 1-7. Make Your Code Plug-and-Play Using GameComponents

## The Problem

You want to separate part of your application into a GameComponent class. This will ensure reusability of the component in other applications.

## The Solution

Certain parts of your applications can be separated from the rest of your application. In an XNA application, most such parts need to be updated or drawn, such as a particle or billboard system (see recipes 3-11 and 3-12).

One step in the correct direction is to create a separate class for such a part. In your main XNA Game class, you will then need to create an instance of this class, initialize it, update it from within the Update method, and, if applicable, render it to the screen from within the Draw method. Therefore, you will want your new class to have its own Initialize, (Un)LoadContent, Update, and Draw methods so you can easily call them from within your main XNA Game class.

If you find yourself defining these methods in your new class, it might be a nice idea to make your new class inherit from the GameComponent class. If you do this, you can add it to the Components list of your Game. This will cause the Initialize method of your newly defined class to be called after the Initialize class of your main Game class finishes. Furthermore, each time the Update method of your main Game class finishes, the Update method of your newly defined GameComponent class will be called automatically.

If your component should also render something, you should inherit from the
DrawableGameComponent class instead of from the GameComponent class. This will expect your
component to also contain a Draw method, which will be called after the Draw method of your
main Game class finishes.

---

**Note** At the end of the Initialize method in your main Game class, you'll notice the call to base.
Initialize. It is this line that starts calling the Initialize methods of all the GameComponent classes of
your Game class. You can find the same kind of call at the end of the other methods in your main Game class,
which will call the corresponding methods of all GameComponent classes currently registered in your Game.

---

## How It Works

As an example, the billboarding code of recipe 3-11 will be separated into a GameComponent
class. Even better, because this code also needs to render something to the screen, you will
make it a DrawableGameComponent class.

### Creating a New (Drawable)GameComponent

Add a new class file to your project by right-clicking your project and selecting Add ➤
New File. Select Class in the upcoming dialog box; I called my new class BillboardGC. In the
new file that is presented to you, you'll want to add the XNA using lines so you have access to
all XNA functionality in your new class, which can be done very easily by copying the using
block of your main Game class into the new class.

Next, make sure you make your new class inherit from the GameComponent class or the
DrawableGameComponent class, as shown in the first line of the following code snippet. Add all
the code of the component, and separate it nicely between the Initialize, (Un)LoadContent,
Update, and Draw methods of your new class.

The following example shows how this can be done for the billboarding code of recipe
3-11. Some methods such as CreateBBVertices have not been fully listed, because in this
recipe you should focus on the Initialize, LoadContent, Update, and Draw methods.

```
class BillboardGC : DrawableGameComponent
{
    private GraphicsDevice device;

    private BasicEffect basicEffect;
    private Texture2D myTexture;
    private VertexPositionTexture[] billboardVertices;
    private VertexDeclaration myVertexDeclaration;
    private List<Vector4> billboardList = new List<Vector4>();

    public Vector3 camPosition;
    public Vector3 camForward;
    public Matrix viewMatrix;
    public Matrix projectionMatrix;
```

```
public BillboardGC(Game game) : base(game)
{
}

public override void Initialize()
{
    device = Game.GraphicsDevice;
    base.Initialize();
}

protected override void LoadContent()
{
    basicEffect = new BasicEffect(device, null);
    myTexture = Game.Content.Load<Texture2D>("billboardtexture");
    AddBillboards();
    myVertexDeclaration = new VertexDeclaration(device, ➥
    VertexPositionTexture.VertexElements);
}

public override void Update(GameTime gameTime)
{
    CreateBBVertices();
    base.Update(gameTime);
}

    .
    .
    .


public override void Draw(GameTime gameTime)
{
    //draw billboards
    .
    .
    .

}
}
```

■**Note** As you can see in the Initialize method, your component can access the main Game class. This allows your component to access the public fields of the main Game class, such as Game.GraphicsDevice and Game.Content.

## Using Your New GameComponent

Now that you have defined your GameComponent, you should add it to the list of GameComponent classes of your main Game class. Once added, its main methods will automatically be called.

The easiest way to do this is to create a new instance of your GameComponent and add it immediately to the Components list. An ideal place to do this is in the constructor of your main Game class:

```
public Game1()
{
    graphics = new GraphicsDeviceManager(this);
    Content.RootDirectory = "Content";

    Components.Add(new BillboardGC(this));
}
```

This will cause the Initialize and LoadContent methods to be called at startup and the Update and Draw methods of the new class to be called each time the Update and Draw methods of your main Game class have finished.

In some cases, you will need to update some public variables of the component. In the case of the billboarding component, you'll need to update the camPosition and camForward variables so the component can adjust its billboards and the View and Projection matrices so they can be rendered correctly to the screen. Therefore, you'll want to keep a link to your component by adding this variable to your main Game class:

```
BillboardGC billboardGC;
```

Then store a link to your component before storing it in the Components list:

```
public Game1()
{
    graphics = new GraphicsDeviceManager(this);
    Content.RootDirectory = "Content";

    billboardGC = new BillboardGC(this);
    Components.Add(billboardGC);
}
```

Now in the Update method of your main Game class, you can update these four variables inside your component. At the end of the Update method of your main Game class, the Update method of all components is called, allowing the billboarding component to update its billboards:

```
protected override void Update(GameTime gameTime)
{
    .
    .
    .
```

```
    billboardGC.camForward = quatCam.Forward;
    billboardGC.camPosition = quatCam.Position;
    billboardGC.viewMatrix = quatCam.ViewMatrix;
    billboardGC.projectionMatrix = quatCam.ProjectionMatrix;

    base.Update(gameTime);
}
```

The Draw method of your main Game class is even simpler: just clear the screen before calling the Draw method of all the components:

```
protected override void Draw(GameTime gameTime)
{
    device.Clear(ClearOptions.Target | ClearOptions.DepthBuffer, ➥
    Color.CornflowerBlue, 1, 0);
    base.Draw(gameTime);
}
```

The last line will cause the Draw method of the billboarding component to be called, rendering the billboards to the screen.

---

■**Tip**  The next recipe shows a much cleaner approach to update the variables of your GameComponents.

---

## The Code

*All the code is available for download at www.apress.com.*

The Initialize, LoadContent, Update, and Draw methods of the GameComponent and main Game class were listed earlier in the text.

# 1-8. Allow Your GameComponents to Communicate with Each Other by Implementing GameServices

## The Problem

As explained in recipe 1-6, you can separate parts of your code into reusable GameComponent classes. Examples of such components can be a camera, particle system, user input processing, billboard engine, and more.

One of the main benefits of using GameComponent classes is that you can easily switch between game functionalities, for example, camera modes. Changing from a first-person camera to a quaternion camera (see recipe 2-4) involves changing just one line of code in the Initialize method of your main Game class.

Using GameComponent classes to achieve this is one thing, but you need to make sure you don't have to change the rest of your code (which uses the camera) when you switch from one component to another.

This recipe uses some more advanced .NET and object-oriented functionality.

## The Solution

You will make both your camera components subscribe to the same interface, such as the (self-defined) ICameraInterface interface. When you initialize your camera component, you let your Game class know that from now on Game contains a component that implements the ICameraInterface interface. In XNA words, the component registers itself as the GameService of the ICameraInterface type.

Once this has been done, the rest of your code can simply ask the Game class for the current ICameraInterface service. The Game class will return the camera that is currently providing the ICameraInterface service. This means your calling code never needs to know whether it is actually a first-person camera or a quaternion camera.

## How It Works

An *interface* is some kind of contract that you make your class (your GameComponent, in this case) sign. An interface contains a list of functionality (nonconcrete methods and/or properties, actually) that the class should minimally support. When your class is subscribed to an interface, it promises that it implements the methods listed in the definition of the interface.

This is how you define the ICameraInterface interface used in this recipe:

```
interface ICameraInterface
{
    Vector3 Position { get;}
    Vector3 Forward { get;}
    Vector3 UpVector { get;}

    Matrix ViewMatrix { get;}
    Matrix ProjectionMatrix { get;}
}
```

---

■**Note** The methods used here are getter methods, introduced in C# 2.0. They are methods, but act to the outside world as read-only public properties. For example, the Position method should return a Vector3 object.

---

Any class wanting to subscribe to ICameraInterface should implement these five getter methods.

For the rest of your code, it isn't of any importance to know whether the current camera is a first-person or quaternion camera. The only thing that matters is that the camera can produce valid View and Projection matrices and maybe some other directional vectors. So, it suffices for your main Game class to have a camera class that subscribes to ICameraInterface.

## Making Your GameComponent Subscribe to an Interface

In this example, you will have two camera components. Because they don't need to draw anything to the screen, a DrawableGameComponent is not necessary, so inherit from the GameComponent class. Also, make your component subscribe to ICameraInterface:

```
class QuakeCameraGC : GameComponent, ICameraInterface
{
    .
    .
    .
}
```

---

■**Note**  Although a class can inherit from only one parental class (the GameComponent class, in this case), it can subscribe to multiple interfaces.

---

Next, you need to make sure your class actually lives up to its contract by implementing the methods described in the interface. In the case of the QuakeCamera and Quaternion classes described in recipe 2-3 and recipe 2-4, this is already the case. See the accompanying code for this recipe for the minor changes in turning them into two GameComponent classes.

## Subscribing to the ICameraInterface Service

In your Game class, you should have one and only one camera component that provides the ICameraInterface service at a time. When you activate a camera component, it should let your main Game class know it is the current implementation of ICameraInterface, so your main Game class knows it should pass this camera to the rest of the code in case it is asked for the current provider of ICameraInterface.

You do this by registering it as a GameService in the Services collection of the main Game class:

```
public QuakeCameraGC(Game game) : base(game)
{
    game.Services.AddService(typeof(ICameraInterface), this);
}
```

You add the this object (the newly created first-person camera component) to the list of interfaces, and you indicate it provides the ICameraInterface service.

**Usage**

Whenever your main Game code needs the current camera (for example, to retrieve the View and Projection matrices), you should ask the main Game class to give you the current implementation of ICameraInterface. On the object that is returned, you can access all the fields defined in the ICameraInterface definition.

```
protected override void Draw(GameTime gameTime)
{
    device.Clear(ClearOptions.Target | ClearOptions.DepthBuffer, ➥
    Color.CornflowerBlue, 1, 0);

    ICameraInterface camera;
    camera = (ICameraInterface)Services.GetService(typeof(ICameraInterface));

    cCross.Draw(camera.ViewMatrix, camera.ProjectionMatrix);

    base.Draw(gameTime);
}
```

You ask your main Game class to return the class that provides the ICameraInterface interface. Since the GetService method is capable of returning any type of object, you need to help the compiler a bit by specifying the type of interface the object should be cast to.

Note that the code inside this Draw method never knows whether it is talking to a first-person camera or a quaternion camera. All that matters is that it supports the functionality listed in the ICameraInterface definition. The beauty of this approach is that you can easily swap between camera modes—somewhere in the Update method, for example—with the rest of your code not even noticing this change.

---

■**Note** You can also define a camera as a global variable and store a link to the currently active implementation of ICameraInterface in the Initialize method of the main Game class.

---

## Using Multiple GameComponents

GameServices are especially useful to ensure interoperability between multiple GameComponent classes. In case you have a camera GameComponent providing the ICameraInterface service, other GameComponent classes can access this by querying the ICameraInterface service from the main Game class.

This means you don't have to provide any hard links between the different components, such as the ugly main Update method of the previous recipe. In case you have created a camera GameComponent that supplies the ICameraInterface service, you can query this service from any other GameComponent, such as from the Initialize method of the billboard GameComponent created in recipe 1-6:

```
public override void Initialize()
{
    device = Game.GraphicsDevice;
    camera = (ICameraInterface)Game.Services.GetService(typeof(ICameraInterface));

    base.Initialize();
}
```

Next, the Update and Draw methods of the billboarding component can access the required fields from the camera. All your main Game needs to do is instantiate the camera and billboarding components. The camera will subscribe itself to the ICameraInterface service, allowing the billboarding component to retrieve the camera.

The camera will automatically be called to update itself, after which the billboarding component will be asked to do the same. The billboarding component is able to access the camera through the ICameraInterface service, and finally the billboarding component is kindly asked to draw itself. This whole process requires two lines of code in your main Game class, plus you can easily swap between camera modes!

### Changing the Updating Order of Your GameComponents

If you have a component that requires the output of another component, such as in this case where the billboarding component needs your camera component, you may want to be able to specify that the camera component should be updated first. You can do this before adding the component to the Components list of the main Game class:

```
public Game1()
{
    graphics = new GraphicsDeviceManager(this);
    Content.RootDirectory = "Content";

    //GameComponent camComponent = new QuakeCameraGC(this);
    GameComponent camComponent = new QuatCamGC(this);
    GameComponent billComponent = new BillboardGC(this);

    camComponent.UpdateOrder = 0;
    billComponent.UpdateOrder = 1;

    Components.Add(camComponent);
    Components.Add(billComponent);
}
```

First, you create your camera and billboarding components. Before adding them to the Components list, you set their updating order, with a lower number indicating the component that should be updated first.

Using GameComponent classes and GameServices, in order to switch between two camera modes, you need to change only the line that adds the camera component. In the previous code, the quaternion mode is activated. If you want to switch to Quake mode, simply uncomment the line that adds the QuakeCamera GameComponent class, and comment the line that adds the QuatCam GameComponent class. The remainder of the code doesn't need to be changed, because all it needs is the ICameraInterface service, provided by one of the GameComponent classes.

## The Code

> All the code is available for download at www.apress.com.

The Game1 constructor displayed previously is all the code needed to get your camera and billboarding working. The Initialize, (Un)LoadContent, Update, and Draw methods of your main Game class are empty.

When your camera component is created, it subscribes itself to the ICameraInterface service:

```
public QuakeCameraGC(Game game) : base(game)
{
    game.Services.AddService(typeof(ICameraInterface), this);
}
```

Whenever any code of your project requires the camera, you can ask your main Game to return the service that implements ICameraInterface:

```
ICameraInterface camera;
camera = (ICameraInterface)Services.GetService(typeof(ICameraInterface));
cCross.Draw(camera.ViewMatrix, camera.ProjectionMatrix);
```

# 1-9. Save and Load Data to or from a File

## The Problem

You need some kind of saving mechanism for your game.

## The Solution

Although saving or loading data is usually one of the last steps involved in creating a game, you definitely want to have some sort of saving mechanism for your game. Basically, XNA uses the default .NET file I/O mechanisms, meaning you can create/open/delete files quite easily. Furthermore, using the XmlSerializer class, it is incredibly easy to save your data to disk and to reload it afterward.

The only problem that needs to be tackled is finding a location to save the data to disk that is valid for PCs and for the Xbox 360 and Zune. You can solve this problem by using a StorageDevice, which needs to be created first.

---

■**Note**  The concept of creating a StorageDevice might seem complex. Don't let that turn you away, though, because the rest of the recipe (starting from "Saving Data to Disk") is very simple and powerful and is not restricted only to XNA, because it is default .NET functionality.

---

## How It Works

Before you can save data to disk, you'll need a valid location to which you have access to write. The solution is provided by creating a StorageDevice, which asks the user on the Xbox 360 console where to store the data. However, you need to make sure you're not making multiple save/load calls to the StorageDevice at the same time, so you'll need to keep track of its activity:

```
bool operationPending = false;
```

### Creating a StorageDevice Asynchronously

This process involves opening the Xbox Guide, which would block your whole program until the user closes the Guide. To solve this, this process has been made asynchronous. This concept is explained in recipe 8-5.

The Guide requires the GamerServicesComponent to be added to your game (see recipe 8-1), so add the following line to your Game1 constructor:

```
public Game1()
{
    graphics = new GraphicsDeviceManager(this);
    Content.RootDirectory = "Content";

    Components.Add(new GamerServicesComponent(this));
}
```

Next, each time the Update method is called, you will check whether the user wants to save data. If this is the case, you will call Guide.BeginShowStorageDeviceSelector, which will open a dialog box so the user can select where the data should be saved. The program doesn't halt at this line, however, because this would stall your whole program until the user closes the dialog box. Instead, this method expects you to pass as the first argument another method, which should be called once the user exits the dialog box:

```
KeyboardState keyState = Keyboard.GetState();
if (!Guide.IsVisible && !operationPending)
    if (keyState.IsKeyDown(Keys.S))
    {
        operationPending = true;
        Guide.BeginShowStorageDeviceSelector(FindStorageDevice, "saveRequest");
    }
```

If the user presses the S button, the dialog box will open, but the code will continue immediately without waiting for the user's response. Notice that you've set the operationPending variable to true, so the first if check of the preceding code will be evaluated negatively until you've set it to false when the operation eventually completes (see the next code snippet).

Your program will continue to run while the dialog box is being displayed on the screen. Once the user has made a selection and closed the dialog box, the FindStorageDevice method you specified as the first argument will be called. This means you'll have to define this method, or your compiler will complain:

```
private void FindStorageDevice(IAsyncResult result)
{
    StorageDevice storageDevice = Guide.EndShowStorageDeviceSelector(result);
    if (storageDevice != null)
        SaveGame(storageDevice);
}
```

The result of `BeginShowStorageDeviceSelector` is received as the argument by this method. If you pass this result to the `Guide.EndShowStorageDeviceSelector` method, you will get the selected data storage. However, if the user canceled the operation, the result will be null, so you have to check for this. If the resulting `StorageDevice` is valid, you pass this to the `SaveGame` method, which you'll define in a moment.

But first, imagine what would happen if you also allowed the user to perform a second operation for which the user needs to specify a data location, such as when loading data. This would require you to define a second method, `FindStorageDeviceForLoading`, for example. A cleaner way would be to specify an identifier to your asynchronous call, which you can check for in the `FindStorageDevice` method. Your `Update` method would contain this block of code:

```
KeyboardState keyState = Keyboard.GetState();
if (!Guide.IsVisible && !operationPending)
{
    if (keyState.IsKeyDown(Keys.S))
    {
        operationPending = true;
        Guide.BeginShowStorageDeviceSelector(FindStorageDevice, "saveRequest");
    }
    if (keyState.IsKeyDown(Keys.L))
    {
        operationPending = true;
        Guide.BeginShowStorageDeviceSelector(FindStorageDevice, "loadRequest");
    }
}
```

As you can see, in both cases, a dialog box will be displayed, which will call the `FindStorageDevice` method after it closes. The difference is that this time you're specifying an identifier, which you can check for in the `FindStorageDevice` method:

```
private void FindStorageDevice(IAsyncResult result)
{
    StorageDevice storageDevice = Guide.EndShowStorageDeviceSelector(result);
    if (storageDevice != null)
    {
        if (result.AsyncState == "saveRequest")
            SaveGame(storageDevice);
        else if (result.AsyncState == "loadRequest")
            LoadGame(storageDevice);
    }
}
```

Depending on the identity of the call, you will call the `SaveGame` or `LoadGame` method.

## Saving Data to Disk

Once you have a valid StorageDevice, you can easily specify a name for the data file that will be written to disk:

```
private void SaveGame(StorageDevice storageDevice)
{
    StorageContainer container = storageDevice.OpenContainer("BookCodeWin");
    string fileName = Path.Combine(container.Path, "save0001.sav");

    FileStream saveFile = File.Open(fileName, FileMode.Create);
}
```

This will create a file called save0001.sav. If it exists, it will be overwritten.

---

**Note** On a PC, this file will be created in a map located in the My Documents\SavedGames folder.

---

Once you have a valid file name and have opened the file, you can save your file using default .NET functionality. Imagine the data you would want to save looks like this:

```
public struct GameData
{
    public int ActivePlayers;
    public float Time;
}
```

All you need to do is create an XmlSerializer, which is capable of converting your data into XML and saving this to disk:

```
XmlSerializer xmlSerializer = new XmlSerializer(typeof(GameData));
xmlSerializer.Serialize(saveFile, gameData);
saveFile.Close();
container.Dispose();
operationPending = false;
```

You indicate the XmlSerializer should be capable of serializing GameData objects, after which you stream your GameData object to file with a single command! Don't forget to close the file stream and container, or your program will keep them locked. Also reset the operationPending variable to false, so your Update method will listen for any new save or load requests from the user.

For this to work, you need to link to the System.IO and System.Xml.Serialization namespaces, which can be done easily by adding these lines to your using block at the very top of your code:

```
using System.IO;
using System.Xml.Serialization;
```

The last line requires you to add a reference to System.Xml, which can be done by opening the Project menu and selecting Add Reference. Highlight System.Xml, as shown in Figure 1-5, and hit OK.

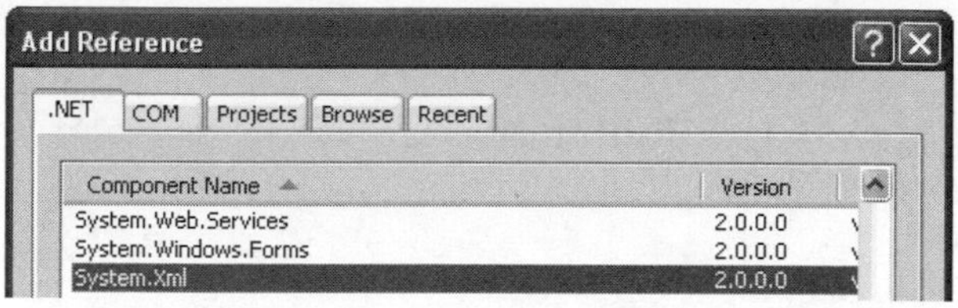

**Figure 1-5.** *Adding a reference to System.Xml*

## Loading Data from Disk

You load data from disk in the same way as you save data to disk, just a bit opposite. You check whether the file exists, and if it does, you open it. Once again, you create an XmlSerializer, but this time around you use it to deserialize a GameData object from the file stream. This single line loads all data from the file and transforms this data into a valid GameData object!

```
private void LoadGame(StorageDevice storageDevice)
{
    StorageContainer container = storageDevice.OpenContainer("BookCodeWin");
    string fileName = Path.Combine(container.Path, "save0001.sav");
    if (File.Exists(fileName))
    {
        FileStream saveFile = File.Open(fileName, FileMode.Open);
        XmlSerializer xmlSerializer = new XmlSerializer(typeof(GameData));

        gameData = (GameData)xmlSerializer.Deserialize(saveFile);
        saveFile.Close();
        operationPending = false;
    }
    container.Dispose();
}
```

# The Code

*All the code is available for download at www.apress.com.*

The Update method simply checks whether the user wants to save or load a file and opens the Guide dialog box:

```
protected override void Update(GameTime gameTime)
{
    GamePadState gamePadState = GamePad.GetState(PlayerIndex.One);
    if (gamePadState.Buttons.Back == ButtonState.Pressed)
        this.Exit();
```

```
    KeyboardState keyState = Keyboard.GetState();
    if (!Guide.IsVisible && !operationPending)
    {
        if (keyState.IsKeyDown(Keys.S))
        {
            operationPending = true;
            Guide.BeginShowStorageDeviceSelector(FindStorageDevice, "saveRequest");
        }
        if (keyState.IsKeyDown(Keys.L))
        {
            operationPending = true;
            Guide.BeginShowStorageDeviceSelector(FindStorageDevice, "loadRequest");
        }
    }

    gameData.Time += (float)gameTime.ElapsedGameTime.TotalSeconds;

    base.Update(gameTime);
}
```

Once the Guide has been closed by the user, the FindStorageDevice method is called. This method in return calls the SaveData or LoadData method, depending on the identity of the asynchronous call. You can find this FindStorageDevice method entirely in the previous code; only the SaveGame method has not yet been listed in full:

```
private void SaveGame(StorageDevice storageDevice)
{
    StorageContainer container = storageDevice.OpenContainer("BookCodeWin");
    string fileName = Path.Combine(container.Path, "save0001.sav");

    FileStream saveFile = File.Open(fileName, FileMode.Create);
    XmlSerializer xmlSerializer = new XmlSerializer(typeof(GameData));

    xmlSerializer.Serialize(saveFile, gameData);
    saveFile.Close();
    container.Dispose();
    operationPending = false;

    log.Add("Game data saved!");
}
```

■ ■ ■

# CHAPTER 2

# Setting Up Different Camera Modes in Your 3D World

In a 3D application, the camera is one of the most elementary components. The camera represents the viewpoint of the user in your 3D world. XNA renders your 3D world to the screen as it is seen by the camera. So before you can ask XNA to render the content of your 3D scene to the screen, you first need to specify the position and viewing direction of your camera.

This chapter starts off with some fundamental topics you need to master before you can create any 3D application.

The second part of this chapter covers some more advanced examples, such as camera fly-bys, quadtrees, octrees, ROAM, and post-processing. The last recipe shows how you can create your own content importer.

Specifically, the recipes in this chapter cover the following:

- Learning about the purpose of the camera in a 3D application and how you can define one (recipe 2-1)

- Rotating and moving your camera through your 3D scene based on user input (recipes 2-2, 2-3, 2-4, and 2-6)

- Not wasting the power of your graphics card by making sure you're not rendering parts of the scene that are not in sight of the camera (recipes 2-5, 2-9, 2-10, and 2-11)

- Performing smooth fly-bys in your 3D world (recipe 2-7)

- Using a skybox to add a nice background to your 3D scene (recipe 2-8)

- Polishing your game by using post-processing effects to enhance the final image (recipes 2-12 and 2-13)

- Coding your custom content importer, allowing you to use self-defined asset files in the content pipeline (recipe 2-14)

# 2-1. Set Up the Camera: Position, Target, and View Frustum

## The Problem

Before you can render your 3D world to the screen, you need set up your camera. You do this by specifying the View and Projection matrices. Before rendering, both matrices are needed so the graphics card can correctly transform your 3D world to your 2D screen.

## The Solution

Setting up your camera in your 3D world comes down to specifying two matrices.

You can save the camera position and direction in a single matrix, which is called the *View matrix*. To create the View matrix, XNA needs to know the Position, Target, and Up vectors of your camera.

You can also save the *view frustum*, which is the part of the 3D world that is actually seen by the camera, in another matrix, which is called the *Projection matrix*.

## How It Works

The View matrix holds the definition of the camera position and the direction into which it is looking. You can create this matrix by a simple call to the `Matrix.CreateLookAt` method:

```
viewMatrix = Matrix.CreateLookAt(camPosition, camTarget, camUpVector);
```

This method takes three vectors as arguments: the Position, Target, and Up vectors of the camera. The Position vector is pretty intuitive, because it indicates where you want to position your camera in your 3D world. Next, you need to specify another point in your 3D world where you want your camera to look. This pretty much defines the viewing direction, so what do you need the Up vector for?

Consider following example: your head (OK, actually your eyes) is your camera. You'll try to define a camera that has the same position and direction as your head. The first vector is easy to find: the Position vector would be the position of your head in the 3D scene. Next, the Target vector is not too difficult either; let's suppose you are looking at the X in Figure 2-1. In this case, the position of that X in this book would be the Target vector of your camera. So far so good, but at this moment, there are still lots of ways you can hold your head at the same position to look at the X!

**Figure 2-1.** *The target of your camera*

With only the Position and Target vectors defined, you can still rotate your head around the point between your two eyes, for example, by standing upside down. While you're trying to do this, the position of your head will remain the same and the position of the target will remain the same, but the resulting image you see will be totally different because everything gets rotated. That's why you need to define which way is up for your camera.

Once you know the position of your camera, where you want it to look, and which direction is considered to be up for the camera, the camera is said to be "uniquely defined." The View matrix, unique to these three vectors, can be constructed using the `Matrix.CreateLookAt` method as follows:

```
Matrix viewMatrix;
Vector3 camPosition = new Vector3(10, 0, 0);
Vector3 camTarget = new Vector3(0, 0, 0);
Vector3 camUpVector = new Vector3(0, 1, 0);

viewMatrix = Matrix.CreateLookAt(camPosition, camTarget, camUpVector);
```

---

■**Note**  Although the Position and Target vectors of the camera point to real points in 3D space, the Up vector indicates the Up *direction*. For example, say a camera is at position (300,0,0) and looking toward point (200,0,0). If you want to indicate that the camera's Up vector is simply pointing upward, you pass the (0,1,0) Up vector and not the point above the camera in 3D space, which would be the (300,1,0) point in this example.

---

---

■**Note**  XNA provides shortcuts for the most commonly used vectors, such as `Vector3.Up` for (0,1,0), `Vector3.Forward` for (0,0,–1), and `Vector3.Right` for (1,0,0). To make you more familiar with 3D vectors, all vectors you'll find in the first recipes of this chapter are written in full.

---

The other matrix that is required by XNA is the Projection matrix. You can think of this matrix as the magic thing that maps all points from 3D space into your 2D window, but I would rather you see it as the matrix that holds information related to the lens of the camera.

Let's first look at Figure 2-2, displaying on the left side the part of a 3D scene that is in sight of a camera, which has, as you can see, the shape of a pyramid. On the right, you can find a 2D cross section of this pyramid.

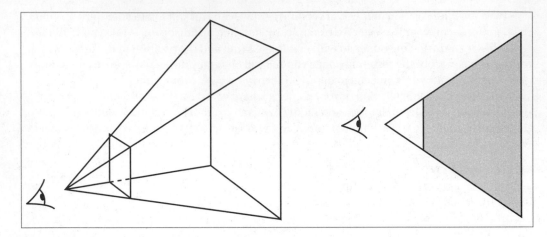

**Figure 2-2.** *The view frustum of a camera, 3D and cross section*

The pyramid minus the top on the left side of the image is called the *view frustum*. Of all objects you instruct XNA to render, only those that are inside this volume are actually rendered to the screen.

XNA can create such a view frustum for you, which is stored in the Projection matrix. You can create one by calling the `Matrix.CreatePerspectiveFieldOfView` method:

```
projectionMatrix = Matrix.CreatePerspectiveFieldOfView(viewAngle, aspectRatio,
nearPlane, farPlane);
```

The first argument you need to pass to the `Matrix.CreatePerspectiveFieldOfView` method is the viewing angle. This corresponds to half the opening angle of the pyramid, as displayed on the right of Figure 2-2. If you try to find out what the viewing angle of your own eyes is by placing your hands next to your eyes, you'll find a value around 90 degrees. Since PI radians equal 180 degrees, 90 degrees equal PI/2 radians. Because you need to specify half the viewing angle, you need to pass PI/4 as the first argument.

---

**■Note**  Usually, you will want to use a viewing angle that corresponds to the viewing angle of human sight when rendering a 3D scene to the screen. However, in some cases you may want to specify other viewing angles. These are usually cases where you are rendering the scene into a texture, for example, as seen by a light. In the case of a light, the larger viewing angle can mean a larger area being lit. For an example, see recipe 3-13.

---

The next argument you need to specify has nothing to do with the "source," which is the frustum, but instead with the "destination," which is the screen. It is the aspect ratio of the 2D window into which the 3D scene will be rendered. Ideally, this will correspond to the ratio of your back buffer, which you can find this way:

```
float aspectRatio = graphics.GraphicsDevice.Viewport.AspectRatio;
```

When using a square window of width and height—300, for example—the division will equal 1. However, it will be larger when rendering into a full-screen window of 800 × 600 pixels and will be even larger when rendering full-screen to a wide-screen laptop or HDTV. If you wrongly passed 1.0 instead of 800/600 as the aspect ratio for an 800 × 600 window, the resulting image would be stretched horizontally.

The two last arguments again have to do with the view frustum of Figure 2-2. Imagine there is an object extremely close to the camera. This object would block the entire sight, and chances are the whole window would be covered by one solid color. To avoid such cases, XNA allows you to define a plane in the pyramid, close to the top. Everything between the top of the pyramid (your camera) and this plane will not be drawn. It is said to be "clipped away." This plane is called the *near* clipping plane, and you can specify the distance between your camera and its near clipping plane as the third argument of the `CreatePerspectiveFieldOfView` method.

---

■**Note**  The term *clipping* is used to indicate that something is not drawn to improve the frame rate of the program.

---

The same story can be told for objects that are positioned very far from the camera; these objects will probably look really tiny, but they still require almost the same processing time of your graphics card to be rendered. So again, objects farther away than a second plane will also be clipped away. This second plane is called the *far* clipping plane and is the final boundary of your view frustum—the volume of your 3D scene that will be rendered to your 2D window. You can specify the distance between the camera and this far clipping plane as the last argument of the `Matrix.CreatePerspectiveFieldOfView` method.

---

■**Caution**  Even when working with a very simple 3D scene, do not set the far clipping plane too far. Setting the far clipping plane distance to some crazy value like 100000 will result in severe visual artifacts. Cards with a 16-bit depth buffer (see the "The Z-Buffer (or Depth Buffer)" section of this recipe) will have $2^{16} = 65{,}535$ possible depth values. Even if the depth distribution is linear, if two objects are competing for a certain pixel and the distance between both objects is smaller than 100k/65,535 = 1.53 units, your graphics card will not be able to decide which object is closer to the camera.

In reality, this is much, much worse, because the scale is quadratic, resulting in the last three quarters of your whole scene seeming to have the same distance to the camera. Therefore, the distance between your near and far clipping plane should stay below a few hundred. This distance should even be smaller if the depth buffer has less than 16-bit resolution.

A typical symptom of this problem would be that all your objects seem to have jagged edges.

---

## Usage

You will want the View matrix to be updated during the update phase of your application, because the position and direction of your camera will depend on user input. The Projection matrix needs to be changed only whenever the aspect ratio of the window changes, for example, when switching from windowed to full-screen mode.

Once you have calculated the View and Projection matrices, you need to pass them to the effect you are using to render a certain object, as you can see in the Draw method of the following code. This allows the shaders on your graphics card to transform all vertices of your 3D scene to their corresponding pixels in your window.

## The Code

*All the code is available for download at* www.apress.com.

The following example will show how to create a View matrix and a Projection matrix. Say you have an object located somewhere at the world space origin point—the (0,0,0) point—and you want to position your camera +10 units on the positive x-axis, with the positive y-axis as the Up vector. Furthermore, you want to render your 3D scene to an 800 × 600 window and want all triangles closer to the camera than 0.5f and farther away than 100.0f to be clipped away. This is what your code will look like:

```
using System;
using System.Collections.Generic;
using System.Linq;
using Microsoft.Xna.Framework;
using Microsoft.Xna.Framework.Audio;
using Microsoft.Xna.Framework.Content;
using Microsoft.Xna.Framework.GamerServices;
using Microsoft.Xna.Framework.Graphics;
using Microsoft.Xna.Framework.Input;
using Microsoft.Xna.Framework.Media;
using Microsoft.Xna.Framework.Net;
using Microsoft.Xna.Framework.Storage;

namespace BookCode
{
    public class Game1 : Microsoft.Xna.Framework.Game
    {
        GraphicsDeviceManager graphics;
        BasicEffect basicEffect;
        GraphicsDevice device;
        CoordCross cCross;

        Matrix viewMatrix;
        Matrix projectionMatrix;
```

```
public Game1()
{
    graphics = new GraphicsDeviceManager(this);
    Content.RootDirectory = "Content";
}
```

The Projection matrix will need to be changed only when the aspect ratio of the target window changes. If this is not going to happen, you have to define it only once, such as during the initialization phase of your program.

```
protected override void Initialize()
{
    base.Initialize();

    float viewAngle = MathHelper.PiOver4;
    float aspectRatio = graphics.GraphicsDevice.Viewport.AspectRatio;
    float nearPlane = 0.5f;
    float farPlane = 100.0f;
    projectionMatrix = Matrix.CreatePerspectiveFieldOfView(viewAngle, ➥
    aspectRatio, nearPlane, farPlane);
}

protected override void LoadContent()
{
    device = graphics.GraphicsDevice;
    basicEffect = new BasicEffect(device, null);
    cCross = new CoordCross(device);
}

protected override void UnloadContent()
{
}
```

User input that moves the camera will make you want to change the View matrix, so an ideal moment to change it is in the update phase.

```
protected override void Update(GameTime gameTime)
{
    if (GamePad.GetState(PlayerIndex.One).Buttons.Back == ➥
    ButtonState.Pressed)
        this.Exit();

    Vector3 camPosition = new Vector3(10, 10, -10);
    Vector3 camTarget = new Vector3(0, 0, 0);
    Vector3 camUpVector = new Vector3(0, 1, 0);
    viewMatrix = Matrix.CreateLookAt(camPosition, camTarget, camUpVector);

    base.Update(gameTime);
}
```

Then pass the Projection and View matrices to the Effect that will be drawing the scene. In this recipe, I'm rendering a coordinate cross so you can see where the (0,0,0) origin point of the 3D world is. The code that actually renders the coordinate cross is in the CoordCross.cs file.

```
protected override void Draw(GameTime gameTime)
{
    device.Clear(ClearOptions.Target | ClearOptions.DepthBuffer, ➥
    Color.CornflowerBlue, 1, 0);

    basicEffect.World = Matrix.Identity;
    basicEffect.View = viewMatrix;
    basicEffect.Projection = projectionMatrix;
    basicEffect.Begin();
    foreach (EffectPass pass in basicEffect.CurrentTechnique.Passes)
    {
        pass.Begin();
        cCross.DrawUsingPresetEffect();
        pass.End();
    }
    basicEffect.End();

    base.Draw(gameTime);
}
}
}
```

## Extra Reading

The previous two matrices are all XNA needs to correctly render your 3D scene to the 2D window on your screen. Going from 3D to 2D involves certain challenges, which are all taken care of by XNA. However, if you want to be able to create and debug medium- to large-sized 3D applications, a clear understanding of what is going on under the hood is necessary.

### The Z-Buffer (or Depth Buffer)

A first challenge lies in specifying which object of your 3D scene will occupy a certain pixel of the final image. When going from 3D space to 2D window space, there can be multiple objects that you want displayed on the same pixel, as shown in Figure 2-3. A pixel on your 2D window corresponds to a ray of points in your 3D world, which is explained in more detail in recipe 4-14. For one pixel, this ray is shown as the dotted line in Figure 2-3, which hits two objects. In this case, the pixel should obviously get the color of object A, since object A is closer to the camera than object B.

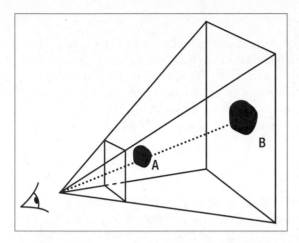

**Figure 2-3.** *Multiple objects competing for the same pixel*

However, if object B gets drawn first, the corresponding pixel in the frame buffer will be assigned the color of object B first. At the next moment, object A is drawn, and now, the graphics card decides whether the pixel needs to be overwritten by the color of object A.

To solve this problem, inside the graphics card a second image is stored, with the same size as the window. At the moment a color is assigned to a pixel of the frame buffer, the distance between the camera and the object is stored in this second image. This distance is a value between 0 and 1, with 0 corresponding to the distance between the camera and the near clipping plane and 1 corresponding to the distance between the camera and the far clipping plane. Because of this, this second image is called the *depth buffer* or *z-buffer*.

So, how does this solve the problem? At the moment object B is drawn, the z-buffer is checked. Because object B is the first object being drawn, the z-buffer will be empty. As a result, all corresponding pixels of your frame buffer get the color of object B. Also, the same pixels in the z-buffer get a value according to the distance between the camera and object B.

The next moment, object A is drawn. For each pixel that could be occupied by object A, the z-buffer is checked first. The z-buffer will already contain a value for the pixels overlapping with object B. But the distance stored in the z-buffer is larger than the distance between the camera and object A, so the graphics card knows it should overwrite the pixel with the color of object A!

# 2-2. Specify the Target of Your Camera

## The Problem

When you define your View matrix, one of the arguments you need to specify is the Target vector. This vector sets the rotation of your camera, which can be challenging to provide.

## The Solution

When rotating the camera, the position of the camera will remain the same. Since the positioning and targeting of the camera are specified by the View matrix (recipe 2-1) and this View matrix is based on the Position, Target, and Up vectors of the camera, the rotation will be achieved by changing the Target point of the camera, as well as the Up vector. You can find the Target vector by taking the usual (0,0,–1) Forward vector and applying your rotation to this vector, which will result in the new Target point of your camera. You can use the same approach to find the Up vector.

## How It Works

As shown in recipe 1-1, a camera needs its Position, Target, and Up vectors before it is uniquely defined. If you want to rotate your camera at a certain point in 3D space, the Position vector remains the same, but the Target vector and probably also the Up vector will change.

Given the rotation angles around the three axes, one approach would be to calculate the Target position by hand. This would, however, lead to very complex calculations, while a much cleaner and faster approach is possible.

### Easiest Example: Camera in Origin, Rotation Along the Up Vector

Let's examine the case where the camera is in the (0,0,0) coordinate origin. It is looking at the (0,0,–1) Forward direction with the default (0,1,0) Up vector as the Up vector. In this case, you could get this code:

```
Vector3 cameraPosition = new Vector3(0, 0, 0);
Vector3 cameraTarget = new Vector3(0, 0, -1);
Vector3 cameraUpVector = new Vector3(0, 1, 0);

viewMatrix = Matrix.CreateLookAt(cameraPosition, ➡
cameraTarget, cameraUpVector);
```

Say you want a View matrix that holds a rotation of 45 degrees along the Up vector. If your head were the camera, this would result in turning your head to the right for 45 degrees. When calculating the new View matrix, your Position vector as well as the Up vector would remain the same, but you need to find your new Target vector. You can find the Target vector by "transforming" the default (0,0,–1) Target vector by the 45-degree rotation. This means you're going to find the vector that is the rotated version of the original Target vector. This is the code you need:

```
Matrix cameraRotation = Matrix.CreateRotationY(MathHelper.PiOver4);
Vector3 cameraPosition = new Vector3(0, 0, 0);
Vector3 cameraUpVector = new Vector3(0, 1, 0);
Vector3 cameraOriginalTarget = new Vector3(0, 0, -1);

Vector3 cameraRotatedTarget = ➡
Vector3.Transform(cameraOriginalTarget, cameraRotation);
viewMatrix = Matrix.CreateLookAt(cameraPosition, ➡
cameraRotatedTarget, cameraUpVector);
```

**Note** Matrices are powerful objects that can represent any kind of transformation. A matrix can represent a rotation, translation, scaling, or any combination of these transformations. You can find more examples in recipe 4-2.

The first line creates a matrix that describes a rotation around the Up axis of 45 degrees, which corresponds to PI/4 radians. The second-to-last line transforms your original (0,0,–1) Target vector by the rotation matrix and stores the rotated Target vector in the cameraRotatedTarget variable, which is used to create the new View matrix.

**Note** This transformation is nothing magic; it's the multiplication between the vector and a matrix, which simply comes down to 16 multiplications and 12 summations between ordinary numbers.

## Second Example: Camera at Origin, Arbitrary Rotation

Now, let's examine an example that is a bit more complex. Instead of rotating your camera along the Up vector, you will rotate it over an arbitrary axis. Without making this example less general, let's rotate for 45 degrees over the (1,0,0) Right vector. Again, if your head is the camera, this will result in looking up for 45 degrees.

Because you're rotating only your camera, the Position vector will remain unchanged. Your Target vector, as in the previous example, will be changed, because your camera needs to be directed toward a different point.

In this case, however, the Up vector will also change. In the previous example of turning your head to the right, there's no change in the Up axis of your head. In the current example, when moving your head so you're looking up, both the Up vector of your head as well as its Target need to be changed.

Transforming your Up vector is done the same way as for the Forward vector: you have the rotation stored in a matrix and define the original Up vector. Next, you transform the original vector by the rotation matrix to obtain the new, transformed Up vector. This is your code:

```
Matrix cameraRotation = Matrix.CreateRotationX(MathHelper.PiOver4);
Vector3 cameraPosition = new Vector3(0, 0, 0);
Vector3 cameraOriginalUpVector = new Vector3(0, 1, 0);
Vector3 cameraOriginalTarget = new Vector3(0, 0, -1);

Vector3 cameraRotatedTarget = ➡
Vector3.Transform(cameraOriginalTarget, cameraRotation);
Vector3 cameraRotatedUpVector = ➡
Vector3.Transform(cameraOriginalUpVector, cameraRotation);
viewMatrix = Matrix.CreateLookAt(cameraPosition, ➡
cameraRotatedTarget, cameraRotatedUpVector);
```

Here the "arbitrary" rotation matrix is simply a rotation around the x-axis, so you can still easily visualize it. The same code, however, is capable of handling any rotation, such as the following one, which combines a rotation over the three axes. The following code generates a matrix that combines a rotation of –45 degrees over the z-axis (camera rotated counter-clockwise), 22.5 degrees over the y-axis (camera rotated to the left), and 90 degrees over the x-axis (camera rotated down):

```
Matrix cameraRotation = ➥
Matrix.CreateRotationX(MathHelper.PiOver2)* ➥
Matrix.CreateRotationY(MathHelper.Pi/8.0f)* ➥
Matrix.CreateRotationZ(-MathHelper.PiOver4);
```

The position of the camera is unchanged, while you have to find the rotated versions of the Forward and Up vectors for your camera.

### Third Example: Camera at a Specified Point, Arbitrary Rotation

In the most general case, you want to set an arbitrary rotation on the camera and specify the position of the camera at a certain point in 3D space. To start with, imagine you position your camera at the (10,20,30) point in 3D space, without rotation. Quite simply, the Position vector of your camera would be (10,20,30).

Without rotation, you want the camera to look in the (0,0,–1) Forward direction.

---

**Note** Keep in mind that you have to specify the Target point, not the Target direction! Indicating (0,0,–1) as the Target vector would be wrong, because this would make your camera always look at the (0,0,–1) point. Imagine that later you want to move your camera to the (–10,20,30) point, for example. If you still specify (0,0,–1) as the Target vector, the camera would still be looking at the (0,0,–1) point, so the direction the camera is looking has been changed!

---

To make the camera at position (10,20,30) look in the (0,0,–1) direction, you need to specify (10,20,29) as the Target vector. You can find this vector by summing your camera position and the target direction, like this:

```
Vector3 cameraPosition = new Vector3(10, 20, 30);
Vector3 cameraOriginalTarget = new Vector3(0, 0, -1);
cameraTargetPoint = cameraPosition + cameraOriginalTarget;
```

Now, it's time to combine everything you've seen so far during this recipe. You will define a camera at position (10,20,30) with an arbitrary rotation. The Position vector will remain (10,20,30). For the Target vector, you again start from the Forward (0,0,–1) direction. To find the Forward direction after the rotation has been applied to it, you transform it by the rotation matrix. Finally, to find the Target vector so the camera positioned at (10,20,30) will be looking in this rotated direction, you need to add (10,20,30) to this rotated direction. The Up vector is found the same way, so this is the final code you get:

```
Matrix cameraRotation = ➥
Matrix.CreateRotationX(MathHelper.PiOver2)* ➥
Matrix.CreateRotationY(MathHelper.Pi/8.0f)* ➥
Matrix.CreateRotationZ(-MathHelper.PiOver4);
Vector3 cameraPosition = new Vector3(10, 20, 30);
Vector3 cameraOriginalTarget = new Vector3(0, 0, -1);
Vector3 cameraOriginalUpVector = new Vector3(0, 1, 0);

Vector3 cameraRotatedTarget = ➥
Vector3.Transform(cameraOriginalTarget, cameraRotation);
Vector3 cameraFinalTarget = cameraPosition + cameraRotatedTarget;

Vector3 cameraRotatedUpVector = ➥
Vector3.Transform(cameraOriginalUpVector, cameraRotation);
Vector3 cameraFinalUpVector = cameraPosition + cameraRotatedUpVector;

viewMatrix = Matrix.CreateLookAt(cameraPosition, ➥
cameraFinalTarget, cameraFinalUpVector);
```

## Moving a Rotated Camera Forward/Sideways

Now that you have your camera at the position you want and looking into the correct direction, moving the camera forward can be a new challenge. If you want the camera to move forward, simply adding the (0,0,–1) Forward vector to the Position vector will not work, because you first need to find out what the Forward vector is relative to the rotated camera. You've already done this in the first example of this recipe by transforming the (0,0,–1) Forward vector by the rotation matrix. Once you have this, you can simply add this to the Position vector:

```
float moveSpeed = 0.5f;
Vector3 cameraOriginalForward = new Vector3(0,0,-1);
Vector3 cameraRotatedForward = Vector3.Transform(cameraOriginalForward,
cameraRotation);
cameraPosition += moveSpeed * cameraRotatedForward;
```

Changing the value of moveSpeed will increase/decrease the speed of your camera's movement, because this value is multiplied by the rotated Forward direction.

The same way, you can let your camera move sideways. Instead of starting from the (0,0,–1) Forward vector, you start with the (1,0,0) Right vector, which again first needs to be transformed so you get the Right vector relative to the current camera's rotation:

```
float moveSpeed = 0.5f;
Vector3 cameraOriginalRight = new Vector3(1, 0, 0);
Vector3 cameraRotatedRight = Vector3.Transform(cameraOriginalRight, cameraRotation);
cameraPosition += moveSpeed * cameraRotatedRight;
```

## The Code

*All the code is available for download at www.apress.com.*

For this approach, your camera needs to keep track only of its current position and rotation. The View matrix will need to be updated only if either of them changes. These changes will usually result from a user input, for which you can find two detailed approaches in recipe 2-3 and recipe 2-4. As with each matrix that needs initialization, you first set the cameraRotation matrix to the Identity matrix, which is the unity element for matrix multiplication.

```
protected override void Initialize()
{
    float viewAngle = MathHelper.PiOver4;
    float aspectRatio = graphics.GraphicsDevice.Viewport.AspectRatio;
    float nearPlane = 0.5f;
    float farPlane = 100.0f;
    projectionMatrix = Matrix.CreatePerspectiveFieldOfView(viewAngle, aspectRatio,
            nearPlane, farPlane);

    cameraPosition = new Vector3(-5, 7, 14);
    cameraRotation = Matrix.CreateRotationX(-MathHelper.Pi/8.0f)* ➥
    Matrix.CreateRotationY(-MathHelper.Pi/8.0f);
    UpdateViewMatrix();
    base.Initialize();
}

protected override void Update(GameTime gameTime)
{
    if (GamePad.GetState(PlayerIndex.One).Buttons.Back == ButtonState.Pressed)
        this.Exit();

    MoveCameraForward();

    base.Update(gameTime);
}

private void MoveCameraForward()
{
    float moveSpeed = 0.05f;
    Vector3 cameraOriginalForward = new Vector3(0, 0, -1);
    Vector3 cameraRotatedForward = ➥
    Vector3.Transform(cameraOriginalForward, cameraRotation);
    cameraPosition += moveSpeed * cameraRotatedForward;
    UpdateViewMatrix();
}
```

```
private void UpdateViewMatrix()
{
    Vector3 cameraOriginalTarget = new Vector3(0, 0, -1);
    Vector3 cameraOriginalUpVector = new Vector3(0, 1, 0);

    Vector3 cameraRotatedTarget = ➥
    Vector3.Transform(cameraOriginalTarget, cameraRotation);
    Vector3 cameraFinalTarget = cameraPosition + cameraRotatedTarget;

    Vector3 cameraRotatedUpVector = ➥
    Vector3.Transform(cameraOriginalUpVector, cameraRotation);

    viewMatrix = Matrix.CreateLookAt(cameraPosition, ➥
    cameraFinalTarget, cameraRotatedUpVector);
}


protected override void Draw(GameTime gameTime)
{
    graphics.GraphicsDevice.Clear(Color.CornflowerBlue);

    //render coordcross using specified View and Projection matrices
    cCross.Draw(viewMatrix, projectionMatrix);

    base.Draw(gameTime);
}
```

# Extra Reading

## The Order of Matrix Multiplication

See recipe 4-2.

## Choosing the Coordinate System

The vectors for the Forward (0,0,–1) and Up (0,1,0) directions used previously are the "offi-cial" XNA vectors for these directions and can also be obtained using the Vector3.Forward and Vector3.Up shortcuts. They are only a convention, however; if you want, you can define a totally different coordinate system for your application. An example would be to use (0,0,1) as the Up direction, (0,1,0) as the Forward direction, and (1,0,0) as the Right direction, but it is totally up to you to decide what coordinate axes you want to use for your project.

There is, however, one rule the three vectors have to obey. In XNA, the x-, y-, and z-axes are expected to form a right-handed (RH) coordinate system. This means that once you know two axes, you can always find the direction of the third axis. Stretch your thumb and your index finger of your right hand. Next, bend your middle finger for 90 degrees, so it is perpendicular to your index finger and thumb. Now, imagine your three fingers are the axis of your coordinate system. If you have an RH coordinate system, there must be a way you map the x-axis of your coordinate system on your thumb, your y-axis on your index finger, and your z-axis on your middle finger.

For the axes described in the first paragraph here, this corresponds to your thumb pointing to the right and your middle finger up (no offense intended). To represent the "official" XNA coordinate system, hold your thumb to the right (positive x-axis = right) and your index finger up (positive y-axis = up). Now, you see that your middle finger points backward (positive z-axis = backward), so that's why the minus sign is in the (0,0,–1) official Forward vector!

# 2-3. Create a First-Person Shooter Camera: A Quake-Style Camera

## The Problem

You want to create a camera that behaves just like in most first-person shooters. You want to use the mouse to rotate the camera, while you can move the camera using the keyboard.

## The Solution

Starting from the camera approach presented in recipe 2-2, you will update the position and the rotation of the camera whenever input from the user is detected. The rotation matrix of your camera will be changed according to the movement of the mouse. A key press on the Up or Down button will result in the position of your camera moving forward/backward, and pressing the Left or Right button will make your camera strafe left/right.

## How It Works

Usually, in a first-person game, the player is free to rotate to the left or to the right and is also unlimited in looking up or down. These movements correspond to rotations around the Up and Right vectors, respectively, or even more detailed in rotations around the (0,1,0) and (1,0,0) directions.

A rotation around the Forward vector, however, is not allowed. This would result in the player bending his neck to the left or right and is not used in first-persons, except maybe when the player has been shot and is lying on the floor.

Before you move on, it might be useful to read the section "Order of Matrix Multiplications" in recipe 4-2 in Chapter 4. The bottom line of this discussion is that the order of multiplication does matter, because when you combine two rotations, the axes of the second rotation are changed by the first rotation.

This impact of the first rotation on the second axis is called *Gimbal lock*; it can sometimes be a real pain, but it can sometimes also be what you want. In this case of a first-person camera, you're in luck: you will first rotate your camera along the vertical Up axis and next rotate along the Right vector. The first rotation rotates your Right vector nicely, which you can visualize by standing up and stretching your right arm. If you turn to the right, your arm turns with you, and now, you can nicely rotate around the direction of your arm to look down or up.

In short, you will need to store two variables: the amount of rotation around the Up direction and the amount of rotation around the Right direction. Next, when you need to calculate the total rotation, you combine both rotations using the "rotation around Right *after* rotation around Up." Once that you know the total rotation, you can simply plug this into the code of the previous recipe!

Now that you know the concept behind first-person camera rotation, you still need to relate user input to the two variables that hold the amount of rotation. Here, the example of mouse input is given. You will determine the change of the mouse position between two update cycles and change the variables accordingly. So, you'll need these variables:

```
float leftrightRot;
float updownRot;
Vector3 cameraPosition;
Matrix viewMatrix;
MouseState originalMouseState;
```

A MouseState contains the position of the mouse cursor, as well as some bits that indicate whether a mouse button has been clicked since the last call to Mouse.GetState(). Give both variables a starting value in your Initialize method:

```
leftrightRot = 0.0f;
updownRot = 0.0f;
cameraPosition = new Vector3(1,1,10);
UpdateViewMatrix();
Mouse.SetPosition(Window.ClientBounds.Width / 2, ➥
Window.ClientBounds.Height / 2);
originalMouseState = Mouse.GetState();
```

You first set the rotation values to zero and position your camera at a starting point of your choice. You will soon create an UpdateViewMatrix method, which is used here simply to initialize the viewMatrix variable.

Next, you set the mouse cursor to the center of the screen to start with. The last line stores the MouseState, which contains the position of your centered mouse pointer, so during the next update cycle, you can check whether there's any difference between this state and the new one, which would indicate the mouse has been moved.

Let's take a look at the update routine. As said before, you'll first check the new MouseState to see whether there's any difference with the one stored in the originalMouseState. If there is a difference, the rotation values are updated accordingly, and the mouse pointer is returned to the center of the window:

```
float rotationSpeed = 0.005f;
MouseState currentMouseState = Mouse.GetState();
if (currentMouseState != originalMouseState)
{
    float xDifference = currentMouseState.X - originalMouseState.X;
    float yDifference = currentMouseState.Y - originalMouseState.Y;
    leftrightRot -= rotationSpeed * xDifference;
    updownRot -= rotationSpeed * yDifference;
```

```
    Mouse.SetPosition(Window.ClientBounds.Width / 2, ➥
    Window.ClientBounds.Height / 2);
}
UpdateViewMatrix();
```

The rotationSpeed variable defines how fast the camera will rotate. You find the horizontal and vertical difference of the mouse coordinate between the new and previous positions, and you adjust the rotations around the Right and Up vectors accordingly.

The last line resets the mouse pointer to the center of the window.

---

■**Note**  Another approach could have been that you store the currentMouseState in the originalMouseState so it is ready to be compared to the new currentMouseState in the next update cycle. However, this would become useless if the mouse cursor is moved toward an edge of the screen. If the mouse cursor, for example, hits the right edge of the screen, there will be no difference in the X position of the mouse cursor when the user moves the mouse even more to the right. Repositioning the mouse cursor to the center of the screen solves this problem.

---

At the end, you call the UpdateViewMatrix method, which will update the viewMatrix variable according to the new rotation values. The code of the UpdateViewMatrix method follows and, except for the first line, you can find a detailed explanation of it in the previous recipe. Based on a matrix that stores the rotation of the camera and the position of the matrix, the method calculates the Target and Up vectors, which are needed to create the View matrix:

```
Matrix cameraRotation = Matrix.CreateRotationX(updownRot) * ➥
Matrix.CreateRotationY(leftrightRot);

Vector3 cameraOriginalTarget = new Vector3(0, 0, -1);
Vector3 cameraOriginalUpVector = new Vector3(0, 1, 0);

Vector3 cameraRotatedTarget = ➥
Vector3.Transform(cameraOriginalTarget, cameraRotation);
Vector3 cameraFinalTarget = cameraPosition + cameraRotatedTarget;

Vector3 cameraRotatedUpVector = ➥
Vector3.Transform(cameraOriginalUpVector, cameraRotation);
Vector3 cameraFinalUpVector = cameraPosition + cameraRotatedUpVector;

viewMatrix = Matrix.CreateLookAt(cameraPosition, ➥
cameraFinalTarget, cameraFinalUpVector);
```

The first line could use some explanation. The Right vector here is the (1,0,0) vector, so it is directed along the x-axis. That's why you use the CreateRotationX method to create this rotation. The Up vector here is the (0,1,0) vector, so you use the CreateRotationY method to create the left/right rotation. About the order of multiplication: M1*M2 means "M1 after M2," so here this becomes "Up/Down rotation *after* Left/Right rotation." For more information on the order of matrix multiplication, see recipe 4-2 in Chapter 4.

This will make your camera rotate when you move your mouse cursor. Next, you want the camera to move forward when you press the Forward button. In the update routine, you will first detect the key presses and react to this by specifying which vector to add to the camera position:

```
KeyboardState keyState = Keyboard.GetState();
if (keyState.IsKeyDown(Keys.Up))
    AddToCameraPosition(new Vector3(0, 0, -1));
if (keyState.IsKeyDown(Keys.Down))
    AddToCameraPosition(new Vector3(0, 0, 1));
if (keyState.IsKeyDown(Keys.Right))
    AddToCameraPosition(new Vector3(1, 0, 0));
if (keyState.IsKeyDown(Keys.Left))
    AddToCameraPosition(new Vector3(-1, 0, 0));
```

Pressing the Up key results in the Forward vector being added to the camera position, pressing the Down key results in the Forward vector being subtracted from the camera position, and so on. However, before you can add these vectors to the camera position, you still need to rotate them by the camera rotation. For more information on this, see the previous recipe. This is handled by the AddToCameraPosition method:

```
private void AddToCameraPosition(Vector3 vectorToAdd)
{
    float moveSpeed = 0.5f;
    Matrix cameraRotation = Matrix.CreateRotationX(updownRot) * ➡
    Matrix.CreateRotationY(leftrightRot);
    Vector3 rotatedVector = Vector3.Transform(vectorToAdd, cameraRotation);
    cameraPosition += moveSpeed * rotatedVector;
    UpdateViewMatrix();
}
```

First, you calculate the camera rotation matrix, as shown in the UpdateViewMatrix method. Then you rotate the specified vector according to this rotation matrix. Next, the rotated vector is multiplied by a variable that lets you set the speed at which your camera will move, and the Position of the camera is actually changed. Finally, you call the UpdateViewMatrix method, which creates a new View matrix that takes the new camera position into account.

## The Code

*All the code is available for download at www.apress.com.*

To create a first-person camera, you will need to keep track of four variables: the amounts of rotation around the Up and Right vectors, the position of your camera, and the MouseState that corresponds to the mouse cursor centered in the window. A key press or movement of the mouse will be detected in the update cycle, which triggers the changes to these variables and results in a new View matrix being created, based on the new values.

```
protected override void Initialize()
{
    base.Initialize();

    float viewAngle = MathHelper.PiOver4;
    float aspectRatio = (float)this.Window.ClientBounds.Width / ➥
    (float)this.Window.ClientBounds.Height;
    float nearPlane = 0.5f;
    float farPlane = 100.0f;
    projectionMatrix = ➥
    Matrix.CreatePerspectiveFieldOfView(viewAngle, ➥
    aspectRatio, nearPlane, farPlane);

    leftrightRot = 0.0f;
    updownRot = 0.0f;
    cameraPosition = new Vector3(1,1,10);
    UpdateViewMatrix();
    Mouse.SetPosition(Window.ClientBounds.Width / 2, ➥
    Window.ClientBounds.Height / 2);
    originalMouseState = Mouse.GetState();
}

protected override void Update(GameTime gameTime)
{
    if (GamePad.GetState(PlayerIndex.One).Buttons.Back == ➥
    ButtonState.Pressed)
        this.Exit();

    float rotationSpeed = 0.005f;

    MouseState currentMouseState = Mouse.GetState();
    if (currentMouseState != originalMouseState)
    {
        float xDifference = currentMouseState.X - ➥
        originalMouseState.X;
        float yDifference = currentMouseState.Y - ➥
        originalMouseState.Y;
        leftrightRot -= rotationSpeed * xDifference;
        updownRot -= rotationSpeed * yDifference;
        Mouse.SetPosition(Window.ClientBounds.Width / 2, ➥
        Window.ClientBounds.Height / 2);

        UpdateViewMatrix();
    }
```

```
        KeyboardState keyState = Keyboard.GetState();
        if (keyState.IsKeyDown(Keys.Up))
            AddToCameraPosition(new Vector3(0, 0, -1));
        if (keyState.IsKeyDown(Keys.Down))
            AddToCameraPosition(new Vector3(0, 0, 1));
        if (keyState.IsKeyDown(Keys.Right))
            AddToCameraPosition(new Vector3(1, 0, 0));
        if (keyState.IsKeyDown(Keys.Left))
            AddToCameraPosition(new Vector3(-1, 0, 0));


        base.Update(gameTime);
    }

    private void AddToCameraPosition(Vector3 vectorToAdd)
    {
        float moveSpeed = 0.5f;
        Matrix cameraRotation = Matrix.CreateRotationX(updownRot) * ➥
        Matrix.CreateRotationY(leftrightRot);
        Vector3 rotatedVector = Vector3.Transform(vectorToAdd, ➥
        cameraRotation);
        cameraPosition += moveSpeed * rotatedVector;
        UpdateViewMatrix();
    }

    private void UpdateViewMatrix()
    {
        Matrix cameraRotation = Matrix.CreateRotationX(updownRot) * ➥
        Matrix.CreateRotationY(leftrightRot);

        Vector3 cameraOriginalTarget = new Vector3(0, 0, -1);
        Vector3 cameraOriginalUpVector = new Vector3(0, 1, 0);

        Vector3 cameraRotatedTarget = ➥
        Vector3.Transform(cameraOriginalTarget, cameraRotation);
        Vector3 cameraFinalTarget = cameraPosition + ➥
        cameraRotatedTarget;

        Vector3 cameraRotatedUpVector = ➥
        Vector3.Transform(cameraOriginalUpVector, cameraRotation);
        Vector3 cameraFinalUpVector = cameraPosition + ➥
        cameraRotatedUpVector;

        viewMatrix = Matrix.CreateLookAt(cameraPosition, ➥
        cameraFinalTarget, cameraRotatedUpVector);
    }
```

### The QuakeCamera Class

Because it is often quite useful to have a first-person camera mode readily available, I have separated the code from this chapter into a class. This class is used as the camera in many of the 3D examples found elsewhere in this book and is easy to integrate into one of your own projects.

## 2-4. Create a Freelancer-Style Camera: Full 3D Rotation Using Quaternions

### The Problem

You want to create a camera that is able to rotate in every possible way, for example, to create a flight game. You will need rotations around three axes to do this, but because of Gimbal lock (each rotation has an impact on the other rotations), this becomes very difficult, if not impossible.

### The Solution

Combining several rotations around multiple axes causes Gimbal lock to occur, which will in this case lead to incorrect results. Using a quaternion to store the rotation of the camera can help you avoid this problem.

### How It Works

When you combine two rotations around two different axes, Gimbal lock will occur. This happens because the first rotation will also rotate the second axis, as explained in recipe 4-2. In this recipe, you want to rotate your camera around your x-, y-, and z-axes. This would imply, however, that the second axis is rotated by the first rotation and that the third axis is rotated by the combination of the first two axes. So, it's hard to imagine what is going to be the final result.

A property of rotations is that there always exists a single rotation that has the same result as the combination of multiple rotations. So, the trick you need here is to define only a single axis of rotation around which your camera will be rotated. This can be any axis: it does not have to be one of the x-, y-, or z-axes. This axis and the amount of rotation will be stored in a variable, which is called a *quaternion*.

A quaternion is perfect to store a rotation, because a quaternion can store an axis and a number that can hold the amount of degrees to rotate around that axis.

The next question is, how can you calculate this axis? You don't. It will be created for you automatically during the process. You just need to specify a starting axis, and this axis will be updated every time the user moves the mouse, as you will see in the next example.

Say you start with the Up axis of your camera as the rotation axis and with 0 degrees of rotation, so you're looking forward. Next, on some user input, you want the camera to rotate around its Right vector. This Right vector first gets rotated with the current camera rotation, but because this is over 0 angles, the Right vector remains same. This Right vector becomes the current rotation axis. The camera is rotated over this axis, and the camera is looking up a bit.

The next user input wants the camera to be rotated along its Forward axis. This axis first is rotated along the current rotation of the camera, which now no longer is zero but contains a rotation around the Right axis. Both rotations are combined, and the resulting single axis of rotation and the amount of rotation is stored in the camera quaternion. This rotation now becomes the current rotation of the camera.

For each new input of the user, the same procedure happens: the Forward/Right/Up/Down/. . . vector gets rotated by the current rotation axis of the camera, and the combination of this new rotation and the current camera rotation is stored as the new camera rotation into the camera quaternion, after which the camera is rotated over this new rotation.

Luckily, this whole story translates to some easy code. To begin with, you'll allow a rotation over only a single axis (around the Right axis):

```
float updownRotation = 0.0f;
KeyboardState keys = Keyboard.GetState();
if (keys.IsKeyDown(Keys.Up))
    updownRotation = 1.5f;
if (keys.IsKeyDown(Keys.Down))
    updownRotation = -1.5f;

Quaternion additionalRotation = ➥
Quaternion.CreateFromAxisAngle(new Vector3(1, 0, 0), updownRotation);
cameraRotation = cameraRotation * additionalRotation;
```

First, user input decides whether the camera should be rotated upward or downward. Next, a new quaternion is created that holds this axis and the amount of rotation around this axis. Finally, this new rotation is combined with the current rotation of the camera, and the result is stored as the new camera rotation.

---

■**Note** The word *quaternion* alone usually makes programmers shiver. I've encountered many articles and sites that present quaternions almost as if they were dark magic, impossible to understand or visualize. This is, however, completely untrue. A quaternion is used to store a rotation around an axis, so it needs to be capable of storing this axis and the amount of degrees to rotate around it. An axis is defined by three numbers, and the amount of degrees can of course be defined by one number. So if you had to store such rotation, the easiest way to store one would be to just store four numbers. Guess what a quaternion actually is? Simply, it's four numbers. Nothing magic. The math behind their operations closely resembles complex magic, though.

---

To allow you to rotate the camera any way you want, you need to be able to rotate it along a second axis. This rotation needs to be stored in the additionalRotation variable from the previous code, by multiplying the rotation around the first axis by the rotation around this second axis:

```
float updownRotation = 0.0f;
float leftrightRotation = 0.0f;
KeyboardState keys = Keyboard.GetState();
```

```
if (keys.IsKeyDown(Keys.Up))
    updownRotation = 0.05f;
if (keys.IsKeyDown(Keys.Down))
    updownRotation = -0.05f;
if (keys.IsKeyDown(Keys.Right))
    leftrightRotation = -0.05f;
if (keys.IsKeyDown(Keys.Left))
    leftrightRotation = 0.05f;

Quaternion additionalRotation =
Quaternion.CreateFromAxisAngle(new Vector3(1, 0, 0), updownRotation)*
Quaternion.CreateFromAxisAngle(new Vector3(0, 1, 0), leftrightRotation);
cameraRotation = cameraRotation * additionalRotation;
```

---

■**Note** As with matrix multiplication, the order in which you multiply quaternions is important. To see an example of why it's important, read recipe 4-2 on the order of matrix multiplications. You have to keep this in mind when multiplying quaternions, as you're doing here. However, for quaternions there is an exception to this rule when both rotational axes are perpendicular to each other, as is the case in the line where you calculate the `additionalRotation` variable. This means whether you first rotate around the (1,0,0) Right vector and then around the (0,1,0) Up vector, or you rotate the other way around, the result will be the same. This is *not* the case for the line where you calculate the `cameraRotation` variable, because both axes are not perpendicular to each other. So, here it is important you write `cameraRotation*additionalRotation`.

---

■**Note** In matrix multiplications, * means *after* (see Recipe 4-2). Because things would otherwise be too easy, * in quaternion multiplication means *before*. So, the line `cameraRotation = cameraRota-tion * additionalRotation` comes down to `cameraRotation` before `additionalRotation`, meaning that the axis stored in the `additionalRotation` variable will first be rotated around the axis stored in the `cameraRotation` variable.

---

Once this rotation matrix has been found, the camera's View matrix can be constructed using the technique shown in recipe 2-2:

```
private void UpdateViewMatrix()
{
    Vector3 cameraOriginalTarget = new Vector3(0, 0, -1);
    Vector3 cameraOriginalUpVector = new Vector3(0, 1, 0);

    Vector3 cameraRotatedTarget = ➥
    Vector3.Transform(cameraOriginalTarget, cameraRotation);
    Vector3 cameraFinalTarget = cameraPosition + ➥
    cameraRotatedTarget;
```

```
    Vector3 cameraRotatedUpVector = ➡
    Vector3.Transform(cameraOriginalUpVector, cameraRotation);

    viewMatrix = Matrix.CreateLookAt(cameraPosition, ➡
    cameraFinalTarget, cameraRotatedUpVector);
}
```

Moving the camera—for example, when the user presses an arrow key—can be done by first rotating the movement vector by the camera rotation and then by adding this transformed vector to the current camera position:

```
float moveSpeed = 0.5f;
Vector3 rotatedVector = ➡
Vector3.Transform(vectorToAdd, cameraRotation);
cameraPosition += moveSpeed * rotatedVector;
UpdateViewMatrix();
```

## The Code

*All the code is available for download at* www.apress.com.

Because this type of camera is usually used in space games, the code presented in this section is immediately useful if you are creating a space shooter and the 3D world needs to be rendered as shown by the pilot inside the spacecraft. The user needs to be able to control the rotation of the camera by the keyboard or mouse, and the camera moves automatically forward. The example of keyboard control will be given; you can find how to use the mouse for this in recipe 2-3.

To implement a quaternion-based camera system, only two variables are necessary: the current position and the rotation of the camera.

```
protected override void Initialize()
{
    cCross = new CoordCross();
    base.Initialize();

    float viewAngle = MathHelper.PiOver4;
    float aspectRatio = graphics.GraphicsDevice.Viewport.AspectRatio;
    float nearPlane = 0.5f;
    float farPlane = 100.0f;
    projectionMatrix = ➡
    Matrix.CreatePerspectiveFieldOfView(viewAngle, ➡
    aspectRatio, nearPlane, farPlane);

    cameraPosition = new Vector3(-1, 1, 10);
    cameraRotation = Quaternion.Identity;
    UpdateViewMatrix();
}
```

```
protected override void Update(GameTime gameTime)
{
    if (GamePad.GetState(PlayerIndex.One).Buttons.Back == ➥
    ButtonState.Pressed)
        this.Exit();

    float updownRotation = 0.0f;
    float leftrightRotation = 0.0f;
    KeyboardState keys = Keyboard.GetState();

    if (keys.IsKeyDown(Keys.Up))
        updownRotation = 0.05f;
    if (keys.IsKeyDown(Keys.Down))
        updownRotation = -0.05f;
    if (keys.IsKeyDown(Keys.Right))
        leftrightRotation = -0.05f;
    if (keys.IsKeyDown(Keys.Left))
        leftrightRotation = 0.05f;

    Quaternion additionalRotation = ➥
    Quaternion.CreateFromAxisAngle(new Vector3(1, 0, 0), ➥
    updownRotation) * Quaternion.CreateFromAxisAngle(new ➥
    Vector3(0, 1, 0), leftrightRotation);
    cameraRotation = cameraRotation * additionalRotation;

    AddToCameraPosition(new Vector3(0, 0, -1));

    base.Update(gameTime);
}

private void AddToCameraPosition(Vector3 vectorToAdd)
{
    float moveSpeed = 0.05f;
    Vector3 rotatedVector = Vector3.Transform(vectorToAdd, ➥
    cameraRotation);
    cameraPosition += moveSpeed * rotatedVector;
    UpdateViewMatrix();
}

private void UpdateViewMatrix()
{
    Vector3 cameraOriginalTarget = new Vector3(0, 0, -1);
    Vector3 cameraOriginalUpVector = new Vector3(0, 1, 0);
```

```
    Vector3 cameraRotatedTarget = ➥
    Vector3.Transform(cameraOriginalTarget, cameraRotation);
    Vector3 cameraFinalTarget = cameraPosition + cameraRotatedTarget;

    Vector3 cameraRotatedUpVector = ➥
    Vector3.Transform(cameraOriginalUpVector, cameraRotation);

    viewMatrix = Matrix.CreateLookAt(cameraPosition, ➥
    cameraFinalTarget, cameraRotatedUpVector);
}
```

# Extra Reading

## Camera Following an Object

You can use the code presented earlier to create a space game where the camera is positioned inside the cockpit of a spacecraft. However, if you want to position the camera behind the spacecraft, you will need other code, which you can find here.

In this case, the position and rotation you will store correspond to the spacecraft, not to the camera. The position of the camera will be calculated based on the position of the spacecraft. For the spacecraft, you can use the code presented earlier, which will allow the spacecraft to rotate in any arbitrary direction and fly forward. Only now, you want the camera to be positioned a bit behind the spacecraft.

Remember, if you want to define the View matrix of a camera, you need three vectors: the Position of the camera, the Target of the camera, and the Up vector of the camera. You can find more information on this in recipe 2-1.

If you want to position the camera behind the spacecraft, you will want the camera to look at the spacecraft. So, you already know the Target vector for your View matrix: it's the position of the spacecraft. The Up direction of the camera is the same as the Up direction of the spacecraft. This vector can be found by taking the (0,1,0) vector that is the default Up vector and rotating it with the spacecraft rotation.

The last vector that needs to be explained is the Position of the camera. You want the camera to be positioned a bit behind the spacecraft. Since the (0,0,–1) vector is generally taken as the Forward vector, (0,0,1) indicates the Behind vector. First, this vector needs to be rotated with the spacecraft rotation, so this Behind vector actually becomes the Behind vector relative to the spacecraft. Then, you need to add this vector to the position of the spacecraft so the resulting position of the camera will move along when the position of the spacecraft changes.

This is how it's done:

```
protected override void Update(GameTime gameTime)
{
    if (GamePad.GetState(PlayerIndex.One).Buttons.Back == ➥
    ButtonState.Pressed)
        this.Exit();
```

```
    float updownRotation = 0.0f;
    float leftrightRotation = 0.0f;
    KeyboardState keys = Keyboard.GetState();

    if (keys.IsKeyDown(Keys.Up))
        updownRotation = 0.05f;
    if (keys.IsKeyDown(Keys.Down))
        updownRotation = -0.05f;
    if (keys.IsKeyDown(Keys.Right))
        leftrightRotation = -0.05f;
    if (keys.IsKeyDown(Keys.Left))
        leftrightRotation = 0.05f;


    Quaternion additionalRotation = ➥
    Quaternion.CreateFromAxisAngle(new Vector3(1, 0, 0), ➥
    updownRotation) * Quaternion.CreateFromAxisAngle(new ➥
    Vector3(0, 1, 0), leftrightRotation);
    spacecraftRotation = spacecraftRotation * additionalRotation;

    AddToSpacecraftPosition(new Vector3(0, 0, -1));

    base.Update(gameTime);
}

private void AddToSpacecraftPosition(Vector3 vectorToAdd)
{
    float moveSpeed = 0.05f;
    Vector3 rotatedVector = Vector3.Transform(vectorToAdd, spacecraftRotation);
    spacecraftPosition += moveSpeed * rotatedVector;
    UpdateViewMatrix();
}
```

In the UpdateViewMatrix method, the actual camera position is calculated as being behind the spacecraftPosition:

```
private void UpdateViewMatrix()
{
    Vector3 cameraOriginalPosition = new Vector3(0, 0, 1);
    Vector3 cameraRotatedPosition = ➥
    Vector3.Transform(cameraOriginalPosition, spacecraftRotation);
    Vector3 cameraFinalPosition = spacecraftPosition + cameraRotatedPosition;

    Vector3 cameraOriginalUpVector = new Vector3(0, 1, 0);
    Vector3 cameraRotatedUpVector = ➥
    Vector3.Transform(cameraOriginalUpVector, spacecraftRotation);
```

```
    viewMatrix = Matrix.CreateLookAt(cameraFinalPosition, ➡
    spacecraftPosition, cameraRotatedUpVector);
}
```

And in the `Draw` cycle, you need to rotate and translate your spacecraft according to its current rotation and position:

```
Matrix worldMatrix = Matrix.CreateScale(0.001f, 0.001f, ➡
0.001f)*Matrix.CreateFromQuaternion(spacecraftRotation)* ➡
Matrix.CreateTranslation(spacecraftPosition);
spacecraftModel.CopyAbsoluteBoneTransformsTo(modelTransforms);
foreach (ModelMesh mesh in spacecraftModel.Meshes)
{

    foreach (BasicEffect effect in mesh.Effects)
    {
        effect.EnableDefaultLighting();
        effect.World = modelTransforms[mesh.ParentBone.Index] * worldMatrix;
        effect.View = viewMatrix;
        effect.Projection = projectionMatrix;
    }
    mesh.Draw();
}
```

Notice how the World matrix of the `Model` depends on the rotation of the spacecraft stored in the quaternion and depends on the position. You can find more about rendering and positioning an object in 3D space by setting its World matrix in Chapter 4.

# 2-5. Check Whether an Object Is in Sight of the Camera

## The Problem

You want to check whether an object is in sight of the camera to determine whether the object should be drawn.

## The Solution

XNA supports this functionality in the shape of the `BoundingFrustum` class, which corresponds to the volume of the 3D world currently in sight of the camera. You can create one by passing the View and Projection matrices, after which you can easily check whether an object is contained in this `BoundingFrustum` class.

# How It Works

The camera's frustum is the volume that is in sight of the camera and has the shape of a pyramid with its top cut off, as you can see in Figure 2-4. Its shape and boundaries are defined by the viewing angle of the camera and by the near and far clipping planes as defined by the Projection matrix. Its actual location and the orientation of the 3D space are defined by the View matrix. For more information on this, see recipe 2-1.

You should ask XNA to render only the objects that are (partially) contained in this volume; otherwise, they are just wasting the processing power of your graphics card. So, you need a way to detect whether an object is inside this frustum.

The XNA Framework contains the complete functionality to do this in the form of the BoundingFrustum class. You can simply create the BoundingFrustum class of your camera by specifying the View and Projection matrices of your camera:

```
BoundingFrustum cameraFrustum = new BoundingFrustum(viewMatrix * projectionMatrix);
```

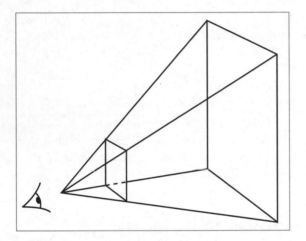

**Figure 2-4.** *Camera's view frustum*

A BoundingFrustum object allows you to use its Contain method (which you can pass a Vector3) and a BoundingSphere or a BoundingBox to test whether it is contained in the camera's frustum. This method will return a ContainmentType object, which can have one of three values:

- Contains: The object tested for is completely contained in the frustum.

- Intersects: The object tested for is partially contained in the frustum, and thus the object intersects the frustum.

- Disjoint: The object tested for is completely outside the frustum.

### Checking Whether a Single Point in 3D Space Is in Sight of the Camera

To check whether a single point in 3D space is in sight of the camera, all you have to do is pass this point to the Contains method:

```
Vector3 pointToTest = new Vector3(0, 0, 0);
BoundingFrustum cameraFrustum = ➡
new BoundingFrustum(fpsCam.ViewMatrix * fpsCam.ProjectionMatrix);
ContainmentType containmentType = cameraFrustum.Contains(pointToTest);

if (containmentType != ContainmentType.Disjoint)
{
    Window.Title = "Point inside frustrum";
    graphics.GraphicsDevice.Clear(Color.CornflowerBlue);
}
else
{
    Window.Title = "Point outside frustrum";
    graphics.GraphicsDevice.Clear(Color.Red);
}
```

Here, you check whether the (0,0,0) point is inside your camera frustum. You print the result to the window title and change the background color accordingly.

## Checking Whether an Object Is in Sight of the Camera

If you want to check whether an object is in sight of the camera, one approach would be to perform the previous check for each vertex of the model. This would of course be very time consuming. A faster way (albeit less precise) would be to define a volume that completely contains this object and then check whether this volume is (at least partially) contained in the view frustum. In this case, you have to do only one simple check to see whether the model is in sight of the camera. The simplest volume you can think of, which would completely contain the object, is a sphere.

XNA already supports complete functionality to create this surrounding volume in the form of the BoundingSphere class. Use the LoadModelWithBoundingSphere method explained in recipe 4-5 to load your Model and have its BoundingSphere stored in its Tag property:

```
myModel = XNAUtils.LoadModelWithBoundingSphere(ref ➡
modelTransforms, "content/tiny", content);
```

---

■**Tip** Because the Tag attribute of a Model can store any kind of data structure, you can use it to store any data belonging to the Model itself, such as the BoundingSphere, textures, and such. Even more, you can define a new struct that can hold all of these and store the struct in the Tag attribute!

---

Now that you have this bounding volume, you can test whether it is inside the view of the camera using this code:

```
BoundingFrustum cameraSight = ➥
new BoundingFrustum(fpsCam.ViewMatrix* fpsCam.ProjectionMatrix);
ContainmentType containmentType = ➥
cameraSight.Contains( (BoundingSphere)myModel.Tag);

if (containmentType != ContainmentType.Disjoint)
{
    Window.Title = "Point inside frustum";
    graphics.GraphicsDevice.Clear(Color.CornflowerBlue);
}
else
{
    Window.Title = "Point outside frustum";
    graphics.GraphicsDevice.Clear(Color.Red);
}
```

### Checking Objects That Have a World Matrix Set

In almost all cases, your Model will not be drawn around the (0,0,0) point but will be rotated, scaled, or moved to someplace else in the 3D world by setting a World matrix. For more information on this, see recipe 4-2. Obviously, the bounding volume around this object needs to be rotated/scaled/moved together with the object so it still fits nicely around the model. This is done by transforming the BoundingSphere by the World matrix of the model:

```
Matrix worldMatrix = Matrix.CreateScale(0.01f, 0.01f, 0.01f) * ➥
Matrix.CreateTranslation(5, 0, 0);
BoundingFrustum cameraSight = ➥
new BoundingFrustum(fpsCam.ViewMatrix * fpsCam.ProjectionMatrix);
BoundingSphere origSphere = (BoundingSphere)myModel.Tag;
BoundingSphere transSphere = origSphere.Transform(worldMatrix);

ContainmentType containmentType = cameraSight.Contains(transSphere);

if (containmentType != ContainmentType.Disjoint)
{
    Window.Title = "Model inside frustum";
    graphics.GraphicsDevice.Clear(Color.CornflowerBlue);

    myModel.CopyAbsoluteBoneTransformsTo(modelTransforms);
    foreach (ModelMesh mesh in myModel.Meshes)
    {
        foreach (BasicEffect effect in mesh.Effects)
```

```
    {
        effect.EnableDefaultLighting();
        effect.World = modelTransforms[mesh.ParentBone.Index] * worldMatrix;
        effect.View = fpsCam.ViewMatrix;
        effect.Projection = fpsCam.ProjectionMatrix;
    }
    mesh.Draw();
}
}
else
{

    Window.Title = "Model outside frustum";
    graphics.GraphicsDevice.Clear(Color.Red);
}
```

---

■**Note**  See Chapter 3 to learn how to render `Models`.

---

The main change here is the line where you call the `origSphere.Transform` method. This method gives you the same `BoundingSphere` but transformed with the World matrix. In this case, `transSphere` will be 100 times smaller than `origSphere`, and its center will be moved 5 units along the x-axis.

Only if the resulting sphere collides with the camera frustum will you render the `Model`.

## The Code

*All the code is available for download at* `www.apress.com`.

The following code will render a model at a certain point in 3D space, only if it is in sight of the camera:

```
protected override void LoadContent()
{
    device = graphics.GraphicsDevice;
    basicEffect = new BasicEffect(device, null);
    cCross = new CoordCross(device);

    myModel = XNAUtils.LoadModelWithBoundingSphere(ref ➥
    modelTransforms, "content/tiny", content);
}
```

```
protected override void Draw(GameTime gameTime)
{
    Matrix worldMatrix = Matrix.CreateScale(0.01f,0.01f,0.01f)* ➥
    Matrix.CreateTranslation(5, 0, 0);
    BoundingFrustum cameraSight = new ➥
    BoundingFrustum(fpsCam.ViewMatrix * fpsCam.ProjectionMatrix);
    BoundingSphere origSphere = (BoundingSphere)myModel.Tag;
    BoundingSphere transSphere = origSphere.Transform(worldMatrix);

    ContainmentType containmentType = cameraSight.Contains(transSphere);

    if (containmentType != ContainmentType.Disjoint)
    {
        Window.Title = "Model inside frustum";
        graphics.GraphicsDevice.Clear(Color.CornflowerBlue);

        //draw model
        myModel.CopyAbsoluteBoneTransformsTo(modelTransforms);
        foreach (ModelMesh mesh in myModel.Meshes)
        {
            foreach (BasicEffect effect in mesh.Effects)
            {
                effect.EnableDefaultLighting();
                effect.World = modelTransforms[mesh.ParentBone.Index] * ➥
                worldMatrix;
                effect.View = fpsCam.ViewMatrix;
                effect.Projection = fpsCam.ProjectionMatrix;
            }
            mesh.Draw();
        }
    }

    else
    {
        Window.Title = "Model outside frustum";
        graphics.GraphicsDevice.Clear(Color.Red);
    }

    //draw coordcross
    cCross.Draw(fpsCam.ViewMatrix, fpsCam.ProjectionMatrix);

    base.Draw(gameTime);
}
```

## Extra Reading

This recipe presented a useful way to check whether points or objects are in sight of the camera. However, when you have a larger scene containing plenty of objects, your application can become very slow if you need to perform this test for every single object in your scene. In recipe 2-9, a more robust solution is presented that can handle more complex scenes.

# 2-6. Detect Camera Collision Against Models, Walls, or Terrains

## The Problem

You want to detect when the camera is close to solid objects to prevent it from entering an object.

## The Solution

To predict a collision between the camera and a model, you can represent the camera as a BoundingSphere, of which you can use the Contains method to check whether it collides with a BoundingSphere or BoundingBox of the model. For user-defined grids, such as a wall or terrain, you have to find the exact 3D coordinate at any position of a triangle of that wall or terrain.

## How It Works

The problem of camera collision can be separated into camera collision with a Model or with a triangle grid of which the height of each vertex is known.

### Camera-Model Collision

For this case, you will represent your camera as a sphere, which you don't want to collide with the model. This allows you to set the minimum distance between the model and the camera simply by adjusting the radius of the sphere.

To detect collision between the camera sphere and the model, you will also need a sphere or box that surrounds this model. Such a sphere can be calculated by the LoadModelWithBoundingSphere method, which is described in recipe 4-5 and stores this sphere in the Tag property of the Model. This Tag property can store any kind of object inside the Model object and is thus perfectly suited for storing something like the Model's BoundingSphere. Load your Model like this in your LoadContent method:

```
myModel = XNAUtils.LoadModelWithBoundingSphere(ref ➡
modelTransforms, "tiny", content);
```

You will want to test for a collision whenever you move your camera or the model. If you detected a collision, you will want to undo the last change to your camera by resetting its position to the previous value. In your Update method, make sure you save this previous value:

```
protected override void Update(GameTime gameTime)
{
    GamePadState gamePadState = GamePad.GetState(PlayerIndex.One);
    if (gamePadState.Buttons.Back == ButtonState.Pressed)
        this.Exit();

    MouseState mouseState = Mouse.GetState();
    KeyboardState keyState = Keyboard.GetState();

    Vector3 lastCamPos = fpsCam.Position;
    fpsCam.Update(mouseState, keyState, gamePadState);

    base.Update(gameTime);
}
```

After updating the camera, you should construct a sphere around the new position of the camera. This is how you create a sphere around your camera that will keep the minimum distance to 1.0 unit:

```
float minimumDistance = 1.0f;
BoundingSphere cameraSphere = new BoundingSphere(fpsCam.Position, minimumDistance);
```

Now that you have both the updated camera sphere and the sphere around your Model, you can test whether both spheres intersect. If they do intersect, reset the camera to its previous position:

```
BoundingSphere origModelSphere = (BoundingSphere)myModel.Tag;
BoundingSphere transModelSphere = ➥
XNAUtils.TransformBoundingSphere (origModelSphere, worldMatrix);

if (cameraSphere.Contains(transModelSphere) != ➥
ContainmentType.Disjoint)
    fpsCam.Position = lastCamPos;
```

If the Model has a World matrix that moves it to another location in space or scales it, you should also move and/or scale the surrounding sphere. You do this using the TransformBoundingSphere.

The remainder of the code will test whether the camera is not closer than 1.0 unit to the bounding sphere around the model.

## Camera-Terrain Collision

If you want to detect whether your camera is close to a grid of vertices you defined yourself, such as a terrain, you have to do some kind of triangle collision detection. The approach described in this chapter works if the horizontal and vertical coordinates of the vertices of the grid are all equidistant.

If the height of each vertex is stored in the Y coordinate, this means the distance between the X and Z coordinates of all vertices is the same. Because of this, for each position of the camera, you'll know exactly above which quad the camera is positioned. For example, if the position of the camera is (10.3f,8.7f,5.1f), you know the camera is somewhere above the quad defined by the vertices (10, . . . ,5), (11, . . . ,5), (10, . . . ,6), and (11, . . . ,6). The three dots indicate the height of these vertices, which you defined when creating the grid. You will have them stored in a separate array, or you should be able to access them from a vertex buffer (which is less preferred, performancewise, since the data would need to be transferred back from your graphics card).

However, what you want to know is the height difference between your camera and the terrain beneath the camera. The simplest solution would be to clamp the camera's position to the nearest vertex and check whether the camera is above the height of the terrain at that vertex. If the camera is below the terrain, adjust its height accordingly:

```
protected override void Update(GameTime gameTime)
{
    GamePadState gamePadState = GamePad.GetState(PlayerIndex.One);
    if (gamePadState.Buttons.Back == ButtonState.Pressed)
        this.Exit();

    MouseState mouseState = Mouse.GetState();
    KeyboardState keyState = Keyboard.GetState();

    fpsCam.Update(mouseState, keyState, gamePadState);

    float treshold = 3.0f;
    float terrainHeight = ➥
    terrain.GetClippedHeightAt(fpsCam.Position.X, -fpsCam.Position.Z);
    if (fpsCam.Position.Y < terrainHeight + treshold)
    {
        Vector3 newPos = fpsCam.Position;
        newPos.Y = terrainHeight + treshold;
        fpsCam.Position = newPos;
    }

    base.Update(gameTime);
}
```

The GetClippedHeightAt method returns the height at the vertex of a Terrain object. To learn about the GetClippedHeightAt method, read recipe 5-9. You can set the lower bound of the height difference between your camera and the terrain by changing the threshold value. The code will make sure the height of your camera is always adjusted so there is a height difference of threshold between your camera and your terrain.

■**Note** The GetClippedHeightAt method expects a positive value for both arguments, because they are used as indices to look up values from a matrix. Because the Forward direction is along the negative z-axis, you want to negate the Z component of the position to make it positive.

As the height is retrieved from a neighboring vertex, this code will cause your camera to hop each time you cross a triangle, because the GetClippedHeightAt method will return a different value. To make sure the transitions are smooth, you may want to use the GetExactHeightAt method of the Terrain object, as explained in recipe 5-9. This method will give the height of the point exactly below the camera for any point on your terrain:

```
float terrainHeight = terrain.GetExactHeightAt(fpsCam.Position.X, ➥
-fpsCam.Position.Z);
```

You will appreciate this enhancement whenever your camera or Model is moving slowly over the terrain.

### Camera-Wall Collision

A wall in general consists of only two triangles, so this is a simplified case of the camera-terrain collision. You can use the same approach used in the GetExactHeightAt method described in recipe 5-9 to find the exact 3D point of the wall in front of the camera.

## The Code

*All the code is available for download at* www.apress.com.

The Update method has been listed completely in the previous text.

# 2-7. Create a Camera Fly-by Action

## The Problem

You want to move your camera smoothly from one position to another in the 3D world. Of course, you also want the target of the camera to transition smoothly during the process.

In detail, you want a mechanism that moves your camera in a smooth curve from a starting position and target to a destination position and target. This movement should start and end smoothly. After this process, you want to be able to pick up your camera for regular use and use it as a first-person camera without any glitches.

## The Solution

This process will require a time variable, which will be 0 when the camera is at its starting position and 1 when the camera has reached its destination position.

By specifying a third position where you want the camera to be in the middle of the operation, you can define a Bezier curve. A Bezier curve is a smooth curve that passes through the beginning and ending positions and gets attracted very closely to any additional points specified in between, such as this third position. By giving such a Bezier curve the current value of a time variable between 0 and 1, the Bezier curve will return the position on the curve at the time specified.

The position of the target will be linearly interpolated between the start and destination targets. As a result, the camera will move on a curve from the start position to the destination position, while at the same time, its target moves over the line that connects the start target and the final target.

To use the code of the first-person camera, you cannot simply change the position and target of the camera, because it calculates the target based on the position of the target and the rotation around the Up and Right axes. So, you will also adjust the rotation values of your camera.

After you have everything working, the smooth starting and ending of the process will be obtained by using the `MathHelper.SmoothStep` method.

---

**Note** You can use the `Curve` class included in the XNA Framework to script complex camera paths, but it is not yet mature enough (or overly complex, if you will) to be used for a camera fly-by, because it misses some trivial functionality. For example, the class does not support 3D points, and it wants you to manually set the tangent vectors in each of the key points of the `Curve` class. Anyway, the only part of this recipe that can be replaced by the `Curve` functionality is the Bezier method. The other 90 percent of this recipe is also useful if you want to use the `Curve` functionality of the XNA Framework instead of this Bezier approach.

---

## How It Works

For a Bezier camera fly-by, you need to keep track of these variables:

```
float bezTime = 1.0f;
Vector3 bezStartPosition;
Vector3 bezMidPosition;
Vector3 bezEndPosition;
Vector3 bezStartTarget;
Vector3 bezEndTarget;
```

The `bezTime` variable holds the process of your fly-by. When starting a fly-by action, you set this to 0. While running, you increment it during your update phase until it reaches 1. A value larger than 1 means that the fly-by has finished.

During your fly-by action, you need to keep track of some positions, such as the starting and ending positions and targets, but you also need to calculate a midpoint in order to get a smooth curve. All of these will be specified at the start of the fly-by action.

In the following code, you can find the method that triggers a fly-by action. All it needs are the beginning and final camera positions and targets:

```
private void InitBezier(Vector3 startPosition, Vector3 startTarget, ➡
 Vector3 endPosition, Vector3 endTarget)
{
    bezStartPosition = startPosition;
    bezEndPosition = endPosition;
```

```
    bezMidPosition = (bezStartPosition + bezEndPosition) / 2.0f;
    Vector3 midShiftDirecton = new Vector3(1, 1, 0)*2;

    Vector3 cameraDirection = endPosition - startPosition;
    Vector3 perpDirection = Vector3.Cross(upV, cameraDirection);
    perpDirection.Normalize();

    Vector3 midShiftDirecton = new Vector3(0, 1, 0) + perpDirection;
    bezMidPosition += cameraDirection.Length() * midShiftDirecton;

    bezStartTarget = startTarget;
    bezEndTarget = endTarget;

    bezTime = 0.0f;
}
```

All the startPosition, endPosition, startTarget, and endTarget arguments can immediately be stored in their corresponding global variables.

The midPosition, which is an extra position you will insert between the starting and ending positions to bend the curve, needs to be calculated. You can do this by first calculating the position exactly in the middle of the starting and ending positions and then taking the mean of these two positions. To deviate the curve a bit to the side, you will shift this position away from the straight line between the start and final camera positions by adding a direction perpendicular to that line.

You can find the direction perpendicular to two directions by taking the cross product of these two directions. In this case, you want the direction perpendicular to the straight camera direction, as well as the Up vector. You first calculate the straight camera direction, which you do as you would find any other direction: by taking the final position and subtracting the original position. Then you take the cross product of this direction and the Up direction, and you find the direction perpendicular to both directions.

If you moved the midpoint into this direction, you would get a nice curve if the starting and ending points are close to each other. But if the distance between them is large, your curve would be very flat. You can solve this by multiplying this amount of shifting by the distance between the starting and ending positions. This distance is found by taking the length of the vector between the ending and starting points.

Finally, you set the bezTime variable to 0, indicating the fly-by has started.

Once your fly-by has been initialized, you should update it every frame by calling the UpdateBezier method:

```
private void UpdateBezier()
{
    bezTime += 0.01f;
    if (bezTime > 1.0f)
        return;
```

```
Vector3 newCamPos = Bezier(bezStartPosition, ➡
bezMidPosition,  bezEndPosition, bezTime);
Vector3 newCamTarget = Vector3.Lerp(bezStartTarget, bezEndTarget, bezTime);

float updownRot;
float leftrightRot;
AnglesFromDirection(newCamTarget - newCamPos, out updownRot, out leftrightRot);

fpsCam.UpDownRot = updownRot;
fpsCam.LeftRightRot = leftrightRot;
fpsCam.Position = newCamPos;
}
```

This method starts by incrementing the progress counter slightly. If the value is larger than 1, you know the fly-by has finished and the method returns.

Otherwise, the next lines, which contain the remainder of this recipe, are executed. First, the next position of your camera is obtained from the Bezier curve by passing the bezTime variable, which indicates how far you are in the fly-by action. Next, you find the current target by interpolating between the startTarget and finalTarget positions. You can find more information on linear interpolation in recipe 5-9.

If you want to use this together with your first-person camera code, you will need to calculate the resulting updownRot and leftrightRot values, which is done by calling the AnglesFromDirection method. This method takes in three arguments: the direction the camera will be facing (if you subtract the camera position from the target position, you obtain the viewing direction) and the two angles you want to know. By passing them as an "out" argument, the method will change the values, and the values will be stored into the variables of this method. Finally, you update your camera with the new position and rotation.

## Bezier Curve

The first line calls the Bezier method, which has to return the position on the curve, based on the bezTime variable, which will always contain a value between 0 and 1. The function needs the three points that define the curve, but you have already calculated these in the InitBezier method.

For a Bezier curve, defined on three points, you can find the position at any given time t using this function:

$$P(t) = P_{start} * (1 - t)^2 + 2 * P_{mid} * (1 - t) * t + P_{final} * t^2$$

This, of course, looks incredibly difficult, but in fact it's not. Let's see what this would give in the beginning, at t = 0. You would get $P(0) = P_{start} * 1^2 + 2 * P_{mid} * 1 * 0 + P_{final} * 0^2$, which is simply $P_{start}$! At the end of the fly-by action, when t = 1, you get $P(1) = P_{start} * 0^2 + 2 * P_{mid} * 0 * 1 + P_{final} * 1^2$, which is $P_{final}$, as it should be. For all values of t between 0 and 1, the resulting position will be somewhere between the starting and ending points, while the second term somewhat pulls the point toward the midpoint.

In this case, t will be the value of bezTime. The following method calculates the previous formula:

```
private Vector3 Bezier(Vector3 startPoint, Vector3 midPoint, ➥
Vector3 endPoint, float time)
{
    float invTime = 1.0f - time;
    float timePow = (float)Math.Pow(time, 2);
    float invTimePow = (float)Math.Pow(invTime, 2);

    Vector3 result = startPoint * invTimePow;
    result += 2 * midPoint * time * invTime;
    result += endPoint * timePow;

    return result;
}
```

The invTime is nothing more than the $(1 - t)$ term in the formula, so the invTimePow is the $(1 - t)^2$ term. The result variable yields the final outcome of the formula, and this position is returned to the calling code.

### Finding the Rotation

When you take another look at the last lines of code of the UpdateBezier method, you see that the next position of the camera is calculated using the Bezier method and the next target using simple linear interpolation (see recipe 5-9).

This would do for the simplest fly-by action, because you can immediately create a View matrix from this position and target (see recipe 2-1). But after the fly-by has finished, you want to be able to pick up camera movement right where the fly-by left the camera. The position is automatically stored, but the rotation variables are not. So if you take the camera and target position you just calculated and find the corresponding leftrightRotation and updownRotation, you can store these so they are immediately useful for your first-person camera code. Moreover, this will allow the first-person camera to pick up the camera where the fly-by left it, without producing a single glitch.

This is exactly what is done by the AnglesFromDirection method. It takes as an argument the direction a camera is facing and calculates the updownRot and leftrightRot values. Both values are passed to the method as an "out" argument, which means the changes will be passed back to the calling code, so the changes the method makes to these changes are stored in the variables of the calling method.

```
private void AnglesFromDirection(Vector3 direction, ➥
out float updownAngle, out float leftrightAngle)
{
    Vector3 floorProjection = new Vector3(direction.X, 0, direction.Z);
    float directionLength = floorProjection.Length();
    updownAngle = (float)Math.Atan2(direction.Y, directionLength);
    leftrightAngle = -(float)Math.Atan2(direction.X, -direction.Z);
}
```

Recipe 4-17 explains in detail how to find the rotation angle corresponding to a direction. In this case, you have to find two angles, because the direction is in 3D. Start by finding the leftrightRot angle. Figure 2-5 shows the XZ plane containing the camera and the target. The diagonal line is the direction the camera is facing, and the X and Z lines are simply the X and Z components of that vector. In a triangle with a 90-degree angle, if you want to find the angle of a corner, all you need to do is take the arctangent of the side opposite the corner, divided by the shortest side next to the corner. In this case, this comes down to X divided by Z. The Atan2 function allows you to specify both values instead of their division, because this removes an ambiguity. This is how you find the leftrightRot angle.

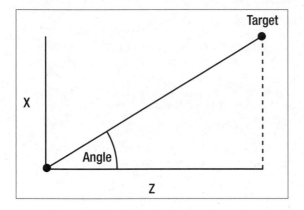

**Figure 2-5.** *Finding the leftrightRot angle*

To find the updownAngle, you can use Figure 2-6. Here, the dashed line shows the direction the camera is looking. You want to find the angle between the Up Y component and the projection of the direction on the XZ floor plane. So, you pass these to the Atan2 method, and you receive the updownAngle.

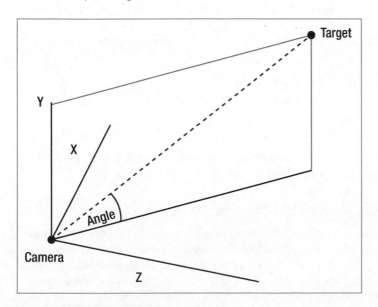

**Figure 2-6.** *Finding the updownAngle*

## Usage

Make sure you call your `UpdateBezier` method from your `Update` method:

```
UpdateBezier();
```

Now, all you have to do to start a fly-by is call the `InitBezier` method!

```
if (bezTime > 1.0f)
    InitBezier(new Vector3(0,10,0), new Vector3(0,0,0), ➥
    new Vector3(0, 0, -20), new Vector3(0, 0, -10));
```

When you want to integrate your fly-by with your user camera, you can start from your camera's position and target easily:

```
if (bezTime > 1.0f)
    InitBezier(fpsCam.Position, fpsCam.Position + fpsCam.Forward * ➥
    10.0f, new Vector3(0, 0, -20), new Vector3(0, 0, -10));
```

You can see I have placed the starting target 10 units in front of the starting position. This will often give a smoother result, because otherwise the camera would have to make a sharp turn when tracking the target.

## Smooth Start and Acceleration

By constantly increasing the `bezTime` from 0 to 1 by a fixed amount, the speed at which the camera moves over the Bezier curve is a constant. This will result in a rather uncomfortable starting and ending. What you really want is to have the `bezTime` first rise slowly from 0 to 0.2 and then rise pretty fast to 0.8, while slowing down again during the last part between 0.8 and 1. This is exactly what `MathHelper.SmoothStep` does: you give it a constantly increasing value between 0 and 1, and it will return a value between 0 and 1 that has a smooth starting and ending!

The only place where you need this is in the `UpdateBezier` method, so replace the middle two lines with this code:

```
float smoothValue = MathHelper.SmoothStep(0, 1, bezTime);
Vector3 newCamPos = Bezier(bezStartPosition, bezMidPosition, ➥
bezEndPosition, smoothValue);
Vector3 newCamTarget = Vector3.Lerp(bezStartTarget, bezEndTarget, smoothValue);
```

The `smoothValue` variable will hold this smoothed value between 0 and 1, which will be passed to the methods, instead of the constantly increasing `bezTime` variable.

## Solving Incorrect/Fast Camera Rotation at the End of the Fly-by

This part of the recipe addresses a problem that can occur in some cases. One of such cases is shown in the left part of Figure 2-7, where the path of the camera position and the curve of the target are shown from above. In the beginning, the camera will be looking to the left, until both curves cross. At this point, the camera will suddenly be switched, so it is looking to the right! You can correct this situation by simply shifting the midpoint of the curve to the left, instead of to the right. This way, you get a curve as shown in the right part, where the starting camera will start by looking to the right and doesn't have to be switched to the left.

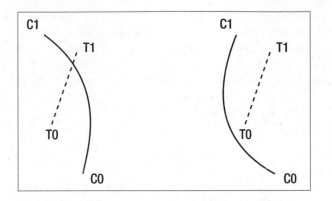

**Figure 2-7.** *Incorrect and correct choices of the fly-by curve*

So, how can you know which side you have to move the midpoint to? Refer to the upper-left and upper-right images of Figure 2-8, which show two cases that can cause trouble. The dashed line shows the path of the target, and the solid line indicates the straight path of the camera.

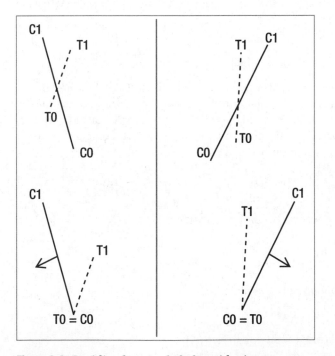

**Figure 2-8.** *Deciding how to shift the midpoint*

In these two cases, the midpoint should be shifted to another direction. This can be detected by taking the cross product between the two directions. In both cases, it will result in a vector perpendicular to the plane; however, in one case, it will point up, and in the other case, it will point down. Let's suppose it is pointing upward and call it the upVector. Next, if you take a cross product of this upVector and the camera direction, you will get a vector that is perpendicular to the camera direction and the upVector. The direction of this final vector will depend on whether the upVector is pointing upward or downward, which again depends on the way the position and target paths cross each other. Since it is perpendicular to the position path and the upVector, it can immediately be used to shift the midpoint.

So, use this code to find the correct midpoint for your curve, in the InitBezier method:

```
bezMidPosition = (bezStartPosition + bezEndPosition) / 2.0f;
Vector3 cameraDirection = endPosition - startPosition;
Vector3 targDirection = endTarget - startTarget;
Vector3 upVector = Vector3.Cross(new Vector3(targDirection.X, ➥
0, targDirection.Z), new Vector3(cameraDirection.X, 0, ➥
cameraDirection.Z));
Vector3 perpDirection = Vector3.Cross(upVector, cameraDirection);
perpDirection.Normalize();
```

The upVector is found by taking the cross product of the position path and the target path, both projected in the XZ plane by setting the Y component to 0 (this way, you get the same lines as shown in the images!). You find the direction perpendicular to this upVector and the position path by taking the cross product of them.

When you've found this perpendicular direction, you can shift your midpoint into that direction, like you've done earlier:

```
Vector3 midShiftDirecton = new Vector3(0, 1, 0) + perpDirection;
bezMidPosition += cameraDirection.Length() * midShiftDirecton;
```

That's it. There is, however, a case when this will not work. If the targDirection and the cameraDirection are parallel to each other, or the upVector and the cameraDirection are parallel to each other, the cross method will fail, resulting in the perpDirection variable being (0,0,0), which will cause an error when you normalize this vector. So, you will detect this case and take care of the problem by setting an arbitrary value:

```
if (perpDirection == new Vector3())
    perpDirection = new Vector3(0, 1, 0);
```

Put this code before the line that normalizes the perpDirection.

## The Code

*All the code is available for download at www.apress.com.*

This method initiates your variables to start a new fly-by action:

```
private void InitBezier(Vector3 startPosition, ➥
Vector3 startTarget, Vector3 endPosition, Vector3 endTarget)
{
    bezStartPosition = startPosition;
    bezEndPosition = endPosition;
```

```
    bezMidPosition = (bezStartPosition + bezEndPosition) / 2.0f;
    Vector3 cameraDirection = endPosition - startPosition;
    Vector3 targDirection = endTarget - startTarget;
    Vector3 upVector = Vector3.Cross(new Vector3(targDirection.X, 0, ➥
    targDirection.Z), new Vector3(cameraDirection.X, 0, ➥
    cameraDirection.Z));
    Vector3 perpDirection = Vector3.Cross(upVector, cameraDirection);

    if (perpDirection == new Vector3())
        perpDirection = new Vector3(0, 1, 0);
    perpDirection.Normalize();

    Vector3 midShiftDirecton = new Vector3(0, 1, 0) + perpDirection;
    bezMidPosition += cameraDirection.Length() * midShiftDirecton;

    bezStartTarget = startTarget;
    bezEndTarget = endTarget;

    bezTime = 0.0f;
}
```

While running, the `UpdateBezier` should be called each frame to calculate the new position and rotation of your camera:

```
private void UpdateBezier()
{
    bezTime += 0.01f;
    if (bezTime > 1.0f)
        return;

    float smoothValue = MathHelper.SmoothStep(0, 1, bezTime);
    Vector3 newCamPos = Bezier(bezStartPosition, bezMidPosition, ➥
    bezEndPosition, smoothValue);
    Vector3 newCamTarget = Vector3.Lerp(bezStartTarget, bezEndTarget, smoothValue);

    float updownRot;
    float leftrightRot;
    AnglesFromDirection(newCamTarget - newCamPos, out updownRot, out leftrightRot);

    fpsCam.UpDownRot = updownRot;
    fpsCam.LeftRightRot = leftrightRot;
    fpsCam.Position = newCamPos;
}
```

The position is calculated by the Bezier method:

```
private Vector3 Bezier(Vector3 startPoint, Vector3 midPoint, ➥
Vector3 endPoint, float time)
{
    float invTime = 1.0f - time;
    float timePow = (float)Math.Pow(time, 2);
    float invTimePow = (float)Math.Pow(invTime, 2);


    Vector3 result = startPoint * invTimePow;
    result += 2 * midPoint * time * invTime;
    result += endPoint * timePow;

    return result;
}
```

And the rotation is found by this method:

```
private Vector3 Bezier(Vector3 startPoint, Vector3 midPoint, ➥
Vector3 endPoint, float time)
{
    float invTime = 1.0f - time;
    float timePow = (float)Math.Pow(time, 2);
    float invTimePow = (float)Math.Pow(invTime, 2);

    Vector3 result = startPoint * invTimePow;
    result += 2 * midPoint * time * invTime;
    result += endPoint * timePow;

    return result;
}
```

# 2-8. Remove the Solid Background Color: Skybox

## The Problem

You want to add background scenery to your scene so you will no longer see any of the solid color you're clearing your window to at the beginning of each frame.

## The Solution

Instead of having to fill each part of your scene with objects, you can simply draw a large cube, decorate the inside of the cube with textures of a landscape or room interior, and put your camera inside this cube.

# How It Works

You can load a skybox into your scene in several ways. The simplest way is to import one from a Model file, together with its textures and optional effects. If you want full control of what's going on, you can also define the cube yourself. I'll also show an HLSL example on how this can be done via one single TextureCube, demonstrating the use of the texCUBE HLSL intrinsic function.

These two techniques are used in both cases:

- The cube must always be drawn around the camera, and the camera must always remain exactly in the center of the skybox. This way, when the user moves the camera, the distance between the camera and the cube will remain the same, which gives the impression that it's infinitely far away.

- You should disable writing to the z-buffer while rendering the skybox so you don't have to scale your skybox to fit around your scene. Make sure you enable writing to the z-buffer again after rendering the skybox, though.

## Loading a Skybox from a File

A quick fix would be to simply import your skybox from a model file. You can use the sample that comes with the DirectX SDK for this. It includes an .x file, together with its six textures. Copy it to your project map, and import the .x file into your project. Finally, add the skyboxModel and skyboxTransforms variables to your project:

```
Model skyboxModel;
Matrix[] skyboxTransforms;
```

And load the model as explained in recipe 4-1 in your LoadContents method:

```
skyboxModel = content.Load<Model>("skybox");
skyboxTransforms = new Matrix[skyboxModel.Bones.Count];
```

All you have to do now is render the skybox as if it were a normal Model (see recipe 4-1):

```
skyboxModel.CopyAbsoluteBoneTransformsTo(skyboxTransforms);
foreach (ModelMesh mesh in skyboxModel.Meshes)
{
    foreach (BasicEffect effect in mesh.Effects)
    {
        effect.World = skyboxTransforms[mesh.ParentBone.Index];
        effect.View = fpsCam.ViewMatrix;
        effect.Projection = fpsCam.ProjectionMatrix;
    }
    mesh.Draw();
}
```

This will simply render the skybox into your scene as a big box. However, when you move your camera around, you will get closer to the box, you will zoom into the textures, and you will feel that the illusion of a sky far away from the camera is completely fake. To solve this, the skybox must seem to be infinitely far away from the camera so that when the camera is moved, the textures of the skybox don't grow any larger.

This can be obtained by making sure the camera always remains in the center of the skybox. In other words, you always need to make sure the camera remains in the center of the skybox by moving your skybox to the position of your camera and setting a World matrix (see recipe 4-2), like this:

```
effect.World = skyboxTransforms[mesh.ParentBone.Index] * ➡
Matrix.CreateTranslation(fpsCam.Position);
```

Now, when you run this code, the landscape of the skybox will seem to stay at the same position regardless of where you move your camera, which gives the impression that it is infinitely far away.

The next problem you'll probably encounter is that you can clearly see the edges of the cube. This is because of the way XNA samples textures near their edges. By setting the texture addressing mode to Clamp (see recipe 5-2 for more information on textures and their addressing modes), you make sure the edges near the border of the texture are clamped to the color of the border pixel:

```
device.SamplerStates[0].AddressU = TextureAddressMode.Clamp;
device.SamplerStates[0].AddressV = TextureAddressMode.Clamp;
```

Running this should give a much smoother result at the edges of the cube.

## Drawing Other Objects in the Scene

Without any objects inside the cube, your scene does not look too nice. When you load other objects into the scene, you have to consider something else: the size of the skybox. How can you make your skybox large enough so it contains all your objects but still have it be inside a reasonable distance so it will not be clipped away by the Projection matrix?

In this case, size really doesn't matter. You will draw the skybox at any size you want, just before anything else and while making sure XNA doesn't write to the depth buffer. This way, anything else you render later will be rendered to the scene as if the skybox weren't even there.

This is how it works: whether you draw a box with lowest point (–1,–1,–1) and highest point (1,1,1) or with points (–100,–100,–100) and (100,100,100), they will both look the same if you put the camera in the middle. So, you're safe to simply draw the skybox at the size it comes in the model file. But if the box is small, it will hide all your objects behind it, right? That's why you are going to disable writing to the depth buffer while rendering the skybox. This way, after drawing the skybox as the first object, the depth buffer will still be empty! So, all objects drawn later will be rendered, not knowing the skybox has already been drawn, and the pixels corresponding to the object will get the color of the objects. For more information on the z-buffer, see the last paragraph of recipe 2-1.

So, you need to add this extra line before drawing the skybox:

```
device.RenderState.DepthBufferWriteEnable = false;
```

Make sure you turn the z-buffer back on after you've drawn the skybox, or your whole scene will be mixed up:

```
device.RenderState.DepthBufferWriteEnable = true;
```

## Manually Defining a Skybox

Loading a skybox from a file doesn't give you full control over all its aspects. For example, the skybox loaded earlier in this chapter uses six different textures, which causes the model to be split up into six different meshes, all of which require a different call to `DrawPrimitives` just to draw two triangles. If there's one thing that slows down an XNA application, it's a lot of `DrawPrimitives` calls that each render a small amount of triangles (see recipe 3-4 and recipe 3-11 in Chapter 3).

Although six calls extra probably won't make a huge difference, since you will now define the vertices of the skybox yourself, you will make sure the whole skybox uses only one texture so the whole skybox can be drawn in one `DrawPrimitives` call. Instead of using a `Texture2D` to store such a texture, you will use a `TextureCube`. This simply is a 2D image, composed of the six images of the walls of the skybox, and it looks like Figure 2-9.

**Figure 2-9.** *Six sides of a skybox combined into one image*

Add variables to hold `TextureCube`, `Effect`, and `VertexBuffer` to your project:

```
VertexBuffer skyboxVertexBuffer;
TextureCube skyboxTexture;
Effect skyboxEffect;
```

And fill the effect and texture in the LoadContent method:

```
effect = content.Load<Effect>("skyboxsample");
skyboxTexture = content.Load<TextureCube>("skyboxtexture");
```

You will create the skyboxsample effect file at the end of this recipe.

---

**Tip** You can create your own TextureCube images using the DirectX Texture tool that comes with the DirectX SDK. After installing the SDK, you should find a shortcut to this utility in your Start menu. You can simply select File ➤ New and then choose Cubemap Texture. Next, you can select which of the six sides is displayed by selecting the side from the View ➤ Cube Map Face menu. Alternatively, you can define the contents of the sides during runtime. For more information on this, see recipe 3-7.

---

By defining each vertex manually, it is possible to draw a skybox using a single DrawPrimitives call. Of course, the vertices need to contain Position data, and because you'll want the triangles to be covered with the skybox texture, you want to add texture coordinate information to the vertices. However, you'll be using the texCUBE HLSL intrinsic function to sample the color data from TextureCube, and it doesn't need any texture coordinate data. You'll learn more details about the texCUBE intrinsic later in this recipe.

The XNA Framework, however, does not come with a vertex format that can store only a position. You could of course simply use a more complex vertex format, such as the VertexPositionColor struct, and leave the color data empty. This will, however, still cause this color data to be sent to your graphics card, which simply wastes some bandwidth. To keep things clean, you'll create the simplest vertex format possible, one that holds only positional data. See recipe 5-12 for how to define your own vertex formats:

```
public struct VertexPosition
{
    public Vector3 Position;
    public VertexPosition(Vector3 position)
    {
        this.Position = position;
    }
    public static readonly VertexElement[] VertexElements =
    {
        new VertexElement( 0, 0, VertexElementFormat.Vector3, ➥
        VertexElementMethod.Default, ➥
        VertexElementUsage.Position, 0 )
    };

    public static readonly int SizeInBytes = sizeof(float) * 3;
}
```

This struct defines a custom vertex format, capable of storing only one Vector3 that will hold the Position data. When defining the vertices of the skybox, it is necessary to take the winding order of the triangles into account, or some faces will be culled away. To learn more about culling, see recipe 5-6. When the camera is inside the skybox, none of the faces should be culled away, so all triangles must be wound in clockwise order, as seen by the camera inside the box. To make things easier, I have given the eight corner points of the cube a name, relative to the camera in the center of the cube:

```
Vector3 forwardBottomLeft = new Vector3(-1, -1, -1);
Vector3 forwardBottomRight = new Vector3(1, -1, -1);
Vector3 forwardUpperLeft = new Vector3(-1, 1, -1);
Vector3 forwardUpperRight = new Vector3(1, 1, -1);

Vector3 backBottomLeft = new Vector3(-1, -1, 1);
Vector3 backBottomRight = new Vector3(1, -1, 1);
Vector3 backUpperLeft = new Vector3(-1, 1, 1);
Vector3 backUpperRight = new Vector3(1, 1, 1);
```

Next, you'll actually define the triangles, using the Vector3s defined earlier. The cube has six faces, which are defined by two triangles each, so you'll need to define 6*2*3 = 36 vertices. After defining all vertices, you send them to the memory on the graphics card by putting them in a VertexBuffer, as described in recipe 5-4:

```
VertexPosition[] vertices = new VertexPosition[36];
int i = 0;

//face in front of the camera
vertices[i++] = new VertexPosition(forwardBottomLeft);
vertices[i++] = new VertexPosition(forwardUpperLeft);
vertices[i++] = new VertexPosition(forwardUpperRight);

vertices[i++] = new VertexPosition(forwardBottomLeft);
vertices[i++] = new VertexPosition(forwardUpperRight);
vertices[i++] = new VertexPosition(forwardBottomRight);

//face to the right of the camera
vertices[i++] = new VertexPosition(forwardBottomRight);
vertices[i++] = new VertexPosition(forwardUpperRight);
vertices[i++] = new VertexPosition(backUpperRight);

vertices[i++] = new VertexPosition(forwardBottomRight);
vertices[i++] = new VertexPosition(backUpperRight);
vertices[i++] = new VertexPosition(backBottomRight);

//face behind the camera
vertices[i++] = new VertexPosition(backBottomLeft);
vertices[i++] = new VertexPosition(backUpperRight);
vertices[i++] = new VertexPosition(backUpperLeft);
```

```
vertices[i++] = new VertexPosition(backBottomLeft);
vertices[i++] = new VertexPosition(backBottomRight);
vertices[i++] = new VertexPosition(backUpperRight);

//face to the left of the camera
vertices[i++] = new VertexPosition(backBottomLeft);
vertices[i++] = new VertexPosition(backUpperLeft);
vertices[i++] = new VertexPosition(forwardUpperLeft);

vertices[i++] = new VertexPosition(backBottomLeft);
vertices[i++] = new VertexPosition(forwardUpperLeft);
vertices[i++] = new VertexPosition(forwardBottomLeft);

//face above the camera
vertices[i++] = new VertexPosition(forwardUpperLeft);
vertices[i++] = new VertexPosition(backUpperLeft);
vertices[i++] = new VertexPosition(backUpperRight);

vertices[i++] = new VertexPosition(forwardUpperLeft);
vertices[i++] = new VertexPosition(backUpperRight);
vertices[i++] = new VertexPosition(forwardUpperRight);

//face under the camera
vertices[i++] = new VertexPosition(forwardBottomLeft);
vertices[i++] = new VertexPosition(backBottomRight);
vertices[i++] = new VertexPosition(backBottomLeft);

vertices[i++] = new VertexPosition(forwardBottomLeft);
vertices[i++] = new VertexPosition(forwardBottomRight);
vertices[i++] = new VertexPosition(backBottomRight);

skyboxVertexBuffer = new VertexBuffer(device, vertices.Length * ➥
VertexPosition.SizeInBytes, BufferUsage.WriteOnly);
skyboxVertexBuffer.SetData<VertexPosition>(vertices);
```

## HLSL

With your vertices defined, you're ready to move on to the HLSL part of this recipe. Since a
TextureCube is nothing more than a 2D texture, you can use the normal texture and sampler
definition:

```
Texture xCubeTexture;
sampler CubeTextureSampler = sampler_state
{
    texture = <xCubeTexture>;
    magfilter = LINEAR;
```

```
    minfilter = LINEAR;
    mipfilter=LINEAR;
    AddressU = clamp;
    AddressV = clamp;
};
```

This texture will be sampled by the texCUBE intrinsic in the pixel shader in a moment, which takes two arguments. The first argument is the texture sampler it needs to sample the color from. The second argument specifies where to sample the texture. Instead of requiring the usual 2D texture coordinates, the texCUBE intrinsic takes the direction from the center of the cube to the 3D position on the cube where the color is needed. The texCUBE intrinsic then calculates the corresponding texture coordinates for you.

This has some advantages. Because your camera will always be in the center of the cube, this direction is nothing more than the 3D position of the pixel for which color is wanted! Also, because you're dealing with a direction, there's no need to scale this argument, because, for example, the (1,3,–2) direction is the same as the (10,30,–20) direction.

So, for each vertex of the cube, the vertex shader needs to pass its 3D position to the pixel shader (next to the 2D screen position, which it should calculate in all cases):

```
//------- Technique: Skybox --------
struct SkyBoxVertexToPixel
{
    float4 Position         : POSITION;
    float3 Pos3D        : TEXCOORD0;
};

SkyBoxVertexToPixel SkyBoxVS( float4 inPos : POSITION)
{
    SkyBoxVertexToPixel Output = (SkyBoxVertexToPixel)0;
    float4x4 preViewProjection = mul (xView, xProjection);
    float4x4 preWorldViewProjection = mul (xWorld, preViewProjection);

    Output.Position = mul(inPos, preWorldViewProjection);
    Output.Pos3D = inPos;

    return Output;
}
```

You can see that the vertex shader requires only the position of each vertex, which is provided by the vertices you defined in your XNA code. By multiplying this 3D position with the combination of the World, View, and Projection matrices, this position is mapped to its 2D screen position. The original position of the vertex is passed to the pixel shader in the Output. Pos3D member, because it is required by the texCUBE intrinsic.

---

■**Note** Unlike in most cases when you need the original 3D position available in the pixel shader, this time the 3D position is not multiplied with the World matrix, because you need the direction from the center of the cube to the vertex, which equals "vertex position minus center position." Because of the way you defined the vertices of your cube, in the original space (called *model space*), the position of the center is (0,0,0), so the direction simply becomes the vertex position!

---

Next in line is the pixel shader, which receives only this direction. It needs to find the corresponding color, which needs to be sent to the frame buffer:

```
struct SkyBoxPixelToFrame
{
    float4 Color : COLOR0;
};


SkyBoxPixelToFrame SkyBoxPS(SkyBoxVertexToPixel PSIn)
{
    SkyBoxPixelToFrame Output = (SkyBoxPixelToFrame)0;

    Output.Color = texCUBE(CubeTextureSampler, PSIn.Pos3D);

    return Output;
}
```

Since you already calculated the direction between the pixel and the center of the cube in the vertex shader, you can immediately pass this as the second argument to the texCUBE intrinsic, which samples the corresponding color from the texture. This color is sent to the frame buffer.

## The Code

*All the code is available for download at www.apress.com.*

### The XNA Code

Put this struct at the very top of your namespace:

```
public struct VertexPosition
{
    public Vector3 Position;
    public VertexPosition(Vector3 position)
    {
        this.Position = position;
    }
```

```
    public static readonly VertexElement[] VertexElements =
    {
        new VertexElement( 0, 0, VertexElementFormat.Vector3, ➥
        VertexElementMethod.Default, ➥
        VertexElementUsage.Position, 0 )
    };

    public static readonly int SizeInBytes = sizeof(float) * 3;
}
```

This method defines the 36 vertices required to render the six faces of your cube:

```
private void CreateSkyboxVertexBuffer()
{
    Vector3 forwardBottomLeft = new Vector3(-1, -1, -1);
    Vector3 forwardBottomRight = new Vector3(1, -1, -1);
    Vector3 forwardUpperLeft = new Vector3(-1, 1, -1);
    Vector3 forwardUpperRight = new Vector3(1, 1, -1);

    Vector3 backBottomLeft = new Vector3(-1, -1, 1);
    Vector3 backBottomRight = new Vector3(1, -1, 1);
    Vector3 backUpperLeft = new Vector3(-1, 1, 1);
    Vector3 backUpperRight = new Vector3(1, 1, 1);

    VertexPosition[] vertices = new VertexPosition[36];
    int i = 0;

    //face in front of the camera
    vertices[i++] = new VertexPosition(forwardBottomLeft);
    vertices[i++] = new VertexPosition(forwardUpperLeft);
    vertices[i++] = new VertexPosition(forwardUpperRight);

    vertices[i++] = new VertexPosition(forwardBottomLeft);
    vertices[i++] = new VertexPosition(forwardUpperRight);
    vertices[i++] = new VertexPosition(forwardBottomRight);

    //face to the right of the camera
    vertices[i++] = new VertexPosition(forwardBottomRight);
    vertices[i++] = new VertexPosition(forwardUpperRight);
    vertices[i++] = new VertexPosition(backUpperRight);

    vertices[i++] = new VertexPosition(forwardBottomRight);
    vertices[i++] = new VertexPosition(backUpperRight);
    vertices[i++] = new VertexPosition(backBottomRight);
```

```
    //face behind the camera
    vertices[i++] = new VertexPosition(backBottomLeft);
    vertices[i++] = new VertexPosition(backUpperRight);
    vertices[i++] = new VertexPosition(backUpperLeft);

    vertices[i++] = new VertexPosition(backBottomLeft);
    vertices[i++] = new VertexPosition(backBottomRight);
    vertices[i++] = new VertexPosition(backUpperRight);

    //face to the left of the camera
    vertices[i++] = new VertexPosition(backBottomLeft);
    vertices[i++] = new VertexPosition(backUpperLeft);
    vertices[i++] = new VertexPosition(forwardUpperLeft);

    vertices[i++] = new VertexPosition(backBottomLeft);
    vertices[i++] = new VertexPosition(forwardUpperLeft);
    vertices[i++] = new VertexPosition(forwardBottomLeft);

    //face above the camera
    vertices[i++] = new VertexPosition(forwardUpperLeft);
    vertices[i++] = new VertexPosition(backUpperLeft);
    vertices[i++] = new VertexPosition(backUpperRight);

    vertices[i++] = new VertexPosition(forwardUpperLeft);
    vertices[i++] = new VertexPosition(backUpperRight);
    vertices[i++] = new VertexPosition(forwardUpperRight);


    //face under the camera
    vertices[i++] = new VertexPosition(forwardBottomLeft);
    vertices[i++] = new VertexPosition(backBottomRight);
    vertices[i++] = new VertexPosition(backBottomLeft);

    vertices[i++] = new VertexPosition(forwardBottomLeft);
    vertices[i++] = new VertexPosition(forwardBottomRight);
    vertices[i++] = new VertexPosition(backBottomRight);

    skyboxVertexBuffer = new VertexBuffer(device, vertices.Length * ➥
    VertexPosition.SizeInBytes, BufferUsage.WriteOnly);
    skyboxVertexBuffer.SetData<VertexPosition>(vertices);
}
```

Add this code in your Draw method to render the triangles using your custom effect:

```
graphics.GraphicsDevice.Clear(ClearOptions.Target | ➥
ClearOptions.DepthBuffer, Color.Black, 1, 0);
```

```
device.RenderState.DepthBufferWriteEnable = false;
skyboxEffect.CurrentTechnique = skyboxEffect.Techniques["SkyBox"];
skyboxEffect.Parameters["xWorld"].SetValue( ➥
Matrix.CreateTranslation(fpsCam.Position));
skyboxEffect.Parameters["xView"].SetValue(fpsCam.ViewMatrix);
skyboxEffect.Parameters["xProjection"].SetValue(fpsCam.ProjectionMatrix);
skyboxEffect.Parameters["xCubeTexture"].SetValue(skyboxTexture);
skyboxEffect.Begin();
foreach (EffectPass pass in skyboxEffect.CurrentTechnique.Passes)
{
    pass.Begin();

    device.VertexDeclaration = new VertexDeclaration(device, ➥
    VertexPosition.VertexElements);
    device.Vertices[0].SetSource(skyboxVertexBuffer, 0, VertexPosition.SizeInBytes);
    device.DrawPrimitives(PrimitiveType.TriangleList, 0, 12);

    pass.End();
}
skyboxEffect.End();
device.RenderState.DepthBufferWriteEnable = true;
```

## The HLSL Code

Here's the HLSL code:

```
float4x4 xWorld;
float4x4 xView;
float4x4 xProjection;

Texture xCubeTexture;
sampler CubeTextureSampler = sampler_state
{
    texture = <xCubeTexture>;
    magfilter = LINEAR;
    minfilter = LINEAR;
    mipfilter=LINEAR;
    AddressU = clamp;
    AddressV = clamp;
};

//------- Technique: Skybox --------
struct SkyBoxVertexToPixel
{
    float4 Position        : POSITION;
    float3 Pos3D          : TEXCOORD0;
};
```

```
SkyBoxVertexToPixel SkyBoxVS( float4 inPos : POSITION)
{
    SkyBoxVertexToPixel Output = (SkyBoxVertexToPixel)0;
    float4x4 preViewProjection = mul (xView, xProjection);
    float4x4 preWorldViewProjection = mul (xWorld, preViewProjection);

    Output.Position = mul(inPos, preWorldViewProjection);
    Output.Pos3D = inPos;

    return Output;
}

struct SkyBoxPixelToFrame
{
    float4 Color : COLOR0;
};

SkyBoxPixelToFrame SkyBoxPS(SkyBoxVertexToPixel PSIn)
{
    SkyBoxPixelToFrame Output = (SkyBoxPixelToFrame)0;

    Output.Color = texCUBE(CubeTextureSampler, PSIn.Pos3D);

    return Output;
}


technique SkyBox
{
    pass Pass0
    {
        VertexShader = compile vs_1_1 SkyBoxVS();
        PixelShader  = compile ps_1_1 SkyBoxPS();
    }
}
```

# 2-9. Draw Only the Parts of the Scene That Are in Sight of the Camera: Octree

## The Problem

If you use the method presented in recipe 2-5 to check for each Model if it is in sight of the camera, the application will slow down a lot if it contains a huge amount of objects. You want a scalable approach that will determine whether parts of the scene have to be drawn and that will render only those parts that are in sight of the camera.

## The Solution

Define a giant cube that contains your whole 3D world and all the models in it. If the cube contains more than a specified number of Models, split up the cube into smaller child cubes. If one of the child cubes contains too many Models, also split up this cube into smaller child cubes, and continue this process until each cube contains no more than a specified amount of Models or until the size of the cube becomes too small.

During the drawing phase, the big cube asks its child cubes to check whether they're in sight of the camera. If a child cube is not in sight, it doesn't have to draw its Models. If it is in sight and does have child cubes of its own, it should simply forward this Draw call to its child cubes, until a cube is reached that is in sight and has no child cubes. As a result, only the final cubes that are in sight of the camera will render their models.

## How It Works

First, you have to decide how many models you want to have at most in a cube. Here, a maximum number of five models will be used.

Whenever a cube that already contains this maximum number of five Models gets another Model assigned, the cube has to be split up into smaller child cubes. The only way to divide a cube into smaller cubes that are all identical would be to divide it into eight cubes, as shown in Figure 2-10.

Because all eight child cubes perfectly fit in their parent cube and each of the child cubes can again be split into eight smaller cubes, you end up with a tree-like structure. Since each parent node has eight child nodes, this structure is called an *octal-tree*, or *octree* for short.

Figures 2-11 and 2-12 show the principle of operation. Take a look at Figure 2-11. This octree contains more than five models, so the parent cube had to be split up into its eight child cubes. You can see that one child cube already has five models in it.

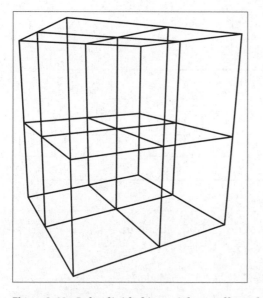

**Figure 2-10.** *Cube divided into eight smaller cubes*

Now, consider the case when an additional model needs to be added to the cube that already contains five models. This cube would have to be split into its eight child cubes, and its six models would have to be sent to the correct child cubes, as depicted in Figure 2-12.

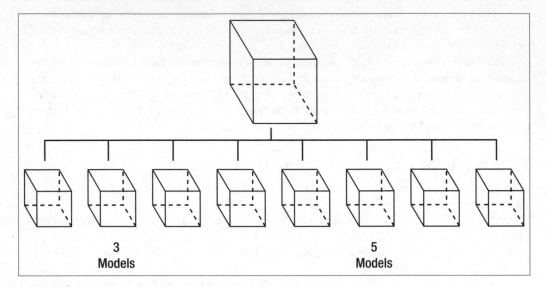

**Figure 2-11.** *Octree before adding another Model*

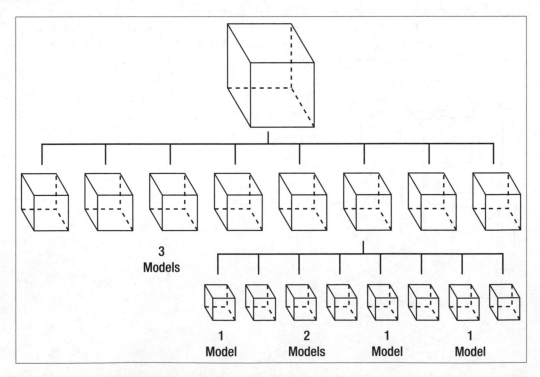

**Figure 2-12.** *Octree after adding another Model*

The benefit of using an octree is that the main program needs to ask the root cube only to draw. This cube will determine whether it's in sight of the camera. If it is, it will propagate the call to its child nodes, which will draw its models if it contains any or propagate the call further to its own child cubes. This way, the octree will decide for itself which nodes to render.

## The DrawableModel Class

To be able to correctly draw a Model, each cube of the octree also needs to remember the World matrix belonging to each Model. This World matrix also contains the position of the Model in the 3D world, so storing the World matrix and the Model is enough for the octree to determine to which child cube the Model belongs.

Coding an octree really becomes easy when using classes. In this case, you'll define a new class, DrawableModel, which will be a definition for objects that contain a model together with its World matrix. For each model you want to store in your octree, a DrawableModel object will be created, which stores this object and its World matrix. It is this object that will actually be stored in a cube of the octree. You will also define a Draw action for this class, which will be called by the cube if the cube detects it is in sight of the camera.

To create a new class, go to your Solution Explorer, right-click your project's name, and select Add ➤ New Item. In the dialog box that appears, select Class, and type **DrawableModel** as the name.

A new file will open, which you'll immediately want to add the XNA references to, or otherwise, you won't be able to use the classes defined by the XNA Framework:

```
using Microsoft.Xna.Framework;
using Microsoft.Xna.Framework.Audio;
using Microsoft.Xna.Framework.Content;
using Microsoft.Xna.Framework.Graphics;
using Microsoft.Xna.Framework.Input;
using Microsoft.Xna.Framework.Storage;
```

I've already discussed two properties of the DrawableModel class: the Model and the World matrix. You'll also store the transformation matrices to allow animation (see recipe 4-9), store the position, and store an ID number that will be used to identify the object. After creating an object of the DrawableModel class, the object will receive its unique ID number, and this ID will be passed to your main application, which allows you to change the World matrix of a particular object.

So, add these four variables inside the class:

```
class DrawableModel
{
    private Matrix worldMatrix;
    private Model model;
    private Matrix[] modelTransforms;
    private Vector3 position;
    private int modelID;
}
```

In the case of the DrawableModel class, the constructor will have three arguments: the Model, the worldMatrix, and the ID number. The position doesn't have to be specified, because the position is actually contained inside the World matrix, together with scaling and rotation values. Put the constructor method inside your class:

```
public DrawableModel(Model inModel, Matrix inWorldMatrix, int inModelID)
{
    model = inModel;
    modelTransforms = new Matrix[model.Bones.Count];
    worldMatrix = inWorldMatrix;
    modelID = inModelID;
    position = new Vector3(inWorldMatrix.M41, inWorldMatrix.M42, inWorldMatrix.M43);
}
```

You can see the position is actually the last row of elements of the World matrix.

---

**■Note**  You can also obtain the position contained in a matrix by calling the Decompose method on that matrix. The translation component of the transformation contained in the matrix corresponds to the position where the Model will be rendered.

---

Next, you will add the Draw method to the class, which will draw the model using its World matrix and transformation matrices:

```
public void Draw(Matrix viewMatrix, Matrix projectionMatrix)
{
    model.CopyAbsoluteBoneTransformsTo(modelTransforms);
    foreach (ModelMesh mesh in model.Meshes)
    {
        foreach (BasicEffect effect in mesh.Effects)
        {
            effect.EnableDefaultLighting();
            effect.World = modelTransforms[mesh.ParentBone.Index] * worldMatrix;
            effect.View = viewMatrix;
            effect.Projection = projectionMatrix;
        }
        mesh.Draw();
    }
}
```

This concludes the main actions of this class. However, up until now, it is not yet possible for the main program to access the private attributes. Although you could get away with making them public instead of private, this is considered evil, because this allows outside code to read *and* write these properties. The nice way to provide access to these properties is through a getter method:

```
public Vector3 Position { get { return position; } }
public Model Model { get { return model; } }
public int ModelID { get { return modelID; } }
```

Getter methods were introduced in .NET 2.0. They are small methods that simply return the corresponding property. You'll see their use in a few minutes. For now, note the outside program can retrieve only the values of these properties; they cannot be set from the outside, and that's exactly how things should be.

There's one more property you don't have access to from the outside: worldMatrix. You must provide the main program with a way to update the object's worldMatrix property. So here, you will define not only a getter method but also a setter method. In this case, this setter method's usage will be twofold: it will change the value of the worldMatrix property, and it will also extract the new position from this new worldMatrix and store it in the position property:

```
public Matrix WorldMatrix
{
    get { return worldMatrix; }
    set
    {
        worldMatrix = value;
        position = new Vector3(value.M41, value.M42, value.M43);
    }
}
```

The getter method allows the main program to read the worldMatrix property. The setter method receives the new worldMatrix from the main program in the value variable. This variable is stored in the worldMatrix variable, and the position is extracted from it.

This concludes the DrawableModel class. You have defined a class, which can store a model together with its worldMatrix. The model can be drawn using the current worldMatrix. The main program can update the worldMatrix.

## The OcTreeNode Class

Now that you have a definition of a complete storage object, you can start work on your octree. The tree will consist of nodes that correspond to the cubes of the octree. You will define a second class, OcTreeNode, which describes such a node. Each node can store DrawableModel objects and can have eight child nodes.

Create a new class, OcTreeNode, as shown earlier. This class contains a few more properties:

```
private const int maxObjectsInNode = 5;
private const float minSize = 5.0f;

private Vector3 center;
private float size;
List<DrawableModel> modelList;
private BoundingBox nodeBoundingBox;
```

```
OcTreeNode nodeUFL;
OcTreeNode nodeUFR;
OcTreeNode nodeUBL;
OcTreeNode nodeUBR;
OcTreeNode nodeDFL;
OcTreeNode nodeDFR;
OcTreeNode nodeDBL;
OcTreeNode nodeDBR;
List<OcTreeNode> childList;

private static int modelsDrawn;
private static int modelsStoredInQuadTree;
```

The first line defines how many models you want a cube to store before it is split up into eight child cubes. Before a cube is split up, you will check whether the future cubes would not become too small, so that's why you need the second property.

Next, each node needs to keep track of a few things, such as the position of its center and its size. Each node will be able to store a few (five, actually) DrawableModel objects, which are stored in the modelList. To check whether the cube is in sight of the camera, each cube will also store a BoundingBox, so containment between the cube and the camera frustum can easily be checked for.

Next is the list of eight child nodes. I've given them full names, such as nodeUFL, which stands for "node Upper Forward Left," and nodeDBR, which is "node Down Back Right." You'll find this useful when you get to the part where you define their positions. In almost all other cases, however, you'll want to use them in a list. Feel free to remove either or both ways to your liking later.

Each OcTreeNode you create will hold its own copy of the variables discussed here. The last two variables, however, are static variables, which means these variables are shared among all OcTreeNode objects. So when one OcTreeNode object changes one of these variables, all other OcTreeNode objects see this change. You'll want to use the modelsDrawn variable to check that your octree is actually working, and the modelsStoredInQuadTree is necessary to find a new ID for each model added to the tree.

The first method to add is the constructor method, which actually creates an OcTreeNode object. All that is needed is the position of the center of the new cube and its size:

```
public OcTreeNode(Vector3 center, float size)
{
    this.center = center;
    this.size = size;
    modelList = new List<DrawableModel>();
    childList = new List<OcTreeNode>(8);

    Vector3 diagonalVector = new Vector3(size / 2.0f, size / 2.0f, size / 2.0f);
    nodeBoundingBox = new BoundingBox(center - diagonalVector, ➥
    center + diagonalVector);
}
```

The center and size are stored in the private variables, while both the modelList and childList are instantiated.

---

■**Tip**  Since you know the cube will have at most eight child nodes, you can specify this number in the constructor method of the List. The nicest thing about a List is that you don't *have* to specify its maximum capacity, but if you do specify it, the List doesn't have to be resized when you add an element to it.

---

Finally, you also create the BoundingBox corresponding to this cube. The constructor of a BoundingBox takes two points, which are positioned diagonally to each other. For a cube with side length 10, you could specify the points (–5,–5,–5) and (5,5,5) if the center of the cube is the (0,0,0) point. If the center is located somewhere else, you need to add this center to the position of both points. This is done in the last line of the constructor method.

Now would be a nice time to define the method that creates the eight child nodes. The method will be used shortly hereafter.

```
private void CreateChildNodes()
{
    float sizeOver2 = size / 2.0f;
    float sizeOver4 = size / 4.0f;

    nodeUFR = new OcTreeNode(center + new Vector3(sizeOver4, ➥
    sizeOver4, -sizeOver4), sizeOver2);
    nodeUFL = new OcTreeNode(center + new Vector3(-sizeOver4, ➥
    sizeOver4, -sizeOver4), sizeOver2);
    nodeUBR = new OcTreeNode(center + new Vector3(sizeOver4, ➥
    sizeOver4, sizeOver4), sizeOver2);
    nodeUBL = new OcTreeNode(center + new Vector3(-sizeOver4, ➥
    sizeOver4, sizeOver4), sizeOver2);
    nodeDFR = new OcTreeNode(center + new Vector3(sizeOver4, ➥
    -sizeOver4, -sizeOver4), sizeOver2);
    nodeDFL = new OcTreeNode(center + new Vector3(-sizeOver4, ➥
    -sizeOver4, -sizeOver4), sizeOver2);
    nodeDBR = new OcTreeNode(center + new Vector3(sizeOver4, ➥
    -sizeOver4, sizeOver4), sizeOver2);
    nodeDBL = new OcTreeNode(center + new Vector3(-sizeOver4, ➥
    -sizeOver4, sizeOver4), sizeOver2);

    childList.Add(nodeUFR);
    childList.Add(nodeUFL);
    childList.Add(nodeUBR);
    childList.Add(nodeUBL);
    childList.Add(nodeDFR);
    childList.Add(nodeDFL);
    childList.Add(nodeDBR);
    childList.Add(nodeDBL);
}
```

First, the eight child cubes are created, and then they are added to the childList. As shown earlier, to create a new node, you have to specify only its center and size. The length of the sides of the child cubes is half the size of the parent cube. To find the center position of the child cube, you start from the center position of the parent cube and add the correct vector. For example, to find this vector for the nodeUpperForwardLeft, you have to add a positive Y value (Up) and negative X and Z values (Left and Forward, respectively).

These child nodes must not be created automatically once the parent node is created, because each child node would then also create its child nodes, and this would go on indefinitely. So, this method needs to be called only if a new model gets added to the node and the node already contains its maximum number of models. This is what's done in the AddDrawableModel method, which you can find here:

```
private void AddDrawableModel(DrawableModel dModel)
{
    if (childList.Count == 0)
    {
        modelList.Add(dModel);

        bool maxObjectsReached = (modelList.Count > maxObjectsInNode );
        bool minSizeNotReached = (size > minSize);
        if (maxObjectsReached && minSizeNotReached)
        {
            CreateChildNodes();
            foreach (DrawableModel currentDModel in modelList)
            {
                Distribute(currentDModel);
            }
            modelList.Clear();
        }
    }
    else
    {
        Distribute(dModel);
    }
}
```

This method gets the DrawableModel object, which needs to be added to the node. First, you check whether the node already has child nodes, which would be indicated by the childList having more than zero elements. If this is not the case, you add the DrawableModel object to the modelList of the node. After this has been done, you check whether the node now contains too many DrawableModel objects. You also check whether the current cube is still large enough to be divided into child cubes.

If both are true, you create the child nodes of this cube and distribute (with the Distribute method) each DrawableModel object in the modelList of the node between the child nodes. This Distribute method is explained below. When all models have been distributed among the child nodes, you clear the modelList. Otherwise, this node would draw the model, as well as the child node, so the model would be drawn twice!

If the node already has been split up into child nodes, the DrawableModel object is immediately distributed to the correct child node.

So in fact, the Distribute method does the difficult part. This method receives the DrawableModel object, which it has to send to one of the child nodes by comparing its position to the center of the parent cube. After all, it's not so difficult, partly because you can immediately access the position of the DrawableModel:

```
private void Distribute(DrawableModel dModel)
{
    Vector3 position = dModel.Position;
    if (position.Y > center.Y)              //Up
        if (position.Z < center.Z)      //Forward
            if (position.X < center.X)  //Left
                nodeUFL.AddDrawableModel(dModel);
            else                        //Right
                nodeUFR.AddDrawableModel(dModel);
        else                            //Back
            if (position.X < center.X)  //Left
                nodeUBL.AddDrawableModel(dModel);
            else                        //Right
                nodeUBR.AddDrawableModel(dModel);
    else                                //Down
        if (position.Z < center.Z)      //Forward
            if (position.X < center.X)  //Left
                nodeDFL.AddDrawableModel(dModel);
            else                        //Right
                nodeDFR.AddDrawableModel(dModel);
        else                            //Back
            if (position.X < center.X)  //Left
                nodeDBL.AddDrawableModel(dModel);
            else                        //Right
                nodeDBR.AddDrawableModel(dModel);
}
```

Very nice, but until now, you have defined only private methods, meaning the main program cannot access your nodes to add Models. So, you will now define the Add method, which can be called by the main program:

```
public int Add(Model model, Matrix worldMatrix)
{
    DrawableModel newDModel = ➥
    new DrawableModel(model, worldMatrix, modelsStoredInQuadTree++);
    AddDrawableModel(newDModel);
    return newDModel.ModelID;
}
```

This method simply expects a model and its worldMatrix from the caller. The method will create a DrawableModel object that stores both arguments. Also, the DrawableModel object will receive its unique ID. This comes from the modelsStoredInQuadTree variable, which will be incremented by 1 each time a model is added to the octree. Because this static variable is shared between all nodes and is always incremented, each new DrawableModel will receive a different ID number, which is 1 more than the ID number of the previous DrawableModel. Next, the newly created DrawableModel is added to the octree.

This ID is returned to the main program, which is quite important, as you'll see in the "Updating the World Matrix of a Certain Model" section.

That will be all regarding the structure of your octree! At the end of this recipe, you'll find some code that renders the borders of each cube so you can actually see what's happening. There's one last part of functionality you need to add: the functionality that lets you draw the whole tree. This Draw method will need the viewMatrix, projectionMatrix, and cameraFrustum. You could calculate the cameraFrustum from both matrices, but then this would need to be done for each cube, so it's faster when you calculate the frustum once and pass it on to the child nodes.

```
public void Draw(Matrix viewMatrix, Matrix projectionMatrix, ➥
BoundingFrustum cameraFrustum)
{
    ContainmentType cameraNodeContainment = cameraFrustum.Contains(nodeBoundingBox);
    if (cameraNodeContainment != ContainmentType.Disjoint)
    {
        foreach (DrawableModel dModel in modelList)
        {
            dModel.Draw(viewMatrix, projectionMatrix);
            modelsDrawn++;
        }

        foreach (OcTreeNode childNode in childList)
            childNode.Draw(viewMatrix, projectionMatrix, cameraFrustum);
    }
}
```

This is what happens: you first check the kind of containment between the camera frustum and the BoundingBox of the current cube. If they have absolutely nothing in common, this cube does not have to be drawn, and neither do its children.

If they do share some volume, all DrawableModel objects in the cube need to be drawn. If the node has child nodes, the Draw request is passed on to these nodes, which will check for themselves whether they are in sight of the camera.

## Usage: Main Program

This recipe is nice in theory, but how does this all work? It's quite simple, actually. In your main program, you have to define only one node: the ocTreeRoot variable. This is the one parent cube that contains all other cubes:

```
OcTreeNode ocTreeRoot;
```

Initialize it in your Initialize method:

```
ocTreeRoot = new OcTreeNode(new Vector3(0, 0, 0), 21);
```

For the center of the cube, you specify the center of your 3D world: the (0,0,0) point. As the second argument, you specify the maximum size of your whole 3D world. Usually, you'll take a value a few orders of magnitude larger than the 21 I'm using here in this demonstration.

Once you have the root of your octree initialized, you can add your models to it. This can be anywhere after your model has been loaded. In the following code, this will be done in the LoadContent method, but you're free to add models to your octree at any time in your program.

```
myModel = content.Load<Model>("tiny");
```

```
int[] modelIDs = new int[8];
modelIDs[0] = ocTreeRoot.Add(myModel, Matrix.CreateScale(0.01f, ➥
0.01f, 0.01f) * Matrix.CreateTranslation(1, 5, 5));
modelIDs[1] = ocTreeRoot.Add(myModel, Matrix.CreateScale(0.01f, ➥
0.01f, 0.01f) * Matrix.CreateTranslation(5, 4, -1));
modelIDs[2] = ocTreeRoot.Add(myModel, Matrix.CreateScale(0.01f, ➥
0.01f, 0.01f) * Matrix.CreateTranslation(10, -4, -1));
modelIDs[3] = ocTreeRoot.Add(myModel, Matrix.CreateScale(0.01f, ➥
0.01f, 0.01f) * Matrix.CreateTranslation(1, 4, -3));
modelIDs[4] = ocTreeRoot.Add(myModel, Matrix.CreateScale(0.01f, ➥
0.01f, 0.01f) * Matrix.CreateTranslation(5, 4, -3));
modelIDs[5] = ocTreeRoot.Add(myModel, Matrix.CreateScale(0.01f, ➥
0.01f, 0.01f) * Matrix.CreateTranslation(10, -4, -3));
modelIDs[6] = ocTreeRoot.Add(myModel, Matrix.CreateScale(0.01f, ➥
0.01f, 0.01f) * Matrix.CreateTranslation(8, 8, -3));
modelIDs[7] = ocTreeRoot.Add(myModel, Matrix.CreateScale(0.01f, ➥
0.01f, 0.01f) * Matrix.CreateTranslation(10, 8, -3))
```

This adds eight models to your octree and stores their ID numbers in the modelIDs array (which will be numbers from 0 to 7).

During the draw phase of your program, you simply have to call the Draw method of the octree root! This call will be propagated to all of its children and to their children, until the models are actually drawn. Remember that only the contents of the cubes in sight of the camera are drawn!

```
BoundingFrustum cameraFrustum = new BoundingFrustum(fpsCam.ViewMatrix ➥
* fpsCam.ProjectionMatrix);
ocTreeRoot.Draw(fpsCam.ViewMatrix, fpsCam.ProjectionMatrix, cameraFrustum);
```

## Updating the World Matrix of a Certain Model

During the process of your application, you will want to be able to update the World matrices of your models. This is why your main program needs to keep track of the ID number of a model you store in the octree: you need to be able to change the World matrix of the model with that ID.

To extend your octree so it allows changing World matrices, two more methods are needed in the OcTreeNode class. This is the first one, which is public, so it can be called by the main program:

```
public void UpdateModelWorldMatrix(int modelID, Matrix newWorldMatrix)
{
    DrawableModel deletedModel = RemoveDrawableModel(modelID);
    deletedModel.WorldMatrix = newWorldMatrix;
    AddDrawableModel(deletedModel);
}
```

■**Note** This approach was chosen here because it uses only the RemoveDrawableModel and AddDrawableModel methods, which are needed anyway. In reality, you won't want to delete and create a new object each time you need to update a World matrix. Instead, you'll want some other kind of mechanism, for example, storing all matrices in one big list, so you can directly update its contents from within your main program.

As you can see, the main program can indicate the ID of the model it wants to change, together with the new World matrix. First, this ID will be passed to the RemoveDrawableModel method, which searches the octree for the DrawableModel with this ID. If it is found, it is removed from the modelList of its cube, and the DrawableModel is returned. The World matrix of the DrawableModel is updated and added again to the octree.

That's very nice, but it's clear the difficult work is in the RemoveDrawableModel method, which you can find here:

```
private DrawableModel RemoveDrawableModel(int modelID)
{
    DrawableModel dModel = null;

    for (int index = 0; index < modelList.Count; index++)
    {
        if (modelList[index].ModelID == modelID)
        {
            dModel = modelList[index];
            modelList.Remove(dModel);
        }
    }

    int child = 0;
    while ((dModel == null) && (child < childList.Count))
    {
        dModel = childList[child++].RemoveDrawableModel(modelID);
    }

    return dModel;
}
```

This method takes the ID it needs to find and first checks whether the model is in its own modelList. If it is, the DrawableModel is stored in the dModel variable, and it is removed from the modelList.

---

■**Note**  In this case, you're not using a foreach loop to cycle through the contents of the modelList, because you're changing the contents of the list, which is not allowed in a foreach loop.

---

If the model was found, dModel is no longer null, so the while loop is not triggered, and the DrawableModel is returned.

If the DrawableModel was not found in the modelList of the node, you will check in the eight child nodes. This is done in the while loop, where, as long as the DrawableModel has not been found and not all eight child nodes have been searched, the next child node will be searched.

That's quite something, but now you're able to update the World matrices of your models in your octree from within your main program. This will be done in the update phase of your program, like this:

```
time += 0.01f;
Vector3 startingPos = new Vector3(1, 5, 5);
Vector3 moveDirection = new Vector3(0, 0, -1);
Matrix newWMatrix = Matrix.CreateScale(0.01f, 0.01f, ➥
0.01f)*Matrix.CreateTranslation(startingPos+time*moveDirection);
int modelToChange = 0;
ocTreeRoot.UpdateModelWorldMatrix(modelToChange, newWMatrix);
```

This will make the model with ID 0 move in the (0,0,–1) Forward direction.

## Checking Whether It Works: Number of Models Drawn

It's time to check whether everything is working fine. The OcTreeNode class contains a variable modelsDrawn, which is static, meaning that it is the same for all nodes of your quadtree. It is increased in the Draw method only if a model is actually drawn.

It is a private variable, so you cannot yet access it from outside the octree. You could change it to public, but here, you can find another example of a getter-plus-setter method, which can be added your OcTreeNode class:

```
public int ModelsDrawn { get { return modelsDrawn; } set { modelsDrawn = value; } }
```

During the drawing phase of your program, you will want to set this value to 0 before you draw the octree. When the rendering of the octree has been completed, this variable will hold the number of models actually drawn to the screen, so you can output it, for example, to the title bar of the window:

```
ocTreeRoot.ModelsDrawn = 0;
BoundingFrustum cameraFrustum = ➥
new BoundingFrustum(fpsCam.ViewMatrix * fpsCam.ProjectionMatrix);
ocTreeRoot.Draw(fpsCam.ViewMatrix, fpsCam.ProjectionMatrix, cameraFrustum);
Window.Title = string.Format("Models drawn: {0}", ocTreeRoot.ModelsDrawn);
```

When a cube containing a model leaves the sight of the camera, you'll see the number of models drawn decreasing.

## Checking Whether It Works: Rendering the Borders of the Cube

If you want to check the structure of your octree, you can use the DrawBoundingBox method inside my XNAUtils class to render the borders of the BoundingBox:

```
public void DrawBoxLines(Matrix viewMatrix, Matrix projectionMatrix, ➥
GraphicsDevice device, BasicEffect basicEffect)
{
    foreach (OcTreeNode childNode in childList)
        childNode.DrawBoxLines(viewMatrix, projectionMatrix, ➥
        device, basicEffect);


    if (childList.Count == 0)
        XNAUtils.DrawBoundingBox(nodeBoundingBox, device, ➥
        basicEffect, Matrix.Identity, viewMatrix, ➥
        projectionMatrix);
}
```

This method checks whether the node has any children. If it does, it passes the call to each of its children. When the call has reached one of the ending nodes, the node will render its BoundingBox using the DrawBoundingBox method.

To render the lines of all boxes of your octree, you simply have to call the DrawBoxLines of the root node in the Draw method of your main program, which will propagate the call to all of its child nodes:

```
ocTreeRoot.DrawBoxLines(fpsCam.GetViewMatrix(), ➥
fpsCam.GetProjectionMatrix(), basicEffect);
```

The DrawBoundingBox method used here is a quick-and-dirty method that renders the borders of a cube. It's dirty because the vertices and indices are all created each and every frame again. It's quick because it does not need additional variables to be stored in the node, so the method can be added or dropped without a problem. Because rendering the borders of a BoundingBox can be useful in many scenarios, I have included it as one of the methods in the XNAUtils class:

```
public static void DrawBoundingBox(BoundingBox bBox, ➥
GraphicsDevice device, BasicEffect basicEffect, Matrix worldMatrix, ➥
Matrix viewMatrix, Matrix projectionMatrix)
{
    Vector3 v1 = bBox.Min;
    Vector3 v2 = bBox.Max;

    VertexPositionColor[] cubeLineVertices = new VertexPositionColor[8];
    cubeLineVertices[0] = new VertexPositionColor(v1, Color.White);
    cubeLineVertices[1] = new VertexPositionColor(new Vector3(v2.X, ➥
    v1.Y, v1.Z), Color.Red);
    cubeLineVertices[2] = new VertexPositionColor(new Vector3(v2.X, ➥
    v1.Y, v2.Z), Color.Green);
    cubeLineVertices[3] = new VertexPositionColor(new Vector3(v1.X, ➥
    v1.Y, v2.Z), Color.Blue);

    cubeLineVertices[4] = new VertexPositionColor(new Vector3(v1.X, ➥
    v2.Y, v1.Z), Color.White);
    cubeLineVertices[5] = new VertexPositionColor(new Vector3(v2.X, ➥
    v2.Y, v1.Z), Color.Red);
    cubeLineVertices[6] = new VertexPositionColor(v2, Color.Green);
    cubeLineVertices[7] = new VertexPositionColor(new Vector3(v1.X, ➥
    v2.Y, v2.Z), Color.Blue);

    short[] cubeLineIndices = { 0, 1, 1, 2, 2, 3, 3, 0, 4, 5, 5, 6, ➥
    6, 7, 7, 4, 0, 4, 1, 5, 2, 6, 3, 7 };

    basicEffect.World = worldMatrix;
    basicEffect.View = viewMatrix;
    basicEffect.Projection = projectionMatrix;
    basicEffect.VertexColorEnabled = true;
    device.RenderState.FillMode = FillMode.Solid;
    basicEffect.Begin();
    foreach (EffectPass pass in basicEffect.CurrentTechnique.Passes)
    {
        pass.Begin();
        device.VertexDeclaration = new VertexDeclaration(device, ➥
        VertexPositionColor.VertexElements);
        device.DrawUserIndexedPrimitives<VertexPositionColor>➥
        (PrimitiveType.LineList, cubeLineVertices, 0, 8, ➥
        cubeLineIndices, 0, 12);
        pass.End();
    }
    basicEffect.End();
}
```

■**Tip**  You can use this method as an example of the usage of an indexed LineList. First, the eight corner points are stored in an array. Next, you have an array of indices that point to this vertex array. Every 2 numbers in the index array define 1 line, so the 24 indices define the 12 lines of a cube. For more information on rendering primitives, see recipe 5-1.

## The Code

*All the code is available for download at* www.apress.com.

The DrawableModel class contains all the information and functionality required to render a Model to the 3D scene:

```
class DrawableModel
{
    private Matrix worldMatrix;
    private Model model;
    private Matrix[] modelTransforms;
    private Vector3 position;
    private int modelID;

    public Matrix WorldMatrix
    {
        get { return worldMatrix; }
        set
        {
            worldMatrix = value;
            position = new Vector3(value.M41, value.M42, value.M43);
        }
    }


    public Vector3 Position { get { return position; } }
    public Model Model { get { return model; } }
    public int ModelID { get { return modelID; } }

    public DrawableModel(Model inModel, Matrix inWorldMatrix, int inModelID)
    {
        model = inModel;
        modelTransforms = new Matrix[model.Bones.Count];
        worldMatrix = inWorldMatrix;
        modelID = inModelID;
        position = new Vector3(inWorldMatrix.M41, inWorldMatrix.M42, ➥
        inWorldMatrix.M43);
    }
```

```
public void Draw(Matrix viewMatrix, Matrix projectionMatrix)
{
    model.CopyAbsoluteBoneTransformsTo(modelTransforms);
    foreach (ModelMesh mesh in model.Meshes)
    {
        foreach (BasicEffect effect in mesh.Effects)
        {
            effect.EnableDefaultLighting();
            effect.World = modelTransforms[mesh.ParentBone.Index] * worldMatrix;
            effect.View = viewMatrix;
            effect.Projection = projectionMatrix;
        }
        mesh.Draw();
    }
}
}
```

The OcTreeNode class can store a link to each model contained in a node, and it contains all the functionality to check whether the node is in sight of the camera and to add/remove models to/from the node:

```
class OcTreeNode
{
    private const int maxObjectsInNode = 5;
    private const float minSize = 5.0f;

    private Vector3 center;
    private float size;
    List<DrawableModel> modelList;
    private BoundingBox nodeBoundingBox;

    OcTreeNode nodeUFL;
    OcTreeNode nodeUFR;
    OcTreeNode nodeUBL;
    OcTreeNode nodeUBR;
    OcTreeNode nodeDFL;
    OcTreeNode nodeDFR;
    OcTreeNode nodeDBL;
    OcTreeNode nodeDBR;
    List<OcTreeNode> childList;

    public static int modelsDrawn;
    private static int modelsStoredInQuadTree;

    public int ModelsDrawn { get { return modelsDrawn; } ➥
    set { modelsDrawn = value; } }
```

```
public OcTreeNode(Vector3 center, float size)
{
    this.center = center;
    this.size = size;
    modelList = new List<DrawableModel>();
    childList = new List<OcTreeNode>(8);

    Vector3 diagonalVector = new Vector3(size / 2.0f, size / 2.0f, size / 2.0f);
    nodeBoundingBox = new BoundingBox(center - diagonalVector, ➥
    center + diagonalVector);
}

public int Add(Model model, Matrix worldMatrix)
{
    DrawableModel newDModel = new DrawableModel(model, ➥
    worldMatrix, modelsStoredInQuadTree++);
    AddDrawableModel(newDModel);
    return newDModel.ModelID;
}

public void UpdateModelWorldMatrix(int modelID, Matrix newWorldMatrix)
{
    DrawableModel deletedModel = RemoveDrawableModel(modelID);
    deletedModel.WorldMatrix = newWorldMatrix;
    AddDrawableModel(deletedModel);
}

private DrawableModel RemoveDrawableModel(int modelID)
{
    DrawableModel dModel = null;

    for (int index = 0; index < modelList.Count; index++)
    {

        if (modelList[index].ModelID == modelID)
        {
            dModel = modelList[index];
            modelList.Remove(dModel);
        }
    }

    int child = 0;
    while ((dModel == null) && (child < childList.Count))
    {
        dModel = childList[child++].RemoveDrawableModel(modelID);
    }
```

```
        return dModel;
}

private void AddDrawableModel(DrawableModel dModel)
{
    if (childList.Count == 0)
    {
        modelList.Add(dModel);

        bool maxObjectsReached = (modelList.Count > maxObjectsInNode);
        bool minSizeNotReached = (size > minSize);
        if (maxObjectsReached && minSizeNotReached)
        {
            CreateChildNodes();
            foreach (DrawableModel currentDModel in modelList)
            {
                Distribute(currentDModel);
            }
            modelList.Clear();
        }
    }
    else
    {
        Distribute(dModel);
    }
}

private void CreateChildNodes()
{
    float sizeOver2 = size / 2.0f;
    float sizeOver4 = size / 4.0f;

    nodeUFR = new OcTreeNode(center + new Vector3(sizeOver4, ➡
    sizeOver4, -sizeOver4), sizeOver2);
    nodeUFL = new OcTreeNode(center + new Vector3(-sizeOver4, ➡
    sizeOver4, -sizeOver4), sizeOver2);
    nodeUBR = new OcTreeNode(center + new Vector3(sizeOver4, ➡
    sizeOver4, sizeOver4), sizeOver2);
    nodeUBL = new OcTreeNode(center + new Vector3(-sizeOver4, ➡
    sizeOver4, sizeOver4), sizeOver2);
    nodeDFR = new OcTreeNode(center + new Vector3(sizeOver4, ➡
    -sizeOver4, -sizeOver4), sizeOver2);
    nodeDFL = new OcTreeNode(center + new Vector3(-sizeOver4, ➡
    -sizeOver4, -sizeOver4), sizeOver2);
    nodeDBR = new OcTreeNode(center + new Vector3(sizeOver4, ➡
    -sizeOver4, sizeOver4), sizeOver2);
```

```
        nodeDBL = new OcTreeNode(center + new Vector3(-sizeOver4, ➥
        -sizeOver4, sizeOver4), sizeOver2);

        childList.Add(nodeUFR);
        childList.Add(nodeUFL);
        childList.Add(nodeUBR);
        childList.Add(nodeUBL);
        childList.Add(nodeDFR);
        childList.Add(nodeDFL);
        childList.Add(nodeDBR);
        childList.Add(nodeDBL);
    }

    private void Distribute(DrawableModel dModel)
    {
        Vector3 position = dModel.Position;
        if (position.Y > center.Y)              //Up
            if (position.Z < center.Z)      //Forward
                if (position.X < center.X)  //Left
                    nodeUFL.AddDrawableModel(dModel);
                else                        //Right
                    nodeUFR.AddDrawableModel(dModel);
            else                            //Back
                if (position.X < center.X)  //Left
                    nodeUBL.AddDrawableModel(dModel);
                else                        //Right
                    nodeUBR.AddDrawableModel(dModel);
        else                                //Down
            if (position.Z < center.Z)      //Forward
                if (position.X < center.X)  //Left
                    nodeDFL.AddDrawableModel(dModel);
                else                        //Right
                    nodeDFR.AddDrawableModel(dModel);
            else                            //Back
                if (position.X < center.X)  //Left
                    nodeDBL.AddDrawableModel(dModel);
                else                        //Right
                    nodeDBR.AddDrawableModel(dModel);
    }

    public void Draw(Matrix viewMatrix, Matrix projectionMatrix, ➥
    BoundingFrustum cameraFrustum)
    {
        ContainmentType cameraNodeContainment = ➥
        cameraFrustum.Contains(nodeBoundingBox);
        if (cameraNodeContainment != ContainmentType.Disjoint)
```

```
        {
            foreach (DrawableModel dModel in modelList)
            {
                dModel.Draw(viewMatrix, projectionMatrix);
                modelsDrawn++;
            }

            foreach (OcTreeNode childNode in childList)
                childNode.Draw(viewMatrix, projectionMatrix, cameraFrustum);
        }
    }

    public void DrawBoxLines(Matrix viewMatrix, ➡
    Matrix projectionMatrix, GraphicsDevice device, ➡
    BasicEffect basicEffect)
    {
        foreach (OcTreeNode childNode in childList)
            childNode.DrawBoxLines(viewMatrix, projectionMatrix, ➡
            device, basicEffect);

        if (childList.Count == 0)
            XNAUtils.DrawBoundingBox(nodeBoundingBox, device, ➡
            basicEffect, Matrix.Identity, viewMatrix, ➡
            projectionMatrix);
    }
}
```

In your main XNA project, you can store all your Models, together with their World matrices, inside your octree:

```
protected override void LoadContent()
{
    device = graphics.GraphicsDevice;
    cCross = new CoordCross(device);
    basicEffect = new BasicEffect(device, null);

    myModel = content.Load<Model>("content/tiny");

    int[] modelIDs = new int[8];
    modelIDs[0] = ocTreeRoot.Add(myModel, Matrix.CreateScale(0.01f, ➡
    0.01f, 0.01f) * Matrix.CreateTranslation(1, 5, 5));
    modelIDs[1] = ocTreeRoot.Add(myModel, Matrix.CreateScale(0.01f, ➡
    0.01f, 0.01f) * Matrix.CreateTranslation(5, 4, -1));
    modelIDs[2] = ocTreeRoot.Add(myModel, Matrix.CreateScale(0.01f, ➡
    0.01f, 0.01f) * Matrix.CreateTranslation(10, -4, -1));
    modelIDs[3] = ocTreeRoot.Add(myModel, Matrix.CreateScale(0.01f, ➡
    0.01f, 0.01f) * Matrix.CreateTranslation(1, 4, -3));
```

```
modelIDs[4] = ocTreeRoot.Add(myModel, Matrix.CreateScale(0.01f, ➥
0.01f, 0.01f) * Matrix.CreateTranslation(5, 4, -3));
modelIDs[5] = ocTreeRoot.Add(myModel, Matrix.CreateScale(0.01f, ➥
0.01f, 0.01f) * Matrix.CreateTranslation(10, -4, -3));
modelIDs[6] = ocTreeRoot.Add(myModel, Matrix.CreateScale(0.01f, ➥
0.01f, 0.01f) * Matrix.CreateTranslation(8, 8, -3));
modelIDs[7] = ocTreeRoot.Add(myModel, Matrix.CreateScale(0.01f, ➥
0.01f, 0.01f) * Matrix.CreateTranslation(10, 8, -3));
}
```

With all Models stored inside your octree, you can render them using a simple call. By passing in the view frustum, the octree can make sure it doesn't render any Models that aren't in the range of the camera:

```
BoundingFrustum cameraFrustum = new BoundingFrustum(fpsCam.ViewMatrix ➥
 * fpsCam.ProjectionMatrix);
ocTreeRoot.Draw(fpsCam.ViewMatrix, fpsCam.ProjectionMatrix, cameraFrustum);
```

If you want to update the World matrix of a Model, simply use the UpdateModelWorldMatrix method defined earlier:

```
ocTreeRoot.UpdateModelWorldMatrix(modelToChange, newWorldMatrix);
```

## Extra Reading

The octree presented in this recipe is a basic one, but it should allow you to grasp the idea of space divisioning. The code has a few rough edges, though; for example, asking to change the World matrix of a modelID that is not present in the octree will cause an error.

Also, the DeleteDrawableModel could be improved, because now the whole octree is searched until eventually the object is found. It would be better to store the positions of all models in one list so the octree can be crawled more efficiently to find the existing DrawableModel. Alternatively, the ID given by the octree can already indicate in which direction the tree should be crawled.

Furthermore, this approach allows you to store (and more specifically, draw) only those models that contain an effect, because the code of the Draw method in the DrawableModel is very specific. A more general approach would be to define a virtual DrawableObject class that could be stored in the tree and a few classes that inherit from this virtual class.

Again, although fully functional, the main objective behind this recipe is to make you familiar with the concept of an octree. With only the strictly necessary functionality added, the whole structure is already big enough for an introduction to octrees.

The domain of object culling is huge. This recipe showed you a basic example of an octree, which in itself is a very simple form of object culling because it culls away only those objects that are clearly not in sight of the camera because they are not inside the view frustum of the camera. More advanced solutions exist in the domain of occlusion culling, where the 3D world is divided into regions corresponding to the 3D world itself. For example, to store the objects inside a house, volumes corresponding to the rooms are used instead of symmetrical cubes. These rooms are connected to each other at positions corresponding to the doors. This way, you can perform checks to see whether a room is actually in sight of the camera or whether a wall or closed door is blocking the sight.

# 2-10. Use a Quadtree to Hide Parts of a Grid That Are Not in Sight

## The Problem

Terrain rendering is one of the most elementary parts of creating a game. However, using the approach described in recipe 5-8, you will not be able to create huge terrains without noticing severe drops in your frame rate.

## The Solution

You can ease the workload of rendering a large terrain by using a quadtree. This is similar to an octree, because you will keep dividing your terrain into smaller quads until all of these quads are no larger than a specified size.

Such a process in shown on the left side of Figure 2-13. A 16×16 quad is split up into 4 quads, which are then again split into 4 quads.

The main benefit of using a quadtree is that when it comes to rendering your terrain, you render only those quads that are in sight of the camera. You do this by detecting which quads intersect with the camera frustum. This is shown in the right part of Figure 2-13, where the quads that should be drawn have been filled with gray.

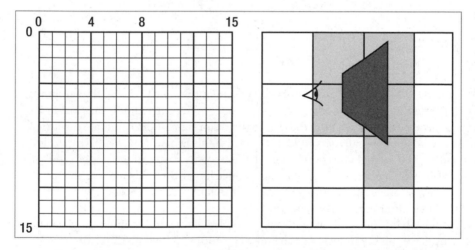

**Figure 2-13.** *Splitting a large quad into smaller quads (left) and quads intersecting with the camera frustum (right)*

A quadtree is a simplified version of an octree. A quad needs to be divided only into four smaller quads, while an octree node needs to be divided into eight child cubes. An octree also needs to keep track of the position of all objects inside it, while a quadtree doesn't have to deal with this.

## How It Works

Create a new class, which will represent one quad, a node of your quadtree:

```
namespace BookCode
{
    class QTNode
    {
        private BoundingBox nodeBoundingBox;

        private bool isEndNode;
        private QTNode nodeUL;
        private QTNode nodeUR;
        private QTNode nodeLL;
        private QTNode nodeLR;

        private int width;
        private int height;
        private GraphicsDevice device;
        private BasicEffect basicEffect;
        private VertexBuffer nodeVertexBuffer;
        private IndexBuffer nodeIndexBuffer;
        private Texture2D grassTexture;

        public static int NodesRendered;
    }
}
```

Let's discuss the variables each node will need to remember. The first one, the bounding box, is quite important. It is the smallest box, so all vertices of the current node are inside the box. Each frame, you will check whether the current box is in sight of the camera. The current node should forward the Draw call to its child nodes only if this is true.

When creating a quadtree, you should specify the maximum size of the nodes. The isEndNode variable will store whether the current node is larger than this maximum size. If it is larger, the node should create four child nodes, stored in nodeUL to nodeLR, where UL stands for UpperLeft and LR stands for LowerRight.

If the node has no child nodes, the node will actually have to draw some triangles when isEndNode is true. To do this, you will need to know its width and height. You'll also need a link to the graphics device and a working BasicEffect, as well as a VertexBuffer and an IndexBuffer together with a Texture to render the triangles to the screen (see recipe 5-8).

A node is created by calling its constructor method, like this one:

```
public QTNode(VertexPositionNormalTexture[,] vertexArray, ➥
GraphicsDevice device, Texture2D grassTexture, int maxSize)
{
    this.device = device;
    this.grassTexture = grassTexture;
    basicEffect = new BasicEffect(device, null);
```

```
    width = vertexArray.GetLength(0);
    height = vertexArray.GetLength(1);
    nodeBoundingBox = CreateBoundingBox(vertexArray);

    isEndNode = width <= maxSize;
    isEndNode &= height <= maxSize;
    if (isEndNode)
    {
        VertexPositionNormalTexture[] vertices = ➥
        Reshape2Dto1D<VertexPositionNormalTexture>(vertexArray);
        int[] indices = TerrainUtils.CreateTerrainIndices(width, height);
        TerrainUtils.CreateBuffers(vertices, indices, ➥
        out nodeVertexBuffer, out nodeIndexBuffer, device);
    }
    else
    {
        CreateChildNodes(vertexArray, maxSize);
    }
}
```

A node needs a 2D array containing all of its vertices, together with a link to the device
and texture, as well as the size after which the nodes should stop splitting themselves into
child nodes.

Links to the device and texture are immediately stored inside the node. The width and
height of the current node are extracted from the 2D array containing the vertices. Given all
vertices of this node, you calculate the bounding box using the CreateBoundingBox method
that you'll define in a minute.

Finally, you check whether the width and height of the current node are smaller than the
maximum size. If this is the case, you create a valid VertexBuffer and IndexBuffer from the
vertices of the current node. If the node is larger than the maximum size, you split the node
into four child nodes.

### Creating the BoundingBox

Given the 2D array containing the vertices, you can easily store all their positions inside a list.
The CreateFromPoints method of the BoundingBox class can generate a BoundingBox from this
list of positions:

```
private BoundingBox CreateBoundingBox(VertexPositionNormalTexture[,] vertexArray)
{

    List<Vector3> pointList = new List<Vector3>();
    foreach (VertexPositionNormalTexture vertex in vertexArray)
        pointList.Add(vertex.Position);

    BoundingBox nodeBoundingBox = BoundingBox.CreateFromPoints(pointList);
    return nodeBoundingBox;
}
```

### Generating the VertexBuffer and IndexBuffer

You can use the `CreateVertices` and `CreateIndices` methods explained in recipe 5-8, which create a `VertexBuffer` and an `IndexBuffer` given a 1D array of vertices. This means you'll have to reshape your 2D array into a 1D array first, which you can do using this method:

```
private T[] Reshape2Dto1D<T>(T[,] array2D)
{
    int width = array2D.GetLength(0);
    int height = array2D.GetLength(1);
    T[] array1D = new T[width * height];

    int i = 0;
    for (int z = 0; z < height; z++)
        for (int x = 0; x < width; x++)
            array1D[i++] = array2D[x, z];

    return array1D;
}
```

This generic method accepts a 2D array of a type T (`VertexPositionNormalTexture` in your case), finds its size, and copies its contents into a 1D array.

---

**Note** Generic functions were introduced in .NET in version 2.0. When calling a generic method, you specify between brackets which type should replace T, like this:

```
VertexPositionNormalTexture[] vertices = ➥
Reshape2Dto1D<VertexPositionNormalTexture>(vertexArray);
```

---

### Splitting a Node into Four Child Nodes

If the node is too large, it should be divided into four child nodes. The challenge here is that the four child nodes will not each be equal in size. On the left side of Figure 2-13, you see that a 16×16 grid cannot be separated into four 8×8 grids. If each of the child nodes stored only 8×8 vertices, it would not be possible to render triangles between the eighth and ninth column or row, leaving gaps there. In Figure 2-13, this problem has been solved by making the top-left node one row and column larger than the others.

For unpaired-sized quads, this problem doesn't exist: a 9×9 quad can be divided into four quads of 5×5 vertices, as shown in the top-left of Figure 2-13.

The question that remains is, how you can calculate the number of vertices to store in each quad? As an example, how can you know that 16 should be split in 9 and 8, while 9 should be split in 5 and 5? The first value can, for example, be found by dividing the parent size by 2, taking the lower integer (which is done for free when dividing integers!), and adding 1 to the result. The other value is found by dividing the parent size by 2, taking the lower integer, and subtracting this from the parent size.

As an example, 16 divided by 2 is 8. Add 1, and you get 9 as the first value. Then, 16 divided by 2 is 8, and 16 minus 8 gives you 8.

Here's a second example: 9 divided by 2 is 4.5, which becomes 4. Add 1, and you get 5 as the first value. Next, 9 divided by 2 is 4.5, which becomes 4; 9 minus 4 gives you 5.

Once you know the sizes of the child quads to be created, you can use this code to create them. For each of the four child quads, you first copy the appropriate vertices, needed to create a QTNode object:

```
private void CreateChildNodes(VertexPositionNormalTexture[,] ➥
vertexArray, int maxSize)
{
    VertexPositionNormalTexture[,] ulArray = ➥
    new VertexPositionNormalTexture[width / 2 + 1, height / 2 + 1];
    for (int w = 0; w < width / 2 + 1; w++)
        for (int h = 0; h < height / 2 + 1; h++)
            ulArray[w, h] = vertexArray[w, h];
    nodeUL = new QTNode(ulArray, device, grassTexture, maxSize);

    VertexPositionNormalTexture[,] urArray = ➥
    new VertexPositionNormalTexture[width - (width / 2), ➥
    height / 2 + 1];
    for (int w = 0; w < width - (width / 2); w++)
        for (int h = 0; h < height / 2 + 1; h++)
            urArray[w, h] = vertexArray[width / 2 + w, h];
    nodeUR = new QTNode(urArray, device, grassTexture, maxSize);

    VertexPositionNormalTexture[,] llArray = ➥
    new VertexPositionNormalTexture[width / 2 + 1, ➥
    height - (height / 2)];
    for (int w = 0; w < width / 2 + 1; w++)
        for (int h = 0; h < height - (height / 2); h++)
            llArray[w, h] = vertexArray[w, height / 2 + h];
    nodeLL = new QTNode(llArray, device, grassTexture, maxSize);

    VertexPositionNormalTexture[,] lrArray = ➥
    new VertexPositionNormalTexture[width - (width / 2), ➥
    height - (height / 2)];
    for (int w = 0; w < width - (width / 2); w++)
        for (int h = 0; h < height - (height / 2); h++)
            lrArray[w, h] = vertexArray[width / 2 + w, height / 2 + h];
    nodeLR = new QTNode(lrArray, device, grassTexture, maxSize);
}
```

## Rendering Your Quad Tree

With all the creating and splitting functionality implemented, you're ready to render your quadtree. You need to make sure you render only the quads that are in sight of the camera.

In your main application, you want to call only the Draw method of the root node of your quadtree to render all nodes that are in sight of the camera.

The root node should check whether it is in sight of the camera. If it isn't, it should do nothing. If it is, it should pass on the Draw call to each of its four child nodes.

Each of the child nodes should do the same: detect whether they are in sight, and if they are, pass the call on to their child nodes until the smallest nodes are reached. If these are in sight, they should actually render a grid from their vertices:

```
public void Draw(Matrix worldMatrix, Matrix viewMatrix, Matrix ➥
projectionMatrix, BoundingFrustum cameraFrustum)
{
    BoundingBox transformedBBox = ➥
    XNAUtils.TransformBoundingBox(nodeBoundingBox, worldMatrix);
    ContainmentType cameraNodeContainment = cameraFrustum.Contains(transformedBBox);
    if (cameraNodeContainment != ContainmentType.Disjoint)
    {
        if (isEndNode)
        {
            DrawCurrentNode(worldMatrix, viewMatrix, projectionMatrix);
        }
        else
        {
            nodeUL.Draw(worldMatrix, viewMatrix, projectionMatrix, cameraFrustum);
            nodeUR.Draw(worldMatrix, viewMatrix, projectionMatrix, cameraFrustum);
            nodeLL.Draw(worldMatrix, viewMatrix, projectionMatrix, cameraFrustum);
            nodeLR.Draw(worldMatrix, viewMatrix, projectionMatrix, cameraFrustum);
        }
    }
}
```

Notice that this method expects the camera's frustum to be passed by the calling method, because it is used to check whether it intersects with the bounding box of the current quad, which would indicate the node is in sight of the camera.

If this call reaches one of the end nodes that is in sight of the camera, the DrawCurrentNode method is called, which should render the specific quad. This code is taken straight from recipe 5-8:

```
private void DrawCurrentNode(Matrix worldMatrix, ➥
Matrix viewMatrix, Matrix projectionMatrix)
{
    basicEffect.World = worldMatrix;
    basicEffect.View = viewMatrix;
    basicEffect.Projection = projectionMatrix;
    basicEffect.Texture = grassTexture;
    basicEffect.VertexColorEnabled = false;
    basicEffect.TextureEnabled = true;
```

```
basicEffect.EnableDefaultLighting();
basicEffect.DirectionalLight0.Direction = new Vector3(1, -1, 1);
basicEffect.DirectionalLight0.Enabled = true;
basicEffect.AmbientLightColor = new Vector3(0.3f, 0.3f, 0.3f);
basicEffect.DirectionalLight1.Enabled = false;
basicEffect.DirectionalLight2.Enabled = false;
basicEffect.SpecularColor = new Vector3(0, 0, 0);

basicEffect.Begin();
foreach (EffectPass pass in basicEffect.CurrentTechnique.Passes)
{
    pass.Begin();

    device.Vertices[0].SetSource(nodeVertexBuffer, 0, ➥
    VertexPositionNormalTexture.SizeInBytes);
    device.Indices = nodeIndexBuffer;
    device.VertexDeclaration = new VertexDeclaration(device, ➥
    VertexPositionNormalTexture.VertexElements);
    device.DrawIndexedPrimitives(PrimitiveType.TriangleStrip, ➥
    0, 0, width * height, 0, (width * 2 * (height - 1) - 2));

    pass.End();
}
basicEffect.End();

NodesRendered++;

//XNAUtils.DrawBoundingBox(nodeBoundingBox, device, basicEffect, ➥
worldMatrix, viewMatrix, projectionMatrix);
}
```

Each time this code is executed, the NodeRendered variable is incremented. Because it is a static variable, it is shared among all nodes of the quadtree, so at the end of the drawing process, it will contain the total number of nodes actually rendered.

You can uncomment the last line, which will render the outlines of the BoundingBox objects of all nodes that are being rendered, allowing you to verify whether your quadtree is working correctly.

## Initializing Your Quad Tree

With your QTNode class completed, you're ready to create your quadtree. Using much of the code from recipe 5-8, you start from a 2D texture containing height data. You then create a 1D array of VertexPositionNormalTexture elements. Because you want to use the GenerateNormalsFromTriangleStrip method, explained in recipe 5-7, to add correct normals to them, you first need to create a list of indices. Add this code to your LoadContent method:

```
Texture2D grassTexture = content.Load<Texture2D>("grass");

Texture2D heightMap = content.Load<Texture2D>("heightmap");
int width = heightMap.Width;
int height = heightMap.Height;

float[,] heightData = TerrainUtils.LoadHeightData(heightMap);
VertexPositionNormalTexture[] vertices = ➥
TerrainUtils.CreateTerrainVertices(heightData);
int[] indices = TerrainUtils.CreateTerrainIndices(width, height);
vertices = TerrainUtils.GenerateNormalsForTriangleStrip(vertices, indices);
VertexPositionNormalTexture[,] vertexArray = ➥
Reshape1Dto2D<VertexPositionNormalTexture>(vertices, width, height);

rootNode = new QTNode(vertexArray, device, grassTexture, 64);
```

Finally, you end up with a 1D array of vertices. The constructor of your QTNode, however, requires a 2D array, so the last lines call the Reshape1Dto2D method, which you find here:

```
private T[,] Reshape1Dto2D<T>(T[] vertices, int width, int height)
{
    T[,] vertexArray = new T[width, height];
    int i=0;
    for (int h = 0; h < height; h++)
        for (int w = 0; w < width; w++)
            vertexArray[w, h] = vertices[i++];

    return vertexArray;
}
```

Once again, this is a generic method, so it allows you to transform *any* 1D array to a 2D array.

With this 2D array of vertices available, add this final line to your LoadContent method:

```
rootNode = new QTNode(vertexArray, device, grassTexture, 64);
```

This single line generates your whole quadtree. You pass in the 2D array of vertices and a maximum size of 64. As long as the size of your quads is larger than 64, they will keep on being split up in child quads.

## Using Your Quad Tree

In your XNA project, you can put these lines in the Draw method:

```
QTNode.NodesRendered = 0;
BoundingFrustum cameraFrustum = new BoundingFrustum(fpsCam.ViewMatrix ➥
* fpsCam.ProjectionMatrix);
rootNode.Draw(Matrix.CreateTranslation(-250,-20,250), ➥
fpsCam.ViewMatrix, fpsCam.ProjectionMatrix, cameraFrustrum);
Window.Title = string.Format("{0} nodes rendered", QTNode.NodesRendered);
```

The first and last lines are for debugging purposes only, because they will result in the total number of quads actually rendered being printed to the title bar of your window.

The second line creates the camera's frustum, required by each node of your quadtree to detect whether it is in sight of the camera. The third line actually initiates the Draw call, which will crawl through all nodes of your quadtree and render only the visible end nodes.

## The Code

*All the code is available for download at www.apress.com.*

You can find all the code of the QTNode class in the previous sections. In your main XNA project, this could be your LoadContent method:

```
protected override void LoadContent()
{
    device = graphics.GraphicsDevice;
    cCross = new CoordCross(device);

    Texture2D grassTexture = content.Load<Texture2D>("grass");

    Texture2D heightMap = content.Load<Texture2D>("heightmap");
    int width = heightMap.Width;
    int height = heightMap.Height;

    float[,] heightData = TerrainUtils.LoadHeightData(heightMap);
    VertexPositionNormalTexture[] vertices = ➥
    TerrainUtils.CreateTerrainVertices(heightData);
    int[] indices = TerrainUtils.CreateTerrainIndices(width, height);
    vertices = TerrainUtils.GenerateNormalsForTriangleStrip(vertices, indices);
    VertexPositionNormalTexture[,] vertexArray = ➥
    Reshape1Dto2D<VertexPositionNormalTexture>(vertices, width, height);

    rootNode = new QTNode(vertexArray, device, grassTexture, 64);
}
```

This Draw method will render all visible quads of your terrain:

```
protected override void Draw(GameTime gameTime)
{
    graphics.GraphicsDevice.Clear(Color.CornflowerBlue);

    cCross.Draw(fpsCam.ViewMatrix, fpsCam.ProjectionMatrix);

    QTNode.NodesRendered = 0;
    BoundingFrustum cameraFrustrum = new ➥
    BoundingFrustum(fpsCam.ViewMatrix * fpsCam.ProjectionMatrix);
```

```
rootNode.Draw(Matrix.CreateTranslation(-250,-20,250), ➥
    fpsCam.ViewMatrix, fpsCam.ProjectionMatrix, cameraFrustrum);
Window.Title = string.Format("{0} nodes rendered", QTNode.NodesRendered);

    base.Draw(gameTime);
}
```

## Extra Reading

This recipe introduced you to the basics of quad trees. The quad tree presented here has some drawbacks:

- The loading time is quite significant.

- The number of DrawPrimitives calls can be huge, slowing down the application.

- A lot of quads will still be rendered when the camera is looking flat over the terrain.

All of these problems have multiple solutions. I cannot list them all in detail here, because they could easily fill an entire book on terrain rendering. However, I will discuss the causes of these three main problems so you are free to come up with your own solution.

The loading time is caused by the copying of vertices in smaller arrays that happens each time a quad is divided into four smaller quads. The reshaping also causes huge overhead. This problem is typically one that can be solved by doing the quadtree generation in a custom content processor so that during runtime only the vertex and index buffers need to be streamed from a binary file. See recipe 5-13 on the (de)serialization of a terrain.

The second issue creates problems because the graphics card wants to perform long-lasting jobs without being interrupted. It is far better to render 1 million triangles in one go than to render 1,000 triangles 1,000 times. You can solve this problem by decreasing the number of DrawPrimitives calls. One approach would be to detect whether all four child nodes of a parent node are visible. If all four nodes are visible, render the parent node instead of the four child nodes. This will render the same triangles using one DrawPrimitives call instead of four.

The last problem causes a huge number of triangles to be rendered, because quads that are very far from the camera will render the same amount of triangles as the quads close to the camera. You can solve this problem by rendering the distant quads in lower detail using what are referred to as *level-of-detail* (LOD) algorithms. This can be quite a challenge.

For another, totally different approach of dealing with large terrain, read the next recipe. It is important to keep in mind that you can mix the techniques from both recipes, because almost all terrain engines use a quadtree, a ROAM engine, or a combination of both. You can, for example, divide your terrain in patches, control these patches using a quadtree, but then render them using the ROAM algorithm described in the next recipe. This combines the control of a quadtree with the power of ROAM.

# 2-11. Create a Real-Time Camera-Dependant Optimally Adapting Mesh (ROAM) Terrain

## The Problem

Although you can use a quadtree mechanism as described in recipe 2-10 to make sure that XNA renders only those patches of the terrain that are in sight of the camera, this approach is not optimal. The patches that are far away from the camera are still rendered in the same high detail as the patches close to the camera. Some of the triangles that are being rendered will occupy less than even a single pixel on the screen.

Therefore, you want a Level-Of-Detail (LOD) approach so that parts of the terrain that are far away from the camera are rendered in less detail. When you render your terrain using different levels of detail, you will notice cracks at the boundaries between these levels.

## The Solution

This recipe introduces you to a powerful technique where you start from two triangles spanning your whole terrain. On each iteration of the algorithm, each triangle will calculate its distance to the camera and decide for itself whether it should be split up into two triangles. At the end, you end up with a mesh that is optimally adapted to the current camera position.

This terrain mesh needs to be updated each time the position or rotation of the camera is changed. To remain optimal for the new camera situation, each triangle will also need to be able to decide whether it should merge with its neighbors in order to reduce the detail level again.

## How It Works

The goal of this recipe is to start with two triangles spanning the entire terrain and create an algorithm where each triangle decides for itself whether it should split or merge depending on the current camera view.

Before you can really start, you need to find a triangle layout that can be split and merged very easily. In the recipes that deal with terrain thus far, I've been using a fixed-grid quad-based mesh. If you split such a quad of two triangles to increase the detail, each quad of two triangles would need to be split in four quads of eight triangles, as shown on the right side of Figure 2-14. Adding six extra triangles is already quite a large step.

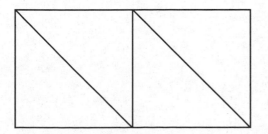 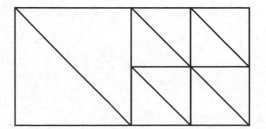

**Figure 2-14.** *Increasing the level of detail in a quad-based layout*

Furthermore, cracks would be visible on the border between two quads of different detail levels, as shown in Figure 2-15. This image shows the 3D representation of the right part of Figure 2-14. You would need to do some stitching to fix such a crack, which is neither easy nor clean.

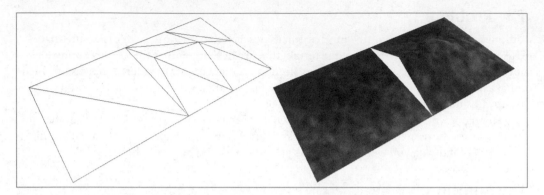

**Figure 2-15.** *3D view of the different levels of detail showing a crack in the quad-based terrain*

Therefore, this recipe will use a radically different triangle layout. Instead of working per quad, you will work per triangle. Whenever a triangle needs to increase its detail level, you will simply split the triangle in two, as shown in Figure 2-16 from left to right. This allows you to increase the detail from two triangles to four triangles, which is a more controlled step.

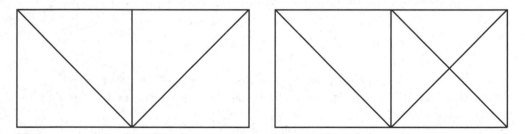

**Figure 2-16.** *Increasing the level of detail in a triangle-based layout*

Furthermore, this splitting will not cause a crack in the terrain. In some cases, you can keep splitting triangles this way without creating cracks in your terrain. As an example, the left side of Figure 2-17 shows three more safe splits.

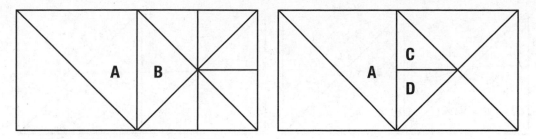

**Figure 2-17.** *Three more safe splits (left), one split causing a crack in the terrain (right)*

However, the right side of Figure 2-17 shows that splitting triangle B into C and D will create a crack in your terrain. Figure 3-18 shows this crack in 3D.

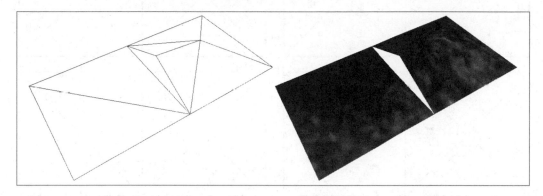

**Figure 2-18.** *3D view of a crack caused by different levels of detail in the triangle layout*

Luckily, you can avoid this. To avoid cracks when splitting a triangle, you should do the following:

- Make sure its parent triangle has also been split.

- Also split the triangle sharing the same long side.

Figure 2-19 shows this process if you want to split triangle A. In the top-left image, the dotted line indicates the split you want to make. According to the second rule here, the triangle sharing the same long side (triangle B) should be split first, as shown by the dotted line in the top-right image. According to the first rule, however, before triangle B can be split, you first need to split triangle B's parent (triangle D) into triangles B and C, as shown by the dotted line in the middle-left image. Before triangle D can be split, however, you need to split triangle E. Luckily, triangle E has no parent triangle, so you can split triangle E, after which you can split triangle D, as shown in the middle-right image. You can now safely split triangle B, as shown in the bottom-left image, and finally make the requested split of triangle A, as shown in the bottom-right image.

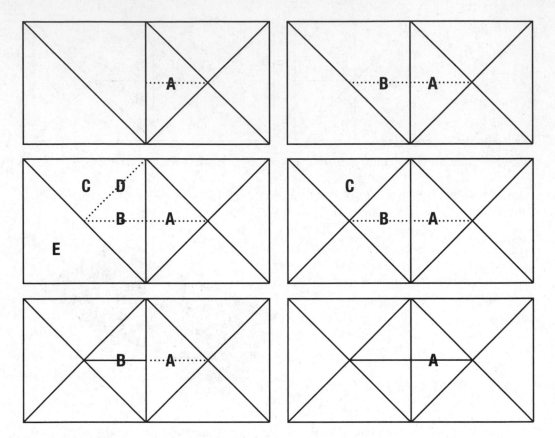

**Figure 2-19.** *Split process in the per-triangle layout*

So much for the splitting. For the terrain to remain optimal (meaning using as few triangles as possible) whenever the camera is moved, in addition to splitting your triangles you should also be able to merge themselves. When the two triangles A and B are merged into one, the two facing triangles, C and D, should also be merged into one in order to avoid cracks. Figure 2-20 illustrates this.

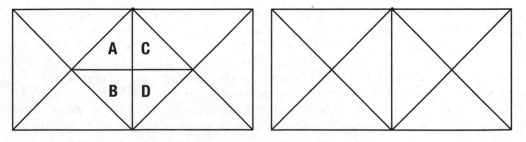

**Figure 2-20.** *Merge process in the per-triangle layout*

## Initialization

Let's convert this into some code. You start by loading an image containing a height map and creating a `VertexBuffer` based on this image, as done in recipe 5-8. In this recipe, both the length and width of the image must be (a power of 2 + 1). Either you create a height map of this size or you start from a height map with sizes that are a power of 2 and copy the last row and column. To keep the focus, this recipe expects you to have a height map of sizes (power of 2 + 1), although you can also find the `LoadHeightDataAndCopyLastRowAndColumn` method in the code of this recipe.

Add this code to your `LoadContent` class, which loads the image and creates the corresponding `VertexBuffer`, as explained in recipe 5-8:

```
Texture2D heightMap = Content.Load<Texture2D>("heightmap");
heightData = LoadHeightData(heightMap);

myVertexDeclaration = new VertexDeclaration(device, ➥
VertexPositionNormalTexture.VertexElements);
VertexPositionNormalTexture[] terrainVertices = CreateTerrainVertices();
int[] terrainIndices = CreateTerrainIndices();
terrainVertices = GenerateNormalsForTriangleStrip(terrainVertices, terrainIndices);
terrainVertexBuffer = new VertexBuffer(device, ➥
VertexPositionNormalTexture.SizeInBytes * terrainVertices.Length, ➥
BufferUsage.WriteOnly);
terrainVertexBuffer.SetData(terrainVertices);
```

## The Triangle Class

You will create a `Triangle` class, which is capable of making all decisions and actions by itself. Add a new class to your project by right-clicking your project in the Solution Explorer and selecting Add ➤ New Item. In the resultant dialog box, select Class, and name your file `Triangle.cs`.

In the almost empty file you get, you should first add some variables you need to store for each triangle. These variables store the links to the three neighboring, child, and parent triangles:

```
Triangle lNeigh;
Triangle rNeigh;
Triangle bNeigh;

Triangle parent;
Triangle lChild;
Triangle rChild;
```

Figure 2-21 illustrates these relationships.

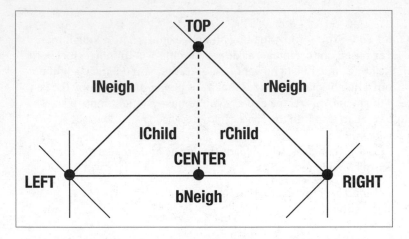

**Figure 2-21.** *Triangle-to-triangle relationships*

You'll need to keep track of some other variables:

```
Vector3 lPos;
Vector3 centerPos;

int tInd;
int lInd;
int rInd;

public bool split = false;
public bool addedToMergeList = false;
```

The two Vector3s will contain the 3D position of the left point and center point (see Figure 2-21) of the triangle, which are needed to determine whether it's worth it to split the triangle. The indices will be needed when the triangle should be rendered. The split Boolean will indicate whether the triangle is currently split, and the addedToMergeList Boolean will be needed only to make sure some calculations are not done twice for the same triangle.

Some of these variables will already be defined by the constructor, which is called whenever you create a new Triangle object:

```
public Triangle(Triangle parent, Vector2 tPoint, Vector2 lPoint, Vector2 rPoint, ➥
float[,] heightData)
{

    int resolution = heightData.GetLength(0);
    tInd = (int)(tPoint.X + tPoint.Y * resolution);
    lInd = (int)(lPoint.X + lPoint.Y * resolution);
    rInd = (int)(rPoint.X + rPoint.Y * resolution);
```

```
        lPos = new Vector3(lPoint.X, ➥
        heightData[(int)lPoint.X, (int)lPoint.Y], -lPoint.Y);
        Vector2 center = (lPoint+rPoint)/2;
        centerPos = new Vector3(center.X, heightData[(int)center.X,➥
        (int)center.Y], -center.Y);

        this.parent = parent;
        if (Vector2.Distance(lPoint, tPoint) > 1)
        {
            lChild = new Triangle(this, center, tPoint, lPoint, heightData);
            rChild = new Triangle(this, center, rPoint, tPoint, heightData);
        }
    }
}
```

As you can see, when creating a new Triangle object, you will need to specify its parent and its top-left and top-right points. Furthermore, since the triangle structure will be used to render a terrain, each of its points represents a 3D position. Therefore, when creating a new Triangle object, you also need to specify a 2D array that contains the height values of the entire terrain. This array is first used to find the indices of the three corners (see recipe 5-8 to learn how to find the indices for a grid of vertices) and then of the 3D positions corresponding to the left corner and the center point.

Finally, you store the link to the parent and check whether the current triangle can still be split up. If the triangle is large enough, you create two child triangles and store their links. Note that the center point is the top (right-angled) point for both child triangles. To verify this and the other points, see Figure 2-21.

## Defining the Two Base Triangles

With the general structure of the Triangle class defined, you're ready to define the two base triangles, covering your entire terrain. You will start by rendering only these two triangles in the first frame. Then, each time the Update method is called, you will decide whether to split the triangles drawn in the previous frame. Therefore, you'll need to keep track of the list of triangles that should currently been drawn. Add this variable to the top of your code:

```
List<Triangle> triangleList;
```

Let's move to the end of the LoadContent method, where you'll create the Triangle structure. First you'll define a resolution variable, which is only a debugging variable. Usually, you'll want to render a terrain of the same size as your height image, but when debugging, it can prove useful to use only a section of this image. Although the image that comes with the code of this recipe measures 1025×1025 pixels, for now you will use only a 33×33 subset.

These lines define the left triangle:

```
int terrainSize = 32;
Triangle leftTriangle = new Triangle(null, new Vector2(0, 0), ➥
new Vector2(terrainSize, 0), new Vector2(0, terrainSize), heightData);
```

The base triangle has no parent triangle. As second, third, and fourth arguments, you pass the three corner points of the triangle, which correspond to the corner points of your entire terrain. Finally, you pass the 2D array containing the height values.

Note that when this line will be executed, the constructor of the `Triangle` class is called. This means that, upon creation, this triangle will by itself create two child triangles, which in their turn will create two child triangles. This process continues until all triangles with a size as small as two height map points have been created.

The right triangle is defined exactly the same way, only with different corner positions:

```
Triangle rightTriangle = new Triangle(null, new Vector2(terrainSize, terrainSize), ➥
new Vector2(0, terrainSize), new Vector2(terrainSize, 0), heightData);
```

## Adding the Links

For all the decisions and actions you will implement into the `Triangle` class, each `Triangle` will need access to its parent, neighboring, and child `Triangles`. Therefore, the next step is to add these links.

Each `Triangle` has already stored a link to its parent and child triangles, but it still needs to know the links to its three neighbors. The trick is that a `Triangle` that knows its three neighbors can figure out the three neighbors of its child triangles. When started from earlier, this mechanism will automatically calculate the neighbors of all triangles in your structure. Start by adding this method to the `Triangle` class:

```
public void AddNeighs(Triangle lNeigh, Triangle rNeigh, Triangle bNeigh)
{
    this.lNeigh = lNeigh;
    this.rNeigh = rNeigh;
    this.bNeigh = bNeigh;
}
```

The `Triangle` expects you to pass links to its three neighbors, which are stored. Next, in case the `Triangle` has children, you want to figure out the neighbors of the child triangles so that you can pass the call on to the child triangles, which will in turn pass the correct neighbors to their children until all `Triangles` in the entire structure have stored a link to their three neighbors:

```
if (lChild != null)
{
    Triangle bNeighRightChild = null;
    Triangle bNeighLeftChild = null;
    Triangle lNeighRightChild = null;
    Triangle rNeighLeftChild = null;

    if (bNeigh != null)
    {
        bNeighLeftChild = bNeigh.lChild;
        bNeighRightChild = bNeigh.rChild;
    }
```

```
    if (lNeigh != null)
        lNeighRightChild = lNeigh.rChild;
    if (rNeigh != null)
        rNeighLeftChild = rNeigh.lChild;

    lChild.AddNeighs(rChild, bNeighRightChild, lNeighRightChild);
    rChild.AddNeighs(bNeighLeftChild, lChild, rNeighLeftChild);
}
```

All you need to do is initiate the process by calling this method on the two base triangles. Add this code to the end of the LoadContent method:

```
leftTriangle.AddNeighs(null, null, rightTriangle);
rightTriangle.AddNeighs(null, null, leftTriangle);
```

Each base triangle is the only neighbor of the other. These two simple calls will propagate through your entire structure until all Triangles have stored the correct links to their three neighbors.

## Moving In: The triangleList and the IndexBuffer

With the initialization phase finished, you're ready to step forward. For each iteration of the ROAM algorithm, you'll start with a list of triangles that were drawn in the previous frame. During the iteration, you want to update this list so triangles that require higher detail are split up (replaced by their two child triangles) and so that triangles that are too detailed are merged with their respective three neighbors (see Figure 2-20). The iteration cycle finishes by each Triangle in the list storing its indices in a list, which is then uploaded to the graphics card into a buffer. Therefore, you'll need a small method inside the Triangle class that allows each Triangle to add its indices to a list:

```
public void AddIndices(ref List<int> indicesList)
{
    indicesList.Add(lInd);
    indicesList.Add(tInd);
    indicesList.Add(rInd);
}
```

Let's get back to the main code file. Since you'll be uploading this list of indices frequently, you'll want to use a DynamicIndexBuffer (see recipe 5-5). Because of this, you'll need to keep a copy of your indices locally in the indicesList. Add these three variables to the top of your code:

```
List<Triangle> triangleList;
List<int> indicesList;
DynamicIndexBuffer dynTerrainIndexBuffer;
```

Next, you start the process by adding your two base Triangles to your list and then storing their indices in another list by adding this code to the end of your LoadContent method:

```
triangleList = new List<Triangle>();
triangleList.Add(leftTriangle);
triangleList.Add(rightTriangle);

indicesList = new List<int>();
foreach (Triangle t in triangleList)
    t.AddIndices(ref indicesList);
```

Now that you have this list of indices, you're ready to transfer the list to the DynamicIndexBuffer:

```
dynTerrainIndexBuffer = new DynamicIndexBuffer(device, typeof(int), ➥
indicesList.Count, BufferUsage.WriteOnly);
dynTerrainIndexBuffer.SetData(indicesList.ToArray(), 0, indicesList.Count, ➥
SetDataOptions.Discard);
dynTerrainIndexBuffer.ContentLost += new EventHandler(dynIndexBuffer_ContentLost);
```

As explained in recipe 5-5, you need to specify a method that is called whenever the device is lost. This means you also need to specify this dynIndexBuffer_ContentLost method, which is capable of copying the indices from local memory to the graphics card:

```
private void dynIndexBuffer_ContentLost(object sender, EventArgs e)
{
    dynTerrainIndexBuffer.Dispose();
    dynTerrainIndexBuffer.SetData(indicesList.ToArray(), 0, indicesList.Count,➥
    SetDataOptions.Discard);
}
```

### Drawing the Triangles in Your triangleList

Later, you'll be adding and removing triangles from your triangleList. For now, you'll start by defining a simple method that renders the triangles contained in your triangleList. It is completely explained in recipe 5-8.

```
private void DrawTerrain()
{
    int width = heightData.GetLength(0);
    int height = heightData.GetLength(1);

    device.RenderState.FillMode = FillMode.Solid;
    device.RenderState.AlphaBlendEnable = false;

    basicEffect.World = Matrix.Identity;
    basicEffect.View = fpsCam.ViewMatrix;
    basicEffect.Projection = fpsCam.ProjectionMatrix;
    basicEffect.Texture = grassTexture;
    basicEffect.TextureEnabled = true;
```

```
basicEffect.Begin();
foreach (EffectPass pass in basicEffect.CurrentTechnique.Passes)
{
    pass.Begin();

    device.Vertices[0].SetSource(terrainVertexBuffer, 0, ➡
    VertexPositionNormalTexture.SizeInBytes);
    device.Indices = dynTerrainIndexBuffer;
    device.VertexDeclaration = myVertexDeclaration;
    int noTriangles = triangleList.Count;
    device.DrawIndexedPrimitives(PrimitiveType.TriangleList, 0, 0,➡
    width * height, 0, noTriangles);

    pass.End();
}
basicEffect.End();
```

Don't forget to call this method from within your Draw method:

```
DrawTerrain();
device.Indices = null;
```

The last line is required because you cannot change the contents of a `DynamicIndexBuffer` while it is set as active on the graphics card.

## ROAM Iteration

With the triangle structure completely initialized and the triangles currently stored in the `triangleList` collection being rendered to the screen each frame, you're ready to focus on the ROAM mechanism itself. Each iteration, you start from the triangles drawn in the previous iteration, and you need to decide which triangles to split and which to merge, depending on the current camera situation. The following are the steps involved in each ROAM iteration. Note that all these lists are emptied at the beginning of each iteration, with the obvious exception of the `triangleList`. Although it might seem easy to take some steps together, it is not, and the reason will be explained during the following paragraphs.

1. Start with the `triangleList` calculated during the previous iteration.

2. For each triangle in the list, check whether it should be split in two, and add those to the `splitList` collection. Keep track of the other triangles in the `remainderList`.

3. Split all triangles in the `splitList`, where each triangle adds its two child triangles to the `newTriangleList`. This `newTriangleList` will become the new `triangleList` at the very end of the iteration.

4. Check each triangle inside the `remainderList` whether it should be merged, and if so, add its parent triangle to the `mergeList`. Add the others to a `leftoverList`.

5. Add each parent triangle inside the `mergeList` to the `newTriangleList`.

6. For each triangle in the leftoverList, add it to the newTriangleList if it still needs to be added.

7. Save the newTriangleList in the triangleList so it is ready to be used by the next iteration.

8. Upload the indices of the triangles inside the triangleList to the DynamicIndexBuffer so these triangles will be rendered to the screen.

This entire process (except for step 8) is handled by the UpdateTriangles method you can find next. Obviously, you still need to code the methods used by the UpdateTriangles method. The UpdateTriangles method needs to be put in your main game file, because it needs access to the triangleList.

```
private void UpdateTriangles()
{
    List<Triangle> splitList = new List<Triangle>();
    List<Triangle> mergeList = new List<Triangle>();
    List<Triangle> remainderList = new List<Triangle>();
    List<Triangle> leftoverList = new List<Triangle>();
    List<Triangle> newTriangleList = new List<Triangle>(triangleList.Count);

    Matrix worldViewProjectionMatrix = Matrix.Identity * fpsCam.ViewMatrix * ➥
    fpsCam.ProjectionMatrix;
    BoundingFrustum cameraFrustum = ➥
    new BoundingFrustum(worldViewProjectionMatrix);

    foreach (Triangle t in triangleList)
        t.CreateSplitList(ref splitList, ref remainderList, ➥
        ref worldViewProjectionMatrix, ref cameraFrustum);

    foreach (Triangle t in splitList)
        t.ProcessSplitList(ref newTriangleList);

    foreach (Triangle t in remainderList)
        t.CreateMergeList(ref mergeList, ref leftoverList, ➥
        ref worldViewProjectionMatrix, ref cameraFrustum);

    foreach (Triangle t in mergeList)
        t.ProcessMergeList(ref newTriangleList, ref worldViewProjectionMatrix, ➥
        ref cameraFrustum);

    foreach (Triangle t in leftoverList)
        t.ProcessRemainders(ref newTriangleList);

    triangleList = newTriangleList;
    triangleList.TrimExcess();
}
```

## Creating the splitList

Before you can create the splitList, each Triangle should be able to decide for itself whether it should be split up. A Triangle will base itself on the screen distance between its left corner point and its center point (see Figure 2-21). The screen distance is the number of pixels on the screen that are between each point, and it will be larger for triangles closer to the camera than for triangles farther away from the camera. Only if this screen distance is larger than a certain threshold should the triangle need to be split up. All of this is decided by the ShouldSplit method, which should be put inside the Triangle class:

```
public bool ShouldSplit(ref Matrix wvp, ref BoundingFrustum bf)
{
    bool shouldSplit = false;
    if (bf.Contains(centerPos) != ContainmentType.Disjoint)
    {
        Vector4 lScreenPos = Vector4.Transform(lPos, wvp);
        Vector4 aScreenPos = Vector4.Transform(centerPos, wvp);
        lScreenPos /= lScreenPos.W;
        aScreenPos /= aScreenPos.W;

        Vector4 difference = lScreenPos - aScreenPos;
        Vector2 screenDifference = new Vector2(difference.X, difference.Y);

        float threshold = 0.1f;
        if (screenDifference.Length() > threshold)
            shouldSplit = true;
    }

    return shouldSplit;
}
```

You start by checking whether the center point is in sight of the camera (see recipe 2-5). If it isn't, the triangle shouldn't be split. If it is in sight of the camera, you find the screen positions of the left and center points. This is done exactly as in each 3D vertex shader: by transforming the 3D position with the WorldViewProjection matrix, which is the combination of the World, View, and Projection matrices. Since the result will be a Vector4, you need to divide the X, Y, and Z components by the W component before the X, Y and Z components contain meaningful values. The X,Y coordinates of the resulting value will then contain the X,Y coordinates of the screen position, both within the [–1,1] range. So, you extract these X,Y coordinates and find the screen distance, screenDifference.Length(), by subtracting the screen positions of the left and center point.

Only if screenDifference.Length() is larger than a specified threshold will the triangle decide for itself that it should split. This means that lowering the value of the threshold variable will increase the overall detail of the terrain.

---

■**Note**  In this case, if the distance is less than 1/20 of the screen size, the triangle is split up. This is still a rather high threshold. See the last paragraph of this recipe for some thoughts on this.

---

Now that each `Triangle` can decide for itself whether to split, you're almost ready to create the `splitList`. However, here you need to keep the discussion of the introduction of this recipe in mind: when a triangle needs to be split, you also need to split its bottom neighbor, as well as its parent (see the discussion at Figure 2-19). You do this by using the following method, which should also be added to the `Triangle` class:

```
public void PropagateSplit(ref List<Triangle> splitList)
{
    if (!split)
    {
        split = true;
        splitList.Add(this);
        if (bNeigh != null)
            bNeigh.PropagateSplit(ref splitList);
        if (parent != null)
            parent.PropagateSplit(ref splitList);
    }
}
```

This method sets the `split` variable to `true`, adds the current triangle to the `splitList`, and propagates the call to its bottom neighbor and parent.

This propagation is the reason the `CreateSplitList` and `ProcessSplits` steps cannot be done together; otherwise, you could add a triangle to the `newTriangleList` that would later be split because its child or bottom neighbor splits. This would result in the triangle as well as its two child triangles being drawn.

---

■**Note** It's important to first check whether the `split` variable is `false` and to set it to `true` as soon as possible. Otherwise, this mechanism would keep looping because two triangles sharing the long side would continuously keep calling this method on each other.

---

Now, you're finally ready to code the simple `CreateSplitList` method, which is called by the `UpdateTriangles` method in the main game code:

```
public void CreateSplitList(ref List<Triangle> splitList, ➥
ref List<Triangle> remainderList, ref Matrix wvp, ref BoundingFrustum bf)
{
    bool hasSplit = false;
    if ((lChild != null) && (!split))
    {
        if (ShouldSplit(ref wvp, ref bf))
        {
            PropagateSplit(ref splitList);
            hasSplit = true;
        }
    }
```

```
    if (!hasSplit)
        remainderList.Add(this);
}
```

If the triangle has not yet been split, can be split, and should be split, its PropagateSplit method is called. Otherwise, it is added to the remainderList.

### Processing the splitList

Now that you have gathered a list of all triangles that should be split, it's easy to code the ProcessSplitList method. Each triangle that should be split should add its two child triangles to the newTriangleList. However, because of propagation, it is possible that one or both child triangles by themselves are split. Such a child triangle should not be added to the newTriangleList, because the child triangle will take care of its own when its ProcessSplitList method is called.

Add the ProcessSplitList method to your Triangle class:

```
public void ProcessSplitList(ref List<Triangle> toDrawList)
{
    if (!rChild.split)
        toDrawList.Add(rChild);
    if (!lChild.split)
        toDrawList.Add(lChild);
}
```

### Creating the mergeList

Next, each triangle inside the remainderList should check whether its parent triangle should merge. According to the introduction of this recipe and according to Figure 2-20, the parent should first perform some checks to decide whether it is actually allowed to merge. This is determined by the CanMerge method, which you should also put inside your Triangle class:

```
public bool CanMerge()
{
    bool cannotMerge = false;
    if (lChild != null)
        cannotMerge |= lChild.split;
    if (rChild != null)
        cannotMerge |= rChild.split;
    if (bNeigh != null)
    {
        if (bNeigh.lChild != null)
            cannotMerge |= bNeigh.lChild.split;
        if (bNeigh.rChild != null)
            cannotMerge |= bNeigh.rChild.split;
    }

    return !cannotMerge;
}
```

As discussed in the introduction, a parent triangle is not allowed to merge when one of its child triangles is currently split or when one of the child triangles of its bottom neighbor is split.

The next method will check whether a triangle should actually merge:

```
public bool CheckMerge(ref List<Triangle> mergeList, ref Matrix wvp, ➡
ref BoundingFrustum bf)
{
    bool shouldMerge = false;
    if (!addedToMergeList)
    {
        if (CanMerge())
        {
            if (!ShouldSplit(ref wvp, ref bf))
            {
                shouldMerge = true;
                if (bNeigh != null)
                    if (bNeigh.ShouldSplit(ref wvp, ref bf))
                        shouldMerge = false;
            }
        }
    }
}
```

Since it is actually the child triangles that nominate their parents to merge, this method can be called twice during one iteration. Therefore, the shouldMerge variable will be used to indicate whether the triangle has already been added to the mergeList this iteration.

If it isn't, you first check whether the triangle can merge. If this is allowed, you check whether it actually *should* merge, in other words, whether it should not be split.

Finally, because of rounding errors, it is possible that a triangle decides that it should split while its bottom neighbor does not, which would result in a crack. Therefore, you make sure both the current triangle and its bottom neighbor think the same about merging (see Figure 2-20).

If the triangle should merge, the following code is executed, which you should put at the end of the CheckMerge method:

```
if (shouldMerge)
{
    addedToMergeList = true;
    mergeList.Add(this);
    if (bNeigh != null)
    {
        bNeigh.addedToMergeList = true;
        mergeList.Add(bNeigh);
    }
}

return addedToMergeList;
```

You start by setting the addedToMergeList variable to true, so this triangle will not execute this method again when it is called by its second child. Next, the triangle is added to the mergeList. Furthermore, if the triangle has a bottom neighbor, you also add this neighbor to the mergeList to avoid cracks. You also set its addedToMergeList variable to true, so this mechanism is not done again for that triangle.

In some cases, you've set the addedToMergeList variable to true, but you still need to reset it to false at the very beginning of an iteration. An ideal place to do this is in the CreateSplitList method, because this method is called on all triangles in the triangleList. So, add this line as the first line in the CreateSplitList method:

```
addedToMergeList = false;
```

With both methods defined, it's easy to code the CreateMergeList, which is called by the main program code. Add the method to your Triangle class as well:

```
public void CreateMergeList(ref List<Triangle> mergeList, ➥
ref List<Triangle> leftoverList, ref Matrix wvp, ref BoundingFrustum bf)
{
    bool cannotMerge = true;
    if (parent != null)
        cannotMerge = !parent.CheckMerge(ref mergeList, ref wvp, ref bf);

    if (cannotMerge)
        leftoverList.Add(this);
}
```

If the current triangle has a parent, you call its CheckMerge method, which was explained previously. If allowed and needed, the parent triangle as well as its bottom neighbor are added to the mergeList. If not, the correct child triangle is added to the leftoverList.

**Processing the mergeList**

Luckily, there's not too much you need to do with the parents that decided they should merge; they just need to reset their split variable to false and add themselves to the newTriangleList:

```
public void ProcessMergeList(ref List<Triangle> toDrawList, ref Matrix wvp, ➥
ref BoundingFrustum bf)
{
    split = false;
    toDrawList.Add(this);
}
```

**Processing the leftoverList**

It's even easier to process the contents of the leftoverList, because they simply need to add themselves to the newTriangleList. However, because of split propagation, it is possible that the current triangle has been split in the meantime, so it first needs to check this:

```
public void ProcessLeftovers(ref List<Triangle> toDrawList)
{
    if (!split)
        toDrawList.Add(this);
}
```

### Updating the Indices

With the entire ROAM mechanism implemented in the previous section, the triangles that should now be rendered are stored in the triangleList. You still need to gather their indices and transfer them to the DynamicIndexBuffer on the graphics card. Add this method to your main Game class:

```
private void UpdateIndexBuffer()
{
    indicesList.Clear();
    foreach (Triangle t in triangleList)
        t.AddIndices(ref indicesList);

    if (dynTerrainIndexBuffer.SizeInBytes / sizeof(int) < indicesList.Count)
    {
        dynTerrainIndexBuffer.Dispose();
        dynTerrainIndexBuffer = new DynamicIndexBuffer(device, typeof(int), ➥
        indicesList.Count, BufferUsage.WriteOnly);
        }
        dynTerrainIndexBuffer.SetData(indicesList.ToArray(), 0, indicesList.Count, ➥
        SetDataOptions.Discard);
}
```

The first lines gather the indices. Next, you transfer them to the DynamicIndexBuffer. However, it takes some time to re-create a new DynamicIndexBuffer. Therefore, you first check whether the current buffer is large enough to store the current list of indices. Only in case the current buffer is too small will you create a new one that's large enough. You detect how many integers the buffer can currently accommodate by finding its size and dividing this size by the number of bytes occupied by an integer.

---

■**Note**  See recipe 5-5 for more details about how to create and use the DynamicIndexBuffer.

---

## Usage

In your Update method, make sure you call the UpdateTriangles method to update your triangleList, as well as the UpdateIndexBuffer method, which transfers the indices to your graphics card:

```
UpdateTriangles();
UpdateIndexBuffer();
```

That's it for the basic ROAM implementation. The remainder of this recipe shows how you can debug your triangle structure using an orthogonal Projection matrix; it also discusses performance.

**Orthogonal Projection Matrix**

Since the ROAM triangle structure is more complicated than most other approaches, you need a powerful way to visualize in real time what exactly is going on, something like what is shown in Figure 2-22.

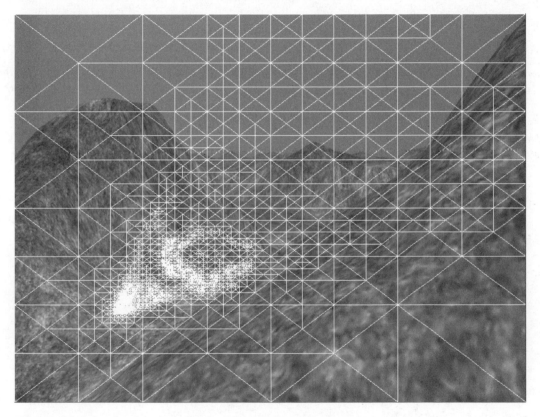

**Figure 2-22.** *Orthogonal grid rendered on top of ROAM terrain*

You should see two things in Figure 2-22. First, you should notice a vast ROAM-powered terrain that reaches out very far, yet the mountains close to the camera are rendered in nice detail. Second, rendered in white on top of that, you should notice the outlines of the triangles that are being rendered. These are the same triangles that render the terrain, with two changes:

- Only their edges are being rendered.

- They are rendered as viewed from above the terrain.

Looking at the white grid, you can tell where the camera is positioned on the terrain and where it is looking: near the camera, a large amount of triangles is being rendered, corresponding to the dense white spot at the bottom-left of the white overlay. The part of the terrain in sight of the camera decreases in detail as the distance to the camera increases. Parts that are outside the sight of the camera are rendered with as few triangles as possible.

In this section, you'll learn how to render the grid. Since you already know the indices of the triangles, you just need to render the same triangles again, only using a different View matrix and Projection matrix (see recipe 2-1).

You could simply define the position of the camera high above the center of your terrain looking straight down. This would, however, not give the desired result shown in Figure 2-22. The reason is that when using a regular Projection matrix, a triangle near the border of the screen appears smaller than the same triangle in the middle of the screen. This is caused by the pyramidal shape of the camera's view frustum, as shown in the left side of Figure 2-23. This projection causes an object to grow larger on your screen as it approaches the camera. Of the two dots on the left side, the one closer to the camera will look larger than the one at the back of the frustum. In the case of the grid, a regular Projection matrix will cause a rounding of the grid near the borders of the screen.

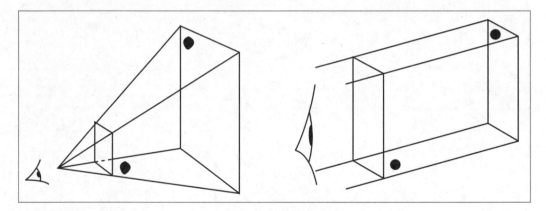

**Figure 2-23.** *Regular camera frustum (left) and orthogonal camera frustum (right)*

What you want is a camera frustum as shown on the right side of Figure 2-23, which is called an *orthographic frustum*. All objects of the same size occupy the same area on the screen in this frustum: both dots on the right side of Figure 2-23 will look equally large on the screen.

### Creating the View and Projection Matrices

Start by adding both matrices to the top of your code:

```
Matrix orthoView;
Matrix orthoProj;
```

Since this top-down camera never changes position or orientation, you can safely define both in the LoadContent method without ever having to change them again:

```
orthoView = Matrix.CreateLookAt(new Vector3(terrainSize / 2,➥
100, -terrainSize / 2), new Vector3(terrainSize / 2, 0, -terrainSize / 2),➥
Vector3.Forward);
orthoProj = Matrix.CreateOrthographic(terrainSize, terrainSize, 1, 1000);
```

Since you're in fact only changing the lens of the camera, the View matrix is defined as usual: you position it above the center of the terrain, making it look straight down to the center of the terrain. Since you'll be using an orthogonal Projection matrix, it doesn't even matter how high above the terrain you position your camera: the triangles will have the same size, no matter what their distance to the camera is.

As you can see, it's fairly easy to define an orthographic Projection matrix: you just need to specify the width and height of the view frustum in World units, as well as the near and far projection distances. For these last two values, you just need to make sure your terrain is between them.

That's it! With your matrices defined and your triangles and indices ready, you can immediately render the grid.

### Rendering the Orthogonal Grid

Since you need the same triangles to render the grid as you need to render your terrain, you can use almost the same method that renders your terrain to render your grid. The most important changes are that you're using your newly defined View and Projection matrices. Furthermore, you're setting the FillMode render state to WireFrame, so you're rendering only the borders of your triangles:

```
private void DrawOrthoGrid()
{
    int width = heightData.GetLength(0);
    int height = heightData.GetLength(1);

    device.RenderState.FillMode = FillMode.WireFrame;
    basicEffect.World = Matrix.Identity;
    basicEffect.View = orthoView;
    basicEffect.Projection = orthoProj;
    basicEffect.TextureEnabled = false;

    device.RenderState.AlphaBlendEnable = true;
    float color = 0.4f;
    device.RenderState.BlendFactor = new ➥
    Color(new Vector4(color, color, color, color));
    device.RenderState.SourceBlend = Blend.BlendFactor;
    device.RenderState.DestinationBlend = Blend.InverseBlendFactor;

    basicEffect.Begin();
    foreach (EffectPass pass in basicEffect.CurrentTechnique.Passes)
    {
        pass.Begin();
```

```
        device.Vertices[0].SetSource(terrainVertexBuffer, 0, !➥
        VertexPositionNormalTexture.SizeInBytes);
        device.Indices = dynTerrainIndexBuffer;
        device.VertexDeclaration = myVertexDeclaration;
        int noTriangles = indicesList.Count / 3;
        device.DrawIndexedPrimitives(PrimitiveType.TriangleList, 0, 0, ➥
        width * height, 0, noTriangles);

        pass.End();
    }
    basicEffect.End();
    device.RenderState.AlphaBlendEnable = false;
}
```

Because the bright white lines can be very distracting, you might want to blend in some of the terrain. This is a useful application of the BlendFactor render state: since you cannot define an alpha value for each vertex (or you would have to create a custom VertexFormat and vertex shader), you're just using a fixed alpha value for all the triangles being rendered. The BlendFactor accepts a color, and each color is made transparent by the amount indicated by the BlendFactor color.

Don't forget to call this method from within your Draw method after you've rendered your terrain:

```
DrawOrthoGrid();
```

## The Code

*All the code is available for download at www.apress.com.*

## Extra Reading

You can find entire books on LOD terrain algorithms. Although the mechanism presented in the previous pages provides a fully working ROAM implementation, I could fill the remainder of this book with possible improvements. To give you something to think about, I will briefly discuss some obvious performance improvements.

In the previous code, the ROAM process is started from within the Update method. This means that the entire mechanism is executed 60 times each second, which is far too often. For a start, the ROAM mechanism should be executed only whenever the camera is moved or rotated. In most cases, this will already cut down the calculation cost to a more bearable level.

Furthermore, the ROAM process is ideally suited to be split up into different steps. During the first cycle, you could create the splitList, process this splitList during the next cycle, and so on. Even more, complex steps (such as creating the splitList) can be split up over multiple cycles. This allows you to specify a maximum allowed time budget to spend on the algorithm each frame, which allows you to easily throttle the resources allocated to the ROAM mechanism.

Finally, because of its split nature, each step of the ROAM algorithm itself can be split into multiple parts, which can be run in parallel in different threads. This means that the algorithm can optimally benefit from multicore processors.

It is also important to note that this approach can be used in conjunction with a quadtree. Instead of using single triangles, the ROAM mechanism can be used to determine whether entire patches of the terrain should be drawn in low or high detail.

# 2-12. Set Up a Post-Processing Framework

## The Problem

You want to add a 2D post-processing effect to the final image of your XNA program, such as a blur, ripple, shock, sniper zoom, edge enhancement, or other post-processing effect.

## The Solution

You will first render your 2D or 3D scene to the screen. At the end of the Draw phase, before the contents of the back buffer are presented to the screen, you are going to hijack the contents of this back buffer and store it in a 2D image, as explained in recipe 3-8.

Next, you will render this 2D image to the screen, but you will send it through a custom pixel shader, which is the interesting part of this recipe. Inside the pixel shader, you can manipulate each pixel of the image individually.

You could do this by using a simple SpriteBatch as you would any other 2D image to the screen (see recipe 3-1), but a SpriteBatch does not support alpha blending for effects with multiple passes (like the effect shown in the next recipe). To solve this and create a framework that supports all post-processing effects, you will manually define two triangles that span the whole screen and cover these two triangles with the final image. This way, you can use any pixel shader to process the pixels of the final image.

If you want to combine multiple post-processing effects, you can render the resulting image of each into a RenderTarget2D variable instead of to the back buffer. Only the final result of the last effect should be rendered to the back buffer, of which the contents are eventually presented to the screen.

## How It Works

First, you'll need to add a few variables to your program. These include ResolveTexture2D, which you'll use to hijack the contents of the back buffer (see recipe 3-8), and RenderTarget2D, which you will use to queue multiple effects. You'll also need an effect file that contains your post-processing technique(s).

```
VertexPositionTexture[] ppVertices;
RenderTarget2D targetRenderedTo;
ResolveTexture2D resolveTexture;
Effect postProcessingEffect;
float time = 0;
```

Because you have to define two triangles that span the whole screen, you should define their vertices:

```
private void InitPostProcessingVertices()
{
    ppVertices = new VertexPositionTexture[4];
    int i = 0;
    ppVertices[i++] = new VertexPositionTexture(new ➡
    Vector3(-1, 1, 0f), new Vector2(0, 0));
    ppVertices[i++] = new VertexPositionTexture(new ➡
    Vector3(1, 1, 0f), new Vector2(1, 0));
    ppVertices[i++] = new VertexPositionTexture(new ➡
    Vector3(-1, -1, 0f), new Vector2(0, 1));
    ppVertices[i++] = new VertexPositionTexture(new ➡
    Vector3(1, -1, 0f), new Vector2(1, 1));
}
```

This method defines four vertices for the quad, rendered by two triangles as a
TriangleStrip (see recipe 5-1). At this point, it might be helpful to remember that screen
coordinates are specified within the [–1,1] region, while texture coordinates are specified
within the [0,1] region.

---

■**Note** Even when using pretransformed coordinates (in screen space instead of 3D space), make sure
you think about backface culling (see recipe 5-6). When using pretransformed coordinates, your eyes are the
camera, so you need to make sure you define your triangles clockwise on your screen. This is done by the
previous code: the first triangle is defined from the top left, over to the top right, and then to the bottom left.

---

You can see that the positions are defined immediately in screen coordinates, where the
(–1,1) point corresponds to the top-left corner of your window and where the (1,–1) point
corresponds to the bottom-right corner. You also specify that the (0,0) top-left corner of the
texture should be positioned at the (–1,1) top-left corner of your window and that the (1,1)
bottom-right corner of the texture should be positioned at the bottom-right corner of your
window. If you render this quad to the screen, the image you specify will cover your whole
window.

---

■**Note** Because your window is only 2D, you could argue you don't need the third coordinate in the position
of these vertices. However, for each pixel put on the screen, XNA keeps track of its distance to the camera in
the depth buffer, and that is what this third coordinate is used for. By specifying 0 as distance, you indicate
the image is drawn as close to the camera as possible (to be more exact, you indicate it is drawn on the near
clipping plane).

---

Don't forget to call this method from your `Initialize` method:

```
InitPostProcessingVertices();
```

The three last variables should be initialized in the `LoadContent` method:

```
PresentationParameters pp = GraphicsDevice.PresentationParameters;
targetRenderedTo = new RenderTarget2D(device, pp.BackBufferWidth, ➥
pp.BackBufferHeight, 1, device.DisplayMode.Format);
resolveTexture = new ResolveTexture2D(device, pp.BackBufferWidth, ➥
pp.BackBufferHeight, 1, device.DisplayMode.Format);
postProcessingEffect = content.Load<Effect>("content/postprocessing");
```

See recipe 3-8 for more information on render targets. Important in this case is that the new render target has the same properties as your window; it needs to have the same width, height, and color format, which you can retrieve from the `PresentationParameters` structure of your graphics device. This way, you can simply retrieve its texture, post-process it, and send the result to the screen, without having to do any scaling or color-mapping operations. Because you'll use the resulting texture only in its full scale, you don't need any mipmaps (see the note in recipe 3-7). This means you need only one mipmap level, which comes down to the texture in its original size. You also load the effect file containing your post-processing technique(s).

With the variables loaded, you can start the real work. After you've rendered your scene as usual, you want to call a method that hijacks the contents of the back buffer, manipulates it, and sends the result to the back buffer again. This is exactly what the `PostProcess` method does:

```
private void PostProcess()
{
    device.ResolveBackBuffer(resolveTexture, 0);
    Texture2D textureRenderedTo = resolveTexture;
}
```

The first line resolves the current contents of the back buffer into a `ResolveTexture2D`, in this case the variable `resolveTexture`. It contains the scene as it would have been sent to the screen. You save this as a normal `Texture2D`, called `textureRenderedto`.

Next, you'll draw the `textureRenderedTo` in the quad covering your whole window by using a post-processing effect. In this simple recipe, you'll be defining an effect, called `Invert`, that inverts the color of every pixel in the image:

```
postProcessingEffect.CurrentTechnique = postProcessingEffect.Techniques["Invert"];
postProcessingEffect.Begin();
postProcessingEffect.Parameters["textureToSampleFrom"]. ➥
SetValue(textureRenderedTo);
foreach (EffectPass pass in postProcessingEffect.CurrentTechnique.Passes)
```

```
{
    pass.Begin();
    device.VertexDeclaration = new VertexDeclaration(device, ➥
    VertexPositionTexture.VertexElements);
    device.DrawUserPrimitives<VertexPositionTexture> ➥
    (PrimitiveType.TriangleStrip, ppVertices, 0, 2);
    pass.End();
}
postProcessingEffect.End();
```

You start by selecting the post-processing technique you want to use for drawing your final image to the screen, and you start the effect.

Next, you pass the textureRenderedTo to your graphics card so your effect can sample from it. Finally, for each pass of your post-processing technique, you instruct your graphics card to render the two triangles that cover your entire window. You will code your effect so the two triangles display the image, manipulated in some way of your choice.

---

■**Note**  When drawing an object from a 3D world, you always need to set the World, View, and Projection matrices as done in many recipes of this book. These matrices allow the vertex shader in your graphics card to map the 3D coordinates from the object to the correct pixels on your screen. In this case, however, you've already defined the positions of your two triangles in screen space! So, there is no need for setting these matrices, because now the vertex shader will not change the positions of the vertices and instead will simply pass them to the pixel shader, as you'll see in the HLSL code.

---

Don't forget to call this method at the end of your Draw method:

```
PostProcess();
```

## HLSL

Only one final step remains: defining the post-processing technique itself in HLSL. There's no need to worry, because the HLSL used here is very easy. So, open a new file, and call it postprocessing.fx. I'll put its contents here in one piece:

```
texture textureToSampleFrom;
sampler textureSampler = sampler_state
{
    texture = <textureToSampleFrom>;
    magfilter = POINT;
    minfilter = POINT;
    mipfilter = POINT;
};
```

```
struct PPVertexToPixel
{
    float4 Position : POSITION;
    float2 TexCoord    : TEXCOORD0;
};
struct PPPixelToFrame
{
    float4 Color     : COLOR0;
};

PPVertexToPixel PassThroughVertexShader(float4 inPos: POSITION0, ➥
float2 inTexCoord: TEXCOORD0)
{
    PPVertexToPixel Output = (PPVertexToPixel)0;
    Output.Position = inPos;
    Output.TexCoord = inTexCoord;
    return Output;
}

//------- PP Technique: Invert --------
PPPixelToFrame InvertPS(PPVertexToPixel PSIn) : COLOR0
{
    PPPixelToFrame Output = (PPPixelToFrame)0;

    float4 colorFromTexture = tex2D(textureSampler, PSIn.TexCoord);
    Output.Color = 1-colorFromTexture;

    return Output;
}

technique Invert
{
    pass Pass0
    {
        VertexShader = compile vs_1_1 PassThroughVertexShader();
        PixelShader  = compile ps_1_1 InvertPS();
    }
}
```

This code could have been a little bit shorter, but I want to keep the structure of all HLSL code presented in this book the same. At the bottom is the technique definition, indicating the name of the technique as well as the vertex shader and pixel shader it uses. Above that are the vertex shader and pixel shader, and at the top of the code are the variables that you can set from within your XNA application. For this simple example, you can set only the 2D image you've hijacked from your back buffer before it was sent to the screen.

Next, you set up a texture sampler stage in your graphics card, which is the variable you will actually use later in your pixel shader to sample colors from. You link this sampler to the texture you just defined and indicate what to do if your code asks for the color of a coordinate that does not correspond 100 percent to a pixel. Here you specify your sampler stage should simply take the color of the nearest pixel.

---

**Note** A texture coordinate is a `float2`, with X and Y values between 0 and 1. Because these numbers are floats, almost any operation on them will result in a very small rounding error. This means that when you use such a coordinate to sample from a texture, most texture coordinates will not exactly correspond to a pixel in the texture but will be very close to one. This is why you need to indicate what the texture sampler should do in such a case.

---

Next, you define two structs: one that holds the information that is sent from the vertex shader to the pixel shader. This information is nothing more than the screen position of the pixel and where the texture needs to be sampled to obtain the color for that pixel. The second struct holds the output of the pixel shader. For each pixel, the pixel shader needs to calculate only the color.

The vertex shader allows you to manipulate the data in each vertex you've sent to the graphics card to construct triangles from. One of the most important tasks of the vertex shader in 3D applications is to transform the 3D coordinates to 2D screen coordinates. In the case of post-processing effects, the vertex shader is not really useful, because you've already defined the positions vertices of the two triangles in screen coordinates! So, you simply want the vertex shader to forward its input position to its output.

Next, you come to the pixel shader, which is the interesting part of a post-processing effect. For each pixel that needs to be drawn to the screen, this method is called, allowing you to change the color of that pixel. In the pixel shader, first an empty output structure is created, simply called `Output`. Next, the color is sampled from the `textureSampler` at the texture coordinate that was sent to the pixel shader. If your pixel shader simply output this color, the resulting output image would be the same as the input image, since each pixel of your window would sample its color from the original location of the original image. So, you'll want to change something to the coordinate that is being sampled from or to the color that is retrieved from the original image, which is done in the next paragraph.

The `colorFromTexture` variable contains four values (for red, green, blue, and alpha) between 0 and 1. In this example, you invert these values by subtracting them from 1. You save this inverted color in the `Output` structure and return it.

When you run your code, your normal scene will be hijacked into the `textureRenderedTo` texture, and the color of each of its pixels will be inverted before it's finally drawn to the screen.

## Queuing Multiple Post-Processing Effects

A few additions to the code allow you to queue multiple post-processing effects. In your `Draw` method, you'll create a list that contains the post-processing techniques you want to be applied to the image before it is sent to the screen, and you'll pass this list to the PostProcess method:

```
List<string> ppEffectsList = new List<string>();
ppEffectsList.Add("Invert");
ppEffectsList.Add("Invert");
PostProcess(ppEffectsList);
```

At this moment, you have defined only the Invert technique, so for this simple example you'll use this technique twice. By inverting an inverted image, you should again obtain the original image. How exciting is that?

You have to adjust your PostProcess method so it accepts this list of effects as an argument. As you can see, the beginning of the method has to be extended to allow for the queuing:

```
public void PostProcess(List<string> ppEffectsList)
{
    for (int currentTechnique = 0; ➡
    currentTechnique < ppEffectsList.Count; currentTechnique++)
    {
        device.SetRenderTarget(0, null);
        Texture2D textureRenderedTo;

        if (currentTechnique == 0)
        {
            device.ResolveBackBuffer(resolveTexture, 0);
            textureRenderedTo = resolveTexture;
        }
        else
        {
            textureRenderedTo = targetRenderedTo.GetTexture();
        }

        if (currentTechnique == ppEffectsList.Count - 1)
            device.SetRenderTarget(0, null);
        else
            device.SetRenderTarget(0, targetRenderedTo);

        postProcessingEffect.CurrentTechnique = ➡
        postProcessingEffect.Techniques[ppEffectsList[currentTechnique]];
        postProcessingEffect.Begin();

        postProcessingEffect.Parameters["textureToSampleFrom"]. ➡
        SetValue(textureRenderedTo);
        foreach (EffectPass pass in postProcessingEffect.CurrentTechnique.Passes)
```

```
            {
                pass.Begin();
                device.VertexDeclaration = new ➡
                VertexDeclaration(device, ➡
                VertexPositionTexture.VertexElements);
                device.DrawUserPrimitives<VertexPositionTexture> ➡
                (PrimitiveType.TriangleStrip, ppVertices, 0, 2);
                pass.End();
            }
        postProcessingEffect.End();
    }
}
```

The idea behind this method is shown in Figure 2-24. Basically, for each effect in your list, you will retrieve the current contents of the RenderTarget into a texture and render it again into the RenderTarget using the current effect. There are two exceptions on this basic rule.

First, for the first effect, hijack the contents of the back buffer, instead of the contents of the RenderTarget. Finally, for the last effect, render the result into the back buffer, so it will be rendered to the screen. This process is displayed in Figure 2-24.

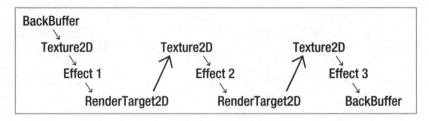

**Figure 2-24.** *Queuing multiple post-processing effects*

The previous code shows how it's done. If it's the first technique, store the contents of the back buffer into textureRenderedTo. Otherwise, get the contents of RenderTarget and store it into textureRenderedTo. Either way, textureRenderTo will contain what was drawn last. As explained in recipe 3-8, before calling GetTexture on RenderTarget, you must have activated another RenderTarget, which is done by the very first line of the method.

Next, you check whether the current technique is the last one in the list. If it is, you set the back buffer as the current render target by passing null in the device.SetRenderTarget method (you can leave this line out, as it was done at the beginning of the method). Otherwise, you reset your custom RenderTarget2D as the active render target.

The remainder of the code has remained the same.

As a second simple example of a post-processing technique, you can change the color value depending on the time. Add this line to the top of the .fx file:

```
float xTime;
```

It's a variable that can be set in your XNA app and can be read from within your HLSL code. Add this code to the end of your .fx file:

```
//------- PP Technique: TimeChange --------
PPPixelToFrame TimeChangePS(PPVertexToPixel PSIn) : COLOR0
{
    PPPixelToFrame Output = (PPPixelToFrame)0;

    Output.Color = tex2D(textureSampler, PSIn.TexCoord);
    Output.Color.b *= sin(xTime);
    Output.Color.rg *= cos(xTime);
    Output.Color += 0.2f;

    return Output;
}

technique TimeChange
{
    pass Pass0
    {
        VertexShader = compile vs_1_1 PassThroughVertexShader();
        PixelShader  = compile ps_2_0 TimeChangePS();
    }
}
```

For each pixel of the image, the blue color component is multiplied with a sine that depends on the xTime variable, and the red and green color components will be multiplied by the cosine of the same variable. Remember, a sine and cosine produce a wave between –1 and +1, and all negative values for color components will be clipped to 0.

Use this technique to render the final image:

```
List<string> ppEffectsList = new List<string>();
ppEffectsList.Add("Invert");
ppEffectsList.Add("TimeChange");
postProcessingEffect.Parameters["xTime"].SetValue(time);
PostProcess(ppEffectsList);
```

Note you set the xTime value to a certain value, kept in time. You need to specify this time variable in your XNA code:

```
float time;
```

Also, update its value in the Update method:

```
time += gameTime.ElapsedGameTime.Milliseconds / 1000.0f;
```

When you run this, you'll see the colors of your image change over time. It's not too nice yet, but you're changing pixel color values based only on their original colors. See the next recipe, where the colors of the surrounding pixels are also taken into account when defining the final color of a pixel.

## The Code

*All the code is available for download at www.apress.com.*

The following are the vertices that define the quad you'll use to display the resulting full-screen image:

```
private void InitPostProcessingVertices()
{
    ppVertices = new VertexPositionTexture[4];
    int i = 0;
    ppVertices[i++] = new VertexPositionTexture(new ➥
    Vector3(-1, 1, 0f), new Vector2(0, 0));
    ppVertices[i++] = new VertexPositionTexture(new ➥
    Vector3(1, 1, 0f), new Vector2(1, 0));
    ppVertices[i++] = new VertexPositionTexture(new ➥
    Vector3(-1, -1, 0f), new Vector2(0, 1));
    ppVertices[i++] = new VertexPositionTexture(new ➥
    Vector3(1, -1, 0f), new Vector2(1, 1));
}
```

In your Draw method, you should render your scene as usual. After rendering, define which post-processing effects you want to be performed, and pass this list to the PostProcess method:

```
protected override void Draw(GameTime gameTime)
{
    device.Clear(ClearOptions.Target|ClearOptions.DepthBuffer, ➥
    Color.CornflowerBlue, 1, 0);

    //draw model
    Matrix worldMatrix = Matrix.CreateScale(0.01f, 0.01f, 0.01f) * ➥
    Matrix.CreateTranslation(0, 0, 0);
    myModel.CopyAbsoluteBoneTransformsTo(modelTransforms);
    foreach (ModelMesh mesh in myModel.Meshes)
    {
        foreach (BasicEffect effect in mesh.Effects)
        {
            effect.EnableDefaultLighting();
            effect.World = modelTransforms[mesh.ParentBone.Index] * worldMatrix;
            effect.View = fpsCam.ViewMatrix;
            effect.Projection = fpsCam.ProjectionMatrix;
        }
        mesh.Draw();
    }

    //draw coordcross
    cCross.Draw(fpsCam.ViewMatrix, fpsCam.ProjectionMatrix);
```

```
List<string> ppEffectsList = new List<string>();
ppEffectsList.Add("Invert");
ppEffectsList.Add("TimeChange");
postProcessingEffect.Parameters["xTime"].SetValue(time);
PostProcess(ppEffectsList);

base.Draw(gameTime);
}
```

At the end of the Draw method, you call the PostProcess method, which hijacks the back buffer and renders the image to the screen using one or more of your post-processing effects:

```
public void PostProcess(List<string> ppEffectsList)
{
    for (int currentTechnique = 0; ➡
    currentTechnique < ppEffectsList.Count; currentTechnique++)
    {
        device.SetRenderTarget(0, null);
        Texture2D textureRenderedTo;

        if (currentTechnique == 0)
        {
            device.ResolveBackBuffer(resolveTexture, 0);
            textureRenderedTo = resolveTexture;
        }
        else
        {
            textureRenderedTo = targetRenderedTo.GetTexture();
        }

        if (currentTechnique == ppEffectsList.Count - 1)
            device.SetRenderTarget(0, null);
        else
            device.SetRenderTarget(0, targetRenderedTo);

        postProcessingEffect.CurrentTechnique = ➡
        postProcessingEffect.Techniques[ppEffectsList[currentTechnique]];
        postProcessingEffect.Begin();
                    postProcessingEffect.Parameters["textureToSampleFrom"]. ➡
        SetValue(textureRenderedTo);
        foreach (EffectPass pass in postProcessingEffect.CurrentTechnique.Passes)
        {
            pass.Begin();
            device.VertexDeclaration = new ➡
            VertexDeclaration(device, VertexPositionTexture.VertexElements);
```

```
            device.DrawUserPrimitives<VertexPositionTexture> ➥
            (PrimitiveType.TriangleStrip, ppVertices, 0, 2);
            pass.End();
        }
        postProcessingEffect.End();
    }
}
```

In your HLSL file, make sure you bind your texture sampler stage to your textureToSampleFrom variable:

```
float xTime;

texture textureToSampleFrom;
sampler textureSampler = sampler_state
{
    texture = <textureToSampleFrom>;
    magfilter = POINT;
    minfilter = POINT;
    mipfilter = POINT;
};

struct PPVertexToPixel
{
    float4 Position : POSITION;
    float2 TexCoord    : TEXCOORD0;
};
struct PPPixelToFrame
{
    float4 Color     : COLOR0;
};

PPVertexToPixel PassThroughVertexShader(float4 inPos: POSITION0, ➥
float2 inTexCoord: TEXCOORD0)
{
    PPVertexToPixel Output = (PPVertexToPixel)0;
    Output.Position = inPos;
    Output.TexCoord = inTexCoord;
    return Output;
}


//------- PP Technique: Invert --------
PPPixelToFrame InvertPS(PPVertexToPixel PSIn) : COLOR0
{
    PPPixelToFrame Output = (PPPixelToFrame)0;
```

```
    float4 colorFromTexture = tex2D(textureSampler, PSIn.TexCoord);
    Output.Color = 1-colorFromTexture;

    return Output;
}


technique Invert
{
    pass Pass0
    {
        VertexShader = compile vs_1_1 PassThroughVertexShader();
        PixelShader  = compile ps_1_1 InvertPS();
    }
}


//------- PP Technique: TimeChange --------
PPPixelToFrame TimeChangePS(PPVertexToPixel PSIn) : COLOR0
{
    PPPixelToFrame Output = (PPPixelToFrame)0;


    Output.Color = tex2D(textureSampler, PSIn.TexCoord);
    Output.Color.b *= sin(xTime);
    Output.Color.rg *= cos(xTime);
    Output.Color += 0.2f;

    return Output;
}

technique TimeChange
{
    pass Pass0
    {
        VertexShader = compile vs_1_1 PassThroughVertexShader();
        PixelShader  = compile ps_2_0 TimeChangePS();
    }
}
```

# 2-13. Create a Blur/Glow Post-Processing Effect

## The Problem

You want to add a blurred look to your final image, or you want to add a glow to the objects in your scene.

## The Solution

Both effects are post-processing effects. See the previous recipe to learn how you can set up a post-processing framework. The glow effect was chosen because it demonstrates how to blend the outputs of multiple shader passes together.

You can obtain a blurred effect by calculating for each pixel the mean color value of some of the surrounding pixels and then replacing the original color of the pixel by this mean value. For example, if the grid in Figure 2-25 were an image that needed to be blurred, how would you calculate the resulting color value of pixel 9?

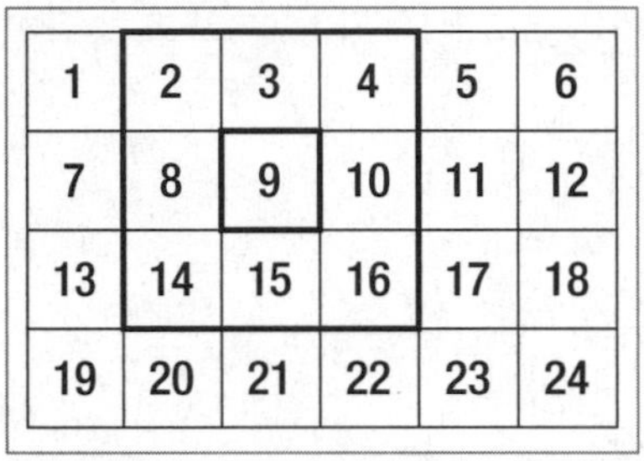

1 2 3 4 5 6
7 8 9 10 11 12
13 14 15 16 17 18
19 20 21 22 23 24

**Figure 2-25.** *Calculating the mean color value of a pixel in a 2D texture*

You find the mean of nine numbers by summing the nine numbers and dividing the result by 9. You find the mean color in the same way: by summing the colors of pixels 2 to 4, summing pixels 8 to 10 and pixels 14 to 16, and then dividing the result by the number of pixels, which is 9.

If all the pixels are white except pixel 9, as is the case in the left part of Figure 2-26, this would have the result that the color of pixel 9 is spread out over pixels 2 to 4, 8 to 10, and 14 to 16, which causes pixel 9 to "expand." However, the color of pixel 9 itself is weakened, because it is also replaced by the mean of the colors of its surrounding pixels. This is shown in the middle part of Figure 2-26. To obtain a glow, you blend in the original image, which would somewhat restore the original color of pixel 9. So, you end up with pixel 9 having its original color and the pixels surrounding pixel 9 having a bit of the color of pixel 9, which makes it seem like pixel 9 has a glow, as shown in the right part of Figure 2-26.

1 2 3 4 5 6
7 8 9 10 11 12
13 14 15 16 17 18
19 20 21 22 23 24

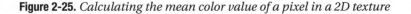

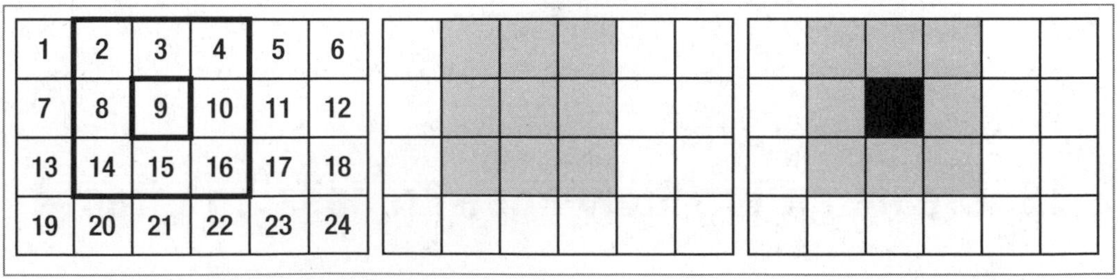

**Figure 2-26.** *Creating a glow*

## How It Works

There are a few caveats, however. To get a nice blur, you need to average over a lot of pixels around the center pixel to get a nice result. A much better way would be to first blur the image horizontally by averaging over just a few pixels on the same row as the center pixel. Next, you would take the result and blur this result vertically by averaging over a few pixels on the same column as the center pixel. This would give you two 1D averages, instead of one 2D average, which would require you to average over many more pixels to get a nice result.

Second, you should decide which pixels to average over. You get the best results by giving the pixels close to the pixel of interest more importance than the pixels farther away. This is called giving them more "weight." For your convenience, I have calculated some offsets and weights corresponding to a Gaussian, which corresponds to blurring as it happens in nature.

Look at the following list, which contains the distances to pixels that will be taken into account. The first entry has 0 offset, meaning the color of the center pixel itself will be taken into account. The second entry has a 0.005 offset, which will result in the sampling of a pixel very close to the center pixel. To make things symmetrical, you will sample the two pixels that are 0.005 away both to the left and right from the center pixel, and you will give both colors a weight of 0.102 in the final color, as you can see in the second list. Next, you'll sample the left and right pixels that are 0.0117 away from the center pixel, and you'll give them a little less weight, 0.0936. You continue like this until you get pretty far away from the center pixel and thus also assign little weight to these outliers.

```
float positions[] =
{
    0.0f,
    0.005,
    0.01166667,
    0.01833333,
    0.025,
    0.03166667,
    0.03833333,
    0.045,
};

float weights[] =
{
    0.0530577,
    0.1028506,
    0.09364651,
    0.0801001,
    0.06436224,
    0.04858317,
    0.03445063,
    0.02294906,
};
```

It's important to note that if you add the weights of all points you'll take into account together, their sum should equal 1. This makes sure no color gets lost or added in the image.

■**Note** The center pixel seems to have a small weight in comparison to the other pixels that are sampled. However, because +0 and −0 are the same, the center pixel will be taken into account twice, effectively doubling its weight and making it the pixel that will have the most influence on the final result.

You will also be using an xBlurSize variable so you can tweak the width of the blurring effect from within your XNA application:

```
float xBlurSize = 0.5f;
```

You can already create the empty body for the HorBlur effect, based on the previous recipe:

```
//------- PP Technique: HorBlur --------
PPPixelToFrame HorBlurPS(PPVertexToPixel PSIn) : COLOR0
{
    PPPixelToFrame Output = (PPPixelToFrame)0;

    return Output;
}

technique HorBlur
{
    pass Pass0
    {
        VertexShader = compile vs_1_1 DefaultVertexShader();
        PixelShader  = compile ps_2_0 HorBlurPS();
    }
}
```

The actual effect is defined in the pixel shader. For each surrounding pixel from the list defined earlier, you will sample the color and multiply it by its assigned weight. For symmetry, you will do this on both sides of the center pixel. Finally, you add all colors together.

You find the locations of the surrounding pixels by starting from the TexCoord of the center pixel and adding the value from the positions array as the horizontal texture coordinate:

```
PPPixelToFrame HorBlurPS(PPVertexToPixel PSIn) : COLOR0
{
    PPPixelToFrame Output = (PPPixelToFrame)0;

    for (int i = 0; i < 8; i++)
    {
        float4 samplePos = tex2D(textureSampler, PSIn.TexCoord + ➥
        float2(positions[i], 0)*xBlurSize);
        samplePos *= weights[i];
```

```
        float4 sampleNeg = tex2D(textureSampler, PSIn.TexCoord - ➥
        float2(positions[i], 0)*xBlurSize);
        sampleNeg *= weights[i];
        Output.Color += samplePos + sampleNeg;
    }

    return Output;
}
```

You can see that the xBlurSize variable can be used to increase/decrease the distance between the pixel of interest and its neighbors.

Now inside your XNA application, you simply have to assign a value to this variable and activate the effect:

```
List<string> ppEffectsList = new List<string>();
ppEffectsList.Add("HorBlur");

postProcessor.Parameters["xBlurSize"].SetValue(0.5f);
postProcessor.PostProcess(ppEffectsList);
```

## Vertical Blur

Now that you have the horizontal blur, it's quite easy to create the vertical blur. Instead of adding the value from the positions array to the horizontal texture coordinate, you should add it to the vertical texture coordinate, selecting the pixels on the same column as the pixel of interest:

```
//------- PP Technique: VerBlur --------
PPPixelToFrame VerBlurPS(PPVertexToPixel PSIn) : COLOR0
{
    PPPixelToFrame Output = (PPPixelToFrame)0;

    for (int i = 0; i < 8; i++)
    {
        float4 samplePos = tex2D(textureSampler, PSIn.TexCoord + ➥
        float2(0, positions[i])*xBlurSize);
        samplePos *= weights[i];
        float4 sampleNeg = tex2D(textureSampler, PSIn.TexCoord - ➥
        float2(0, positions[i])*xBlurSize);
        sampleNeg *= weights[i];
        Output.Color += samplePos + sampleNeg;
    }

    return Output;
}
```

```
technique VerBlur
{
    pass Pass0
    {
        VertexShader = compile vs_1_1 PassThroughVertexShader();
        PixelShader  = compile ps_2_0 VerBlurPS();
    }
}
```

You will get a nicely blurred image by combining the horizontal and vertical blurs:

```
List<string> ppEffectsList = new List<string>();
ppEffectsList.Add("HorBlur");
ppEffectsList.Add("VerBlur");

postProcessor.Parameters["xBlurSize"].SetValue(0.5f);
postProcessor.PostProcess(ppEffectsList);
```

## The Glow Effect

As explained in the introduction of this recipe, you can obtain a glow effect by starting from the blended image and blending in the original image a bit. This way, the original contours will be sharpened.

This requires you to have the blurred image present in the back buffer, so during a second pass, you can blend in the original image. Therefore, you will define a new technique, a glow, that has as a first pass the vertical blur and as a second pass a blend-in pass:

```
technique VerBlurAndGlow
{
    pass Pass0
    {
        VertexShader = compile vs_1_1 PassThroughVertexShader();
        PixelShader  = compile ps_2_0 VerBlurPS();
    }
    pass Pass1
    {
        AlphaBlendEnable = true;
        SrcBlend = SrcAlpha;
        DestBlend = InvSrcAlpha;
        PixelShader  = compile ps_2_0 BlendInPS();
    }
}
```

The second pass is new. You can see three render states are changed at the beginning of the pass: you enable alpha blending and set the alpha function. You'll learn more about this alpha function in a few minutes. The effect will start with the first pass, so the blurred image will be present in the back buffer. Next, the second pass will be started, allowing you to blend in the original image over the image in the back buffer.

This is the pixel shader for the second pass:

```
//------- PP Technique: VerBlurAndGlow --------
PPPixelToFrame BlendInPS(PPVertexToPixel PSIn) : COLOR0
{
    PPPixelToFrame Output = (PPPixelToFrame)0;

    float4 finalColor = tex2D(originalSampler, PSIn.TexCoord);
    finalColor.a = 0.3f;

    Output.Color = finalColor;
    return Output;
}
```

Here, you sample the color of the pixel of the original image and adjust its alpha (transparency) value. When blending in XNA, the final color is found using this rule:

```
finalColor=sourceBlend*sourceColor+destBlend*destColor
```

In the technique definition, you've set `sourceBlend` to `SourceAlpha`. This means `sourceBlend` equals the alpha value of the color you want to blend in, which is 0.3f, as you've defined in the previous code. Furthermore, you've set `destBlend` to `InvSourceAlpha`, meaning 1 – SourceAlpha. So, `destBlend` will be 1 – 0.3f = 0.7f.

In summary, 70 percent of the final color will be taken from the color already present in the back buffer (in which the blurred image of the first pass is stored). The remaining 30 percent will be taken from the new color you want to write to the back buffer, which, in this case, is sampled from the original image.

You haven't yet defined the `originalSampler`. Add it to the top of your effect file:

```
texture originalImage;
sampler originalSampler = sampler_state
{
    texture = <originalImage>;
    magfilter = LINEAR;
    minfilter = LINEAR;
    mipfilter = LINEAR;
};
```

In your XNA project, you should store the original image that you hijacked from the back buffer into this `originalImage` variable. Luckily, using the framework created in the previous chapter, you can do this easily during the first effect:

```
if (currentTechnique == 0)
{
    device.ResolveBackBuffer(resolveTexture, 0);
    textureRenderedTo = resolveTexture;
    ppEffect.Parameters["originalImage"].SetValue(textureRenderedTo);
}
```

The last line sends the original image to your HLSL effect.

Now that all your effects are ready, this code will first blur your image vertically. Afterward, this result will first be horizontally blurred by the first pass of the VerBlurAndGlow effect. After the first pass, the blurred image will remain inside the frame buffer, allowing you to blend in the original image!

```
List<string> ppEffectsList = new List<string>();
ppEffectsList.Add("HorBlur");
ppEffectsList.Add("VerBlurAndGlow");

postProcessor.Parameters["xBlurSize"].SetValue(0.5f);
postProcessor.PostProcess(ppEffectsList);
```

## The Code

*All the code is available for download at www.apress.com.*

As for all post-processing effects, you need to bind the texture sampler stage to the image containing your scene. The glow effect also expects you to store the original image inside the originalImage variable.

```
float xTime;
float xBlurSize = 0.5f;

texture textureToSampleFrom;
sampler textureSampler = sampler_state
{
    texture = <textureToSampleFrom>;
    magfilter = LINEAR;
    minfilter = LINEAR;
    mipfilter = LINEAR;
};

texture originalImage;
sampler originalSampler = sampler_state
{
    texture = <originalImage>;
    magfilter = LINEAR;
    minfilter = LINEAR;
    mipfilter = LINEAR;
};

float positions[] =
{
    0.0f,
    0.005,
    0.01166667,
    0.01833333,
```

```
    0.025,
    0.03166667,
    0.03833333,
    0.045,
};

float weights[] =
{
    0.0530577,
    0.1028506,
    0.09364651,
    0.0801001,
    0.06436224,
    0.04858317,
    0.03445063,
    0.02294906,
};

struct PPVertexToPixel
{
    float4 Position : POSITION;
    float2 TexCoord    : TEXCOORD0;
};
struct PPPixelToFrame
{
    float4 Color    : COLOR0;
};

PPVertexToPixel PassThroughVertexShader(float4 inPos: POSITION0, ➥
float2 inTexCoord: TEXCOORD0)

{
    PPVertexToPixel Output = (PPVertexToPixel)0;
    Output.Position = inPos;
    Output.TexCoord = inTexCoord;
    return Output;
}

//-------- PP Technique: HorBlur --------
PPPixelToFrame HorBlurPS(PPVertexToPixel PSIn) : COLOR0
{
    PPPixelToFrame Output = (PPPixelToFrame)0;
```

```
    for (int i = 0; i < 8; i++)
    {
        float4 samplePos = tex2D(textureSampler, PSIn.TexCoord + ➥
        float2(positions[i], 0)*xBlurSize);
        samplePos *= weights[i];
        float4 sampleNeg = tex2D(textureSampler, PSIn.TexCoord - ➥
        float2(positions[i], 0)*xBlurSize);
        sampleNeg *= weights[i];
        Output.Color += samplePos + sampleNeg;
    }

    return Output;
}


technique HorBlur
{
    pass Pass0
    {
        VertexShader = compile vs_1_1 PassThroughVertexShader();
        PixelShader  = compile ps_2_0 HorBlurPS();
    }
}

//------- PP Technique: VerBlur --------
PPPixelToFrame VerBlurPS(PPVertexToPixel PSIn) : COLOR0
{
    PPPixelToFrame Output = (PPPixelToFrame)0;

    for (int i = 0; i < 8; i++)
    {
        float4 samplePos = tex2D(textureSampler, PSIn.TexCoord + ➥
        float2(0, positions[i])*xBlurSize);
        samplePos *= weights[i];
        float4 sampleNeg = tex2D(textureSampler, PSIn.TexCoord - ➥
        float2(0, positions[i])*xBlurSize);
        sampleNeg *= weights[i];
        Output.Color += samplePos + sampleNeg;
    }

    return Output;
}
```

```
technique VerBlur
{
    pass Pass0
    {
        VertexShader = compile vs_1_1 PassThroughVertexShader();
        PixelShader  = compile ps_2_0 VerBlurPS();
    }
}

//------- PP Technique: VerBlurAndGlow --------
PPPixelToFrame BlendInPS(PPVertexToPixel PSIn) : COLOR0
{
    PPPixelToFrame Output = (PPPixelToFrame)0;

    float4 finalColor = tex2D(originalSampler, PSIn.TexCoord);
    finalColor.a = 0.3f;

    Output.Color = finalColor;
    return Output;
}


technique VerBlurAndGlow
{
    pass Pass0
    {
        VertexShader = compile vs_1_1 PassThroughVertexShader();
        PixelShader  = compile ps_2_0 VerBlurPS();
    }
    pass Pass1
    {
        AlphaBlendEnable = true;
        SrcBlend = SrcAlpha;
        DestBlend = InvSrcAlpha;
        PixelShader  = compile ps_2_0 BlendInPS();
    }
}
```

## Extra Reading

Every finished game contains a set of post-processing effects, because they have the potential of bringing that extra touch to the final image. Although the blur effect is a relatively easy concept, some sort of blurring or glowing is almost always used to cover some imperfections near the edges of 3D objects.

A whole range of post-processing effects exists, but with the glow effect that uses multiple passes and alpha blending, you know the basics behind most of them.

# 2-14. Write a Custom Content Importer

## The Problem

You want to load a file of a custom format into your XNA project through the content pipeline. Because the extension and/or the structure of your file will be different from the file formats known to XNA, the default XNA content pipeline does not know how to import and process your file into a useful game object.

## The Solution

You will write a custom content importer, capable of reading in the file from disk and formatting the useful data into an object, ready to be processed by a content processor. Therefore, this recipe assumes you already know how to create your own content processor. You are encouraged to read the introduction to the content pipeline in recipe 3-9.

This recipe will focus on the custom importer only. The ContentImporter should read in the data from disk and format it into an object. In this recipe, you will read in two Vector3s that have been stored in a comma-separated values (CSV) file and transform them into a View matrix. This example was chosen because a View matrix needs some processing calculations to be constructed, and the XNA framework comes with a default TypeWriter and TypeReader capable of serializing and deserializing Matrix objects. This allows the recipe to put its focus on loading a file from disk, writing a content importer, and accepting the data in a custom content processor.

Have a look at Figure 5-27 for the visualization of the focus of this recipe. The custom importer will read in data from a CSV file and create a CSVImporterToProcessor objcct storing the useful data extracted from the file. The custom CSVMatrixProcessor will process the data in this CSVImporterToProcessor object class into a Matrix object. From then on, XNA's default TypeWriter and TypeReader for a Matrix object will take care of the serializing and deserializing. See recipe 4-15 and recipe 4-16 for information about coding your own TypeWriters and TypeReaders.

Because both the importer and processor are invoked at compile time, you might wonder what good it is to split up the processing task between the importer and the processor. For example, wouldn't it be much simpler to just define a method that reads in a CSV file and shapes this data immediately into a Matrix object, instead of having two methods and an intermediate CSVMatrixProcessor object?

The benefit of splitting things up is that you can reuse a processor for multiple importers (or vice versa). For example, the XNA Framework comes with a processor capable of transforming a NodeContent object into a ModelContent object. If you import a model from a different format from .x or .fbx, all you have to do is write an importer that creates a NodeContent from your file, with the default ModelProcessor taking your job from there.

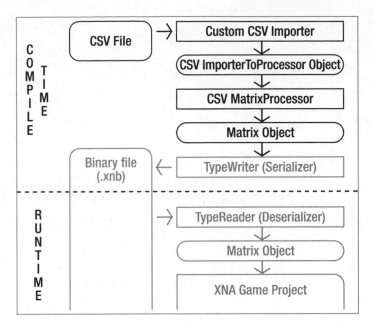

**Figure 2-27.** *Defining a custom content importer and its place in the content pipeline*

## How It Works

Start at the beginning by defining the CSV using a simple text editor. This is what my CSV file looks like:

```
-5;5;8;
0;2;0;
```

These are the position and target of the view matrix you'll construct in this recipe.

### Intermediate Class

Next, go through the checklist presented in recipe 3-9. I called my pipeline project CSVToViewMatrixPipeline. Don't do anything at step 4 of recipe 3-9; you'll be coding a few additional methods. At the end of this recipe, you can find the full code of the content pipeline project.

First, you'll need an object that can be used to store the data read in from disk. This object will be the output of the content importer and the input of the content processor (which will use its contents to construct a View matrix). Add the custom CSVImporterToProcessor class, which can store two Vector3s:

```
public class CSVImporterToProcessor
{
    private Vector3 position;
    private Vector3 target;
```

```
public Vector3 Position { get { return position; } }
public Vector3 Target { get { return target; } }

public CSVImporterToProcessor(Vector3 position, Vector3 target)
{
    this.position = position;
    this.target = target;
}
}
```

This class is capable of storing two Vector3s. The two getter methods allow the processor to access this data. The importer will need to provide all the data when calling the constructor method.

## The ContentImporter

The ContentImporter will actually read in the data from the file, so make sure that, at the top of your file, you've linked to the namespace containing them (this was explained in step 3 of recipe 3-9, introducing the content pipeline):

using System.IO;

You're ready to code your custom importer. Add its empty body:

```
[ContentImporter(".csv", DefaultProcessor = "CSVMatrixProcessor")]
public class CSVImporter : ContentImporter<CSVImporterToProcessor>
{
    public override CSVImporterToProcessor Import(string filename, ➥
    ContentImporterContext context)
    {
    }
}
```

The attribute indicates this class is a content importer capable of handling .csv files and that by default its output should be processed by the CSVHeightMapProcessor (which you will create in a moment). In the next line, you specify that this importer will generate a CSVImporterToProcessor object.

At compile time, the importer receives the file name of the .csv file to be imported and should transform it into a CSVImporterToProcessor object. Start by opening the file and reading in the first line, as done by the first two lines in the code that follows. To separate the value between ; you should use the simple Strip method, which in this case returns an array of three strings, with each string holding a number for our camera position. The next three lines convert these strings to float numbers, which are in the end used to create the position Vector3.

```
StreamReader file = new StreamReader(filename);

string line = file.ReadLine();
string[] lineData = line.Split(';');
float x = float.Parse(lineData[0]);
float y = float.Parse(lineData[1]);
float z = float.Parse(lineData[2]);
Vector3 position = new Vector3(x,y,z);
```

You read the second line from the file and convert it into the target Vector3 in exactly the same way:

```
line = file.ReadLine();
lineData = line.Split(';');
x = float.Parse(lineData[0]);
y = float.Parse(lineData[1]);
z = float.Parse(lineData[2]);
Vector3 target = new Vector3(x,y,z);
```

Now, you have all the data ready to create a CSVImporterToProcessor object:

```
CSVImporterToProcessor finalData = new CSVImporterToProcessor(position, target);
return finalData;
```

This object will be sent to the processor the user selects to process the asset. Obviously, the processor should be capable of taking a CSVImporterToProcessor object as input.

## Receiving the Data in a Content Processor

Because the CSVImporterToProcessor class is a custom class, you'll need to create a custom processor. This sample processor will process the CSVImporterToProcessor object into a Matrix object. See the first recipes of this chapter for information on how to construct a View matrix based on the position and target of a camera:

```
[ContentProcessor]
public class CSVMatrixProcessor : ContentProcessor<CSVImporterToProcessor, Matrix>
{
    public override Matrix Process(CSVImporterToProcessor input, ➥
    ContentProcessorContext context)
    {
        Vector3 up = new Vector3(0, 1, 0);
        Vector3 forward = input.Target - input.Position;
        Vector3 right = Vector3.Cross(forward, up);
        up = Vector3.Cross(right, forward);

        Matrix viewMatrix = Matrix.CreateLookAt(input.Position, input.Target, up);
        return viewMatrix;
    }
}
```

You indicate this processor is capable of transforming a `CSVImporterToProcessor` object into a `Matrix` object. The `position` and `target` inside the `CSVImporterToProcessor` object are used to create the View matrix. XNA knows by default how to serialize/deserialize a `Matrix` object to/from the binary file and load the resulting `Matrix` object in your XNA game project, so you don't have to code a custom `TypeWriter` and `TypeReader`.

## Usage

When you make sure you fulfill all nine steps of recipe 3-9, you should be able to import `.csv` files into your project. When you select such an imported `.csv` file in your Solution Explorer, you should notice in the Properties window that the file will be imported by your `CSVImporter`, as shown in Figure 2-28. Also, because you indicated this to be the default processor, the `CSVMatrixProcessor` is chosen as the processor.

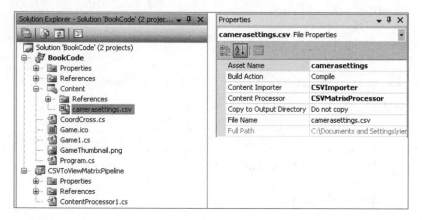

**Figure 2-28.** *Selecting the content importer and content processor*

Once the `.csv` file has been imported, all you need to load a View matrix from a `.csv` file is just one line of code:

```
protected override void LoadContent()
{
    viewMatrix = Content.Load<Matrix>("camerasettings");
}
```

## The Code

*All the code is available for download at www.apress.com.*

Since the entire content pipeline is rather short, I'll list it here in one piece. The first block links to the necessary namespaces. The first class inside the namespace is the `CSVImporterToProcessor` class, which is capable of storing all the required data, from the importer to the processor. Next is the `ContentImporter` class itself, which is capable of reading in a .csv file and storing the useful data inside such a CSVImporterToProcessor object. The last block is a content processor, capable of creating a View matrix based on the contents of a CSVImporterToProcessor object. Since XNA comes with a TypeWriter and TypeReader capable of handling a Matrix object, that's all you need for a fully functional content pipeline. If your processor creates an object of a custom class, see recipes 4-15 and 4-16 for information on how to create your own TypeWriter and TypeReader.

```
using System;
using System.Collections.Generic;
using System.Linq;
using Microsoft.Xna.Framework;
using Microsoft.Xna.Framework.Graphics;
using Microsoft.Xna.Framework.Content.Pipeline;
using Microsoft.Xna.Framework.Content.Pipeline.Graphics;
using Microsoft.Xna.Framework.Content.Pipeline.Processors;
using System.IO;
using Microsoft.Xna.Framework.Content;
using Microsoft.Xna.Framework.Content.Pipeline.Serialization.Compiler;

namespace CVSToViewMatrixPipeline
{
    public class CSVImporterToProcessor
    {
        private Vector3 position;
        private Vector3 target;

        public Vector3 Position { get { return position; } }
        public Vector3 Target { get { return target; } }

        public CSVImporterToProcessor(Vector3 position, Vector3 target)
        {
            this.position = position;
            this.target = target;
        }
    }

    [ContentImporter(".csv", DefaultProcessor = "CSVMatrixProcessor")]
    public class CSVImporter : ContentImporter<CSVImporterToProcessor>
    {
        public override CSVImporterToProcessor Import(string filename, ➥
        ContentImporterContext context)
        {
            StreamReader file = new StreamReader(filename);
```

```
                    string line = file.ReadLine();
                    string[] lineData = line.Split(';');
                    float x = float.Parse(lineData[0]);
                    float y = float.Parse(lineData[1]);
                    float z = float.Parse(lineData[2]);
                    Vector3 position = new Vector3(x,y,z);

                    line = file.ReadLine();
                    lineData = line.Split(';');
                    x = float.Parse(lineData[0]);
                    y = float.Parse(lineData[1]);
                    z = float.Parse(lineData[2]);
                    Vector3 target = new Vector3(x,y,z);

                    CSVImporterToProcessor finalData = new ➥
                    CSVImporterToProcessor(position, target);
                    return finalData;
                }
            }

    [ContentProcessor]
    public class CSVMatrixProcessor : ContentProcessor<CSVImporterToProcessor, ➥
    Matrix>
    {
        public override Matrix Process(CSVImporterToProcessor input, ➥
        ContentProcessorContext context)
        {
            Vector3 up = new Vector3(0, 1, 0);
            Vector3 forward = input.Target - input.Position;
            Vector3 right = Vector3.Cross(forward, up);
            up = Vector3.Cross(right, forward);

            Matrix viewMatrix = Matrix.CreateLookAt(input.Position, input.Target, ➥
            up);
            return viewMatrix;
        }
    }
}
```

■ ■ ■

# CHAPTER 3

# Working with 2D Images/Textures in XNA 3.0

**W**hether your game will be 2D or 3D, it will definitely use a vast amount of images. Where 2D games need a whole set of canvas and character images, 3D games use images to cover the triangles that make up their 3D objects.

There are many other cases where you'll need images while creating a game. Presenting the user with a nice-looking menu interface and saving a screenshot to disk are just some examples. Special 2D images can be required as input to very advanced effects.

This chapter covers how to load, create, show, and manipulate images in XNA. The first recipes are aimed at 2D games because they mainly focus on rendering 2D images to the screen. You'll also find two recipes that introduce you to the content pipeline, a major component of the XNA Framework. The more advanced recipes in this chapter show some uses of 2D images in a 3D game world, supported by HLSL code fragments.

Specifically, the recipes in this chapter cover the following:

- Loading, scaling, rotating, drawing, and blending 2D images to the screen using the user-friendly `SpriteBatch` class (recipes 3-1, 3-2, 3-3, and 3-4)

- Rendering text to the screen (recipe 3-5)

- Making your game more appealing by adding a nice-looking menu interface (recipe 3-6)

- Mastering the more advanced functionality of the `Texture2D` class by manually defining their colors, saving an image to disk, and saving the contents of your back buffer into an image before it is sent to the screen (recipes 3-7 and 3-8)

- Finding out why the content pipeline is an important component of the XNA Framework and how you can benefit from it; extending an existing content processor is used to introduce the content pipeline (recipes 3-9 and 3-10)

- Using the billboarding and particle effects to add some nice-looking effects produced by 2D images to your 3D game world (recipes 3-11 and 3-12)

- Learning how you can capture your scene using one camera and rendering its result into the scene as seen by another camera using projective texturing (recipe 3-13)

# 3-1. Display 2D Images: Load and Render Images Using the SpriteBatch Class

## The Problem

You want to render 2D images to the screen to create a 2D game or as part of the user interface of a 3D game. You want an easy interface so you can specify the position on the screen where the image should be displayed.

## The Solution

The XNA Framework provides functionality that is capable of rendering images in a very performant way, in the form of the SpriteBatch class.

The SpriteBatch class has been designed with ease of use as a priority, which will be shown in this recipe. Still, the SpriteBatch class is very powerful, as it also allows you to choose among several ways of optimization, which you can find explained in detail in recipe 3-4.

---

■**Note**  Because each image is a quad, it can be rendered as two triangles, which are covered with the 2D image as texture. The SpriteBatch class does this automatically for you. Because you'll actually be rendering triangles, using the SpriteBatch class allows you to take full advantage of hardware acceleration.

---

## How It Works

In graphics programming, 2D images are usually called *sprites*. However, when a 2D image is used to cover a surface, it is called a *texture*. So when discussing the image on the screen, I'll be talking about sprites. When I'm discussing the colors required to render the sprite, I'll be talking about textures.

### Loading a Texture

XNA's Game Studio (GS) supports drag-and-drop functionality, allowing you to easily import textures into your project. GS supports an extensive list of image formats. First, locate the Content entry of your project in the Solution Explorer at the top-right of your window. You can simply drag an image file from Windows Explorer onto this Content item.

You can also do this manually by right-clicking the Content entry in the Solution Explorer and selecting Add ➤ Add Existing Item, as shown in Figure 3-1.

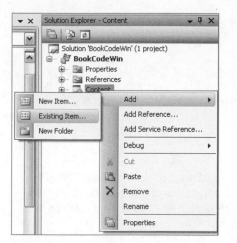

**Figure 3-1.** *Adding a new image to your XNA project*

Next, you need to add a variable to your project, which comes down to giving a name to the image you just imported for use in your code; this allows you to access the image from within your code. Add this line to your class variables:

```
Texture2D myTexture;
```

And add the following to your class variables, at the top of your code:

```
namespace BookCode
{
    public class Game1 : Microsoft.Xna.Framework.Game
    {
        GraphicsDeviceManager graphics;
        GraphicsDevice device;
        SpriteBatch spriteBatch;
        Texture2D myTexture;

        public Game1()
        {
            graphics = new GraphicsDeviceManager(this);
            Content.RootDirectory = "Content";
        }
```

---

**Note** The `device` variable is just a shortcut you may want to create for `GraphicsDevice`, because you will use it very often. Because you need to relink to `GraphicsDevice` every time your application recovers focus (for example, after a minimizing operation), you should put the `device = graphics.GraphicsDevice;` line in the `LoadContent` method.

---

Next, you will actually link the variable to the image, which should be done in the LoadContent method. If the file name of your image is image1.jpg or image1.png, the asset name will be image1.

```
myTexture = content.Load<Texture2D>("image1");
```

This will make the content pipeline (see recipe 3-9) load the image file from disk and process it into a workable variable.

### Putting the Image on the Screen

In XNA, it's easy to put an image on the screen. This is done using a SpriteBatch object. To make things easier for beginners, a SpriteBatch object is already declared by default when you create a new XNA game project, and it is already instantiated in the LoadContent method.

---

■**Caution** Creating a new SpriteBatch object takes time and a lot of resources. Therefore, never create a new SpriteBatch object for each frame; rather, reuse one SpriteBatch object you created at the startup of your application.

---

In the Draw method of your application, you want the SpriteBatch object to draw your texture:

```
spriteBatch.Begin();
spriteBatch.Draw(myTexture, new Vector2(50, 100), Color.White);
spriteBatch.End();
```

This will render your image to the screen. The second argument allows you to specify where you want it to be positioned on the screen. More specifically, you can define on which pixel of your window you want the top-left corner of the image to be positioned. The top-left corner of your window corresponds to the (0,0) point, so in this case there will be 50 pixels between the left border of the window and your image, and there will be 100 pixels between the top border of your window and your image. You find more information about the last argument at the end of this recipe.

### Rendering Multiple Images to the Screen

If you want to render multiple sprites to the screen, obviously you first need to import their textures into the project and link them to a variable, as shown previously. As its name implies, a single SpriteBatch object can render a batch of sprites to the screen. This example uses two separate image files and expects them to be already imported into your XNA project and linked to two texture variables, as discussed in the "Loading a Texture" section. Each of these textures is drawn to two different positions on the screen, resulting in four sprites being drawn to the screen:

```
spriteBatch.Begin();
spriteBatch.Draw(myTexture, new Vector2(50, 100), Color.White);
spriteBatch.Draw(anotherTexture, new Vector2(70, 100), Color.White);
spriteBatch.Draw(anotherTexture, new Vector2(70, 200), Color.White);
spriteBatch.Draw(myTexture, new Vector2(100, 200), Color.White);
spriteBatch.End();
```

## Drawing an Image into a Rectangle

Using another overload of the `spriteBatch.Draw` method, you can immediately specify the target rectangle on the screen, indicating where the image should be rendered. If the target rectangle does not have the same size as the image, the image will be scaled automatically to fit in the target rectangle.

This code defines a target rectangle having the same size as your window, starting at the top-left (0,0) corner. As a result, the image will be stretched over your entire screen, which is useful if you want to render a background:

```
spriteBatch.Begin();
PresentationParameters pp = device.PresentationParameters;
spriteBatch.Draw(myTexture, new Rectangle(0, ➡
0, pp.BackBufferWidth, pp.BackBufferHeight), Color.White);
spriteBatch.End();
```

Note that the images are rendered to the screen only at the moment you call `spriteBatch.End()`. This timing allows XNA to sort the images optimally. See recipe 3-4 for more information on this.

## Color Modulation

Until now, you've been using `Color.White` as an argument in the `spriteBatch.Draw` call. The color of each pixel of the image will be multiplied by this color before it is drawn to the screen.

For example, if you specify `Color.Blue`, the red and green color channels of each pixel in your texture will be multiplied by 0, while the blue color channel will be multiplied by 1. This will completely remove the red and green components of your image. If your image consists of only red pixels, all pixels will turn black, because the red component is multiplied by 0.

If you specify `Color.Purple`, the red color channel is multiplied by 1, the green channel by 0, and the blue channel by 1. So, in the example of the red image, the colors remain unchanged.

The `Color.White` argument is composed of red, green, and blue, so the red, green, and blue color channels will be multiplied by 1. As a result, your image will be drawn to the screen in its original colors.

You will want to specify other values than `Color.White` to slightly decrease a color strength or to strengthen, for example, the blue color by decreasing the strength of the red and green color channels.

---

■**Tip** The "Rotation and Scaling" article of the series of 2D XNA tutorials on my site `www.riemers.net` contains an example of how color modulation can be useful.

---

### Using the SpriteBatch Class in a 3D Application

Whenever you activate the SpriteBatch to render images, the SpriteBatch will modify some settings of the graphics card. When you render some 3D objects afterwards, chances are these new settings will have an undesirable impact on your 3D renderings. Therefore, you may want the SpriteBatch to save the original settings of the graphics card, so it can restore them once it has finished:

```
spriteBatch.Begin(SpriteBlendMode.None, SpriteSortMode.Texture, ➥
  SaveStateMode.SaveState);
```

## The Code

> *All the code is available for download at www.apress.com.*

This simple program renders a single image to the screen. Note the definition and initialization of the myTexture variable and how it is rendered to the screen in the Draw method:

```
using System;
using System.Collections.Generic;
using System.Linq;
using Microsoft.Xna.Framework;
using Microsoft.Xna.Framework.Audio;
using Microsoft.Xna.Framework.Content;
using Microsoft.Xna.Framework.GamerServices;
using Microsoft.Xna.Framework.Graphics;
using Microsoft.Xna.Framework.Input;
using Microsoft.Xna.Framework.Media;
using Microsoft.Xna.Framework.Net;
using Microsoft.Xna.Framework.Storage;

namespace BookCode
{
    public class Game1 : Microsoft.Xna.Framework.Game
    {
        GraphicsDeviceManager graphics;
        GraphicsDevice device;
        SpriteBatch spriteBatch;
        Texture2D myTexture;

        public Game1()
        {
            graphics = new GraphicsDeviceManager(this);
            Content.RootDirectory = "Content";
        }
```

```
protected override void Initialize()
{
    base.Initialize();
}

protected override void LoadContent()
{
    device = graphics.GraphicsDevice;
    spriteBatch = new SpriteBatch(GraphicsDevice);
    myTexture = Content.Load<Texture2D>("smile");
}

protected override void UnloadContent()
{
}

protected override void Update(GameTime gameTime)
{
    if (GamePad.GetState(PlayerIndex.One).Buttons.Back == ➡
    ButtonState.Pressed)
        this.Exit();

    base.Update(gameTime);
}

protected override void Draw(GameTime gameTime)
{
    device.Clear(ClearOptions.Target | ➡
    ClearOptions.DepthBuffer, Color.CornflowerBlue, ➡
    1, 0);

    spriteBatch.Begin();
    spriteBatch.Draw(myTexture, new Vector2(50, 100), Color.White);
    spriteBatch.End();

    base.Draw(gameTime);
    }
    }
}
```

## Moving an Image Using Keyboard Input

In XNA, it's also very easy to read out which keyboard keys are currently pressed. In this short section, we will move our image using keyboard input. First, we need to keep track of the position of our image, which is done by creating a variable for it. This line should be added next to the other four variables in your project:

```
Vector2 position = new Vector2(200, 100);
```

You see that we immediately set a default position for our image. Let's use this position in our Draw method:

```
spriteBatch.Draw(myTexture, position, Color.White);
```

This code should run without any problem, displaying the image at a fixed position. Next, let's read from our keyboard. Since this should be done frequently, it should be done in the Update method. Place the following line in the Update method to read the current state of all keys on the keyboard:

```
KeyboardState keyState = Keyboard.GetState();
```

Finally, we can use this keyState variable to check which keys are pressed and change our image position accordingly:

```
if (keyState.IsKeyDown(Keys.Right))
    position.X++;
if (keyState.IsKeyDown(Keys.Left))
    position.X--;
if (keyState.IsKeyDown(Keys.Down))
    position.Y++;
if (keyState.IsKeyDown(Keys.Up))
    position.Y--;
```

# 3-2. Rotate, Scale, and Mirror an Image

## The Problem

You want to rotate, scale, or mirror an image before rendering it to the screen.

## The Solution

The different overloads of the Draw method provided by the SpriteBatch class (see the previous recipe) allow you to do this easily.

## How It Works

### Rotating/Scaling/Mirroring an Image

The SpriteBatch.Draw method has a few useful overloads. The most complex overload is shown here, and the possible arguments will be discussed next:

```
public void Draw (
        Texture2D texture,
        Vector2 position,
        Nullable<Rectangle> sourceRectangle,
        Color color,
        float rotation,
```

```
       Vector2 origin,
       Vector2 scale,
       SpriteEffects effects,
       float layerDepth
)
```

The first two arguments, as well as the fourth argument, have already been discussed in the previous recipe, because they specify the texture that needs to be drawn and the screen position where you want the top-left corner of the image to be positioned.

The sourceRectangle argument allows you to draw only a section of an image to the screen. This is useful if you have stored multiple images into a single image, as discussed in recipe 3-3. If you want to simply display the whole image, you should specify null for this argument.

## Rotation

Using the rotation argument, you can rotate the image before it is drawn to the screen. You need to specify the angle in radians, so if you want to rotate your image clockwise over 20 degrees, you can specify MathHelper.ToRadians(20), which will do the conversion for you.

---

■**Note**  2*PI radians correspond to 360 degrees, so PI radians correspond to 180 degrees. So if you want to rotate over 20 degrees, you can also specify MathHelper.PI/180.0f*20.0f as an argument.

---

The origin argument allows you to specify which point in the image you want to be positioned on the screen at the position you've specified in the second argument. By default, this is (0,0). For example, if you specify (0,0) for both arguments, the top-left pixel of the image will be placed in the top-left corner of the screen, as indicated in the top-left image of Figure 3-2.

**Figure 3-2.** *Image origin (offset) argument*

If you have a 64×64 image and you specify (0,0) as the screen position and (32,32) as the image origin, the center point of the image will be positioned at the top-left corner of the screen, as shown in the top-middle image of Figure 3-2.

If you specify (32,32) for both arguments, the center position of the image will be positioned at the (32,32) screen coordinate, as shown in the top-right image. Note that this yields the same effect as in the top-left case.

More important, the position you specify as the image origin will be taken as the rotation origin. In the top-left case, where you specified (0,0) as the image origin, the image will be rotated around this point, as shown in the bottom-left image of Figure 3-2. If you specify (32,32) as the image origin, the image will be rotated around its center point, as shown in the bottom-right image. Notice the difference between the bottom-left and bottom-right images.

### Scaling

If you want to make your image larger/smaller before it is drawn to the screen, you can specify this in the scale argument. By default, the scaling value is 1, meaning the image should be rendered in its original size. Because this argument accepts a Vector2, you can stretch the image differently in the horizontal and vertical directions. For example, specifying (0.5f, 2.0f) will shrink the width to half of the original width, while the height is stretched to double the original image height.

### Mirroring

The effects argument allows you to mirror the image horizontally or vertically. As with most flags, you can also specify both using SpriteEffects.FlipHorizontally|SpriteEffects. FlipVertically, which has the same effect as rotating the image over 180 degrees.

### Layer Depth

The last argument allows you to specify which layer the image is on, which is useful when you want multiple images to be drawn on top of each other. You can find more information on this in the next two recipes.

## The Code

*All the code is available for download at www.apress.com.*

The following simple code example enables all default effects on the image before rendering it to the screen:

```
protected override void Draw(GameTime gameTime)
{
    device.Clear(ClearOptions.Target | ClearOptions.DepthBuffer, ➥
    Color.CornflowerBlue, 1, 0);

    spriteBatch.Begin();
    spriteBatch.Draw(myTexture, new Vector2(50, 100), null, ➥
    Color.White, MathHelper.ToRadians(20), new Vector2(32, 32), ➥
    new Vector2(0.5f, 2.0f), SpriteEffects.FlipVertically, 0);
    spriteBatch.End();
```

```
    base.Draw(gameTime);
}
```

The functionality covered in these 2 recipes should allow you to create some basic 2D games. For a hands-on series of tutorials that use only this functionality to create a complete 2D game, you can read the 2D Series of XNA Tutorials on my site at www.riemers.net.

# 3-3. Render Transparent Images Using Layers

## The Problem

In most cases, you will want to render multiple images on top of each other. The main problem is that all images are full rectangles, so they will cover the images rendered earlier. You also need to make sure you render the background images first.

## The Solution

Using XNA, you can specify the layer, or the *depth* of the images that should be rendered. When you call the SpriteBatch.Draw method, XNA can order images, so the images on the deepest layer will be rendered first.

Most image formats support transparency. This means that in addition to the red, green, and blue color information, they also carry alpha information. When transparency is enabled, transparent regions of an image will show the image underneath.

In XNA, you can also specify a color, which will be treated as transparent. This is useful for images that don't have any transparency information encoded.

## How It Works

### Simple Transparency

The SpriteBatch class is capable of dealing with images that contain transparency information. This is necessary in most cases, such as when you draw a 2D image of a grass terrain and you want to draw an image of a rock on top of that. Say this rock image is a simple white image with a rock in its center. If you draw this rock image over your grass, you would also see the white background of the rock image on top of the grass!

So, what you need to do is set the image background to transparent. This way, when you render the rock image over the grass, the transparent regions of the rock image will get the color of the grass underneath it. Note that each pixel of the image needs to specify whether that pixel should be transparent or not. This extra information is called the *alpha* value and is stored next to the red, green and blue channels in the alpha channel.

If you want XNA to take the transparency of your image into account, you need to enable alpha blending (see the "Alpha Blending" section later in this recipe) using the SpriteBatch. Begin() method:

```
spriteBatch.Begin(SpriteBlendMode.AlphaBlend);
spriteBatch.Draw(myTexture, Vector2.Zero, Color.White);
spriteBatch.End();
```

## Using Color Key Transparency

For images that don't have transparency information, you can specify a color that will be treated as transparent. You do this by setting the color key inside the properties of your image. To do this, select your image in your Solution Explorer so its properties are shown on the bottom-right of your window, as shown in Figure 3-3. Find Color Key Color, and change it to the color of your choice (you might need to expand the Content Processor entry before this property shows up). Wherever this color is found in your image, it will be treated as completely transparent. Make sure color keying is enabled by setting Color Key Enabled to True.

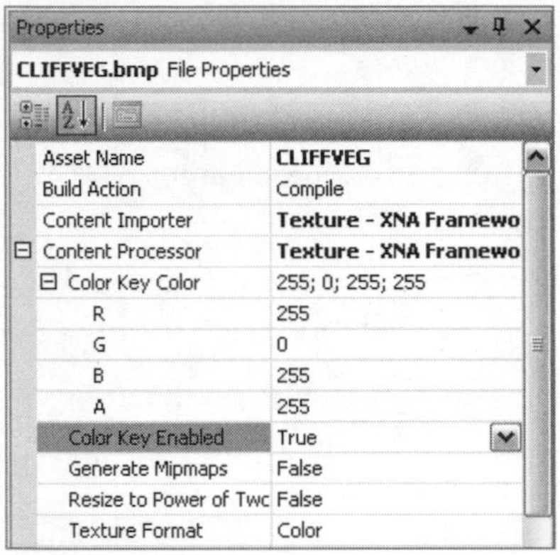

**Figure 3-3.** *Setting the Color Key Color property of the texture*

## Using Multiple Layers

If you want to blend multiple images over each other, you somehow have to indicate which image should be on top. In XNA, for each image you render, you can specify the layer (or image depth) as a number between 0 and 1. Layer 1 indicates the bottom layer, which will be rendered first, while layer 0 will be rendered last, on top of all other layers. You can specify this value as the last argument of the SpriteBatch.Draw method.

You have to enable sorting by layer by setting the correct SpriteSortMode in the SpriteBatch.Begin method, as shown in the following code snippet.

As an example, the following code will first cover the entire screen with grass. Because this is the bottom texture, you can safely set the layer value for these images to 1. Next, you will render some cliffs, which should be put over the grass. Therefore, you should render them to a layer smaller than 1, where you can specify any float value between 0 and 1:

```
Rectangle grassRec = new Rectangle(240, 121, 40, 40);
Rectangle leftRec = new Rectangle(40, 121, 80, 40);
Rectangle topleftRec = new Rectangle(40, 0, 80, 80);
Rectangle topRec = new Rectangle(240, 0, 40, 80);
Rectangle toprightRec = new Rectangle(320, 0, 80, 80);
Rectangle rightRec = new Rectangle(320, 121, 80, 40);
```

```
Rectangle bottomrightRec = new Rectangle(320, 281, 80, 120);
Rectangle bottomRec = new Rectangle(240, 281, 40, 120);
Rectangle bottomleftRec = new Rectangle(40, 281, 80, 120);
Rectangle centerRec = new Rectangle(240, 201, 80, 40);

spriteBatch.Begin(SpriteBlendMode.AlphaBlend, ➥
SpriteSortMode.BackToFront, SaveStateMode.None);

for (int x = 0; x < 10; x++)
    for (int y = 0; y < 10; y++)
        spriteBatch.Draw(myTexture, new Vector2(x * 40, y * 40), ➥
        grassRec, Color.White, 0, Vector2.Zero, 1, ➥
        SpriteEffects.None, 1);


spriteBatch.Draw(myTexture, new Vector2(40, 120), leftRec, ➥
Color.White, 0, Vector2.Zero, 1, SpriteEffects.None, 0.5f);
spriteBatch.Draw(myTexture, new Vector2(40, 40), topleftRec, ➥
Color.White, 0, Vector2.Zero, 1, SpriteEffects.None, 0.5f);
spriteBatch.Draw(myTexture, new Vector2(120, 40), topRec, Color.White, ➥
0, Vector2.Zero, 1, SpriteEffects.None, 0.5f);
spriteBatch.Draw(myTexture, new Vector2(160, 40), toprightRec, ➥
Color.White, 0, Vector2.Zero, 1, SpriteEffects.None, 0.5f);
spriteBatch.Draw(myTexture, new Vector2(160, 120), rightRec, ➥
Color.White, 0, Vector2.Zero, 1, SpriteEffects.None, 0.5f);
spriteBatch.Draw(myTexture, new Vector2(160, 160), bottomrightRec, ➥
Color.White, 0, Vector2.Zero, 1, SpriteEffects.None, 0.5f);
spriteBatch.Draw(myTexture, new Vector2(120, 160), bottomRec, ➥
Color.White, 0, Vector2.Zero, 1, SpriteEffects.None, 0.5f);
spriteBatch.Draw(myTexture, new Vector2(40, 160), bottomleftRec, ➥
Color.White, 0, Vector2.Zero, 1, SpriteEffects.None, 0.5f);
spriteBatch.Draw(myTexture, new Vector2(120, 120), centerRec, ➥
Color.White, 0, Vector2.Zero, 1, SpriteEffects.None, 0.5f);

spriteBatch.End();
```

The 100 grass tiles are rendered using the double for loop. The nine images composing the cliff, as well as the grass tile, are stored in one image file, of which parts are displayed at the left of Figure 3-4. Therefore, the code first declares the rectangles in this image file where each of the subimages can be found. By specifying such a rectangle as the third argument, XNA will cut the correct subimage from the complete image. The final result is shown on the right of the image.

**Figure 3-4.** *One image containing multiple images (left) and another blending them over a grassy surface (right)*

Because the grass has layer value 1.0f and the cliff images have layer value 0.5f, XNA knows it should first render the grass, followed by the cliff.

Make sure you have set SpriteSortMode to BackToFront in the SpriteBatch.Begin method so XNA actually knows it should order the sprites by layer before rendering them:

```
spriteBatch.Begin(SpriteBlendMode.AlphaBlend, ➥
SpriteSortMode.BackToFront, SaveStateMode.None);
```

### Alpha Blending

The transparency of pixels doesn't have to be "all or nothing," as is the case with the cliff images, where a pixel either has to be drawn in its own color or is completely transparent. A pixel can also have a transparency value of, for example, 70 percent. In the example of a car driving over your grass, the gray windows of your car could have 70 percent transparency. This way, when you render your car over the grass, the final color of the windows will be 30 percent gray and 70 percent the color of the grass behind it. You can find more information on this in recipe 2-13. This is called *alpha blending*, as you're obtaining the final color by blending in two colors.

### SpriteBlendModes

By default, alpha blending is enabled when drawing with the SpriteBatch class. However, you can turn off alpha blending (try this to see the difference!) or set the mode to Additive blending.

In the latter case, every color you render to a pixel is added to the color that was already present in that pixel. So using this mode, if you draw a blue pixel over a red pixel, you get a purple pixel. If you draw a green rectangle over this purple pixel, you get a green rectangle containing a white pixel. This mode is used for effects such as fire or explosions, which are composed of many sprites and are additively blended, as you can read in recipe 3-12.

XNA allows you to set the blending mode of the SpriteBatch class as an argument in the SpriteBatch.Begin method, where you specify one of these SpriteBlendMode states:

- SpriteBlendMode.None turns off the blending and will render the image to the screen neglecting any transparency information it carries and thus overwriting any images already present in deeper layers.

- SpriteBlendMode.AlphaBlend uses a portion of the existing color and a portion of the color contained in the new image, corresponding to the alpha value specified in the image. This corresponds to the example on the car windows.

- SpriteBlendMode.Additive adds the color of the new image to the color already present in the frame buffer.

## The Code

*All the code is available for download at www.apress.com.*

All code required in the Draw method was listed previously.

## Extra Reading

The menu system explained in recipe 3-6 is using alpha blending and multiple layers.

# 3-4. Consider Performance When Using the SpriteBatch Class

## The Problem

When using the SpriteBatch class incorrectly, your application will run terribly slowly if you want to render a large amount of images.

## The Solution

As already mentioned in recipe 3-1, creating a new SpriteBatch class each frame or beginning and ending your SpriteBatch class between each image of your render will kill your performance. But there are more subtle aspects you should know about.

## How It Works

### Performance Optimization: Sprite Sorting Modes

The Begin method of a SpriteBatch class allows you to set a SpriteSortMode. But before I go through the different modes, you need to know how your graphics card likes to work and certainly what it dislikes.

Drawing a 2D image to the screen is done by drawing two triangles and filling them with the colors found in a texture. Your graphics card likes rendering a huge amount of triangles at once, without being disturbed. However, whenever you need to change the texture, you're disturbing your graphics card. In other words, rendering 100 images from the same texture will go much faster than rendering 100 images from 100 different textures. This means that you can improve your performance by making sure you change the active texture as few times as possible.

With this in mind, you can read a discussion on the possible sprite sorting modes you can specify as an argument to the SpriteBatch.Begin method:

- Deferred: This is the default SpriteSortMode. You'll almost never want to use it, though, because actually no sorting is involved. Whenever you add a sprite to the batch by calling the SpriteBatch.Draw method, the sprite is simply put on top of the stack. At the moment you call the SpriteBatch.End method, all sprites on the stack are drawn in the order the sprites were put on the stack.

- Texture: Usually, for optimal performance and ease, you'll want to use this mode. At the moment you call the SpriteBatch.End method, all images you have put on the stack are sorted by texture, before XNA actually asks your graphics card to render them. This way, your graphics card can draw all triangles using the same texture in one run, and you will reduce the number of times you have to disturb your graphics card to change the texture. However, in cases where you're using alpha transparency, this can cause trouble, and you'll want to use one of the next modes.

- BackToFront: When using alpha blending, you want the objects that are the farthest away to be drawn first. To see why, read the previous recipe. To this end, the SpriteBatch.Draw method, which adds an image to the SpriteBatch class, has an overload that accepts a layerDepth. Using this float, you can specify which layer the image should be drawn on, where 1.0f indicates the layer that is the farthest away (which will, for example, contain your grass) and 0.0f indicates the layer that is the closest by (which you can, for example, render your rock in). You can specify any number in between. When using the BackToFront mode, whenever you call the SpriteBatch.End method, the images in the SpriteBatch will be sorted so the farthest layer is drawn first.

- FrontToBack: This is opposite of the previous mode, so the images on the closest layer are drawn first. Because each pixel drawn on the screen will never need to be overwritten (because all following images are behind the ones drawn), this yields the best performance. However, this will not work with alpha blending (see the previous recipe) and will give great performance only if all images use the same texture! If the texture needs to be swapped ten times to draw the closest layer, your performance will be a lot worse than when using the Texture mode.

- Immediate: In contradiction to all other modes, in this mode XNA will not wait for a call to the SpriteBatch.End method to render all images in the SpriteBatch class. As long as you add images that use the same texture to the SpriteBatch by calling SpriteBatch.Draw, the SpriteBatch will put them on a stack. However, at the moment you ask to draw a sprite that uses another texture, the sprites on the current stack will be drawn first immediately.

Using the first four modes, only at the call to SpriteBatch.End, the sprites will be sorted, the render states will be set, and the triangles and textures will be sent to the graphics card. This allows you to use multiple objects of the SpriteBatch class and add new sprites to them in a random order, or even draw 3D objects using their own render states.

Using the `Immediate` mode, however, the render states will be set at the moment you call the `SpriteBatch.Begin` method, and the sprites will be rendered after the call to `SpriteBatch.Draw`. This means you have the opportunity to change the render states in between! This way, you can access more alpha blending modes or even draw the sprites using a custom pixel shader! However, while drawing images using the `Immediate` mode, you should not render anything else, such as 3D objects, because you will probably change the render states while doing so. When you want to continue drawing sprites with your `SpriteBatch`, the render states will not be reset, so you will be rendering sprites using the render states and pixel shader of the 3D object.

## Performance Optimization: Storing Multiple Images in One Image File

As discussed in the previous section, the one thing you want when rendering a large number of sprites is that your graphics card has to change the active texture as little as possible. The `SpriteSortingMode.Texture` already helps a lot, but for a complete game you will need hundreds of different images, which will cause your graphics card to switch hundreds of times between textures, making it quite angry.

A useful approach is to store images that are somewhat related to each other into one big image, like the one shown on the left of Figure 3-4. This way, you can use the `sourceRectangle` argument of the `SpriteBatch.Draw` method to specify which part of the big image contains the image you actually want to draw, as shown in the code fragment of recipe 3-3.

In the image shown in Figure 3-4, each subimage contains 40×40 pixels. This code of recipe 3-3 defines a few rectangles that indicate where the subimages are positioned in the large image file. Specifying one of these rectangles as the third argument in the `SpriteBatch.Draw` method will cause only this subimage to be drawn to the screen.

## Using Multiple SpriteBatches

As you've seen up until now, the `SpriteBatch` is quite a powerful object. You could batch the images of an entire game into a single `SpriteBatch` and have them sorted and rendered to the screen easily. However, there are cases when you might want to use multiple `SpriteBatch` classes.

Say you're creating a flight game, with planes firing rockets at each other. Of course, you have multiple types of planes and rockets. You can store all possible rotations of a single plane or rocket into one big texture map, which will reduce the total number of textures needed.

You want some smoke behind the engines of the planes, slowly fading away, and a lot of smoke in a trail after the rockets, of course. If you render all these images using a single `SpriteBatch`, you have a problem: you want all the images to be sorted by texture to get optimal performance. However, you need the planes and rockets to be drawn first, so after that, you can nicely blend over your smoke sprites. This would require your sprites to be sorted by their `layerDepth`!

The solution is in using two objects of the `SpriteBatch` class: `planeBatch` and `smokeBatch`. At the beginning of your `Draw` method, you call the `Begin` method of both `SpriteBatch` classes. Next, for each plane or rocket, you add the plane or rocket image to the `planeBatch` and the smoke behind the plane or rocket to the `smokeBatch`.

The `planeBatch` can be sorted by `Texture`, and the `smokeBatch` can be sorted using `BackToFront`. After all images have been added to the batches, you first call the `End` method of the `planeBatch`, which will cause all the plane and rocket images to be sorted by texture, and they will be drawn to the screen with nice performance. Next, you `End` the `smokeBatch`, which will cause the smoke sprites to be blended nicely over the image.

So, you have optimal performance for rendering your planes, and yet the blending is done correctly!

# 3-5. Display Text

## The Problem

You want to render some text, for example, to display some instructions or the current score.

## The Solution

The `SpriteBatch` class, which is discussed in the first four recipes of this chapter, is also capable of rendering text. This is done almost the same way as with textures. Instead of importing a `Texture2D`, you'll import a `SpriteFont`, which contains the type of font and font size you want to use. Next, you can render your text using the `SpriteBatch.DrawString` method.

## How It Works

First you need to create a `SpriteFont` file. You do this by clicking the Content entry of your XNA project (see Figure 3-1) and selecting Add ➤ New item. Select Sprite Font from the dialog box, give your font a name (such as ourFont), and click Add.

You should be presented with an XML page. The most important line is where you set the `FontName` property. Change this to the font you want your text to be rendered in. The next property allows you to select the font size, although you can scale this later.

---

**Note**  You can specify any TrueType font that is installed on your computer. To see the list of installed fonts, open the `C:\WINDOWS\FONTS` map (for example, by clicking the Start button, selecting Run, and typing this map name). The Font Name column displays all the fonts you can specify. For example, if the font name is Times New Roman (TrueType), you can specify Times New Roman as the `FontName` property for your font.

---

**Note**  When compiling your code on another PC, the font has to be installed on this computer, or you will get an error.

---

**Caution**  As with all art assets, make sure you check the copyright on the font before distributing your program.

---

With the `SpriteFont` file created, you should add a `SpriteFont` variable to your class:

```
SpriteFont myFont;
```

which you should initialize in the `LoadContent` method:

```
myFont = Content.Load<SpriteFont>("ourFont");
```

Make sure you specify the name of the file you just created between the brackets. With your `SpriteFont` object loaded, you're ready to render some text in your `Draw` method:

```
spriteBatch.Begin();
string myString = "Elapsed seconds: " + gameTime.TotalGameTime.Seconds.ToString();
spriteBatch.DrawString(myFont, myString, new Vector2(50, 20), Color.Tomato);
spriteBatch.End();
```

---

■**Caution** If you use another overload of the `SpriteBatch.Begin` method, make sure you specify `SpriteBlendMode.AlphaBlend` as the first argument. Otherwise, the pixels surrounding the letters will not be transparent, rendering your letters as solid blocks of the color you specified!

---

## String Length

You can query a `spriteFont` to find out how many pixels a certain string would occupy on the screen. This information can be useful to scale or cut off a string that is too long. You get both the horizontal and vertical size of the string:

```
Vector2 stringSize = myFont.MeasureString(myString);
```

## Overloads

`SpriteBatch.DrawString` has some other overloads that accept the same arguments as the `SpriteBatch.Draw` method. See recipe 3-2 for their explanations.

```
spriteBatch.DrawString(myFont, secondString, new Vector2(50, 100), Color.White, 0, ➡
new Vector2(0,0), 0.5f, SpriteEffects.None, 0);
```

## StringBuilder

Instead of just accepting strings, the `spriteBatch.DrawString` method also accepts a `StringBuilder` object. `StringBuilder` objects should be used if you're doing lots of modifications to a string, such as appending lots of strings together in a loop. First add a `StringBuilder` variable to the top of your code so you don't have to re-create one in each frame:

```
StringBuilder stringBuilder = new StringBuilder();
```

When you want to use the method, first clear it by setting its length to 0. After that, create your string, and pass the `StringBuilder` to the `SpriteBatch.DrawString` method:

```
stringBuilder.Length = 0;
stringBuilder.Append("StringBuilder example: ");
for (int i = 0; i < 10; i++)
    stringBuilder.Append(i);
spriteBatch.DrawString(myFont, stringBuilder, new Vector2(50, 180), Color.White➥
, 0, new Vector2(0, 0), 0.5f, SpriteEffects.None, 0);
```

## The Code

*All the code is available for download at* www.apress.com.

Your SpriteFont object is initialized in the LoadContent method, together with the SpriteBatch,
which is loaded by default:

```
protected override void LoadContent()
{
    device = graphics.GraphicsDevice;
    spriteBatch = new SpriteBatch(GraphicsDevice);
    myFont = Content.Load<SpriteFont>("ourFont");
}
```

These two objects are all you need to render some text in your Draw method:

```
protected override void Draw(GameTime gameTime)
{
    device.Clear(ClearOptions.Target | ClearOptions.DepthBuffer, ➥
    Color.CornflowerBlue, 1, 0);

    spriteBatch.Begin();
    string myString = "Elapsed seconds: " + ➥
    gameTime.TotalGameTime.Seconds.ToString();
    spriteBatch.DrawString(myFont, myString, new Vector2(50, 20), Color.Tomato);
    spriteBatch.End();

    base.Draw(gameTime);
}
```

# 3-6. Create a 2D Menu Interface

## The Problem

You want to create a 2D menu interface, which allows you to easily add new menus and
specify their items. The menus should allow the user to scroll through the different items and
menus using the controller/keyboard. You want to be able to define nice transition effects
when the user browses from one menu to another.

# The Solution

You will create a new class, MenuWindow, which will keep track of all things related to a menu, such as the current state of the menu, the items in the menu, the background image, and more. This class allows the main program to easily create multiple instances of such a MenuWindow and to add items to these instances. The items will be displayed using plain text with a font of your liking that's installed on your system.

To allow transitions, a window will have states such as Starting and Ending, as well as the Active and Inactive states. The controller/keyboard state is passed to the Active MenuWindow, which lets the main program know whether the user has selected one of its items by passing the selected menu to the main program.

Giving the MenuWindow the capability of storing and displaying a background image will greatly enhance the final result, which can be even improved by using some post-processing effects (see recipe 2-12).

# How It Works

The main program will create a number of MenuWindow objects, of which each item will link to another MenuWindow object. So first, you have to define the MenuWindow class.

### The MenuWindow Class

Create a new class called MenuWindow. Each menu should be capable of storing its items. For each item, the text as well as the menu it points to must be stored. So, define this little struct in your MenuWindow class:

```
private struct MenuItem
{
    public string itemText;
    public MenuWindow itemLink;

    public MenuItem(string itemText, MenuWindow itemLink)
    {
        this.itemText = itemText;
        this.itemLink = itemLink;
    }
}
```

Each menu will always be in one of these four states:

- Starting: The menu has just been selected and is fading in.

- Active: The menu is the only one showing on the screen and will process user input.

- Ending: An item in this menu has been selected, so this menu is fading out.

- Inactive: If the menu is not in one of the three previous states, it should not be drawn.

Therefore, you'll need an enum to indicate the state, which can be put outside the class:

```
public enum WindowState { Starting, Active, Ending, Inactive }
```

Next are the variables needed for the class to work properly:

```
private TimeSpan changeSpan;
private WindowState windowState;
private List<MenuItem> itemList;
private int selectedItem;
private SpriteFont spriteFont;
private double changeProgress;
```

changeSpan will indicate how long a fade-in or fade-out transition takes. Then you need some variables to hold the current state of the menu, the list of menu items, and which of the items is currently selected. The changeProgress variable will hold a value between 0 and 1 to indicate how far the fading progress is in case of the Starting or Ending state.

The constructor will simply initialize these values:

```
public MenuWindow(SpriteFont spriteFont)
{
    itemList = new List<MenuItem>();
    changeSpan = TimeSpan.FromMilliseconds(800);
    selectedItem = 0;
    changeProgress = 0;
    windowState = WindowState.Inactive;
    this.spriteFont = spriteFont;
}
```

You indicate that a transaction between two menus should be completed in 800 milliseconds, and a menu starts in Inactive mode. You can read all about the SpriteFont class and how to render text in the previous recipe.

Next, you need a method that allows you to add items to the menu:

```
public void AddMenuItem(string itemText, MenuWindow itemLink)
{
    MenuItem newItem = new MenuItem(itemText, itemLink);
    itemList.Add(newItem);
}
```

The item's caption, as well as the menu that needs to be activated when the user selects the item, is passed in by the main program. A new MenuItem is created and added to the itemList.

You also need a method that will activate an Inactive menu:

```
public void WakeUp()
{
    windowState = WindowState.Starting;
}
```

Like almost any component in an XNA application, this class will also need to be updated:

```
public void Update(double timePassedSinceLastFrame)
{
    if ((windowState == WindowState.Starting) || (windowState == ➥
    WindowState.Ending))
        changeProgress += timePassedSinceLastFrame / changeSpan.TotalMilliseconds;

    if (changeProgress >= 1.0f)
    {
        changeProgress = 0.0f;
        if (windowState == WindowState.Starting)
            windowState = WindowState.Active;
        else if (windowState == WindowState.Ending)
            windowState = WindowState.Inactive;
    }
}
```

This method will receive the number of milliseconds that have passed since the last update call (usually, this will be 1000/60 milliseconds; see recipe 1-6). If the menu is in transition mode, the changeProgress variable is updated, so after the number of milliseconds stored in changeSpan (800, as you specified earlier), this value reaches 1.

When this value reaches 1, the transition is over, and the state either has to be changed from Starting to Active or has to be changed from Ending to Inactive.

Finally, you want some code that renders the menu. When the menu is Active, the items should be displayed, starting from, for example, position (300,300), with each item 30 pixels below the previous item.

When the menu is in Starting mode, the items should fade in (their alpha value should increase from 0 to 1) and move from the left of the screen to their final position. When in Ending mode, the items should fade out (their alpha value should decrease), and they should move to the right.

```
public void Draw(SpriteBatch spriteBatch)
{
    if (windowState == WindowState.Inactive)
        return;

    float smoothedProgress = MathHelper.SmoothStep(0,1,(float)changeProgress);

    int verPosition = 300;
    float horPosition = 300;
    float alphaValue;

    switch (windowState)
    {
        case WindowState.Starting:
            horPosition -= 200 * (1.0f - (float)smoothedProgress);
            alphaValue = smoothedProgress;
```

```
        break;
    case WindowState.Ending:
        horPosition += 200 * (float)smoothedProgress;
        alphaValue = 1.0f - smoothedProgress;
        break;
    default:
        alphaValue = 1;
        break;
        }

for (int itemID = 0; itemID < itemList.Count; itemID++)
{

    Vector2 itemPostition = new Vector2(horPosition, verPosition);
    Color itemColor = Color.White;

    if (itemID == selectedItem)
        itemColor = new Color(new Vector4(1,0,0,alphaValue));
    else
        itemColor = new Color(new Vector4(1,1,1,alphaValue));

    spriteBatch.DrawString(spriteFont, ➥
    itemList[itemID].itemText, itemPostition, itemColor, ➥
    0, Vector2.Zero, 1, SpriteEffects.None, 0);
    verPosition += 30;
    }
}
```

When in Starting or Ending state, the changeProgress value will increase linearly from 0 to 1, which is OK but will not give smooth starts or endings. The MathHelper.SmoothStep method smoothens this curve, so the transitions will start and end smoothly.

The case structure adjusts the horizontal position and alpha values for the menu items, in case the menu is in Starting or Ending mode. Next, for each item in the menu, the caption is rendered to the screen at the correct position. For more information on rendering text, see the previous recipe. If the item is not the selected item, its text is drawn in white, while the selected item will be drawn in red.

That's it for the basics of the MenuWindow class!

In your main program, you simply need a list to store all your menus:

```
List<MenuWindow> menuList;
```

In your LoadContent method, you can create your menus and add them to the menuList. Next, you can add items to the menus, allowing you to specify which menu should be activated next in case the user selects the item.

```
MenuWindow menuMain = new MenuWindow(menuFont, "Main Menu", backgroundImage);
MenuWindow menuNewGame = new MenuWindow(menuFont, "Start a New Game", bg);
```

```
menuList.Add(menuMain);
menuList.Add(menuNewGame);

menuMain.AddMenuItem("New Game", menuNewGame);
menuNewGame.AddMenuItem("Back to Main menu", menuMain);

menuMain.WakeUp();
```

This will create two menus, each containing an item that links to the other menu. After you're done initializing your menu structure, the mainMenu is activated, bringing it in the Starting state.

Now you need to update all your menus during the update cycle of your program:

```
foreach (MenuWindow currentMenu in menuList)
    currentMenu.Update(gameTime.ElapsedGameTime.TotalMilliseconds);
```

and render them during the draw phase of your program:

```
spriteBatch.Begin();
foreach (MenuWindow currentMenu in menuList)
    currentMenu.Draw(spriteBatch);
spriteBatch.End();
```

When you run this code, the main menu should come fading in from the left. You can't yet move to the other menu, simply because you aren't processing any user input yet.

### Allowing the User to Navigate Through the Menus

You will extend your MenuWindow class with a method that processes user input. Note that this method will be called only on the currently active menu:

```
public MenuWindow ProcessInput(KeyboardState lastKeybState, ➥
KeyboardState currentKeybState)
{
    if (lastKeybState.IsKeyUp(Keys.Down) && currentKeybState.IsKeyDown(Keys.Down))
        selectedItem++;

    if (lastKeybState.IsKeyUp(Keys.Up) && currentKeybState.IsKeyDown(Keys.Up))
        selectedItem--;

    if (selectedItem < 0)
        selectedItem = 0;

    if (selectedItem >= itemList.Count)
        selectedItem = itemList.Count-1;
```

```
    if (lastKeybState.IsKeyUp(Keys.Enter) && currentKeybState.IsKeyDown(Keys.Enter))
    {
        windowState = WindowState.Ending;
        return itemList[selectedItem].itemLink;
    }
    else if (lastKeybState.IsKeyDown(Keys.Escape))
        return null;
    else
        return this;
}
```

A lot of interesting stuff is happening here. First, you check whether the up or down key is pressed. When the user presses a button, the IsKeyUp for that key remains true as long as the key remains pressed! So, you need to check whether that button wasn't already pressed the previous time.

If the up or down key is pressed, you change the selectedItem variable accordingly. If it has gone out of bounds, you bring it back into a reasonable range.

The following lines contain the whole navigation mechanism. You should note that this method has to return a MenuWindow object to the main program. Since this method will be called only on the currently active menu, this allows the menu to pass the newly selected menu to the main program. If the user didn't select any item, the menu will stay active and should return itself, which is done at the last line. This way, the main program knows which menu is the active menu after input processing.

So, if the user presses the Enter button, the currently active menu is moved from Active to Ending mode, and the menu to which the selected item links is returned to the main program. If the user presses the Escape button, null is returned, which will be captured later to exit the application. If nothing is selected, the menu returns itself, informing the main program that this menu is still the active one.

This method needs to be called from the main program, which needs to keep track of two more variables:

```
MenuWindow activeMenu;
KeyboardState lastKeybState;
```

The first variable holds the menu that is currently active and should be initialized to the mainMenu in the LoadContent method. The lastKeybState should be initialized in the Initialize method.

```
private void MenuInput(KeyboardState currentKeybState)
{
    MenuWindow newActive = activeMenu.ProcessInput(lastKeybState, currentKeybState);

    if (newActive == null)
        this.Exit();
    else if (newActive != activeMenu)
        newActive.WakeUp();

    activeMenu = newActive;
}
```

This method calls the `ProcessInput` method of the currently active menu and passes it the previous and current keyboard state. As discussed previously, this method will return `null` if the user presses the Escape button, so if this is the case, the application quits. Otherwise, if the method returns a menu different from the active menu, this indicates the user has made a selection. In this case, the newly selected menu is moved from the `Inactive` to the `Starting` state by calling its `WakeUp` method. Either way, the menu that was returned contains the active menu at this moment, so it needs to be stored in the `activeMenu` variable.

Make sure you call this method from within the `Update` method. Running this code will allow you to switch nicely between both menus.

## Adding a Menu Title and Background Image to the Menu

The mechanism works, but what good is a menu without a background image? Add these two variables to the `MenuWindow` class:

```
private string menuTitle;
private Texture2D backgroundImage;
```

which need to be filled in the `Initialize` method:

```
public MenuWindow(SpriteFont spriteFont, string menuTitle, ➥
Texture2D backgroundImage)
{
    //...
    this.menuTitle = menuTitle;
            this.backgroundImage = backgroundImage;

}
```

Displaying the title should be easy. However, rendering the background image could be troublesome if your menus use different background images. What you want is that in both `Active` and `Ending` states, the image is displayed. When in `Starting` mode, the new background image should be blended over the previous one. When blending a second image over a first image, you need to make sure your first image was actually drawn first! This is not easy, because it will involve changing the drawing order of the menus.

An easier approach is to use the `layerDepth` argument (see recipe 3-3) of the `SpriteBatch`. `Draw` method. When in `Active` or `Ending` mode, the image will be drawn at distance 1, the "deepest" layer. In `Starting` mode, the image will be drawn at depth 0.5f, and all text will be drawn at distance 0. When using `SpriteSortMode.BackToFront`, first the `Active` or `Ending` menu at depth 1 will be drawn. Next, if applicable, the `Starting` menu will be drawn (blending over the image already there) and finally all text renderings.

In the `Draw` method of your `MenuWindow` class, keep track of these two variables:

```
float bgLayerDepth;
Color bgColor;
```

These will contain the `layerDepth` and transparency value for the background image, which are set in the `switch` structure:

```
switch (windowState)
{
    case WindowState.Starting:
        horPosition -= 200 * (1.0f - (float)smoothedProgress);
        alphaValue = smoothedProgress;
        bgLayerDepth = 0.5f;
        bgColor = new Color(new Vector4(1, 1, 1, alphaValue));
        break;
    case WindowState.Ending:
        horPosition += 200 * (float)smoothedProgress;
        alphaValue = 1.0f - smoothedProgress;
        bgLayerDepth = 1;
        bgColor = Color.White;
        break;
    default:
        alphaValue = 1;
        bgLayerDepth = 1;
        bgColor = Color.White;
        break;
}
```

where Color.White is the same as Color(new Vector4(1, 1, 1, 1)), meaning full alpha value. If a menu is in Starting or Ending state, the alphaValue is calculated. Next, you use this transparency value to render the title and render the background image as well.

```
Color titleColor = new Color(new Vector4(1, 1, 1, alphaValue));
spriteBatch.Draw(backgroundImage, new Vector2(), null, bgColor, 0, ➥
Vector2.Zero, 1, SpriteEffects.None, bgLayerDepth);
spriteBatch.DrawString(spriteFont, menuTitle, new Vector2(horPosition, ➥
 200), titleColor,0,Vector2.Zero, 1.5f, SpriteEffects.None, 0);
```

You can see the title text has been scaled to 1.5f, which will make it larger than the regular items of the menu.

Finally, you need to make sure in the Draw method of your main program you set SpriteSortMode to BackToFront:

```
spriteBatch.Begin(SpriteBlendMode.AlphaBlend, ➥
SpriteSortMode.BackToFront, SaveStateMode.None);
```

## Moving from the Menu to the Game

At this point you can create some nice-looking menus, but how can you actually make a menu item start the game? This can be done using dummy menus, which need to be stored in the main program. For example, if you want your Start New Game menu to contain items to start an Easy, a Normal, or a Hard game, add these menus:

```
MenuWindow startGameEasy;
MenuWindow startGameNormal;
MenuWindow startGameHard;
bool menusRunning;
```

In your LoadContent method, you can instantiate these variables with null arguments and link them to items in menuNewGame:

```
startGameEasy = new MenuWindow(null, null, null);
startGameNormal = new MenuWindow(null, null, null);
startGameHard = new MenuWindow(null, null, null);

menuNewGame.AddMenuItem("Easy", startGameEasy);
menuNewGame.AddMenuItem("Normal", startGameNormal);
menuNewGame.AddMenuItem("Hard", startGameHard);
menuNewGame.AddMenuItem("Back to Main menu", menuMain);
```

This will add four items to your New Game menu. All you have to do next is detect whether either of the dummy menus has been selected. So, expand your MenuInput method a bit:

```
private void MenuInput(KeyboardState currentKeybState)
{
    MenuWindow newActive = activeMenu.ProcessInput(lastKeybState, currentKeybState);

    if (newActive == startGameEasy)
    {
        //set level to easy
        menusRunning = false;
    }
    else if (newActive == startGameNormal)
    {
        //set level to normal
        menusRunning = false;
    }

    else if (newActive == startGameHard)
    {
        //set level to hard
        menusRunning = false;
    }
    else if (newActive == null)
        this.Exit();
    else if (newActive != activeMenu)
        newActive.WakeUp();

    activeMenu = newActive;
}
```

You can use this `menusRunning` variable to make sure you're not updating/drawing your menus when the user is in the game:

```
if (menusRunning)
{
    spriteBatch.Begin(SpriteBlendMode.AlphaBlend, ➥
    SpriteSortMode.BackToFront, SaveStateMode.None);
    foreach (MenuWindow currentMenu in menuList)
        currentMenu.Draw(spriteBatch);
    spriteBatch.End();

    Window.Title = "Menu running ...";
}
else
{
    Window.Title = "Game running ...";
}
```

## The Code

*All the code is available for download at* www.apress.com.

### The MenuWindow Class

Here are some easy and necessary methods:

```
public MenuWindow(SpriteFont spriteFont, string menuTitle, ➥
Texture2D backgroundImage)
{
    itemList = new List<MenuItem>();
    changeSpan = TimeSpan.FromMilliseconds(800);
    selectedItem = 0;
    changeProgress = 0;
    windowState = WindowState.Inactive;


    this.spriteFont = spriteFont;
    this.menuTitle = menuTitle;
    this.backgroundImage = backgroundImage;
}

public void AddMenuItem(string itemText, MenuWindow itemLink)
{
    MenuItem newItem = new MenuItem(itemText, itemLink);
    itemList.Add(newItem);
}
```

```
public void WakeUp()
{
    windowState = WindowState.Starting;
}
```

Next, here are the methods that update the menu. Note that the ProcessInput method is called only on the currently active menu.

```
public void Update(double timePassedSinceLastFrame)
{
    if ((windowState == WindowState.Starting) || (windowState == ➥
        WindowState.Ending))
        changeProgress += timePassedSinceLastFrame / changeSpan.TotalMilliseconds;

    if (changeProgress >= 1.0f)
    {
        changeProgress = 0.0f;
        if (windowState == WindowState.Starting)
            windowState = WindowState.Active;
        else if (windowState == WindowState.Ending)
            windowState = WindowState.Inactive;
    }
}

public MenuWindow ProcessInput(KeyboardState lastKeybState, ➥
KeyboardState currentKeybState)
{
    if (lastKeybState.IsKeyUp(Keys.Down) && currentKeybState.IsKeyDown(Keys.Down))
        selectedItem++;

    if (lastKeybState.IsKeyUp(Keys.Up) && currentKeybState.IsKeyDown(Keys.Up))
        selectedItem--;

    if (selectedItem < 0)
        selectedItem = 0;


    if (selectedItem >= itemList.Count)
        selectedItem = itemList.Count-1;

    if (lastKeybState.IsKeyUp(Keys.Enter) && currentKeybState.IsKeyDown(Keys.Enter))
    {
        windowState = WindowState.Ending;
        return itemList[selectedItem].itemLink;
    }
```

```
        else if (lastKeybState.IsKeyDown(Keys.Escape))
            return null;
        else
            return this;
}
```

And finally, here is the method that actually renders the menu:

```
public void Draw(SpriteBatch spriteBatch)
{
    if (windowState == WindowState.Inactive)
        return;

    float smoothedProgress = MathHelper.SmoothStep(0,1,(float)changeProgress);

    int verPosition = 300;
    float horPosition = 300;
    float alphaValue;
    float bgLayerDepth;
    Color bgColor;

    switch (windowState)
    {
        case WindowState.Starting:
            horPosition -= 200 * (1.0f - (float)smoothedProgress);
            alphaValue = smoothedProgress;
            bgLayerDepth = 0.5f;
            bgColor = new Color(new Vector4(1, 1, 1, alphaValue));
            break;
         case WindowState.Ending:
            horPosition += 200 * (float)smoothedProgress;
            alphaValue = 1.0f - smoothedProgress;
            bgLayerDepth = 1;
            bgColor = Color.White;
            break;
        default:
            alphaValue = 1;
            bgLayerDepth = 1;
            bgColor = Color.White;
            break;
    }

    Color titleColor = new Color(new Vector4(1, 1, 1, alphaValue));
    spriteBatch.Draw(backgroundImage, new Vector2(), null, ➥
    bgColor, 0, Vector2.Zero, 1, SpriteEffects.None, bgLayerDepth);
    spriteBatch.DrawString(spriteFont, menuTitle, ➥
    new Vector2(horPosition, 200), titleColor,0,Vector2.Zero, ➥
    1.5f, SpriteEffects.None, 0);
```

```
    for (int itemID = 0; itemID < itemList.Count; itemID++)
    {
        Vector2 itemPostition = new Vector2(horPosition, verPosition);
        Color itemColor = Color.White;

        if (itemID == selectedItem)
            itemColor = new Color(new Vector4(1,0,0,alphaValue));
        else
            itemColor = new Color(new Vector4(1,1,1,alphaValue));

        spriteBatch.DrawString(spriteFont, ➥
        itemList[itemID].itemText, itemPostition, itemColor, ➥
        0, Vector2.Zero, 1, SpriteEffects.None, 0);
        verPosition += 30;
    }
}
```

## Main Program

You can create the structure of your menus in the LoadContent method. Your Update method should call the Update method of each menu and call the MenuInput method:

```
protected override void Update(GameTime gameTime)
{
    if (GamePad.GetState(PlayerIndex.One).Buttons.Back == ButtonState.Pressed)
        this.Exit();

    KeyboardState keybState = Keyboard.GetState();

    if (menusRunning)
    {
        foreach (MenuWindow currentMenu in menuList)
            currentMenu.Update(gameTime.ElapsedGameTime.TotalMilliseconds);
        MenuInput(keybState);
    }
    else
    {
    }


    lastKeybState = keybState;

    base.Update(gameTime);
}
```

This MenuInput method passes user input to the currently active menu and receives the menu that is active after the user input has been processed:

```
private void MenuInput(KeyboardState currentKeybState)
{
    MenuWindow newActive = activeMenu.ProcessInput(lastKeybState, currentKeybState);

    if (newActive == startGameEasy)
    {
        //set level to easy
        menusRunning = false;
    }
    else if (newActive == startGameNormal)
    {
        //set level to normal
        menusRunning = false;
    }
    else if (newActive == startGameHard)
    {
        //set level to hard
        menusRunning = false;
    }
    else if (newActive == null)
        this.Exit();
    else if (newActive != activeMenu)
        newActive.WakeUp();

    activeMenu = newActive;
}
```

## Extra Reading

Although this mechanism is sufficient for a basic menu implementation, for a completely finished game design the MenuWindow class should be an abstract class so menus cannot be instances of that class. Instead, you could create a new class for menus and a class for your game, which both inherit from the MenuWindow class. This way, the keyboard handling and drawing is completely handled by the mechanism, and the ugly menuRunning variable is no longer required. This is the basis of the menus sample on the http://creators.xna.com site.

# 3-7. Create a Texture, Define the Color of Each Pixel, Save a Texture to a File

## The Problem

You want to create a new texture from scratch and manually define the color of each pixel of the texture. This can be useful when you want to let the user create an image or generate an artificial image such as a depth map or noise map.

You want to save this or another texture to a file, for example, to generate a screenshot of your application or for debugging purposes.

## The Solution

Setting the color contents of an image is directly supported by the XNA Framework, as is saving the texture to a file in a format of your choice.

You can set and change the contents of a texture by calling the SetData method of the texture, which accepts an array containing the color value for each pixel.

You can save a texture to a file on disk using its Save method.

## How It Works

You should first create an array, holding the color for each pixel in the image:

```
int textureWidth = 512;
int textureHeight = 512;

Color[] textureColors = new Color[textureWidth* textureHeight];
int i = 0;
for (int ver = 0; ver < textureHeight; ver++)
    for (int hor=0; hor<textureWidth; hor++)
    {
        float red = (float)hor / (float)textureWidth;
        float green = 0;
        float blue = (float)ver / (float)textureHeight;
        float alpha = 1;

        textureColors[i++] = new Color(new Vector4(red, green, blue, alpha));
    }
```

The first three lines create an array that can store colors for a texture with a resolution of 512×512 pixels. Next, the code fills each pixel separately using the double for loop. Using this filling order, you start at the top-left corner. When incrementing the index, the pixels are scanned from left to right and then from top to bottom.

Finally, you need to actually create the texture and load the contents of your array into the texture's memory:

```
Texture2D newTexture = new Texture2D(device, textureWidth, ➥
textureHeight, 1, TextureUsage.None, SurfaceFormat.Color);
```

After the device and the resolution of the image, you need to specify the number of mipmaps (see the following note) that you want to be generated. The next argument allows you to set TextureUsage. By selecting TextureUsage.AutoGenerateMipMap, XNA will automatically generate the number of mipmaps you've specified. Keep in mind that the width and height of your image should be powers of 2 if you want to work with mipmaps.

---

■**Note**  A mipmapped image contains multiple resolutions of the image. This is beneficial in a lot of cases. Imagine you are rendering a 3D scene, with a textured box so far away from the camera that it occupies only a single pixel of your window. To determine the color of this box, your graphics card will still calculate what it considers the right texture coordinate at which to sample the texture. When you move your camera a little bit, this will probably give a slightly different texture coordinate, which might correspond to a totally different color in the texture. As a result, moving the camera a little bit might cause the box to aggressively change color, resulting in a flickering pixel on your screen whenever you move your camera. A solution to this was found by storing multiple resolution versions of an image in the image. For an image of 64×64 pixels, if you enable mipmapping, XNA will also create a 32×32 version, a 16×16 version, an 8×8, a 4×4, and a 2×2 up to a 1×1 version inside the image. Now, in case of the box being very far away, XNA will use the 1×1 mipmap of the image. As a result, a slight change in the position of the camera will still result in a different texture coordinate. However, this change in texture coordinate will not result in a change of color, as the entire texture (of 1×1 pixels) has the same color! This means the pixel on the screen corresponding to the box will now keep a constant color.

---

The last argument specifies the format of the pixels in the texture. This is necessary so XNA can allocate enough memory to store the texture. Also, when retrieving the values of the texture, this is the format you can expect, or when you write data to a texture as you're doing here, you must provide the data in this format.

Finally, you can simply store the Color array in the texture:

```
newTexture.SetData<Color>(textureColors);
```

That's all there is to it. Saving a texture to a file is even easier:

```
myTexture.Save("savedtexture.jpg", ImageFileFormat.Jpg);
```

The last argument specifies how you want your file to be formatted/compressed. Make sure the extension of your file name corresponds to this format, or you might run into trouble when trying to open the file with an external image viewer.

When you run your code, the file will be created in the same map as your executable. By default, this is in the \bin\x86\Debug map.

## The Code

*All the code is available for download at* www.apress.com.

This method creates a texture, fills it with color data, and returns it:

```
private Texture2D DefineTextureColors()
{
    int textureWidth = 512;
    int textureHeight = 512;
```

```
Color[] textureColors = new Color[textureWidth* textureHeight];
int i = 0;
for (int ver = 0; ver < textureHeight; ver++)
    for (int hor=0; hor<textureWidth; hor++)
    {
        textureColors[i++] = new ➥
        Color(new Vector4((float)hor / (float)textureWidth, ➥
        0, (float)ver / (float)textureHeight, 1));
    }

Texture2D newTexture = new Texture2D(device, textureWidth, ➥
textureHeight, 1, ResourceUsage.None, SurfaceFormat.Color);
newTexture.SetData<Color>(textureColors);

return newTexture;
}
```

The preceding method should be called from the LoadContent method, because it requires the device to be instantiated:

```
protected override void LoadContent()
{
    device = graphics.GraphicsDevice;
    spriteBatch = new SpriteBatch(GraphicsDevice);

    myTexture = DefineTextureColors();
    myTexture.Save("savedtexture.jpg", ImageFileFormat.Jpg);
}
```

# 3-8. Render the Scene into a Texture

## The Problem

You want to store the contents of the screen in a texture, which, for example, allows you to save a screenshot into a file. As another example, you may want to render the scene into a texture to be used as a depth map/refraction map or as input for a post-processing effect.

## The Solution

The easiest solution is using the device.ResolveBackBuffer method, which writes the current contents of the back buffer into a texture.

However, if you want the scene to be rendered into a texture only, or into a texture of a size you want to specify, you should first change the render target from the screen to one you define in memory using the device.SetRenderTarget method. Once the scene has been completely rendered to that target, you can store its contents into a texture.

## How It Works

The easiest approach is to render the scene to the screen and copy the contents of the back buffer into a ResolveTexture2D. Therefore, you first need to create a ResolveTexture2D object, capable of storing the contents of the back buffer. This means its size and format have to be the same as the size and format of the back buffer. Add this code to your LoadContent method to create your ResolveTexture2D object:

```
PresentationParameters pp = device.PresentationParameters;
resolveTexture = new ResolveTexture2D(device, pp.BackBufferWidth, ➡
pp.BackBufferHeight, 1, device.DisplayMode.Format);
```

The first line retrieves the current PresentationParameters, containing all details about the current configuration of the graphical device. These include the current width, height, and data format of the current back buffer. The second line creates a ResolveTexture2D object, based on these settings.

With your ResolveTexture2D object created, you can use it to store the current contents of the back buffer. In your Draw method, at a point where you want to capture the contents of the back buffer, add these lines:

```
device.ResolveBackBuffer(resolveTexture);
resolveTexture.Save("output.bmp", ImageFileFormat.Bmp);
```

This will store the current contents of the back buffer in your resolveTexture variable. Because the ResolveTexture2D inherits from the Texture2D class, you can use it in any way you would use a normal Texture2D. In this example, the texture is saved to file.

---

■**Caution**  Because of hardware constraints, after calling the device.ResolveBackBuffer method, the contents of the back buffer are discarded!

---

### Using a Custom Render Target of Size Equal to the Screen

Instead of rendering to the back buffer, you can define a custom RenderTarget2D and activate this before rendering. This way, nothing will be drawn on the screen while the custom render target is active. A render target is exactly what the name implies: it is a piece of memory on the graphics card that can be used to render to. After all rendering is done, you will again copy the contents of this render target into a texture.

Add the variable that will hold the render target:

```
RenderTarget2D renderTarget;
```

and instantiate it in the LoadContent method:

```
PresentationParameters pp = device.PresentationParameters;
renderTarget = new RenderTarget2D(device, pp.BackBufferWidth, ➡
pp.BackBufferHeight, 1, device.DisplayMode.Format);
```

You define the width and height of your render target, indicate how many mipmap levels it should have (see the note on mipmaps in recipe 3-6), and set the data format of the render target. In this example, you're using the same values as your current back buffer.

---

**■Note** As always, mipmapping (see the note in the previous recipe) can be done only if the width/height of your texture is a power of 2. So if you get an error when you specify any other number of mipmaps than 1, this might be the cause.

---

Once you have initialized your render target, you can set it as the active render target in your Draw method using the following line. Anything you render after this line will be rendered onto your custom render target:

```
device.SetRenderTarget(0, renderTarget);
```

See recipe 6-10 for an explanation of and example on the first argument of this method. You should place this line before the Clear call in your Draw method, because the contents of your render target need to be cleared before you render anything to it. Next, you render the whole scene, and after all rendering has been finished, you want to copy the contents of the render target into a texture. Before you can do this, though, you need to deactivate it by activating another render target. In this code, you set the default back buffer (which will be presented to your screen) as the active render target by specifying null as the second argument:

```
device.SetRenderTarget(0, null);
Texture2D resolvedTexture = renderTarget.GetTexture();
```

Since you've activated the default back buffer, anything you render from now on will be rendered to the screen as usual. In addition, the last line loads the contents you've rendered to the custom render target into the resolvedTexture variable. Make sure you do things in this order:

1. First, activate your custom render target.

2. Clear the custom render target (if needed).

3. Render what needs to be drawn into this render target.

4. Deactivate the custom render target by activating another render target.

5. Store the contents of your custom render target into a texture.

### Setting a Custom Render Target of Size Not Equal to the Screen

You can also choose to render to a render target that has a different size than that of the screen. This can often be useful, for example, for intermediate steps during post-processing effects. Steps such as blurring, intensity, and edge detection can be done on a smaller image, reducing the work the graphics card has to do.

If the ratio between width and height is the same as that of the window (in other words, as of the default back buffer), this is not a problem.

If you want to set a render target with a different width/height ratio than your window, your Projection matrix for the window will not be valid for your render target any longer, because it was created using the width/height ratio of your screen (see recipe 2-1). This means you'll have to define a new Projection matrix that corresponds to your custom render target:

```
PresentationParameters pp = device.PresentationParameters;
int width = pp.BackBufferWidth / 2;
int height = pp.BackBufferHeight / 4;
renderTarget = new RenderTarget2D(device, width, height, 1, ➥
device.DisplayMode.Format);
rendertargetProjectionMatrix = ➥
Matrix.CreatePerspectiveFieldOfView(MathHelper.PiOver4, ➥
(float)width / (float)height, 0.5f, 100.0f);
```

First you define the resolution you want the render target to have and create the corresponding render target and Projection matrix.

The width of your new render target will be half the width of your window, while its height will be a quarter of the window height. As such, the ratio of this render target is different from the ratio of your window. If you used your old Projection matrix instead of this new one, the whole scene would look like it had been squashed together vertically.

Now whenever you're rendering the scene into the new render target, you have to indicate you want to use your rendertargetProjectionMatrix instead of the Projection matrix corresponding to the window.

## The Code

*All the code is available for download at* www.apress.com.

Initialize a RenderTarget2D object, and set it to a resolution you want. Note that if you save its contents into a texture, the size of the texture will be the same as the render target.

```
protected override void LoadContent()
{
    device = graphics.GraphicsDevice;
    basicEffect = new BasicEffect(device, null);
    cCross = new CoordCross(device);
    spriteBatch = new SpriteBatch(device);

    PresentationParameters pp = device.PresentationParameters;
    int width = pp.BackBufferWidth / 2;
    int height = pp.BackBufferHeight / 4;
    renderTarget = new RenderTarget2D(device, width, height, 1, ➥
    device.DisplayMode.Format);
    rendertargetProjectionMatrix = ➥
    Matrix.CreatePerspectiveFieldOfView(MathHelper.PiOver4, ➥
    (float)width / (float)height, 0.5f, 100.0f);
}
```

In the `Draw` method, you activate your custom render target, clear it, render into it, deactivate it, and save its contents into a texture. Important to note is that you use your `rendertargetProjectionMatrix` to render 3D objects into your custom render target (shown in the following code). Optionally, this texture is displayed on the screen using a `SpriteBatch`:

```
protected override void Draw(GameTime gameTime)
{
    device.SetRenderTarget(0, renderTarget);
    device.Clear(ClearOptions.Target | ClearOptions.DepthBuffer, ➥
    Color.CornflowerBlue, 1, 0);

    cCross.Draw(fpsCam.ViewMatrix, rendertargetProjectionMatrix);

    device.SetRenderTarget(0, null);
    Texture2D resolvedTexture = renderTarget.GetTexture();

    graphics.GraphicsDevice.Clear(Color.Tomato);
    spriteBatch.Begin();
    spriteBatch.Draw(resolvedTexture, new Vector2(100, 100), Color.White);
    spriteBatch.End();

    base.Draw(gameTime);
}
```

# 3-9. Extend the Image Content Processor

## The Problem

You want to extend the default image content importer, to manipulate some pixel values, for example. Or, you're looking for an introduction to the content pipeline.

## The Solution

Since XNA already comes with a content importer that takes an image file as its source and creates a `Texture2D` object as its end product, all you have to do is extend the content processor.

Specific to this recipe, you can simply call the `ReplaceColor` method of the `PixelBitmapContent` helper class, which is provided by the content pipeline framework.

---

■**Note**  If you're simply interested in alpha color keying, the image content processor automatically changes the pixels with magenta to fully transparent. This recipe mainly serves as an introduction to extending a content importer.

---

# How It Works

This recipe will be written as an introduction to the content pipeline and, more specifically, to extending an existing content processor. Therefore, it is important you keep the general flow-chart of the content pipeline in mind, which is displayed in Figure 3-5.

## The Content Pipeline

Before you can use an image file in your XNA project, you need to load it from a file. This involves reading the bytes, selecting the useful data, and running this data through a decompressing algorithm if needed.

The same is true for other art assets, such as 3D models. Their data needs to be loaded from a file, and after a lot of data manipulations, a Model object needs to be created based on this data.

This whole process that starts by a file on disk and results in an object ready to be used by your XNA project is taken care of by the content pipeline of XNA. Actually, each type of art asset has its own content pipeline. As you can see in Figure 3-5, a complete content pipeline for a specific type of object consists of an importer, a processor, a serializer, and a deserializer.

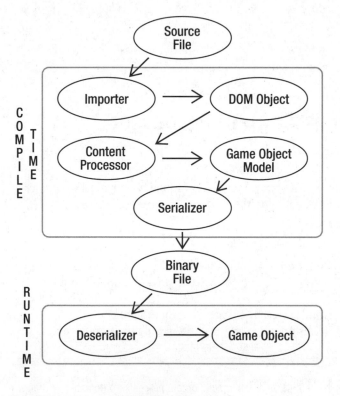

**Figure 3-5.** *The content pipeline flowchart*

At compile time (your project is compiled each time you press F5), the source file is read in from disk, its content is processed, and the result is serialized into an .xnb binary file on disk. You can find these binary files in the Content submap of the map your .exe file is in.

When the game is run (after compiling, when running the game on Xbox or Zune or when double-clicking the `.exe` file), this `.xnb` binary file is deserialized, so all the useful information becomes readily available, without any further need of processing. The obvious advantage of this approach is that all processing needs to be done only once (at compile time), instead of each time when the game is run. A second advantage is that the `.xnb` files are platform independent, so they can be used on the PC, Xbox 360, and Zune.

Let's dissect the compile stage a bit more, because it is executed each time you compile your project. The compile stage is divided into three substages:

- The *importer*, which reads the source file and extracts the useful data from the file. This data is stored in a standard format specific for the kind of data. For a model, this standard format is a `NodeContent` object, while for an image, this is a `TextureContent` object. Such standard formats are called *DOM objects*. You can find a list of default DOM objects in Table 3-1, but you can also define your own types (see recipe 5-11).

- The *processor*, which actually does all the processing on the data contained in the DOM object and generates an object as it could be used in a game. In case of a `Model`, for example, the processor can add normal data, calculate tangents, set effects on the model, and much more.

- The *serializer*, or `TypeWriter`, defines how the `.xnb` binary file needs to be generated from the output of the processor.

This approach has an additional advantage in that if you want to change something in the compile stage, you probably have to change only one of the three substages. For example, if you have created a `Model` in a format that is not natively supported by the XNA Framework, all you have to do is write a new importer, which reads your file and creates a `NodeContent` object from the data contained in it. You can leave the rest of the work to the default content pipeline components, because the default processor for the `NodeContent` will take your object from there.

During runtime, there's only one small stage that needs to be executed:

- The deserializer, or `TypeReader`, defines how the game object can again be constructed from the binary data stream stored in the `.xnb` file. Because no processing calculations need to be done here, this really takes almost no time in comparison to what is being done at compile time.

XNA comes with a lot of default content importers and content processors. Combining `TextureImporter` and `TextureProcessor`, you can import almost any image format into your XNA project. Combining the `XImporter` or `FbxImporter` with `ModelImporter`, you can import `.x` or `.fbx` models on disk into your XNA project.

---

**Note** This is one example where the separation between the importer and the processor proves useful. Both `XImporter` and `FbxImporter` load data from disk and format the data into a simple `NodeContent` object, which is in both cases passed to `ModelProcessor`, which does the heavy work.

---

**Table 3-1.** *The Default Content Importers and Processors in the XNA Framework*

| Content Importer | Input (File) | Output (DOM Object) |
|---|---|---|
| TextureImporter | .bmp, .dds, .dib, .hdr, .jpg, .pfm, .png, .ppm, .tga | TextureContent |
| XImporter | .x | NodeContent |
| FbxImporter | .fbx | NodeContent |
| EffectImporter | .fx | EffectContent |
| FontDescriptionImporter | .spritefont | FontDescription |
| XmlImporter | .xml | User-defined |
| XACT Project | .xap | Audio project |

| Content Processor | Input (DOM Object) | Output (Game OM) |
|---|---|---|
| TextureProcessor | TextureContent | TextureContent |
| ModelProcessor | NodeContent | ModelContent |
| EffectProcessor | EffectContent | CompiledEffect |
| PassThroughProcessor | Any | Any |
| FontDescriptionProcessor | FontDescription | SpriteFontContent |
| FontTextureProcessor | TextureContent | SpriteFontContent |
| FontTextureProcessor | Texture2DContent | SpriteFontContent |

The XNA content pipeline comes with default serializers that can write those objects into a binary file at compile time and with default deserializers that can re-create your objects from such a binary file at runtime.

## Using the Default Content Pipeline Framework Components

The key to writing/extending a content processor is in using the default objects as much as possible so you can reuse the components already in the content pipeline.

In this recipe, you will extend the default TextureProcessor so you can perform some changes on the image data before it is loaded into your XNA project. During compile time, you want the image to be read from file and its contents to be shaped in a 2D array so it becomes an image, and you want to change some pixels and save the resulting image to an .xnb file.

When it comes to running your project, the .xnb file will be read from file, containing the changes you made.

For the first part, reading the file from disk and transforming it into a 2D array of colors (whatever the format of the image file might be), you should use the default importer for textures.

Next, however, you will need to extend TextureProcessor. Because this recipe focuses on setting up a custom content pipeline, you will simply switch all pixels with a certain color to another color. For a more realistic texture processor, see the next recipe.

You will want to make sure the final product of your processor is a TextureContent object so you can use the default serializer to save it as an .xnb file and use the default deserializer to load that .xnb file into the game during game startup.

Figure 3-6 shows this whole process. Locate the processor you're going to extend, as well as the components you'll borrow from XNA.

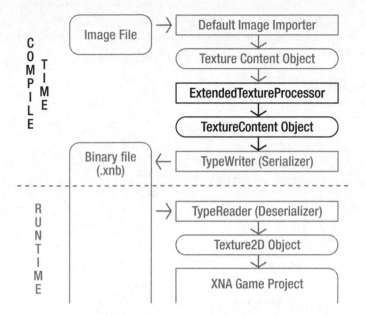

**Figure 3-6.** *The location in the content pipeline of the processor you'll overwrite*

I'll show images like Figure 3-6 throughout this book each time you'll be working on a content pipeline so you can easily visualize on which parts you'll be working.

## Extending an Existing Content Processor

To extend an already existing content processor, a few short initialization steps are required. Although the steps will be straightforward for the experienced .NET programmer, I will list them here so you can refer to this section from all other recipes that involve extending a content processor. If you follow this list, you shouldn't have any trouble getting your custom content pipeline to work. Each step in the list will be explained in the following sections.

1. Add a new content pipeline project to your solution.

2. In the new project, add a reference to `Microsoft.XNA.Framework.Content.Pipeline`.

3. Add the pipeline namespaces to the `using` block.

4. Indicate which part you're going to extend (which method you're going to override).

5. Compile the new content pipeline project.

6. Add the newly created assembly to your main project.

7. Select the newly created processor to process an asset.

8. Set the project dependencies.

9. And after everything has been initialized, code the method you've created in step 4.

**Adding a New Content Pipeline Project to Your Solution**

To extend or create a new content importer/processor, you need to add a new project to your solution. To do this, find your Solution Explorer at the top-right of the screen, right-click your solution (the top entry in the list), and select Add ➤ New Project, as shown in Figure 3-7. In the dialog box that appears, select Content Pipeline Extension Library, and give your project a name that suits the purpose of your processor, as shown in Figure 3-8.

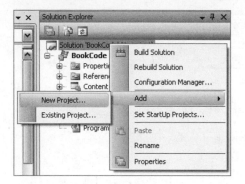

**Figure 3-7.** *Adding a new project to your solution*

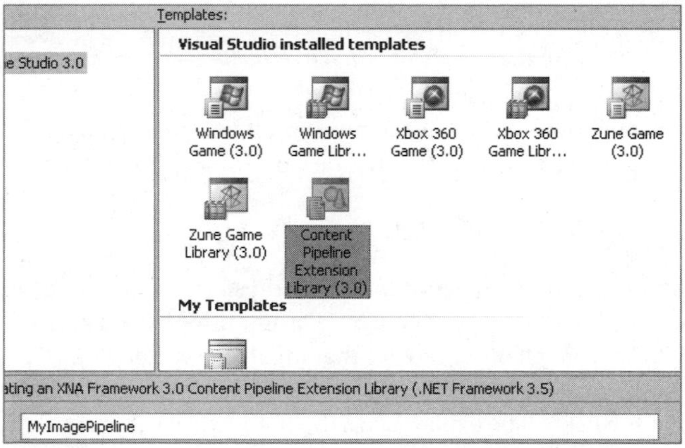

**Figure 3-8.** *Creating a content pipeline extension library*

You should be presented with a new file, containing the namespace you just defined, as well as a default `Processor` class. Also note that your new project has been added to your solution in your Solution Explorer, as shown in Figure 3-9.

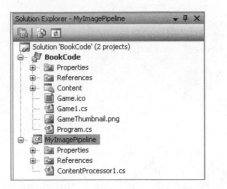

**Figure 3-9.** *Content pipeline project added to solution*

### Adding a Reference to Microsoft.XNA.Framework.Content.Pipeline

In the new project, make sure you add a reference to `Microsoft.XNA.Framework.Content.Pipeline` (version 3.0.0.0). First highlight the new project in the Solution Explorer as shown in Figure 3-9. Next, open the Project menu and select Add Reference. From the list, add the correct reference, as shown in Figure 3-10.

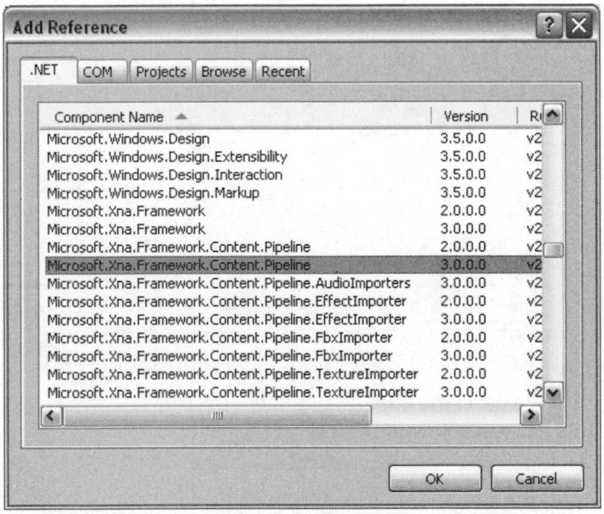

**Figure 3-10.** *Selecting the XNA pipeline reference*

### Adding the Pipeline Namespaces to the using Block

You will also want your compiler to link to the newly available namespaces so all of their functionality will be available to you. Make sure these lines are in your `using` block (the last three lines probably are already present):

```
using System.IO;
using Microsoft.Xna.Framework.Content;
using Microsoft.Xna.Framework.Content.Pipeline.Serialization.Compiler;
using Microsoft.Xna.Framework.Content.Pipeline;
using Microsoft.Xna.Framework.Content.Pipeline.Graphics;
using Microsoft.Xna.Framework.Content.Pipeline.Processors;
```

### Indicating Which Part You're Going to Extend

The document already contains a lot of comments and a sample ContentProcessor. Replace the entire namespace with the following code (note that the name of the namespace must be the same as the name you gave to your pipeline project in Figure 3-7), and indicate the specific input and output of your new processor. All this custom processor does is ask its base class (the default texture processor) to process its input, so this new ContentProcessor will behave the same way as the default texture processor.

```
namespace MyImagePipeline
{
    [ContentProcessor(DisplayName = "ExtendedExample")]
    public class ExtentedTextureProcessor : TextureProcessor
    {
        public override TextureContent ➥
        Process(TextureContent input, ContentProcessorContext context)
        {
            return base.Process(input, context);
        }
    }
}
```

In this recipe, you're going to extend the default TextureProcessor, so you need to inherit from the TextureProcessor class. Because of this, your Process method receives a TextureContent object and is supposed to produce a TextureContent object as output.

In a few minutes, you'll be coding a real Process method for your custom processor; for now it passes only the input it receives to the base class, being the default TextureProcessor.

---

■**Note** ExtendedExample will be the name of your new custom processor. If you omit the DisplayName tag and simply put in the [ContentProcessor] attribute, your new processor will have the name of your class, ExtendedTextureProcessor in this case.

---

■**Note** Make sure you put in the [ContentProcessor] attribute. If you don't put it in, XNA will not consider this class as a content processor. As a result, your processor will not show up when browsing through the list of available content processors in step 7 in the earlier list of steps.

---

### Compiling the New Content Pipeline Project

During the next step, you're going to link the assemblies of this new project to your main project, so you first need to compile the project into an assembly. Pressing F6 will do this; pressing F5 will build the assembly and afterward run the whole solution.

---

**Note**  This can take a few seconds; you can check the bottom-left corner of your window for information about the progress.

---

### Adding the Newly Created Assembly to Your Main Project

Now that you have assembled your custom processor, you still need to let your main game project know this new processor exists. Therefore, in your Solution Explorer, find the Content entry, and open it. Right-click References, and select Add Reference, as shown in Figure 3-11.

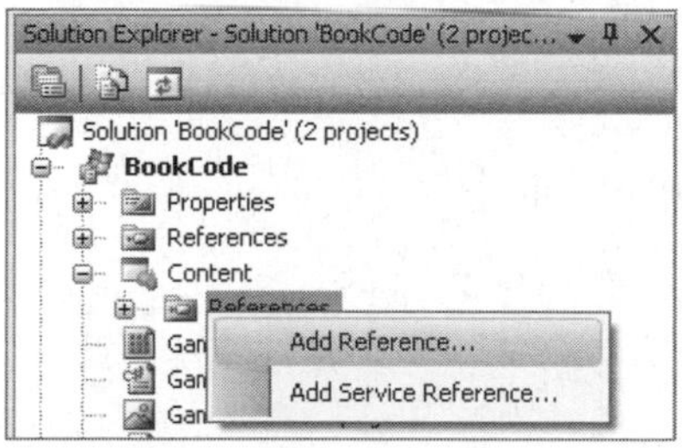

**Figure 3-11.** *Adding a reference to your custom content pipeline project*

In the dialog box that appears, go to the Projects tab, and select your content pipeline project from the list, as shown in Figure 3-12.

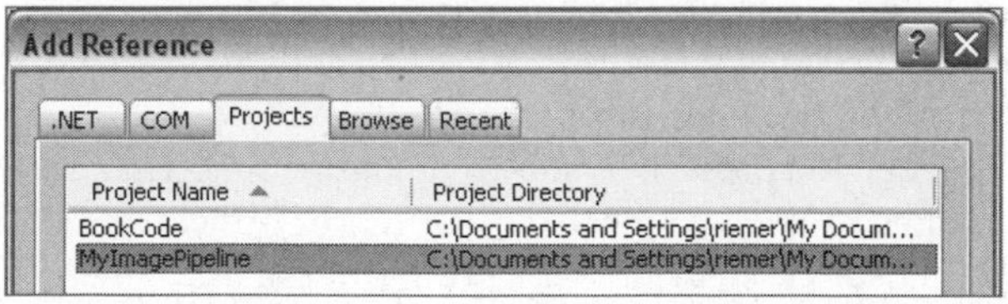

**Figure 3-12.** *Selecting your content pipeline project*

---

**Note**  If your content pipeline project is not in the list, you must have skipped the previous step.

---

**Selecting the Newly Created Processor to Process an Image File**

When you import an image into your GS project (see recipe 3-1), you should now be able to select your newly created content processor to process the image. To do this, select the image in your Content folder, and select the content processor in the Property box at the bottom-right of your screen, as shown in Figure 3-13.

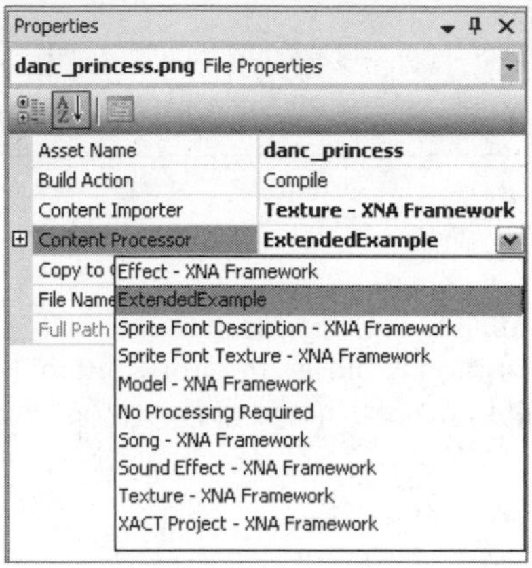

**Figure 3-13.** *Selecting your own content processor to process an image*

Now when you compile your project, your custom processor will be used to process the contents of your image file!

**Setting Project Dependencies**

For each change you make to your custom content processor project, you have to recompile that project manually before your main project will see the changes. To solve this, you will indicate your main project depends on your content project, so each time you recompile your main project, the content project will be compiled first (if you made some changes to it since the last time you compiled).

You set the project dependencies by right-clicking your main project in your Solution Explorer and selecting Project Dependencies. In the dialog box that appears, you need to indicate your main project depends on your second project, as shown in Figure 3-14. This will make sure whenever you press F5 in your main project, your content processor project's `.dll` file is built before your main project.

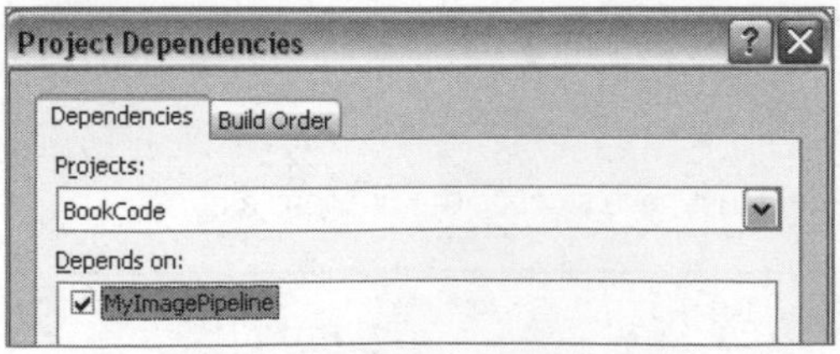

**Figure 3-14.** *Accessing project dependencies*

## Extending the Default Texture Processor

Now everything has been initialized, you're ready to code your processor so it does something custom.

You have created a class, ExtendedTextureProcessor, that inherits from the default TextureProcessor class, and you have declared you will override the Process method of that class. As with all content processor methods, this method is called Process and receives a DOM object (in the case of TextureProcessor, this will be a TextureContent object, as you can see in Table 3-1) and a ContentProcessorContext object. This context object can be used to create nested builds. For example, when importing a Model from file, this object could contain the names of all texture files that also need to be loaded, together with the model. You can learn more about this in recipe 4-12.

As you can see in Table 3-1, in the case of a TextureProcessor, you need to return a TextureContent object. The case of a texture is special (and simple) as the processor's input and output have the same type. The processor you currently have simply routes its input to its base class:

```
[ContentProcessor(DisplayName = "ExtendedExample")]
public class ExtentedTextureProcessor : TextureProcessor
{
    public override TextureContent Process(TextureContent input, ➥
    ContentProcessorContext context)
    {
        return base.Process(input, context);
    }
}
```

This will cause the input to be processed by the Process method of the TextureProcessor class (this is possible, because you inherited from the default TextureProcessor class) and returns the resulting image to your method, so it is ready to be further processed as you like. For now, you simply send it immediately to the output, so your processor will give the same result as the default TextureProcessor would.

---

**Note**  The case of the TextureProcessor is special, because the type of the input and output objects is the same. In this case, you could drop the line that passes the input to the base.Process method, because the input is already useful as output. In more complex cases, however, you will want the base. Process method to convert the input object to a workable output model for you. For example, if you extend the model processor, you will first want the base.Process method to convert the input NodeContent to a ModelContent object for you, because this involves a lot of work. Once you have this default ModelContent object, you're free to extend/change it to your liking. See recipe 4-12 for an example on extending the model processor.

---

In this recipe, however, you don't want to route the input immediately to the output, because you're interested in changing some of the color values. One of the benefits of using standard DOM objects is that you can use the default content pipeline methods that have been defined for these objects. For example, the TextureContent class has a useful ConvertBitmapType method that changes the type of format the contents of the texture is stored in. The next line changes the contents of the texContent object to colors:

```
TextureContent texContent = base.Process(input, context);
texContent.ConvertBitmapType(typeof(PixelBitmapContent<Color>));
```

Because the TextureContent class is abstract, the texContent object will in reality be a TextureContent2D object in case of a 2D image but can also be a TextureContent3D or TextureContentCube object. This means the image can have multiple faces, as well as multiple mipmaps (see the note on mipmaps in recipe 3-7). The next line selects the first face and the first mipmap, which will be the only face and mipmap level available in case of a simple 2D texture.

```
PixelBitmapContent<Color> image = (PixelBitmapContent<Color>)input.Faces[0][0];
```

The PixelBitmapContent class has a very useful method, ReplaceColor, which replaces all pixels of a specified color in the image to another color:

```
Color colorToReplace = Color.Black;
Color toReplace = new Color(81, 92, 164);
image.ReplaceColor(toReplace, Color.Yellow);
```

That's all the functionality you'll build in for your custom processor at this time. All you have to do is return the altered TextureContent object:

```
return texContent;
```

During compile time, this object will be sent to the serializer, which will save the object into a binary .xnb file at compile time. At runtime, this binary file will be loaded by the deserializer, which will create a Texture2D object from it (in case your image file contains a simple 2D image).

Now make sure you import an image into your main XNA project, select your self-made processor to process this image, and load it into a Texture2D object in your LoadContent method:

```
myTexture = Content.Load<Texture2D>("image");
```

## Multiple Faces/Mipmaps

In this case, you're inheriting from the TextureContent processor, which will generate mipmaps (instead of, for example, the SpriteTextureProcessor). For more information on mipmaps, see the note in recipe 3-7. If the imported image is a cube image, the texture will also have six faces. To make this recipe complete, the following code shows how to scroll through the faces and mipmaps:

```
for (int face = 0; face < texContent.Faces.Count; face++)
{
    MipmapChain mipChain = texContent.Faces[face];
    for (int mipLevel = 0; mipLevel < mipChain.Count; mipLevel++)
    {
        PixelBitmapContent<Color> image = ➥
        (PixelBitmapContent<Color>)input.Faces[face][mipLevel];
        Color toReplace = new Color(81, 92, 164);
        image.ReplaceColor(toReplace, Color.Yellow);
    }
}
```

The first index on the Faces property is the face of the image. Standard 2D images will have only one face, while cube textures will have six faces. The second index indicates the mipmap level. Non-mipmapped images will have only one level.

This code sets the color of your choice (in this case, black) to white for each mipmap level for each face of the texture.

## The Code

*All the code is available for download at* www.apress.com.

Here you can find all the code you need for extending a default content importer. You should put this code in a new project you have added to your solution. Remember, for this code to work, you need to have added a reference to Microsoft.XNA.Framework.Content.Pipeline to that new project.

```
using System;
using System.Collections.Generic;
using System.Linq;
using Microsoft.Xna.Framework;
using Microsoft.Xna.Framework.Graphics;
using Microsoft.Xna.Framework.Content.Pipeline;
using Microsoft.Xna.Framework.Content.Pipeline.Graphics;
using Microsoft.Xna.Framework.Content.Pipeline.Processors;
using System.IO;
using Microsoft.Xna.Framework.Content;
using Microsoft.Xna.Framework.Content.Pipeline.Serialization.Compiler;


namespace MyImagePipeline
{
    [ContentProcessor(DisplayName = "ExtendedExample")]
    public class ExtentedTextureProcessor : TextureProcessor
    {
```

```
public override TextureContent Process(TextureContent input, ➡
ContentProcessorContext context)
{
    TextureContent texContent = base.Process(input, context);
    texContent.ConvertBitmapType(typeof(PixelBitmapContent<Color>));

    for (int face = 0; face < texContent.Faces.Count; face++)
    {
        MipmapChain mipChain = texContent.Faces[face];
        for (int mipLevel = 0; mipLevel < mipChain.Count; mipLevel++)
        {
            PixelBitmapContent<Color> image = (PixelBitmapContent<Color>) ➡
            input.Faces[face][mipLevel];
            Color toReplace = new Color(81, 92, 164);
            image.ReplaceColor(toReplace, Color.Yellow);
        }
    }

    return texContent;
}
    }
}
```

# 3-10. Extend the Image Content Processor: Grayscale Conversion and Processor Parameters

## The Problem

You want to extend the image processor to gain access to the color values of each individual pixel. Also, you want to be able to change some important parameters of your processor from within your main XNA project.

## The Solution

In the previous recipe, you can find exactly how to extend an existing content processor. This will allow you to access and change individual pixel values.

All public variables you declare in your Processor class are configurable from within the Properties box of an asset, processed by your processor.

## How It Works

Start by going through the initialization steps explained in recipe 3-9. Use the following code, copied from that recipe, which gives you access to all images inside the image file you loaded (some image files, such as a texCube, contain multiple images):

```
namespace GrayContentPipeline
{
    [ContentProcessor(DisplayName = "GrayScaleProcessor")]
    public class ExtentedTextureProcessor : TextureProcessor
    {
        public override TextureContent ➥
        Process(TextureContent input, ContentProcessorContext context)
        {
            TextureContent texContent = base.Process(input, context);
            texContent.ConvertBitmapType(typeof(PixelBitmapContent<Color>));

            for (int face = 0; face < input.Faces.Count; face++)
            {
                MipmapChain mipChain = input.Faces[face];
                for (int mipLevel = 0; mipLevel < mipChain.Count; mipLevel++)
                {
                    ...
                }
            }

            return texContent;
        }
    }
}
```

Inside the inner for loop, you have access to all faces of the image. Here, you will first cast the current face to a PixelBitmapContent object, allowing you to access each pixel individually. You can also immediately create a second one, which you will use to store the new colors:

```
PixelBitmapContent<Color> oldImage = ➥
(PixelBitmapContent<Color>)input.Faces[face][mipLevel];
PixelBitmapContent<Color> grayImage = new ➥
PixelBitmapContent<Color>(oldImage.Width, oldImage.Height);
```

■**Note** For this example, you could get away with simply overwriting the old colors with the new ones. However, for many image-processing techniques, in order to calculate the new color of a pixel, you will still need access to the original colors of the surrounding pixels. This is no problem if you separate the new image from the old image.

Next, you can scan through all pixels of the image and retrieve the original color:

```
for (int x = 0; x < oldImage.Width; x++)
    for (int y = 0; y < oldImage.Height; y++)
    {
        Color oldColor = oldImage.GetPixel(x, y);
    }
```

Once you know the original color, you can define the corresponding grayscale color. Instead of simply taking the average of the three color components, in imaging people usually assign more importance to the green color channel, because the human eye is more sensitive to this color. Also, when you retrieve the color, each color channel value will be indicated as an integer value between 0 and 255. However, when you want to create a new color, you need to specify your colors as floats between 0 and 1. This means you need to divide the original values by 255 in the for loop:

```
Color oldColor = oldImage.GetPixel(x, y);
float grayValue = oldColor.R * 0.299f / 255.0f;
grayValue += oldColor.G * 0.596f / 255.0f;
grayValue += oldColor.B * 0.211f / 255.0f;
float alpha = oldColor.A / 255.0f;

Color grayColor = new Color(grayValue, grayValue, grayValue, alpha);
grayImage.SetPixel(x, y, newColor);
```

This will replace all pixels of your image with their corresponding grayscale values. After the double for loop, which scans through all pixels, make sure you copy the new colors onto the current image face:

```
input.Faces[face][mipLevel] = grayImage;
```

### Debugging Content Processors

Often, you'll feel the need to debug your content pipeline. This might be trickier than debugging a normal project, because breakpoints and more of the like will be ignored at compile time. You have to manually attach a debugger to your content project.

For example, if you want to debug your project at the center pixel of your image, you can use this code:

```
if ((x == oldImage.Width / 2) && (y == oldImage.Height / 2))
{
    System.Diagnostics.Debugger.Launch();
}
```

When you compile your project, Visual Studio will prompt you to specify which debugger you want to use. Select New Instance of Visual Studio.

Once the debugger has been launched, you'll want to call System.Diagnostics.Debugger.Break(); wherever you want to place additional breakpoints.

### Defining Processor Parameters

By adding public variables to your Processor class, you can make your processor much more flexible. For example, add this to the top of your Processor class:

```
public float interpolation = 0.8f;
```

When you compile your project, you will be able to set this value from within your main XNA project, as shown in Figure 3-15.

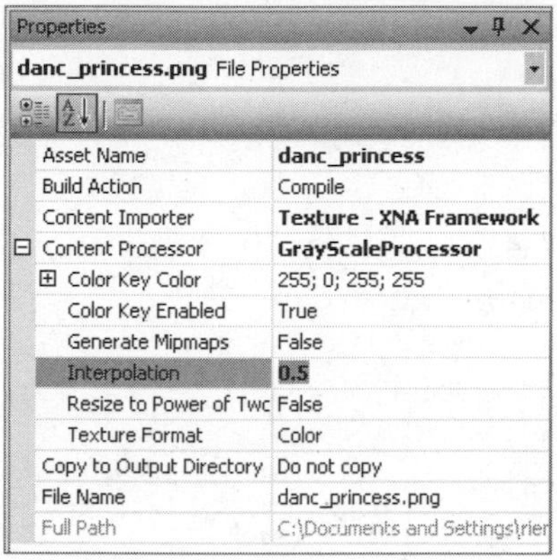

**Figure 3-15.** *Configuring the parameters of your custom processor*

---

■**Note**  Depending on your computer's locale settings, you will need to use a comma or a point as the decimal separator, or XNA Game Studio 3.0 will complain that you've entered an invalid value.

---

You can use this variable as any other inside your content processor. In this example, you can use it to interpolate between the normal, colored image and the new, grayscale image. If the interpolation value is 0, the colored pixels will be stored inside the new image. If the value is 1, the grayscale values will be stored inside the new image.

```
Color grayColor = new Color(grayValue, grayValue, grayValue, alpha);
Color newColor = Color.Lerp(oldColor, grayColor, interpolation);
grayImage.SetPixel(x, y, newColor);
grayImage.SetPixel(x, y, newColor);
```

## The Code

*All the code is available for download at www.apress.com.*

Here you find the full code for the grayscale image processor:

```
namespace GrayContentPipeline
{
    [ContentProcessor(DisplayName = "GrayScaleProcessor")]
    public class ExtentedTextureProcessor : TextureProcessor
    {
        private float interpolation = 0.8f;
        public float Interpolation
```

```
        {
            get { return interpolation; }
            set { interpolation = value; }
        }

        public override TextureContent Process(TextureContent input, ➥
        ContentProcessorContext context)
        {
            TextureContent texContent = base.Process(input, context);
            texContent.ConvertBitmapType(typeof(PixelBitmapContent<Color>));

            for (int face = 0; face < input.Faces.Count; face++)
            {
                MipmapChain mipChain = input.Faces[face];
                for (int mipLevel = 0; mipLevel < mipChain.Count; mipLevel++)
                {
                    PixelBitmapContent<Color> oldImage = ➥
                     (PixelBitmapContent<Color>)input.Faces[face][mipLevel];
                    PixelBitmapContent<Color> grayImage = ➥
                    new PixelBitmapContent<Color>(oldImage.Width, oldImage.Height);

                    for (int x = 0; x < oldImage.Width; x++)
                        for (int y = 0; y < oldImage.Height; y++)
                        {
                            Color oldColor = oldImage.GetPixel(x, y);
                            float grayValue = oldColor.R * 0.299f / 255.0f;
                            grayValue += oldColor.G * 0.596f / 255.0f;
                            grayValue += oldColor.B * 0.211f / 255.0f;
                            float alpha = oldColor.A / 255.0f;

                            Color grayColor = new Color(grayValue, grayValue, ➥
                            grayValue, alpha);
                            Color newColor = Color.Lerp(oldColor, grayColor, ➥
                            interpolation);
                            grayImage.SetPixel(x, y, newColor);
                        }

                    input.Faces[face][mipLevel] = grayImage;
                }
            }

            return texContent;
        }
    }
}
```

# 3-11. Make Your Scene More Impressive with Billboarding: Render 2D Images in a 3D World So They Always Face the Camera

## The Problem

To look impressive, a 3D world needs to contain a lot of objects, especially when dealing with outdoor scenes. For example, you will need hundreds, if not thousands, of trees, or your forest will not look real. However, it is out of the question that you would render a couple hundred trees as full 3D models, because this would slow down your application tremendously.

You can also use billboarding in smaller quantities, for example, to render laser beams or bullets. This is usually done in conjunction with a particle engine (see recipe 3-12).

## The Solution

You can solve this problem by replacing the 3D object with a 2D image. However, when the camera is positioned next to the 2D image, the viewer will of course notice it's simply a 2D image, as you can see in the left part of Figure 3-16, where five 2D images are positioned in the 3D world.

**Figure 3-16.** *2D images in a 3D scene: not billboarded (left), billboarded (right)*

To solve this, for each image you will want to define two triangles in 3D space that will display the image, and you will want to rotate these triangles so the image is facing the camera. This is shown in the right part of Figure 3-16, where the same five 2D images are rotated so they are facing the camera. If the images will contain trees and their borders will be transparent instead of black, this would already give a nice result, while the images on the left would not.

The XNA Framework contains functionality that calculates the rotated positions of the six corner points of the two triangles of each image, by means of the `Matrix.CreateBillboard` method, but you can get a significant speed boost by performing these calculations in a vertex shader, which is explained in the second part of this recipe.

## How It Works

As an interface of your forest or particle engine, you want to define only the position in the 3D world where you want the center of your 2D image to be positioned and the size of the 2D image in your 3D world. So, you want to keep a list that contains the 3D position as well as the size for each of your 2D images:

```
List<Vector4> billboardList = new List<Vector4>();
Texture2D myTexture;
VertexPositionTexture[] billboardVertices;
```

You see the billboards will be stored as a Vector4: three floats for the 3D position of the center and an additional float to hold the size of the billboard.

For each billboarded 2D image, you will need to calculate the six corner points of the two triangles that will hold the image in 3D space. These vertices will be stored in the variable on the last line. The myTexture variable holds the texture (or textures) the graphics card will use to sample the colors from.

---

■**Tip** As explained in recipe 3-4, the fastest way to render from multiple textures is by storing them in one large texture file so the graphics card doesn't need to switch textures while it's doing its job!

---

Load the texture into this variable as explained in recipe 3-1 by putting the following line in the LoadContent method:

```
myTexture = content.Load<Texture2D>("billboardtexture");
```

Next, you will want to add a simple method that allows you to easily add billboards to your scene:

```
private void AddBillboards()
{
    billboardList.Add(new Vector4(-20, -10, 0, 10));
    billboardList.Add(new Vector4(0, 0, 0, 5));
    billboardList.Add(new Vector4(20, 10, 0, 10));
}
```

For now, this method adds only three billboards to the scene. As the fourth component indicates, you want the size of the middle billboard to be four times smaller than that of the other two, because the length of its sides is two times smaller. Don't forget to call this method from the Initialize method:

```
AddBillboards();
```

Next, you need to calculate the positions of the six corner points of the two triangles that will display the image in your 3D scene. Billboarding comes in two main flavors: spherical billboarding and cylindrical billboarding. Spherical billboarding is used mainly in particle engines, while cylindrical billboarding is used for rendering trees, people, and more. Read on to learn why.

## Calculating the Six Corner Points for Spherical Billboarding

**Tip** If you're into HLSL, you can skip to the "Performance Considerations: Part 2" section of this recipe, because performing the billboarding calculations on the GPU can give your application a huge speed boost. The section called "Performance Considerations: Part 1" is also worth reading.

Now that you've defined the center locations of your billboards, it's up to you to calculate the six corner points of the triangles surrounding the center point:

```
private void CreateBBVertices()
{
    billboardVertices = new VertexPositionTexture[billboardList.Count * 6];

    int i = 0;
    foreach (Vector4 currentV4 in billboardList)
    {
        Vector3 center = new Vector3(currentV4.X, currentV4.Y, currentV4.Z);
        float scaling = currentV4.W;

        //add rotated vertices to the array
    }
}
```

The code shown previously will first create an array that is capable of storing six vertices for the two triangles of each of your billboards. Next, for each of your billboards stored in the billboardList, you find the center and the size. The remaining part of the for loop will be the code that actually calculates the position of the six vertices.

For each 2D image, you will need to define two triangles so you can define a quad or rectangle in 3D space that holds the 2D image. This means you will need to define six vertices, of which only four are unique. Since they need to display a texture, you want a VertexPositionTexture to hold each of them.

Since the billboardList contains the center position of each quad, you want all of the vertices to have the same distance to the center. In this example, you will add/subtract 0.5f offsets to/from the X and Y components of the center to obtain the positions of corner points. For example, the following three positions hold the offsets from the center position defining one triangle, where DL is DownLeft and UR is UpRight:

```
Vector3 posDL = new Vector3(-0.5f, -0.5f, 0);
Vector3 posUR = new Vector3(0.5f, 0.5f, 0);
Vector3 posUL = new Vector3(-0.5f, 0.5f, 0);
```

If you add the center position of the billboard to each of these positions, you get the positions of the corners of one triangle in 3D space. However, these positions will remain the same, no matter what the position of the camera is. So if you move your camera next to the triangle, you'll see the side of the triangle, as on the left side of Figure 3-16. You want the triangle to always face the camera, so you need to perform some kind of rotation on these offsets, depending on the position of the camera. This can get quite mathematical, but luckily XNA can immediately generate a matrix for you that you can use to transform these offsets. Add this line in the for loop:

```
Matrix bbMatrix = Matrix.CreateBillboard(center, quatCam.Position, ➥
quatCam.UpVector, quatCam.Forward);
```

To be able to create this billboard matrix that rotates the positions of the triangles so the image is facing the camera, XNA needs to know the position of both the quad and the camera, as well as the Forward vector of your camera. Because you want spherical billboarding to rotate your image so it is facing up relative to the camera, you also need to specify this Up vector.

**Note** When you rotate your camera upside down, the quads will be rotated so they still remain upward relative to the camera. To demonstrate this, the sample code uses a simple arrow that points upward as the texture. Also, to allow you to rotate the camera unrestrictedly in the sample, the quaternion camera of recipe 2-4 was chosen instead of the quake camera of recipe 2-3.

Once you have this matrix, you can find the rotated offsets by transforming them with this matrix:

```
Vector3 posDL = new Vector3(-0.5f, -0.5f, 0);
Vector3 billboardedPosDL = Vector3.Transform(posDL*scaling, bbMatrix);
billboardVertices[i++] = new VertexPositionTexture(billboardedPosDL, ➥
new Vector2(1, 1));
```

The first line defines the static offset, not taking the camera position into account. You also specified the size you want your quad to be, so now you'll use this value. Multiply the offset by the scaling value so the quad will have the size you specified in the AddBillboards method. Now that you know your offset between the corner and the center, you actually transform it by the matrix. Finally, you store this transformed position, together with the correct texture coordinate, into the vertices array.

If you do this for all three positions of a triangle, the resulting triangle will be facing the camera.

**Note** You apply the transformation only to the offsets: the translation of the vertices toward its center position in 3D space is performed automatically by the matrix transformation! That's one of the reasons you had to specify the center position of the quad when you created the bbMatrix.

You need to perform this transformation for each of the offsets. Since the two triangles each share two points, you need to perform only four transformations. This is what the CreateBBVertices method looks like:

```
private void CreateBBVertices()
{
    billboardVertices = new VertexPositionTexture[billboardList.Count * 6];

    int i = 0;
    foreach (Vector4 currentV4 in billboardList)
    {
        Vector3 center = new Vector3(currentV4.X, currentV4.Y, currentV4.Z);
        float scaling = currentV4.W;

        Matrix bbMatrix = Matrix.CreateBillboard(center, ➡
        quatCam.Position, quatCam.UpVector, quatCam.Forward);

        //first triangle
        Vector3 posDL = new Vector3(-0.5f, -0.5f, 0);
        Vector3 billboardedPosDL = Vector3.Transform(posDL * scaling, bbMatrix);
        billboardVertices[i++] = new ➡
        VertexPositionTexture(billboardedPosDL, new Vector2(1, 1));
        Vector3 posUR = new Vector3(0.5f, 0.5f, 0);
        Vector3 billboardedPosUR = Vector3.Transform(posUR * scaling, bbMatrix);
        billboardVertices[i++] = new ➡
        VertexPositionTexture(billboardedPosUR, new Vector2(0, 0));
        Vector3 posUL = new Vector3(-0.5f, 0.5f, 0);
        Vector3 billboardedPosUL = Vector3.Transform(posUL * scaling, bbMatrix);
        billboardVertices[i++] = new ➡
        VertexPositionTexture(billboardedPosUL, new Vector2(1, 0));

        //second triangle: 2 of 3 corner points already calculated!
        billboardVertices[i++] = new ➡
        VertexPositionTexture(billboardedPosDL, new Vector2(1, 1));
        Vector3 posDR = new Vector3(0.5f, -0.5f, 0);
        Vector3 billboardedPosDR = Vector3.Transform(posDR * scaling, bbMatrix);
        billboardVertices[i++] = new ➡
        VertexPositionTexture(billboardedPosDR, new Vector2(0, 1));
        billboardVertices[i++] = new ➡
        VertexPositionTexture(billboardedPosUR, new Vector2(0, 0));
    }
}
```

For each entry in billboardList, this method will calculate four points in 3D space, so the resulting quad is facing the camera.

Make sure you call this method each time the camera's position or rotation changes, because the rotations of all your billboards have to be adjusted accordingly! To be safe, you can call it at the end of the Update method.

### Rendering from the Vertex Array

Once you have all vertices containing the correct 3D position and texture coordinate, you can render them to the screen in the Draw method, as explained in recipe 5-1:

```
//draw billboards
basicEffect.World = Matrix.Identity;
basicEffect.View = quatMousCam.ViewMatrix;
basicEffect.Projection = quatMousCam.ProjectionMatrix;
basicEffect.TextureEnabled = true;
basicEffect.Texture = myTexture;

basicEffect.Begin();
foreach (EffectPass pass in basicEffect.CurrentTechnique.Passes)
{
    pass.Begin();
    device.VertexDeclaration = new VertexDeclaration(device, ➥
    VertexPositionTexture.VertexElements);
    device.DrawUserPrimitives<VertexPositionTexture> ➥
    (PrimitiveType.TriangleList, billboardVertices, 0, ➥
    billboardList.Count*2);
    pass.End();
}
basicEffect.End();
```

You want to render from the billboardVertices array, whose vertices describe a list of triangles. Since each 2D image is a quad, it requires two triangles to be drawn, so you will be rendering a total of billboardList.Count*2 triangles. Since you're rendering a TriangleList, this number equals billboardVertices.Length/3.

### Performance Considerations: Part 1

When playing around with billboards, you can easily get yourself into situations where you need to render thousands of billboards. You can, for example, define a few thousand billboards like this:

```
private void AddBillboards()
{
    int CPUpower = 10;
    for (int x = -CPUpower; x < CPUpower; x++)
        for (int y = -CPUpower; y <CPUpower; y++)
            for (int z = -CPUpower; z < CPUpower; z++)
                billboardList.Add(new Vector4(x, y, z, 0.5f));
}
```

This will completely fill a cube starting from (–10,–10,–10) to (9,9,9) with billboards of side length 0.5f, all at a distance of 1 unit from each other, already totaling a whopping 8,000 billboards! If this doesn't run smoothly on your PC, try reducing the CPU power value, so fewer billboards will be drawn.

Your PC is able to render this many billboards only because you are using one big vertex array to store them all. This way, your graphics card can process the whole task of drawing the 16,000 triangles in one big, single run, which keeps your graphics card happy.

The sample code also includes a minor variation of the code presented previously. In that code, for each billboard, a new vertex array is created and filled with the six vertices for that billboard, exactly the same way as shown previously. Then, for each billboard, the graphics card is issued to render two triangles from the six vertices, and the whole process starts over again.

With almost the same workload for the CPU, the graphics card now receives 8,000 calls to render two triangles, so in this task the GPU will be disturbed 7,999 times, making it quite angry.

Using this approach, I was able to set CPUpower only to 3 before I got some serious hiccups in the frame rate. This corresponds to only 216 billboards drawn!

So, the bottom line is, as always, keep your graphics card happy by letting it do its work in one big run. Always try to render your scene from as few vertex buffers/textures as possible.

## Calculating the Six Corner Points for Cylindrical Billboarding

In some cases, you do not want the quad to be rotated so it exactly faces the camera. For example, if you are creating a forest using 2D images of trees, you want each image to be rotated along only the axis of the tree's trunk. Using spherical billboarding as you've done previously, the billboards are rotated along the three axes, so they completely face the camera.

Imagine the case where you have some images of trees and you move the camera exactly above them. Using spherical billboarding, you will get a result as shown in the upper-left part of Figure 3-17. At the bottom-left part of the same image, you see that in order to get the quads facing the camera, the trees are rotated in quite an unnatural way. This will give some very strange effects when the camera is moved over the forest.

What you want is that the quads holding the images of the trees are rotated only along the Up vector of the tree, as shown in the bottom-right part of Figure 3-17. In the 3D view, this will give a result as shown in the upper-right part of the image.

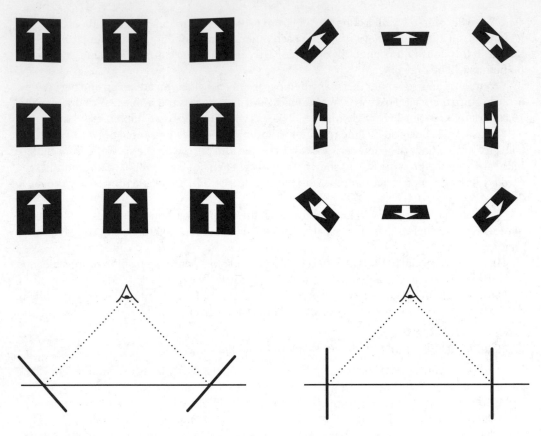

**Figure 3-17.** *Spherical billboarding (left), cyclindrical billboarding (right)*

---

■**Note** This kind of billboarding is labeled *cylindrical*, because when you position the camera inside a lot of such billboarded images, they will create a cylindrical tunnel. This is caused by the fact that they are allowed to be rotated along only one direction. Figure 3-18 shows such a tunnel.

---

The code to calculate the corner points of each billboard is almost the same as in the first part of this recipe. You only need to use another billboarding matrix, which can be created using the Matrix.CreateConstrainedBillboard method:

```
Matrix bbMatrix = Matrix.CreateConstrainedBillboard(center, ➥
quatCam.Position, new Vector3(0, 1, 0), quatCam.Forward, null);
```

As an extra constraint to the rotation, you can now specify the single direction around which the billboard is allowed to rotate. For a tree, this will be the (0,1,0) Up vector. To make the rotation more accurate when the camera is very close to the object, you can also specify the Up vector of the camera.

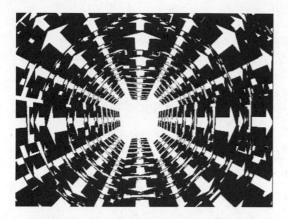

**Figure 3-18.** *Even more cylindrical billboarding*

## Performance Considerations: Part 2

The first part of this recipe showed how you can create a billboarding engine in XNA code. However, this approach puts a lot of stress on your CPU and is highly inefficient for your graphics card, as you can read here.

Say you want to render 1,000 billboarded 2D images in your 3D scene. Whenever the camera changes position, you need to recalculate the positions of the four corner points of each of your images so they are again facing the camera. Targeting an update rate of 60 updates/second, this comes down to calculating 4,000 3D positions 60 times each second, which has to be done on the CPU. Furthermore, for each frame a complete array of 6,000 vertices needs to be created to hold the two triangles needed to display each billboard.

The CPU is a general-purpose processor, not really optimized for this kind of calculation. A task like this will cripple the CPU, severely limiting whatever else you need the CPU for, such as general game logic.

Moreover, each frame this updated vertex buffer needs has to be sent to the graphics card! This requires the graphics card to put this data in nonoptimal memory and puts a lot of traffic on your PCI-express (or AGP) bus.

Wouldn't it be incredible if you just had to store the 3D center position and size of each billboard only one time in the fast static memory on your graphics card and have your GPU (the calculation unit on your graphics card) perform all the billboarding calculations instead of the CPU? Keep in mind that your GPU is optimized for vector operations, making it an order of magnitude faster at doing these calculations than your CPU. This combines the following important benefits:

- One-time-only traffic on your PCI-express (or AGP) bus

- Calculation time *much* shorter (because the GPU is optimized for these kind of calculations)

- Absolutely *no* billboarding calculations done on the CPU, leaving the CPU free to do more important work

And it introduces no drawbacks. This is almost starting to sound like a cheap infomercial!

## Preparing Your Code for HLSL Billboarding

You can still use a list to keep track of your billboards, so you can use the AddBillboards method without any modification. The CreateBBVertices method, however, will be simplified, because all billboarding calculations will be done in the vertex shader on the GPU.

A billboard will still be drawn using two quads, so for each billboard you will still need to pass six vertices to the GPU. So, what exactly do you want the vertex shader to do?

- You want the vertex shader to compute the 3D rotated coordinates of each of the six vertices surrounding a billboard so the billboard is facing the camera.

To do this, the vertex shader needs to know the following information about each vertex:

- The 3D position of the center of the billboard to which the vertex belongs

- Some kind of information identifying which corner point the current vertex is of the billboard so the vertex shader can calculate the corresponding offset from the center

- The usual texture coordinates, so they can be passed to the pixel shader that will use them to sample at the right location from the texture

---

**■Note** Obviously, your vertex shader also needs to know the location of the camera in 3D space before it can rotate the billboards so they are facing the camera. This camera position is the same for all vertices, however, and should therefore be set as an XNA-to-HLSL variable, instead of storing this position inside each vertex.

---

This means that one part of the information carried by all six vertices belonging to a billboard will be the same: the 3D position of the center of the billboard. As information that identifies the vertex as one of the four corner points, you could, for example, pass a number between 0 and 3, where 0 means, for example, the top-left corner points and 3 the bottom-right corner points.

However, you are already passing this kind of information to the vertex shader by means of the texture coordinate! Indeed, a (0,0) texture coordinate indicates the current vertex is the top-left corner point, and a (1,0) texture coordinate indicates a top-right corner point.

As a summary: for each billboard you want to draw, you need to render two triangles, so you need to pass six vertices to the vertex shader. These six vertices will carry the same positional data: the center of the billboard. Each of the six vertices will also carry its specific texture coordinate, required for correctly texturing the two triangles, but in this case the texture coordinate will also be used by the vertex shader to determine which corner point the current vertex is, so the vertex shader can calculate the offset of the current vertex to the center of the billboard.

So in your XNA code, adjust the CreateBBVertices method so it generates these vertices and stores them in an array:

```
private void CreateBBVertices()
{
    billboardVertices = new VertexPositionTexture[billboardList.Count * 6];

    int i = 0;
    foreach (Vector4 currentV4 in billboardList)
    {
        Vector3 center = new Vector3(currentV4.X, currentV4.Y, currentV4.Z);

        billboardVertices[i++] = new VertexPositionTexture(center, ➨
        new Vector2(0, 0));
        billboardVertices[i++] = new VertexPositionTexture(center, ➨
        new Vector2(1, 0));
        billboardVertices[i++] = new VertexPositionTexture(center, ➨
        new Vector2(1, 1));

        billboardVertices[i++] = new VertexPositionTexture(center, ➨
        new Vector2(0, 0));
        billboardVertices[i++] = new VertexPositionTexture(center, ➨
        new Vector2(1, 1));
        billboardVertices[i++] = new VertexPositionTexture(center, ➨
        new Vector2(0, 1));
    }
}
```

For each billboard in your list, you add six vertices to your array. Each of these vertices contains the center position of the billboard, as well as its correct texture coordinate.

The great news is that you have to call this method only once at the beginning of your application, since the contents of this array don't need to be updated when the camera is changed! So, call it, for example, from the Initialize method, after the call to the AddBillboards method:

```
AddBillboards();
CreateBBVertices();
```

Now that your vertices are ready to be transferred to the GPU, it's time to start coding the vertex shader. Let's start with the case of cylindrical billboarding, because it's a tiny bit easier than spherical billboarding.

---

■**Note**  You could definitely benefit from storing this data in the memory on the graphics card, since you won't be updating its contents. You do this by creating a VertexBuffer from your billboardVertices array. See recipe 5-4 on how to create a VertexBuffer.

---

## Vertex Shader for Cylindrical Billboarding

As with all HLSL code in this book, let's start with the variables passed from your XNA application to your shaders, the texture stages, and the vertex/pixel shader output structures:

```
//------- XNA interface --------
float4x4 xView;
float4x4 xProjection;
float4x4 xWorld;
float3 xCamPos;
float3 xAllowedRotDir;

//------- Texture Samplers --------
Texture xBillboardTexture;
sampler textureSampler = sampler_state { texture = <xBillboardTexture>; ➥
magfilter = LINEAR; minfilter = LINEAR; mipfilter=LINEAR; ➥
AddressU = CLAMP; AddressV = CLAMP;};

struct BBVertexToPixel
{
    float4 Position : POSITION;
    float2 TexCoord   : TEXCOORD0;
};
struct BBPixelToFrame
{
    float4 Color    : COLOR0;
};
```

As always when you need to render a 3D world to a 2D screen, you need World, View, and Projection matrices. To perform the billboarding calculations, you also need to know the current position of the camera. Since you'll start with cylindrical billboarding, you need to define around which axis the image is allowed to be rotated.

You'll need only one texture stage, to put the actual image on the two triangles. For each vertex, the vertex shader will produce the mandatory 2D screen coordinate, as well as the corresponding texture coordinate. For each pixel, the pixel shader will output the color.

In case of billboarding, the vertex shader is responsible for calculating the offsets to the center. Let's start with some shader code that adds only the offsets to the vertices; the real billboarding will build on this code:

```
//------- Technique: CylBillboard --------
BBVertexToPixel CylBillboardVS(float3 inPos: POSITION0, ➥
float2 inTexCoord: TEXCOORD0)
{
    BBVertexToPixel Output = (BBVertexToPixel)0;

    float3 center = mul(inPos, xWorld);
```

```
    float3 upVector = float3(0,1,0);
    float3 sideVector = float3(1,0,0);

    float3 finalPosition = center;
    finalPosition += (inTexCoord.x-0.5f)*sideVector;
    finalPosition += (0.5f-inTexCoord.y)*upVector;

    float4 finalPosition4 = float4(finalPosition, 1);

    float4x4 preViewProjection = mul (xView, xProjection);
    Output.Position = mul(finalPosition4, preViewProjection);

    Output.TexCoord = inTexCoord;

    return Output;
}
```

For each vertex, the vertex shader receives the position and texture coordinate you
defined in your XNA application. Note that this position is the 3D position of the center of
the billboard. The multiplication with the World matrix allows you to define a global World
matrix so you can rotate/scale/translate all your billboards at once. The final center position is
stored in a variable called center, which will be the same for the six vertices belonging to one
billboard.

Next, a static Side vector and an Up vector are defined. These are the vectors that will
offset the individual vertex from the center of the billboard. Take a look at how you want to
offset the six vertices from the center in Figure 3-19, where the two triangles for a billboard are
shown. Note the four texture coordinates outside the two triangles and the six vertex indices
inside the corners of the triangles.

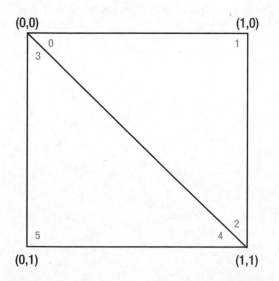

**Figure 3-19.** *Offset between the six vertices and the center*

The next code block calculates the final 3D position of the specific vertex. First, you start from the center position. Next, you want to find out whether the current vector needs to be offset to the (-1,0,0) Left direction or the (1,0,0) Right direction. You can find this by looking at the X texture coordinate of Figure 3-19: a vertex with texture coordinate (0,0) is the top-left vertex, so it needs to be shifted to the left. A vertex with texture coordinate (1,0) is the top-right vertex, so it needs to be shifted to the right.

All of this is coded in one simple line: first you subtract 0.5f from the X texture coordinate. This will give –0.5f if the vertex is a left vertex and +0.5f if the vertex is on the right of the center. By multiplying this by the (+1,0,0) vector, you will get (–0.5f,0,0) for a left vertex and (+0.5f,0,0) for a right vertex!

The same approach holds for the Y texture coordinate: a (0,0) texture coordinate means top-left vertex, and (0,1) means bottom left. So if the Y texture coordinate is 0, you have a top vertex; if it is 1, you have a bottom vertex.

You add both the correct Side and Up offsets to the center position, and you end up with the correct 3D position of the specific vertex.

That's it for the code specific to this recipe. All you have to do now is transform this 3D position to 2D screen space as usual by transforming it with the ViewProjection matrix. Before you can transform this `float3` by a 4×4 matrix, you need to make it a `float4`, by adding a 1 as the fourth coordinate.

When you use the pixel shader belonging to this technique, all your billboards will be nice-looking quads, but they all are parallel to each other. This is because you haven't yet used the camera location in the code that calculates the offsets, which you'll want to use to rotate your triangles so they are facing the camera.

This obviously cannot be achieved by using static Up and Side vectors in the vertex shader. Cylindrical billboarding is a bit easy, because you already define the Up vector of the billboard: it is the allowed rotation direction, passed to the shader by the XNA app in the `xAllowedRotDir` variable.

An example of two billboards, holding, for example, two trees, is shown in the left part of Figure 3-20. Since you specify the allowed rotational direction in your XNA application as the Up vector of the trees, you already know the Up vector you will use in your vertex shader.

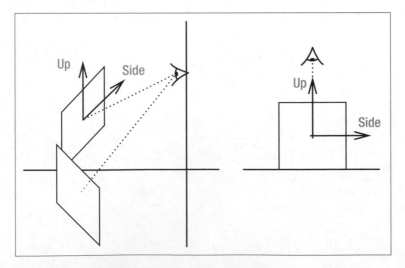

**Figure 3-20.** *Two images cyclindrically billboarded*

The Side vector of the billboard is not known a priori. But, as always, you can find this. To this end, you need to know the Eye vector, which is the vector going from the eye toward the center of the billboard and is shown as a dotted line in Figure 3-20. One thing you know about the Side vector is that it is perpendicular to both the Eye vector and the Up vector, as shown in the right side of Figure 3-20, displaying the same as the left part of the image from a different angle.

You can always find the vector that is perpendicular to two other vectors by taking the cross product of these two vectors (see recipe 5-7), so this is how you can find the Side vector.

Translated into HLSL code, the inner clockwork of the vertex shader becomes the following:

```
float3 center = mul(inPos, xWorld);
float3 eyeVector = center - xCamPos;

float3 upVector = xAllowedRotDir;
upVector = normalize(upVector);
float3 sideVector = cross(eyeVector, upVector);
sideVector = normalize(sideVector);

float3 finalPosition = center;
finalPosition += (inTexCoord.x-0.5f)*sideVector;
finalPosition += (0.5f-inTexCoord.y)*upVector;
```

You can find the Eye vector as you would find any vector going from point A to point B: by taking B – A. As discussed, the Up vector for your billboard is the allowed rotational direction, to be specified by your XNA code. Since the Side vector is perpendicular to the Eye vector and the Up vector, you can find it by taking the cross product of both vectors.

You need to make sure both Side and Up vectors have unity length (otherwise you have no control over the final size of your billboard), so you normalize both vectors.

Once you know the Up and Side vectors of your billboard, you can reuse the same code from earlier that transforms the 3D position to a 2D screen coordinate. Now your vertex shader uses the current position of the camera to calculate the final 3D position of the vertices, so your vertices will change their position whenever the camera is moved!

### Finishing Off the Billboarding Technique: Pixel Shader and Technique Definition

Now that your vertex shader is capable of calculating the correct 3D coordinates for the vertices, all you need to do is put the texture over the triangles in the pixel shader:

```
BBPixelToFrame BillboardPS(BBVertexToPixel PSIn) : COLOR0
{
    BBPixelToFrame Output = (BBPixelToFrame)0;
    Output.Color = tex2D(textureSampler, PSIn.TexCoord);
    return Output;
}
```

And of course here is the definition of the technique:

```
technique CylBillboard
{
    pass Pass0
    {
        VertexShader = compile vs_1_1 CylBillboardVS();
        PixelShader  = compile ps_1_1 BillboardPS();
    }
}
```

That will be all for the moment. All you need to do is import this HLSL file (which I called
bbEffect.fx) into your project and load it into a variable in your LoadContent method:

```
bbEffect = content.Load<Effect>("bbEffect");
```

Now in your Draw method, you can set the required XNA-to-HLSL variables and finally
render the billboards!

```
bbEffect.CurrentTechnique = bbEffect.Techniques["CylBillboard"];
bbEffect.Parameters["xWorld"].SetValue(Matrix.Identity);
bbEffect.Parameters["xProjection"].SetValue(quatMousCam.ProjectionMatrix);
bbEffect.Parameters["xView"].SetValue(quatMousCam.ViewMatrix);

bbEffect.Parameters["xCamPos"].SetValue(quatMousCam.Position);
bbEffect.Parameters["xAllowedRotDir"].SetValue(new Vector3(0,1,0));
bbEffect.Parameters["xBillboardTexture"].SetValue(myTexture);

bbEffect.Begin();
foreach (EffectPass pass in bbEffect.CurrentTechnique.Passes)
{
    pass.Begin();
    device.VertexDeclaration = new VertexDeclaration(device, ➡
    VertexPositionTexture.VertexElements);
    device.DrawUserPrimitives<VertexPositionTexture> ➡
    (PrimitiveType.TriangleList, billboardVertices, 0, billboardList.Count*2);
    pass.End();
}
bbEffect.End();
```

Note where you indicate, for example, the (0,1,0) Up direction as the rotational direction
for your billboards.

If your PC is equipped with a separate graphics card, you should be able to render many
more billboards now than with the XNA-only version.

## Vertex Shader for Spherical Billboarding

The difference between cylindrical and spherical billboarding is that in spherical billboarding each billboard has to completely face the camera. In the words of your vertex shader

code, both the Up and the Side vector have to be perfectly perpendicular to the Eye vector (in Cylindrical billboarding, only the Side vector was perpendicular to the Eye vector).

The challenge in spherical billboarding is that you also need to find the Up vector, because this no longer is known a priori as was the case in cylindrical billboarding. To help you out, you will need to know the Up vector of the camera.

Since you want the billboard to completely face the camera, you can say that the Side vector of the billboard will need to be perpendicular to the Eye vector and also to the Up vector of the camera. To demonstrate this, I've colored the plane of the Eye and CamUp vectors in the left part of Figure 3-21 so you can see that the Side vector is perpendicular to this plane. Since they are perpendicular, you already know how to find the Side vector: it's the cross product between the Eye vector and the CamUp vectors:

```
float3 sideVector = cross(eyeVector,xCamUp);
sideVector = normalize(sideVector);
```

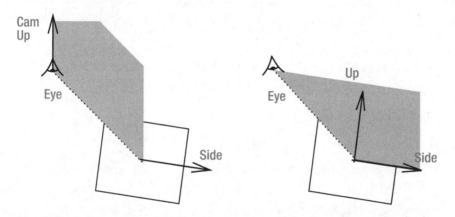

**Figure 3-21.** *Finding Side and Up vectors for spherical billboarding*

Now that you know the Side vector, you can also find the Up vector of the billboard: it is the vector that is perpendicular to the Side vector and the Eye vector. I've colored the plane of the Side and Eye vectors in the right part of Figure 3-21, so you can again try to visualize this. This means that the Up vector of the billboard is nothing more than the cross product of the Eye and Side vectors:

```
float3 upVector = cross(sideVector,eyeVector);
upVector = normalize(upVector);
```

This is all that needs to be changed when going from cylindrical to spherical billboarding! Just make sure you've defined the xCamUp variable . . .

```
float3 xCamUp;
```

. . . and a new technique:

```
technique SpheBillboard
{
    pass Pass0
    {
        VertexShader = compile vs_1_1 SpheBillboardVS();
        PixelShader  = compile ps_1_1 BillboardPS();
    }
}
```

. . . and since you can use the same pixel shader, you're ready to go!

Be sure to call the correct technique from within your XNA project and to set the xCamUp parameter:

```
bbEffect.CurrentTechnique = bbEffect.Techniques["SpheBillboard"];
bbEffect.Parameters["xWorld"].SetValue(Matrix.Identity);
bbEffect.Parameters["xProjection"].SetValue(quatCam.ProjectionMatrix);
bbEffect.Parameters["xView"].SetValue(quatCam.ViewMatrix);

bbEffect.Parameters["xCamPos"].SetValue(quatCam.Position);
bbEffect.Parameters["xCamUp"].SetValue(quatCam.UpVector);
bbEffect.Parameters["xBillboardTexture"].SetValue(myTexture);
```

## The Code

*All the code is available for download at* www.apress.com.

Note that you can find sample code for the main four flavors of billboarding and the code for the addendum to this recipe:

- *XNA—only code*: Spherical billboarding
- *XNA—only code*: Cylindrical billboarding
- *XNA + HLSL code*: Spherical billboarding
- *XNA + HLSL code*: Cylindrical billboarding
- *XNA + HLSL code*: Sizeable spherical billboarding

The code presented here is representative for the XNA+HLSL spherical billboarding flavor. First you have the method that defines where to put billboards:

```
private void AddBillboards()
{
    int CPUpower = 10;
    for (int x = -CPUpower; x < CPUpower; x++)
        for (int y = -CPUpower; y <CPUpower; y++)
            for (int z = -CPUpower; z < CPUpower; z++)
                billboardList.Add(new Vector4(x, y, z, 0.5f));
}
```

And here is the code that transforms this into a vertex array:

```
private void CreateBBVertices()
{
    billboardVertices = new VertexPositionTexture[billboardList.Count * 6];

    int i = 0;
    foreach (Vector4 currentV4 in billboardList)
    {
        Vector3 center = new Vector3(currentV4.X, currentV4.Y, currentV4.Z);

        billboardVertices[i++] = new VertexPositionTexture(center, ➥
        new Vector2(1, 1));
        billboardVertices[i++] = new VertexPositionTexture(center, ➥
        new Vector2(0, 0));
        billboardVertices[i++] = new VertexPositionTexture(center, ➥
        new Vector2(1, 0));

        billboardVertices[i++] = new VertexPositionTexture(center, ➥
        new Vector2(1, 1));
        billboardVertices[i++] = new VertexPositionTexture(center, ➥
        new Vector2(0, 1));
        billboardVertices[i++] = new VertexPositionTexture(center, ➥
        new Vector2(0, 0));
    }
}
```

The following code invokes the correct technique, sets its parameters, and renders from the array:

```
bbEffect.CurrentTechnique = bbEffect.Techniques["SpheBillboard"];
bbEffect.Parameters["xWorld"].SetValue(Matrix.Identity);
bbEffect.Parameters["xProjection"].SetValue(quatMousCam.ProjectionMatrix);
bbEffect.Parameters["xView"].SetValue(quatMousCam.ViewMatrix);

bbEffect.Parameters["xCamPos"].SetValue(quatMousCam.Position);
bbEffect.Parameters["xAllowedRotDir"].SetValue(new Vector3(0,1,0));
bbEffect.Parameters["xBillboardTexture"].SetValue(myTexture);
bbEffect.Parameters["xCamUp"].SetValue(quatMousCam.UpVector);

bbEffect.Begin();
foreach (EffectPass pass in bbEffect.CurrentTechnique.Passes)
{
    pass.Begin();
    device.VertexDeclaration = new VertexDeclaration(device, ➥
    VertexPositionTexture.VertexElements);
```

```
device.DrawUserPrimitives<VertexPositionTexture> ➥
(PrimitiveType.TriangleList, billboardVertices, 0, billboardList.Count*2);
pass.End();
}
bbEffect.End();
```

On the HLSL part, you have the vertex shader:

```
BBVertexToPixel SpheBillboardVS(float3 inPos: POSITION0, ➥
float2 inTexCoord: TEXCOORD0)
{
    BBVertexToPixel Output = (BBVertexToPixel)0;

    float3 center = mul(inPos, xWorld);
    float3 eyeVector = center - xCamPos;

    float3 sideVector = cross(eyeVector,xCamUp);
    sideVector = normalize(sideVector);
    float3 upVector = cross(sideVector,eyeVector);
    upVector = normalize(upVector);

    float3 finalPosition = center;
    finalPosition += (inTexCoord.x-0.5f)*sideVector*0.5f;
    finalPosition += (0.5f-inTexCoord.y)*upVector*0.5f;

    float4 finalPosition4 = float4(finalPosition, 1);

    float4x4 preViewProjection = mul (xView, xProjection);
    Output.Position = mul(finalPosition4, preViewProjection);

    Output.TexCoord = inTexCoord;

    return Output;
}
```

And here is the trivial pixel shader:

```
BBPixelToFrame BillboardPS(BBVertexToPixel PSIn) : COLOR0
{
    BBPixelToFrame Output = (BBPixelToFrame)0;
    Output.Color = tex2D(textureSampler, PSIn.TexCoord);
    return Output;
}
```

## Passing Additional Information

In case you want to set the size of the billboards generated by your vertex shader or pass
other information from your XNA app to your vertex shader, you somehow need to be able

to add this information to the information contained in each vertex. You could do this by using, for example, VertexPositionNormalTexture and storing the size in a component in the Normal vector.

However, this would simply move the problem, and you would meet the same problem again when you needed to pass real Normal data with your vertex data. So in order to remain general, you want to create your own vertex format, which can hold positional texture as well as some additional data. For more information on creating your custom vertex format, see recipe 5-13.

```
public struct VertexBillboard
{
    public Vector3 Position;
    public Vector2 TexCoord;
    public Vector4 AdditionalInfo;
    public VertexBillboard(Vector3 Position, Vector2 TexCoord, ➥
    Vector4 AdditionalInfo)
    {
        this.Position = Position;
        this.TexCoord = TexCoord;
        this.AdditionalInfo = AdditionalInfo;
    }
    public static readonly VertexElement[] VertexElements = new VertexElement[]
    {
        new VertexElement(0, 0, VertexElementFormat.Vector3, ➥
        VertexElementMethod.Default, ➥
        VertexElementUsage.Position, 0),
        new VertexElement(0, 12, VertexElementFormat.Vector2, ➥
        VertexElementMethod.Default, ➥
        VertexElementUsage.TextureCoordinate, 0), ➥
        new VertexElement(0, 20, VertexElementFormat.Vector4, ➥
        VertexElementMethod.Default, ➥
        VertexElementUsage.TextureCoordinate, 1),
    };
    public static readonly int SizeInBytes = sizeof(float) * (3 + 2 + 4);
}
```

You see this format accepts an additional Vector4, called AdditionalInfo, next to the usual Position and TexCoord information. You identify this extra Vector4 as another TextureCoordinate. To distinguish both TextureCoordinates, notice that they differ in the last argument, which is the index. This means the real texture coordinate can be accepted in the vertex shader as TEXCOORD0 and the additional Vector4 as TEXCOORD1 (see recipe 5-13).

Next, you replace every occurrence of VertexPositionTexture with your newly defined VertexBillboarding (you'll want to use Ctrl+H in XNA Game Studio to do this). Finally, you can adjust your CreateBBVertices method and pass up to four additional float values with every vertex:

```
private void CreateBBVertices()
{
    billboardVertices = new VertexBillboard[billboardList.Count * 6];

    int i = 0;
    foreach (Vector4 currentV4 in billboardList)
    {
        Vector3 center = new Vector3(currentV4.X, currentV4.Y, currentV4.Z);


        billboardVertices[i++] = new VertexBillboard(center, ➥
        new Vector2(1, 1), new Vector4(0.8f, 0.4f, 0, 0));
        billboardVertices[i++] = new VertexBillboard(center, ➥
        new Vector2(0, 0), new Vector4(0.8f, 0.4f, 0, 0));
        billboardVertices[i++] = new VertexBillboard(center, ➥
        new Vector2(1, 0), new Vector4(0.8f, 0.4f, 0, 0));

        billboardVertices[i++] = new VertexBillboard(center, ➥
        new Vector2(1, 1), new Vector4(0.8f, 0.4f, 0, 0));
        billboardVertices[i++] = new VertexBillboard(center, ➥
        new Vector2(0, 1), new Vector4(0.8f, 0.4f, 0, 0));
        billboardVertices[i++] = new VertexBillboard(center, ➥
        new Vector2(0, 0), new Vector4(0.8f, 0.4f, 0, 0));
    }
}
```

In this example, you will make the size of the billboard changeable. The first argument of the extra Vector4, 0.8f in this case, will be used to scale the width of the billboards, and the second argument, 0.4f in this case, will scale the height. This will result in the width of your billboards being twice their height.

That's it for the XNA code; all you have to do is accept this extra Vector4 in your vertex shader as TEXCOORD1:

```
BBVertexToPixel SpheBillboardVS(float3 inPos: POSITION0, ➥
float2 inTexCoord: TEXCOORD0, float4 inExtra: TEXCOORD1)
```

Now you can access the extra Vector4 as the inExtra variable throughout your vertex shader. Use it to scale the width and the height of your billboards:

```
finalPosition += (inTexCoord.x-0.5f)*sideVector*inExtra.x;
finalPosition += (0.5f-inTexCoord.y)*upVector*inExtra.y;
```

This sample uses only the x and y values of the float4, while you can also access the z and w values if required. You can find the resulting code in the samples.

# 3-12. Create a 3D Explosion Effect/Simple Particle System

## The Problem

You want to create a nice-looking 3D explosion effect somewhere in your 3D world.

## The Solution

You can create an explosion effect by additively blending a lot of small fireball images (called *particles*) over each other. You can see such a fireball particle in Figure 3-22. Note that a single particle is very dark. However, if you add a lot of them on top of each other, you'll get a very convincing explosion.

**Figure 3-22.** *Single explosion particle*

At the start of the explosion, all of these particles are at the origin of the explosion, which will result in a bright fireball because the colors of all images are added together. You will obtain this using additive blending when rendering the particles.

As time goes by, the particles should move away from the origin. Additionally, you'll want each of the particle images to get smaller and lose their color (fade away) while they're moving away from the center.

A nice 3D explosion can take between 50 and 100 particles. Because these images are simple 2D images displayed in a 3D world, each of these images needs to be billboarded, so this recipe will build on the results of recipe 3-11.

You'll be building a real shader-based particle system. Each frame, the age of each particle is calculated. Its position, color, and size are calculated depending on the current age of the particle. Of course, you'll want all of these calculations to happen on the GPU so your CPU remains available for more important calculations.

## How It Works

As mentioned previously, this chapter will reuse the code of recipe 3-11, so a basic understanding of spherical billboarding is recommended. For each particle, you'll again define six vertices, which you'll want to define only once so they can be transferred to the graphics card and remain there untouched. For each vertex, you'll want the following data to be available to the vertex shader in the GPU:

- The original 3D position center of the billboard at the start of the explosion (required for billboarding) (Vector3 = three floats)

- The texture coordinates (required for billboarding) (Vector2 = two floats)

- The time at which the particle was created (one float)

- How long you want the particle to stay alive (one float)

- The direction in which you want the particle to move (Vector3 = three floats)

- A random value, which will be used to make each particle behave uniquely (one float)

From this data, the GPU can calculate everything it needs to know, based on the current time. For example, it can calculate how long the particle has been alive. When you multiply this age by the direction of the particle, you can find how far it's off the original position of the particle, which was the center of the explosion.

You will need a vertex format that is able to store all this data for each vertex. You'll use a Vector3 to store the position; a Vector4 to store the second, third, and fourth items; and another Vector4 to store the last two items. Create a custom vertex format that can store this data, as explained in recipe 5-13:

```
public struct VertexExplosion
{
    public Vector3 Position;
    public Vector4 TexCoord;
    public Vector4 AdditionalInfo;
    public VertexExplosion(Vector3 Position, ➥
    Vector4 TexCoord, Vector4 AdditionalInfo)
    {
        this.Position = Position;
        this.TexCoord = TexCoord;
        this.AdditionalInfo = AdditionalInfo;
    }
    public static readonly VertexElement[] VertexElements = new VertexElement[]
    {
        new VertexElement(0, 0, VertexElementFormat.Vector3, ➥
        VertexElementMethod.Default, VertexElementUsage.Position, 0),
        new VertexElement(0, 12, VertexElementFormat.Vector4, ➥
        VertexElementMethod.Default, ➥
        VertexElementUsage.TextureCoordinate, 0),
        new VertexElement(0, 28, VertexElementFormat.Vector4, ➥
        VertexElementMethod.Default, ➥
        VertexElementUsage.TextureCoordinate, 1),
    };
    public static readonly int SizeInBytes = sizeof(float) * (3 + 4 + 4);
}
```

This looks a lot like the vertex format defined in recipe 3-11, except that it stores a Vector4 instead of a Vector2 as the second argument, allowing two more floats to be passed on to your vertex shader for each vertex. To create the random directions, you'll need a randomizer, so add this variable to your XNA class:

```
Random rand;
```

You need to initialize this, such as in the Initialize method of your Game class:

```
rand = new Random();
```

Now all is set so you can start creating your vertices. The method that generates the vertices is based on recipe 3-11:

```
private void CreateExplosionVertices(float time)
{
    int particles = 80;
    explosionVertices = new VertexExplosion[particles * 6];

    int i = 0;
    for (int partnr = 0; partnr < particles; partnr++)
    {
        Vector3 startingPos = new Vector3(5,0,0);

        float r1 = (float)rand.NextDouble() - 0.5f;
        float r2 = (float)rand.NextDouble() - 0.5f;
        float r3 = (float)rand.NextDouble() - 0.5f;
        Vector3 moveDirection = new Vector3(r1, r2, r3);
        moveDirection.Normalize();

        float r4 = (float)rand.NextDouble();
        r4 = r4 / 4.0f * 3.0f + 0.25f;

        explosionVertices[i++] = new VertexExplosion(startingPos, ➥
        new Vector4(1, 1, time, 1000), new Vector4(moveDirection, r4));
        explosionVertices[i++] = new VertexExplosion(startingPos, ➥
        new Vector4(0, 0, time, 1000), new Vector4(moveDirection, r4));
        explosionVertices[i++] = new VertexExplosion(startingPos, ➥
        new Vector4(1, 0, time, 1000), new Vector4(moveDirection, r4));

        explosionVertices[i++] = new VertexExplosion(startingPos, ➥
        new Vector4(1, 1, time, 1000), new Vector4(moveDirection, r4));
        explosionVertices[i++] = new VertexExplosion(startingPos, ➥
        new Vector4(0, 1, time, 1000), new Vector4(moveDirection, r4));
        explosionVertices[i++] = new VertexExplosion(startingPos, ➥
        new Vector4(0, 0, time, 1000), new Vector4(moveDirection, r4));
    }
}
```

This method should be called whenever you want to initiate a new explosion, and it will receive the current time from the calling method. First, you define how many particles you want in your explosion and create an array that can hold six vertices for each particle. Next, you create these vertices. For each particle, you first store the startingPos, where you can indicate where you want to position the center of your explosion.

Next, you want to give each of your particles a unique direction. You can do this by generating two random values in the [0,1] region and by subtracting 0.5f from them so they are shifted to the [–0.5f,+0.5f] region. You create a Vector3 based on these values and normalize the Vector3 to make all random directions of equal length.

---

■**Tip**  This normalization is recommended, because the (0.5f,0.5f,0.5f) vector is longer than the (0.5f,0, 0) vector. So if you increment the position with this first vector, this particle would go much faster than if you used the second vector as the direction. As a result, the explosion would spread like a cube instead of like a sphere.

---

Next, you find another random value, which will be used to add some uniqueness to each particle, because the speed and size of the particle will be adjusted by this value. A random value between 0 and 1 is asked, and it is scaled into the [0.25f,1.0f] region (who wants a particle of speed 0 anyway?).

Finally, you add the six vertices for each particle to the array of vertices. Note that each of the six vertices stores the same information, except for the texture coordinate, which will be used by the billboarding code in your vertex shader to define the offset between each vertex and the center of the billboard.

## HLSL

Now that you have your vertices ready, it's time to start coding your vertex and pixel shader. As usual, you start with the variables passed from XNA to your HLSL code, the texture samplers, and the output structures of your vertex shader and pixel shader:

```
//------- XNA interface --------
float4x4 xView;
float4x4 xProjection;
float4x4 xWorld;
float3 xCamPos;
float3 xCamUp;
float xTime;

//------- Texture Samplers --------
Texture xExplosionTexture;
sampler textureSampler = sampler_state { texture = <xExplosionTexture>; ➥
 magfilter = LINEAR; minfilter = LINEAR; mipfilter=LINEAR; ➥
AddressU = CLAMP; AddressV = CLAMP;};
```

```
struct ExpVertexToPixel
{
    float4 Position : POSITION;
    float2 TexCoord : TEXCOORD0;
    float4 Color    : COLOR0;
};
struct ExpPixelToFrame
{
    float4 Color    : COLOR0;
};
```

Because you will billboard each particle of your explosion, you will need the same variables as in the recipe on billboarding. This time, you will also need your XNA application to store the current time in the xTime variable so your vertex shader can calculate how long each particle has been alive.

As in recipe 3-11, your vertex shader will pass the 2D screen coordinate of the vertex, together with the texture coordinate to the pixel shader. Because you'll want the particles to fade away after some time, you'll also want to pass some color information from your vertex shader to your pixel shader. As usual, your pixel shader will calculate only the color of each pixel.

## Vertex Shader

Your vertex shader will need to billboard the vertices, so you can use this method, which contains the useful spherical billboarding code of recipe 3-11:

```
//------- Technique: Explosion --------
float3 BillboardVertex(float3 billboardCenter, float2 cornerID, float size)
{
    float3 eyeVector = billboardCenter - xCamPos;

    float3 sideVector = cross(eyeVector,xCamUp);
    sideVector = normalize(sideVector);
    float3 upVector = cross(sideVector,eyeVector);
    upVector = normalize(upVector);

    float3 finalPosition = billboardCenter;
    finalPosition += (cornerID.x-0.5f)*sideVector*size;
    finalPosition += (0.5f-cornerID.y)*upVector*size;

    return finalPosition;
}
```

In a nutshell, you pass the center of the billboard to this method, together with the texture coordinate (required to identify the current vertex) and how big you want the billboard to be. The method returns the billboarded 3D position of the vertex. For more information, see recipe 3-11.

Now it's time for the vertex shader, which will make use of the method defined previously:

```
ExpVertexToPixel ExplosionVS(float3 inPos: POSITION0, ➥
float4 inTexCoord: TEXCOORD0, float4 inExtra: TEXCOORD1)
{
    ExpVertexToPixel Output = (ExpVertexToPixel)0;

    float3 startingPosition = mul(inPos, xWorld);

    float2 texCoords = inTexCoord.xy;
    float birthTime = inTexCoord.z;
    float maxAge = inTexCoord.w;
    float3 moveDirection = inExtra.xyz;
    float random = inExtra.w;
}
```

This vertex shader receives the Vector3 and the two Vector4s you stored for each vertex. First, the content of this data is stored in some more meaningful variables. The position of the center of the billboard was stored in the Vector3. You defined the x and y components of the first Vector4 to contain the texture coordinate, and the third and fourth components stored the time at which the particle was created and how long it should be visible. The last Vector4 contained the direction in which you want the particle to move and an extra random float.

At this moment, you can find how long the particle has been alive by subtracting the birthTime from the current time, stored in the xTime variable. However, when working with time spans, you always want to work with relative values between 0 and 1, where 0 means the beginning of the time span and 1 means the end of the time span. So, you'll want to divide the age by the maximum age at which the particle should "die":

```
float age = xTime - birthTime;
float relAge = age/maxAge;
```

Always check stuff like this for yourself: when the particle is really new, xTime will be the same as birthTime, and relAge will be 0. When the particle is nearing its end, the age will almost equal maxAge, and the relAge variable will almost equal 1.

Let's first adjust the size of the particle according to its age. You want each particle of the explosion to start big and then get smaller as it gets older. However, you don't want it to completely shrink away, so for example you can use this code:

```
float size = 1-relAge*relAge/2.0f;
```

This looks a bit scary, but it's more understandable if you visualize it, as is done in the left part of Figure 3-23. For each relAge of the particle on the horizontal axis, you can find the corresponding size on the vertical axis. For example, at relAge = 0, the size will be 1, and at relAge = 1, the size will be 0.5f.

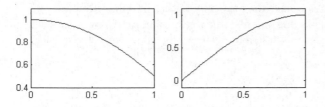

**Figure 3-23.** *Size in function of relAge; displacement in function of relAge*

However, `relAge` continues to increase after it has become 1. This means size will become negative (as you can see in the following code, this will cause the image to stretch in the opposite direction). So, you will want to saturate this value between 0 and 1.

Because particles of size 1 are too small in your application, simply scale them up by multiplying them by a number, 5 in this case. To make each particle unique, you'll also multiply the size by the random value of the particle, so each particle has its own starting (and this ending) size:

```
float sizer = saturate(1-relAge*relAge/2.0f);
float size = 5.0f*random*sizer;
```

Now that you have the size decreasing as the particle gets older, the next thing to calculate is the 3D location of the center of the particle. You know the original 3D location (the center of the explosion), as well as the direction in which the particle has to move. All you need to know is how far the particle has been moved into this direction. Of course, this also corresponds to the age of the particle. An easy approach would be to assume the particle keeps on moving at a constant speed, but in reality this speed decreases after a while.

Take a look at the right part of Figure 3-23. The horizontal axis again represents the age of your particle, while the vertical axis indicates how far the particle has moved from the center of the explosion. You see that first the distance increases linearly, but after a while, the distance increases a bit more slowly, and at the end the distance does not change that much anymore. This means that at the beginning the speed will remain constant and that at the end the speed of the particle will almost be 0.

You're in luck—this curve is simply one quarter of a sine wave. For any given `relAge` between 0 and 1, you can find the corresponding displacement of the curve using this function:

```
float totalDisplacement = sin(relAge*6.28f/4.0f);
```

A whole sine wave period stretches from 0 to 2*pi=6.28. Since you want only a quarter of that period, you divide by 4. Now for `relAge` going from 0 to 1, `totalDisplacement` will have a value corresponding to the curve in the right part of Figure 3-23.

---

**■Note**  While the sine works perfectly in this case, it isn't the mathematical equivalent of what's happening in reality. I've chosen the sine as the simple paragraph that would otherwise need to be replaced by two pages of math, which would draw your attention away from the code too much. The correct approach for finding the current displacement is discussed in detail in the 2D explosion tutorial on my site.

---

You will want to multiply this value to make the particle move a bit farther from the center. In this example, a factor of 3 is a nice value, but feel free to experiment. Larger values will cause larger explosions. Also, this value is multiplied by the random value, so each particle will move at a unique speed:

```
float totalDisplacement = sin(relAge*6.28f/4.0f)*3.0f*random;
```

Once you know how much the particle has moved in its direction at the given time, you can easily find its current 3D position:

```
float3 billboardCenter = startingPosition + totalDisplacement*moveDirection;
billboardCenter += age*float3(0,-1,0)/1000.0f;
```

The last line adds some gravitational force to the explosion. Because the xTime variable will contain the current time in milliseconds, this line pulls the particles down one unit each second.

---

■Tip  If you want to explode a moving object, such as an airplane, you simply need to add a line that pulls all particles into the direction the object was moving. You'll need to pass this direction as an additional TEXCOORD2 variable inside your vertices.

---

Now that you have the 3D location of the center of the billboard and its size, you're ready to pass these values to your billboarding method:

```
float3 finalPosition = BillboardVertex(billboardCenter, texCoords, size);
float4 finalPosition4 = float4(finalPosition, 1);

float4x4 preViewProjection = mul (xView, xProjection);
Output.Position = mul(finalPosition4, preViewProjection);
```

This code comes from recipe 3-11. Start by calculating your billboarded position. As always, this 3D position needs to be transformed to 2D screen space by multiplying it by a 4×4 matrix, but before this can be done, the float3 needs to be converted to a float4. You store the final 2D screen coordinate in the mandatory Position field of the Output structure.

That's it for the position. This should already give a nice result, but of course things will look much nicer when you blend your particles away as they near their end. When the particle is still fresh, you want it to be completely visible. When it reaches relAge = 1, you want it to become completely transparent.

To achieve this, you can use a linear degradation, but the result will look nicer when you use a curve as in the left part of Figure 3-23. Only this time, you want it to stretch from 1 to 0, so there's no need to divide by 2:

```
float alpha = 1-relAge*relAge;
```

So, now you can define the modulation color of the particle:

```
Output.Color = float4(0.5f,0.5f,0.5f,alpha);
```

In your pixel shader, you'll multiply each pixel color of the particle by this color. This will adjust its alpha value to the value you've calculated here, so the particles will become more transparent as time goes by. The RGB components of the colors will also be softened by a factor of 2; otherwise, you would too easily see the separate particles.

Don't forget to pass the texture coordinates to the pixel shader so it knows which corner of the billboard corresponds to which corner of the texture:

```
Output.TexCoord = texCoords;
return Output;
```

## Pixel Shader

That's it for the vertex shader; luckily, the pixel shader is easy in comparison to the vertex shader:

```
ExpPixelToFrame ExplosionPS(ExpVertexToPixel PSIn) : COLOR0
{
    ExpPixelToFrame Output = (ExpPixelToFrame)0;
    Output.Color = tex2D(textureSampler, PSIn.TexCoord)*PSIn.Color;
    return Output;
}
```

For each pixel, you find the corresponding color from the texture, and you multiply this color by the modulation color you've calculated in your vertex shader. This modulation color reduces the brightness and sets the alpha value corresponding to the current age of the particle.

Here's the trivial technique definition:

```
technique Explosion
{
    pass Pass0
    {
        VertexShader = compile vs_1_1 ExplosionVS();
        PixelShader  = compile ps_1_1 ExplosionPS();
    }
}
```

## Setting Technique Parameters in XNA

In your XNA code, don't forget to set all the XNA-to-HLSL variables:

```
expEffect.CurrentTechnique = expEffect.Techniques["Explosion"];
expEffect.Parameters["xWorld"].SetValue(Matrix.Identity);
expEffect.Parameters["xProjection"].SetValue(quatMousCam.ProjectionMatrix);
expEffect.Parameters["xView"].SetValue(quatMousCam.ViewMatrix);
```

```
expEffect.Parameters["xCamPos"].SetValue(quatMousCam.Position);
expEffect.Parameters["xExplosionTexture"].SetValue(myTexture);
expEffect.Parameters["xCamUp"].SetValue(quatMousCam.UpVector);
expEffect.Parameters["xTime"]. ➥
SetValue((float)gameTime.TotalGameTime.TotalMilliseconds);
```

## Additive Blending

Because this technique relies heavily on blending, you need to set the render states correctly before rendering. You can read more about alpha blending in recipes 2-13 and 3-3.

In this case, you want to use additive blending so the colors of all explosion images are added together on top of each other. You can achieve this by setting these render states before actually rendering the triangles:

```
device.RenderState.AlphaBlendEnable = true;
device.RenderState.SourceBlend = Blend.SourceAlpha;
device.RenderState.DestinationBlend = Blend.One;
```

The first line enables alpha blending. For each pixel drawn, the color will be determined using this rule:

$$finalColor=sourceBlend*sourceColor+destBlend*destColor$$

With the render states you set previously, this becomes the following:

$$finalColor=sourceAlpha*sourceColor+1*destColor$$

Note that your graphics card will render each pixel many times, because you are rendering lots of explosion images near and on top of each other (and you will disable writing to the depth buffer). So when your graphics card has already rendered 79 of the 80 particles and now has to render the final particle, it will do this for each pixel it has to render:

1. Find the current color of that pixel stored in the frame buffer, and multiply its three color channels by 1 (corresponding to 1*destColor in the earlier rule).

2. Take the color that was newly calculated by the pixel shader for the last particle, and multiply its three color channels by the alpha channel, which depended on the current age of the particle (corresponding to sourceAlpha*sourceColor in the earlier rule).

3. Sum both colors, and save the resulting color to the frame buffer (finalizing the rule).

In the beginning of the particle (relAge=0), sourceAlpha will equal 1, so your additive blending will result in a bright explosion. At the end of the particle (relAge=1), newAlpha will be 0, and the particle will have no effect on the scene.

---

**■Note** For a second example on this blending rule, see recipe 2-13.

---

## Disabling Writing to the Depth Buffer

You still have to think about one last aspect. In case the particle closest to the camera is drawn first, all particles behind that one will not be drawn (and this will not be blended in)! So when you render your particles, you could turn off the z-buffer test for each pixel and render your particles as the last element of your scene. This is, however, not a very good idea, because when the explosion happens very far from the camera and there is a building between the explosion and the camera, the explosion will be rendered as if it were before the building!

A better solution would be to render your scene as normal first and then to turn off z-buffer writing and render the particles as the last element of your scene. This way, you solve both problems:

- Each pixel of each particle is checked against the current contents of the z-buffer (which contains depth information about your existing scene). In case there is an object already drawn between the explosion and the camera, the pixels of the explosion will not pass the z-buffer test and will not be rendered.

- Since the particles don't change the z-buffer, the second particle will be rendered even if the first particle is in front of it (of course, if there isn't another object between the explosion and the camera).

This is the code that helps you out:

```
device.RenderState.DepthBufferWriteEnable = false;
```

Next, render the triangles holding the particles of your explosion:

```
expEffect.Begin();
foreach (EffectPass pass in expEffect.CurrentTechnique.Passes)
{
    pass.Begin();
    device.VertexDeclaration = new VertexDeclaration(device, ➥
    VertexExplosion.VertexElements);
    device.DrawUserPrimitives<VertexExplosion> ➥
    (PrimitiveType.TriangleList, explosionVertices, 0, ➥
    explosionVertices.Length / 3);
    pass.End();
}
expEffect.End();
```

After you're done rendering your explosion, be sure to enable z-buffer writing again before you start rendering your next frame:

```
device.RenderState.DepthBufferWriteEnable = true;
```

And call the CreateExplosionVertices method whenever you want to start a new explosion! In this example, the method is called when the user presses the spacebar:

```
if ((keyState.IsKeyDown(Keys.Space)))
    CreateExplosionVertices((float) ➥
    gameTime.TotalGameTime.Tot  alMilliseconds);
```

## The Code

*All the code is available for download at www.apress.com.*

Here's the XNA method that generates the vertices for the explosion:

```
private void CreateExplosionVertices(float time)
{
    int particles = 80;
    explosionVertices = new VertexExplosion[particles * 6];

    int i = 0;
    for (int partnr = 0; partnr < particles; partnr++)
    {
        Vector3 startingPos = new Vector3(5,0,0);

        float r1 = (float)rand.NextDouble() - 0.5f;
        float r2 = (float)rand.NextDouble() - 0.5f;
        float r3 = (float)rand.NextDouble() - 0.5f;
        Vector3 moveDirection = new Vector3(r1, r2, r3);
        moveDirection.Normalize();

        float r4 = (float)rand.NextDouble();
        r4 = r4 / 4.0f * 3.0f + 0.25f;

        explosionVertices[i++] = new VertexExplosion(startingPos, ➥
        new Vector4(1, 1, time, 1000), new Vector4(moveDirection, r4));
        explosionVertices[i++] = new VertexExplosion(startingPos, ➥
        new Vector4(0, 0, time, 1000), new Vector4(moveDirection, r4));
        explosionVertices[i++] = new VertexExplosion(startingPos, ➥
        new Vector4(1, 0, time, 1000), new Vector4(moveDirection, r4));

        explosionVertices[i++] = new VertexExplosion(startingPos, ➥
        new Vector4(1, 1, time, 1000), new Vector4(moveDirection, r4));
        explosionVertices[i++] = new VertexExplosion(startingPos, ➥
        new Vector4(0, 1, time, 1000), new Vector4(moveDirection, r4));
        explosionVertices[i++] = new VertexExplosion(startingPos, ➥
        new Vector4(0, 0, time, 1000), new Vector4(moveDirection, r4));
    }
}
```

And here's your complete Draw method:

```
protected override void Draw(GameTime gameTime)
{
    device.Clear(ClearOptions.Target | ClearOptions.DepthBuffer, Color.Black, 1, 0);

    cCross.Draw(quatCam.ViewMatrix, quatCam.ProjectionMatrix);
```

```
    if (explosionVertices != null)
    {
        //draw billboards
        expEffect.CurrentTechnique = expEffect.Techniques["Explosion"];
        expEffect.Parameters["xWorld"].SetValue(Matrix.Identity);
        expEffect.Parameters["xProjection"].SetValue(quatCam.ProjectionMatrix);
        expEffect.Parameters["xView"].SetValue(quatCam.ViewMatrix);

        expEffect.Parameters["xCamPos"].SetValue(quatCam.Position);
        expEffect.Parameters["xExplosionTexture"].SetValue(myTexture);
        expEffect.Parameters["xCamUp"].SetValue(quatCam.UpVector);
        expEffect.Parameters["xTime"]. ➥
        SetValue((float)gameTime.TotalGameTime.TotalMilliseconds);

        device.RenderState.AlphaBlendEnable = true;
        device.RenderState.SourceBlend = Blend.SourceAlpha;
        device.RenderState.DestinationBlend = Blend.One;
        device.RenderState.DepthBufferWriteEnable = false;

        expEffect.Begin();
        foreach (EffectPass pass in expEffect.CurrentTechnique.Passes)
        {
            pass.Begin();
            device.VertexDeclaration = new ➥
            VertexDeclaration(device, ➥
            VertexExplosion.VertexElements);
            device.DrawUserPrimitives<VertexExplosion> ➥
            (PrimitiveType.TriangleList, explosionVertices, 0, ➥
            explosionVertices.Length / 3);
            pass.End();
        }
        expEffect.End();

        device.RenderState.DepthBufferWriteEnable = true;
    }

    base.Draw(gameTime);
}
```

On the HLSL part, you have your vertex shader:

```
ExpVertexToPixel ExplosionVS(float3 inPos: POSITION0, ➥
float4 inTexCoord: TEXCOORD0, float4 inExtra: TEXCOORD1)
{
    ExpVertexToPixel Output = (ExpVertexToPixel)0;

    float3 startingPosition = mul(inPos, xWorld);
```

```
    float2 texCoords = inTexCoord.xy;
    float birthTime = inTexCoord.z;
    float maxAge = inTexCoord.w;
    float3 moveDirection = inExtra.xyz;
    float random = inExtra.w;

    float age = xTime - birthTime;
    float relAge = age/maxAge;

    float sizer = saturate(1-relAge*relAge/2.0f);
    float size = 5.0f*random*sizer;

    float totalDisplacement = sin(relAge*6.28f/4.0f)*3.0f*random;
    float3 billboardCenter = startingPosition + totalDisplacement*moveDirection;
    billboardCenter += age*float3(0,-1,0)/1000.0f;

    float3 finalPosition = BillboardVertex(billboardCenter, texCoords, size);
    float4 finalPosition4 = float4(finalPosition, 1);

    float4x4 preViewProjection = mul (xView, xProjection);
    Output.Position = mul(finalPosition4, preViewProjection);

    float alpha = 1-relAge*relAge;
    Output.Color = float4(0.5f,0.5f,0.5f,alpha);

    Output.TexCoord = texCoords;

    return Output;
}
```

Your vertex shader uses the BillboardVertex method that you can find earlier in this recipe, and at the end of this recipe you can also find the simple pixel shader, together with the technique definition.

# 3-13. Create a Mirror: Projective Texturing

## The Problem

You want to create a mirror in your scene, for example, to create a rear mirror for a racing game. You can also use this technique to create a reflection map.

## The Solution

First, you'll render the scene, as it is seen by the mirror, into a texture. Next, you'll render the scene as seen by the camera (including the empty mirror), and finally you'll put the texture on the mirror.

To render the scene as seen by the mirror, you will want to define a second camera, called the *mirror camera*. You can find this mirror camera's Position, Target, and Up vectors by mirroring the normal camera Position, Target, and Up vectors over the mirror plane. When you look at the scene through this mirror camera, you'll see the same as what should be displayed on the mirror. Figure 3-24 displays this principle.

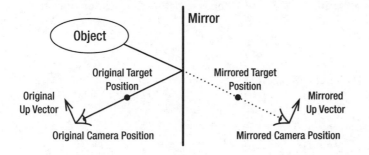

**Figure 3-24.** *Mirroring principle*

After you have stored this result in a texture, you'll render the scene as seen by the normal camera and put the texture on the mirror using projective texturing, which makes sure the correct pixel is mapped to the correct position on the mirror.

This approach will fail if there are objects between the mirror camera and the mirror itself. You can solve this problem by defining the mirror plane as a clip plane, so all objects behind the mirror are clipped away.

## How It Works

Start by adding these variables to your project:

```
RenderTarget2D renderTarget;
Texture2D mirrorTexture;
VertexPositionTexture[] mirrorVertices;
Matrix mirrorViewMatrix;
```

The renderTarget and mirrorTexture variables are required because you'll need to render the scene as seen by the mirror into a custom render target, as explained in recipe 3-8. To create the mirror camera, you'll need to define a mirror View matrix. Since you want to actually put your mirror in the scene, you'll need some vertices that define the location of the mirror.

The renderTarget variable needs to be initialized in the LoadContent method. For more information on setting up and using custom render targets, see recipe 3-8.

```
PresentationParameters pp = device.PresentationParameters;
int width = pp.BackBufferWidth;
int height = pp.BackBufferHeight;
renderTarget = new RenderTarget2D(device, width, height, 1, ➥
device.DisplayMode.Format);
```

**Tip** If you want, you can decrease the width and height of your render target. This way, it will cost less effort from your graphics card, but the resulting mirrored image will look coarser.

With the custom `renderTarget` initialized, the next step is to define the location of your mirror:

```
private void InitMirror()
{
    mirrorVertices = new VertexPositionTexture[4];
    int i = 0;

    Vector3 p0 = new Vector3(-3, 0, 0);
    Vector3 p1 = new Vector3(-3, 6, 0);
    Vector3 p2 = new Vector3(6, 0, 0);

    Vector3 p3 = p1 + p2 - p0;

    mirrorVertices[i++] = new VertexPositionTexture(p0, new Vector2(0,0));
    mirrorVertices[i++] = new VertexPositionTexture(p1, new Vector2(0,0));
    mirrorVertices[i++] = new VertexPositionTexture(p2, new Vector2(0,0));
    mirrorVertices[i++] = new VertexPositionTexture(p3, new Vector2(0,0));

    mirrorPlane = new Plane(p0, p1, p2);
}
```

Although you can use this technique to create a mirror of arbitrary shape, in this example you'll create a simple rectangular mirror. You'll use the mirror surface to display the contents of the custom render target. You'll draw the two triangles defining the rectangle using a `TriangleStrip`, so four vertices will be enough.

In 3D space, you need only three points to uniquely define a rectangle. This method allows you to specify three corner points—p0, p1, and p2—of the mirror, and the code will calculate the last point p3. This makes sure the four points are in one plane. The line of interest in the method is short for this:

```
Vector3 p3 = p0 + (p1 - p0) + (p2 - p0);
```

The four vertices are created from these four positions. This technique doesn't require any texture coordinates to be passed to the vertex shader (see later in the vertex shader), but because I'm too lazy to define a `VertexPosition` struct in this recipe, I'm simply passing in some arbitrary texture coordinates, for example (0,0), because they won't be used anyway (see recipe 5-13 on how to create custom vertex formats).

**Note** Because all the Z coordinates in this example are 0, this mirror will be in the XY plane.

## Constructing the View Matrix of the Mirror Camera

Next, you will want to create a mirror View matrix, which you'll use to render the scene as seen by the mirror. To create this mirror View matrix, you will need the Position, Target, and Up vectors of the mirror camera. The Position, Target, and Up vectors of this mirror View matrix are the same as the normal camera but mirrored over the mirror plane, as you can see in Figure 3-24.

```
private void UpdateMirrorViewMatrix()
{
    Vector3 mirrorCamPosition = MirrorVector3(mirrorPlane, fpsCam.Position);
    Vector3 mirrorTargetPosition = MirrorVector3(mirrorPlane, ➥
    fpsCam.TargetPosition);

    Vector3 camUpPosition = fpsCam.Position + fpsCam.UpVector;
    Vector3 mirrorCamUpPosition = MirrorVector3(mirrorPlane, camUpPosition);
    Vector3 mirrorUpVector = mirrorCamUpPosition - mirrorCamPosition;

    mirrorViewMatrix = Matrix.CreateLookAt(mirrorCamPosition, ➥
    mirrorTargetPosition, mirrorUpVector);
}
```

The Position and TargetPosition values can simply be mirrored, because they are absolute positions in 3D space. The Up vector, however, indicates a direction, which cannot immediately be mirrored. First you need to reshape this Up direction into a 3D location, somewhere above your camera. You can do this by adding the Up direction to the 3D location of your camera.

Since this is a 3D location, you can mirror it over your mirror plane. What you obtain is the 3D location somewhere above your mirror camera, so you subtract the position of your mirror camera to obtain the Up direction of your mirror camera!

Once you know the Position, Target, and Up directions of your mirror camera, you can create the View matrix for your mirror camera.

The MirrorVector3 method will mirror the Vector3 passed to it over the plane. For now, because the mirror created during this recipe is in the XY plane, all you need to do to find the mirrored position is change the sign of the Z component:

```
private Vector3 MirrorVector3(Plane mirrorPlane, Vector3 originalV3)
{
    Vector3 mirroredV3 = originalV3;
    mirroredV3.Z = -mirroredV3.Z;
    return mirroredV3;
}
```

You can find the real method that allows mirroring over an arbitrary plane in a moment, but the math in that method could draw your attention away from the bigger picture.

Now call the UpdateMirrorViewMatrix method from within your Update method:

```
UpdateMirrorViewMatrix();
```

## Rendering the Scene As Seen by the Mirror

Now that you're sure your mirror View matrix will be correct at any moment, you're ready to render your scene, as seen by the mirror, using this mirror View matrix. Because you will need to render your scene twice (one time as seen by the mirror, then again as seen by the normal camera), it's a good idea to refactor your code that actually draws your scene into a separate method:

```
private void RenderScene(Matrix viewMatrix, Matrix projectionMatrix)
{
    Matrix worldMatrix = Matrix.CreateScale(0.01f, 0.01f, 0.01f) * ➥
    Matrix.CreateTranslation(0, 0, 5);
    myModel.CopyAbsoluteBoneTransformsTo(modelTransforms);
    foreach (ModelMesh mesh in myModel.Meshes)
    {
        foreach (BasicEffect effect in mesh.Effects)
        {
            effect.EnableDefaultLighting();
            effect.World = modelTransforms[mesh.ParentBone.Index] * worldMatrix;
            effect.View = viewMatrix;
            effect.Projection = projectionMatrix;
        }
        mesh.Draw();
    }

        //draw other objects of your scene ...
}
```

This method should render your whole scene, using the View and Projection matrices you specify as arguments.

In your Draw method, add this code that activates your custom render target and renders the whole scene as seen by the mirror using the mirror View matrix into the custom render target. After that has been done, you deactivate your custom render target by setting the back buffer as the active render target (see recipe 3-9), and you store the contents of the custom render target into a texture:

```
//render scene as seen by mirror into render target
device.SetRenderTarget(0, renderTarget);
graphics.GraphicsDevice.Clear(Color.CornflowerBlue);
RenderScene(mirrorViewMatrix, fpsCam.ProjectionMatrix);

//deactivate custom render target, and save its contents into a texture
device.SetRenderTarget(0, null);
mirrorTexture = renderTarget.GetTexture();
```

**Note** In the case of a mirror, you want to use the same Projection matrix to render to the custom target as you use to render your normal scene. If, for example, the angle of your normal Projection matrix is wider than the matrix of the render target, the coordinates you will calculate in your shaders will all be mixed up.

Now that that has been saved, you clear the back buffer of the screen and render your scene as seen by the normal camera, in other words, using the normal View matrix:

```
//render scene + mirror as seen by user to screen
graphics.GraphicsDevice.Clear(Color.Tomato);
RenderScene(fpsCam.ViewMatrix, fpsCam.ProjectionMatrix);
RenderMirror();
```

The last line calls the method that will add the mirror to your scene. In this example, the mirror is simply a rectangle defined by two triangles, of which the color will be sampled from the texture containing the scene as seen by the mirror. Since the mirror should display only the correct part of this texture, you cannot simply put the image on the rectangle; instead, you have to create an HLSL technique for this.

## HLSL

As always, you should start by defining the variables passed from your XNA application to your shaders, the texture samplers, and the output structures of your vertex and pixel shader:

```
//------- XNA interface --------
float4x4 xWorld;
float4x4 xView;
float4x4 xProjection;
float4x4 xMirrorView;

//------- Texture Samplers --------
Texture xMirrorTexture;
sampler textureSampler = sampler_state { texture = <xMirrorTexture>; ➥
magfilter = LINEAR; minfilter = LINEAR; mipfilter=LINEAR; ➥
AddressU = CLAMP; AddressV = CLAMP;};

struct MirVertexToPixel
{
    float4 Position : POSITION;
    float4 TexCoord    : TEXCOORD0;
};
struct MirPixelToFrame
{
    float4 Color      : COLOR0;
};
```

As always, you'll need World, View, and Projection matrices so you can calculate the 2D screen position of each of your 3D vertices. Additionally, you'll also need the View matrix of your mirror camera, which will be used in your vertex shader to calculate the correct corresponding texture coordinate for each vertex of your mirror.

Your technique will require the texture containing the scene as seen by the mirror camera. It will find the color of each pixel of the mirror by sampling from this texture at the correct texture coordinate.

The output of the vertex shader will be this texture coordinate, as well as the usual 2D screen coordinate of the current vertex. As usual, your pixel shader will have to calculate only the color of each pixel.

## Vertex Shader

Next in line is the vertex shader. As always, the vertex shader has to calculate the 2D screen coordinate for each vertex. You do this by multiplying the 3D position of the vertex by the WorldViewProjection matrix.

```
//------- Technique: Mirror --------
MirVertexToPixel MirrorVS(float4 inPos: POSITION0)
{
    MirVertexToPixel Output = (MirVertexToPixel)0;

    float4x4 preViewProjection = mul(xView, xProjection);
    float4x4 preWorldViewProjection = mul(xWorld, preViewProjection);
    Output.Position = mul(inPos, preWorldViewProjection);
}
```

In the mirror technique, for each vertex of the mirror, the vertex shader also has to calculate to which pixel in the xMirrorTexture that vertex corresponds. To visualize this, say you want to find to which pixel in the xMirrorTexture the upper-left corner vertex of the mirror corresponds. The key in finding the answer is in looking at the mirror from the mirror camera. You need to find at which 2D coordinate the mirror camera has saved that vertex in the xMirrorTexture. This is exactly what you get if you transform the 3D coordinate of the vertex by the WorldViewProjection matrix of the mirror camera.

```
float4x4 preMirrorViewProjection = mul (xMirrorView, xProjection);
float4x4 preMirrorWorldViewProjection = mul(xWorld, preMirrorViewProjection);
Output.TexCoord = mul(inPos, preMirrorWorldViewProjection);

return Output;
```

**Note**  The word Mirror in this code does not imply an additional matrix; it simply means the matrix belongs to the mirror camera instead of the normal camera. As an example, xMirrorView is *not* the View matrix multiplied by a Mirror matrix; it is simply the View matrix of the mirror camera.

## Pixel Shader

Now in your pixel shader, for each of the four vertices of the mirror, you have the corresponding texture coordinate available. The only remaining problem is that the range in which you have them is not what you want. As you know, texture coordinates range between 0 and 1, as shown on the left of Figure 3-25. Screen coordinates, however, range from −1 to 1, as shown on the right of Figure 3-25.

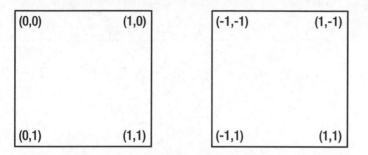

**Figure 3-25.** *Texture coordinates (left), screen coordinates (right)*

Luckily, it's easy to remap from the [-1,1] range to the [0,1] range. For example, you can divide by 2, so the range becomes [-0.5,0.5]. Then add 0.5, so the range becomes [0,1].

Also, since you're dealing with a float4 (homogeneous) coordinate, before you can use the first three components, you need to divide them by the fourth coordinate. This is what's being done in the first part of the pixel shader:

```
MirPixelToFrame MirrorPS(MirVertexToPixel PSIn) : COLOR0
{
    MirPixelToFrame Output = (MirPixelToFrame)0;

    float2 ProjectedTexCoords;
    ProjectedTexCoords[0] = PSIn.TexCoord.x/PSIn.TexCoord.w/2.0f +0.5f;
    ProjectedTexCoords[1] = -PSIn.TexCoord.y/PSIn.TexCoord.w/2.0f +0.5f;
    Output.Color = tex2D(textureSampler, ProjectedTexCoords);

    return Output;
}
```

The – sign in the line that calculates the second texture coordinate is needed because the scene needs to drawn upside down into the frame buffer, so you need to compensate for that. The final line looks up the corresponding color in the xMirrorTexture, and this color is returned by the pixel shader.

■**Note** The first two components indicate the 2D screen position; you need a fourth component to divide the first three components by, but what is this third coordinate? It actually is the 2D depth. In other words, it is the value that is entered into the z-buffer of the graphics card. It's a value between 0 and 1, where 0 indicates a vertex on the near clipping plane and 1 a vertex at the far clipping plane. Before the pixel shader is called to calculate the color of a pixel, the graphics card first determines whether the pixel should be drawn, based on the current depth value in the z-buffer for that pixel. For more information on the z-buffer, read the last part of recipe 2-1.

What remains is the technique definition:

```
technique Mirror
{
    pass Pass0
    {
        VertexShader = compile vs_1_1 MirrorVS();
        PixelShader  = compile ps_2_0 MirrorPS();
    }
}
```

## Using the Technique in XNA

You still need the DrawMirror method in your XNA project, which will actually render the rectangle using the newly created technique:

```
private void RenderMirror()
{
    mirrorEffect.Parameters["xWorld"].SetValue(Matrix.Identity);
    mirrorEffect.Parameters["xView"].SetValue(fpsCam.ViewMatrix);
    mirrorEffect.Parameters["xProjection"].SetValue(fpsCam.ProjectionMatrix);
    mirrorEffect.Parameters["xMirrorView"].SetValue(mirrorViewMatrix);
    mirrorEffect.Parameters["xMirrorTexture"].SetValue(mirrorTexture);

    mirrorEffect.Begin();
    foreach (EffectPass pass in mirrorEffect.CurrentTechnique.Passes)
    {
        pass.Begin();
        device.VertexDeclaration = new VertexDeclaration(device, ➥
        VertexPositionTexture.VertexElements);
        device.DrawUserPrimitives<VertexPositionTexture> ➥
        (PrimitiveType.TriangleStrip, mirrorVertices, 0, 2);
        pass.End();
    }
    mirrorEffect.End();
}
```

The regular World, View, and Projection matrices are set, as well as the xMirrorView matrix and the xMirrorTexture containing the scene as seen by the mirror. The two triangles of the rectangle are drawn as a TriangleStrip. You'll need to have imported the .fx file into your XNA project and to have linked it to the mirrorEffect variable.

## Arbitrary Mirror Plane

In the previous example, a special mirror plane was chosen, so it was easy to mirror points. In real cases, however, you'll want to be able to define arbitrary mirror planes. Improving the MirrorVector3 method so it is capable of mirroring any point in 3D space over an arbitrary plane will allow you to do this:

```
private Vector3 MirrorVector3(Plane mirrorPlane, Vector3 originalV3)
{
    float distV3ToPlane = mirrorPlane.DotCoordinate(originalV3);
    Vector3 mirroredV3 = originalV3 - 2 * distV3ToPlane * mirrorPlane.Normal;
    return mirroredV3;
}
```

First you want to know the shortest possible distance between the point and the plane, which can be calculated by the DotCoordinate method of the plane the mirror is in (it is the distance from the point perpendicular to the plane). If you multiply the Normal vector of the plane by this distance and subtract the resulting vector from the point, you end up exactly on the plane. You don't want to end on the plane; you want to move your point twice as far! So, you double this vector and subtract it from your original point coordinate.

This code allows you to use a mirror based on any three points.

## Defining a Mirror Clipping Plane

One big problem still remains: in case there are objects *behind* the mirror, these objects will be seen by the mirror camera and thus stored in the mirrorTexture. Finally, when your Mirror pixel shader samples colors from this texture, these objects will be shown on the mirror, while in reality these objects are behind the mirror and thus should in no case be shown on the mirror.

The solution to this problem is in defining a user clip plane. This is done by defining a plane and letting XNA know that all objects on one side of that plane must not be drawn. Of course, this plane should be the plane your mirror is in, so all objects behind the mirror are not drawn.

However, the four coefficients of a clip plane have to be defined in clip space (so your graphics card has an easy time deciding which objects to render and which ones to clip away). To map them from 3D space to clip space, you have to transform them by the inverse-transpose of the ViewProjection matrix, like this:

```
private void UpdateClipPlane()
{
    Matrix camMatrix = mirrorViewMatrix * fpsCam.ProjectionMatrix;
    Matrix invCamMatrix = Matrix.Invert(camMatrix);
    invCamMatrix = Matrix.Transpose(invCamMatrix);
```

```
        Vector4 mirrorPlaneCoeffs = new Vector4(mirrorPlane.Normal, mirrorPlane.D);
        Vector4 clipPlaneCoeffs = Vector4.Transform(-mirrorPlaneCoeffs, invCamMatrix);
        clipPlane = new Plane(clipPlaneCoeffs);
}
```

First you calculate this inverse-transpose matrix. Next, you retrieve the four coefficients of your mirror plane, defined in 3D. You map them to clip space by transforming them with the inverse-transpose matrix, and you use the resulting coefficients to create the clipping plane.

Note the – sign indicates which side of the plane should be culled away. This all has to do with the direction of the normal of the plane, which is defined by the order in which you defined the points p0, p1, p2, and p3 you used to define the plane.

Since this `clipPlane` variable depends on the `viewMatrix`, it should be updated every time the position of the camera changes, so call it from within the `Update` method:

```
UpdateClipPlane();
```

All you need to do next is pass the clip plane to your graphics card and activate it before you render your scene as seen by your mirror camera. Remember to disable it before rendering the scene as seen by the normal camera, because the objects behind the mirror could be in sight of the normal camera and thus should be displayed:

```
//render scene as seen by mirror into render target
device.SetRenderTarget(0, renderTarget);
device.Clear(ClearOptions.Target | ClearOptions.DepthBuffer, ➥
Color.CornflowerBlue, 1, 0);
device.ClipPlanes[0].Plane = clipPlane;
device.ClipPlanes[0].IsEnabled = true;
RenderScene(mirrorViewMatrix, fpsCam.ProjectionMatrix);
device.ClipPlanes[0].IsEnabled = false;
```

---

■**Note** When you take a close look, the image you see in the mirror might seem like a slightly blurred version of the original scene. This is because the calculated texture coordinates will almost never correspond to an exact pixel number, so your graphics card will average between the closest pixels. This averaging corresponds to a blurring operation (see recipe 2-13).

---

## The Code

*All the code is available for download at www.apress.com.*

To initialize this technique, you'll of course need to load the `.fx` file into an `Effect` variable, and you'll need to define your mirror:

```
private void InitMirror()
{
    mirrorVertices = new VertexPositionTexture[4];
    int i = 0;
```

```
    Vector3 p0 = new Vector3(-3, 0, 1);
    Vector3 p1 = new Vector3(-3, 6, 0);
    Vector3 p2 = new Vector3(6, 0, 0);

    Vector3 p3 = p1 + p2 - p0;

    mirrorVertices[i++] = new VertexPositionTexture(p0, new Vector2(0,0));
    mirrorVertices[i++] = new VertexPositionTexture(p1, new Vector2(0,0));
    mirrorVertices[i++] = new VertexPositionTexture(p2, new Vector2(0,0));
    mirrorVertices[i++] = new VertexPositionTexture(p3, new Vector2(0,0));

    mirrorPlane = new Plane(p0, p1, p2);
}
```

Each time the position of the camera is changed, you'll need to update the mirrorViewMatrix and the clipPlane variables, because they depend on the normal View matrix:

```
private void UpdateMirrorViewMatrix()
{
    Vector3 mirrorCamPosition = MirrorVector3(mirrorPlane, fpsCam.Position);
    Vector3 mirrorTargetPosition = MirrorVector3(mirrorPlane, ➥
    fpsCam.TargetPosition);

    Vector3 camUpPosition = fpsCam.Position + fpsCam.UpVector;
    Vector3 mirrorCamUpPosition = MirrorVector3(mirrorPlane, camUpPosition);
    Vector3 mirrorUpVector = mirrorCamUpPosition - mirrorCamPosition;

    mirrorViewMatrix = Matrix.CreateLookAt(mirrorCamPosition, ➥
    mirrorTargetPosition, mirrorUpVector);
}

private Vector3 MirrorVector3(Plane mirrorPlane, Vector3 originalV3)
{
    float distV3ToPlane = mirrorPlane.DotCoordinate(originalV3);
    Vector3 mirroredV3 = originalV3 - 2 * distV3ToPlane * mirrorPlane.Normal;
    return mirroredV3;
}

private void UpdateClipPlane()
{
    Matrix camMatrix = mirrorViewMatrix * fpsCam.ProjectionMatrix;
    Matrix invCamMatrix = Matrix.Invert(camMatrix);
    invCamMatrix = Matrix.Transpose(invCamMatrix);
```

```
      Vector4 mirrorPlaneCoeffs = new Vector4(mirrorPlane.Normal, mirrorPlane.D);
      Vector4 clipPlaneCoeffs = Vector4.Transform(-mirrorPlaneCoeffs, invCamMatrix);
      clipPlane = new Plane(clipPlaneCoeffs);
}
```

During your drawing phase, you'll first render the scene as seen by the mirror camera into a texture, clear the screen, and render the scene as seen by the normal camera. After that, you'll render the mirror:

```
protected override void Draw(GameTime gameTime)
{
      //render scene as seen by mirror into render target
      device.SetRenderTarget(0, renderTarget);
      device.Clear(ClearOptions.Target | ClearOptions.DepthBuffer, ➡
      Color.CornflowerBlue, 1, 0);
      device.ClipPlanes[0].Plane = clipPlane;
      device.ClipPlanes[0].IsEnabled = true;
      RenderScene(mirrorViewMatrix, fpsCam.ProjectionMatrix);
      device.ClipPlanes[0].IsEnabled = false;

      //deactivate custom render target, and save its contents into a texture
      device.SetRenderTarget(0, null);
      mirrorTexture = renderTarget.GetTexture();

      //render scene + mirror as seen by user to screen
      graphics.GraphicsDevice.Clear(Color.Tomato);
      RenderScene(fpsCam.ViewMatrix, fpsCam.ProjectionMatrix);
      RenderMirror();

      base.Draw(gameTime);
}
```

The mirror is rendered as a simple rectangle using the mirror technique, which extracts the colors from the mirrorTexture variable:

```
private void RenderMirror()
{
      mirrorEffect.Parameters["xWorld"].SetValue(Matrix.Identity);
      mirrorEffect.Parameters["xView"].SetValue(fpsCam.ViewMatrix);
      mirrorEffect.Parameters["xProjection"].SetValue(fpsCam.ProjectionMatrix);
      mirrorEffect.Parameters["xMirrorView"].SetValue(mirrorViewMatrix);
      mirrorEffect.Parameters["xMirrorTexture"].SetValue(mirrorTexture);

      mirrorEffect.Begin();
      foreach (EffectPass pass in mirrorEffect.CurrentTechnique.Passes)
      {
```

```
        pass.Begin();
        device.VertexDeclaration = new VertexDeclaration(device, ➥
        VertexPositionTexture.VertexElements);
        device.DrawUserPrimitives<VertexPositionTexture> ➥
        (PrimitiveType.TriangleStrip, mirrorVertices, 0, 2);
        pass.End();
    }
    mirrorEffect.End();
}
```

For each 3D vertex of your mirror, your vertex shader calculates the 2D screen coordinate, as well as the corresponding location in the xMirrorTexture:

```
MirVertexToPixel MirrorVS(float4 inPos: POSITION0)
{
    MirVertexToPixel Output = (MirVertexToPixel)0;

    float4x4 preViewProjection = mul(xView, xProjection);
    float4x4 preWorldViewProjection = mul(xWorld, preViewProjection);
    Output.Position = mul(inPos, preWorldViewProjection);

    float4x4 preMirrorViewProjection = mul (xMirrorView, xProjection);
    float4x4 preMirrorWorldViewProjection = mul(xWorld, preMirrorViewProjection);
    Output.TexCoord = mul(inPos, preMirrorWorldViewProjection);

    return Output;
}
```

Your pixel shader divides this coordinate by the homogeneous coordinate and maps this location from the [–1,1] render target range to the [0,1] texture range. Using the resulting texture coordinate, the color at the correct location in the xMirrorTexture is sampled and returned:

```
MirPixelToFrame MirrorPS(MirVertexToPixel PSIn) : COLOR0
{
    MirPixelToFrame Output = (MirPixelToFrame)0;

    float2 ProjectedTexCoords;
    ProjectedTexCoords[0] = PSIn.TexCoord.x/PSIn.TexCoord.w/2.0f +0.5f;
    ProjectedTexCoords[1] = -PSIn.TexCoord.y/PSIn.TexCoord.w/2.0f +0.5f;
    Output.Color = tex2D(textureSampler, ProjectedTexCoords);

    return Output;
}
```

# CHAPTER 4

■■■

# Working with Models

**W**hat good is a game without any objects? It would be quite impossible, however, to manually specify the shapes of all objects you use in your game. Luckily, XNA can load Models that have been created in specific modeling applications and have been saved to disk. Once you've loaded them into your XNA project, you can move and rotate your Models around in your scene and even animate them!

The first recipes of this chapter explain how to load a Model from a file and how to position it correctly in your 3D world. Next, you'll find a detailed discussion on the structure of a Model object, allowing you to make your Models come to life by animating them.

Furthermore, this chapter presents some different collision detection mechanisms, because most games rely heavily on this. These checks range from some very fast, volume-based checks to the most detailed per-triangle check.

Because some of the advanced recipes require a custom content processor for the Models, this chapter demonstrates how to extend the default Model processor and how to pass objects of custom classes using a custom-built TypeWriter and a custom-built TypeReader.

You'll definitely need some models to make your 3D world come alive. However, if you use an orthogonal Projection matrix (see recipe 2-13), a 2D game can also use Models.

Specifically, the recipes in this chapter cover the following:

- Loading 3D Models from files; scaling, rotating, moving, and drawing them into your 3D world (recipes 4-1, 4-2, and 4-6)

- Polishing the movement of your Models by making sure they are always facing the direction they're going to and by adding acceleration (recipes 4-3 and 4-4)

- Letting the user select Models using the pointer on the screen (recipe 4-19)

- Making your Models come alive by visualizing their structure and animating them (recipes 4-8 and 4-9)

- Checking for collisions between your Models by using some fast mechanisms (recipes 4-10 and 4-11)

- Learning how you can detect collisions on the finest level of detail, by checking for collisions for each triangle of your Model (recipe 4-18)

- Rendering your Model using your own HLSL effects because the BasicEffect class no longer suits your needs (recipes 4-7 and 4-12)

- Extending the Model processor so you can access much more useful data in your XNA project (recipes 4-13, 4-14, 4-15, and 4-16)

- Learning how you can store objects of your custom class inside a Model when it is loaded and processed in your custom Model processor, by coding your own TypeWriter and TypeReader (recipes 4-15 and 4-16)

- Making your Models nicely follow the slopes of your terrain (recipe 4-17)

# 4-1. Load and Render a Model Using the BasicEffect Class

## The Problem

Since it is quite impossible to manually define all points of a complex 3D object, these objects are created by artists in 3D modeling software packages. Such a model can be saved to a file. You want to be able to load such a model from a file and render the model to your XNA scene.

## The Solution

The XNA Framework comes with all the functionality you need to do this. XNA provides a default Model content pipeline, capable of loading models from .x and .fbx files. As explained for images in recipe 3-1, you can simply drag and drop a Model onto your project's Content folder in the Solution Explorer and link it to a variable in your XNA project's code. This Model variable comes with the functionality you need to easily render the model to your 3D scene.

## How It Works

First you need to import the .x or .fbx file into XNA Game Studio. As with images, you can do this by selecting the file in Windows Explorer and dragging it onto the Content entry below your project's name in the Solution Explorer of XNA Game Studio. Alternatively, you can right-click this Content entry in the Solution Explorer and select Add ➤ Existing Item, as shown in Figure 4-1. Next, browse to the .x or .fbx file, and select it.

---

■**Note** When you click the newly added model file in your Solution Explorer, the Properties box at the bottom-right of the Game Studio window should indicate XNA will use its default content importer and processor to load the file. Read recipes 4-12 to 4-16 for information on how to create your own model processors.

---

Now that you have the object added to your project, you should link it to a Model variable. Add this variable to the top of your code:

```
Model myModel;
```

**Figure 4-1.** *Adding a Model to your project*

And bind the model to the variable. The ideal place to do this is in the `LoadContent` method:

```
myModel = Content.Load<Model>("tank");
```

**Note** The name of the asset, `tank` in this case, defaults to the part of the file name before the extension. If you want, you can change the name of the asset by selecting the source file in the Solution Explorer and changing the Asset Name property in the bottom-right corner.

Now that you have the `Model` fully loaded from a file and associated with a variable in your code, you can easily draw it to your scene by adding the following code to the `Draw` method. This is the only code you need to render a `Model` to your scene; the remainder of this recipe provides some background information on what the code does.

```
//draw model
modelTransforms = new Matrix[myModel.Bones.Count];
Matrix worldMatrix = Matrix.CreateScale(0.01f, 0.01f, 0.01f);
myModel.CopyAbsoluteBoneTransformsTo(modelTransforms);
foreach (ModelMesh mesh in myModel.Meshes)
{
    foreach (BasicEffect effect in mesh.Effects)
    {
        effect.EnableDefaultLighting();
        effect.World = modelTransforms[mesh.ParentBone.Index] * worldMatrix;
        effect.View = fpsCam.ViewMatrix;
        effect.Projection = fpsCam.ProjectionMatrix;
    }
    mesh.Draw();
}
```

## Structure of a Model

In most cases, you'll want to be able to rotate or move some parts of a model, for example, the arm of a person. To allow this, most models are divided into members. For each such member, you'll want to know two things:

- *The geometrical data*: You'll want to know the vertices, which contain the information about corners of all triangles that make up this member of the Model. This information describes the position, color, normal, and much more of all vertices.

- *How to connect the member to its parent member*: In the example of the person and the arm, you'll want to specify the arm is connected to the person at the position of the person's shoulder.

The geometrical data of each member is stored as a ModelMesh object in the ModelMeshCollection of the Model, which you can find in its Meshes property. The positional data of the member is stored as a Bone object in the ModelBoneCollection of the Model, which you can find in the Bones collection of the Model. Each ModelMesh object contains a reference to a Bone object. Such a Bone object contains a reference to a parent Bone and where it should connect to this parent Bone. This way, you can link all the Bone objects to each other, as described in detail in recipes 4-8 and 4-9. In recipe 4-9, you can also find the explanation for the CopyAbsoluteBoneTransformsTo method.

### ModelMeshes and Bones

A ModelMesh contains the geometrical information of one solid member of the model, which is not separable into smaller members. For example, a laptop would not be a good ModelMesh, because you will want to open/close the screen and open/close the DVD tray. A better way would be to have one ModelMesh for the bottom part of the laptop, a second ModelMesh for the screen, and a third ModelMesh for the DVD tray.

Because all ModelMeshes need to be associated to a Bone, next to your three ModelMeshes you'll also have three Bones. You'll want to define the Bone associated with the base of the laptop as the root Bone, because the base of the laptop can be thought of as the laptop's origin. The Bone associated with the ModelMesh of the screen indicates the position where the screen connects to the base. Similarly, the Bone associated with the ModelMesh of the DVD tray also points to the root Bone, while indicating the position of the DVD tray relative to the laptop's base.

### ModelMeshes and ModelMeshParts

You have defined a single ModelMesh and associated Bone for your screen, which is excellent because the screen itself contains no rotatable/movable parts. However, you'll probably want to render the plastic border of the screen using an effect that uses a fixed texture, while you'll want to render your LCD using a totally different effect. For example, this effect should fetch its colors from another texture, or maybe you even want to add some reflective glow.

This is where the ModelMeshParts come into play. Each ModelMesh can include multiple ModelMeshParts, which can be rendered using a different texture, material, and/or effect. This means that each ModelMeshPart contains its geometry and a link to the effect it wants to render this geometry with.

▪**Note**  If you're not familiar with effects, you can think of them as definitions of the color that should be given to the pixels that are being rendered. Should the pixels respond to lighting, be transparent, or get their color from another image? See Chapter 6 for examples on how to make your pixels respond correctly to lighting. Recipe 3-13 contains an example of getting color from another image, which is already quite a mathematical effect.

## Two Nested for Loops

The structure of the Model explains why you need the two for loops to render the whole model. First, you cycle through the ModelMeshes of the Model. Each ModelMesh contains one or more ModelMeshParts, which can all have a different effect. So, you would expect the second for loop to scroll through all ModelMeshParts of the current ModelMesh, setting the parameters of their own effect. However, if multiple ModelMeshParts were to use the same effect, this would cause the same effect to be set twice, which is clearly a waste of time. To avoid this, the ModelMesh keeps track of all unique effects used by its ModelMeshParts. It is this list that is being scrolled through in the second for loop.

Finally, after all effects used by a ModelMesh have been configured, you call the Draw method on the ModelMesh object, which causes all ModelMeshParts of the ModelMesh objects to be drawn using their specified effect.

▪**Note**  Recipe 4-8 contains an example of scrolling through the ModelMeshParts of a ModelMesh, instead of through its effects.

## Minor Performance Improvement

The code presented earlier causes the array of Bones to be reinstantiated during each call of the Draw method. A better way would be to instantiate and fill the array only one time, immediately after the model gets loaded. So, move that line to the LoadContent method:

```
myModel = content.Load<Model>("tank");
modelTransforms = new Matrix[myModel.Bones.Count];
```

## The Code

*All the code is available for download at www.apress.com.*

First, load your Model and initialize its Bone array in the LoadContent method:

```
protected override void LoadContent()
{
    device = graphics.GraphicsDevice;
    basicEffect = new BasicEffect(device, null);
```

```
    myModel = Content.Load<Model>("tank");
    modelTransforms = new Matrix[myModel.Bones.Count];
}
```

Next, render your Model in the Draw method:

```
protected override void Draw(GameTime gameTime)
{
    device.Clear(ClearOptions.Target | ClearOptions.DepthBuffer, ➥
    Color.CornflowerBlue, 1, 0);

    //draw model
    Matrix worldMatrix = Matrix.CreateScale(0.01f, 0.01f, 0.01f);
    myModel.CopyAbsoluteBoneTransformsTo(modelTransforms);
    foreach (ModelMesh mesh in myModel.Meshes)
    {
        foreach (BasicEffect effect in mesh.Effects)
        {
            effect.EnableDefaultLighting();
            effect.World = modelTransforms[mesh.ParentBone.Index] * worldMatrix;
            effect.View = fpsCam.ViewMatrix;
            effect.Projection = fpsCam.ProjectionMatrix;
        }
        mesh.Draw();
    }

    base.Draw(gameTime);
}
```

# 4-2. Set Different World Matrices for Different Objects, Combining World Matrices

## The Problem

What good is a model when you can't move it around your scene? You want to move, rotate, and/or scale each object separately before rendering it to your 3D world.

## The Solution

You can do this by setting the World matrix of the object. A matrix is nothing magical; it is an object that can store any kind of transformation (such as a move, rotate, or scale operation). You can easily create a transformation matrix using one of these basic methods that come with the XNA Framework:

- `Matrix.CreateTranslation`
- `Matrix.CreateScale`
- `Matrix.CreateRotationX-Y-Z`

The first method creates a matrix holding a translation, where you can define how much you want to move your model in the X, Y, and Z directions. The second method allows you to scale your model, while the last method returns a matrix holding a rotation around the x-, y-, or z-axis, respectively.

You can combine multiple transformations by multiplying their matrices, but you have to multiply them in the correct order, as shown in this recipe.

## How It Works

When rendering a model to the screen as presented in the previous recipe, the model will be drawn so its origin point collides with the (0,0,0) 3D world origin. One of the most trivial things you'll want to do with your model is move it around the 3D scene.

This is quite easy to do. In your Draw method, define a time variable that represents the number of seconds (use milliseconds for precision, and then divide them by 1,000) that have elapsed since the start of your program. Next, you'll define a matrix that holds a translation along the x-axis. The amount of translation will depend on the current time:

```
float time = (float)gameTime.TotalRealTime.TotalMilliseconds/1000.0f;
Matrix worldMatrix = Matrix.CreateTranslation(time, 0, 0);
```

When set as the World matrix, this matrix will cause the model to be moved one unit each second along the x-axis. This code renders your model using the defined World matrix:

```
myModel.CopyAbsoluteBoneTransformsTo(modelTransforms);
foreach (ModelMesh mesh in myModel.Meshes)
{
    foreach (BasicEffect effect in mesh.Effects)
    {
        effect.EnableDefaultLighting();
        effect.World = modelTransforms[mesh.ParentBone.Index] * worldMatrix;
        effect.View = fpsCam.GetViewMatrix();
        effect.Projection = fpsCam.GetProjectionMatrix();
    }
    mesh.Draw();
}
```

To keep all parts of your Model at their correct positions, the Bone transform needs to be part of the World matrix (see recipe 4-9 for more information on bone transformations). Only this time, you combine this Bone transformation with the translation matrix you just defined by multiplying both matrices. Make sure you put your World matrix on the right side of the multiplication, because in matrix math, the order of multiplication is very important (see the remainder of this recipe for more information and examples). When you run this code, your model should slowly move along the x-axis.

The same holds for scaling and rotation. Try using this World matrix:

```
Matrix worldMatrix = Matrix.CreateScale(time);
```

At startup, when time = 0, the model will be invisibly small and will grow as time increases. After one second, the model will reach its original size. After that, the model will continue growing.

Next, try using this World matrix:

```
Matrix worldMatrix = Matrix.CreateRotationY(time);
```

which will continuously rotate the model around the Up y-axis.

## Combining Multiple Transformations

Usually, you'll want to combine multiple transformations to use as the World matrix for your model. For example, you may want to move your character to a position in your 3D world, rotate it so it's looking into the direction it is running, and scale it up because it has just found a power-up.

As a small example, try this World matrix:

```
Matrix worldMatrix = Matrix.CreateTranslation(time, 0, 0) * ➥
Matrix.CreateRotationY(time/10.0f);
```

This will combine a rotation and a translation. This combination will be used as the World matrix for your model. However, you can combine both transformations in a different way, like this:

```
Matrix worldMatrix = Matrix.CreateRotationY(time / 10.0f) * ➥
Matrix.CreateTranslation(time, 0, 0);
```

As you should clearly see after running the program 30 seconds or so, both results are totally different. As mentioned before, in matrix math, the order of multiplication is all-important, as I will discuss in the next section of this recipe.

## The Order of Matrix Multiplication

In matrix math, multiplying matrix M1 by matrix M2 generally *doesn't* yield the same result as multiplying matrix M2 by matrix M1. In the following sections, I'll discuss all possible combinations.

There is one rule (or trick, if you will) you should always remember: in matrix multiplication, M1*M2 means "M1 *after* M2."

### Rotation Combined with Another Rotation

The order in which you multiply your rotations to obtain the final rotation is important. This is because when you first rotate around axis A1 and then around axis A2, the rotation around axis A1 will have changed axis A2 before you start rotating around axis A2!

As an example, let's say M1 holds a rotation around the Right vector of 90 degrees and M2 holds a rotation around the Up vector of 90 degrees.

Let's first look at the M1*M2 case, which means "rotation around Right *after* rotation around Up." Think about what would happen if the object were to be rotated. In this case, at any moment you can find your Right vector by stretching out your right arm. You start by rotating around your Up vector for 90 degrees, so you're looking to the left, as shown on the left of Figure 4-2. When you take a look at your Right arm, you'll (I hope) see that it has been rotated with you! So now, when you rotate around your Right vector, you end up lying face down, as shown in the right part of Figure 4-2.

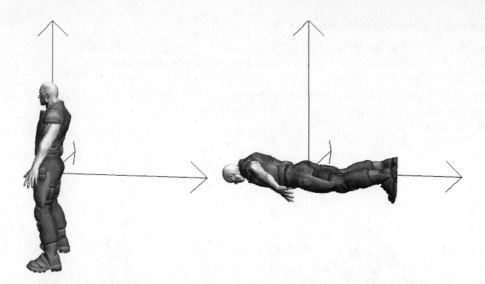

**Figure 4-2.** *Rotation around Right after rotation around Up*

Next, let's take the second case, which is M2*M1, or "rotation around Up *after* rotation around Right." You start again in your original position. You first rotate around your Right direction, which results in you lying face down, as shown in the left part of Figure 4-3. Now, your Up vector is horizontal, in the same direction as the World's Forward vector. When you rotate around it, you end up lying on your side, as shown in the right part of Figure 4-3!

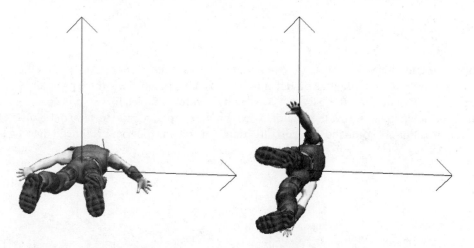

**Figure 4-3.** *Rotation around Up after rotation around Right*

As you can see, M1*M2 and M2*M1 have completely different results, because when combining two rotations, the axis of the second rotation is affected by the first rotation.

### Rotation Combined with a Translation

In this case, the order of multiplication is again important. In this example, M3 holds a rotation around the Up vector of 90 degrees, and M4 holds a translation of ten units along the positive x-axis.

In the M3*M4 case, meaning "rotation after translation," the model is first moved toward its position. Once it has arrived there, the model is rotated along the Up vector. Both steps are shown in Figure 4-4.

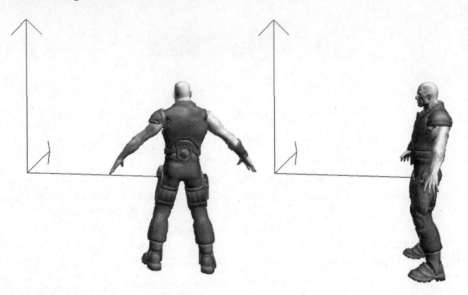

**Figure 4-4.** *Rotation after translation*

Things are different in the M4*M3 case. When asking for translation after rotation, first the whole coordinate system (including the model and the x-axis) is rotated along the Up vector for 90 degrees, as shown on the left of Figure 4-5. Next, the model is moved for ten units over the rotated x-axis. Keep in mind that the original x-axis has been rotated, and instead of being the Right direction, it has become the Forward direction! This means the Model is moved over the World's Forward z-axis.

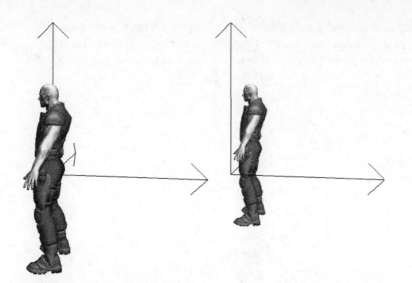

**Figure 4-5.** *Translation after rotation*

## Scaling Combined with a Translation

The same is true for a scaling combined with a translation. As an example for this case, M5 will hold a scaling of factor 0.5, while M6 will again hold a translation of ten units along the x-axis.

In the M5*M6 case, you're asking to perform the scaling after the translation. So first, the model is moved ten units to the right along the x-axis, and afterward it is scaled down, as shown in Figure 4-6.

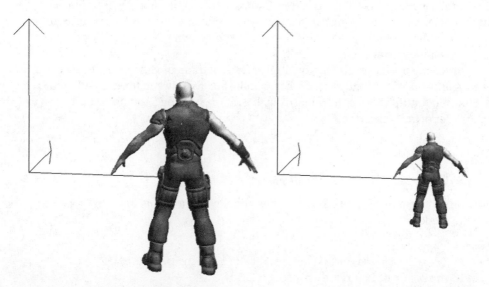

**Figure 4-6.** *Scaling after translation*

When setting M6*M5 as the World matrix, you're first scaling down the whole coordinate system (yes, again including the model and x-axis). Next, the small model is moved for ten units over the downscaled x-axis. Since the axis has been downscaled by factor 0.5, ten down-scaled units correspond to only five original units! This results in the model being moved less far away, as shown in Figure 4-7.

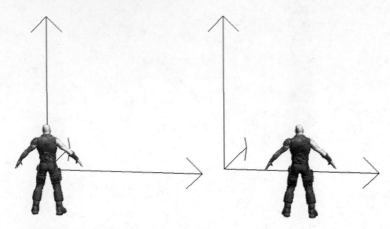

**Figure 4-7.** *Translation after scaling*

### Safe Combinations

Luckily, you can use some transformations without having to think about the order of multiplication.

For example, it's safe to combine two translations, because the model will simply be moved twice. Also, when combining two scaling transformations, the order is not important. For example, whether you first scale up two times and then down ten times or first down ten and then up two times yields the same result.

Finally, a scaling operation also has no impact on a rotation, or vice versa, because you're scaling down only the coordinate system's axis, but the angles between the axes still remain 90 degrees. So when multiplying a scaling matrix with a matrix holding a rotation, you're free to choose the order of multiplication.

## The Code

*All the code is available for download at* www.apress.com.

The following code combines a rotation and translation matrix and sets the resulting World matrix on the model:

```
//draw model
float time = (float)gameTime.TotalRealTime.TotalMilliseconds/1000.0f;
Matrix worldMatrix = Matrix.CreateScale(0.005f)* ➡
Matrix.CreateRotationY(time / 10.0f) * Matrix.CreateTranslation(time, 0, 0);
myModel.CopyAbsoluteBoneTransformsTo(modelTransforms);
foreach (ModelMesh mesh in myModel.Meshes)
```

```
{
    foreach (BasicEffect effect in mesh.Effects)
    {
        effect.EnableDefaultLighting();
        effect.World = modelTransforms[mesh.ParentBone.Index] * worldMatrix;
        effect.View = fpsCam.ViewMatrix;
        effect.Projection = fpsCam.ProjectionMatrix;
    }
    mesh.Draw();
}
```

# 4-3. Find the Rotation Angle Corresponding to a Direction

## The Problem

By setting a World matrix before rendering your Model (as explained in the previous recipe), you can position your Model anywhere in your 3D scene.

When you move your Model from point A to point B, you need to make sure it is rotated toward the correct direction.

This is often obtained in a natural way, for example, when dealing with a World matrix containing a rotation. However, if you simply move your Model by means of storing its previous and current 3D position, you will have to rotate your Model manually.

## The Solution

You should first calculate the direction to which the Model is being moved. Starting from the X and Z coordinates of this direction, it is fairly easy to retrieve the angle.

## How It Works

Given a direction, you want to know how much you should rotate the Model so it is facing into this direction. Given the direction shown on the right side of Figure 4-8, you want to find the angle between Z and this direction.

The solution is quite easy once you've remembered some basic trigonometry math. Given the triangle shown on the left of Figure 4-8, you can find the angle α by taking the arc tangent (atan) of S divided by L. In the words of the right part of Figure 4-8, you can find the rotation angle by taking the atan of the X component of the direction, divided by the Z direction of the component.

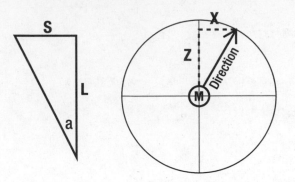

**Figure 4-8.** *Calculating the rotation angle from the direction*

The drawback of the atan method is that it returns values only between +90 degrees and –90 degrees (which is caused by the fact that when dividing two negative numbers, the – sign is lost).

Luckily, the .NET Framework also provides the Atan2 method to which you can provide your X and Z values separately. This allows the method to return a value between –180 and 180 degrees, providing a rotation that is uniquely defined over a full circle.

This simple method calculates the rotation angle corresponding to the current and previous positions of a model:

```
private float CalculateRotation(Vector3 oldPos, Vector3 newPos, float lastRot)
{
    Vector3 direction = newPos - oldPos;
    if ((direction.X == 0) && (direction.Z == 0))
        return lastRot;
    else
        return (float)Math.Atan2(direction.X,direction.Z);
}
```

First you find the direction from the old to the new position, allowing you to calculate the corresponding angle. If the model has stopped or if it is moved vertically, both the X and Z components of the direction will be 0 and the Atan2 method will return a useless value. If this is the case, you return the last rotation, so a stopped model will keep its rotation.

## Usage

You should use the angle you calculated to create a rotation around the Up y-axis so the front of the model is facing the direction it is going. When creating the World matrix, you should first translate the Model to its 3D position and then rotate it. This means you need to put the rotation to the left of the translation in the multiplication (see recipe 4-2). Look at the following example, where the last position of your Model should be stored in the position variables and the angle variable has been calculated by the CalculateRotation method explained previously:

```
worldMatrix = Matrix.CreateTranslation(position);
worldMatrix = Matrix.CreateRotationY(angle) * worldMatrix;
worldMatrix = Matrix.CreateScale(0.005f) * worldMatrix;
```

In this case, first the coordinate system of the model is moved toward the final 3D position of the center of the model. Next, the Y rotation of this recipe is applied, rotating the coordinate system. After this, it shrinks. Because this is a scaling matrix, it can be swapped from place with the adjacent Y rotation matrix, not with the translation matrix (see recipe 4-2).

As a result, the Model will be moved to its location, rotated, and shrunk afterward.

### The Code

*All the code is available for download at www.apress.com.*

You can find the CalculateRotation method in one piece a few paragraphs earlier.

# 4-4. Use Acceleration to Control Velocity

## The Problem

You want to make your models accelerate nicely, instead of going instantly from total stop to full speed, and vice versa. Figure 4-9 shows the kind of speed increase you want.

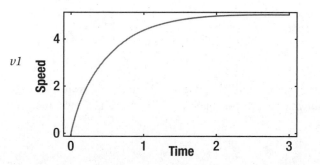

**Figure 4-9.** *The speed of your Model in function of time*

## The Solution

By adding acceleration, you can define how fast your model can speed up. It is the amount of speed you will add to the current speed of your model each frame.

## How It Works

You will need to keep track of the position and rotation of your Model, because you'll need to know which direction is Forward. In this example, you will let the model rotate only around its Up y-axis and move only the X and Z coordinates of its position. See recipe 4-17 if you want your Model to move over a surface, based solely on the X and Z coordinates.

Also, because the next speed of your model will depend on the current speed, you will need to keep track of the current speed. Instead of just storing the speed as a number, you will store the velocity vector. This velocity vector contains the direction the model is currently going to, while its length indicates the speed. So, add these three variables to your class:

```
Vector3 modelPosition = new Vector3();
float modelYRot = 0;
Vector3 modelVelocity = new Vector3();
```

You can also define the maximal acceleration and turning speed of your Model:

```
const float modelMaxAcceleration = 30.0f;
const float modelMaxTurnSpeed = 0.002f;
```

In your Update method, retrieve the amount of seconds elapsed since the last frame, and detect how the user wants the Model to move:

```
float elapsedSeconds = (float)gameTime.ElapsedGameTime.Milliseconds / 1000.0f;
float forwardReq = 0;
float angleReq = 0;

if (keyState.IsKeyDown(Keys.Up))
    forwardReq += 1.0f;
if (keyState.IsKeyDown(Keys.Down))
    forwardReq -= 1.0f;
if (keyState.IsKeyDown(Keys.Left))
    angleReq += 1.0f;
if (keyState.IsKeyDown(Keys.Right))
    angleReq -= 1.0f;
```

The forwardReq value will be positive if the user wants the Model to accelerate Forward. It will be negative if the model should slow down or accelerate backward. The angleReq contains whether the Model should turn left or right.

### Acceleration on Ice

This piece of code adds the basics of acceleration:

```
Matrix rotMatrix = Matrix.CreateRotationY(angle);
Vector3 forwardDir = Vector3.Transform(new Vector3(0, 0, -1), rotMatrix);

velocity = velocity + elapsedTime * forwardReq * maxAccel *forwardDir;

modelPosition += velocity;
modelYRot += rotationReq * maxRotSpeed * velocity.Length();
```

The first two lines calculate the current Forward vector of the Model, which is needed to know into which direction to accelerate the Model. This Forward vector is found by rotating the default (0,0,–1) Forward vector over the Up y-axis.

The second line, which calculates the velocity, is the most important one. You start from the previous velocity, while the second term adds a new vector based on the user input. The more time that has passed since the last frame, the more you need to adjust this velocity. Furthermore, the larger the acceleration the user requested, the more you need to adjust the velocity. As a last factor, you take the maximum acceleration of the `Model` into account. You multiply all three factors together, giving you a value indicating how much you need to adjust your velocity this frame. Because you need a `Vector3` to add to the velocity, you multiply this value with `forwardDir` to obtain the vector you want to add to your velocity for this frame.

In the end, this `Vector3` is added to the position of your `Model`, and the rotation of your `Model` is adjusted. The faster your model is moving, the faster it will rotate.

When you use this code, you will notice two flaws. First, your `Model` will never slow down, and it doesn't have a maximum speed. You want the speed to increase as shown in Figure 4-9 and saturate at a certain maximum speed. Using this code, your `Model` will keep on speeding up at the same pace.

Second, if the `Model` is going pretty fast into a direction, after you rotate the `Model`, it will still be going in the same direction. That's pretty nice if your `Model` is moving over an ice plane, but in general this is not what you want.

## Adding Friction

In reality, the speed of your `Model` will decrease because of the friction between the `Model` and the air, surface, and, when applicable, internal mechanical frictions. When you stop accelerating your `Model`, friction will cause the speed to decrease until your `Model` reaches a full stop. When you keep on accelerating, friction will cause the speed to saturate at a certain level.

You can obtain friction by reducing the previous speed before building on top of it. The next line adds friction to your `Model`:

```
velocity = velocity * (1 - friction * elapsedTime) + elapsedTime * ➥
forwardReq * maxAccel *forwardDir;
```

The more time between the last frame and this frame, the more impact friction should have on your `Model`, so you multiply the friction value by the amount of time that has passed.

### Keeping Only the Forward Component

Although your Model will accelerate in a more natural way now, it still moves a bit awkwardly whenever it is rotated (unless you're creating a space or an ice-skidding game). Generally, you want your Model to move only along its Forward direction.

To this end, you want to know how much the current velocity vector is along the Forward direction of the Model. This is exactly what a *dot product* does: it projects your Velocity (V) vector on the Forward vector (F), as shown in Figure 4-10, and returns the length of this projected vector (M).

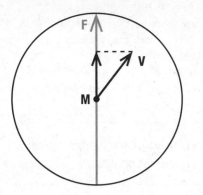

**Figure 4-10.** *Projecting the Velocity vector on the Forward vector*

So, after you've updated your velocity, use this code:

```
float forwardSpeed = Vector3.Dot(velocity, forwardDir);
velocity = forwardSpeed * forwardDir;

modelPosition += velocity * elapsedTime;
modelYRot += rotationReq * maxRotSpeed * forwardSpeed;
```

The forwardSpeed variable indicates the length of the Forward component of the Velocity vector. You multiply this value by the Forward direction and store this as the new Velocity vector. This way, you are sure the Model will move along its Forward direction only.

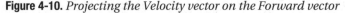

■**Note** An extra advantage of the forwardSpeed variable is that it will be positive whenever the Model is going forward and negative whenever it is going backward. This is in contradiction to velocity.Length(), which always returns a positive value.

## The Code

*All the code is available for download at www.apress.com.*

The Accelerate method listed next adjusts the position, velocity, and rotation of your Model, taking acceleration into account. You will probably want to add these together with the maximum acceleration and rotation speed inside a model structure. Furthermore, you need to pass the user input, as well as the friction value.

```
private float Accelerate(ref Vector3 position, ref float angle, ➥
ref Vector3 velocity, float forwardReq, float rotationReq, ➥
float elapsedTime, float maxAccel, float maxRotSpeed, float friction)
{
    Matrix rotMatrix = Matrix.CreateRotationY(angle);
    Vector3 forwardDir = Vector3.Transform(new Vector3(0, 0, -1), rotMatrix);

    velocity = velocity * (1 - friction * elapsedTime) + ➥
    elapsedTime * forwardReq * maxAccel *forwardDir;

    float forwardSpeed = Vector3.Dot(velocity, forwardDir);
    velocity = forwardSpeed * forwardDir;

    modelPosition += velocity * elapsedTime;
    modelYRot += rotationReq * maxRotSpeed * forwardSpeed;

    return forwardSpeed;
}
```

The method returns the forwardSpeed variable, which is negative if the model is going backward.

## Extra Reading

You can extend this introduction to object acceleration by allowing multiple accelerations to have an impact on the Model, for example, the gravity. You can do this by summing the accelerations and taking this sum as forwardDir.

# 4-5. Construct the Global BoundingSphere Around a Model

## The Problem

The BoundingSphere of a Model is the smallest sphere that completely surrounds the Model. In many cases, such as collision detecting, size determination, and more, it is very useful to have this global BoundingSphere.

## The Solution

You can access the BoundingSphere of each ModelMesh of your Model. Using the BoundingSphere.CreateMerged method, you can weld these all together and obtain one BoundingSphere surrounding your entire Model.

However, because these separate BoundingSpheres are defined relative to the Bone matrix of each ModelMesh, you need to take the transformation inside the Bone matrix into account.

## How It Works

You will create a method that loads an asset into a Model variable, initializes its Bone matrix array, and saves the global BoundingBox into the Tag property of the Model.

---

■**Tip**  You can use the Tag property of the Model to store any object. In this example, you'll use it to store the BoundingSphere. The Tag property will be used intensively throughout this chapter.

---

```
private Model LoadModelWithBoundingSphere(ref Matrix[] ➡
modelTransforms, string asset, ContentManager content)
{
    Model newModel = content.Load<Model>(asset);

    modelTransforms = new Matrix[newModel.Bones.Count];
    newModel.CopyAbsoluteBoneTransformsTo(modelTransforms);

    return newModel;
}
```

This method does the trivial parts required to load a Model, as explained in recipe 4-1. Before returning the Model, though, you want to scroll through all ModelMeshes of the Model to look at their BoundingSpheres (which are created by the default Model processor at compile time, as explained in recipe 4-13).

```
foreach (ModelMesh mesh in newModel.Meshes)
{
    BoundingSphere origMeshSphere = mesh.BoundingSphere;
}
```

You want to weld all of these spheres together to obtain the global BoundingSphere of the whole Model. You can do this by creating and keeping track of a new BoundingSphere and merging it with all these smaller spheres:

```
BoundingSphere completeBoundingSphere = new BoundingSphere();
foreach (ModelMesh mesh in newModel.Meshes)
{
    BoundingSphere origMeshSphere = mesh.BoundingSphere;
    completeBoundingSphere = ➡
    BoundingSphere.CreateMerged(completeBoundingSphere, ➡
    origMeshSphere);
}
```

As a result, completeBoundingSphere will be a sphere containing all the smaller spheres.

However, when you retrieve a BoundingSphere of a ModelMesh, it is defined in the local space of the ModelMesh. For example, the BoundingSphere of the torso of a person will measure 80 cm. Next, the BoundingSphere of the head Model will measure only 30 cm. If you simply merge these two together, you will again obtain the sphere of 80 cm, because the smaller sphere is completely included in the larger one.

To merge them correctly, you first need to move the sphere of the head to the correct position on top of the torso and then merge this moved sphere with the larger sphere. This will result in an even larger sphere of 110 cm that includes both spheres.

In XNA terms, this means you first need to transform the BoundingSphere of the new ModelMesh with the transformation contained in its Bone matrix (see the last part of recipe 4-1) before merging it with the completeBoundingSphere, like this:

```
BoundingSphere completeBoundingSphere = new BoundingSphere();
foreach (ModelMesh mesh in newModel.Meshes)
{
    BoundingSphere origMeshSphere = mesh.BoundingSphere;
    BoundingSphere transMeshSphere = ➥
    XNAUtils.TransformBoundingSphere(origMeshSphere, ➥
    modelTransforms[mesh.ParentBone.Index]);
    completeBoundingSphere = ➥
    BoundingSphere.CreateMerged(completeBoundingSphere, ➥
    transMeshSphere);
}
newModel.Tag = completeBoundingSphere;
```

The correctly merged BoundingSphere will be stored in the Tag property of your Model.

---

■**Note** The BoundingSphere.Transform method that comes with the XNA Framework doesn't take any rotations contained in the matrix into account; therefore, I have included an extended version in my XNAUtils file, which you can find in the sample code.

---

## Usage

Whenever you need to retrieve your global BoundingSphere from inside the Tag property, you need to cast it to a BoundingSphere object first, because the Tag property really can store anything, and you need to remind your compiler what you stored in there:

```
BoundingSphere bSphere = (BoundingSphere)myModel.Tag;
```

## The Code

*All the code is available for download at www.apress.com.*

This is the method that completely initializes a Model and stores its BoundingSphere inside its Tag property:

```
private Model LoadModelWithBoundingSphere(ref Matrix[] ➥
modelTransforms, string asset, ContentManager content)
{
    Model newModel = content.Load<Model>(asset);

    modelTransforms = new Matrix[newModel.Bones.Count];
    newModel.CopyAbsoluteBoneTransformsTo(modelTransforms);

    BoundingSphere completeBoundingSphere = new BoundingSphere();
    foreach (ModelMesh mesh in newModel.Meshes)
    {
        BoundingSphere origMeshSphere = mesh.BoundingSphere;
        BoundingSphere transMeshSphere = ➥
        XNAUtils.TransformBoundingSphere(origMeshSphere, ➥
        modelTransforms[mesh.ParentBone.Index]);
        completeBoundingSphere = ➥
        BoundingSphere.CreateMerged(completeBoundingSphere, ➥
        transMeshSphere);
    }
    newModel.Tag = completeBoundingSphere;

    return newModel;
}
```

# 4-6. Scale the Model to a Predefined Size

## The Problem

When loading a Model from disk, often it will look very large or very tiny. You want to immediately scale it to a size you can define.

## The Solution

First you should create the global BoundingSphere of the Model, as explained in the previous recipe. Once you know this sphere, you know the current size of your Model.

From this size, you can find how much you should scale your Model up/down before rendering it. Alternatively, you can store this scaling operation in the matrix of the root Bone, as this scaling will be applied to all matrices of all Bones in your Model (see recipe 4-9).

## How It Works

Often, when working with models created with different tools or models found on the Internet, you cannot make any assumptions about the size of the model. So, it would be nice if you could load the model and scale it to the size you want.

The following code calculates how much the model needs to be scaled down, depending on your liking. It expects the global BoundingSphere to be stored inside the Tag property of the Model, as explained in the previous recipe.

```
private Matrix[] AutoScale(Model model, float requestedSize)
{
    BoundingSphere bSphere = (BoundingSphere)model.Tag;
    float originalSize = bSphere.Radius * 2;
    float scalingFactor = requestedSize / originalSize;

    model.Root.Transform = model.Root.Transform * Matrix.CreateScale(scalingFactor);

    Matrix[] modelTransforms = new Matrix[model.Bones.Count];
    model.CopyAbsoluteBoneTransformsTo(modelTransforms);

    return modelTransforms;
}
```

You need to pass the model to this method and indicate how large you want the final model to be.

The method starts by retrieving the global BoundingSphere of the Model (explained in recipe 4-5). You need to double the radius of a sphere to find the size of the sphere, which, in the case of this bSphere, corresponds to the original size of the loaded model. Next, you find how much the model needs to be scaled by dividing this value by the requested size.

You can use this scaling factor to create a matrix from. When you set this matrix as the World matrix when rendering the Model, your Model will be scaled down to the size you wanted.

### Applying the Scaling to the Root Bone

Well-made models link all their submeshes to their root bone. This means that all you have to scale is the matrix of this root bone (see recipe 4-9 for more information), and all ModelMeshes of the Model will automatically be scaled down by this factor.

You can obtain this by multiplying this Root matrix by a scaling matrix, based on the scalingFactor you calculated before, and storing the resulting matrix back into the model.

Because you've changed the contents of the Bone matrices of your Model, you have to extract the new version of the modelTransforms matrices so these are returned.

---

■**Note**  A nicer way would be to do this in a custom Model processor using a configurable variable. See recipe 4-12 on how to extend the default Model processor and recipe 3-10 on processor parameters.

---

## The Code

*All the code is available for download at www.apress.com.*

In your LoadContent method, all the code you need to load and scale your Model are these two lines:

```
myModel = XNAUtils.LoadModelWithBoundingSphere(ref modelTransforms, ➥
"tank", Content);
modelTransforms = AutoScale(myModel, 10.0f);
```

When it comes to rendering your Model, you can use your normal code, since the scaling has been stored in the Root bone of your Model. This way, each time you call the Model.CopyAbsoluteBoneTransformsTo method, all resulting matrices will include this scaling operation, causing all parts of the Model to be scaled before they are rendered to the screen.

```
Matrix worldMatrix = Matrix.Identity;
myModel.CopyAbsoluteBoneTransformsTo(modelTransforms);
foreach (ModelMesh mesh in myModel.Meshes)
{
    foreach (BasicEffect effect in mesh.Effects)
    {
        effect.EnableDefaultLighting();
        effect.World = modelTransforms[mesh.ParentBone.Index] * worldMatrix;
        effect.View = fpsCam.ViewMatrix;
        effect.Projection = fpsCam.ProjectionMatrix;
    }
    mesh.Draw();
}
```

Remember, you can find more information on Bones in recipes 4-1 and 4-9 and on World matrices in recipe 4-2.

# 4-7. Render a Model Using Custom Effects and Custom Textures (Easy Approach)

## The Problem

When you load a model into your XNA project using the code explained in recipe 4-1, you will be rendering the model to your scene using a BasicEffect instance. Although this will render the model just fine in simple cases, often you'll want to render the model using a different, custom effect.

## The Solution

By casting the effects contained in the model to BasicEffect objects, you can obtain all information about the effects, such as texture and material information. After you have copied these properties to somewhere safe, you can overwrite the effect with an effect of your choice.

---

■**Note** You can also do this in a cleaner way by writing a custom content processor, as discussed in recipe 4-12. If you just need a quick way or if you are interested in the structure of an Effect object, read on.

---

## How It Works

First, you'll need to load a model, together with a custom effect with which you want to render the model. Both should be loaded using the content pipeline:

```
protected override void LoadContent(bool loadAllContent)
{
    if (loadAllContent)
    {
        device = graphics.GraphicsDevice;
        basicEffect = new BasicEffect(device, null);

        myModel = content.Load<Model>("forklift");
        modelTransforms = new Matrix[myModel.Bones.Count];

        customEffect = content.Load<Effect>("bwcolor");
    }
}
```

The simple custom effect in this example will render the model using grayscale values.

Because the effects are stored in the ModelMeshes of a Model, you can easily overwrite them with your custom effect. However, all information held in the original effect will be lost! Such information includes textures and material color information.

Before overwriting the default effect of the model, you'll want to store this information, because your custom effect will need to know, for example, which textures to use.

You will create a method that takes in a Model and a custom effect. It will replace all effects in the model with copies of your custom effect. Finally, to demonstrate how to store the original data, the method will return an array of all textures used by the original effects, so you can feed them to your own effect. In this example, all effects are overridden by your custom effect, but a small adaptation suffices to override only the effect of a particular ModelMeshPart:

```
private Texture2D[] ChangeEffect(ref Model model, Effect newEffect)
{
}
```

Because you want the changes made to the model to be permanent, you'll want the model to be passed by reference (hence the ref in front of the first variable). Otherwise, a local copy would be made for the method, and all changes made to this copy would not be seen by the calling code.

First, you'll want to make a copy of all textures used by the original effects:

```
List<Texture2D> textureList = new List<Texture2D>();

foreach (ModelMesh mesh in model.Meshes)
    foreach (ModelMeshPart modmeshpart in mesh.MeshParts)
    {
        BasicEffect oldEffect = (BasicEffect)modmeshpart.Effect;
        textureList.Add(oldEffect.Texture);                    ;
    }
```

```
Texture2D[] textures = textureList.ToArray();
return textures;
```

You create a list to store the textures and scroll through the different ModelMeshParts of each ModelMesh in your Model. Such a ModelMeshPart contains a link to the effect it uses to be drawn with. You downcast this effect to a BasicEffect object so you can access its properties, such as the texture. For each effect in the model, you append the texture to your list of textures.

After all textures have been gathered, you reshape your list into an array and return this array to the calling code.

All you have to do now is overwrite the original effect with a copy of your custom effect, so add this line in the second foreach loop:

```
modmeshpart.Effect = newEffect.Clone(device);
```

---

■**Note** You use the Clone method to create a copy of the effect for each part of the model. You will want to use copies; otherwise, all ModelMeshParts would share the same effect. By giving each ModelMeshPart its own copy of the effect, each ModelMeshPart can, for example, use a different texture.

---

Call this method from your LoadContent method after both the model and the custom effect have been loaded:

```
modelTextures = ChangeEffect(ref myModel, customEffect);
```

When it comes to drawing the model, you now have the possibility to define each of the parameters of your custom effect separately:

```
int i = 0;
Matrix worldMatrix = Matrix.CreateScale(0.01f);
myModel.CopyAbsoluteBoneTransformsTo(modelTransforms);

foreach (ModelMesh mesh in myModel.Meshes)
{
    foreach (Effect currentEffect in mesh.Effects)
    {
        currentEffect.Parameters["xWorld"]. ➡
        SetValue(modelTransforms[mesh.ParentBone.Index]*worldMatrix);
        currentEffect.Parameters["xView"].SetValue(fpsCam.ViewMatrix);
        currentEffect.Parameters["xProjection"].SetValue(fpsCam.ProjectionMatrix);
        currentEffect.Parameters["xTexture"].SetValue(modelTextures[i++]);
    }
    mesh.Draw();
}
```

Note how you can pass the original effect information to your custom effect, such as the texture in this example.

### Scrolling Through ModelMeshParts Instead of Through Effects

The previous for loop scrolls through all effects used by one ModelMesh. Because this can give problems if you want to set the effect for a specific ModelMeshPart, you can scroll through the ModelMeshParts of the ModelMesh, instead of through its effects:

```
int i = 0;
Matrix worldMatrix = Matrix.CreateScale(0.01f);
myModel.CopyAbsoluteBoneTransformsTo(modelTransforms);
foreach (ModelMesh mesh in myModel.Meshes)
{
    foreach (ModelMeshPart part in mesh.MeshParts)
    {
        Effect currentEffect = part.Effect;
                        currentEffect.Parameters["xWorld"]. ➥
        SetValue(modelTransforms[mesh.ParentBone.Index] * worldMatrix);
        currentEffect.Parameters["xView"].SetValue(fpsCam.ViewMatrix);
        currentEffect.Parameters["xProjection"].SetValue(fpsCam.ProjectionMatrix);
        currentEffect.Parameters["xTexture"].SetValue(modelTextures[i++]);
    }
    mesh.Draw();
}
```

### Storing All Original Information

If you want to store more than the texture information, you can simply store the original effects instead of only the textures in a list:

```
BasicEffect[] originalEffects;
```

In the ChangeEffect method, add the original effects to the list:

```
BasicEffect oldEffect = (BasicEffect)modmeshpart.Effect;
effectList.Add(oldEffect);
```

When setting the parameters of your custom effect, you can easily access original information like this:

```
currentEffect.Parameters["xTexture"].SetValue(originalEffects[i++].Texture);
```

# The Code

*All the code is available for download at www.apress.com.*

In your LoadContent method, load the model and your custom effect:

```
protected override void LoadContent()
{
    device = graphics.GraphicsDevice;
    basicEffect = new BasicEffect(device, null);
    cCross = new CoordCross(device);
```

```
    myModel = Content.Load<Model>("tank");
    modelTransforms = new Matrix[myModel.Bones.Count];
    customEffect = Content.Load<Effect>("bwcolor");
    originalEffects = ChangeEffect(ref myModel, customEffect);
}
```

The last line replaces all effects in the Model file with copies of your custom effect, which is done in this method:

```
private BasicEffect[] ChangeEffect(ref Model model, Effect newEffect)
{
    List<BasicEffect> effectList = new List<BasicEffect>();

    foreach (ModelMesh mesh in model.Meshes)
        foreach (ModelMeshPart modmeshpart in mesh.MeshParts)
        {
            BasicEffect oldEffect = (BasicEffect)modmeshpart.Effect;
            effectList.Add(oldEffect);
            modmeshpart.Effect = newEffect.Clone(device);
        }

    BasicEffect[] effects = effectList.ToArray();
    return effects;
}
```

When rendering the model, you can access the stored information like this:

```
int i = 0;
Matrix worldMatrix = Matrix.CreateScale(0.01f);
myModel.CopyAbsoluteBoneTransformsTo(modelTransforms);
foreach (ModelMesh mesh in myModel.Meshes)
{

    foreach (ModelMeshPart part in mesh.MeshParts)
    {
        Effect currentEffect = part.Effect;
                        currentEffect.Parameters["xWorld"]. ➥
        SetValue(modelTransforms[mesh.ParentBone.Index] * worldMatrix);
        currentEffect.Parameters["xView"].SetValue(fpsCam.ViewMatrix);
        currentEffect.Parameters["xProjection"].SetValue(fpsCam.ProjectionMatrix);
        currentEffect.Parameters["xTexture"].SetValue(originalEffects[i++].Texture);
    }
    mesh.Draw();
}
```

# 4-8. Visualize the Bone Structure of a Model

## The Problem

As discussed in the last part of recipe 4-1, a Model usually contains a lot of members, called ModelMeshes. The positional relations between these ModelMeshes are contained within the Bone structure of a Model object. This Bone structure defines how and where all ModelMeshes are attached to each other and how much each ModelMesh is rotated and/or scaled relative to its parent ModelMesh.

Before you can move on to making a Model come alive, you need to know which ModelMeshes are attached to which Bone, and you need to visualize the Bone structure.

## The Solution

Models are composed from ModelMeshes. These ModelMeshes contain all the data needed to render a certain part of the Model. It contains all the vertices, indices, textures, effects, and more, as you can read in the second part of recipe 4-1.

However, a ModelMesh does not contain any information about its position in the Model. For example, a frontRightDoor ModelMesh of a car Model will contain all information about the vertices and textures it requires to be drawn, but it will not include information about where it needs to be drawn relative to the center of the car.

This information is stored in the Bones collection of a Model. Each ModelMesh links to a Bone, so XNA can find out where to position the ModelMesh relative to the center of the Model. A Bone contains nothing more than a transformation matrix, holding the position of the ModelMesh relative to its parent ModelMesh. For example, the ModelMesh of the hull of the car would point to a Bone holding a 0 translation, because the hull of the car is the main part of the car. The frontRightDoor ModelMesh would link to a Bone holding a transformation storing the position of the front right door relative to the center of the car hull.

You can extend this even further. An advanced car model will also have a separate frontRightWindow ModelMesh, which will also have its own Bone to which it will link. This Bone will hold the position of the side window, relative to center of the front right door. Figure 4-11 shows a corresponding Bone structure.

I added a *B* to the end of each name to remind you that those are Bone objects. To allow such a structure, each Bone object keeps a link to its parent Bone, as well as links to all of its child Bone objects.

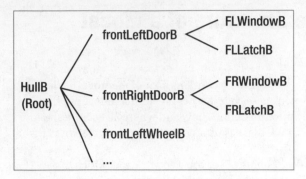

**Figure 4-11.** *Bone hierarchy in a car Model*

In this recipe, you will walk through this structure and write out all Bone objects to a file, in a similar way as shown in Figure 4-11. You'll also scroll through all ModelMeshes of the Model and indicate to which Bone they are linking.

## How It Works

Luckily, you can easily see which ModelMeshes are defined in a Model by setting a breakpoint after the line that loads the Model. You can do this by clicking the sidebar to the left of your code or by using this code:

```
myModel = Content.Load<Model>("tank");
modelTransforms = new Matrix[myModel.Bones.Count];
System.Diagnostics.Debugger.Break();
```

When you run the code, the program will halt at the last line, and in the bottom-left corner of your screen you can browse to your model and see which ModelMeshes it contains, as shown in Figure 4-12.

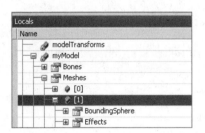

**Figure 4-12.** *Browsing through the runtime variables*

This can still be confusing and very time consuming for two reasons: for each ModelMesh you'll need to look up which Bone it links to, and you'll have to browse through the Bones collection of the Model to get an overview of the Bone hierarchy.

In this recipe, you'll write some code that generates a simple text file, containing the Bone structure as well as the ModelMesh-to-Bone relationships. This following listing is the output for the dwarf model that ships with the DirectX SDK:

```
Model Bone Information
----------------------
- Name : DXCC_ROOT
  Index: 0
    - Name : null
      Index: 1
        - Name : Drawf
          Index: 2
            - Name : Sword_new
              Index: 3
                - Name : Sword_newShape
                  Index: 4
            - Name : backpack_new
              Index: 5
                - Name : backpack_newShape
                  Index: 6
            - Name : Body1
              Index: 7
                - Name : Body1Shape
                  Index: 8
            - Name : Armor_new
              Index: 9
                - Name : Armor_newShape
                  Index: 10
            - Name : Face_gear_new
              Index: 11
                - Name : Face_gear_newShape
                  Index: 12
            - Name : Head_new
              Index: 13
                - Name : Head_newShape
                  Index: 14
        - Name : side
          Index: 15
        - Name : front
          Index: 16
        - Name : top
          Index: 17
        - Name : persp
          Index: 18
```

```
Model Mesh Information
----------------------
- ID  : 0
  Name: Sword_newShape
  Bone: Sword_newShape (4)
- ID  : 1
  Name: backpack_newShape
  Bone: backpack_newShape (6)
- ID  : 2
  Name: Body1Shape
  Bone: Body1Shape (8)
- ID  : 3
  Name: Armor_newShape
  Bone: Armor_newShape (10)
- ID  : 4
  Name: Face_gear_newShape
  Bone: Face_gear_newShape (12)
- ID  : 5
  Name: Head_newShape
  Bone: Head_newShape (14)
```

At the bottom, you see the dwarf model has six ModelMeshes, parts of the Model that you can render separately (see recipe 4-1). Each of them links to its own Bone. You see you can move the sword and backpack separately, but unfortunately it is impossible to move an arm or a leg of the dwarf, because they aren't provided as separate ModelMeshes.

Bad luck—this Model doesn't allow basic animation. Let's take a look at the structure of anther model, for example, the tank model found on the XNA Creators Club site:

```
Model Bone Information
----------------------
- Name : tank_geo
  Index: 0
    - Name : r_engine_geo
      Index: 1
        - Name : r_back_wheel_geo
          Index: 2
        - Name : r_steer_geo
          Index: 3
            - Name : r_front_wheel_geo
              Index: 4
    - Name : l_engine_geo
      Index: 5
        - Name : l_back_wheel_geo
          Index: 6
        - Name : l_steer_geo
          Index: 7
            - Name : l_front_wheel_geo
              Index: 8
```

```
           - Name : turret_geo
             Index: 9
                - Name : canon_geo
                  Index: 10
                - Name : hatch_geo
                  Index: 11


Model Mesh Information
----------------------
- ID  : 0
  Name: r_back_wheel_geo
  Bone: r_back_wheel_geo (2)
- ID  : 1
  Name: r_front_wheel_geo
  Bone: r_front_wheel_geo (4)
- ID  : 2
  Name: r_steer_geo
  Bone: r_steer_geo (3)
- ID  : 3
  Name: r_engine_geo
  Bone: r_engine_geo (1)
- ID  : 4
  Name: l_back_wheel_geo
  Bone: l_back_wheel_geo (6)
- ID  : 5
  Name: l_front_wheel_geo
  Bone: l_front_wheel_geo (8)
- ID  : 6
  Name: l_steer_geo
  Bone: l_steer_geo (7)
- ID  : 7
  Name: l_engine_geo
  Bone: l_engine_geo (5)
- ID  : 8
  Name: canon_geo
  Bone: canon_geo (10)
- ID  : 9
  Name: hatch_geo
  Bone: hatch_geo (11)
- ID  : 10
  Name: turret_geo
  Bone: turret_geo (9)
- ID  : 11
  Name: tank_geo
  Bone: tank_geo (0)
```

In this case, you see you have a different ModelMesh for almost all of the physically separate parts! You have four ModelMeshes for the wheels, two for the steering mechanisms, one for the turret, and one for the canon. Even the hatch is separately drawable. Since all ModelMeshes have their own Bones, they all can be transformed separately! You see, for example, that the ModelMesh of the canon is attached to Bone 10. Changing the matrix of Bone 10 will change the rotation or position of the canon. You'll learn more about this in the next recipe.

## Gathering the Model Information

The following method will write the Model information to a file:

```
private void WriteModelStructure(Model model)
{
    StreamWriter writer = new StreamWriter("modelStructure.txt");

    writer.WriteLine("Model Bone Information");
    writer.WriteLine("---------------------");

    ModelBone root = model.Root;
    WriteBone(root, 0, writer);

    writer.WriteLine();
    writer.WriteLine();

            writer.WriteLine("Model Mesh Information");
            writer.WriteLine("---------------------");

            foreach (ModelMesh mesh in model.Meshes)
        WriteModelMesh(model.Meshes.IndexOf(mesh), mesh, writer);

    writer.Close();
}
```

Because you'll be writing text to a file, you'll create a StreamWriter. For this to work, you will need to link to the System.IO namespace by adding this line to the very top of your code file:

```
using System.IO;
```

Next, you'll write a header to the file and call the WriteBone method for the root Bone of your Model. This method, which you'll create in two minutes, will write down the information of this Bone and pass this call on to all of its child Bone objects so all Bone objects will be written to the file.

After writing the second header to file, you scroll through all ModelMeshes of the Model and pass them to the WriteModelMesh method, which will write all information regarding the ModelMesh to file.

## WriteBone Method

This method writes the name (or null, if this hasn't been specified) as well as its index to the file. At the end, the method calls itself for each of the current Bone's child Bone objects. This way, you have to call this method only once for the root Bone of the Model, which will cause all Bone objects connected to the root Bone to be listed.

```
private void WriteBone(ModelBone bone, int level, StreamWriter writer)
{
    for (int l = 0; l < level; l++)
        writer.Write("\t");
    writer.Write("- Name : ");
    if ((bone.Name == "") || (bone.Name == "null"))
        writer.WriteLine("null");
    else
        writer.WriteLine(bone.Name);

    for (int l = 0; l < level; l++)
        writer.Write("\t");
    writer.WriteLine("  Index: " + bone.Index);

    foreach (ModelBone childBone in bone.Children)
        WriteBone(childBone, level + 1, writer);
}
```

## WriteModelMesh Method

This simple method writes the ID and name of each ModelMesh in the Model to the file and, most important, the name and ID of the Bone to which it is attached. You'll need this in the next recipe, when you'll want to animate your Model:

```
private void WriteModelMesh(int ID, ModelMesh mesh, StreamWriter writer)
{
    writer.WriteLine("- ID  : " + ID);
    writer.WriteLine("  Name: " + mesh.Name);
    writer.Write("  Bone: " + mesh.ParentBone.Name);
    writer.WriteLine(" (" + mesh.ParentBone.Index + ")");
}
```

# Usage

Simply call the WriteModelStructure method once you've loaded your Model:

```
myModel = Content.Load<Model>("tank");
modelTransforms = new Matrix[myModel.Bones.Count];
WriteModelStructure(myModel);
```

When you run this code, the structure of your `Model` will be written to the `modelStructure.txt` file, which you can find in the same map in which your `.exe` file resides. By default, this is in the `\bin\x86\Debug` map.

### The Code

*All the code is available for download at www.apress.com.*

The `WriteModelStructure`, `WriteBone`, and `WriteModelMesh` methods were all listed completely in the previous text.

# 4-9. Make the Bones Move Individually: Model Animation

## The Problem

You want to be able to move each part of a `Model` separately. For example, you want to lower the side window or rotate a wheel of a car.

## The Solution

As explained in recipe 4-1, a `Model` consists of separately drawable `ModelMeshes`. Each `ModelMesh` is attached to a `Bone`. These `Bones` are attached to each other, at the position described by their matrices.

Each `Model` has a root `Bone` to which all other `Bone` objects are connected, directly or indirectly. Figure 4-11 shows an example of such a structure.

If you apply a transformation to the root `Bone` of that image—for example, a scaling—each of its child `Bone` objects (and their child `Bone` objects) will automatically be transformed the same way. As a second example, if you add a rotation to the matrix stored in the `frontRightDoor` `Bone` of Figure 4-11, only the door itself, its window, and its latch will be rotated, which is exactly what you want.

## How It Works

Before you can animate a `Model`, you need to get an overview of the `Bone` structure of the `Model`. The previous recipe explained how you can visualize this `Bone` structure and see which `ModelMeshes` are linking to which `Bone` objects.

Let's examine the `Bone` structure of the tank found on the XNA Creators Club site. Its structure is also listed in the previous recipe. You have one root `Bone`. When you scale this `Bone`'s matrix, you will be scaling the whole tank. Next, you see, for example, the turret `Bone`, which is a child `Bone` of the root. If you rotate this `Bone`, each `ModelMesh` that links to this `Bone` or one of its child `Bone` objects will be rotated. So if you rotate the turret `Bone`'s matrix, the turret itself, the canon, and the hatch are rotated, because they are attached to the turret.

At this point, this is what you should have remembered:

- All separately drawable, and thus transformable, parts of the Model are stored as different ModelMesh objects.

- Each ModelMesh object links to a Bone object.

- Each Bone object stores the position, rotation, and scaling of the Bone relative to its parent.

- When you set a transformation to a Bone, this transformation will also be applied to all the Bone's child Bone objects.

## Necessity of the CopyAbsoluteBoneTransformsTo Method (Additional Explanation)

The property described in the last point of the previous list doesn't come for free. Before drawing each ModelMesh, you need to set its World matrix, because you want the ModelMesh to be positioned at the correct location in 3D space. The problem is that this World matrix should define where the ModelMesh should be positioned, relative to the 3D origin. However, the Bone matrix contains the position of the ModelMesh, relative to the origin of its parent ModelMesh!

The canon of the tank will once again be used as an example. The canon's Bone matrix will contain a translation, such as (0,0,–2): two units Forward relative to the origin of its parent, the tank's turret.

Imagine you simply set this matrix as the World matrix for the canon's ModelMesh. As with all translation matrices set as a World matrix, this will cause the canon ModelMesh to be rendered at the position contained in the translation matrix, relative to the (0,0,0) main 3D origin. As a result, the canon will be rendered with the (0,0,–2) as its origin.

However, this is not what you want! You want the turret's origin to be positioned at position (0,0,–2) relative to the origin of its parent, the turret.

So before drawing the canon, you need to combine its Bone with its parent's Bone (you do this by multiplying the two matrices held by the Bones). Furthermore, this needs to be forwarded up to the root node, because in this case the resulting matrix still needs to be transformed with the Bone of the turret's parent, the tank's hull. This way, you obtain a matrix containing the position of the canon's origin, relative to the root origin of the tank.

Since the matrix you eventually obtain is relative to the origin of the tank, it's called the *absolute transformation matrix* for the canon.

Luckily, XNA provides functionality for you that automates this task of combining all matrices. Before rendering the Model, you should call the CopyAbsoluteBoneTransformsTo method of the Model. This method will perform all these combinations for you and store the resulting absolute matrices in an array. These absolute matrices no longer contain transformations relative to parent Bones; they will be relative only to the very root of the Model. Hence, you can say the matrices contained in the following modelTransforms array contain the absolute transformations for all ModelMeshes of the tank.

You can use these matrices to set as absolute the World matrix for each ModelMesh of the Model:

```
myModel.CopyAbsoluteBoneTransformsTo(modelTransforms);
foreach (ModelMesh mesh in myModel.Meshes)
{
    foreach (BasicEffect effect in mesh.Effects)
    {
        effect.EnableDefaultLighting();
        effect.World = modelTransforms[mesh.ParentBone.Index];
        effect.View = fpsCam.GetViewMatrix();
        effect.Projection = fpsCam.GetProjectionMatrix();
    }
    mesh.Draw();
}
```

Although it might seem difficult, this brings a huge benefit. In case of the tank, whenever the Bone matrix of the turret is rotated, the (0,0,–2) translation matrix of the canon will also be rotated. This is because when the CopyAbsoluteBoneTransformsTo method finishes, the absolute transformation matrix of the canon's Bone will contain the rotation of its parent Bone matrix. More generally, all child ModelMeshes attached to the turret, such as the canon and the hatch, are rotated automatically once you set a rotation in the Bone matrix of the turret.

### Animating a Specific ModelMesh of the Model

Now that you know all you need to know about the structure of a Model, it's time to actually animate the Model.

In this example, you want to raise only the canon. To do this, look up the ModelMesh part of the canon using the result of the previous recipe and see which Bone it is pointing to. It is the matrix of this Bone you want to add a rotation to.

However, the matrix of that Bone holds the original position of the canon relative to its parent, the turret. If you overwrite this matrix by its rotated version, this original position will be lost (or very hard to find)! It will almost be impossible to animate the canon later, because you'll always want to start from the original matrices.

So, immediately after loading the Model, you need to make a backup of all the original Bone matrices. You want to store the matrices describing the relative position to its parent, so you use the CopyBoneTransformsTo method:

```
Matrix[] originalTransforms = new Matrix[myModel.Bones.Count];
myModel.CopyBoneTransformsTo(originalTransforms);
```

---

■**Note**  For each ModelMesh, you want to store the positions relative to the parent ModelMesh, so you use the CopyBoneTransformsTo method. The CopyAbsoluteBoneTransformsTo method gives you the positions relative to the origin of the Model, as explained in the "Necessity of the CopyAbsoluteBoneTrans-formsTo Method (Additional Explanation)" section earlier.

---

You should place this code in the LoadContent method.

With the original relative matrices stored, you're safe to overwrite the matrices stored in the Bone objects. Add a canonRot variable to your project:

```
float canonRot = 0;
```

And let the user adjust it in the Update method:

```
if (keyState.IsKeyDown(Keys.U))
    canonRot -= 0.05f;
if (keyState.IsKeyDown(Keys.D))
    canonRot += 0.05f;
```

Now that you can control this variable by using the keyboard, put this line in the Draw method, at the line before you calculate the absolute matrices of the Model:

```
Matrix newCanonMat = Matrix.CreateRotationX(canonRot) * originalTransforms[10];
myModel.Bones[10].Transform = newCanonMat;
```

As you can see in the structure of the tank Model listed in the previous recipe, the ModelMesh of the turret points to Bone 10. This code will take the matrix holding the original position of the canon, relative to its parent (the turret), rotate it along the Right vector (to rotate it up/down), and store the combined matrix in the Model. When you run the code at this point, the canon will move up/down corresponding to your keyboard input.

If you want to rotate the whole turret, you need to do the same for the turret's Bone matrix. First add a turretRot variable to your project:

```
float turretRot = 0;
```

Next make it controllable through the keyboard in your Update method:

```
if (keyState.IsKeyDown(Keys.L))
    turretRot += 0.05f;
if (keyState.IsKeyDown(Keys.R))
    turretRot -= 0.05f;
```

And adjust the matrix of the corresponding Bone in the Draw method:

```
Matrix newTurretMat = Matrix.CreateRotationY(turretRot) * originalTransforms[9];
myModel.Bones[9].Transform = newTurretMat;
```

As you can see in the previous Model structure, the Bone corresponding to the turret's ModelMesh has index 9. You first retrieve its original matrix. Next, you rotate the original matrix along the Up y-axis to make it turn left/right, and you set this new matrix as the active matrix for the Bone.

---

**■Note** It doesn't matter whether you change the turret's matrix after you change the canon matrix, or vice versa. The relations between the Bone objects are stored in the absolute matrices only once you call the CopyAbsoluteBoneTransformsTo method.

---

As explained in the previous section of this recipe, by rotating the turret, all of its children (in this case, the hatch and the canon) are also rotated because the Bone matrix of the turret is combined with the matrices of its child Bone objects by the CopyAbsoluteBoneTransformsTo method.

## The Code

*All the code is available for download at* www.apress.com.

After loading the model, you need to make sure you save the original Bone matrices:

```
protected override void LoadContent()
{
    device = graphics.GraphicsDevice;
    basicEffect = new BasicEffect(device, null);
    cCross = new CoordCross(device);


    myModel = Content.Load<Model>("tank");
    modelTransforms = new Matrix[myModel.Bones.Count];
    originalTransforms = new Matrix[myModel.Bones.Count];
    myModel.CopyBoneTransformsTo(originalTransforms);
}
```

During the update phase, you should allow the rotation angles to be changed. You can do this based on the time or on the user input, as shown in this example:

```
KeyboardState keyState = Keyboard.GetState();
if (keyState.IsKeyDown(Keys.U))
    canonRot -= 0.05f;
if (keyState.IsKeyDown(Keys.D))
    canonRot += 0.05f;
if (keyState.IsKeyDown(Keys.L))
    turretRot += 0.05f;
if (keyState.IsKeyDown(Keys.R))
    turretRot -= 0.05f;
```

Finally, before you draw your Model, you should overwrite the original Bone matrices by their rotated version and construct the absolute Bone matrices. These matrices must be used as the active World matrix of each ModelMesh:

```
protected override void Draw(GameTime gameTime)
{
    device.Clear(ClearOptions.Target | ClearOptions.DepthBuffer, ➥
    Color.CornflowerBlue, 1, 0);

    cCross.Draw(fpsCam.ViewMatrix, fpsCam.ProjectionMatrix);
```

```
//draw model
Matrix newCanonMat = Matrix.CreateRotationX(canonRot) * originalTransforms[10];
myModel.Bones[10].Transform = newCanonMat;

Matrix newTurretMat = Matrix.CreateRotationY(turretRot) * originalTransforms[9];
myModel.Bones[9].Transform = newTurretMat;

Matrix worldMatrix = Matrix.CreateScale(0.01f, 0.01f, 0.01f);
myModel.CopyAbsoluteBoneTransformsTo(modelTransforms);
foreach (ModelMesh mesh in myModel.Meshes)
{
    foreach (BasicEffect effect in mesh.Effects)
    {
        effect.EnableDefaultLighting();
        effect.World = modelTransforms[mesh.ParentBone.Index] * worldMatrix;
        effect.View = fpsCam.ViewMatrix;
        effect.Projection = fpsCam.ProjectionMatrix;
    }

    mesh.Draw();
}

base.Draw(gameTime);
}
```

# 4-10. Use BoundingSpheres for Basic Model Collision Detection

## The Problem

You want to check whether two Models collide. If you have many Models in your scene, you cannot afford to perform a detailed, per-triangle check. You want to start with a fast way to check for possible collisions and run finer checks afterward.

## The Solution

When performing a collision check, you'll always find yourself making a trade-off between speed and accuracy. In most cases, you'll want to settle for a combination of checks. During a first pass, you'll want to scan all of your objects for possible collisions using a very fast check and afterward perform detailed tests only for those objects that responded positively on the quick check.

This recipe demonstrates two fast ways to check for possible collisions between two models.

The fastest way is to find the two global BoundingSpheres of the Models and check whether they intersect by calling the Intersect method on one of the spheres.

You can extend this a bit to improve accuracy. Models consist of several ModelMeshes, which store the geometrical information about the different parts of the Model. Each of these ModelMeshes can generate its own BoundingSphere, so you can perform a collision check between each of the BoundingSpheres of the first Model and each of the BoundingSpheres of the second Model. Obviously, this higher accuracy comes at a higher calculating cost.

## How It Works

### Fastest Check

This approach will use the BoundingSphere surrounding the whole Model. If these BoundingSpheres of the two Models intersect, it is possible that both Models collide.

In some cases, this can give very bad results, such as in a skiing game where you want to detect the collision between the two skis of a player. The sphere of a ski is huge in comparison to the ski itself; the ski will occupy less than 1 percent of the volume of the sphere. This check will classify all objects inside the globe (such as the other ski!) as colliding, as illustrated in Figure 4-13.

Nonetheless, this method is used very frequently as the first check because of its speed. It would be a shame to waste processing power to check for collisions between two Models of which the global BoundingSpheres don't even collide.

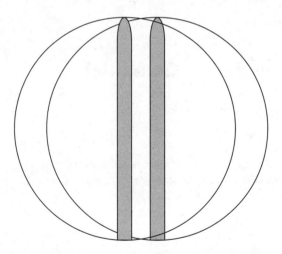

**Figure 4-13.** *Each ski is inside the other's BoundingSphere.*

To perform this fast check, start by loading the Models and generating their global BoundingSphere as explained in recipe 4-5. This BoundingSphere will be stored in the Tag property of the Model:

```
myModel = XNAUtils.LoadModelWithBoundingSphere(ref modelTransforms, ➡
"tank", Content);
```

This BoundingSphere will contain the center of the Model (which doesn't need to be the (0,0,0) point of the Model) as well as its radius.

When you render both Models, you need a different World matrix for each of the Models to have them moved (and/or scaled/rotated) to their correct position in the 3D world. When you move (and/or scale) a model, you also need to move the center (and/or scale the radius) of its BoundingSphere. You can do this using the TransformBoundingSphere of my XNAUtils file. The method takes a BoundingSphere as well as a World matrix. It moves the center and scales the radius of the sphere according to the matrix, and the resulting sphere is returned.

All you need to do to check for a collision between two Models is transform each of the BoundingSpheres by the World matrix of the corresponding Model and check whether the transformed BoundingSpheres intersect.

```
private bool ModelsCollide1(Model model1, Matrix world1, Model model2, ➥
Matrix world2)
{
    BoundingSphere origSphere1 = (BoundingSphere)model1.Tag;
    BoundingSphere sphere1 = XNAUtils.TransformBoundingSphere(origSphere1, world1);

    BoundingSphere origSphere2 = (BoundingSphere)model2.Tag;
    BoundingSphere sphere2 = XNAUtils.TransformBoundingSphere(origSphere2, world2);

    bool collision = sphere1.Intersects(sphere2);
    return collision;
}
```

Because the Tag property of a Model can really contain anything (the Object class is the very root class in C#), you need to tell your compiler in this case that it contains a BoundingSphere by performing a cast. If the transformed BoundingSpheres collide, the method returns true.

## More Accurate, a Bit Slower

Each Model consists of multiple members, of which the geometrical data is stored in the Meshes collection of the Model as explained in recipe 4-1. Each such ModelMesh can generate its own BoundingSphere. The total volume of all these small BoundingSpheres will be much smaller than the volume of the global BoundingSphere of the Model. This is displayed in Figure 4-14. On the right part of that image you can see the separate BoundingSpheres for all parts of the Model.

*v1*

**Figure 4-14.** *Global BoundingSphere vs. multiple smaller BoundingSpheres*

On the left of the image, both BoundingSpheres collide, so the first check would indicate a collision between the Models. On the other hand, none of the BoundingSpheres on the right collide, so this check will correctly indicate that both Models don't collide. The second approach will often give a better result; however, the first case requires only one check, while the second requires (members inside Model1)*(members inside Model2) checks.

This method detects collisions according to the second case:

```
private bool FinerCheck(Model model1, Matrix world1, Model model2, Matrix world2)
{
    if (CoarseCheck(model1, world1, model2, world2) == false)
        return false;

    bool collision = false;
    Matrix[] model1Transforms = new Matrix[model1.Bones.Count];
    Matrix[] model2Transforms = new Matrix[model2.Bones.Count];
    model1.CopyAbsoluteBoneTransformsTo(model1Transforms);
    model2.CopyAbsoluteBoneTransformsTo(model2Transforms);

    foreach (ModelMesh mesh1 in model1.Meshes)
    {
        BoundingSphere origSphere1 = mesh1.BoundingSphere;
        Matrix trans1 = model1Transforms[mesh1.ParentBone.Index] * world1;
        BoundingSphere transSphere1 = ➥
        XNAUtils.TransformBoundingSphere(origSphere1, trans1);

        foreach (ModelMesh mesh2 in model2.Meshes)
        {
            BoundingSphere origSphere2 = mesh2.BoundingSphere;
            Matrix trans2 = model2Transforms[mesh2.ParentBone.Index] * world2;
            BoundingSphere transSphere2 = ➥
            XNAUtils.TransformBoundingSphere(origSphere2, trans2);
```

```
            if (transSphere1.Intersects(transSphere2))
                collision = true;
        }
    }
    return collision;
}
```

You start by performing the fast check. If this check returns false, there is definitely no need to perform the finer check.

If the coarse check indicated a possible collision, you move on. You first set the collision variable to false, which will stay like this until you encounter a collision. Because you'll need to move each small BoundingSphere to its correct location in the Model, you'll need the absolute Bone matrices for both Models.

To perform the check, for each ModelMesh of the first Model, you transform its BoundingSphere to its absolute position in the 3D world. To do this, you need to take into account both the position of the BoundingSphere in the Model and the position of the Model in the 3D world.

Next, you scroll through all parts of Model2 and transform these BoundingSpheres to their absolute position in the 3D world.

For each BoundingSphere of Model1, you check whether there's a collision with any BoundingSphere of Model2, and if there is a collision, you set the collision variable to true.

In the end, the collision variable will indicate whether at least one of the BoundingSpheres of Model1 collided with one of the BoundingSpheres of Model2, so you return this variable.

## Optimization

Because for each part of Model1, all BoundingSpheres of Model2 are transformed each time the same way, this method can obviously be optimized. For example, you can do this by first transforming the BoundingSpheres of Model1 and Model2 once, at the beginning of the method, and storing them in an array. After this, you can simply check for collisions between these transformed BoundingSpheres.

This is what's done in the next version of the FinerCheck method:

```
private bool FinerCheck(Model model1, Matrix world1, Model model2, Matrix world2)
{
    if (CoarseCheck(model1, world1, model2, world2) == false)
        return false;

    Matrix[] model1Transforms = new Matrix[model1.Bones.Count];
    model1.CopyAbsoluteBoneTransformsTo(model1Transforms);
    BoundingSphere[] model1Spheres = ➥
    new BoundingSphere[model1.Meshes.Count];
    for (int i=0; i<model1.Meshes.Count; i++)
    {
        ModelMesh mesh = model1.Meshes[i];
        BoundingSphere origSphere = mesh.BoundingSphere;
```

```
        Matrix trans = model1Transforms[mesh.ParentBone.Index] * world1;
        BoundingSphere transSphere = ➥
        XNAUtils.TransformBoundingSphere(origSphere, trans);
        model1Spheres[i] = transSphere;
    }

    Matrix[] model2Transforms = new Matrix[model2.Bones.Count];
    model2.CopyAbsoluteBoneTransformsTo(model2Transforms);
    BoundingSphere[] model2Spheres = new BoundingSphere[model2.Meshes.Count];
    for (int i = 0; i < model1.Meshes.Count; i++)
    {
        ModelMesh mesh = model2.Meshes[i];
        BoundingSphere origSphere = mesh.BoundingSphere;
        Matrix trans = model2Transforms[mesh.ParentBone.Index] * world2;
        BoundingSphere transSphere = ➥
        XNAUtils.TransformBoundingSphere(origSphere, trans);
        model2Spheres[i] = transSphere;
    }

    bool collision = false;
    for (int i=0; i<model1Spheres.Length; i++)
        for (int j = 0; j < model2Spheres.Length; j++)
            if (model1Spheres[i].Intersects(model2Spheres[j]))
                return true;

    return collision;
}
```

---

**■Note** The CopyAbsoluteBoneTransformsTo method should ideally be called only once after the Bone matrices of a Model have been updated.

---

## The Code

*All the code is available for download at www.apress.com.*

Both the CoarseCheck and FinerCheck methods were listed in one piece earlier. The following Draw method defines two World matrices to position two Models at separate locations. As time goes on, one Model approaches the other. If a collision is detected between them, the background flashes red:

```
protected override void Draw(GameTime gameTime)
{
    //define World matrices
    float time = (float)gameTime.TotalGameTime.TotalMilliseconds / 1000.0f;
    Matrix worldM1 = Matrix.CreateScale(0.01f) * ➥
    Matrix.CreateRotationY(MathHelper.PiOver2) * ➥
    Matrix.CreateTranslation(-10, 0, 0);
    Matrix worldM2 = Matrix.CreateScale(0.01f) * ➥
    Matrix.CreateRotationY(-MathHelper.PiOver2) * ➥
    Matrix.CreateTranslation(10, 3, 0);
    worldM2 = worldM2 * Matrix.CreateTranslation(-time * 3.0f, 0, 0);

    //check for collision
    if (FinerCheck(myModel, worldM1, myModel, worldM2))
    {
        Window.Title = "Collision!!";
        device.Clear(ClearOptions.Target | ClearOptions.DepthBuffer, ➥
        Color.Red, 1, 0);
    }
    else
    {
        Window.Title = "No collision ...";
        device.Clear(ClearOptions.Target | ➥
        ClearOptions.DepthBuffer, Color.CornflowerBlue, 1, 0);
    }

    //render scene
    cCross.Draw(fpsCam.ViewMatrix, fpsCam.ProjectionMatrix);

    DrawModel(myModel, worldM1, modelTransforms);
    DrawModel(myModel, worldM2, modelTransforms);

    base.Draw(gameTime);
}
```

# 4-11. Use Ray-Traced Collision Detection for Small/Fast Objects

## The Problem

Most collision detection approaches will detect collisions only if both objects are physically colliding. However, if you have a small object going very fast through an object, chances are your program does not update fast enough to detect this collision.

As a far too detailed example, consider a bullet shot at a bottle. The bullet will travel at a speed of 5000 km/h toward the bottle, which is only 15 cm wide (that will already be a 1.5 L bottle). Your XNA program updates 60 times each second, so between each update of your program the bullet has traveled 23 meters, as you can learn from this formula:

$$\frac{5000\frac{km}{h}+1000\frac{m}{km}}{3600\frac{sec}{h}+60\frac{updates}{sec}}=23\frac{m}{update}$$

This means there's almost no chance the bullet and the bottle will collide the moment your Update method is called, even when the bullet went straight through your bottle during the last frame.

## The Solution

You can create a Ray between the previous and current positions of the bullet. Next, you can check whether this Ray collides with the BoundingSphere of your object by calling the Intersect method of the Ray or BoundingSphere.

If they collide, the method returns the distance between the collision and the definition point of your Ray (for which you can use the previous position of the bullet). You can use this distance to check whether the collision actually happened between the previous and current positions of the bullet.

## How It Works

This approach requires the global BoundingSphere of a Model to be stored in its Tag property, as explained in recipe 4-5:

```
myModel = XNAUtils.LoadModelWithBoundingSphere(ref modelTransforms, ➥
"tank", Content);
```

You will create a method that receives a Model, its World matrix, and the previous and current positions of the fast object. The model will return whether both objects have collided between the current and previous frames.

```
private bool RayCollision(Model model, Matrix world, ➥
Vector3 lastPosition, Vector3 currentPosition)
{
    BoundingSphere modelSpere = (BoundingSphere)model.Tag;
    BoundingSphere transSphere = TransformBoundingSphere(modelSpere, world);
}
```

First you need to move the BoundingSphere of the Model to the current location of the Model in 3D space. You do this by transforming the BoundingSphere by the World matrix of the Model (as in the previous recipe).

**■Note** If you want to scale the `Model` down before it is rendered to the scene, the scaling transformation will also be contained inside the World matrix. This will cause the previous code to scale the `BoundingSphere` correctly.

Next, you want to find the direction the fast object is going, as well as the distance it covered since the last frame:

```
Vector3 direction = currentPosition - lastPosition;
float distanceCovered = direction.Length();
direction.Normalize();
```

As always, you can find the direction from point A to point B by subtracting A from B. You find the distance between them by calling the `Length` method on this direction. When working with directions, you'll usually want to normalize them so their length becomes 1. Because of this, you need to make sure you normalize after you've stored its length; otherwise, the length will always be 1.

Now that you know one point of the `Ray` as well as its direction, you're ready to create the `Ray`. You want to do this so you can use its `Intersect` method to detect collisions with the `BoundingSphere` of the slow `Model`.

```
Ray ray = new Ray(lastPosition, direction);
```

Now that you have the `Ray` of the bullet, you're ready to finish the method:

```
bool collision = false;
float? intersection = ray.Intersects(transSphere);
if (intersection != null)
    if (intersection <= distanceCovered)
        collision = true;

return collision;
```

First you define a variable `collision`, which will stay `false` unless the fast and slow objects collide. At the end of the method, this variable is returned.

You call the `Intersect` method on the ray and pass it the transformed `BoundingSphere` of the slow `Model`.

The intersection method is a little special. In case of an intersection, it returns the distance between the intersection point and the point used to define the `Ray`. However, if the `Ray` and the sphere don't collide, the method returns null. Hence, you need a `float?` variable instead of a `float`, because it needs to be capable of storing the `null` value.

**■Note** If the collision point is positioned behind the point you used to define the ray, the method also returns `null`. Because of the direction you specified while creating the ray, XNA knows which side of the ray is in front of or behind the point.

If there is a collision between the ray and the sphere and the collision point is in front of the lastPosition point, the intersection will not be null. To verify the collision happened between the previous and the current frame, you check whether the distance between the collision point and the previous position of the fast object is smaller than the distance the object has traveled during the last frame. If this is the case, the fast object has collided with the Model during the last frame.

### More Accurate Approaches

As explained in the previous recipe, because of the use of a BoundingSphere, this approach can detect collisions even if there is no collision in reality.

Again, you can increase accuracy by performing the ray-sphere collision on the smaller BoundingSpheres of the different ModelMeshes of the Model.

### Large and Fast Objects

The approach described previously checks for collision, assuming the fast object is very small, much like a single point in 3D space. This is usually OK, but in cases when the fast object is too large to be modeled as a point, you'll need to represent the fast object as a BoundingSphere. One solution is to perform multiple ray checks based on different points of the BoundingSphere of the fast object, but this gets quite complex.

A faster and much simpler way is to add the radius of the fast object to the radius of the slow object, as shown in Figure 4-15. The figure shows two objects that are on the rim of collision. If you add the small radius to the large radius, the result will be the same. Using this approach, you can again represent the fast object by a single point and use the approach discussed earlier.

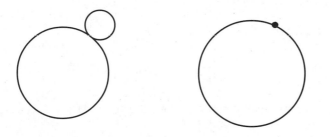

**Figure 4-15.** *Enlarging the BoundingSphere yields the same result.*

# The Code

*All the code is available for download at www.apress.com.*

After loading the slow Model, you'll need to store its BoundingSphere inside its Tag property:

```
protected override void LoadContent()
{
    device = graphics.GraphicsDevice;
    basicEffect = new BasicEffect(device, null);
    cCross = new CoordCross(device);

    myModel = XNAUtils.LoadModelWithBoundingSphere(ref ➥
    modelTransforms, "tank", Content);
}
```

Now that you have the sphere, you can call this method, which will indicate whether a collision has occurred during the last frame:

```
private bool RayCollision(Model model, Matrix world, ➥
Vector3 lastPosition, Vector3 currentPosition)
{
    BoundingSphere modelSpere = (BoundingSphere)model.Tag;
    BoundingSphere transSphere = ➥
    XNAUtils.TransformBoundingSphere(modelSpere, world);

    Vector3 direction = currentPosition - lastPosition;
    float distanceCovered = direction.Length();
    direction.Normalize();

    Ray ray = new Ray(lastPosition, direction);

    bool collision = false;
    float? intersection = ray.Intersects(transSphere);
    if (intersection != null)
        if (intersection <= distanceCovered)
            collision = true;

    return collision;
}
```

# 4-12. Extend the Model Content Processor to Load Custom Effects (Clean Approach)

## The Problem

Instead of changing the effects of a Model at runtime, you want to do this using a custom content processor. This way, the Model is loaded correctly into your XNA project, and you don't have to keep track of all textures and other information contained in the original effects during runtime.

---

**Note** If you're looking for an introduction to extending the default Model processor, it might be better to start with the next recipe instead of this one.

---

## The Solution

Extend the default Model processor and override the ConvertMaterial method, which is called for each MaterialContent encountered in the Model. Override it to deviate all MaterialContent information to a custom material processor.

In this custom material processor, you will create an empty material object from which to start. This allows you to link an effect of your choice to this object. You will also copy any textures from the original MaterialContent into the new object and have the opportunity to set values for all HLSL variables of the effect.

## How It Works

Because this comes down to extending a default content processor, make sure you've read the introduction to the content pipeline in recipe 3-9. Start by creating a new content pipeline project, as explained in detail in the section "Checklist for Extending a Content Processor Using an Object of a Custom Class" of that recipe.

In this case, you will extend the default Model processor, as you can see in Figure 4-16. When the default ModelImporter reads a Model file from disk and creates a NodeContent object, it saves the effects it encounters inside MaterialContent objects. Your extended Model processor will make only some changes to these MaterialContent objects, stored inside the NodeContent. The rest of the NodeContent object will remain untouched.

---

**Note** If you compare Figure 4-15 to Figure 3-6, you can verify that you're also extending the processor. However, because the processor is dealing with Models instead of textures, the input and output will be different, as indicated in both images.

---

By extending the Process method, you gain full control of the contents of the Model object, before it is loaded into your XNA project. In this case, you want to hijack the way the materials inside the Models are processed, because effects are stored inside the material information. So in step 4 of the checklist presented in recipe 4-9, inside your custom Model processor class, you don't have to override the Process method as shown in that example, but the ConvertMaterial method. This method is called by the default Process method each time a material is encountered in the Model that needs loading.

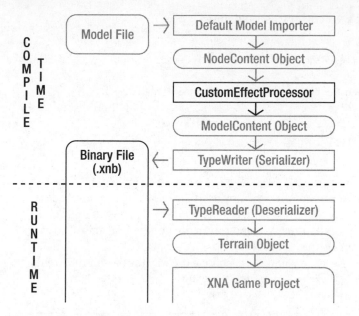

**Figure 4-16.** *Custom Model processor in the content pipeline*

So, replace the dummy `Process` method you see in your new file with this one:

```
[ContentProcessor]
public class ModelCustomEffectProcessor : ModelProcessor
{
    protected override MaterialContent ➡
    ConvertMaterial(MaterialContent material, ➡
    ContentProcessorContext context)
    {
        return context.Convert<MaterialContent, ➡
        MaterialContent>(material, ➡
        "MaterialCustomEffectProcessor");
    }
}
```

This will create a `ModelCustomEffectProcessor` class that you can select from your drop-down list when importing a `Model` file to process it. This processor will process the geometrical information the same way as the default `ModelProcessor` would, because you are overriding only the `ConvertMaterial` method that is called every time a material is encountered in the `Model`. In the `ConvertMaterial` method, you indicate that the materials should be processed by the `MaterialCustomEffectProcessor`, which you'll define now.

After your `ModelCustomEffectProcessor` class, add this class:

```
[ContentProcessor]
public class MaterialCustomEffectProcessor : MaterialProcessor
{
    public override MaterialContent Process(MaterialContent input, ➥
    ContentProcessorContext context)
    {
        return base.Process(input, context);
    }
}
```

As its attribute indicates, it's a content processor by itself. Instead of processing `Models` or textures, it can process materials. By inheriting from the `MaterialProcessor`, you indicate it will receive a `MaterialContent` as input, process it, and return the updated `MaterialContent`.

This time, you'll want to override the `Process` method of your `MaterialCustomEffectProcessor`, because you want to change the way the `MaterialContent` object is processed.

---

**■Note** In the `ModelCustomEffectProcessor` class, you've overridden the way all `MaterialContent` objects encountered in the `NodeObject` are handled. Similar to this, since textures and effects are stored in `MaterialContent` objects, you can change the way `EffectContent` and `TextureContent` objects are handled by overriding the `BuildEffect` or `BuildTexture` method inside your `MaterialCustomEffectProcessor` class, respectively.

---

For now, the `Process` method simply calls the `Process` method of its base class, the default `MaterialProcessor`, to do its job. Of course, you'll want to change this so you can influence how the `MaterialContent` is processed. For now, change the contents of the `Process` method to this:

```
EffectMaterialContent myMaterial = new EffectMaterialContent();

string map = Path.GetDirectoryName(input.Identity.SourceFilename);
string effectFile = Path.Combine(map, "colorchannels.fx");
myMaterial.Effect = new ExternalReference<EffectContent>(effectFile);
```

This will create an empty `EffectMaterialContent` object and will store a link to an effect file of your choice in it. You do this by first finding the map where the `Model` is stored and then appending the name of your effect file to it. When the compiler reaches this line, it will add the effect to the list of assets that need to be loaded. This will result in the effect being automatically loaded using the default `EffectProcessor` of the XNA Framework; all you have to do is make sure the effect file is stored in the same directory as the model.

Most models carry textures, which you need to transfer from the original MaterialContent object to the new one. The effect used in this example samples color from a texture, called xTexture, and allows you to set the strength of the red, green, and blue color components individually.

Most models come with only one texture per effect, while others use multiple textures (for example, a bump map, as explained in recipe 5-14). Unrelated to the number of textures used by the original effect, this code will feed only the last texture to the xTexture variable of my sample effect, but the code shows you how you can scroll through multiple textures. You can access the Textures collection of the original effect and bind these textures to HLSL texture variables of your custom effect:

```
if (input.Textures != null)
    foreach (string key in input.Textures.Keys)
        myMaterial.Textures.Add("xTexture", input.Textures[key]);
```

If you feel the need to adjust some of the HLSL parameters while loading the Model, this is how to do it:

```
myMaterial.OpaqueData.Add("xRedIntensity", 1.1f);
myMaterial.OpaqueData.Add("xGreenIntensity", 0.8f);
myMaterial.OpaqueData.Add("xBlueIntensity", 0.8f);
```

■**Note** Inside this sample HLSL effect file, the red, green, and blue color components of each pixel are multiplied by these variables. These settings will strengthen the red component while weakening the other components, rendering the model as if it were the sunset. This is also useful as a simple post-processing effect!

Finally, you have to return this newly created MaterialContent. You can try to return it as it is, but it's better to pass this object to the default MaterialProcessor, which will make sure any errors it contains (such as some required fields you didn't specify) are corrected. You can do this by calling the base.Process class or using the more general call shown here. Both have the same effect.

```
return context.Convert<MaterialContent, MaterialContent>(myMaterial, ➥
"MaterialProcessor");
```

This line searches for a processor called MaterialProcessor that accepts a MaterialContent object as input and produces another MaterialContent object. The newly created MaterialObject is passed as input. A polished MaterialObject is returned and will be stored in the Model you receive in your XNA application.

■**Note** Compare this line to the last line of your ConvertMaterial method defined earlier.

## Using the Custom Effect

Import a model into your XNA project, and select your new `ModelCustomEffectProcessor` to process it, as shown in Figure 4-17 (make sure you don't select the `MaterialCustomEffectProcessor`, because this is also shown in the list).

**Figure 4-17.** *Selecting your custom Model processor*

Load it the usual way, in your `LoadContent` method:

```
myModel = content.Load<Model>("tank");
modelTransforms = new Matrix[myModel.Bones.Count];
```

Your model will now contain the effect you specified! When it comes to drawing your model, you can use much cleaner code to set the parameters specific to your effect:

```
myModel.CopyAbsoluteBoneTransformsTo(modelTransforms);
foreach (ModelMesh mesh in myModel.Meshes)
{
    foreach (Effect effect in mesh.Effects)
    {
        effect.Parameters["xWorld"]. ➥
        SetValue(modelTransforms[mesh.ParentBone.Index]);
        effect.Parameters["xView"].SetValue(fpsCam.GetViewMatrix());
        effect.Parameters["xProjection"].SetValue(fpsCam.GetProjectionMatrix());

        effect.Parameters["xRedIntensity"].SetValue(1.2f);
    }
    mesh.Draw();
}
```

This results in a much clearer approach than the one shown in recipe 4-7.

## The Code

*All the code is available for download at www.apress.com.*

First, you indicate you want each MaterialContent object encountered in your Model to be processed by MaterialCustomEffectProcessor, your own material processor. Of course, you also need to define this custom material processor.

```
namespace ModelCustEffectPipeline
{
    [ContentProcessor]
    public class ModelCustomEffectProcessor : ModelProcessor
    {
        protected override MaterialContent ➥
        ConvertMaterial(MaterialContent material, ➥
        ContentProcessorContext context)
        {
            return context.Convert<MaterialContent, ➥
            MaterialContent>(material, ➥
            "MaterialCustomEffectProcessor");
        }
    }


    [ContentProcessor]
    public class MaterialCustomEffectProcessor : MaterialProcessor
    {
        public override MaterialContent Process(MaterialContent ➥
        input, ContentProcessorContext context)
        {
            EffectMaterialContent myMaterial = new EffectMaterialContent();

            string map = Path.GetDirectoryName(input.Identity.SourceFilename);
            string effectFile = Path.Combine(map, "colorchannels.fx");
            myMaterial.Effect = new ExternalReference<EffectContent>(effectFile);

            if (input.Textures != null)
                foreach (string key in input.Textures.Keys)
                    myMaterial.Textures.Add("xTexture", input.Textures[key]);

            myMaterial.OpaqueData.Add("xRedIntensity", 1.1f);
            myMaterial.OpaqueData.Add("xGreenIntensity", 0.8f);
            myMaterial.OpaqueData.Add("xBlueIntensity", 0.8f);

            return context.Convert<MaterialContent, ➥
            MaterialContent>(myMaterial, "MaterialProcessor");
        }
    }
}
```

Next, import your Model into your XNA project, select your custom Model processor to process it, and load it into a variable:

```
protected override void LoadContent()
{
    device = graphics.GraphicsDevice;
    basicEffect = new BasicEffect(device, null);
    cCross = new CoordCross(device);

    myModel = Content.Load<Model>("tank");
    modelTransforms = new Matrix[myModel.Bones.Count];
}
```

When this executes, the Model will have your custom effect loaded. This allows you to immediately set the parameters of the effect before rendering:

```
protected override void Draw(GameTime gameTime)
{
    device.Clear(ClearOptions.Target | ClearOptions.DepthBuffer, ➥
    Color.CornflowerBlue, 1, 0);

    cCross.Draw(fpsCam.ViewMatrix, fpsCam.ProjectionMatrix);

    //draw model
    Matrix worldMatrix = Matrix.CreateScale(0.01f, 0.01f, 0.01f);
    myModel.CopyAbsoluteBoneTransformsTo(modelTransforms);
    foreach (ModelMesh mesh in myModel.Meshes)
    {
        foreach (Effect effect in mesh.Effects)
        {
            effect.Parameters["xWorld"]. ➥
            SetValue(modelTransforms[mesh.ParentBone.Index] * worldMatrix);
            effect.Parameters["xView"].SetValue(fpsCam.ViewMatrix);
            effect.Parameters["xProjection"].SetValue(fpsCam.ProjectionMatrix);

            effect.Parameters["xRedIntensity"].SetValue(1.2f);
        }
        mesh.Draw();
    }

    base.Draw(gameTime);
}
```

# 4-13. Gain Direct Access to Vertex Position Data by Extending the Model Processor

## The Problem

In your XNA project, you want to have access to the position of each vertex inside your Model during runtime. This can be required if you need to do some very precise collision detection or if you want to find certain points of your Model.

Although you can access the VertexBuffer of your Model from your regular XNA code, this approach requires a lot of clumsy code and slows down your application because the vertex data needs to be transferred from your graphics card to your main system memory.

## The Solution

Extend the default Model processor by extracting the data you want and saving this into the polyvalent Tag property of the Model. During this recipe, you will code a custom Model processor that creates an array, containing three Vector3s for each triangle of your Model, and stores this array inside the Tag property of the Model. Because this processor is only an extension of the default Model processor, you can use the default Model importer and TypeWriter, as shown in Figure 4-18.

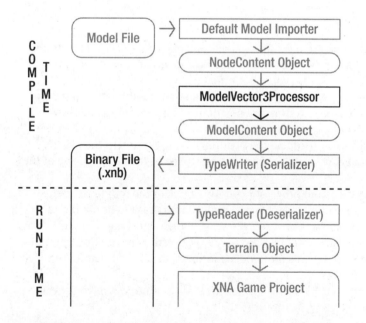

**Figure 4-18.** *Extended Model processor in the content pipeline*

## How It Works

Start by adding a custom pipeline project to your solution, as explained in the section "Check-list for Extending a Content Processor Using an Object of a Custom Class" in recipe 4-15, and give your content project a fancy name.

When it comes to defining your custom processor in step 4 of that recipe, inherit from the default ModelProcessor. Because you want to change something to the Model object itself (you need to store something in its Tag property), you want to override the Process method:

```
[ContentProcessor]
public class ModelVector3Processor : ModelProcessor
{
    public override ModelContent Process(NodeContent input, ➥
    ContentProcessorContext context)
    {
        ModelContent usualModel = base.Process(input, context);

        List<Vector3> vertices = new List<Vector3>();
        vertices = AddVerticesToList(input, vertices);
        usualModel.Tag = vertices.ToArray();

        return usualModel;
    }
}
```

This processor first passes its input to the Process method of its base class, the default ModelProcessor, to do its work. This will result in a default ModelContent object, ready to be serialized into a binary file and loaded into your XNA project.

However, before you return this object, you want to add some custom stuff to it. You start by creating a list that you will use to store the positions of all vertices inside the model. In the next paragraph, you will create the AddVerticesToList method, which will browse through the whole Model structure and add all the positions it encounters to the list. This list is returned, shaped into an array, and this array will be stored in the Tag property of the ModelContent object.

The "input" variable of your custom processor contains a link to the root node of the Model. Next to geometrical and material data, this node will contain links to its child nodes, and so on, until the whole Model has been covered. If you want to create a method that saves all vertices inside a model to the list, it will first have to save the vertices inside the root node and then call itself on all child nodes of this root node, and so on, until all vertices of the Model have been saved into the list.

This is exactly what's being done by the AddVerticesToList method, which you should add inside your ModelVector3Processor class:

```
private List<Vector3> AddVerticesToList(NodeContent node, List<Vector3> vertList)
{
    MeshContent mesh = node as MeshContent;
    if (mesh != null)
    {
        //This node contains vertices, add them to the list
    }

    foreach (NodeContent child in node.Children)
        vertList = AddVerticesToList(child, vertList);

    return vertList;
}
```

A node doesn't have to contain vertices. Sometimes a node serves only as a parent to two or more child nodes, without containing any actual vertex data. This means you should first check whether the node can be cast to a MeshContent object, which would mean it contains vertices. The as keyword tries to perform that cast, but if unsuccessful, the resulting object (mesh, in this case) will contain null. So if the program enters the if block, the cast to a MeshContent object was possible, so you're sure the node contains geometrical data. And of course you want to store these vertices to your list.

---

■**Note**  A node containing no vertex information will simply result in a Bone in the Model object that you receive in your main XNA project. A node that does contain geometrical information will result in both a Bone as well as a ModelMesh that links to this Bone (actually, a ModelMeshPart instead of a ModelMesh).

---

After all vertices of the current node have been stored, you need to call the same method on all child nodes (if any) of the current node so your code crawls through the whole structure of the Model.

Add the code that extracts all positional information from the node and adds it to the list. This code should be put inside the if clause:

```
Matrix absTransform = mesh.AbsoluteTransform;

foreach (GeometryContent geo in mesh.Geometry)
{
    foreach (int index in geo.Indices)
    {
        Vector3 vertex = geo.Vertices.Positions[index];
        Vector3 transVertex = Vector3.Transform(vertex, absTransform);
        vertList.Add(transVertex);
    }
}
```

The positions of all vertices of a node are referenced to the origin of that node. To obtain the position relative to the origin of the root node (= the origin of the future Model), you need to transform the position by the absolute transformation matrix of that node (see recipe 4-9 for more information on this). Each node stores its absolute transformation matrix in its AbsoluteTransform property.

Next, you need to actually find the positional data. All triangles of a Model are drawn from an IndexBuffer, linked to a VertexBuffer (see recipe 5-3). Each index is a number representing a vertex inside the VertexBuffer, so for each triangle you will find three indices.

---

■**Note** All triangles inside the models are rendered as indexed TriangleLists (see recipe 5-3 and recipe 5-4).

---

You scroll through the indices of the node, look up the corresponding vertex from the VertexBuffer, transform the position of this vertex so it becomes relative to the Model's origin instead of to the ModelMesh's origin, and add the resulting position to the list.

After all positions have been added to the list, the list is returned to the parent node, ready to be passed on to the next node until all nodes have added their vertices to the list. After this, the final list is returned to the Process method defined earlier, which reshapes your list into an array and stores it in the Tag property of the Model.

That's it! When you import a Model into XNA using your custom Model processor, you will find an array containing Vector3s in the Tag property of the Model:

```
myModel = content.Load<Model>("tank");
modelTransforms = new Matrix[myModel.Bones.Count];

Vector3[] modelVertices = (Vector3[])myModel.Tag;
System.Diagnostics.Debugger.Break();
```

Because the Tag property can really contain anything, you need to cast it to the type you know that's in there. The last line will cause your program to halt there, so you can check the contents of modelVertices, as shown in Figure 4-19.

| Locals | |
|---|---|
| Name | Value |
| ⊞ ● this | {BookCode.Game1} |
| ⊟ ✓ modelVertices | {Microsoft.Xna.Framework.Vector3[64830]} |
| ⊞ ● [0] | {X:-96,75819 Y:154,481 Z:-120,9981} |
| ⊞ ● [1] | {X:-96,75819 Y:133,2315 Z:-18,6476} |
| ⊞ ● [2] | {X:-96,75819 Y:132,728 Z:-121,3885} |
| ⊞ ● [3] | {X:-96,75819 Y:99,0993 Z:-121,9921} |
| ⊞ ● [4] | {X:-96,75819 Y:100,1859 Z:-21,6862} |
| ⊞ ● [5] | {X:-93,84441 Y:100,2224 Z:-19,1681} |

**Figure 4-19.** *All Vector3s of the Model are accessible at runtime.*

## The Code

*All the code is available for download at* www.apress.com.

Your custom pipeline project contains your custom Model processor. This processor inherits from the default ModelProcessor but overrides its Process method to store all vertices into an array of Vector3s:

```
namespace Vector3Pipeline
{
    [ContentProcessor]
    public class ModelVector3Processor : ModelProcessor
    {
        public override ModelContent Process(NodeContent input, ➥
        ContentProcessorContext context)
        {
            ModelContent usualModel = base.Process(input, context);

            List<Vector3> vertices = new List<Vector3>();
            vertices = AddVerticesToList(input, vertices);
            usualModel.Tag = vertices.ToArray();

            return usualModel;
        }

        private List<Vector3> AddVerticesToList(NodeContent node, ➥
        List<Vector3> vertList)
        {
            MeshContent mesh = node as MeshContent;
            if (mesh != null)
            {
                Matrix absTransform = mesh.AbsoluteTransform;


                foreach (GeometryContent geo in mesh.Geometry)
                {
                    foreach (int index in geo.Indices)
                    {
                        Vector3 vertex = geo.Vertices.Positions[index];
                        Vector3 transVertex = Vector3.Transform(vertex, ➥
                        absTransform);
                        vertList.Add(transVertex);
                    }
                }
            }
```

```
            foreach (NodeContent child in node.Children)
                vertList = AddVerticesToList(child, vertList);

            return vertList;
        }
    }
}
```

# 4-14. Gain Direct Access to Vertex Position Data of Each ModelMesh by Extending the Model Processor

## The Problem

The previous recipe gives you access to the positions of all vertices in a Model, relative to the origin of the Model. However, if you animate a part of the Model, for example, rotate the arm of a person, you'll also want to transform the position of the vertices in the arm, hand, fingers, and (why not?) nails. Using the result of the previous recipe, this is not possible, because the huge list of Vector3s does not contain any information as to which part of the Model the Vector3s belong. They are defined to the origin of the Model.

## The Solution

All separately transformable parts of a Model are stored as ModelMeshes inside the Model. A ModelMesh also has a Tag property, which you can use to store useful information. In this recipe, you will store the positions of all vertices of a ModelMesh inside this Tag property of the ModelMesh.

You will store the positions relative to the origin of the ModelMesh (instead of relative to the origin of the whole Model, as in the previous recipe). When your XNA program updates the Bone matrices of the Model and calculates the absolute matrices (see recipe 4-9), you can transform the positions using the same absolute Bone matrices used to render the Model to obtain the position relative to the Model's origin. As a main benefit over the previous recipe, this time you'll be taking the current transformation of the separate parts into account.

## How It Works

This recipe expands on the code of the previous recipe. Once again, you will be crawling through the whole structure of the Model. Only this time, instead of saving all vertices you encounter into one big array, you will generate separate arrays for each node.

After you have crawled through the whole Model and stored your arrays, you ask the default ModelProcessor to produce a ModelContent from the node as usual. Finally, you scroll through all ModelMeshContents contained in the generated ModelContent and store each array in the Tag property of the corresponding ModelMeshContent.

---

■**Note**  The ModelContent object is the output of a content processor and is written to a binary file. When your application is run, this file is loaded from disk, and the object is transformed into a Model.

---

This processor already takes care of the first part:

```
public override ModelContent Process(NodeContent input, ➥
ContentProcessorContext context)
{
    List<Vector3[]> modelVertices = new List<Vector3[]>();
    modelVertices = AddModelMeshVertexArrayToList (input, modelVertices);
}
```

You create the List to store the separate Vector3 arrays. Next, you pass it together with the root node to the AddModelMeshVertexArrayToList method.

First, the method calls itself, passing its child nodes, so they add their arrays of Vector3s to the list first.

After all children have added their arrays to the list, the AddModelMeshVertexArrayToList method checks whether the current node contains any vertices. If it does, an array of Vector3s containing the positions of all vertices is created and added to the list.

```
private List<Vector3[]> AddModelMeshVertexArrayToList(NodeContent ➥
node, List<Vector3[]> modelVertices)
{
    foreach (NodeContent child in node.Children)
        modelVertices = AddModelMeshVertexArrayToList(child, modelVertices);

    MeshContent mesh = node as MeshContent;

    if (mesh != null)
    {
        List<Vector3> nodeVertices = new List<Vector3>();
        foreach (GeometryContent geo in mesh.Geometry)
        {

            foreach (int index in geo.Indices)
            {
                Vector3 vertex = geo.Vertices.Positions[index];
                nodeVertices.Add(vertex);
            }
        }
        modelVertices.Add(nodeVertices.ToArray());
    }

    return modelVertices;
}
```

---

■**Note** In contradiction to the previous recipe, this time the positions are not transformed. This is because you want to store the positions of the vertices relative to the origin of the part, instead of relative to the whole Model. This will allow you to transform them later with the absolute transformation matrix of the ModelMesh at that moment.

---

---

■**Note** A big difference between this method and the AddVerticesToList method of the previous recipe is that here you first ask the child nodes to add their data to the list before the current node adds its own data. In the previous recipe, first the current node added its data before asking its child nodes to do the same, which might seem more intuitive. However, it is important to save the arrays of the ModelMesh in the same order as ModelMeshes are saved in the Model, so you can simply load your arrays in the ModelMeshes at the end of the Process method.

---

Finally, add this code to the end of your Process method:

```
ModelContent usualModel = base.Process(input, context);

int i = 0;
foreach (ModelMeshContent mesh in usualModel.Meshes)
    mesh.Tag = modelVertices[i++];

return usualModel;
```

With the arrays gathered, you ask the default ModelProcessor to build a default ModelContent object from your nodes. In each of the ModelMeshes, you will store the correct array containing the Vector3s of that ModelMesh (see the earlier note).

However, because things would otherwise be too easy, keep in mind that some Models have ModelMeshes that consist of more than one ModelMeshPart. Each ModelMeshPart will have its own NodeContent, and thus for each ModelMeshPart, your AddModelMeshVertexArrayToList method will have added an array of Vector3s to your List. So in order to be complete, you have to use this code instead of the code shown earlier:

```
ModelContent usualModel = base.Process(input, context);

int i = 0;
foreach (ModelMeshContent mesh in usualModel.Meshes)
{
    List<Vector3> modelMeshVertices = new List<Vector3>();
    foreach (ModelMeshPartContent part in mesh.MeshParts)
```

```
    {
        modelMeshVertices.AddRange(modelVertices[i++]);
    }
    mesh.Tag = modelMeshVertices.ToArray();
}

return usualModel;
```

For all `ModelMeshParts` belonging to one `ModelMesh`, this code adds all `Vector3`s to one list, which it converts to an array and stores in the `Tag` property of the `ModelMesh`.

---

■**Note**  Because all `ModelMeshParts` of one `ModelMesh` are rendered with the same absolute transformation matrix, you can throw all of their `Vector3`s together and still remain compatible with animation
(see recipe 4-9). You might still want to store the vertices of each `ModelMeshPart` in the `Tag` property of that
`ModelMeshPart`, though, for example, to create finer `BoundingSpheres` to allow for finer but still very fast
collision detection.

---

Finally, the resulting `ModelContent` is returned, ready to be serialized into a binary file.

When you import a `Model` using this custom `Model` processor, for each `ModelMesh` of the `Model` you will find an array in its `Tag` property, containing three `Vector3`s for each triangle of the `ModelMesh`. You can load your `Model` as usual in your `LoadContent` method:

```
myModel = Content.Load<Model>("tank");
modelTransforms = new Matrix[myModel.Bones.Count];
```

Each `ModelMesh` of this `Model` now contains its list of `Vector3`s in its `Tag` property. You can access it by letting the compiler know there's an array of `Vector3`s stored in there:

```
Vector3[] modelVertices = (Vector3[])myModel.Meshes[0].Tag;
System.Diagnostics.Debugger.Break();
```

The last line will put a breakpoint in your code so you can verify the `Vector3`s are available at that point.

## The Code

*All the code is available for download at* www.apress.com.

Here's the custom content pipeline:

```
namespace Vector3Pipeline
{
    [ContentProcessor]
    public class ModelVector3Processor : ModelProcessor
```

```
    {
        public override ModelContent Process(NodeContent input, ➥
        ContentProcessorContext context)
        {
            List<Vector3[]> modelVertices = new List<Vector3[]>();
            modelVertices = AddModelMeshVertexArrayToList(input, modelVertices);

            ModelContent usualModel = base.Process(input, context);

            int i = 0;
            foreach (ModelMeshContent mesh in usualModel.Meshes)
            {
                List<Vector3> modelMeshVertices = new List<Vector3>();
                foreach (ModelMeshPartContent part in ➥
                mesh.MeshParts)
                {
                    modelMeshVertices.AddRange(modelVertices[i++]);
                }
                mesh.Tag = modelMeshVertices.ToArray();
            }

            return usualModel;
        }

        private List<Vector3[]> AddModelMeshVertexArrayToList(NodeContent node, ➥
        List<Vector3[]> modelVertices)
        {
            foreach (NodeContent child in node.Children)
                modelVertices = AddModelMeshVertexArrayToList(child, modelVertices);

            MeshContent mesh = node as MeshContent;

            if (mesh != null)
            {
                List<Vector3> nodeVertices = new List<Vector3>();
                foreach (GeometryContent geo in mesh.Geometry)
                {

                    foreach (int index in geo.Indices)
                    {
                        Vector3 vertex = geo.Vertices.Positions[index];
                        nodeVertices.Add(vertex);
                    }
                }
                modelVertices.Add(nodeVertices.ToArray());
            }
```

```
        return modelVertices;
    }
  }
}
```

# 4-15. Gain Direct Access to Vertex Position Data by Defining a Custom TypeWriter and TypeReader

## The Problem

You want to have access to the position of each vertex inside your Model. Instead of one huge list containing three Vector3s for each triangle of the Model, you want a list of Triangle objects, where each Triangle object contains three Vector3s.

Or, more generally, you want to pass an object of a custom class from a custom content processor to your XNA application. The content pipeline will not know how it should serialize and deserialize objects of your new class to and from a binary file, so you have to define your own TypeWriter and TypeReader.

## The Solution

The base code of this recipe will rely heavily on the code from the previous recipe, but this time you'll create a simple Triangle object for each three vertices you encounter. You will add all generated Triangle objects to a list and store this list in the Tag property of the Model.

The main difference is that you will define the Triangle class in your custom content pipeline. The default XNA content pipeline has no idea how it should serialize objects of your custom class to file or how to deserialize it into an object for your XNA project. So, you will define a TypeWriter and TypeReader suited for your new class.

## How It Works

This recipe will be written as an introduction to writing your custom TypeWriter and TypeReader. Therefore, it's useful to take a look at Figure 4-20 to locate the TypeWriter and TypeReader in the content pipeline story.

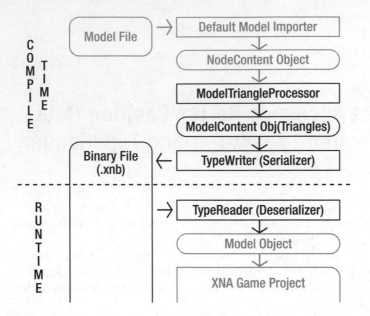

**Figure 4-20.** *Content pipeline with custom Processor, TypeWriter, and TypeReader*

Go through the checklist of recipe 3-9 to create a custom content pipeline project. Add this class to the namespace of your new content pipeline project:

```
public class Triangle
{
    private Vector3[] points;

    public Triangle(Vector3 p0, Vector3 p1, Vector3 p2)
    {
        points = new Vector3[3];
        points[0] = p0;
        points[1] = p1;
        points[2] = p2;
    }

    public Vector3[] Points { get { return points; } }
    public Vector3 P0 { get { return points[0]; } }
    public Vector3 P1 { get { return points[1]; } }
    public Vector3 P2 { get { return points[2]; } }
}
```

This is a very simple class, capable of storing three Vector3s. It provides some getter methods, allowing you to retrieve one Vector3 at a time or an array containing the three Vector3s.

For each triangle of your Model, you want to create an object of this custom class, store all of these objects in an array, and store this array in the Tag property of the Model, so it becomes available to your XNA runtime code.

The Process class is nearly identical to the code of recipe 4-13, only this time you're keep-ing track of a List of Triangle objects, instead of a List of Vector3s. Add your Processor class after your Triangle class:

```
[ContentProcessor]
public class ModelTriangleProcessor : ModelProcessor
{
    public override ModelContent Process(NodeContent input, ➥
    ContentProcessorContext context)
    {
        ModelContent usualModel = base.Process(input, context);

        List<Triangle> triangles = new List<Triangle>();
        triangles = AddVerticesToList(input, triangles);
        usualModel.Tag = triangles.ToArray();

        return usualModel;
    }
}
```

The AddVerticesToList will crawl through the whole Model structure, generate a Triangle object for each three Vector3s encountered, and add all Triangle objects to the List:

```
private List<Triangle> AddVerticesToList(NodeContent node, ➥
List<Triangle> triangleList)
{
    MeshContent mesh = node as MeshContent;
    if (mesh != null)
    {
        Matrix absTransform = mesh.AbsoluteTransform;

        foreach (GeometryContent geo in mesh.Geometry)
        {
            //generate Triangle objects...
        }
    }

    foreach (NodeContent child in node.Children)
        triangleList = AddVerticesToList(child, triangleList);

    return triangleList;
}
```

This code is taken straight from recipe 4-13. You will now code the part that generates Triangle objects for every three Vector3s:

```
int triangles = geo.Indices.Count / 3;
for (int currentTriangle = 0; currentTriangle < triangles; currentTriangle++)
{
    int index0 = geo.Indices[currentTriangle * 3 + 0];
    int index1 = geo.Indices[currentTriangle * 3 + 1];
    int index2 = geo.Indices[currentTriangle * 3 + 2];

    Vector3 v0 = geo.Vertices.Positions[index0];
    Vector3 v1 = geo.Vertices.Positions[index1];
    Vector3 v2 = geo.Vertices.Positions[index2];

    Vector3 transv0 = Vector3.Transform(v0, absTransform);
    Vector3 transv1 = Vector3.Transform(v1, absTransform);
    Vector3 transv2 = Vector3.Transform(v2, absTransform);

    Triangle newTriangle = new Triangle(transv0, transv1, transv2);
    triangleList.Add(newTriangle);
}
```

This code could obviously be shorter, but it would only make the easy code look more difficult.

A Model is drawn from its IndexBuffer, where each index refers to a vertex inside the VertexBuffer (see recipe 5-3 to learn more about indices). First you need to find the total number of triangles in the Model, which equals the number of indices divided by 3.

Next, for each triangle, you first find the indices. Each triangle is defined by three consecutive indices, so first you store these into more meaningful variables. Once you have the indices, you retrieve the corresponding vertices and transform this with the node's absolute transformation matrix (see recipe 4-9) so the positions become relative to the Model's origin instead of relative to the ModelMesh's origin. Finally, you create a new Triangle object based on the three vertices and add the Triangle to your List.

At the end of the Process method, this List is converted into an array of Triangle objects and stored into the Tag property of the Model.

Tada! This is the point where the previous recipes would be finished: you've stored your extra data inside the Tag property of the Model. However, when you import a Model, select this Processor to process the model, and try to compile and run your solution, you should get this error:

```
Unsupported type. Cannot find a ContentTypeWriter implementation for ➡
ModelTriaPipeline.Triangle
```

## Coding Your Custom Content TypeWriter

This error is raised because the content pipeline does not yet know how to serialize a Triangle object to a binary file! So, you will need to code a simple TypeWriter that instructs how such a Triangle object should be serialized. Each time a Triangle object is encountered inside the ModelContent object generated by your Processor, XNA will call this TypeWriter to save the Triangle to the binary file of the Model.

Add this new class to your pipeline project, and make sure you put the code outside your Processor class:

```
[ContentTypeWriter]
public class TriangleTypeWriter : ContentTypeWriter<Triangle>
{
    protected override void Write(ContentWriter output, Triangle value)
    {
        output.WriteObject<Vector3>(value.P0);
        output.WriteObject<Vector3>(value.P1);
        output.WriteObject<Vector3>(value.P2);
    }

    public override string GetRuntimeReader(TargetPlatform targetPlatform)
    {
        return typeof(TriangleTypeReader).AssemblyQualifiedName;
    }
}
```

The first two lines indicate to your pipeline that you will be defining a `ContentTypeWriter` that knows how to serialize objects of the `Triangle` class.

You first need to override the `Write` method, which will receive each `Triangle` object that needs to be saved. This array is passed to the `Write` method as the `value` argument. The `output` variable contains a `ContentWriter` object that allows you to save to the binary file.

When coding a `TypeWriter` for a certain object, you should first think what you need to store about this object, allowing you to re-create the object when it should be loaded from the binary file at program startup. Next, you need to break down the object into more simple objects, until you end up with objects that the content pipeline knows how to serialize.

In the case of a `Triangle`, storing the three `Vector3`s will enable you to re-create the `Triangle` afterward. You're in luck, because the content pipeline already knows how to serialize `Vector3`s, so the `Write` method simply breaks the `Triangle` down into three `Vector3`s and serializes them.

---

**Tip** You can scroll through the different overloads of the `output.Write` method to see which types the default content pipeline knows how to serialize.

---

**Note** You can also use `output.Write(value.P0)`; because the `Vector3` type is by default supported by the default content pipeline. However, the `output.WriteObject` method used in the previous code is more general because it allows writing objects of custom classes for which you already defined a custom `TypeWriter`.

---

The resulting binary file will need to be deserialized each time you start your XNA program. Again, the default content pipeline will not know how to deserialize all Triangle objects it encounters in the binary file, so you'll have to define a custom TypeReader.

To allow your XNA program to find your corresponding custom TypeReader for objects of the Triangle class, your TypeWriter needs to specify the location of the TypeReader in the GetRuntimeReader method.

This GetRuntimeReader method (also defined in the previous code) simply returns a string, specifying where the TypeReader for Triangle objects can be found.

If you run the solution at this point, you'll get an error stating the ModelTriaPipeline.TriangleReader class cannot be found, which is probably because you haven't coded that class yet. So, add this last class to your ModelTriaPipeline namespace:

```
public class TriangleTypeReader : ContentTypeReader<Triangle>
{
    protected override Triangle Read(ContentReader input, Triangle existingInstance)
    {
        Vector3 p0 = input.ReadObject<Vector3>();
        Vector3 p1 = input.ReadObject<Vector3>();
        Vector3 p2 = input.ReadObject<Vector3>();

        Triangle newTriangle = new Triangle(p0, p1, p2);

        return newTriangle;
    }
}
```

You inherit from the ContentTypeReader class and indicate your custom TypeReader will be able to deserialize objects of the Triangle class.

---

**■Note**  Make sure the name of your custom reader is the same as you specified in the GetRuntimeReader method of your writer! Otherwise, XNA will still not be able to find the TypeReader suited for reading serialized Triangle objects.

---

During the startup of your XNA project, the Read method of this class will be called each time a Triangle object is found in a binary file. For each triangle, you stored its three Vector3s. So in your TypeReader, you simply read in the three Vector3s from the binary file, create a Triangle object based on these three Vector3s, and return the Triangle.

### Adding a Reference to Your Content Pipeline Project

With your TypeReader coded, you should be ready to run your solution. However, although this time your project will build correctly, you will get another error when the program is actually run:

```
Cannot find ContentTypeReader ModelTriaPipeline.Triangle, ➥
ModelTriaPipeline, Version=1.0.0.0, Culture=neutral
```

You get this error because your XNA project cannot yet access the `ModelTriaPipeline` namespace in which the `TypeReader` for `Triangle` objects resides. To solve this, you will want to add a reference to your content pipeline project. So, open your main XNA project, and choose Project ➤ Add Reference. In the upcoming dialog box, select the Projects tab. You should see your content pipeline in the list, as shown in Figure 4-21. Select it, and hit OK.

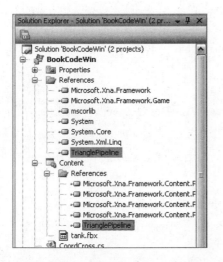

**Figure 4-21.** *Adding a reference to your custom content pipeline project*

---

■**Note** If your content pipeline project is not in the list, make sure you have built your content pipeline project (step 6 in the checklist of recipe 4-9).

---

At this point, you should have added a reference to your content pipeline project for the Content entry in your XNA project, as well as for your XNA project itself, as shown in Figure 4-22. The first reference will allow you to select your custom processor as the processor for your model, while the second reference allows your XNA project to call the `TypeReader` at runtime.

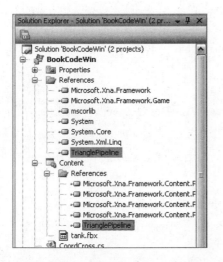

**Figure 4-22.** *Two references to your custom content pipeline project are required.*

When you select the `ModelTriangleProcessor` to process your model and run your solution, your model should now contain an array of `Triangle` objects in its `Tag` property.

## Adding the Content Pipeline Namespace to Your Using Block

In your XNA project, when you want to access the `Triangle` objects stored in the `Tag` property, you'll always have to cast the contents of the `Tag` property to the type you want, which in this case is `Triangle[]` (an array of triangles). However, since the `Triangle` class was defined in another namespace, you need to precede the `Triangle` name by its namespace:

```
ModelTriaPipeline.Triangle[] modelTriangles = ➡
(ModelTriaPipeline.Triangle[])myModel.Tag;
```

That looks rather ugly. If you add your content pipeline namespace (`ModelTriaPipeline` in my case) to the `using` block of your XNA project:

```
using ModelTriaPipeline;
```

From now on all classes of your custom content project will be known to your XNA project, so you can write that last line shorter:

```
Triangle[] modelTriangles = (Triangle[])myModel.Tag;
```

---

■**Note**  The positions stored in the `Triangles` will be references to the origin of the `Model`. To learn how you can use these positions while animating certain parts of the `Model`, see recipe 4-14.

---

## Checklist for Extending a Content Processor Using an Object of a Custom Class

Here you can find the steps required to get your custom content pipeline containing a custom class up and running. As in recipe 4-9, I'll present them as a checklist, so you can easily refer to this list from other chapters. The initialization list of recipe 4-9 is extended by two steps, which were discussed earlier.

1. Add a new content pipeline project to your solution.

2. In the new project, add a reference to `Microsoft.XNA.Framework.Content.Pipeline`.

3. Add the `Pipeline` namespaces to the `using` block.

4. Indicate which part you're going to extend (which method you're going to override).

5. Compile the new content pipeline project.

6. Add the newly created assembly to your main project.

7. Select the newly created processor to process an asset.

8. Set the project dependencies.

9. In your main XNA project, add a reference to your content pipeline project.

10. Add your content pipeline namespace to the `using` block of your main XNA project.

And after everything has been initialized, do the following:

1. Define the custom classes you'll need in your processor.

2. Code the method you've created in step 4.

3. For each of the custom classes you used in your processor, create a `TypeWriter`.

4. For each of the custom classes you used in your processor, create a `TypeReader`.

---

■**Note** Keep in mind that the content importers, processors, and typewriters are invoked only when you compile your project. Therefore, these classes will not be deployed on the Xbox 360 console, and as such both the `TypeReader` class and your custom class will not be known to your main `Game` class. To solve this, move both classes to your main XNA project, and add your main XNA project as a reference to your content pipeline project. See the sample code for this recipe as an example.

---

## The Code

*All the code is available for download at www.apress.com.*

You can see the complete custom content pipeline namespace in the following code. This namespace includes a custom `Model` processor with its helper method, a custom class, a `TypeReader` (to store this custom class to a binary file), and a `TypeReader` (to deserialize objects of your custom class). This `TypeReader` is called each time during startup of your application for every `Triangle` encountered in the binary file.

```
namespace TrianglePipeline
{
    public class Triangle
    {
        private Vector3[] points;

        public Triangle(Vector3 p0, Vector3 p1, Vector3 p2)
        {
            points = new Vector3[3];
            points[0] = p0;
            points[1] = p1;
            points[2] = p2;
        }

        public Vector3[] Points { get { return points; } }
        public Vector3 P0 { get { return points[0]; } }
        public Vector3 P1 { get { return points[1]; } }
        public Vector3 P2 { get { return points[2]; } }
    }
```

```
[ContentProcessor]
public class ModelTriangleProcessor : ModelProcessor
{
    public override ModelContent Process(NodeContent input, ➡
    ContentProcessorContext context)
    {
        ModelContent usualModel = base.Process(input, context);

        List<Triangle> triangles = new List<Triangle>();
        triangles = AddVerticesToList(input, triangles);
        usualModel.Tag = triangles.ToArray();

        return usualModel;
    }

    private List<Triangle> AddVerticesToList(NodeContent node, ➡
    List<Triangle> triangleList)
    {
        MeshContent mesh = node as MeshContent;
        if (mesh != null)
        {
            Matrix absTransform = mesh.AbsoluteTransform;

            foreach (GeometryContent geo in mesh.Geometry)
            {
                int triangles    = geo.Indices.Count / 3;
                for (int currentTriangle = 0; currentTriangle < triangles; ➡
                currentTriangle++)
                {
                    int index0 = geo.Indices[currentTriangle * 3 + 0];
                    int index1 = geo.Indices[currentTriangle * 3 + 1];
                    int index2 = geo.Indices[currentTriangle * 3 + 2];

                    Vector3 v0 = geo.Vertices.Positions[index0];
                    Vector3 v1 = geo.Vertices.Positions[index1];
                    Vector3 v2 = geo.Vertices.Positions[index2];
                    Vector3 transv0 = Vector3.Transform(v0, absTransform);
                    Vector3 transv1 = Vector3.Transform(v1, absTransform);
                    Vector3 transv2 = Vector3.Transform(v2, absTransform);

                    Triangle newTriangle = ➡
                    new Triangle(transv0, transv1, transv2);
                    triangleList.Add(newTriangle);
                }
            }
        }
```

```
        foreach (NodeContent child in node.Children)
            triangleList = AddVerticesToList(child, triangleList);

        return triangleList;
    }
}


[ContentTypeWriter]
public class TriangleTypeWriter : ContentTypeWriter<Triangle>
{
    protected override void Write(ContentWriter output, Triangle value)
    {
        output.WriteObject<Vector3>(value.P0);
        output.WriteObject<Vector3>(value.P1);
        output.WriteObject<Vector3>(value.P2);
    }

    public override string GetRuntimeReader(TargetPlatform targetPlatform)
    {
        return typeof(TriangleTypeReader).AssemblyQualifiedName;
    }
}


public class TriangleTypeReader : ContentTypeReader<Triangle>
{
    protected override Triangle Read(ContentReader input, ➥
    Triangle existingInstance)
    {
        Vector3 p0 = input.ReadObject<Vector3>();
        Vector3 p1 = input.ReadObject<Vector3>();
        Vector3 p2 = input.ReadObject<Vector3>();

        Triangle newTriangle = new Triangle(p0, p1, p2);

        return newTriangle;
    }
}
}
```

In your main XNA project, this is how you load the Model, access its Triangles, and place a breakpoint so you can examine the contents of the modelTriangles array:

```
myModel = Content.Load<Model>("tank");
modelTransforms = new Matrix[myModel.Bones.Count];

Triangle[] modelTriangles = (Triangle[])myModel.Tag;
System.Diagnostics.Debugger.Break();
```

# 4-16. Store Multiple Objects in the Tag Property by Defining a Custom TypeWriter and TypeReader

## The Problem

To allow your Model processor to store objects inside a Model and pass it to your XNA project, XNA provides the Tag property of a Model. As shown in recipes 4-13, 4-14, and 4-15, this Tag property is quite useful to store an array of objects of the same type, such as an array of Vector3s or Triangles. But often you'll want to pass multiple objects, such as the list of Vector3s together with the global BoundingBox of the Model.

## The Solution

Define a custom class, capable of storing all objects you want to pass. Inside your Model processor, create a new object of your class, and fill it with anything you want to pass from your content pipeline to your XNA project. Finally, store the object in the Tag property of the Model.

Because you have defined a custom class, you'll have to define a suitable TypeWriter (see recipe 4-15) so XNA knows how it should serialize the object to a binary file, as well as a TypeReader, which will be called to restore the object from the binary file each time you run your XNA application.

## How It Works

Because you will be extending a content processor and you'll be passing an object of a custom class, make sure you go through the (many, but short) initialization steps listed in the "Checklist for Extending a Content Processor Using an Object of a Custom Class" section of recipe 4-15. In step 1, I called my new content pipeline project TagPipeline. In step 4, I called my processor ExtendedModelProcessor.

```
namespace TagPipeline
{
    [ContentProcessor]
    public class ExtendedModelProcessor : ModelProcessor
    {
        public override ModelContent Process(NodeContent input, ➡
        ContentProcessorContext context)
        {
            return base.Process(input, context);
        }
    }
}
```

With all the initialization done, you're ready to define the new class that should be capable of storing everything you want to pass from your content pipeline to your XNA project. In this example, you'll send an array of all Vector3s used by the Model together with the global BoundingBox of the Model.

At the top of your content pipeline namespace, define a class that can hold both objects:

```
public class TagObject
{
    private Vector3[] positions;
    private BoundingBox boundingBox;

    public TagObject(Vector3[] positions, BoundingBox boundingBox)
    {
        this.positions = positions;
        this.boundingBox = boundingBox;
    }


    public Vector3[] Positions { get { return positions; } }
    public BoundingBox GlobalBoundingBox { get { return boundingBox; } }
}
```

This simple class can store an array of Vector3s and a BoundingBox. It has one constructor that stores the values passed to it in its internal variables. You've also defined two getter methods, allowing you to retrieve the contents of the variables later.

---

■**Note**  Since this class does not contain any behavioral methods, you can choose to use a struct instead of a class.

---

Next, you should start coding your Model processor. It should gather the data you want to pass: the array of Vector3s and the BoundingBox.

```
public override ModelContent Process(NodeContent input, ➡
ContentProcessorContext context)
{
    ModelContent usualModel = base.Process(input, context);

    List<Vector3> vertices = new List<Vector3>();
    vertices = AddVerticesToList(input, vertices);

    BoundingBox bBox = BoundingBox.CreateFromPoints(vertices);

    TagObject myTagObject = new TagObject(vertices.ToArray(), bBox);

    usualModel.Tag = myTagObject;

    return usualModel;
}
```

First you ask the default ModelProcessor to do its job as done many times in the previous recipes, and you store its output in the usualModel variable. Next, you crawl the whole model structure and add all Vector3s you find to a List using the AddVerticesToList method, which is explained in recipe 4-13.

Once you have this List, it's easy to create a BoundingBox from them using the BoundingBox.CreateFromPoints method. This method accepts a collection of Vector3s, which is subscribed to the IEnumerable interface, such as an array or a List.

By reshaping the List into an array, you have everything you need to create an object of your newly defined TagObject class! Finally, you store this object in the Tag property of the Model.

That's it for the first half of this recipe. Make sure you take a five-minute break now. In the second half, you'll code the TypeWriter and the TypeReader for your custom class.

## Coding the TypeWriter and TypeReader

Glad you made it back! When you run the code at this point, XNA will complain because it does not know how to save an object of the TagObject class to a binary file, as in the previous recipe. Add this custom TypeWriter to your content pipeline namespace:

```
[ContentTypeWriter]
public class TagObjectTypeWriter : ContentTypeWriter<TagObject>
{
    protected override void Write(ContentWriter output, TagObject value)
    {
        output.WriteObject<Vector3[]>(value.Positions);
        output.WriteObject<BoundingBox>(value.GlobalBoundingBox);
    }

    public override string GetRuntimeReader(TargetPlatform targetPlatform)
    {
        return typeof(TagObjectTypeReader).AssemblyQualifiedName;
    }
}
```

As explained in recipe 4-15, the first two lines specify this class is a ContentTypeWriter capable of serializing an object of the TagObject class. Again, you want to override two methods: the Write method specifies how a TagObject should be written to a binary file, while the GetRuntimeReader method can be called by XNA so it knows where to find the corresponding TypeReader to reconstruct the object. See recipe 4-15 for more information on this.

The default content pipeline knows how to serialize an array of Vector3s and a BoundingBox, so you can simply ask the framework to serialize these for you. In the GetRuntimeReader method, you indicate you will code a corresponding TypeReader called TagObjectReader in the same namespace.

So far, so good. All you have to do next is code the corresponding TypeReader. As defined
in the GetRuntimeReader method, the TypeReader class should be called TagObjectTypeReader:

```
public class TagObjectTypeReader : ContentTypeReader<TagObject>
{
    protected override TagObject Read(ContentReader input, ➥
    TagObject existingInstance)
    {
        Vector3[] positions = input.ReadObject<Vector3[]>();
        BoundingBox bBox = input.ReadObject<BoundingBox>();

        TagObject restoredTagObject = new TagObject(positions, bBox);
        return restoredTagObject;
    }
}
```

During application startup, for each object of the TagObject class that has been serialized
to a binary file, this method will be called to reconstruct the object. First you read the array of
Vector3s from the file and store it into a variable; next you do the same for the BoundingBox.
Now that you have both objects, re-create the TagObject object and send it over to your XNA
project.

That's easy, but it is quite important you read the objects in the same order you wrote
them to the file! If you first tried to read a BoundingBox, you would create a BoundingBox based
on the first Vector3s of your array! Luckily, the XNA team has managed to build in a protection
for this, so if you screw up the reading order, XNA will complain at compile time.

■**Note** If your solution refuses to compile at this point, go over the ten-point list of recipe 4-15 again.

### Accessing the Data in Your XNA Project

When you run your solution at this point, any model imported using the
ExtendedModelProcessor will contain a TagObject object in its Tag property. As always, since
the Tag property can really contain anything, you first need to cast it to a TagObject object.
From then on, you can easily access its properties:

```
myModel = Content.Load<Model>("tank");
modelTransforms = new Matrix[myModel.Bones.Count];

TagObject modelTag = (TagObject)myModel.Tag;
BoundingBox modelBBox = modelTag.GlobalBoundingBox;
Vector3[] modelVertices = modelTag.Positions;

System.Diagnostics.Debugger.Break();
```

## The Code

*All the code is available for download at* www.apress.com.

For this recipe, the complete content pipeline namespace contains the following:

- The ExtendedModelProcessor Model processor, including the AddVerticesToList helper method

- The custom TagObject class definition

- A custom TypeWriter, capable of serializing objects of the TagObject class

- A custom TypeReader, capable of restoring objects of the TagObject class stored in a binary file

This entire namespace is as follows:

```
namespace TagPipeline
{
    public class TagObject
    {
        private Vector3[] positions;
        private BoundingBox boundingBox;

        public TagObject(Vector3[] positions, BoundingBox boundingBox)
        {
            this.positions = positions;
            this.boundingBox = boundingBox;
        }

        public Vector3[] Positions { get { return positions; } }
        public BoundingBox GlobalBoundingBox { get { return boundingBox; } }
    }

    [ContentProcessor]
    public class ExtendedModelProcessor : ModelProcessor
    {
        public override ModelContent Process(NodeContent input, ➥
        ContentProcessorContext context)
```

```
    {
        ModelContent usualModel = base.Process(input, context);

        List<Vector3> vertices = new List<Vector3>();
        vertices = AddVerticesToList(input, vertices);

        BoundingBox bBox = BoundingBox.CreateFromPoints(vertices);

        TagObject myTagObject = new TagObject(vertices.ToArray(), bBox);

        usualModel.Tag = myTagObject;

        return usualModel;
    }

    private List<Vector3> AddVerticesToList(NodeContent node, ➥
    List<Vector3> vertList)
    {
        MeshContent mesh = node as MeshContent;
        if (mesh != null)
        {
            Matrix absTransform = mesh.AbsoluteTransform;

            foreach (GeometryContent geo in mesh.Geometry)
            {
                foreach (int index in geo.Indices)
                {
                    Vector3 vertex = geo.Vertices.Positions[index];
                    Vector3 transVertex = ➥
                    Vector3.Transform(vertex, absTransform);
                    vertList.Add(transVertex);
                }
            }
        }

        foreach (NodeContent child in node.Children)
            vertList = AddVerticesToList(child, vertList);

        return vertList;
    }
}
```

```
[ContentTypeWriter]
public class TagObjectTypeWriter : ContentTypeWriter<TagObject>
{
    protected override void Write(ContentWriter output, TagObject value)
    {
        output.WriteObject<Vector3[]>(value.Positions);
        output.WriteObject<BoundingBox>(value.GlobalBoundingBox);
    }

    public override string GetRuntimeReader(TargetPlatform targetPlatform)
    {
        return typeof(TagObjectTypeReader).AssemblyQualifiedName;
    }
}


public class TagObjectTypeReader : ContentTypeReader<TagObject>
{
    protected override TagObject Read(ContentReader input, ➥
TagObject existingInstance)
    {
        Vector3[] positions = input.ReadObject<Vector3[]>();
        BoundingBox bBox = input.ReadObject<BoundingBox>();

        TagObject restoredTagObject = new TagObject(positions, bBox);
        return restoredTagObject;
    }
}
}
```

# 4-17. Correctly Tilt a Model According to the Terrain Underneath

## The Problem

When moving a car Model over a terrain, using recipe 4-2 you can adjust the height of the car, and using recipe 5-9 you can find the height of the terrain underneath the car. However, if you do not tilt the car according to the slope underneath the car, the result will not look very nice on hilly parts of the terrain.

You want to correctly position and tilt your car so it is positioned nicely on the terrain.

# The Solution

This problem can be split up into four parts:

1. First, you want to find the positions of the lowest vertices of the four wheels of your Model.

2. Second, you want the height of the terrain exactly underneath these four points.

3. Next, you need to find the rotation along the Forward and Side vectors of the Model to tilt the Model correctly.

4. Finally, you should find the height difference between the model and the terrain and compensate for this difference.

Instead of hacking your way in the runtime program to solve the first step, you should code a small custom Model processor that stores the position of the lowest vector for each ModelMesh of the Model in the Tag properties of the ModelMeshes. Because these lowest points of the four wheels will be moved while the game is running, each update you'll need to transform these positions with the current World positions of these vectors.

To find the exact height at a certain location on a triangle-based surface, you can use the GetExactHeightAt method created in recipe 5-9.

The approach to find the rotation angles are based on a single mathematical rule (which you should have remembered from high school!).

The final step involves adding a vertical translation to the Model's World matrix.

# How It Works

## Coding a Custom Model Processor to Find the Lowest Positions of Each ModelMesh

The first step is to find the positions of the lowest vertices of the wheels of the Model, because these vertices should ultimately connect with the terrain. You will create a Model processor that is a simplified version of the processor coded in recipe 4-14.

For each ModelMesh of the Model, you will store its lowest position in the Tag property of the ModelMesh. Note that you want this position to be defined relative to the origin of the ModelMesh, so this recipe remains valid even when you animate the Bones of the Model (see recipe 4-9).

Start from the code explained in recipe 4-14. Make some minor changes to the Model processor's Process method:

```
public override ModelContent Process(NodeContent input, ➡
ContentProcessorContext context)
{
    List<Vector3> lowestVertices = new List<Vector3>();
    lowestVertices = FindLowestVectors(input, lowestVertices);

    ModelContent usualModel = base.Process(input, context);
```

```
        int i = 0;
        foreach (ModelMeshContent mesh in usualModel.Meshes)
            mesh.Tag = lowestVertices[i++];

        return usualModel;
    }
```

The FindLowestVertices method crawls its way through all the nodes of the Model and stores, for each ModelMesh, the lowest position of the lowestVertices list. Once you have this list, you store each position in the Tag property of its corresponding ModelMesh.

Based on the AddVertices method described in recipe 4-14, the FindLowestVertices method adds its position to the list and passes the list on to all of the node's child nodes:

```
private List<Vector3> FindLowestVectors(NodeContent node, ➥
List<Vector3> lowestVertices)
{
    Vector3? lowestPos = null;
    MeshContent mesh = node as MeshContent;

    foreach (NodeContent child in node.Children)
        lowestVertices = FindLowestVectors(child, lowestVertices);

    if (mesh != null)
        foreach (GeometryContent geo in mesh.Geometry)
            foreach (Vector3 vertexPos in geo.Vertices.Positions)
                if ((lowestPos == null) || (vertexPos.Y < lowestPos.Value.Y))
                    lowestPos = vertexPos;

    lowestVertices.Add(lowestPos.Value);

    return lowestVertices;
}
```

You start by calling this method on the node's children so they also store their lowest position in the list.

Each node, you check whether the node contains any geometrical information. If it does, you scroll through all vertices that define the geometrical shape defined in the node. If the lowestPos is null (it will be null the first time this check is encountered) or if the current position is lower than the one previously stored in lowestPos, you store the current position in lowestPos.

In the end, the vertex with the lowest Y coordinate is stored in lowestPos. You add this to the lowestVertices list and return the list to the parent node.

**■Note** As discussed in recipe 4-14, a ModelMesh first calls this method on its children, and afterward it
adds its own lowest position to the list. A more intuitive approach would have been to have a node first store
its own Vector3 to the list and then call the method on its child node. You have to do it in the order shown
earlier, though, because this is the order the nodes are converted to ModelMeshes by the default Model
processor. In the Process method, this allows you to easily store the correct Vector3 in the Tag property
of the correct ModelMesh.

Make sure you select this Model processor to process the Model you're importing for this
recipe.

### Finding the Absolute 3D Coordinates of the Lowest Positions of the Wheels

In your XNA project, you're ready to store the position of your four wheels. It depends on the
structure of your Model and which ModelMesh corresponds to which wheel. You can use the
code of recipe 4-8 to visualize the structure of your Model.

For each wheel, you should know the ID of the corresponding ModelMesh. Once you know
the ID, you can access the lowest position of each wheel and store it in a variable. Although
you can make the following code four times as compact as shown here using a simple for loop,
I'll always use four separate variables with a somewhat intuitive name for each of the wheels.
The front-left one is abbreviated to fl, the back-right one to br, and so on.

```
int flID = 5;
int frID = 1;
int blID = 4;
int brID = 0;

Vector3 frontLeftOrig = (Vector3)myModel.Meshes[flID].Tag;
Vector3 frontRightOrig = (Vector3)myModel.Meshes[frID].Tag;
Vector3 backLeftOrig = (Vector3)myModel.Meshes[blID].Tag;
Vector3 backRightOrig = (Vector3)myModel.Meshes[brID].Tag;
```

Remember, you need to use the correct IDs for your specific Model, which you can find
using recipe 4-8.

The positions you have stored in the Tag properties of the ModelMeshes are relative to the
origin of the ModelMesh. You want to know them in the same space as your terrain, which is in
absolute 3D space.

A first step toward this goal would be to find the position of your lowest vertices relative
to the origin of the Model, which can be done by transforming them with the absolute transformation matrix of the ModelMesh (see recipe 4-9). Next, because you will probably also use a
World matrix to render the Model at a certain position in the 3D world, you should combine the
Bone matrix of each ModelMesh with the Model's World matrix.

```
myModel.CopyAbsoluteBoneTransformsTo(modelTransforms);
Matrix frontLeftMatrix = modelTransforms[myModel.Meshes[flID].ParentBone.Index];
Matrix frontRightMatrix = modelTransforms[myModel.Meshes[frID].ParentBone.Index];
Matrix backLeftMatrix = modelTransforms[myModel.Meshes[blID].ParentBone.Index];
Matrix backRightMatrix = modelTransforms[myModel.Meshes[brID].ParentBone.Index];

Vector3 frontLeft = Vector3.Transform(frontLeftOrig, frontLeftMatrix * modelWorld);
Vector3 frontRight = Vector3.Transform(frontRightOrig, ➡
frontRightMatrix * modelWorld);
Vector3 backLeft = Vector3.Transform(backLeftOrig, backLeftMatrix * modelWorld);
Vector3 backRight = Vector3.Transform(backRightOrig, backRightMatrix * modelWorld);
```

First, you calculate the absolute transformation matrix for all Bones of the Model (see recipe 4-9). Next, for each wheel, you find the absolute transformation matrix stored in the Bone corresponding to the ModelMesh of the wheel.

Once you know the absolute transformation matrix for each wheel, you combine this matrix with the World matrix of the Model and use the resulting matrix to transform your vertices. The resulting Vector3s contain the absolute world 3D coordinates of the lowest vectors of your Model's wheels.

---

**Note** As explained in detail in recipe 4-2, the order of matrix multiplication is important. Because these vertices are part of the Model, first you're taking the offset between the (0,0,0) absolute 3D origin stored in the World matrix into account, and afterward you're transforming your vertices so they become relative to the Model's origin. Doing things this way, your World matrix has an impact on the Bones of your Model, which is what you want. If you did this the other way around, any rotations contained in the Bones would have an impact on the World matrix. See recipe 4-2 for more information on the order of matrix multiplication.

---

Finally, you're ready to make the four vertices collide with your terrain, because both the positions of your vertices and of your terrain coordinates are in absolute 3D space.

## Retrieving the Height of the Terrain Underneath the Model

Now that you've found the absolute 3D positions of the four wheels, you're almost ready to find the required rotation angles. As a start, you want to find how much you should rotate the Model around its Side vector so the front of the car is lowered or raised. Instead of working with all four points, you're going to base your calculations on two points only. The first point, front, is positioned between the front wheels, while the second point, back, is between the two back wheels, as illustrated in Figure 4-23. You want to find the rotation so the dotted line frontToBack (that connects both points) is aligned with the terrain underneath.

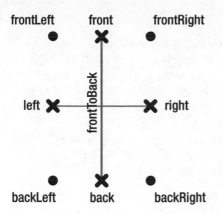

**frontLeft**       **front**       **frontRight**

**left**                      **right**

**backLeft**       **back**       **backRight**

**Figure 4-23.** *Points of interest when tilting a car*

You can find the position of both points easily by taking the average of their neighboring wheels. You can find the vector between them, backToFront, by subtracting them from each other:

```
Vector3 front = (frontLeft + frontRight) / 2.0f;
Vector3 back = (backLeft + backRight) / 2.0f;
Vector3 backToFront = front - back;
```

Remember, you want to find how much you should rotate your car around its Side vector, so its front point is moved upward or downward. Ideally, you want your frontToBack vector to have the same inclination as the terrain slope, as shown in Figure 4-24. The angle you want to calculate is denoted fbAngle in Figure 4-24.

You first need to find the height difference of the terrain at both points. Use the GetExactHeightAt method constructed in recipe 5-9:

```
float frontTerHeight = terrain.GetExactHeightAt(front.X, -front.Z);
float backTerHeight = terrain.GetExactHeightAt(back.X, -back.Z);
float fbTerHeightDiff = frontTerHeight - backTerHeight;
```

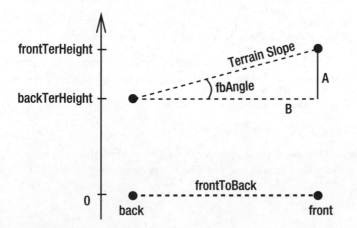

**Figure 4-24.** *Finding the inclination angle*

## Calculating the Rotation Angles

Now that you know the height difference on your terrain, using some trigon math you can find the inclination angle. In a triangle with one corner of 90 degrees, you can find the angle of one of the other corners if you know the length of the opposite side (A in Figure 4-24) and of the neighboring side (B in Figure 4-24). The angle is found by taking the arc tangent (atan) of their lengths. The first length equals the height difference you just calculated, while the second length equals the length of your frontToBack vector!

This is how you find the angle and construct the corresponding rotation around the (1,0,0) Side vector. The resulting rotation is stored in a quaternion (an object useful for storing and combining rotations without Gimbal lock, as explained in recipe 2-4):

```
float fbAngle = (float)Math.Atan2(fbTerHeightDiff, backToFront.Length());
Quaternion bfRot = Quaternion.CreateFromAxisAngle(new Vector3(1, 0, 0), -fbAngle);
```

If you rotate your Model using this rotation, the front and back points of your Model will follow the slope of your terrain!

Obviously, this is only 50 percent of the work, because you'll also want to rotate your model around its Forward vector so its left and right points follow the terrain. Luckily, you can use the same approach and code to find the lrAngle. You simply want to make sure the leftToFront dotted line in Figure 4-23 is aligned to the terrain underneath:

```
Vector3 left = (frontLeft + backLeft) / 2.0f;
Vector3 right = (frontRight + backRight) / 2.0f;
Vector3 rightToLeft = left - right;

float leftTerHeight = terrain.GetExactHeightAt(left.X, -left.Z);
float rightTerHeight = terrain.GetExactHeightAt(right.X, -right.Z);
float lrTerHeightDiff = leftTerHeight - rightTerHeight;

float lrAngle = (float)Math.Atan2(lrTerHeightDiff, rightToLeft.Length());
Quaternion lrRot = Quaternion.CreateFromAxisAngle(new Vector3(0, 0, -1), -lrAngle);
```

Now that you have both rotations, it's easy to combine them by multiplying them. Combine the resulting transformation with the World transformation:

```
Quaternion combRot = fbRot * lrRot;
Matrix rotatedModelWorld = Matrix.CreateFromQuaternion(combRot) * modelWorld;
```

If you use this rotatedModelWorld matrix as the World matrix for rendering your Model, it will be perfectly rotated to fit on your terrain! However, you still need to position it at the correct height.

## Positioning the Model at the Correct Height

Because you're rotating your Model, some wheels will be lower than others. Now that you have calculated your rotations, you can easily find the rotated positions of your wheels:

```
Vector3 rotFrontLeft = Vector3.Transform(frontLeftOrig, ➥
frontLeftMatrix * rotatedModelWorld);
Vector3 rotFrontRight = Vector3.Transform(frontRightOrig, ➥
frontRightMatrix * rotatedModelWorld);
Vector3 rotBackLeft = Vector3.Transform(backLeftOrig, backLeftMatrix * ➥
rotatedModelWorld);
Vector3 rotBackRight = Vector3.Transform(backRightOrig, ➥
backRightMatrix * rotatedModelWorld);
```

Next, you can use the X and Y components of these positions to find out exactly where they should be positioned:

```
float flTerHeight = terrain.GetExactHeightAt(rotFrontLeft.X, -rotFrontLeft.Z);
float frTerHeight = terrain.GetExactHeightAt(rotFrontRight.X, -rotFrontRight.Z);
float blTerHeight = terrain.GetExactHeightAt(rotBackLeft.X, -rotBackLeft.Z);
float brTerHeight = terrain.GetExactHeightAt(rotBackRight.X, -rotBackRight.Z);
```

You know the Y height coordinate of your wheels and you know the Y coordinate of where they should be, so it's easy to calculate how much they're off:

```
float flHeightDiff = rotFrontLeft.Y - flTerHeight;
float frHeightDiff = rotFrontRight.Y - frTerHeight;
float blHeightDiff = rotBackLeft.Y - blTerHeight;
float brHeightDiff = rotBackRight.Y - brTerHeight;
```

However, you've obtained four different values that could be useful for shifting your Model to its correct height. Because you'll be shifting your whole model, there's only one value you can actually use.

The value you actually want depends on your liking. If you want to make sure not a single wheel ever sticks even a millimeter in the ground, take the largest difference. If you don't like having spaces between your Model and the terrain, take the smallest one. Hey, this is my recipe, so I'm taking their average as the final shifting value:

```
float finalHeightDiff = (blHeightDiff + brHeightDiff + flHeightDiff + ➥
frHeightDiff) / 4.0f;
modelWorld = rotatedModelWorld * Matrix.CreateTranslation(new ➥
Vector3(0, -finalHeightDiff, 0));
```

The last line adds a matrix that contains this vertical translation to the World matrix of the Model.

---

■**Note** Here you're putting your newly calculated matrix at the right of the multiplication to make sure the model is moved over the absolute Up axis. If you put it at the left part of the multiplication, the Model would be moved along the Up vector of the Model, which is rotated.

---

That's it. If you render your Model using this World matrix, the Model will follow the slope of the terrain nicely. It's a huge amount of code, but if you put it in a for loop, the amount is already divided by 4. If you're scared it looks a bit heavy on the calculations, keep in mind that these calculations have to be performed only for Models that actually have to be rendered to the screen!

## Preparing for Animation

If you have animated your Model, you can run into some trouble. For example, if you have rotated one of the wheels for 180 degrees, the vector stored in the Tag property of the wheel will contain the highest point of the wheel, instead of the lowest! This will cause your Model's wheel to sink into the ground.

To solve for this, you should reset the Bone matrices of the wheels to their original value before performing the calculations. This is no problem, because you need to store these anyway when doing Model animations (see recipe 4-9); 2, 4, 6, and 8 are the indices of the Bones attached to the four wheels.

```
myModel.Bones[2].Transform = originalTransforms[2];
myModel.Bones[4].Transform = originalTransforms[4];
myModel.Bones[6].Transform = originalTransforms[6];
myModel.Bones[8].Transform = originalTransforms[8];

float time = (float)gameTime.TotalGameTime.TotalMilliseconds / 1000.0f;

Matrix worldMatrix = Matrix.CreateTranslation(new Vector3(10, 0, ➥
-12)); // starting position
worldMatrix = Matrix.CreateRotationY(MathHelper.PiOver4*3)*worldMatrix;
worldMatrix = Matrix.CreateTranslation(0, 0, time)*worldMatrix; //move forward
worldMatrix = Matrix.CreateScale(0.001f)*worldMatrix; //scale down a bit
worldMatrix = TiltModelAccordingToTerrain(myModel, worldMatrix, 5, ➥
1, 4, 0); //do tilting magic
```

## The Code

*All the code is available for download at www.apress.com.*

Here's the code for the content pipeline namespace that will save the lowest vertex of each ModelMesh in its Tag property:

```
namespace ModelVector3Pipeline
{
    [ContentProcessor]
    public class ModelVector3Processor : ModelProcessor
    {
        public override ModelContent Process(NodeContent input, ➥
        ContentProcessorContext context)
        {
            List<Vector3> lowestVertices = new List<Vector3>();
            lowestVertices = FindLowestVectors(input, lowestVertices);
```

```
        ModelContent usualModel = base.Process(input, context);

        int i = 0;
        foreach (ModelMeshContent mesh in usualModel.Meshes)
            mesh.Tag = lowestVertices[i++];

        return usualModel;
    }

    private List<Vector3> FindLowestVectors(NodeContent node, ➥
    List<Vector3> lowestVertices)
    {
        Vector3? lowestPos = null;
        MeshContent mesh = node as MeshContent;

        foreach (NodeContent child in node.Children)
            lowestVertices = FindLowestVectors(child, lowestVertices);

        if (mesh != null)
            foreach (GeometryContent geo in mesh.Geometry)
                foreach (Vector3 vertexPos in geo.Vertices.Positions)
                    if ((lowestPos == null) || ➥
                    (vertexPos.Y < lowestPos.Value.Y))
                        lowestPos = vertexPos;

        lowestVertices.Add(lowestPos.Value);

        return lowestVertices;
    }
}
}
```

The following code is the method that adjusts a given World matrix in such a way that your Model will be titled so it fits nicely on your terrain. You need to pass it the World matrix of the Model, the Model itself, and the four indices of the ModelMeshes that correspond to the four wheels of the Model.

```
private Matrix TiltModelAccordingToTerrain(Model model, ➥
Matrix worldMatrix, int flID, int frID, int blID, int brID)
{
    Vector3 frontLeftOrig = (Vector3)model.Meshes[flID].Tag;
    Vector3 frontRightOrig = (Vector3)model.Meshes[frID].Tag;
    Vector3 backLeftOrig = (Vector3)model.Meshes[blID].Tag;
    Vector3 backRightOrig = (Vector3)model.Meshes[brID].Tag;
```

```
model.CopyAbsoluteBoneTransformsTo(modelTransforms);
Matrix frontLeftMatrix = modelTransforms[model.Meshes[flID].ParentBone.Index];
Matrix frontRightMatrix = modelTransforms[model.Meshes[frID].ParentBone.Index];
Matrix backLeftMatrix = modelTransforms[model.Meshes[blID].ParentBone.Index];
Matrix backRightMatrix = modelTransforms[model.Meshes[brID].ParentBone.Index];

Vector3 frontLeft = Vector3.Transform(frontLeftOrig, ➥
frontLeftMatrix * worldMatrix);
Vector3 frontRight = Vector3.Transform(frontRightOrig, ➥
frontRightMatrix * worldMatrix);
Vector3 backLeft = Vector3.Transform(backLeftOrig, ➥
backLeftMatrix * worldMatrix);
Vector3 backRight = Vector3.Transform(backRightOrig, ➥
backRightMatrix * worldMatrix);

Vector3 front = (frontLeft + frontRight) / 2.0f;
Vector3 back = (backLeft + backRight) / 2.0f;
Vector3 backToFront = front - back;

float frontTerHeight = terrain.GetExactHeightAt(front.X, -front.Z);
float backTerHeight = terrain.GetExactHeightAt(back.X, -back.Z);
float fbTerHeightDiff = frontTerHeight - backTerHeight;

float fbAngle = (float)Math.Atan2(fbTerHeightDiff, backToFront.Length());
Quaternion fbRot = Quaternion.CreateFromAxisAngle(new Vector3(1, 0, 0), ➥
-fbAngle);

Vector3 left = (frontLeft + backLeft) / 2.0f;
Vector3 right = (frontRight + backRight) / 2.0f;
Vector3 rightToLeft = left - right;

float leftTerHeight = terrain.GetExactHeightAt(left.X, -left.Z);
float rightTerHeight = terrain.GetExactHeightAt(right.X, -right.Z);
float lrTerHeightDiff = leftTerHeight - rightTerHeight;


float lrAngle = (float)Math.Atan2(lrTerHeightDiff, rightToLeft.Length());
Quaternion lrRot = Quaternion.CreateFromAxisAngle(new Vector3(0, 0, -1), ➥
-lrAngle);

Quaternion combRot = fbRot * lrRot;
Matrix rotatedModelWorld = Matrix.CreateFromQuaternion(combRot) * worldMatrix;
```

```
Vector3 rotFrontLeft = Vector3.Transform(frontLeftOrig, ➥
frontLeftMatrix * rotatedModelWorld);
Vector3 rotFrontRight = Vector3.Transform(frontRightOrig, ➥
frontRightMatrix * rotatedModelWorld);
Vector3 rotBackLeft = Vector3.Transform(backLeftOrig, ➥
backLeftMatrix * rotatedModelWorld);
Vector3 rotBackRight = Vector3.Transform(backRightOrig, ➥
backRightMatrix * rotatedModelWorld);

float flTerHeight = terrain.GetExactHeightAt(rotFrontLeft.X, -rotFrontLeft.Z);
float frTerHeight = terrain.GetExactHeightAt(rotFrontRight.X, -rotFrontRight.Z);
float blTerHeight = terrain.GetExactHeightAt(rotBackLeft.X, -rotBackLeft.Z);
float brTerHeight = terrain.GetExactHeightAt(rotBackRight.X, -rotBackRight.Z);

float flHeightDiff = rotFrontLeft.Y - flTerHeight;
float frHeightDiff = rotFrontRight.Y - frTerHeight;
float blHeightDiff = rotBackLeft.Y - blTerHeight;
float brHeightDiff = rotBackRight.Y - brTerHeight;

float finalHeightDiff = (blHeightDiff + brHeightDiff + ➥
flHeightDiff + frHeightDiff) / 4.0f;

worldMatrix = rotatedModelWorld * Matrix.CreateTranslation(new ➥
Vector3(0, -finalHeightDiff, 0));

return worldMatrix;
}
```

## Extra Reading

The correctness of this method depends on the correctness of the bottom positions of the wheels. It will work very well on Models with thin tires, because their bottom positions will be positioned exactly on the terrain.

Models with wide tires, on the contrary, can still give some trouble. If the Model processor picks the inner bottom vertices, calculations are done on these positions, and nothing will assure you that the edges of the wheels don't sink into the terrain.

If this is the case and it bothers you, adjust your Model processor so it stores the outer bottom vertices of the wheels in the Tag properties, or specify them manually to the method.

# 4-18. Detect Ray-Model Collisions Using Per-Triangle Checks

## The Problem

You want to check whether a 3D ray collides with a Model. This is required if you want to perform collision detection at the finest level of detail. It can be used as an extension to recipe 4-11 to detect at a high level of detail whether a bullet has hit an object. As shown in the next recipe, this can, for example, also be used to check whether the pointer is currently over a Model.

Even more, this can be used as an ultrafine check for Model-to-Model collisions, because each edge of a triangle corresponds to a Ray that can be tested for collisions with another Model.

This recipe will deal with the most complex case, allowing separate parts of the Model to be transformed individually, to make this recipe compatible with Model animation. These transformations will have an impact on the final position of the vertices of the Model. For example, if a person moves his arm, the final positions of the vertices of the arm are changed. This recipe will take these transformations into account.

Or, you want a crash course in 3D vector math.

## The Solution

This recipe uses a mix of the custom content pipelines created in recipes 4-13 and 4-14, because it stores an array of Triangle objects inside the Tag property of each ModelMesh of the Model. Each Triangle object carries three Vector3s defining a triangle of the ModelMesh.

The benefit of having each ModelMesh carrying its own array of Triangle positions is that you can transform them with the Bone transform of the ModelMesh. Whatever transformation you have currently set on that part of the Model, you can find the Triangle positions in absolute 3D space by transforming them with the absolute transformation matrix of that ModelMesh (see recipes 3-9 and 4-17). This is required, because in most cases the 3D Ray will be defined in absolute 3D space, so you need to know the absolute 3D positions of the vertices if you want to do any kind of comparison between them.

Once you know the absolute 3D position of each triangle of the Model, the problem reduces to a Ray-Triangle check for each Triangle of the Model.

## How It Works

Because the required content pipeline of recipe 4-15 uses a custom class (Triangle), the easiest way is to add the content pipeline project to your solution. You do this by right-clicking your solution and selecting Add ➤ Existing Project. Browse to the map containing the .csproj file of your content pipeline project, and select that file.

The following steps are still required to allow your main XNA project to access the content pipeline project. See recipe 3-9 for more details on steps 1–5. The last two steps allow your XNA project to deserialize the Triangle objects and are explained in recipe 4-15.

6. Add the newly created assembly to your main project.

7. Select the newly created processor to process an asset.

8. Set project dependencies.

9. In your main XNA project, add a reference to your content pipeline project.

10. Add your content pipeline namespace to the using block of your main XNA project.

Be sure not to forget step 7, and select the `ModelMeshTriangleProcessor` to process your imported `Model`. This processor will store an array of `Triangle` objects in the `Tag` property of each `ModelMesh` of the `Model`.

## Transformations

Now that you have access to all vertex positions of the `Model`, you can define a method that checks for Ray-Model collisions:

```
private bool ModelRayCollision(Model model, Matrix modelWorld, Ray ray)
{
    Matrix[] modelTransforms = new Matrix[model.Bones.Count];
    model.CopyAbsoluteBoneTransformsTo(modelTransforms);

    bool collision = false;
    foreach (ModelMesh mesh in model.Meshes)
    {
        Matrix absTransform = modelTransforms[mesh.ParentBone.Index] *modelWorld;
        Triangle[] meshTriangles = (Triangle[])mesh.Tag;

        foreach (Triangle tri in meshTriangles)
        {
            Vector3 transP0 = Vector3.Transform(tri.P0, absTransform);
            Vector3 transP1 = Vector3.Transform(tri.P1, absTransform);
            Vector3 transP2 = Vector3.Transform(tri.P2, absTransform);

            // if (Ray-Triangle collision)
            //     return true;
                }
    }
    return collision;
}
```

The concept is simple enough: you start off by setting `collision = false`. For each part of the `Model`, you will scroll through all of its `Triangle` objects, containing the positions of the triangles. For each `Triangle`, you will check whether that `Triangle` collides with the Ray. If they collide, return true. Simple.

This is the moment to remind you that the positions stored in the `Triangle` objects are relative to the origin of the `ModelMesh`. This means they first have to be transformed by the absolute transformation matrix of the `ModelMesh` to obtain their position relative to the `Model` origin. Next, they need to be transformed by the World matrix of the Model to obtain their position relative to the 3D world (in other words, the absolute positions).

This first transformation looks like a burden, but in fact it offers a huge advantage: if you rotate one ModelMesh of the Model (for example, an arm of a person), this rotation will also be taken into account here. After you transform the positions of the arm vertices by their absolute transformation matrix, you get their position relative to the Model origin, with the rotation taken into account!

In the previous code, you first calculate the absolute transformation matrices for all Bones of the Model. Next, you combine the absolute matrix for the current Bone with the World matrix. You use the resulting matrix to transform each Triangle you find in the ModelMesh to absolute 3D positions.

Finally, for each Triangle of the ModelMesh, you end up with the exact positions in 3D space, taking any animation on the Model and the positioning of the Model into account! That's how far the previous code goes.

## Ray-Triangle Collision

Once you have these absolute positions for each Triangle, you check whether there's a collision between the Triangle and the Ray. Even simpler.

The if (Ray-Triangle collision) will be broken in two parts. First you will find the point where the Ray collides with the plane of the Triangle. Because the Triangle and this intersection point are in the same plane, the problem becomes a 2D problem, as shown in Figure 4-25. Next, you check whether the collision point is inside the triangle.

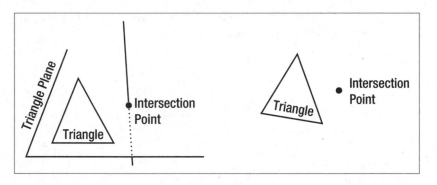

**Figure 4-25.** *Reducing a 3D problem (left) to a 2D problem (right)*

You will code two methods that tackle both parts of the problem. The first method, RayPlaneIntersection, receives a Plane and a Ray and returns the distance of the collision point on the Ray. From this distance you can easily calculate the intersection point between the Ray and the Triangle.

The second method, PointInsideTriangle, receives the three coordinates of a triangle, as well as the coordinate of an extra point (in your case, the intersection point). This method will return whether the point is inside the triangle or not.

If this is the case, you have detected a collision between the Ray and your Model. This is the code that should replace the two lines of pseudocode:

```
Plane trianglePlane = new Plane(transP0, transP1, transP2);
float distanceOnRay = RayPlaneIntersection(ray, trianglePlane);
Vector3 intersectionPoint = ray.Position + distanceOnRay * ray.Direction;
if (PointInsideTriangle(transP0, transP1, transP2, intersectionPoint))
    return true;
```

First you create the triangle plane, based on the three corner points of the triangle. You pass this plane together with the Ray to the RayPlaneIntersection method and receive the location of the intersection point on the Ray, which you use to calculate the position of the intersection point. Finally, you check whether this intersection point is inside the triangle.

---

■**Note**  For more examples on the usage of Ray objects, see recipes 4-11 and 4-19.

---

### Finding the Collision Point Between a Ray and a Plane

You're in luck—the first method is pretty mathematical. Don't worry too much; I've chosen a vector-based approach so you can visualize the process using Figure 4-26.

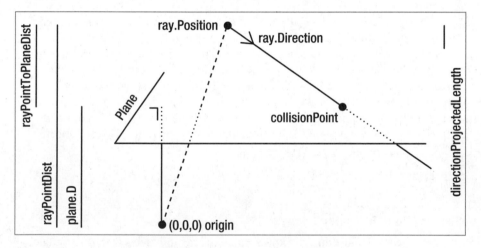

**Figure 4-26.** *Finding the location of the collisionPoint on the Ray*

Given a Ray and a Plane, this method finds the distance from the ray.Direction point to the collisionPoint based on the approach shown in Figure 4-26. Note that all lengths of the variables in the method are shown to the left and right of the image.

```
private float RayPlaneIntersection(Ray ray, Plane plane)
{
    float rayPointDist = -plane.DotNormal(ray.Position);
    float rayPointToPlaneDist = rayPointDist - plane.D;
    float directionProjectedLength = Vector3.Dot(plane.Normal, ray.Direction);
    float factor = rayPointToPlaneDist / directionProjectedLength;
    return factor;
}
```

You start by finding the rayPointDist, which is the length of the projection of the ray.Position on the normal of the plane (the line perpendicular to the plane). The plane.D value equals by definition the shortest distance between the plane and the (0,0,0) origin point, which is the distance along the normal of the plane.

Once you have these two distances along the normal, you can find the distance between the ray.Position point and the plane (that is, rayPointToPlaneDist) by subtracting them from each other.

This shortest distance from the ray.Position point to the plane is the line from ray.Position that goes perpendicularly to the plane, again along the normal of the plane. Now it's time to determine the length of the ray's direction along the plane normal. In other words, if you start in the ray.Position point and you add one ray.Direction, how much closer did you get to the plane?

You can find this length by projecting the ray.Direction on the plane's normal, which is done by taking their dot product. This length is also indicated to the right of Figure 4-26.

You know how much one ray.Direction brings you to the plane and you know how far ray.Position is from the plane, so you can calculate how many times you should add the ray.Direction to the ray.Position point to hit the plane! This factor is what the method returns and can be used to find the exact position of the intersection between the Ray and the Plane. Start from the definition point of the Ray (=ray.Position) and add the Ray's direction multiplied by this factor, and you obtain the position of the collision point. This is done in your ModelRayCollision method:

```
Vector3 intersectionPoint = ray.Position + distanceOnRay * ray.Direction;
```

### Checking Whether a Point Is Inside a Triangle

Luckily, things aren't over yet. Now that you know where the ray intersects with the triangle's plane, you should check whether the intersection point is inside the triangle. Otherwise, the Ray and the Triangle clearly don't collide.

This can again be done using a vector-based approach. Figure 4-27 demonstrates the general idea. If you keep in mind that the collisionPoint is in the same plane as the triangle, the image is not that complicated.

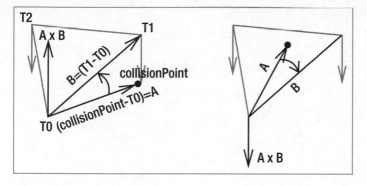

**Figure 4-27.** *Checking whether the collisionPoint is inside the triangle*

In the left part of Figure 4-27, the collisionPoint is outside the triangle. First concentrate on the T0,T1 boundary of the triangle. You want to find out on which side of the boundary the collisionPoint is. Look at vectors A = (collisionPoint – T0) and B = (T1–T0) in the left part of Figure 4-27. If you rotate from A to B, you're rotating in a counterclockwise way.

However, in the right part of Figure 4-27, the collisionPoint is inside the triangle and thus at the other side of the T0,T1 boundary. In this case, when you rotate from A to B, you're rotating in a clockwise way!

This is definitely a way you can check on which side of the boundaries the collisionPoint is. You can take the cross product of A and B, A×B, which will return a vector sticking out of the plane in case of the left part where you're rotating counterclockwise. If you're rotating clockwise, as in the right part of Figure 4-27, this vector will point downward.

This code calculates the A and B vectors and takes their cross product:

```
Vector3 A = point - p0;
Vector3 B = p1 - p0;
Vector3 cross = Vector3.Cross(A, B);
```

Let's take this one step further: the collisionPoint is inside the triangle if it is on the same side of all three boundaries of the triangle. In other words, it's inside the triangle if the three cross vectors are pointing in the same direction.

So in order to check whether the point is inside the triangle, you'll calculate the cross vector for each boundary of the triangle. They are pointing in the same direction when the signs of their components are the same. So, this is the method you end up with:

```
private bool PointInsideTriangle(Vector3 p0, Vector3 p1, Vector3 p2, Vector3 point)
{
    if (float.IsNaN(point.X)) return false;

    Vector3 A0 = point - p0;
    Vector3 B0 = p1 - p0;
    Vector3 cross0 = Vector3.Cross(A0, B0);
```

```
        Vector3 A1 = point - p1;
        Vector3 B1 = p2 - p1;
        Vector3 cross1 = Vector3.Cross(A1, B1);

        Vector3 A2 = point - p2;
        Vector3 B2 = p0 - p2;
        Vector3 cross2 = Vector3.Cross(A2, B2);

        if (CompareSigns(cross0, cross1) && CompareSigns(cross0, cross2))
            return true;
        else
            return false;
}
```

The method receives the corner position of the triangle, as well as the position of the collisionPoint. If the ray was parallel to the plane, no collisionPoint was found, and the point will contain NaNs for all of its components (NaN means Not a Number). If this is the case, it returns false immediately, as a parallel Ray, and Triangle will never intersect in the finite future.

Otherwise, the method continues. For each side of the triangle, you calculate the cross vector. If all cross vectors point in the same direction (meaning the signs of their components are the same), the collisionPoint is inside the triangle!

All that remains is the CompareSigns method, which receives two Vector3s. It needs to check whether the signs of both X components are the same, the signs of both Y components are the same, and the same for the Z components. In short, it checks whether both directions differ less than 90 degrees. This is your code:

```
private bool CompareSigns(Vector3 first, Vector3 second)
{
    if (Vector3.Dot(first, second) > 0)
        return true;
    else
        return false;
}
```

You simply take the dot product between both vectors, which projects one vector on the other. This results in a single value, which will be negative if both vectors differ more than 90 degrees, 0 if they are perpendicular to each other, and positive if they differ less than 90 degrees.

## Performance Considerations

You have to keep in mind that this check needs to be called for each triangle of the Model. Therefore, it is important that it executes as fast as possible. In the following sections, you can find some suggestions to optimize the checks.

## Transform the Ray Instead of the Positions

Inside a ModelMesh, you're transforming each and every position with the absolute transformation matrix of the ModelMesh. This transforms the position to absolute 3D space, so it can be compared to the Ray, which is also defined in absolute 3D space.

It would be better to bring the ray into the ModelMesh coordinate space, because this would have to be done only once for each ModelMesh. As long as the Ray and Triangle positions are in the same coordinate space, they can be compared.

Replace the interior of your ModelRayCollision method with this code:

```
private bool ModelRayCollision(Model model, Matrix modelWorld, Ray ray)
{
    Matrix[] modelTransforms = new Matrix[model.Bones.Count];
    model.CopyAbsoluteBoneTransformsTo(modelTransforms);

    bool collision = false;
    foreach (ModelMesh mesh in model.Meshes)
    {
        Matrix absTransform = modelTransforms[mesh.ParentBone.Index] * modelWorld;
        Triangle[] meshTriangles = (Triangle[])mesh.Tag;

        Matrix invMatrix = Matrix.Invert(absTransform);
        Vector3 transRayStartPoint = Vector3.Transform(ray.Position, invMatrix);
        Vector3 origRayEndPoint = ray.Position + ray.Direction;
        Vector3 transRayEndPoint = Vector3.Transform(origRayEndPoint, invMatrix);
        Ray invRay = new Ray(transRayStartPoint, ➥
        transRayEndPoint - transRayStartPoint);

        foreach (Triangle tri in meshTriangles)
        {
            Plane trianglePlane = new Plane(tri.P0, tri.P1, tri.P2);

            float distanceOnRay = RayPlaneIntersection(invRay, trianglePlane);
            Vector3 intersectionPoint =  invRay.Position + ➥
            distanceOnRay * invRay.Direction;

            if (PointInsideTriangle(tri.P0, tri.P1, tri.P2, intersectionPoint))
                return true;
        }
    }

    return collision;
}
```

Instead of transforming triangle positions into absolute 3D space, you transform the Ray from absolute 3D space to ModelMesh space. It's the opposite transformation of the absTransform, so you invert that matrix. Next, you retrieve both points of the ray, transform them with the inverse matrix, and create a new Ray from the transformed points. Now you have a Ray described in ModelMesh space, so you can compare the Ray to the untransformed vertex positions, which are in the same coordinate space!

As a result, for each ModelMesh you perform two transformations, instead of three for each Triangle inside the ModelMesh!

### First Do a BoundingSphere Check

Instead of scanning for an intersection between the ray and all triangles of the model, it's much better to first check whether the ray collides with the BoundingSphere of a ModelMesh. If this simple and fast check for a ModelMesh returns false, there's no use in checking each triangle of the ModelMesh!

If this fast check returns true, before jumping in to the heavy per-triangle check, it might be a nice idea to check for collisions between the Ray and the smaller BoundingSpheres of all ModelMeshes. Or even better, check with the BoundingSpheres of all ModelMeshParts, if the Model has multiple ModelMeshParts for a ModelMesh.

As you can see, a Model split up in several ModelMeshes not only allows for detailed animation but also has the potential of speeding up your collision checks because you will have more (detailed) BoundingSpheres and thus fewer triangles to check.

## The Code

*All the code is available for download at www.apress.com.*

This is the final method that checks for collisions between a Ray and a Model:

```
private bool ModelRayCollision(Model model, Matrix modelWorld, Ray ray)
{
    Matrix[] modelTransforms = new Matrix[model.Bones.Count];
    model.CopyAbsoluteBoneTransformsTo(modelTransforms);

    bool collision = false;
    foreach (ModelMesh mesh in model.Meshes)
    {
        Matrix absTransform = modelTransforms[mesh.ParentBone.Index] * modelWorld;
        Triangle[] meshTriangles = (Triangle[])mesh.Tag;

        foreach (Triangle tri in meshTriangles)
        {
            Vector3 transP0 = Vector3.Transform(tri.P0, absTransform);
            Vector3 transP1 = Vector3.Transform(tri.P1, absTransform);
            Vector3 transP2 = Vector3.Transform(tri.P2, absTransform);

            Plane trianglePlane = new Plane(transP0, transP1, transP2);
```

```
            float distanceOnRay = RayPlaneIntersection(ray, trianglePlane);
            Vector3 intersectionPoint = ray.Position ➥
            + distanceOnRay * ray.Direction;
            if (PointInsideTriangle(transP0, transP1, transP2, intersectionPoint))
                return true;
        }
    }
    return collision;
}
```

This method calls the `RayPlaneIntersection` method, which returns the position of the collision point between a `Plane` and a `Ray`:

```
private float RayPlaneIntersection(Ray ray, Plane plane)
{
    float rayPointDist = -plane.DotNormal(ray.Position);
    float rayPointToPlaneDist = rayPointDist - plane.D;
    float directionProjectedLength = Vector3.Dot(plane.Normal, ray.Direction);
    float factor = rayPointToPlaneDist / directionProjectedLength;
    return factor;
}
```

The `PointInsideTriangle` method can be used to check whether this collision point is inside the triangle:

```
private bool PointInsideTriangle(Vector3 p0, Vector3 p1, Vector3 p2, Vector3 point)
{
    if (float.IsNaN(point.X))
        return false;

    Vector3 A0 = point - p0;
    Vector3 B0 = p1 - p0;
    Vector3 cross0 = Vector3.Cross(A0, B0);

    Vector3 A1 = point - p1;
    Vector3 B1 = p2 - p1;
    Vector3 cross1 = Vector3.Cross(A1, B1);

    Vector3 A2 = point - p2;
    Vector3 B2 = p0 - p2;
    Vector3 cross2 = Vector3.Cross(A2, B2);

    if (CompareSigns(cross0, cross1) && CompareSigns(cross0, cross2))
        return true;
    else
        return false;
}
```

This verifies that the collision point is on the same side of each boundary of the triangle, by checking whether the cross vectors have the same direction. This is verified in the CompareSigns method:

```
private bool CompareSigns(Vector3 first, Vector3 second)
private bool CompareSigns(Vector3 first, Vector3 second)
{
    if (Vector3.Dot(first, second) > 0)
        return true;
    else
        return false;
}
```

# 4-19. Detect Whether the Pointer Is Over a Model

## The Problem

You want to detect whether the user's pointer is over a Model in your 3D scene.

## The Solution

In XNA, it's easy to retrieve the 2D position of the pointer on the screen. However, this single point on your screen corresponds to a whole Ray in the 3D space of your application, as shown in Figure 4-28.

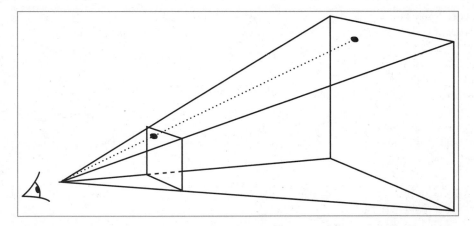

**Figure 4-28.** *The 2D pointer corresponds to a Ray in 3D space.*

As a result, if you want the check which Model the pointer is over, you need to check whether the Ray collides with any Models. Therefore, this recipe will use the code of recipe 4-18.

It's entirely possible that the Ray intersects with multiple Models. This recipe also shows how you can detect which Model is the closest to the screen.

## How It Works

All you have to do is create the 3D pointer Ray and send it together with the Model to the ModelRayCollision method created in recipe 4-18.

You can define a Ray only once you know two points located on the Ray. The two points you're going to use are indicated in Figure 4-28. The first point is the collision of the pointer Ray with the near clipping plane; the second is the collision with the far clipping plane (see recipe 2-1 for more information on clipping planes). You can find their 3D positions by turning the problem around.

If you knew the 3D positions of both points, you would transform them with the ViewProjection matrix to obtain their 2D positions on the screen. However, when you transform a Vector3, the result is another Vector3. Of the resulting Vector3, transformed with the ViewProjection matrix, the X and Y components are the 2D screen position. The third coordinate, the Z component, also contains useful information, because it contains the distance between the camera and the original point, where 0 indicates a point on the near clipping plane and 1 a point on the far clipping plane. It is this distance that is stored in the depth buffer. So in fact, each pixel drawn on your 2D screen by XNA has three coordinates!

This recipe can be used as an example of this. Both points you're looking for share the same pixel on the screen, the same 2D position, so they share the same X and Y components. Because the first point is located on the near clipping plane, its Z component is 0. The second point is located on the far clipping plane, so its Z component is 1. The three coordinates for both points in screen space, in case of a mouse pointer, are as follows:

- (mouseX, mouseY, 0)
- (mouseX, mouseY, 1)

Here they are in code:

```
MouseState mouseState = Mouse.GetState();
Vector3 nearScreenPoint = new Vector3(mouseState.X, mouseState.Y, 0);
Vector3 farScreenPoint = new Vector3(mouseState.X, mouseState.Y, 1);
```

If you go from 3D space to screen space, you transform the 3D point by the ViewProjection matrix. Here you want to transform these points from screen space to 3D space, so you want to transform using the inverse of the ViewProjection matrix. You also need to map the X and Y pointer coordinates into the [–1, 1] region, so you also need the height and width of your screen in pixels.

Luckily, XNA provides the UnProject method that performs exactly this mapping and inverse transformation:

```
Vector3 near3DWorldPoint = device.Viewport.Unproject(nearScreenPoint, ➡
fpsCam.ProjectionMatrix, fpsCam.ViewMatrix, Matrix.Identity);
Vector3 far3DWorldPoint = device.Viewport.Unproject(farScreenPoint, ➡
fpsCam.ProjectionMatrix, fpsCam.ViewMatrix, Matrix.Identity);
```

The two points you get contain the 3D positions of the two points indicated in Figure 4-28!

---

**Note**  You want to know the 3D positions relative to (0,0,0) 3D origin, so you specify Matrix.Identity as the World matrix. The ViewProjection matrix is found by multiplying the View and the Projection matrices. That's why you're specifying both matrices as the second and third arguments.

---

Once you know two points of a Ray, you can create the Ray object:

```
Vector3 pointerRayDirection = far3DWorldPoint - near3DWorldPoint;
pointerRayDirection.Normalize();
Ray pointerRay = new Ray(near3DWorldPoint, pointerRayDirection);
```

With the Ray created, you're ready to detect collisions between the Ray and your Model using the ModelRayCollision method created in the previous recipe:

```
selected = ModelRayCollision(myModel, modelWorld, pointerRay);
```

### Adding a Crosshair to Verify Accuracy

The code presented earlier looks very nice, but what good is it if you can't test it? Let's add an image that shows the position of the pointer. For a brief introduction to rendering images to the screen, see recipe 3-1. Start by storing the 2D screen position of the pointer in a Vector2:

```
pointerPosition = new Vector2(mouseState.X, mouseState.Y);
```

In your LoadContent method, add a SpriteBatch object and a Texture2D holding a transparent crosshair image:

```
spriteBatch = new SpriteBatch(device);
crosshair = content.Load<Texture2D>("cross");
```

And render this image to the screen in the Draw method:

```
spriteBatch.Begin(SpriteBlendMode.AlphaBlend, SpriteSortMode.Deferred, ➥
SaveStateMode.SaveState);
spriteBatch.Draw(cross, mouseCoords, null, Color.White, 0, new ➥
Vector2(7, 7), 1, SpriteEffects.None, 0);
spriteBatch.End();
```

This will allow you to visualize your pointer on the screen. The center point of the image (7,7) will be positioned at the position of the pointer.

### Checking for Multiple Objects

If you have multiple objects located in your scene, it is possible that more than one object is colliding with the Ray. In most cases, you are interested only in the one closest to the camera, because this will be the one that is actually occupying the pixel on the screen.

You can do this by slightly adjusting your ModelRayCollision so it returns the distance to the collision instead of simply true or false. Similar to the Intersect method, you will use a nullable float? variable, so you can return null if there is no collision:

```
private float? ModelRayCollision(Model model, Matrix modelWorld, Ray ray)
{
    Matrix []modelTransforms = new Matrix[model.Bones.Count];
    model.CopyAbsoluteBoneTransformsTo(modelTransforms);

    float? collisionDistance = null;
    foreach (ModelMesh mesh in model.Meshes)
    {
        Matrix absTransform = modelTransforms[mesh.ParentBone.Index]*modelWorld;
        Triangle[] meshTriangles = (Triangle[])mesh.Tag;

        foreach (Triangle tri in meshTriangles)
        {
            Vector3 transP0 = Vector3.Transform(tri.P0, absTransform);
            Vector3 transP1 = Vector3.Transform(tri.P1, absTransform);
            Vector3 transP2 = Vector3.Transform(tri.P2, absTransform);

            Plane trianglePlane = new Plane(transP0, transP1, transP2);

            float distanceOnRay = RayPlaneIntersection(ray, trianglePlane);
            Vector3 intersectionPoint = ray.Position ➥
            + distanceOnRay * ray.Direction;


            if (PointInsideTriangle(transP0, transP1, transP2, intersectionPoint))
                if ((collisionDistance == null) || ➥
                (distanceOnRay < collisionDistance))
                    collisionDistance = distanceOnRay;
        }
    }

    return collisionDistance;
}
```

Each time a collision is detected, you check whether collisionDistance is still null. This will indicate it is the first collision detected, so you store the distance to the collision. From then on, you check whether the distance is less than the distance already known. If this is the case, you overwrite the distance.

The resulting value in the collisionDistance variable will contain the collision closest to the camera, so this is returned. You can use this result to detect which model is closest to the camera.

## The Code

*All the code is available for download at www.apress.com.*

This code creates a 3D Ray describing all points belonging to the pixel indicated by the pointer. This Ray is passed to the ModelRayCollision method of recipe 4-18.

```
Vector3 nearScreenPoint = new Vector3(mouseState.X, mouseState.Y, 0);
Vector3 farScreenPoint = new Vector3(mouseState.X, mouseState.Y, 1);

Vector3 near3DWorldPoint = device.Viewport.Unproject(nearScreenPoint, ➥
fpsCam.ProjectionMatrix, fpsCam.ViewMatrix, Matrix.Identity);
Vector3 far3DWorldPoint = device.Viewport.Unproject(farScreenPoint, ➥
fpsCam.ProjectionMatrix, fpsCam.ViewMatrix, Matrix.Identity);

Vector3 pointerRayDirection = far3DWorldPoint - near3DWorldPoint;
pointerRayDirection.Normalize();
Ray pointerRay = new Ray(near3DWorldPoint, pointerRayDirection);

selected = ModelRayCollision(myModel, worldMatrix, pointerRay);
```

# CHAPTER 5

■■■

# Getting the Most Out of Vertices

**W**hether you're creating a 3D game or some visualization software, in many cases you'll want to render primitives such as points, lines, or triangles. All of these primitives are defined by *vertices*, which are the corners of your triangles or the ends of your lines.

Vertices contain not only a position; they can contain all kinds of data. They can specify which color the corner of your triangle should be rendered in. Or, if you're using a texture to put over your triangle, the vertices should indicate which point of your texture should be mapped to which corner of your triangle. These are only two examples of an almost endless list of data that can be contained in your vertices.

This chapter starts by showing you the basics: how to define vertices and how to render points, lines, or triangles from them. Next in line are texture coordinates and normal data, because most vertices usually store this data.

Next, the chapter covers some powerful functionality provided by XNA, including static and dynamic `VertexBuffers` and `IndexBuffers`, which let you store your vertices in the memory on the graphics card. This is applied in practice when you create a whole 3D terrain defined solely by vertices. Since a terrain (or a grid in general) is quite commonly used in game programming, this chapter deals with some common challenges such as bilinear height determination as well as surface picking. Using Catmull-Rom interpolation, you can even generate extra vertices to make any terrain as detailed as you like!

Since vertices are the data that is sent to your graphics card, this chapter explains why vertex formats are the link between your XNA project, your vertices, and your vertex shader on your graphics card.

Using HLSL, you'll learn how to add bump mapping to your 3D objects to increase the detail of the pixels in your triangles. In the end, you'll even learn how to add an impressive ocean to your 3D world by letting your graphics card manipulate all of your vertices and pixels.

Furthermore, in this chapter you'll learn how to load an object from an XML file into your XNA project.

Specifically, the recipes in this chapter cover the following:

- Understanding what vertices are and how to define them. You'll also learn how to render points, lines, or triangles from your vertices and how to cover your triangles with a texture (recipes 5-1 and 5-2).

- Making the best use of the available memory. You'll remove redundant vertices using indices and store your vertices and indices in the memory of your graphics card by storing them in a `VertexBuffer` and in an `IndexBuffer` (recipes 5-3, 5-4, and 5-5).

- Figuring out why your triangle won't show up! This might be because your graphics card thinks your camera is looking at the back of the triangle, causing it to be non-rendered, or *culled* (see recipe 5-6).

- Storing the correct normal in each of your vertices to allow for correct lighting. You'll also learn how you can calculate all normals at once (recipe 5-7).

- Putting everything you've learned about vertices into practice by creating a textured 3D terrain. You need to be able to calculate the exact height at any point of your terrain, as well as find the point on your terrain that the user's pointer is over (recipes 5-8, 5-9, and 5-10).

- Learning how you load objects from XML files straight into your XNA project (recipe 5-11).

- Learning how you can define vertices of your own format and allowing you to store any data you want in your vertices so you can access this in your vertex shader (recipe 5-12). The vertex format is the glue between your XNA project, your vertices, and your vertex shader on your graphics card.

- Adding an enormous amount of detail to your objects by bump mapping them (recipes 5-13 and 5-14).

- Putting everything you've learned about vertices until now together to create an immersive ocean. Your vertex shader calculates the rolling waves, while the pixel shader adds the required realism (recipe 5-15).

- Given a list of points, learning how you can calculate any number of points on the curve that passes nicely through your predefined points. You'll use this technique to create a racetrack (recipes 5-16 and 5-17).

# 5-1. Render Triangles, Lines, and Points in a 3D World

## The Problem

You want to define a 3D geometrical structure and render it to your screen. This structure can be composed of triangles, lines, or points.

## The Solution

When rendering a 3D geometrical object, you need to define its shape using primitives. Primitives are the most basic geometrical object that can be drawn by XNA, and the most frequently used primitive is the triangle. Any shape, even spheres, can be represented using triangles, if you use enough of them. The XNA Framework can render points, lines, and triangles as primitives.

XNA allows you to define all coordinates of these primitives immediately as 3D coordinates. Once you call the DrawUserPrimitives function, XNA will automatically convert the 3D coordinates into their corresponding screen positions, provided you've specified a valid View matrix and Projection matrix (see recipe 2-1).

## How It Works

To transform 3D coordinates to pixel positions on your screen, XNA needs to know the position of the camera (stored in the View matrix) and some details concerning the lens of the camera (stored in the Projection matrix). If your project doesn't already provide these matrices or you're unsure about their meaning, you might want to read recipe 2-1 and use the camera system from recipe 2-3. Just copy the QuakeCamera.cs file into your project map, and import it into your project. Add the camera system to your project by adding this variable:

```
private QuakeCamera fpsCam;
```

And initialize it in the Initialize method:

```
fpsCam = new QuakeCamera(GraphicsDevice.Viewport);
```

That's it—you now have a working camera system in your project! I explained it in detail in recipes 2-1 and 2-3. The fpsCam object provides the required View and Projection matrices. If you want to let the user move the camera around, pass the user input to your camera by adding these lines to the default Update method of your XNA project:

```
protected override void Update(GameTime gameTime)
{
    GamePadState gamePadState = GamePad.GetState(PlayerIndex.One);
    if (gamePadState.Buttons.Back == ButtonState.Pressed)
        this.Exit();

    MouseState mouseState = Mouse.GetState();
    KeyboardState keyState = Keyboard.GetState();

    fpsCam.Update(mouseState, keyState, gamePadState);

    base.Update(gameTime);
}
```

Instead of going through the list of primitives in alphabetical order, I'll start with the triangle because it is used most often.

### Defining and Rendering a Triangle in Your 3D World

Using XNA, rendering primitives is simple. The few steps needed to render a triangle to the screen are as follows:

1. Define the coordinates and color of the three vertices (corner points) of the triangle, and store them in an array.

2. Set up the effect you want to use to render your triangle.

3. Indicate to your graphics card which kind of data your vertices are carrying.

4. Instruct the graphics card to render the contents of the array to the screen.

### Defining the Vertices

The corner of a triangle is called a *vertex* (the plural form is *vertices*). In this recipe, for each vertex, you want to store a 3D position as well as a color. XNA provides a structure called VertexPositionColor, which can store just that. So, you'll add an array of such objects to your project. Next, you'll also need to specify a VertexDeclaration, which tells the graphics card what kind of information is contained in each vertex.

```
VertexPositionColor[] vertices;
VertexDeclaration myVertexDeclaration;
```

With these variables defined, you'll create a method that first creates this VertexDeclaration and fills the array with three vertices, which should be enough to define your triangle:

```
private void InitVertices()
{
    myVertexDeclaration = new VertexDeclaration(device, ➥
    VertexPositionColor.VertexElements);
    vertices = new VertexPositionColor[3];

    vertices[0] = new VertexPositionColor(new Vector3(-5, 1, 1), Color.Red);
    vertices[1] = new VertexPositionColor(new Vector3(-5, 5, 1), Color.Green);
    vertices[2] = new VertexPositionColor(new Vector3(-3, 1, 1), Color.Blue);
}
```

The VertexDeclaration will be used before instructing your graphics card to render triangles from the vertices. It tells what kind of information can be found in each vertex. This information is described by the VertexElements of the vertex format, which, in this case, will be the position and color.

---

■**Caution** In most cases, you'll use the resulting myVertexDeclaration variable only in the Draw method, where you actually render your triangles. Therefore, it can be tempting to create the variable right there. However, this would cause the myVertexDeclaration variable to be re-created for each frame, which would result in a small slowdown. More importantly, since Xbox 360 uses a "lite" version of the .NET Framework, it will cause your application to crash on Xbox 360 after some undetermined time, making it hard to find out what's causing the crash. Therefore, make sure you always initialize the myVertexDeclaration only once.

---

Next, you specify this 3D position and color for each vertex. In this example, all vertices have the same Z coordinate, so you can expect the triangle to be parallel to the XY plane.

Make sure you call this method from within your LoadContent method.

## Loading the BasicEffect

Before you can render your triangle to the screen, the graphics card first needs to be told what to do with the information it receives. In this example, you want the color you specified to be simply used as the color for that corner. This sounds trivial, but in more complex scenarios you may want to use the information you send to your graphics card for different purposes. This needs to be coded in what is called an *effect*.

Luckily, XNA provides a default effect that makes the graphics card do the most logical and basic things with the information you provide. This effect is called BasicEffect, and you'll need one to get the triangle rendered to your screen. Add this variable to your project:

```
private BasicEffect basicEffect;
```

And initialize it in the LoadContent method:

```
protected override void LoadContent()
{
    device = graphics.GraphicsDevice;
    basicEffect = new BasicEffect(device, null);
    InitVertices();
}
```

---

■**Note**  See Chapter 6 for an introduction to coding your own effect.

---

## Rendering the Triangle to the Screen

---

■**Note**  For demonstrative purposes, I'll use the DrawUserPrimitive method here, although it doesn't perform as well as others of its kind. See recipe 5-4 for a detailed discussion about faster/more complex alternatives.

---

With your vertices defined and your BasicEffect loaded, you're ready to render your triangle to the screen. Obviously, this should be done in the Draw method, which is already provided by the XNA Framework when you start a new project and is called each frame.

Add this code just after you clear the whole scene:

```
device.RenderState.CullMode = CullMode.None;
basicEffect.World = Matrix.Identity;
basicEffect.View = fpsCam.ViewMatrix;
basicEffect.Projection = fpsCam.ProjectionMatrix;
basicEffect.VertexColorEnabled = true;
```

```
basicEffect.Begin();
foreach (EffectPass pass in basicEffect.CurrentTechnique.Passes)
{
    pass.Begin();
    device.VertexDeclaration = myVertexDeclaration;
    device.DrawUserPrimitives<VertexPositionColor> ➥
    (PrimitiveType.TriangleList, vertices, 0, 1);
    pass.End();
}
basicEffect.End();
```

**Tip** This is very elementary code, which is used in this chapter each time custom geometry is rendered from vertices.

Before you can render your triangle, you need to set some values on the BasicEffect effect.

It is possible to move, rotate, or scale your triangle by setting a World transform (see recipe 4-2). For now, you just want the vertices simply to be drawn at the positions you specified, so you set the unity matrix as the World matrix.

The BasicEffect effect also needs to know the View and Projection matrices so the graphics card can take the position of the camera into account and transform all 3D positions of your vertices to their screen positions (see recipe 2-1). Finally, you need to indicate that the BasicEffect effect should actually use the color information you specified.

**Note** If you do not specify where the BasicEffect should sample its color from, it will get its color from the last source specified.

Next, you start the effect. Advanced effects can have multiple passes. Although the BasicEffect effect has only one pass, it's good practice to always loop through all the possible passes.

Once the pass has started, you first need to pass the VertexDeclaration so your graphics card knows which data is contained in the vertices.

Finally, you call the device.DrawUserPrimitives method to render your triangle. The DrawUserPrimitives method takes four arguments. First you need to specify whether you want to render triangles, lines, or points, as well as how they are stored in the array (see the following six sections). Next, you need to pass the array you used to store your vertices. The third argument allows you to specify at which vertex inside the array the graphics card should start drawing from. Because here you want to start drawing from the very first vertex in your array, you specify 0. Finally, you indicate how many primitives XNA should render from the array. Since you've stored only three vertices in the array, you can expect XNA to render only one triangle from them.

Running this code will render your triangle to the screen! As you can see, each corner of the triangle is rendered in the color you specified, with the colors linearly shifted between the corners.

---

■**Note**  The `device.RenderState.CullMode = CullMode.None` code disables culling (see recipe 5-6). Culling can prevent triangles from being drawn, so when beginning 3D programming, you should turn if off.

---

## Rendering Multiple Triangles Using the TriangleList

Now that you've managed to render one triangle, there's no challenge in rendering a few of them. First define their vertices:

```
private void InitVertices()
{
    myVertexDeclaration = new VertexDeclaration(device, ➥
    VertexPositionColor.VertexElements);
    vertices = new VertexPositionColor[12];

    vertices[0] = new VertexPositionColor(new Vector3(-5, 1, 1), Color.Red);
    vertices[1] = new VertexPositionColor(new Vector3(-5, 5, 1), Color.Green);
    vertices[2] = new VertexPositionColor(new Vector3(-3, 1, 1), Color.Blue);

    vertices[3] = new VertexPositionColor(new Vector3(-3, 5, 1), Color.Gray);
    vertices[4] = new VertexPositionColor(new Vector3(-1, 1, 1), Color.Purple);
    vertices[5] = new VertexPositionColor(new Vector3(-1, 5, 1), Color.Orange);

    vertices[6] = new VertexPositionColor(new Vector3(1, 1, 1), Color.BurlyWood);
    vertices[7] = new VertexPositionColor(new Vector3(1, 5, 1), Color.Gray);
    vertices[8] = new VertexPositionColor(new Vector3(3, 1, 1), Color.Green);

    vertices[9] = new VertexPositionColor(new Vector3(3, 5, 1), Color.Yellow);
    vertices[10] = new VertexPositionColor(new Vector3(5, 1, 1), Color.Blue);
    vertices[11] = new VertexPositionColor(new Vector3(5, 5, 1), Color.Red);
}
```

---

■**Tip**  Instead of doing all indexing manually, you can save yourself some time and use an integer that is incremented after each line.

---

With twelve vertices defined, all you have to do is indicate you want to render four triangles from them:

```
device.DrawUserPrimitives<VertexPositionColor> ➥
(PrimitiveType.TriangleList, vertices, 0, 4);
```

If you want to render only the last two triangles, you should mention you want to start rendering from the seventh vertex. Since arrays are 0-based, this vertex has index 6:

```
device.DrawUserPrimitives<VertexPositionColor> ➥
(PrimitiveType.TriangleList, vertices, 6, 2);
```

Indicating only a subset of the vertices can save you some bandwidth because less data is being pushed from your system RAM to your graphics card.

### Rendering Multiple Triangles Using the TriangleStrip

Whenever the triangles you want to render are connected to each other with a side, you can save a lot of memory, and thus bandwidth, by using a TriangleStrip instead of a TriangleList.

Take a look at the six triangles shown in Figure 5-1. Using a TriangleList, this would take 6*3 = 18 vertices. However, only eight of them are unique, so the ten duplicates you're storing and sending to your graphics card are a total waste of the memory, bandwidth, and processing power of your GPU!

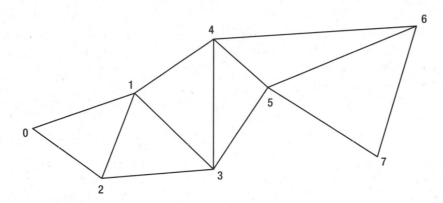

**Figure 5-1.** *Rendering a TriangleStrip*

By specifying you have stored your triangles as a TriangleStrip, XNA will draw the first triangle based on the first three vertices stored in the array. From then on, XNA will create a new triangle for each next vertex, using the new vertex and the previous two. So, the first triangle is defined by vertices 0, 1, and 2; the second triangle is defined by vertices 1, 2, and 3; the third is defined by vertices 2, 3, and 4; and so on.

To render *x* triangles, you need to define *x*+2 vertices. So if you have stored twelve vertices in an array (as done in the InitVertices method earlier), you can render ten triangles as a TriangleStrip using this line:

```
device.DrawUserPrimitives<VertexPositionColor> ➥
(PrimitiveType.TriangleStrip, vertices, 0, 10);
```

**Note**  When defining a `TriangleStrip`, it's impossible to fulfill the culling rule, where you want to define each triangle in a counterclockwise winding order (see recipe 5-6). To solve this, culling is a bit special for `TriangleStrips`. The first triangle needs to be defined in clockwise order, and then the order needs to be flipped to counterclockwise for each triangle (this will automatically be the case!).

### Rendering Multiple Points Using a PointList

In addition to triangles, you can also render lines and points. This involves using the same code; you specify only a different type of primitive.

Simply store a vertex for each point you want to render in an array. If you have stored 12 vertices in an array as shown earlier, this is how you render the 3D points to the screen:

```
device.DrawUserPrimitives<VertexPositionColor> ➥
(PrimitiveType.PointList, vertices, 0, 12);
```

Note that each point will occupy exactly one pixel on your screen, no matter how close/far the camera is from the point. Anyway, you'll need a couple of good eyes to see the pixels.

### Rendering Multiple Lines Using a LineList

The last type of primitive is the line. Strangely enough, you need two points to define a line. An array containing 12 vertices can be used to render 12/2 = 6 lines by calling this method:

```
device.DrawUserPrimitives<VertexPositionColor> ➥
(PrimitiveType.LineList, vertices, 0, 6);
```

### Rendering Multiple Lines Using a LineStrip

As with the triangles, you can also render a strip of lines if they're connected with a point, as shown in Figure 5-2.

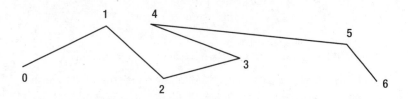

**Figure 5-2.** *Rendering multiple lines as a LineStrip*

Rendering $x$ lines requires $x–1$ vertices, so if you have stored 12 vertices in an array, you can render 11 lines using this method:

```
device.DrawUserPrimitives<VertexPositionColor> ➥
(PrimitiveType.LineStrip, vertices, 0, 11);
```

## Rendering Multiple Triangles Using a TriangleFan

To make this list complete, you can also render triangles that share one point using a TriangleFan. Figure 5-3 shows such a set of triangles. Note that in addition to sharing the central point, each triangle must also share an edge with the next triangle.

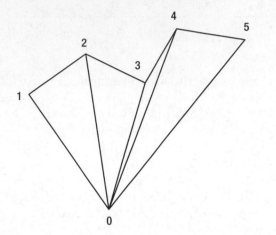

**Figure 5-3.** *Rendering multiple triangles as a TriangleFan*

It takes $x–2$ vertices to render $x$ triangles. This means you can draw ten triangles based on your twelve vertices. The shared point must be stored at position 0 of your array.

---

■**Note**  The TriangleStrip offers the same performance while being much more flexible.

---

```
device.DrawUserPrimitives<VertexPositionColor> ➥
(PrimitiveType.TriangleFan, vertices, 0, 10);
```

# The Code

*All the code is available for download at www.apress.com.*

Because this is the first recipe of this chapter, here you can find all the code you need to render a few triangles as a TriangleStrip:

```
using System;
using System.Collections.Generic;
using System.Linq;
using Microsoft.Xna.Framework;
using Microsoft.Xna.Framework.Audio;
using Microsoft.Xna.Framework.Content;
using Microsoft.Xna.Framework.GamerServices;
```

```csharp
using Microsoft.Xna.Framework.Graphics;
using Microsoft.Xna.Framework.Input;
using Microsoft.Xna.Framework.Media;
using Microsoft.Xna.Framework.Net;
using Microsoft.Xna.Framework.Storage;

namespace BookCode
{
    public class Game1 : Microsoft.Xna.Framework.Game
    {
        GraphicsDeviceManager graphics;
        GraphicsDevice device;
        BasicEffect basicEffect;
        QuakeCamera fpsCam;
        CoordCross cCross;

        VertexPositionColor[] vertices;
        VertexDeclaration myVertexDeclaration;

        public Game1()
        {
            graphics = new GraphicsDeviceManager(this);
            Content.RootDirectory = "Content";
        }

        protected override void Initialize()
        {
            fpsCam = new QuakeCamera(GraphicsDevice.Viewport);
            base.Initialize();
        }

        protected override void LoadContent()
        {
            device = graphics.GraphicsDevice;
            basicEffect = new BasicEffect(device, null);
            InitVertices();
            cCross = new CoordCross(device);
        }

        private void InitVertices()
        {
            myVertexDeclaration = new VertexDeclaration(device, .VertexElements);
            vertices = new VertexPositionColor[12];
```

```
        vertices[0] = new VertexPositionColor(new Vector3(-5, 1, 1), Color.Red);
        vertices[1] = new VertexPositionColor(new Vector3(-5, 5, 1), ➥
        Color.Green);
        vertices[2] = new VertexPositionColor(new Vector3(-3, 1, 1), ➥
        Color.Blue);


        vertices[3] = new VertexPositionColor(new Vector3(-3, 5, 1), ➥
        Color.Gray);
        vertices[4] = new VertexPositionColor(new Vector3(-1, 1, 1), ➥
        Color.Purple);
        vertices[5] = new VertexPositionColor(new Vector3(-1, 5, 1), ➥
        Color.Orange);

        vertices[6] = new VertexPositionColor(new Vector3(1, 1, 1), ➥
        Color.BurlyWood);
        vertices[7] = new VertexPositionColor(new Vector3(1, 5, 1), Color.Gray);
        vertices[8] = new VertexPositionColor(new Vector3(3, 1, 1), ➥
        Color.Green);

        vertices[9] = new VertexPositionColor(new Vector3(3, 5, 1), ➥
        Color.Yellow);
        vertices[10] = new VertexPositionColor(new Vector3(5, 1, 1), ➥
         Color.Blue);
        vertices[11] = new VertexPositionColor(new Vector3(5, 5, 1), Color.Red);
    }

    protected override void UnLoadContent()
    {
    }

    protected override void Update(GameTime gameTime)
    {
        GamePadState gamePadState = GamePad.GetState(PlayerIndex.One);
        if (gamePadState.Buttons.Back == ButtonState.Pressed)
            this.Exit();

        MouseState mouseState = Mouse.GetState();
        KeyboardState keyState = Keyboard.GetState();

        fpsCam.Update(mouseState, keyState, gamePadState);

        base.Update(gameTime);
    }
```

```
protected override void Draw(GameTime gameTime)
{
    device.Clear(ClearOptions.Target | ClearOptions.DepthBuffer, ➥
    Color.CornflowerBlue, 1, 0);

    cCross.Draw(fpsCam.ViewMatrix, fpsCam.ProjectionMatrix);


    //draw triangles
    device.RenderState.CullMode = CullMode.None;
    basicEffect.World = Matrix.Identity;
    basicEffect.View = fpsCam.ViewMatrix;
    basicEffect.Projection = fpsCam.ProjectionMatrix;
    basicEffect.VertexColorEnabled = true;

    basicEffect.Begin();
    foreach (EffectPass pass in basicEffect.CurrentTechnique.Passes)
    {
        pass.Begin();
        device.VertexDeclaration = myVertexDeclaration;
        device.DrawUserPrimitives<VertexPositionColor> ➥
        (PrimitiveType.TriangleStrip, vertices, 0, 10);
        pass.End();
    }
    basicEffect.End();

    base.Draw(gameTime);
}
    }
}
```

# 5-2. Apply a Texture to Your Triangles

## The Problem

You want to render a nicely colored triangle by putting a texture over the triangle.

## The Solution

Your graphics card allows you to specify a 2D image, from which it can sample the colors for your triangle.

This means you'll have to import a 2D image into your XNA project and pass it to the graphics card before rendering your triangles. For each vertex, instead of specifying the color, you'll have to indicate which position in the 2D image corresponds to the vertex.

## How It Works

Start by importing the 2D image into your project, as demonstrated in recipe 3-1. Make sure you link it to a variable in the LoadContent method:

```
myTexture = content.Load<Texture2D>("texture");
```

Next, you should define the vertices of your triangles. As in the previous recipe, you have to specify the 3D position of each vertex. This time, you will not define a color but the position in the 2D texture that should correspond with the vertex. You do this by storing a 2D texture coordinate in each vertex. If each vertex of your triangle corresponds to a 2D texture coordinate, your graphics card will fill the interior of your triangle with the part of the 2D image you specified.

When specifying texture coordinates, you have to keep in mind that the top-left corner of your texture has the (0,0) coordinate, while the top-right corner has the (1,0) coordinate. This means the second coordinate indicates the vertical position, so the bottom-right corner has the (1,1) coordinate. Figure 5-4 shows three regions of a texture that correspond to different texture coordinates.

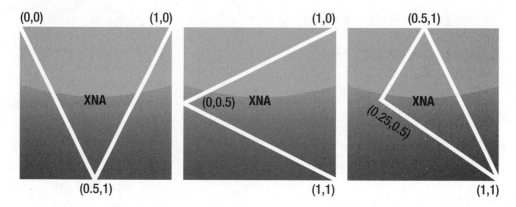
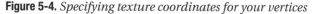

**Figure 5-4.** *Specifying texture coordinates for your vertices*

This means you now have to store a 2D texture coordinate instead of a Color in each vertex. Instead of storing an array containing VertexPositionColor elements, you will now create an array containing VertexPositionTexture elements, which, much as the name implies, can store a 3D position and texture coordinate:

```
private void InitVertices()
{
    vertices = new VertexPositionTexture[9];
    int i = 0;
```

```
vertices[i++] = new VertexPositionTexture(new Vector3(-10, 1, -5), ➥
new Vector2(0,0));
vertices[i++] = new VertexPositionTexture(new Vector3(-7, 5, -5), ➥
new Vector2(0.5f, 1));
vertices[i++] = new VertexPositionTexture(new Vector3(-4, 1, -5), ➥
new Vector2(1,0));

vertices[i++] = new VertexPositionTexture(new Vector3(-3, 1, -5), ➥
new Vector2(0, 0.5f));
vertices[i++] = new VertexPositionTexture(new Vector3(0, 5, -5), ➥
new Vector2(1, 0));
vertices[i++] = new VertexPositionTexture(new Vector3(3, 1, -5), ➥
new Vector2(1, 1));

vertices[i++] = new VertexPositionTexture(new Vector3(4, 1, -5), ➥
new Vector2(0.25f, 0.5f));
vertices[i++] = new VertexPositionTexture(new Vector3(7, 5, -5), new ➥
Vector2(0.5f, 0));
vertices[i++] = new VertexPositionTexture(new Vector3(10, 1, -5), ➥
new Vector2(1, 1));

myVertexDeclaration = new VertexDeclaration(device, ➥
VertexPositionTexture.VertexElements);
}
```

The nine vertices you're defining here have texture coordinates corresponding to the three triangles of Figure 5-4. By specifying these texture coordinates, you indicate the triangles will have the same colors as the triangles in Figure 5-4.

---

**Note** It is important to keep in mind that the actual position in 3D space of the triangles is defined by the Vector3. For example, the first triangle of Figure 5-4 will be rendered upside down in your 3D world, because two vertices have 1 as the Y coordinate and the middle vertex has 5 as the Y texture coordinate. This will cause the word *XNA* in the middle of the texture to be rendered upside down.

---

You also need to inform your graphics card that your vertices now contain a texture coordinate instead of a color. Therefore, you should create a VertexDeclaration based on the VertexElements of the VertexPositionTexture, which you'll pass to the graphics card before rendering the triangle.

With your vertices defined, you're ready to render the three triangles to the screen using a small variation on the code presented in the previous recipe:

```
device.RenderState.CullMode = CullMode.None;
basicEffect.World = Matrix.Identity;
basicEffect.View = fpsCam.ViewMatrix;
basicEffect.Projection = fpsCam.ProjectionMatrix;
basicEffect.Texture = myTexture;
basicEffect.TextureEnabled = true;

basicEffect.Begin();
foreach (EffectPass pass in basicEffect.CurrentTechnique.Passes)
{
    pass.Begin();
    device.VertexDeclaration = myVertexDeclaration;
    device.DrawUserPrimitives<VertexPositionTexture> ➥
    (PrimitiveType.TriangleList, vertices, 0, 3);
    pass.End();
}
basicEffect.End();
```

You need to pass your texture to the graphics card, which is done by setting the texture as the active texture of the BasicEffect. Next, instead of using the colors defined inside the vertices as done in the previous recipe, you specify that the BasicEffect should sample the colors from the texture by setting TextureEnabled to true. Since you're using a different vertex format, you need to pass the new VertexDeclaration to the graphics card.

Finally, you issue your graphics card to render the three textured triangles!

## Texture Addressing Modes

As mentioned earlier, the (0,0) texture coordinate corresponds to the top-left pixel of your texture, while the (1,1) texture coordinate corresponds to the bottom-right pixel.

This doesn't mean you have to use texture coordinates in the [0,1] range, however. For example, it's entirely valid to specify (1.5f, –0.5f) as the texture coordinate. In such cases, you just have to let XNA know how to handle such coordinates by setting the U and V texture addressing modes (where U is the first texture coordinate and V is the second). The following code defines a triangle having U and V coordinates outside the [0,1] region:

```
private void InitVertices()
{
    vertices = new VertexPositionTexture[3];
    int i = 0;

    vertices[i++] = new VertexPositionTexture(new Vector3(-3, -3, -1), ➥
    new Vector2(-0.5f,1.5f));
    vertices[i++] = new VertexPositionTexture(new Vector3(0, 5, -1), ➥
    new Vector2(0.5f, -1.5f));
    vertices[i++] = new VertexPositionTexture(new Vector3(3, -3, -1), ➥
    new Vector2(1.5f,1.5f));

    myVertexDeclaration = new VertexDeclaration(device, ➥
    VertexPositionTexture.VertexElements);
}
```

Next, you need to instruct XNA how it should handle these coordinates by setting the addressing mode of the texture sampler in the graphics card, which is used to sample colors from the texture.

### TextureAddressMode.Clamp

Use this code to set the U and V addressing modes to Clamp:

```
device.SamplerStates[0].AddressU = TextureAddressMode.Clamp;
device.SamplerStates[0].AddressV = TextureAddressMode.Clamp;
```

This addressing mode will cause all texture coordinates to be clamped to the [0,1] region. All coordinates less than 0 will be clamped to 0, while all coordinates greater than 1 will be clamped to 1.

As a result, all the pixels of the triangle having a texture coordinate outside the [0,1] region will get the color of the pixel at the edge of the texture, as shown on the left side of Figure 5-5. The triangle shown in the image corresponds to the triangle having texture coordinates as defined earlier.

This is how your graphics card first maps the texture coordinates before sampling the color from the image:

(–0.5f,1.5f) ➤ (0,1)

(0.5f,–1.5f) ➤ (0.5f,0)

(1.5f,1.5f) ➤ (1,1)

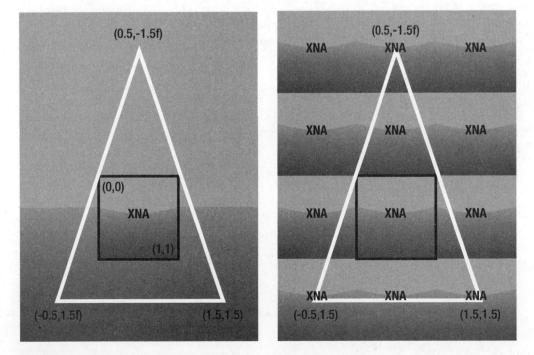

**Figure 5-5.** *Clamp (left) and Wrap (right) texture addressing modes*

### TextureAddressMode.Wrap

Although this is the default texture addressing mode, after using a different one you can reselect wrapping using this code:

```
device.SamplerStates[0].AddressU = TextureAddressMode.Wrap;
device.SamplerStates[0].AddressV = TextureAddressMode.Wrap;
```

Using this addressing mode, the graphics card will keep adding or subtracting 1 from the coordinate until it enters the [0,1] range.

Graphically, this will result in the original texture being copied, as shown in the right part of Figure 5-5.

Here are some example texture coordinate mappings:

(–0.5f,1.5f) ➤ (0.5f,0.5f)

(1.2f,–0.2f) ➤ (0.2f,0.8f)

(–0.7f,–1.2f) ➤ (0.3f,0.8f)

### TextureAddressMode.Mirror

Use this code to set the texture addressing mode to `Mirror`:

```
device.SamplerStates[0].AddressU = TextureAddressMode.Mirror;
device.SamplerStates[0].AddressV = TextureAddressMode.Mirror;
```

This addressing mode will result in the original texture being copied. However, unlike the `Wrapping` mode, the copies are mirrored over the neighboring side with the original texture. So, the copies above and below the original texture are mirrored vertically, while the copies to the left and right of the original texture are mirrored horizontally. The diagonal copies are mirrored along both sides, resulting in the original texture rotated over 180 degrees, as shown on the left side of Figure 5-6.

This mode is quite useful, because it allows you to enlarge your texture without introducing sharp edges, as the `Wrap` method does.

Here are some coordinate mappings:

(–0.5f,1.5f) ➤ (0.5f,0.5f)

(0.5f,–1.5f) ➤ (0.5f,0.5f)

(1.2f,1.7f) ➤ (0.8f,0.3f)

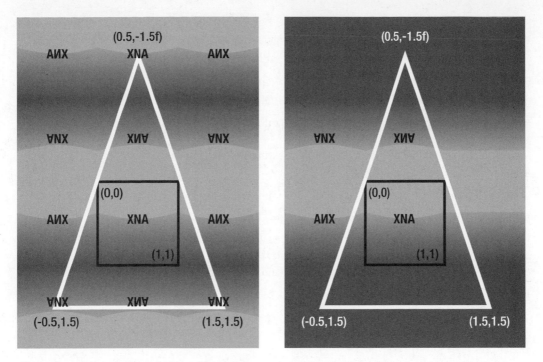

**Figure 5-6.** *Mirror (left) and MirrorOne (right) texture addressing modes*

## TextureAddressMode.MirrorOnce

Alternatively, you can choose to specify the MirrorOnce addressing mode:

```
device.SamplerStates[0].AddressU = TextureAddressMode.MirrorOnce;
device.SamplerStates[0].AddressV = TextureAddressMode.MirrorOnce;
```

This mode mirrors the texture coordinates between the [–1,1] region into the [0,1] region, while all coordinates outside the [–1,1] region are clamped to –1 (for values less than –1) or to 1 (for values greater than 1), as shown on the right of Figure 5-6.

Here are the sample coordinate mappings:

(–0.5f,1.5f) ➤ (0.5f, 1)

(0.5f,–1.5f) ➤ (0.5f, -1)

(1.2f,1.7f) ➤ (1, 1)

## TextureAddressMode.Border

You can also define that you want all the pixels with a texture coordinate outside the [0,1] region to be assigned a color you specify. This color is called the BorderColor and can be set on the SamplerState using this code:

```
device.SamplerStates[0].BorderColor = Color.LightSeaGreen;
device.SamplerStates[0].AddressU = TextureAddressMode.Border;
device.SamplerStates[0].AddressV = TextureAddressMode.Border;
```

This mode is quite useful when debugging, because it clearly indicates all texture coordinates outside the [0,1] region.

No texture mappings are performed; all the pixels with texture coordinates outside the [0,1] region are rendered using the BorderColor.

---

■**Caution**  The Xbox 360 console can only use white as a border color.

---

## The Code

*All the code is available for download at* www.apress.com.

First you need to define your vertices. Since they need to contain their positions in 3D space, as well as their corresponding locations in the texture, you want to use VertexPositionTexture elements. Don't forget to initialize the corresponding VertexDeclaration.

```
private void InitVertices()
{
    vertices = new VertexPositionTexture[3];
    int i = 0;

    vertices[i++] = new VertexPositionTexture(new Vector3(-3, -3, -1), ➥
    new Vector2(-0.5f, 1.5f));
    vertices[i++] = new VertexPositionTexture(new Vector3(0, 5, -1), ➥
    new Vector2(0.5f, -1.5f));
    vertices[i++] = new VertexPositionTexture(new Vector3(3, -3, -1), ➥
    new Vector2(1.5f, 1.5f));

    myVertexDeclaration = new VertexDeclaration(device, ➥
    VertexPositionTexture.VertexElements);
}
```

Once you have your vertices stored in an array and a valid VertexDeclaration, you can set a texture addressing mode and render your triangle(s):

```
protected override void Draw(GameTime gameTime)
{
    device.Clear(ClearOptions.Target | ClearOptions.DepthBuffer, ➥
    Color.CornflowerBlue, 1, 0);

    //draw triangles
    device.RenderState.CullMode = CullMode.None;
    basicEffect.World = Matrix.Identity;
    basicEffect.View = fpsCam.ViewMatrix;
    basicEffect.Projection = fpsCam.ProjectionMatrix;
    basicEffect.Texture = myTexture;
    basicEffect.TextureEnabled = true;
```

```
device.SamplerStates[0].AddressU = TextureAddressMode.Mirror;
device.SamplerStates[0].AddressV = TextureAddressMode.Mirror;

basicEffect.Begin();
foreach (EffectPass pass in basicEffect.CurrentTechnique.Passes)
{
    pass.Begin();
    device.VertexDeclaration = myVertexDeclaration;
    device.DrawUserPrimitives<VertexPositionTexture> ➥
    (PrimitiveType.TriangleList, vertices, 0, 1);
    pass.End();
}
basicEffect.End();

base.Draw(gameTime);
}
```

# 5-3. Remove Redundant Vertices Using Indices

## The Problem

The triangles you want to render share a lot of vertices. Figure 5-7 shows such a situation.

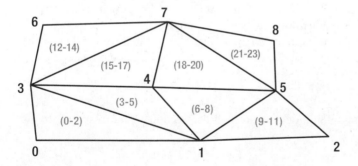

**Figure 5-7.** *Structure that could benefit from using indices*

The eight triangles shown in Figure 5-7 would require 8*3 = 24 vertices to be rendered using a TriangleList. However, you can clearly see this structure contains only nine unique vertices, so the remaining fifteen vertices would be a waste of memory, bandwidth, and vertex processing power on your graphics card.

## The Solution

A better approach is to store the nine unique vertices in an array and send these to the graphics card. Next, you create a list of twenty-four numbers, which refer to one of the nine vertices.

Figure 5-8 shows the big list of twenty-four vertices on the left and the nine vertices with the twenty-four indices on the right. Note that each of the indices links to a vertex.

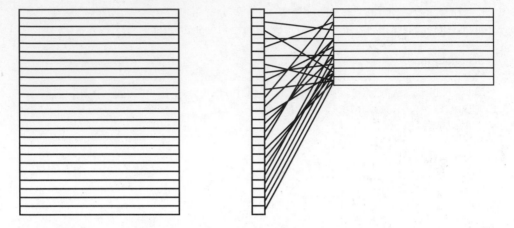

**Figure 5-8.** *Eight triangles drawn from twenty-four vertices (left) or from twenty-four indices pointing to nine vertices (right)*

This brings some important benefits. Since they are just numbers, the 24 indices are very small compared to the vertices, which contain a Vector3, a color, a texture coordinate, and other information you need to store with each vertex. This helps you save on memory and bandwidth. Furthermore, the vertex shader on your graphics card will have to process only nine vertices instead of twenty-four. Of course, these advantages will be quite important when you work with complex structures made from thousands of triangles.

The indices refer to one of the nine vertices, so the triangles are actually drawn based on the indices. Using a TriangleList, you'll need twenty-four indices to render eight triangles.

## How It Works

First you need to define your array of unique vertices. This list (somewhat) corresponds to the structure of Figure 5-7:

```
private void InitVertices()
{
    vertices = new VertexPositionColor[9];

    vertices[0] = new VertexPositionColor(new Vector3(0, 0, 0), Color.Red);
    vertices[1] = new VertexPositionColor(new Vector3(1, 0, 0), Color.Green);
    vertices[2] = new VertexPositionColor(new Vector3(2, 0, 1), Color.Blue);

    vertices[3] = new VertexPositionColor(new Vector3(0, 1, -1), Color.Orange);
    vertices[4] = new VertexPositionColor(new Vector3(1, 1, 0), Color.Olive);
    vertices[5] = new VertexPositionColor(new Vector3(2, 1, 0), Color.Magenta);
```

```
vertices[6] = new VertexPositionColor(new Vector3(0, 2, 0), ➥
Color.Yellow);
vertices[7] = new VertexPositionColor(new Vector3(1, 2, 1), Color.Tomato);
vertices[8] = new VertexPositionColor(new Vector3(2, 2, -1), Color.Plum);

myVertexDeclaration = new VertexDeclaration(device, ➥
VertexPositionColor.VertexElements);
}
```

Now you need to define which vertices should be used to create the triangles. Each of the eight triangles requires three indices to be rendered.

Next, you'll create the list of indices, pointing to these vertices. First add an array to hold these indices:

```
private int[] indices;
```

This method will fill your newly defined array with indices:

```
private void InitIndices()
{
    indices = new int[24];

    indices[0] = 0;
    indices[1] = 3;
    indices[2] = 1;

    indices[3] = 1;
    indices[4] = 3;
    indices[5] = 4;

    indices[6] = 1;
    indices[7] = 4;
    indices[8] = 5;

    indices[9] = 1;
    indices[10] = 5;
    indices[11] = 2;

    indices[12] = 3;
    indices[13] = 6;
    indices[14] = 7;

    indices[15] = 3;
    indices[16] = 7;
    indices[17] = 4;
```

```
indices[18] = 4;
indices[19] = 7;
indices[20] = 5;

indices[21] = 5;
indices[22] = 7;
indices[23] = 8;
}
```

I've split the code up into blocks of three indices so each block corresponds to a triangle. I've also made the list correspond to the gray numbers in Figure 5-7. For example, the upper-left triangle is defined by indices 12 to 14, which point to vertices 3, 6, and 7.

---

■**Note** The triangles have been defined in such a way that the vertices follow each other in a clockwise order. To see why, read recipe 5-6.

---

Don't forget to call this method, for example, from within your `Initialize` method:

```
InitIndices();
```

With your vertices and indices defined, you're ready to send them to your graphics card and render the triangles defined by them:

```
basicEffect.World = Matrix.CreateScale(2.0f);
basicEffect.View = fpsCam.ViewMatrix;
basicEffect.Projection = fpsCam.ProjectionMatrix;
basicEffect.VertexColorEnabled = true;

basicEffect.Begin();
foreach (EffectPass pass in basicEffect.CurrentTechnique.Passes)
{
    pass.Begin();
    device.VertexDeclaration = myVertexDeclaration;
    device.DrawUserIndexedPrimitives<VertexPositionColor> ➥
    (PrimitiveType.TriangleList, vertices, 0, 9, indices, 0, 8);
    pass.End();
}
basicEffect.End();
```

This code is the same as the rendering code of recipe 5-1, except for two lines. The first line sets a scaling transformation of factor 2 as the World matrix, meaning that all vertex positions will be multiplied by 2. So, instead of stretching from 0 to 2, the grid will stretch from 0 to 4. Read recipe 4-2 for more information on World matrices.

Second, and more on topic, you're using the `DrawUserIndexedPrimitives` method, indicating you want to render triangles defined by an array of indices.

You need to indicate the array storing your vertices, as well as how many vertices you'll need from the array and at which position to start. This allows you to use only a portion of the vertices.

Next, you need to specify the array containing your indices and which index your graphics card has to start with. The last argument specifies how many primitives, triangles in this case, you want to render.

---

**■Note** This method supports all primitive types discussed in recipe 5-1. For example, it's entirely possible to render a `TriangleStrip` using indices (see recipe 5-8 for an example) or a `LineList` using indices. However, it's completely useless to use indices for rendering points.

---

### When to Use Indices?

Switching to indices is some kind of optimization, so before moving over to indices, you should first try to render your vertices without indices.

There are cases where using indices will have a negative impact on performance. As an example, imagine five triangles not sharing a single point. Without using indices, you would have to use 15 vertices. Using indices, you also have to define the same 15 vertices, because they're all unique! Even more, you have to define 15 indices, each pointing to its own vertex. So, in this case, you're sending more bytes to your graphics card!

As a rule, you can look at the (number of unique vertices) divided by the (number of triangles). If no vertices are shared among the triangles, this value will be 3. If lots of vertices can be shared, this value will be smaller. The lower this value, the more performance you gain using indices. In the example of Figure 5-7, this value is 9/8 = 1.125, indicating you can gain a lot of performance using indices.

### The Code

*All the code is available for download at www.apress.com.*

Because all the methods used in this recipe were listed in whole in the previous code, I won't list them again here.

# 5-4. Store Your Vertices and Indices in the Memory of Your Graphics Card Using a VertexBuffer and an IndexBuffer

## The Problem

Each time you call the `device.DrawUserPrimitives` method, your vertices are transferred from system RAM to the graphics card. Usually, the majority of this data remains the same between consecutive frames, meaning the same data is transferred each frame again.

Given the huge amount of fast RAM present on today's graphic cards, you can speed up your application by storing your vertices in that video RAM. Vertex data can be transferred much faster from video RAM to the GPU, because the data is sent between chips on the same card. The same holds for indices.

## The Solution

By creating a `VertexBuffer` from your `vertices` array, you're copying the vertex data to video RAM. Once your vertices have been stored in video RAM, you should call the `DrawPrimitives` method (instead of the `DrawUserPrimitives` method used in recipe 5-1), which feeds the vertices from fast video RAM to the GPU.

---

**■Note**  This approach brings the largest improvements when you (almost) never need to update the vertices. When dealing with so-called dynamic vertex data, meaning that it is updated frequently, you should use the `DynamicVertexBuffer`, as explained in the next recipe.

---

## How It Works

Instead of passing an array containing your vertices to the graphics card each time you call the `DrawUserPrimitives` method, you're going to pass the data once and store it in the video RAM. You can do this after you've created the array storing your vertices by loading them into a `VertexBuffer`. Add this `VertexBuffer` to your project:

```
VertexBuffer vertBuffer;
```

Then use this method to generate six vertices, describing two textured triangles as explained in recipe 5-1. At the end of the method, these six vertices are loaded into the `VertexBuffer`, moving them to video RAM:

```
private void InitVertices()
{
    myVertexDeclaration = new VertexDeclaration(device, ➥
    VertexPositionTexture.VertexElements);

    VertexPositionTexture[] vertices = new VertexPositionTexture[6];
    int i = 0;

    vertices[i++] = new VertexPositionTexture(new Vector3(-5.0f, -3, -1), ➥
    new Vector2(-0.5f, 1.5f));
    vertices[i++] = new VertexPositionTexture(new Vector3(-2.5f, 5, -1), ➥
    new Vector2(0.5f, -1.5f));
    vertices[i++] = new VertexPositionTexture(new Vector3(0, -3, -1), ➥
    new Vector2(1.5f, 1.5f));
```

```
vertices[i++] = new VertexPositionTexture(new Vector3(0, -3, -1), ➡
new Vector2(-0.5f, 1.5f));
vertices[i++] = new VertexPositionTexture(new Vector3(2.5f, 5, -1), ➡
new Vector2(0.5f, -1.5f));
vertices[i++] = new VertexPositionTexture(new Vector3(5.0f, -3, -1), ➡
new Vector2(1.5f, 1.5f));

vertBuffer = new VertexBuffer(device, ➡
VertexPositionTexture.SizeInBytes * vertices.Length, BufferUsage.WriteOnly);
vertBuffer.SetData(vertices, 0, vertices.Length);
}
```

When you've defined all your vertices, you create a new VertexBuffer. This translates to
the reservation of memory space on the graphics board. Because of this, you need to specify
a link to the device, as well as the total number of bytes the vertices will occupy. This number
equals (the number of bytes occupied by one vertex) times (the number of vertices you want to
store). In the next section, you can find more details about the last argument.

---

**Note** You certainly don't want to create a new VertexBuffer each frame, so make sure you call
this line only once for each geometrical entity. If you need to overwrite data in a VertexBuffer, never
delete one VertexBuffer and create a new one. Instead, simply load the new data into the existing
VertexBuffer using the SetData method explained in a moment. The only case in which you should delete
a VertexBuffer and replace it with a new one is when you have to increase the number of vertices that can
be stored by the VertexBuffer.

---

With the VertexBuffer created, you're ready to transfer the vertices to their new memory
using the SetData method on the VertexBuffer. Obviously, the SetData needs your vertex array
as the source from which to copy data. The overload shown here can be used if you want to
write only to a part of the VertexBuffer. In such a case, you can indicate the position where
you want to start writing to and how many vertices you want to copy.

---

**Note** If you need to update the contents of your VertexBuffer quite often, you should definitely use a
DynamicVertexBuffer. The SetData method of a DynamicVertexBuffer also has some more powerful
overloads.

---

With the vertex data stored on the graphics card, it's time to render some triangles to
the screen. You can use the same code of recipe 5-1, with two modifications. You will use the
DrawPrimitive method, indicating you're going to render from the active VertexBuffer. Before
you can do this, you need to activate your VertexBuffer.

```
device.RenderState.CullMode = CullMode.None;
basicEffect.World = Matrix.Identity;
basicEffect.View = fpsCam.ViewMatrix;
basicEffect.Projection = fpsCam.ProjectionMatrix;
basicEffect.Texture = myTexture;
basicEffect.TextureEnabled = true;

basicEffect.Begin();
foreach (EffectPass pass in basicEffect.CurrentTechnique.Passes)
{
    pass.Begin();
    device.VertexDeclaration = myVertexDeclaration;
    device.Vertices[0].SetSource(vertBuffer, 0, VertexPositionTexture.SizeInBytes);
    device.DrawPrimitives(PrimitiveType.TriangleList, 0, 2);
    pass.End();
}
basicEffect.End();
```

Inside the pass, as usual you indicate which type of information is stored in each vertex by passing the VertexDeclaration to the device.

The third line of the pass sets your VertexBuffer as the active vertex source for the graphics card. For each vertex, you can store separate information in separate VertexBuffers. In this case, you're using only one VertexBuffer, so you specify index 0. Using the SetSource method, you indicate you want to activate your vertBuffer as the current source for the vertices. You're going to need its data starting from the first vertex, and you need to specify how many bytes one vertex occupies (so the graphics card can cut the byte stream in separate vertices).

Once you've activated your VertexBuffer, render its contents as a TriangleList, starting from the first vertex. The VertexBuffer contains data to draw two triangles.

### Performance Considerations: VertexBuffer Constructor

The constructor of the VertexBuffer allows you to specify a few useful option flags as the last argument. The driver of your graphics card can use this to determine which memory would be the fastest for your usage of your vertex data. Here you can find the possible BufferUsages for creating a VertexBuffer:

- BufferUsage.None: Allows you to write to and read from your VertexBuffer.

- BufferUsage.Points: Indicates that the vertices stored inside the VertexBuffer will be used to render points and sprites.

- BufferUsage.WriteOnly: You promise you will *never* read from data you stored in the VertexBuffer. When used with a VertexBuffer, this allows the driver to put your vertex data in the fastest RAM on your graphics card. Therefore, if you think you'll need access to your vertex data, it's often better to store a local copy of your vertices in your main system RAM instead of calling the GetData method on one of your VertexBuffers.

You can also specify combinations of them, separated by the | bitwise OR operator (which, paradoxically enough, results in a logical AND of the options specified).

## IndexBuffer

If you also want to store your indices on your graphics card, you should use an IndexBuffer next to a VertexBuffer, so add this IndexBuffer variable to your project:

```
IndexBuffer indexBuffer;
```

As a simple example, you'll define the same two triangles as shown earlier, but because they share one point, you'll define only the five unique vertices:

```
private void InitVertices()
{
    myVertexDeclaration = new VertexDeclaration(device, ➥
    VertexPositionTexture.VertexElements);

    VertexPositionTexture[] vertices = new VertexPositionTexture[5];
    int i = 0;

    vertices[i++] = new VertexPositionTexture(new Vector3(-5.0f, -3, -1), ➥
    new Vector2(-0.5f, 1.5f));
    vertices[i++] = new VertexPositionTexture(new Vector3(-2.5f, 5, -1), ➥
    new Vector2(0.5f, -1.5f));
    vertices[i++] = new VertexPositionTexture(new Vector3(0, -3, -1), ➥
    new Vector2(1.5f, 1.5f));
    vertices[i++] = new VertexPositionTexture(new Vector3(2.5f, 5, -1), ➥
    new Vector2(0.5f, -1.5f));
    vertices[i++] = new VertexPositionTexture(new Vector3(5.0f, -3, -1), ➥
    new Vector2(-0.5f, 1.5f));

    vertBuffer = new VertexBuffer(device, ➥
    VertexPositionTexture.SizeInBytes * vertices.Length, BufferUsage.WriteOnly);
    vertBuffer.SetData(vertices, 0, vertices.Length);
}
```

Next, use the InitIndices method to create an array of indices that point to your vertices, and copy them into your IndexBuffer:

```
private void InitIndices()
{
    int[] indices = new int[6];
    int i = 0;
    indices[i++] = 0;
    indices[i++] = 1;
    indices[i++] = 2;

    indices[i++] = 2;
    indices[i++] = 3;
    indices[i++] = 4;
```

```
indexBuffer = new IndexBuffer(device, typeof(int), ➥
indices.Length, BufferUsage.WriteOnly);
indexBuffer.SetData<int>(indices);
}
```

When creating an `IndexBuffer`, you have to specify the type of indices you've used, which will be ints or shorts, and how many you've used of them.

**■Caution**  Some low-end graphics cards allow only 16-bit indices. This will cause errors when you use 32-bit ints as indices. To solve this, store your indices in an array of shorts, and specify you want to create an index buffer of shorts.

**■Tip**  If your vertex array/buffer will never contain more than 32,768 vertices, you should use shorts instead of ints. This will cut the amount of memory your index buffer consumes in half.

Don't forget to call this method during the startup of your project!

When it comes to rendering, you first need to activate your `VertexBuffer` and `IndexBuffer` and then call the `DrawIndexedPrimitives` method to render your triangles from them:

```
device.RenderState.CullMode = CullMode.None;
basicEffect.World = Matrix.Identity;
basicEffect.View = fpsCam.ViewMatrix;
basicEffect.Projection = fpsCam.ProjectionMatrix;
basicEffect.Texture = myTexture;
basicEffect.TextureEnabled = true;

basicEffect.Begin();
foreach (EffectPass pass in basicEffect.CurrentTechnique.Passes)
{
    pass.Begin();
    device.VertexDeclaration = myVertexDeclaration;
    device.Vertices[0].SetSource(vertBuffer, 0, VertexPositionTexture.SizeInBytes);
    device.Indices = indexBuffer;
    device.DrawIndexedPrimitives(PrimitiveType.TriangleList, 0, 0, 5, 0, 2);
    pass.End();
}
basicEffect.End();
```

## The Code

*All the code is available for download at* www.apress.com.

The `InitVertices`, `InitIndices`, and `Draw` methods were all listed earlier.

# 5-5. Store Your Frequently Updated Vertices in a DynamicVertexBuffer

## The Problem

You need to update your vertex data frequently. This will cause slowdowns if you're using the SetData method of the VertexBuffer.

## The Solution

If you're planning to frequently update your vertex data, you should use a DynamicVertexBuffer instead of a normal VertexBuffer. This will cause the data to be stored not in the fastest video RAM but in some memory that is more easily accessible. Therefore, this will result in slightly reduced performance, but changing data frequently inside a normal VertexBuffer would result in a much larger performance hit.

However, as opposed to a normal VertexBuffer, whenever the graphics card is ordered to switch tasks (for example, when switching applications using Alt+Tab), the contents of the DynamicVertexBuffer should be reloaded. You can do this by hooking onto its ContentLost event.

## How It Works

The DynamicVertexBuffer works very much like the normal VertexBuffer. Again, you'll first need an array of vertices that you'll load into your DynamicVertexBuffer, as shown here:

```
private void InitVertices()
{
    myVertexDeclaration = new VertexDeclaration(device, ➥
    VertexPositionTexture.VertexElements);

    vertices = new VertexPositionTexture[6];
    int i = 0;

    vertices[i++] = new VertexPositionTexture(new Vector3(-5.0f, -3, -1), ➥
    new Vector2(-0.5f, 1.5f));
    vertices[i++] = new VertexPositionTexture(new Vector3(-2.5f, 5, -1), ➥
    new Vector2(0.5f, -1.5f));
    vertices[i++] = new VertexPositionTexture(new Vector3(0, -3, -1), ➥
    new Vector2(1.5f, 1.5f));

    vertices[i++] = new VertexPositionTexture(new Vector3(0, -3, -1), ➥
    new Vector2(-0.5f, 1.5f));
    vertices[i++] = new VertexPositionTexture(new Vector3(2.5f, 5, -1), ➥
    new Vector2(0.5f, -1.5f));
    vertices[i++] = new VertexPositionTexture(new Vector3(5.0f, -3, -1), ➥
    new Vector2(1.5f, 1.5f));
```

```
dynVertBuffer = new DynamicVertexBuffer(device, ➥
VertexPositionTexture.SizeInBytes * vertices.Length, BufferUsage.WriteOnly);
dynVertBuffer.SetData(vertices, 0, vertices.Length, SetDataOptions.NoOverwrite);
dynVertBuffer.ContentLost +=new EventHandler(dynVertBuffer_ContentLost);
}
```

The line that actually creates the DynamicVertexBuffer accepts the same arguments as when creating a normal VertexBuffer. The SetData method, however, accepts a new powerful argument, which I'll describe in a moment.

The last line is completely new. If the device gets "lost," then when the graphics card is required by another application, the contents of a DynamicVertexBuffer will be lost. Therefore, you can hook a method to the ContentLost event of the DynamicVertexBuffer. Whenever the DynamicVertexBuffer loses its content, it will fire the ContentLost event. All methods that are hooked to this event will be called, so this is your chance to reload its contents.

In the previous example, you've hooked the dynVertBuffer_ContentLost method to the event. Of course, you still have to define this method. You want the method to simply restore the contents of the buffer:

```
private void dynVertBuffer_ContentLost(object sender, EventArgs e)
{
    dynVertBuffer.SetData(vertices, 0, vertices.Length, SetDataOptions.NoOverwrite);
}
```

**Note** This requires local access to your vertex data. Because a DynamixVertexBuffer is to be used only in cases where your vertex data changes frequently, this should be no problem. Keep in mind that you should never try to read from a (Dynamic)VertexBuffer.

When it comes to rendering, the DynamicVertexBuffer behaves in the same way as a VertexBuffer.

## Performance Considerations: DynamicVertexBuffer.SetData Method

Since a DynamicVertexBuffer is needed in cases when you want to frequently update the vertex data, you can expect the SetData method to be used a lot. Therefore, the SetData method of a DynamicVertexBuffer accepts an extra argument, SetDataOptions.

This argument allows you to specify some interesting options, which can improve the overall speed of your application. By default, whenever you want to overwrite the contents of RAM on the graphics card, your graphics card can't read from that section because it doesn't support simultaneous reading and writing. When writing to a large, important section of memory, this could cause the drawing operation of your graphics card to stall, because it has to wait for your copy operation to be completed.

However, there are two ways you can make sure your graphics card doesn't have to wait for your copy operation to be completed. You can indicate this using the SetDataOptions argument; the following are the possible values:

- `SetDataOptions.None`: This option gives you full control over which parts of the `VertexBuffer` to overwrite. However, as explained previously, this can come at a performance penalty. If the graphics card is rendering from the previous contents of the `VertexBuffer` at the time you issue your `SetData` command, your graphics card has to stall its drawing operation until all the slow copying has been finished!

- `SetDataOptions.Discard`: Using this option, you indicate you don't need the previous contents of the `VertexBuffer` anymore. The data you write using this option will be stored in a new spot in video RAM. Although this is happening, the graphics card can happily continue to render from the old contents. Once the writing has been finished, the graphics card is kindly requested to use the new contents from then on, and the old contents are discarded. In short, the graphics card does not have to wait, but you have to rewrite all the data. (This option cannot be used when programming for Xbox 360. You should use a `DrawUserIndexedPrimitive` call to render frequently changed vertex data on Xbox 360.)

- `SetDataOptions.NoOverwrite`: This is quite powerful but dangerous. Using this option, you promise your graphics card that the part of the `VertexBuffer` you're going to overwrite is currently not being used to render from. Therefore, you can overwrite a specific section of your `VertexBuffer`, while your graphics card doesn't have to wait for the copying to be finished, because it doesn't need that specific part to do its job. This is faster than the `Discard` option, because you do not need to reserve a new section of memory. However, if you break your promise and overwrite data that is currently being rendered from, your application will crash.

# 5-6. Enable Backface Culling: What It Is and What It Can Do for You

## The Problem

In the previous recipes, you can always find the following line inside the `Draw` method:

```
device.RenderState.CullMode = CullMode.None;
```

If you remove this line and move the camera behind the triangles, they will disappear!

Also, when you start defining the vertices of your triangles without understanding backface culling, each triangle you define has a 50 percent chance of not being displayed.

## The Solution

The way you define the vertices of your triangles tells XNA which side you want to be facing the camera.

When rendering a solid object, a human can clearly say which side of each triangle is on the inside or on the outside of the object. To render only the necessary triangles, you could ask XNA to render only the triangles, of which the front side is facing the camera. All the other triangles (of which the front sides are turned away from the camera) are on the back side of the object and are hidden by triangles on the front side!

However, things are not so trivial for a computer. For each triangle you define, you need to indicate which side of it is on the inside or the outside. You do this by defining the three vertices of a triangle in counterclockwise or clockwise order.

## How It Works

When defining vertices, you need to keep the position of the camera in mind. If you want the triangle to be rendered, the order of vertices as seen by the camera must increment in a clockwise manner.

To visualize this, you should imagine a ray going from the camera through the center of the triangle, as shown in Figure 5-9. If the order of vertices (as seen by the camera!) rotates around this center point in a clockwise way as in the left part of the image, XNA considers this triangle as facing the camera; thus, the triangle will be rendered.

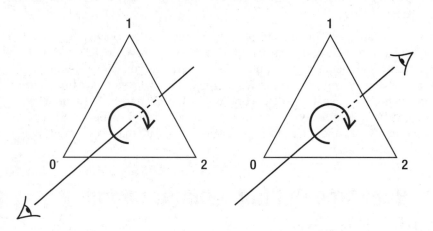

**Figure 5-9.** *Camera in front of (left) and behind (right) the triangle*

If you put the camera behind the same triangle as shown in the right part of Figure 5-9, the order of vertices (again, as seen by the camera!) increments in a counterclockwise way (if you don't see this immediately, read on). XNA will consider this triangle as not facing the camera and will not render it.

Figure 5-10 shows the same situation, but this time shown from the sight of the camera. It should be clear the camera sees the order of vertices on the right side in a counterclockwise way.

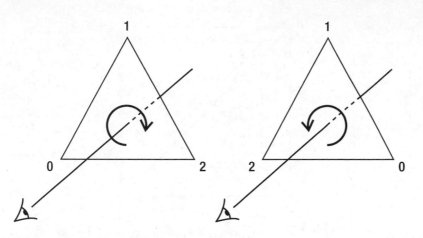

**Figure 5-10.** *Clockwise-defined triangle will be rendered (left); counterclockwise-defined triangle will be culled.*

## Why Do You Need Backface Culling?

The case of a single triangle is useful for showing the principle but does not really show the benefit of backface culling. As mentioned briefly in the introduction to this recipe, backface culling is most interesting when rendering solid objects, such as models or terrains.

Let's discuss a cube as an example. However you rotate your cube, at any one moment you will be able to see only three faces of the cube at a time. This means that the other three faces are simply a waste of the processing power of your graphics card. The triangles not facing the camera should not be drawn.

As an example, say you are holding the cube so you see only its front face, as in the left part of Figure 5-11. Next, take a look at the right of the figure, where one triangle of the front face and one triangle of the back face of the cube have been highlighted.

The numbers indicate the order of the vertices. The six faces consist of twelve triangles, requiring thirty-six vertices to be defined. The numbers in Figure 5-11 indicate which vertices define the two triangles.

---

■**Note** If you are using indices, the cube has only eight unique vertices but still requires thirty-six indices to render the twelve triangles from the eight vertices. The numbers in Figure 5-11 then indicate which indices define the two triangles.

---

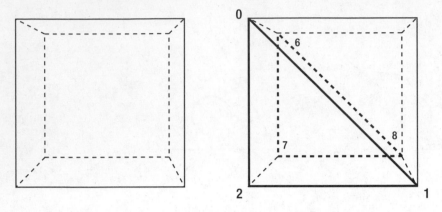

**Figure 5-11.** *Cube: two triangles of the front and back faces of the cube*

The left part of Figure 5-12 shows the ray that is coming from your camera and intersects both triangles at the dots. Focus on the dot that indicates the intersection between the ray and the front triangle. When you follow the vertices of the front triangle in increasing order (going from 0 to 1 to 2), you will see you are making a clockwise rotation around the dot. As a result, XNA will render this triangle.

Now focus on the intersection dot between the ray and the back triangle. When you follow the vertices of the back triangle in increasing order (going from 6 to 7 to 8), you will be making a counterclockwise rotation. So, XNA will be culling this triangle away, which is excellent because it's on the back side of the cube and will be hidden by the front face!

The right part of Figure 5-12 shows the same cube, rotated for 180 degrees, so the front and back faces have changed places. The camera has remained on this side of the page. Now if you follow vertices 6 to 7 to 8, you are making a clockwise rotation around the eye ray. This time, your graphics card will draw this triangle and cull away the other one! It's exactly as it should be.

This is the way your graphics card knows which triangles to cull away. Culling away triangles that are not facing the camera can vastly improve the rendering performance of your application and is activated by default.

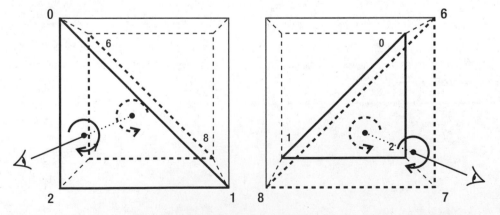

**Figure 5-12.** *Ray from your eye intersecting both triangles*

---

**■Tip** Recipe 5-7 contains an example of a cylinder. Make sure culling is on, and try moving your camera exactly above the cylinder. See what happens!

---

### When and How to Turn Off Culling

Although culling offers a huge benefit when rendering objects consisting of solid surfaces, sometimes you'll want to turn culling off. For example, if you create a building of which a rectangular wall is composed of only two triangles, this wall would look nice from the outside. However, when the camera enters the building, the wall would be culled away, and you would be able to see right through it!

To solve this, you could define two extra triangles for the wall with the opposite winding order, so either way you look at it, two triangles are drawn and two triangles are culled away.

An easier approach is to turn off culling by using this line:

```
device.RenderState.CullMode = CullMode.None;
```

Don't forget to turn culling back on after the code that renders the walls, though, so the rest of your scene is rendered with backface culling enabled.

You'll want to enable culling when rendering solid objects, while you'll want to turn culling off when rendering a surface that can be seen from both sides.

---

**■Tip** When designing and especially when debugging your application, you may want to turn off culling. Doing so removes one of the possibilities of why objects don't get rendered.

---

## The Code

*All the code is available for download at www.apress.com.*

The sample code defines a cube in a clockwise order and a counterclockwise order. When running the counterclockwise version, you'll see that XNA renders only the triangles it actually shouldn't render.

When running the clockwise version, try moving your camera into the cube.

# 5-7. Automatically Calculate the Normals for All Vertices in a VertexBuffer

## The Problem

When rendering your self-defined structure to the 3D world, you notice it isn't lit correctly.

This is because you haven't specified the correct normal vector for each vertex of your structure. A normal is required in each vertex so your graphics card can determine how much light hits the triangle. See Chapter 6 for more information about normals and why they are needed.

Calculating the normal vector for each vertex can seem complicated, because in all structures most vertices are shared among multiple triangles. Therefore, you need a method that automatically calculates the normals for all vertices of your object.

## The Solution

If each vertex will be used by only one triangle, all you have to do is find the normal vector of the triangle (in other words, the vector perpendicular to the triangle) and assign this vector to the vertex.

However, in the case of a structure, all vertices will be shared among several triangles. To obtain a smooth effect, each vertex needs to store the normal that is the average of all normals of the surrounding triangles.

## How It Works

Using this bit of pseudocode, you can find the correct normal in each vector:

1. For each vertex in your structure, find all triangles using that vertex.

2. Calculate the normal vector for these triangles.

3. Average all these normal vectors.

4. Store this averaged normal vector in the vertex.

The averaging step is required, because you'll always want the normal vectors stored in your vertices to be normalized (in other words, have a length of exactly 1).

---

■**Note**  You want the length of your normal vectors to be exactly 1, because this vector will be used in the vertex and pixel shader to calculate lighting factors. A larger normal vector will result in a larger lighting factor than a small vector, while you want the lighting factor to depend only on the angle between the incoming light and the normal, as explained in Chapter 6.

---

You can go on and convert this to real code, but if you swap the order of steps 1 and 2, you can make life much easier:

1. For each triangle in your structure, calculate the normal vector.

2. Add this vector to the normals of the three vertices of the triangle.

    And after this has been done for all triangles, do the following:

3. For each vertex in your structure, normalize its normal vector.

## Calculating the Normal of a Triangle: Definition of the Cross Product

Before continuing, you should know what a normal exactly is. Put quite simply, it is the direction perpendicular to the triangle. This means that in any point of the triangle, the normal is the same. Because the normal is perpendicular to the plane of the triangle, it is also perpendicular to any vector inside the triangle.

So, how can you calculate the normal vector of a single triangle? You do this using a cross product, because the cross product of two vectors returns the vector perpendicular to the plane of the two vectors.

In the case of your triangle, you will take two sides of the triangle as vectors. By taking their cross product, you will obtain the vector perpendicular to the triangle, as indicated by the dotted line in Figure 5-13. However, the length of this normal will be based on the angle between and the length of both sides, so afterward you need to normalize your vector to unity length.

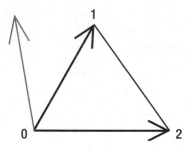

**Figure 5-13.** *Finding the normal vector of a triangle*

Note that `Vector3.Cross(Vec1, Vec2)` is not the same as `Vector3.Cross(Vec2,Vec1)`. Both resulting vectors will be on the same line, but they will have opposite directions. This is because a plane, and thus the previous triangle, has two perpendicular directions: one pointing out of this page and the other pointing into this page.

## The GenerateNormalsForTriangleList Method

When defining a large object, you'll mostly want to define your structure using indices, because this is the only way a vertex can be used by multiple triangles, which allows smooth lighting on your object (see recipe 6-2). Therefore, this recipe will base its calculations on two arrays containing the vertices and indices of your structure:

```
private VertexPositionNormalTexture[] ➥
GenerateNormalsForTriangleList(VertexPositionNormalTexture[] vertices, ➥
int[] indices)
{
}
```

This method receives the array of vertices, which do not yet contain any normal data. It will store the correct normal information inside each vertex and will return the array. Based on the indices, it can determine which vertices are used to create triangles. However, depending on whether you are drawing the triangles as a TriangleList or TriangleStrip, the contents of the indices array will be different, so some lines in the method are different for both cases.

### Calculating Normals for a Structure Rendered As a TriangleList

If the vertices already contain any data for their normals, reset them all to 0:

```
for (int i = 0; i < vertices.Length; i++)
    vertices[i].Normal = new Vector3(0, 0, 0);
```

Next, as indicated in the previous pseudocode, you're going to scroll through all the triangles of the structure and calculate their normals. In a TriangleList, each triangle is defined by three consecutive indices. This means the number of triangles in your structure equals indices.Length/3.

This for loop scrolls through each triangle defined in the indices array:

```
for (int i = 0; i < indices.Length/3; i++)
{
    Vector3 firstVec = vertices[indices[i*3 + 1]].Position - ➡
    vertices[indices[i*3]].Position;
    Vector3 secondVec = vertices[indices[i*3 + 2]].Position - ➡
    vertices[indices[i*3]].Position;
    Vector3 normal = Vector3.Cross(secondVec, firstVec);
    normal.Normalize();

    vertices[indices[i*3]].Normal += normal;
    vertices[indices[i*3 + 1]].Normal += normal;
    vertices[indices[i*3 + 2]].Normal += normal;
}
```

For each triangle, you define the two vectors that are shown in Figure 5-13. As for any vector between point P0 and P1, you find it by subtracting P0 from P1. This is done in the first line, and the second line calculates the vector from P0 to P2.

Next, you find the vector perpendicular to these two vectors by taking their cross product. Don't forget to normalize this result so its length becomes exactly 1.

---

■**Note** Based on the way you defined your indices, you might need to use Vector3.Cross(secondVec, firstVec); instead. As mentioned earlier, this will result in the vector in the opposite direction. If you've defined your vertices in a clockwise order (see recipe 5-6), this code should be OK.

---

Now that you know the normal of the triangle, you simply add it to the normal of each vertex of the triangle. When this for loop finishes, each vertex will store the sum of all normals of the triangles it was used for.

This means you have to bring the length of these large vectors back to 1 by normalizing them:

```
for (int i = 0; i < vertices.Length; i++)
    vertices[i].Normal.Normalize();
```

```
return vertices;
```

With all normals stored in the `vertices` array, you return this array to the calling code.

## Calculating Normals for a Structure Rendered As a TriangleStrip

For a `TriangleStrip`, things are slightly different because each index in the `indices` array creates a new triangle, based on that index and the previous two indices:

```
for (int i = 2; i < indices.Length; i++)
{
    Vector3 firstVec = vertices[indices[i - 1]].Position - ➥
    vertices[indices[i]].Position;
    Vector3 secondVec = vertices[indices[i - 2]].Position - ➥
    vertices[indices[i]].Position;
    Vector3 normal = Vector3.Cross(firstVec, secondVec);
    normal.Normalize();
}
```

Starting from the third index, each index you encounter builds a triangle based on indices i, i-1, and i-2. The previous code scrolls through all the triangles defined by the `indices` array and creates two vectors corresponding to two sides of the triangle.

However, when you defined the indices for your `TriangleStrip`, you automatically swapped the winding order after each triangle (see the note in recipe 5-1). As a result, your so-called `firstVec` and `secondVec` change sides after each triangle. This will have the same effect as changing `firstVec` and `secondVec` in the `Cross` method for each next triangle, which will swap the direction of the resulting normal each time.

You can't do anything about this, but you can compensate for it easily. Just keep track of a Boolean, and switch this value after each triangle. If the value is, say, `true`, you swap the direction of the normal again:

```
bool swappedWinding = false;
for (int i = 2; i < indices.Length; i++)
{
    Vector3 firstVec = vertices[indices[i - 1]].Position - ➥
    vertices[indices[i]].Position;
    Vector3 secondVec = vertices[indices[i - 2]].Position - ➥
    vertices[indices[i]].Position;
    Vector3 normal = Vector3.Cross(firstVec, secondVec);
    normal.Normalize();

    if (swappedWinding)
        normal *= -1;
```

```
    vertices[indices[i]].Normal += normal;
    vertices[indices[i - 1]].Normal += normal;
    vertices[indices[i - 2]].Normal += normal;

    swappedWinding = !swappedWinding;
}
```

The remainder of the code is identical to the method of the previous section, so don't forget about the resetting code at the beginning of the method, as well as the normalization code at the end.

### Making the Method Fail-Safe

The Vector3.Cross method used earlier might give an error if firstVec and secondVec have the same direction. The triangle of this case would be a line instead of a triangle and is called a *ghost triangle* (see the example in recipe 5-8).

In this case, the Vector3.Cross method will return a Vector3 containing three Not-a-Number (NaN) values. If this is the case, don't add that vector to any vertex, or it will become corrupted:

```
if (!float.IsNaN(normal.X))
{
    vertices[indices[i]].Normal += normal;
    vertices[indices[i - 1]].Normal += normal;
    vertices[indices[i - 2]].Normal += normal;
}
```

### Starting from a VertexBuffer and an IndexBuffer

The previous code starts from two arrays containing the vertices and indices. If you already stored them in Buffers in the video RAM (see recipe 5-4) and you haven't kept a local copy, you have to get the data back. This is how you do that:

```
int numberOfVertices = myVertexBuffer.SizeInBytes / ➥
 VertexPositionNormalTexture.SizeInBytes;
VertexPositionNormalTexture[] vertices = new ➥
VertexPositionNormalTexture[numberOfVertices];
myVertexBuffer.GetData(vertices);

int numberOfIndices = myIndexBuffer.SizeInBytes / 4;
int[] indices = new int[numberOfIndices];
myIndexBuffer.GetData(indices);
```

You find the number of vertices in your VertexBuffer by looking at how many bytes it occupies. Since you know how many bytes one vertex occupies, you can find how many of your vertices fit in the VertexBuffer.

You follow the same approach to find the number of indices inside the IndexBuffer, because you know one int occupies 4 bytes.

■**Note** As explained in recipe 5-4, using the GetData on a VertexBuffer or an IndexBuffer is definitely not recommended. Even more, if you've used the BufferUsage.WriteOnly flag to create the buffer, the compiler will throw an error on the GetData method.

## The Code

*All the code is available for download at www.apress.com.*

The following method adds normal data to the vertices stored in the vertices array, if the indices render triangles as a TriangleStrip:

```
private VertexPositionNormalTexture[] ➥
GenerateNormalsForTriangleStrip(VertexPositionNormalTexture[] vertices, ➥
int[] indices)
{
    for (int i = 0; i < vertices.Length; i++)
        vertices[i].Normal = new Vector3(0, 0, 0);

    bool swappedWinding = false;
    for (int i = 2; i < indices.Length; i++)
    {
        Vector3 firstVec = vertices[indices[i - 1]].Position - ➥
        vertices[indices[i]].Position;
        Vector3 secondVec = vertices[indices[i - 2]].Position - ➥
        vertices[indices[i]].Position;
        Vector3 normal = Vector3.Cross(firstVec, secondVec);
        normal.Normalize();

        if (swappedWinding)
            normal *= -1;

        if (!float.IsNaN(normal.X))
        {
            vertices[indices[i]].Normal += normal;
            vertices[indices[i - 1]].Normal += normal;
            vertices[indices[i - 2]].Normal += normal;
        }

        swappedWinding = !swappedWinding;
    }
```

```
    for (int i = 0; i < vertices.Length; i++)
        vertices[i].Normal.Normalize();

    return vertices;
}
```

# 5-8. Create a Terrain Based on a VertexBuffer and an IndexBuffer

## The Problem

Based on a 2D height map, you want to create a terrain and render it in an efficient way.

## The Solution

First you need to have a height map, containing all the height data you want to define your terrain from. This height map will have a certain number of data points in both dimensions; let's call these the *width* and *height* of your future terrain.

Obviously, if you want to build a terrain based on this data, your terrain will be drawn from width*height unique vertices, as shown at the top-right corner of Figure 5-14 (note that the count is 0-based).

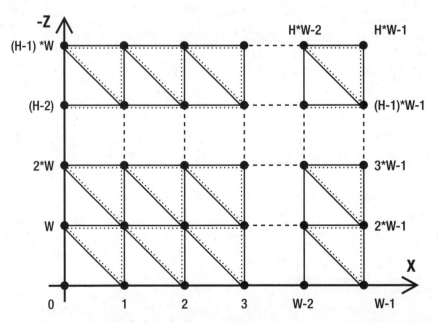

**Figure 5-14.** *Floor grid of a terrain*

To completely cover the whole grid with triangles, you need to render two triangles between each four points of the grid, which are shown as the triangles drawn in the solid and dotted lines in Figure 5-14. You will need (width–1)*2 triangles for one row, yielding (height–1)*(width–1)*2 triangles for the whole terrain.

If you want to determine whether you should use indices to render your terrain, use the rule from recipe 5-3. In this case, (number of unique vertices) divided by (number of triangles) is less than 1, so you should definitely use indices. All vertices that are not on the border are shared by no less than six triangles!

Furthermore, because all triangles share at least one side with each other, you should render the whole pack of triangles as a TriangleStrip instead of a TriangleList.

## How It Works

### Defining the Vertices

Start by defining your vertices. The following method assumes you have access to a heightData variable, which is a 2D array containing the height for all vertices of your terrain. If you don't have such an array available, the LoadHeightData method at the end of this recipe creates such an array based on a 2D image.

```
private VertexPositionNormalTexture[] CreateTerrainVertices()
{
    int width = heightData.GetLength(0);
    int height = heightData.GetLength(1);
    VertexPositionNormalTexture[] terrainVertices = ➥
    new VertexPositionNormalTexture[width * height];

    int i = 0;
    for (int z = 0; z < height; z++)
    {
        for (int x = 0; x < width; x++)
        {
            Vector3 position = new Vector3(x, heightData[x, z], -z);
            Vector3 normal = new Vector3(0, 0, 1);
            Vector2 texCoord = new Vector2((float)x / 30.0f, (float)z / 30.0f);

            terrainVertices[i++] = new VertexPositionNormalTexture(position, ➥
            normal, texCoord);
        }
    }

    return terrainVertices;
}
```

First you find the width and the height of your terrain, based on the dimensions of the heightData array. Next, you create an array that can store all vertices you'll need for your terrain. As discussed earlier, your terrain requires width*height vertices.

Next, you create all vertices using two for loops. The inner for loop creates all vertices for a certain row, and after one row has been finished, the first for loop switches to the next row, until all vertices in all rows have been defined.

Using this looping mechanism, you can immediately use the loop counters as X and Z coordinates. The z value is negated, so the terrain is built in the Forward (–Z) direction. The height value is taken from the heightData array.

For now, you give all vertices a default normal direction, which will soon be replaced by the correct directions using the method explained in the previous recipe. Because you probably want your terrain to be textured, you need to specify a valid texture coordinate. Depending on your texture, you'll want to control its size on the terrain. This example divides by 30, indicating the texture will be repeated every 30 vertices. If you want the texture to be stretched over a larger area of your terrain, divide by a larger number.

Now that you've assembled all this data, you're ready to create your new vertex and store it in the array.

## Defining the Indices

With your vertices defined, you're ready to indicate how you want your triangles to be built by defining the indices array (see recipe 5-3). You are going to define the triangles as a TriangleStrip, where each index indicates a new triangle, based on that index and the previous two indices.

Figure 5-15 shows how you can render your terrain as a TriangleStrip. The first two indices of your array will point to vertices 0 and W. Next, for each vertex of the row, you add that vertex and the corresponding vertex of the next row, until you reach the end of the bottom row. At this moment, you will have defined 2*width indices, corresponding to (2*width–2) triangles, which is exactly enough to cover the whole bottom row with triangles!

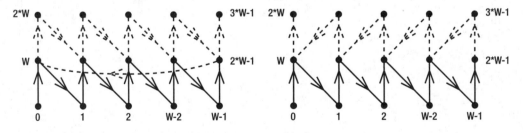

**Figure 5-15.** *Wrong ways to define a terrain using a TriangleStrip*

However, you've defined only your first row. You cannot use the same approach to render the second row, because each index you add defines a new triangle based on the last three indices. At this point, the last index you defined points to vertex (2*W–1). If you started over again for the second row, you would start by adding an index to vertex W, as indicated in the left part of Figure 5-15. However, this would define a triangle based on vertices W, (2*W–1), and (W–1)! This triangle would span the whole length of the first row, and you would not appreciate this in the final result.

You can solve this by defining the second row, starting from the right. However, simply starting from the index you ended with is not a good idea, because the long sides of the triangles of both rows will have a different direction. You want your triangles to have a uniform orientation, as in recipe 5-9.

Figure 5–16 shows how you can solve this problem. Immediately after your index pointing to vertex (2*W–1), you add another index pointing to the same vertex! This will add a triangle based on vertices (W–1) and twice vertex (2*W–1), which will result in a line between vertices (W–1) and (2*W–1). This line was already drawn by the last triangle, so this triangle has no visible result and is called a *ghost triangle*. Next, you add an index pointing to vertex (3*W–1), resulting in a line instead of a triangle because it is based on two indices pointing to the same vertex, (2*W–1). Note that if you define your second row starting from the right, these are the two vertices you would normally begin with; just keep in mind that in fact you're rendering two invisible triangles.

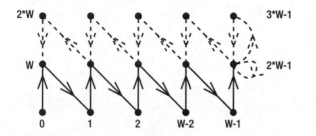

**Figure 5-16.** *Rendering your terrain correctly as a TriangleStrip*

---

■**Note** You could argue that instead of adding the second index pointing to (2*W–1), you could immediately add an index to (3*W–1). However, the extra index pointing to vertex (2*W–1) is required for two reasons. First, if you hadn't added it, only a single triangle would have been added, and you would have interrupted the winding order swapping required for TriangleStrips. Second, this would have added a triangle based on (3*W–1), (2*W–1), and (W–1), which would be visible if there is a height difference between them.

---

This is a method that generates indices defining triangles as a TriangleStrip for a terrain based on a grid:

```
private int[] CreateTerrainIndices()
{
    int width = heightData.GetLength(0);
    int height = heightData.GetLength(1);

    int[] terrainIndices = new int[(width)*2*(height-1)];

    int i = 0;
    int z = 0;
    while (z < height-1)
    {
```

```
        for (int x = 0; x < width; x++)
        {
            terrainIndices[i++] = x + z * width;
            terrainIndices[i++] = x + (z + 1) * width;
        }
        z++;

        if (z < height-1)
        {
            for (int x = width - 1; x >= 0; x--)
            {
                terrainIndices[i++] = x + (z + 1) * width;
                terrainIndices[i++] = x + z * width;
            }
        }
        z++;
    }

    return terrainIndices;
}
```

You start by creating an array, storing all indices required for the terrain. As you can see in Figure 5-16, for each row you'll need to define width*2 triangles. In that example, you have three rows of vertices, but you're rendering only two rows of triangles. This results in a total of width*2*(height–1) indices required.

The z variable in the previous code indicates the current row. You create the first row from left to right. Next, you increment z, indicating you're switching to the next row. The second row is created from right to left, as shown in Figure 5-16, and z is incremented again. The program will cycle through the while loop, until all even rows are created from left to right and all uneven rows are created from right to left.

At the moment z reaches height–1, the while loop is terminated, and the resulting array is returned.

## Normals, VertexBuffer, and IndexBuffer

That's all for the new code of this recipe; all you have to do now is generate the normal data, send the data to your graphics card by creating a VertexBuffer and an IndexBuffer, and, of course, render the triangles.

Add this code to your LoadContents method:

```
myVertexDeclaration = new VertexDeclaration(device, ➥
VertexPositionNormalTexture.VertexElements);
VertexPositionNormalTexture[] terrainVertices = CreateTerrainVertices();
int[] terrainIndices = CreateTerrainIndices();
terrainVertices = GenerateNormalsForTriangleStrip(terrainVertices, terrainIndices);
CreateBuffers(terrainVertices, terrainIndices);
```

The first line is required so your graphics card knows each vertex will be carrying position, normal, and texture coordinate data. I've already discussed the next two methods; they generate all the vertices and indices required to render the terrain. The GenerateNormalsForTriangleStrip method was explained in recipe 5-7; it adds normal data to your terrain vertices so your terrain can be lit correctly. The final method sends your data to your graphics card:

```
private void CreateBuffers(VertexPositionNormalTexture[] vertices, int[] indices)
{
    terrainVertexBuffer = new VertexBuffer(device, ➥
    VertexPositionNormalTexture.SizeInBytes * vertices.Length, ➥
    BufferUsage.WriteOnly);
    terrainVertexBuffer.SetData(vertices);

    terrainIndexBuffer = new IndexBuffer(device, typeof(int), ➥
    indices.Length, BufferUsage.WriteOnly);
    terrainIndexBuffer.SetData(indices);
}
```

You can find an explanation of all the methods and arguments used here in recipe 5-3.

With your data uploaded to your graphics card, it's finally time to render your terrain. This first part of the code correctly sets the variables of your BasicEffect (including lighting; see recipe 6-1), so add it to your Draw method:

```
int width = heightData.GetLength(0);
int height = heightData.GetLength(1);
basicEffect.World = Matrix.Identity;
basicEffect.View = fpsCam.ViewMatrix;
basicEffect.Projection = fpsCam.ProjectionMatrix;
basicEffect.Texture = grassTexture;
basicEffect.TextureEnabled = true;

basicEffect.EnableDefaultLighting();
basicEffect.DirectionalLight0.Direction = new Vector3(1, -1, 1);
basicEffect.DirectionalLight0.Enabled = true;
basicEffect.AmbientLightColor = new Vector3(0.3f, 0.3f, 0.3f);
basicEffect.DirectionalLight1.Enabled = false;
basicEffect.DirectionalLight2.Enabled = false;
basicEffect.SpecularColor = new Vector3(0, 0, 0);
```

As always when rendering a 3D scene to a 2D screen, you'll need to set the World, View, and Projection matrices (see recipes 2-1 and 4-2). Next, you indicate which texture you want to use to add some color to your terrain. The second block sets up one directional light as explained in recipe 6-1. The specular component is turned off (see recipe 6-4), because a grassy terrain is hardly a shiny, metallic material.

With the effect set up, you're ready to render the triangles. This code renders triangles from an indexed TriangleStrip, as explained in recipe 5-3:

```
basicEffect.Begin();
foreach (EffectPass pass in basicEffect.CurrentTechnique.Passes)
{
    pass.Begin();

    device.Vertices[0].SetSource(terrainVertexBuffer, 0, ➥
    VertexPositionNormalTexture.SizeInBytes);
    device.Indices = terrainIndexBuffer;
    device.VertexDeclaration = myVertexDeclaration;
    device.DrawIndexedPrimitives(PrimitiveType.TriangleStrip, 0, 0, ➥
    width * height, 0, width * 2 * (height - 1) - 2);

    pass.End();
}
basicEffect.End();
```

You first set your VertexBuffer and IndexBuffer as active buffers on the graphics card. The VertexDeclaration indicates to the GPU what kind of data to expect and where to find all the necessary information in the large data stream. The DrawIndexedPrimitives renders your TriangleStrip. This requires all width*height vertices to be processed, for a total of width*2*(height–1)–2 triangles to be rendered. To find this last value, look up the total number of indices in your index array. Because you're rendering from a TriangleStrip, the total number of vertices drawn will equal that value minus 2.

## The Code

*All the code is available for download at* www.apress.com.

The last four lines of this LoadContent method generate all the indices needed to render a terrain together with the corresponding vertices. Normal data is added to the vertices, and the final data is stored in a VertexBuffer and an IndexBuffer. Note that the LoadHeightMap method is discussed later in this recipe.

```
protected override void LoadContent()
{
    device = graphics.GraphicsDevice;
    basicEffect = new BasicEffect(device, null);
    cCross = new CoordCross(device);

    Texture2D heightMap = Content.Load<Texture2D>("heightmap");
    heightData = LoadHeightData(heightMap);

    grassTexture = Content.Load<Texture2D>("grass");
```

```
    myVertexDeclaration = new VertexDeclaration(device, ➥
    VertexPositionNormalTexture.VertexElements);
    VertexPositionNormalTexture[] terrainVertices = CreateTerrainVertices();
    int[] terrainIndices = CreateTerrainIndices();
    terrainVertices = GenerateNormalsForTriangleStrip(terrainVertices, ➥
    terrainIndices);
            CreateBuffers(terrainVertices, terrainIndices);
}
```

The vertices are created in this method:

```
private VertexPositionNormalTexture[] CreateTerrainVertices()
{
    int width = heightData.GetLength(0);
    int height = heightData.GetLength(1);
    VertexPositionNormalTexture[] terrainVertices = new ➥
    VertexPositionNormalTexture[width * height];

    int i = 0;
    for (int z = 0; z < height; z++)
    {
        for (int x = 0; x < width; x++)
        {
            Vector3 position = new Vector3(x, heightData[x, z], -z);
            Vector3 normal = new Vector3(0, 0, 1);
            Vector2 texCoord = new Vector2((float)x / 30.0f, (float)z / 30.0f);

            terrainVertices[i++] = new VertexPositionNormalTexture(position, ➥
            normal, texCoord);
        }
    }

    return terrainVertices;
}
```

The indices are generated in this method:

```
private int[] CreateTerrainIndices()
{
    int width = heightData.GetLength(0);
    int height = heightData.GetLength(1);

    int[] terrainIndices = new int[(width) * 2 * (height - 1)];
```

```
int i = 0;
int z = 0;
while (z < height - 1)
{
    for (int x = 0; x < width; x++)
    {
        terrainIndices[i++] = x + z * width;
        terrainIndices[i++] = x + (z + 1) * width;
    }
    z++;


    if (z < height - 1)
    {
        for (int x = width - 1; x >= 0; x--)
        {
            terrainIndices[i++] = x + (z + 1) * width;
            terrainIndices[i++] = x + z * width;
        }
    }
    z++;
}

return terrainIndices;
}
```

The GenerateNormalsForTriangleStrip method that adds normal data to your vertices is explained in recipe 5-7, while this CreateBuffers method stores your data on your graphics card:

```
private void CreateBuffers(VertexPositionNormalTexture[] vertices, int[] indices)
{
    terrainVertexBuffer = new VertexBuffer(device, ➥
    VertexPositionNormalTexture.SizeInBytes * vertices.Length, ➥
    BufferUsage.WriteOnly);
    terrainVertexBuffer.SetData(vertices);

    terrainIndexBuffer = new IndexBuffer(device, typeof(int), ➥
    indices.Length, BufferUsage.WriteOnly);
    terrainIndexBuffer.SetData(indices);
}
```

Finally, the terrain is rendered as a TriangleStrip in this Draw method:

```
protected override void Draw(GameTime gameTime)
{
    device.Clear(ClearOptions.Target | ClearOptions.DepthBuffer, ➥
    Color.CornflowerBlue, 1, 0);
```

```
cCross.Draw(fpsCam.ViewMatrix, fpsCam.ProjectionMatrix);

//draw terrain
int width = heightData.GetLength(0);
int height = heightData.GetLength(1);
basicEffect.World = Matrix.Identity;
basicEffect.View = fpsCam.ViewMatrix;
basicEffect.Projection = fpsCam.ProjectionMatrix;
basicEffect.Texture = grassTexture;
basicEffect.TextureEnabled = true;


basicEffect.EnableDefaultLighting();
basicEffect.DirectionalLight0.Direction = new Vector3(1, -1, 1);
basicEffect.DirectionalLight0.Enabled = true;
basicEffect.AmbientLightColor = new Vector3(0.3f, 0.3f, 0.3f);
basicEffect.DirectionalLight1.Enabled = false;
basicEffect.DirectionalLight2.Enabled = false;
basicEffect.SpecularColor = new Vector3(0, 0, 0);

basicEffect.Begin();
foreach (EffectPass pass in basicEffect.CurrentTechnique.Passes)
{
    pass.Begin();

    device.Vertices[0].SetSource(terrainVertexBuffer, 0, ➥
    VertexPositionNormalTexture.SizeInBytes);
    device.Indices = terrainIndexBuffer;
    device.VertexDeclaration = myVertexDeclaration;
    device.DrawIndexedPrimitives(PrimitiveType.TriangleStrip, ➥
    0, 0, width * height, 0, width * 2 * (height - 1) - 2);

    pass.End();
}
basicEffect.End();

base.Draw(gameTime);
}
```

## Loading a heightData Array from an Image

In most cases, you will not want to specify a heightData array manually, but you will want to load it, for example, from an image. This method loads an image and maps the color of each pixel in the image to a height value:

```
private void LoadHeightData(Texture2D heightMap)
{
    float minimumHeight = 255;
    float maximumHeight = 0;

     int width = heightMap.Width;
    int height = heightMap.Height;

    Color[] heightMapColors = new Color[width * height];
    heightMap.GetData<Color>(heightMapColors);

    heightData = new float[width, height];
    for (int x = 0; x < width; x++)

        for (int y = 0; y < height; y++)
        {
            heightData[x, y] = heightMapColors[x + y * width].R;
            if (heightData[x, y] < minimumHeight) minimumHeight = heightData[x, y];
            if (heightData[x, y] > maximumHeight) maximumHeight = heightData[x, y];
        }

    for (int x = 0; x < width; x++)
        for (int y = 0; y < height; y++)
            heightData[x, y] = (heightData[x, y] - ➥
            minimumHeight) / (maximumHeight - minimumHeight) * 30.0f;
}
```

The first part stores the intensity of the red color channel of each pixel in the heightData array. The bottom part of the method rescales each value in the array, so the lowest value becomes 0 and the maximum value becomes 30.

# 5-9. Calculate the Exact Height of a Terrain Between Vertices Using Bilinear Interpolation

## The Problem

When you're creating a game that uses a terrain, you'll often need to know the exact height of the terrain at a certain point. This will be the case, for example, when moving a Model over the terrain (see recipe 4-17), when finding the collision between the pointer and the terrain (next recipe), or when preventing the camera from crashing into the terrain (see recipe 2-6).

Since you defined the 3D position of each vertex of your terrain in the previous recipe, you already know the exact height at these points. For all positions between the vertices, however, you'll need some kind of interpolation to find the exact height at those positions.

## The Solution

If the point at which you want to know the height collides with a vertex of your terrain, you know the exact height of your terrain at that point. If the point doesn't collide exactly with a vertex, the point is in a triangle of your terrain. Because the triangle is a flat linear surface, you can find the exact height of any point of the triangle by interpolating between the heights of the three vertices defining the triangle.

## How It Works

You start with an X coordinate and a Z coordinate, and you want to know the corresponding Y coordinate of a point on your terrain. You find this by interpolating the heights of the three vertices of the triangle the point is in.

This means you first have to find which triangle the point is in, which is not as trivial as it seems. But first I'll introduce you to interpolation.

### Linear Interpolation

Some kind of interpolation is required if you have access only to data of discrete (that is, separate) points but you want to know the value somewhere in between these points. Such a situation is presented in the left part of Figure 5-17.

For some separate (read: integer) X values, you know the exact Y value. For X=2, you know Y=10, and for X=3, you know Y=30. But you don't know how much Y would be for X=2.7.

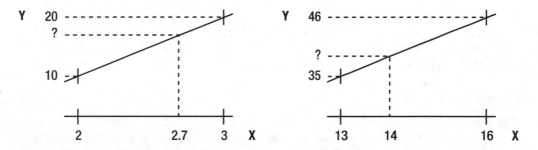

**Figure 5-17.** *Linear interpolation: easy and general example*

Using linear interpolation, you find the Y value for X=2.7 by connecting the exact points with a line, as in Figure 5-17. Linear interpolation always starts by expressing your X value between 0 and 1, where 0 corresponds to the lower X value of which you know the exact Y value (2 in this case) and 1 corresponds to the higher X value (3 in this case). In the example case where you want to find the Y value corresponding to X=2.7, this would yield 0.7, meaning "70 percent between 2 and 3."

In the left part of Figure 5-17, 0 percent corresponds to a Y value of 10, 100 percent corresponds to a Y value of 20, so 70 percent corresponds to Y=17. It's easy to see, but how about the right part of that image? Fourteen gives a relative value of 0.33, because it is 33 percent between 13 and 16. But how much is 33 percent between 35 and 46? Obviously, you want some code to calculate this for you.

First you want some code to find the relative value between 0 and 1. From your X value, you first subtract the lower X value so your minimum value becomes 0. Next, you have to scale it down so your maximum value becomes 1. You can do this by dividing with the difference between the max and min X values. Wow.

This is how it's done for the left part of Figure 5-17:

$$2.7 \Rightarrow \frac{2.7 - \min X}{\max X - \min X} = \frac{2.7 - 2}{3 - 2} = \frac{0.7}{1} = 0.7$$

Next, you do exactly the opposite to find the corresponding Y value: you first scale this value up (by multiplying by the difference between the min and max Y values), and you add the lower Y value:

$$0.7 * (\max Y - \min Y) + \min Y = 0.7 * (20 - 10) + 10 = 0.7 * 10 + 10 = 7 + 10 = 17$$

Here you applied the rule to the "easy" example on the left of Figure 5-17, but you can use this approach to do any linear interpolation. As a more difficult example, let's apply it to the right part of Figure 5-17. In that case, you know X=13 corresponds to Y=35 and X=16 corresponds to Y=46, but you want to know Y for X=14. So, first you find the relative value between 0 and 1:

$$14 \Rightarrow \frac{14 - \min X}{\max X - \min X} = \frac{14 - 13}{16 - 13} = \frac{1}{3} = 0.33$$

Once you know the relative value, you're ready to find the corresponding Y value:

$$0.33 * (\max Y - \min Y) + \min Y = 0.33 * (46 - 35) + 35 = 0.33 * 11 + 35 = 3.67 + 35 = 38.67$$

Finally, we're getting to the floating-point calculations. For the right part of Figure 5-17, you find that X=14 corresponds to Y=38.67. In reality, almost all interpolations will result in a floating-point value, and this approach is up to this task.

---

**Tip** XNA provides functionality to do this interpolation for you if you want to interpolate `Vector2`s, `Vector3`s, or `Vector4`s. For example, if you want to know which `Vector2` is 70 percent between (5,8) and (2,9), you could use `Vector2.Lerp(new Vector2(5,8), new Vector2(2,9), 0.7f)`.

---

## Bilinear Interpolation

In the case of your terrain, for all (X,Z) values, you have defined a vertex for which you know the exact Y value. For all (X,Z) values between these discrete points, you don't know the exact Y value, so you'll have to do some kind of interpolation. This time, you will have to find a relative value between 0 and 1, both for X and for Z.

Once you've found these values, you can calculate the exact Y value in two steps, as shown in this recipe.

**Finding the Relative Values**

Given any (X,Z) coordinate, you need to find the exact height Y on your terrain. You start by finding the relative values for X and Z, using the formula discussed earlier. Only this time, you have to apply it two times because you're working in three dimensions:

```
int xLower = (int)xCoord;
int xHigher = xLower + 1;
float xRelative = (xCoord - xLower) / ((float)xHigher - (float)xLower);

int zLower = (int)zCoord;
int zHigher = zLower + 1;
float zRelative = (zCoord - zLower) / ((float)zHigher - (float)zLower);
```

In your terrain, for each integer value of X and Z, you have defined a vertex, so you know the exact Y value at these points. So for any floating-point value of X, you find the lower X value by casting it to an int (for example, 2.7 will become 2). You find the higher X value by adding 1 to this value (2.7 will get 3 as a higher X value). Knowing the lower and higher bounds, it's easy to find the relative value between 0 and 1 using the formula explained earlier. You do the same for the Z value.

**Finding the minY and maxY Values**

Now that you know your relative values between 0 and 1, the next step is to find the exact Y value. However, you first need to know the minY and maxY values, as you did in the earlier linear interpolation example. These values are the heights in the vertices described by the higher and lower X and Z values. You need to know which triangle your point is over in order to know which vertices you need to use the height from as the Y value.

You know the X and Z coordinates of your point P, so you know the four vertices surrounding your point. It's easy to find their Y coordinates:

```
float heightLxLz = heightData[xLower, zLower];
float heightLxHz = heightData[xLower, zHigher];
float heightHxLz = heightData[xHigher, zLower];
float heightHxHz = heightData[xHigher, zHigher];
```

In this notation, LxHz means "lower X coordinate, higher Z coordinate."

**Determining Which Triangle the (X,Z) Point Is In**

Your four vertices are used to render two triangles of your terrain. However, there are two ways to define them, as shown in Figure 5-18. The way the triangles are rendered affects the height of point P, as you can see in the image.

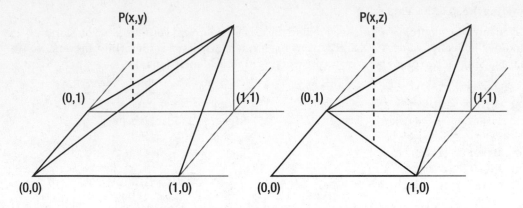

**Figure 5-18.** *Two ways to render two triangles from four vertices*

Although the four vertices of both quads have the same coordinates, you can see that the height of almost any point inside the quad is different in the two cases. As an example, the middle point is highlighted, so you can easily see there's a difference.

For a reason I'll discuss now, the preferred winding order for triangles is as shown in the right image of Figure 5-18.

Using this winding order, it's easy to determine which triangle the point is above. The border between the two triangles is given by the diagonal line. In the right part of the image, this line corresponds to the points with X and Z coordinates if the sum of xRelative + zRelative is exactly 1!

For example, if the point is exactly between the four points, as shown in Figure 5-18, xRelative and zRelative are both 0.5f, so their sum is 1, meaning on the diagonal. If the point is positioned a bit more to the left, xRelative gets smaller, and the sum becomes smaller than 1. The same holds for the Z coordinate. So if this sum is smaller than 1, the (X,Z) coordinate is inside the bottom-left triangle; otherwise, the point is inside the upper-right triangle:

```
bool pointAboveLowerTriangle = (xRelative + zRelative < 1);
```

---

■**Note** Take your time to assure yourself that all triangles defined in Figure 5-16 are rendered as shown in the right part of Figure 5-18.

---

**Finding the Exact Height**

Now that you know the relative values, the heights of the four surrounding vertices, and which triangle the point is in, you're finally ready to calculate the exact height.

If the point is in the bottom-left triangle, thus when pointAboveLowerTriangle is true, the following is how you can find the height of any position in the triangle using bilinear interpolation:

```
finalHeight = heightLxLz;
finalHeight += zRelative * (heightLxHz - heightLxLz);
finalHeight += xRelative * (heightHxLz - heightLxLz);
```

For the single interpolation explained earlier, you started with the Y value of lowestX. Because this is "double" interpolation, you start with the Y value of lowestXlowestZ.

In single interpolation, you added the height difference between maxY and minY, multiplied by the relative X value. In bilinear interpolation, you do this for the zRelative and xRelative values.

In other words, you start with the height of the lower-left vertex. To this height, you add the height difference between this vertex and the vertex with a higher Z coordinate, multiplied by how close the real Z coordinate is to this second vertex. The same holds for the last line: to the height, you add the height difference between the lower-left vertex and the lower-right vertex, multiplied by how close the real X coordinate is to that lower-right vertex.

If the point is inside the upper-right triangle, when pointAboveLowerTriangle is false, things are a bit different, and you'll need this code:

```
finalHeight = heightHxHz;
finalHeight += (1.0f - zDifference) * (heightHxLz - heightHxHz);
finalHeight += (1.0f - xDifference) * (heightLxHz - heightHxHz);
```

As the starting height, you take the upper-right vertex, and you follow the same procedure: you add the height differences, multiplied by the relative distance.

## The Code

*All the code is available for download at www.apress.com.*

This method contains all the code explained earlier. Based on any (X,Z) coordinate, whether integer or floating point, the method returns the exact height above this point. First you check that the point that is requested is on the terrain. If it isn't, you return a default height of 10.

```
public float GetExactHeightAt(float xCoord, float zCoord)
{
    bool invalid = xCoord < 0;
    invalid |= zCoord < 0;
    invalid |= xCoord > heightData.GetLength(0) - 1;
    invalid |= zCoord > heightData.GetLength(1) - 1;
    if (invalid)
        return 10;

    int xLower = (int)xCoord;
    int xHigher = xLower + 1;
    float xRelative = (xCoord - xLower) / ((float)xHigher - (float)xLower);

    int zLower = (int)zCoord;
    int zHigher = zLower + 1;
    float zRelative = (zCoord - zLower) / ((float)zHigher - (float)zLower);
```

```
    float heightLxLz = heightData[xLower, zLower];
    float heightLxHz = heightData[xLower, zHigher];
    float heightHxLz = heightData[xHigher, zLower];
    float heightHxHz = heightData[xHigher, zHigher];

    bool pointAboveLowerTriangle  = (xRelative + zRelative < 1);

    float finalHeight;
    if (pointAboveLowerTriangle )
    {
        finalHeight = heightLxLz;
        finalHeight += zRelative * (heightLxHz - heightLxLz);
        finalHeight += xRelative * (heightHxLz - heightLxLz);
    }
    else
    {
        finalHeight = heightHxHz;
        finalHeight += (1.0f - zRelative) * (heightHxLz - heightHxHz);
        finalHeight += (1.0f - xRelative) * (heightLxHz - heightHxHz);
    }

    return finalHeight;
}
```

# 5-10. Calculate the Collision Point Between the Pointer and the Terrain: Surface Picking

## The Problem

You want to find the exact 3D coordinates on your terrain at the position indicated by your pointer. This is required if you want to indicate a target position on the terrain for your objects to move to or when positioning objects on a terrain.

## The Solution

As discussed in the introduction of recipe 4-19, the 2D point on your screen, indicated by your pointer, corresponds to a Ray in your 3D scene. In this recipe, you will walk over this Ray until you hit the terrain.

You can do this using a binary search algorithm, which is capable of giving you the location of the collision with an accuracy of your choice.

Given the hilliness of a terrain, it is possible that there are multiple collision points between the Ray and the terrain, as shown in Figure 5-20. Therefore, you will want to precede your binary search with a linear search so you make sure you detect the collision closest to the camera.

## How It Works

This method converts the 2D screen position of the pointer into a 3D Ray. It is fully explained in the first part of recipe 4-19.

```
private Ray GetPointerRay(Vector2 pointerPosition)
{
    Vector3 nearScreenPoint = new Vector3(pointerPosition.X, pointerPosition.Y, 0);
    Vector3 farScreenPoint = new Vector3(pointerPosition.X, pointerPosition.Y, 1);

    Vector3 near3DWorldPoint = ➥
    device.Viewport.Unproject(nearScreenPoint, ➥
    moveCam.ProjectionMatrix, moveCam.ViewMatrix, Matrix.Identity);
    Vector3 far3DWorldPoint = ➥
    device.Viewport.Unproject(farScreenPoint, ➥
    moveCam.ProjectionMatrix, moveCam.ViewMatrix, Matrix.Identity);

    Vector3 pointerRayDirection = far3DWorldPoint - near3DWorldPoint;
    Ray pointerRay = new Ray(near3DWorldPoint, pointerRayDirection);

    return pointerRay;
}
```

---

**Note**  In this version, you do not normalize the direction of the Ray. I'll explain this in a moment.

---

Now that you know the pointer Ray, you're ready to detect collisions between the Ray and the terrain.

### Binary Search

The Ray contains a starting point (in this case, where the Ray strikes the near clipping plane), as well as a direction. Figure 5-19 shows the Ray and terrain. The starting point is indicated as point A. The direction of the Ray is the vector between point A and point B.

The general idea behind the binary search is quite intuitive. You start with two points, A and B, of which you're sure that the collision point is located between them. Calculate the point between points A and B to find their midpoint, which is indicated by point 1 in Figure 5-19. You check whether this point is above or below the terrain. If this point is above the terrain (such as in the case of the image), you know the collision point is between point 1 and point B.

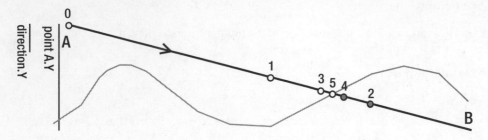

**Figure 5-19.** *Binary search to detect a collision between Ray and the terrain*

You continue. Find point 2, between points 1 and B. This point is below the terrain, so you know the collision point is between point 1 and point 2.

You continue to narrow down. Look at point 3, between point 1 and point 2. This point is again above the terrain, so the collision is between 3 and 2.

Next, point 4 between 3 and 2 is below the terrain, so the collision is between 3 and 4.

Finally, you check point 5, which is between points 3 and 4. You discover that the height of point 5 is very close to the height of the terrain at that (X,Z) position, so you have detected the collision point!

### Finding Point A and Point B

In preparation for the binary search, you need to start with two points, A and B, on your Ray where you're sure the collision point is between them.

You can safely use the starting position of your pointer Ray as point A, because it is the point on the Ray closest to the camera (it is positioned on the near clipping plane; see recipe 4-19).

For now, you'll take the point where the pointer Ray strikes the far clipping plane as point B. This is not a bad choice, because it is the most distant point on the Ray that is still visible with your camera.

As you can see in the GetPointerRay method explained in recipe 4-19, the pointerRay. Direction equals the vector you need to add to go from point A to point B.

### The Binary Search Method

Now that you know point A and the direction to point B, you're ready to detect collisions with the terrain. The binary search algorithm explained earlier, translated into pseudocode, becomes this:

As long as the difference in height between the current point and the terrain below is too large, do the following:

    **a.** Divide the direction of the Ray in half.

    **b.** Add the resulting direction to the current point to obtain the next point.

    **c.** If the next point is also above the terrain, save the next point as the current point.

Imagine this as walking over the Ray each step, and before placing your foot, you check whether your foot is not below the terrain. As long as this isn't the case, you continue while halving your step size after each step. Once you've placed your foot under the terrain, you retract your foot and try putting it half as far, until you end up with your foot exactly on the position of the terrain that collides with the terrain.

In code, this is as follows:

```
private Vector3 BinarySearch(Ray ray)
{
    float accuracy = 0.01f;
    float heightAtStartingPoint = ➥
    terrain.GetExactHeightAt(ray.Position.X, -ray.Position.Z);
    float currentError = ray.Position.Y - heightAtStartingPoint;
    while (currentError > accuracy)
    {
        ray.Direction /= 2.0f;
        Vector3 nextPoint = ray.Position + ray.Direction;
        float heightAtNextPoint = terrain.GetExactHeightAt(nextPoint.X, ➥
        -nextPoint.Z);
        if (nextPoint.Y > heightAtNextPoint)
        {
            ray.Position = nextPoint;
            currentError = ray.Position.Y - heightAtNextPoint;
        }
    }
    return ray.Position;
}
```

You start by calculating the difference in height between the starting point on your Ray and the terrain beneath (or above) that point.

The while will loop until this difference is less than your predefined accuracy of 0.01f. If the difference is still larger, you halve the step size and calculate the next point on the Ray. If this next point is above the terrain, you step to that point and calculate the height difference at that point. If it isn't, do nothing so that the next time the step size is halved again.

After quitting the while loop, ray.Position will contain a position on the Ray where the height difference with the terrain is less than 0.01f.

This is how you can use your method, starting from the rayAB created with the GetPointerRay:

```
pointerPos = BinarySearch(pointerRay);
```

---

■**Caution** If your pointer is not over the terrain, this method will stay forever in its while loop. Therefore, it can be useful to break out of the while loop if a counter value is greater than some threshold, as shown in the code later in this recipe.

---

## Problems with the Binary Search

In most cases, the binary search will do a fine job, but in some case it will just fail miserably, as shown in Figure 5-20.

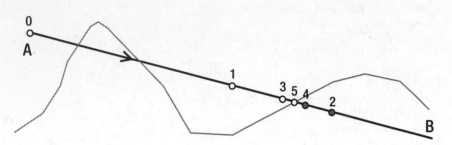

**Figure 5-20.** *Problematic case for the binary search*

Since the binary check does not check the terrain height between point 0 and point 1, the collision between the first hill and the Ray is not detected at all, and the same result (point 5) is returned as a collision between the Ray and the terrain.

To solve this, the binary search should be preceded by a linear search, which is simple in comparison to the binary search.

## Linear Search

In a linear search, you're going to divide your Ray into a few equidistant steps, for example, eight steps, as shown in Figure 5-21.

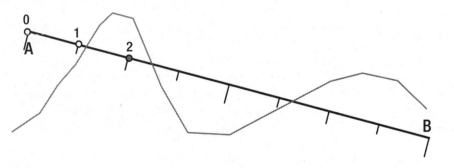

**Figure 5-21.** *Linear search*

You simply walk over your Ray in steps of the same size, until you encounter a point below the terrain. This will not give you an exact result, but at least you will detect that the Ray has collided with the first hill.

Because neither point 1 nor point 2 in Figure 5-21 is really close to the terrain, you will want to use the binary search on the Ray between points 1 and 2 to accurately find the exact collision point.

The LinearSearch method accepts the whole Ray between A and B, divides it into equal steps, and returns the part of the Ray that corresponds to the step during which the collision occurred:

```
private Ray LinearSearch(Ray ray)
{
    ray.Direction /= 300.0f;

    Vector3 nextPoint = ray.Position + ray.Direction;
    float heightAtNextPoint = terrain.GetExactHeightAt(nextPoint.X, -nextPoint.Z);
    while (heightAtNextPoint < nextPoint.Y)
    {
        ray.Position = nextPoint;

        nextPoint = ray.Position + ray.Direction;
        heightAtNextPoint = terrain.GetExactHeightAt(nextPoint.X, -nextPoint.Z);
    }
    return ray;
}
```

In this example, the Ray is divided into no less than 300 steps. Increasing this value will increase the probability of detecting peaks but will require more processing power.

For each point, you calculate the next point and check whether that next point is above or below the terrain. As long as it is above the terrain, continue. If the next point is below the terrain, return the current Ray containing the point before the collision and the step in which the collision occurred.

This Ray can immediately be used to start the BinarySearch method:

```
Ray shorterRay = LinearSearch(pointerRay);
pointerPos = BinarySearch(shorterRay);
```

## Application-Specific Optimization

The linear search will make sure you detect small peaks, while the following binary search will give you the accuracy you want.

In the previous code, you've taken points A and B as the collision points of the pointer Ray with the near and far clipping planes. This is OK, but if the distance between the near and far clipping planes is huge, this Ray can also be huge. This means you'll do a lot of useless checks at a distance way above the terrain or way below the terrain.

Instead, you need to look only at the Ray at the heights where the Ray can possibly collide with the terrain. In the terrain used in this book, the maximum height is 30, while the lowest height is 0. So, it would be better to find the point on your Ray where the Y coordinate is 30 and use this as starting point A. Next, find the point on your Ray with Y=0 and use this as ending point B.

The resulting Ray is constructed by this method:

```
private Ray ClipRay(Ray ray, float highest, float lowest)
{
    Vector3 oldStartPoint = ray.Position;

    float factorH = -(oldStartPoint.Y-highest) / ray.Direction.Y;
    Vector3 pointA = oldStartPoint + factorH * ray.Direction;
```

```
    float factorL = -(oldStartPoint.Y-lowest) / ray.Direction.Y;
    Vector3 pointB = oldStartPoint + factorL * ray.Direction;

    Vector3 newDirection = pointB - pointA;
    return new Ray(pointA, newDirection);
}
```

To find the point on the Ray with a specific Y coordinate, find the difference between this Y value and the Y coordinate of the starting point of the original Ray. If you know the height difference of the direction of the Ray, you know which portion (stored in `factor`) of this Ray you should add to the starting point to arrive at the point of your requested Y value.

---

■**Note** The Y coordinate of `oldStartPoint` is positive, while the Y coordinate of the direction will be negative as the Ray descends. You want `factor` to be a positive value, which explains the − sign.

---

If you start from this resulting Ray, you will need to do a lot fewer checks in your `LinearSearch` to end up with the same peak detection rate.

## The Code

*All the code is available for download at www.apress.com.*

You can easily check for the collision point between your pointer Ray and the terrain using this code:

```
protected override void Update(GameTime gameTime)
{
    GamePadState gamePadState = GamePad.GetState(PlayerIndex.One);
    if (gamePadState.Buttons.Back == ButtonState.Pressed)
        this.Exit();

    MouseState mouseState = Mouse.GetState();
    KeyboardState keyState = Keyboard.GetState();


    Vector2 pointerScreenPos = new Vector2(mouseState.X, mouseState.Y);
    Ray pointerRay = GetPointerRay(pointerScreenPos);

    Ray clippedRay = ClipRay(pointerRay, 30, 0);
    Ray shorterRay = LinearSearch(clippedRay);
    pointerPos = BinarySearch(shorterRay);

    base.Update(gameTime);
}
```

This code first asks the ClipRay method to return the section of the Ray that has Y coordinates between 30 and 0:

```
private Ray ClipRay(Ray ray, float highest, float lowest)
{
    Vector3 oldStartPoint = ray.Position;

    float factorH = -(oldStartPoint.Y-highest) / ray.Direction.Y;
    Vector3 pointA = oldStartPoint + factorH * ray.Direction;

    float factorL = -(oldStartPoint.Y-lowest) / ray.Direction.Y;
    Vector3 pointB = oldStartPoint + factorL * ray.Direction;

    Vector3 newDirection = pointB - pointA;
    return new Ray(pointA, newDirection);
}
```

Next it calls the LinearSearch method to refine the large Ray to a very short Ray, which contains the collision closest to the camera:

```
private Ray LinearSearch(Ray ray)
{
    ray.Direction /= 50.0f;

    Vector3 nextPoint = ray.Position + ray.Direction;
    float heightAtNextPoint = terrain.GetExactHeightAt(nextPoint.X, -nextPoint.Z);
    while (heightAtNextPoint < nextPoint.Y)
    {
        ray.Position = nextPoint;

        nextPoint = ray.Position + ray.Direction;
        heightAtNextPoint = terrain.GetExactHeightAt(nextPoint.X, -nextPoint.Z);
    }
    return ray;
}
```

To pinpoint the collision to a very accurate 3D location, the BinarySearch is called on this short Ray:

```
private Vector3 BinarySearch(Ray ray)
{
    float accuracy = 0.01f;
    float heightAtStartingPoint = ➥
    terrain.GetExactHeightAt(ray.Position.X, -ray.Position.Z);
    float currentError = ray.Position.Y - heightAtStartingPoint;
    int counter = 0;
    while (currentError > accuracy)
```

```
    {
        ray.Direction /= 2.0f;
        Vector3 nextPoint = ray.Position + ray.Direction;
        float heightAtNextPoint = terrain.GetExactHeightAt(nextPoint.X, ➡
        -nextPoint.Z);
        if (nextPoint.Y > heightAtNextPoint)
        {
            ray.Position = nextPoint;
            currentError = ray.Position.Y - heightAtNextPoint;
        }
        if (counter++ == 1000) break;
    }
    return ray.Position;
}
```

Note that if the while loop is iterated for 1,000 times, this code will break out of the while
loop.

# 5-11. Load Data from an XML File

## The Problem

You want to load data from an XML file into your XNA game project. You can do this by reading from the file when your XNA project starts using default .NET file I/O functionality, but this
will not work when running the game on the Xbox 360 console or Zune.

You want the XML file to be serialized into a binary file by the content pipeline so you can
read in the data contained in this binary file in your XNA project.

## The Solution

In the XML file, simply put the object you want to load between <XNAContent> and <Asset>
tags, as done in this sample XML file describing an object of the custom MapData class:

```
<?xml version="1.0" encoding="utf-8"?>
    <XnaContent>
        <Asset Type="XMLDataPLine.MapData">
            <mapName>Battle In The Middle</mapName>
            <numberOfCastles>8</numberOfCastles>
            <allies>
                <Item>Humans</Item>
                <Item>Elves</Item>
                <Item>Dwarves</Item>
            </allies>
        </Asset>
    </XnaContent>
```

**■Tip**  If you don't know how to create an XML file from an object automatically, you can learn how to do this at the end of this recipe.

The XNA Framework comes with a content importer capable of turning the XML file into an object of the class defined in the XML file. Because the object is already finished at this point, you don't need a processor, and the object can immediately be serialized into a binary file.

In this case, the object is of the custom MapData class, so you'll have to define a custom TypeWriter and TypeReader because this is a custom class.

**■Note**  If the XML file describes an object of a class that the content pipeline already knows how to (de-)serialize, you don't have to code a new TypeWriter or TypeReader.

Figure 5-22 shows the full schematic.

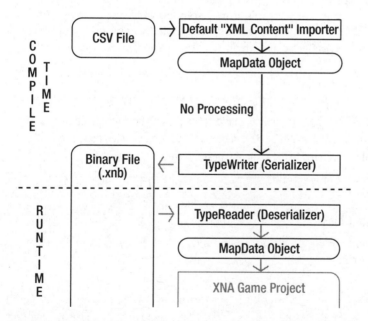

**Figure 5-22.** *No processor is required when importing an object from an XML file.*

## How It Works

Import an .xml file into your XNA game project. In the Solution Explorer, select the file so its properties are shown at the bottom-right corner of the screen. Indicate you want to use the default XML content importer that comes with the XNA Framework, and select No Processing

Required to indicate the output of the importer should be serialized to a file without passing through a processor. Figure 5-23 shows the final Properties window.

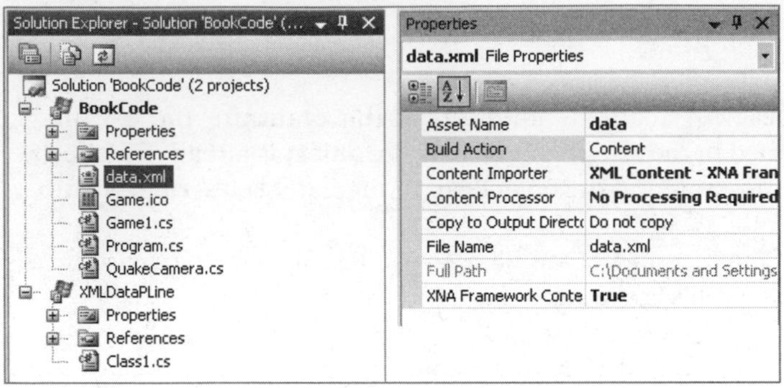

**Figure 5-23.** *Properties of an imported XML file*

If the XML file contains an object of a class that the content pipeline knows how to serialize and deserialize to/from a binary file, you can immediately load the object into a variable in your LoadContent method. In this recipe, however, the MapData class is a custom class, so you'll have to define your own TypeWriter.

Add a new content pipeline project to your solution by going through the ten steps explained in recipe 4-15. This time, however, you will not need to define your custom processor. All you need to do is define the MapData class, together with an appropriate TypeWriter and TypeReader.

---

**■Note**  Make sure you have added a reference to your content pipeline project, both for the Content entry and for your XNA project, as explained in recipe 4-15. This is required so your main project can access the definition of the MapData class, which is stored in the content pipeline project.

---

### Defining the Custom MapData Class

As an example, the MapData class contains a string, an int, and a List of strings. Add this definition to your content pipeline project:

```
public class MapData
{
    public string mapName;
    public int numberOfCastles;
    public List<string> allies = new List<string>();
}
```

---

**■Tip**  Verify the data contained in the previous XML file provides data for these three variables.

---

## Defining a TypeWriter Capable of Serializing an Object of the MapData Class

As explained in recipe 4-15, the TypeWriter needs to serialize exactly enough data from the object so the object can later be reconstructed by the TypeReader. As always, it also should provide the location of the TypeReader to be used:

```
[ContentTypeWriter]
public class MapDataTypeWriter : ContentTypeWriter<MapData>
{
    protected override void Write(ContentWriter output, MapData value)
    {
        output.WriteObject<string>(value.mapName);
        output.WriteObject<int>(value.numberOfCastles);
        output.WriteObject<List<string>>(value.allies);
    }

    public override string GetRuntimeReader(TargetPlatform targetPlatform)
    {
        return typeof(MapDataReader).AssemblyQualifiedName;
    }
}
```

You indicate this TypeWriter will be capable of serializing objects of the MapData class. The default content pipeline knows how to serialize a string, an int, and a List, so you simply serialize them to the binary file. You pass a link to the MapDataReader TypeReader, which you'll define next.

## Defining a TypeReader Capable of Serializing an Object of the MapData Class

This TypeReader simply creates a new MapData object; reads in the string, int, and List (in this correct order!); and stores them inside the MapData object. The filled object is returned and sent to the XNA game project.

```
class MapDataReader : ContentTypeReader<MapData>
{
    protected override MapData Read(ContentReader input, MapData existingInstance)
    {
        MapData map = new MapData();
        map.mapName = input.ReadObject<string>();
        map.numberOfCastles = input.ReadObject<int>();
        map.allies = input.ReadObject<List<string>>();

        return map;
    }
}
```

## Usage

The first line in this LoadContent method is enough to read in the MapData object at runtime. You'll insert a second line, which is a breakpoint in your code so that you can check that the data is actually available:

```
protected override void LoadContent()
{
    MapData loadedMap = Content.Load<MapData>("data");
    System.Diagnostics.Debugger.Break();
}
```

The last line's Break allows you to verify that the loadedMap variable contains the values from the XML file.

---

■**Note**  Keep in mind that the XML file is transformed into a binary file whenever you compile your project (by hitting F5). Whenever the project is started, only the TypeReader is called to construct the MapData object from the binary file. This means that if you change the contents of your XML file, you'll have to recompile in order to apply your changes.

---

## The Code

*All the code is available for download at www.apress.com.*

The custom content pipeline contains only the class definition, the TypeWriter, and the TypeReader, which you can find earlier in the recipe.

## Extra Reading

### Creating an XNA-Compatible XML File from an Existing Object

This section explains how you can store any object of any class as an XML file, which you can load using the default XML importer.

First, you'll need to add these namespaces to your using block so you can use their functionality:

```
using System.Xml;
using Microsoft.Xna.Framework.Content.Pipeline.Serialization.Intermediate;
```

For these lines to work, you'll also need to add the System.XML and Microsoft.XNA. Framework.Content.Pipeline references; you can add them by selecting Project ➤ Add Reference.

Next, either link to your custom content pipeline or manually redefine the MapData class by putting this code outside the namespace of your project:

```
namespace XMLDataPLine
{
    public class MapData
    {
        public string mapName;
        public int numberOfCastles;
        public List<string> allies = new List<string>();
    }
}
```

If you redefine the class manually, make sure you put it in the same namespace as your custom content pipeline (mine was called XMLDataPLine) and that all of the variables are the same.

Next, back in the namespace of your XNA project, make sure you have an object of the MapData class ready:

```
XMLDataPLine.MapData myMap = new XMLDataPLine.MapData();
myMap.mapName = "Battle In The Middle";
myMap.numberOfCastles = 8;
myMap.allies.Add("Humans");
myMap.allies.Add("Elves");
myMap.allies.Add("Dwarves");
```

And use this code to save it into an XNA-compatible XML file, called data.xml:

```
string fileName = "data.xml";
XmlWriter writer = XmlWriter.Create(fileName);
IntermediateSerializer.Serialize<XMLDataPLine.MapData>(writer, myMap, fileName);
writer.Close();
```

When you run this program, the data.xml file will be created in the map where your .exe is located.

---

**■Note**  You can also find this code in the samples.

---

# 5-12. Create Your Own Vertex Format

## The Problem

Vertices are used to store data you send from your XNA project to the shaders on your graphics card. A vertex format contains a description of the data stored in your vertices. The XNA Framework comes with some default vertex formats, ranging from the simple VertexPositionColor to the VertexPositionNormalTexture format.

However, if you're coding a more advanced HLSL effect (such as bump mapping, skinning, particle effects, and so on), you'll find that each vertex will need to store some additional information, such as the tangent in that vertex or some timing data. Packing each vertex with some extra data requires you to define a custom vertex format. Therefore, you will need to define a custom vertex format only when coding custom vertex and pixel shaders.

## The Solution

The vertex format defines what kind of data is stored inside each vertex and thus what kind of data will be accessible to you in the vertex shader. For example, when using VertexPositionColor vertices, the vertex format of the VertexPositionColor struct informs your graphics card that all incoming vertices will carry position and color data and specifies where that data can be found in the data stream.

The vertex format is the link between the vertices in your XNA code and your vertex shader. First, the vertex format describes which data should be positioned where in the data stream. This is shown by the upper gray curves in Figure 5-24, indicating where the Position and Color data of a vertex are placed in the data stream.

Whenever the graphics card needs to render triangles from your vertices, the graphics card needs to be able to separate this stream back into vertices.

Furthermore, it also needs to separate each vertex back into Position and Color data. Again, the vertex format informs the graphics card where it should cut the data stream. This is shown by the lower gray curves in Figure 5-24.

Finally, for each reconstructed vertex, the vertex shader is called with the Position and Color data of that vertex available to the vertex shader.

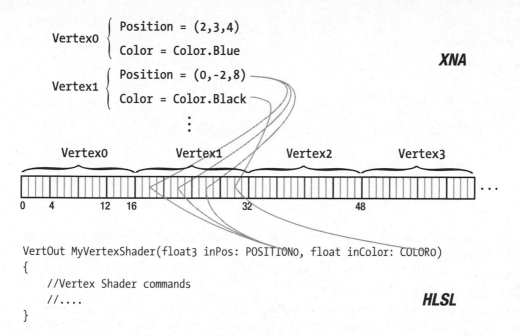

```
VertOut MyVertexShader(float3 inPos: POSITION0, float inColor: COLOR0)
{
    //Vertex Shader commands
    //....
}
```

**Figure 5-24.** *The vertex format describes which data can be found where in the data stream.*

## How It Works

In this recipe, you'll create your own version of the VertexPositionColor struct to learn the basics. In the second part, you'll extend it to a new, custom vertex format.

### Re-creating the VertexPositionColor Struct

In this part, you'll create the MyVertexPositionColor struct (which is the same as the VertexPositionColor struct) to learn the basics.

The VertexPositionColor struct was designed so it is capable of storing all the necessary information described in the introduction of this recipe. It consists of three parts:

- The data for each vertex itself, which is a Vector3 to store the positional data and a Color

- The total size of one vertex so your graphics card can nicely cut the data stream into separate vertices

- The VertexElements description, which is needed to inform the graphics card which kind of data is contained in each vertex and where the graphics card should cut inside the vertices to obtain this data

**Step 1**

Start by adding this struct:

```
public struct MyVertexPositionColor
{
    public Vector3 Position;
    public Color Color;
    public MyVertexPositionColor(Vector3 position, Color color)
    {
        Position = position;
        Color = color;
    }
}
```

This struct is capable of storing a Vector3 for the position and color. This would be enough to create vertices and send them to the graphics card.

**Step 2**

Imagine a stream of vertices is sent to the graphics card. Your graphics card would have a pretty hard time trying to figure out where to split the stream of bytes into vertices. It needs to know the number of bytes occupied by one vertex so it can cut the stream nicely into separate vertices. Add this line to your struct:

```
public static readonly int SizeInBytes = sizeof(float) * (3 + 1);
```

Since this information is the same for all vertices you create based on this struct and you need only to read them, you can make it static readonly.

Each vertex contains a Vector3 and a Color. A Vector3 is composed of three floats, while a Color is stored in one float. So, the total number of bytes occupied by one vertex equals (number of bytes occupied by one float)*(3+1).

---

■**Note**  One float occupies 4 bytes, so you can also replace this value with 4*(3+1) = 16. Make sure you have a look at Figure 5-24 to verify each vertex contains 16 bytes and that each new vertex starts at a byte number that is a multiple of 16. This is how the graphics card knows where to cut the byte stream into separate vertices.

---

As a result of step 2, your graphics card will know how to cut the byte stream it receives into separate vertices.

**Step 3**

Finally, add this code to your struct:

```
public static readonly VertexElement[] VertexElements =
    {
        new VertexElement(0, 0, VertexElementFormat.Vector3, ➡
        VertexElementMethod.Default, VertexElementUsage.Position, 0),
        new VertexElement(0, sizeof(float)*3, ➡
        VertexElementFormat.Color, VertexElementMethod.Default, ➡
        VertexElementUsage.Color, 0),
    };
```

The information describes the kind of data contained within one vertex and at which byte of the vertex it should be positioned. The first entry indicates that each vertex has positional data, and the second indicates that each vertex has Color data. Let's discuss the arguments of each line one by one.

The first argument indicates which data stream the data can be found in. Only advanced applications will use multiple vertex streams, so usually you'll use 0 here.

---

**■Tip**  Multiple vertex streams are useful, for example, if the Color data requires frequent updates while the Position data stays the same. By splitting up the data in two vertex streams, the Position data can remain unchanged on the GPU, so you have to transfer only the Color data from the CPU to GPU.

---

The second argument describes where the data can be found. It is the byte index of the data in a vertex. Because the Position data is the first data inside each vertex, you indicate it can be found at index 0. The Color data, however, can be found after the Position data, so you need to know how many bytes the Position data occupies. The Position data occupies three floats, so you indicate sizeof(float)*3 (because a float occupies 4 bytes, you can also indicate 12 here). Take a look at Figure 5-24: the Color data begins at byte 12.

The third argument indicates in which format the data needs to be saved to the data stream and is the base type of your data. For the Position, you indicate Vector3, and for the Color you indicate the Color type.

The next argument is used only in advanced and specific hardware extensions, such as N-Patching where the number of triangles of a geometry are adjusted based on normals so the overall shading quality of the geometry can be increased.

The fifth argument is quite important, because it indicates to which input of the vertex shader this data should be connected. Take another look at Figure 5-24, and pay special attention to the input arguments of the vertex shader. Both arguments are followed by a semantic POSITION0 and COLOR0. In this example, you link the first data part, containing the Position data, to the POSITION0 semantic. The second data part is linked to the COLOR0 semantic.

The last argument allows you to specify multiple versions of each semantic. It actually refers to the 0 at the end of the POSITION0 and COLOR0 semantics. An example of this is shown in the second half of this recipe.

As a result of step 3, your graphics card will know where to find what data inside each vertex. In this example, it will pass bytes 0 to 11 (3 floats) to the POSITION0 input of the vertex shader. Bytes 12 to 15 (1 float) will be passed to the COLOR0 input of the vertex shader.

### The Complete MyVertexPositionColor Struct

This is what you should have at the moment:

```
public struct MyVertexPositionColor
{
    public Vector3 Position;
    public Color Color;
    public MyVertexPositionColor(Vector3 position, Color color)
    {
        Position = position;
        Color = color;
    }

    public static readonly VertexElement[] VertexElements =
    {
        new VertexElement(0, 0, VertexElementFormat.Vector3, ➥
        VertexElementMethod.Default, VertexElementUsage.Position, 0),
        new VertexElement(0, sizeof(float)*3, ➥
        VertexElementFormat.Color, VertexElementMethod.Default, ➥
        VertexElementUsage.Color, 0),
    };
    public static readonly int SizeInBytes = sizeof(float) * (3 + 1);
}
```

## Using the MyVertexPositionColor Struct

With the struct ready to be used, you can define the vertices and turn them into a VertexBuffer stream, as explained in recipe 5-4. This time, you're using your own vertex format:

```
private void InitVertices()
{
    myVertexDeclaration = new VertexDeclaration(device, ➥
    MyVertexPositionColor.VertexElements);

    MyVertexPositionColor[] vertices = new MyVertexPositionColor[3];
    int i = 0;
```

```
vertices[i++] = new MyVertexPositionColor(new Vector3(1, 1, -1), Color.Red);
vertices[i++] = new MyVertexPositionColor(new Vector3(3, 5, -1), Color.Green);
vertices[i++] = new MyVertexPositionColor(new Vector3(5, 1, -1), Color.Blue);


vertBuffer = new VertexBuffer(device, ➥
MyVertexPositionColor.SizeInBytes * vertices.Length, ➥
BufferUsage.WriteOnly);
vertBuffer.SetData<MyVertexPositionColor>(vertices, 0, vertices.Length);
}
```

The first line creates the VertexDeclaration, which is nothing more than what you coded in step 3 earlier. It will be passed to your graphics card before rendering the triangle.

The middle part of the method creates an array holding three MyVertexPositionColors, defining another silly triangle. For each vertex, you store the position and color. To create a VertexBuffer based on the array, you need to specify how many bytes one vertex occupies, so you pass in MyVertexPositionColor.SizeInBytes.

When it comes to drawing this triangle from the VertexBuffer, you need this code, as explained in recipe 5-4:

```
basicEffect.Begin();
foreach (EffectPass pass in basicEffect.CurrentTechnique.Passes)
{
    pass.Begin();
    device.VertexDeclaration = myVertexDeclaration;
    device.Vertices[0].SetSource(vertBuffer, 0, MyVertexPositionColor.SizeInBytes);
    device.DrawPrimitives(PrimitiveType.TriangleList, 0, 1);
    pass.End();
}
basicEffect.End();
```

Before you render the triangles, you need to pass the VertexElements to the graphics card so it knows how to correctly separate the byte stream into useful data.

## Custom Vertex Format

As a second example, you will create a new vertex format, capable of storing a Position, a Texture coordinate, and an extra Vector4. This allows you to pack four extra values with every vertex sent from your XNA project to your vertex shader; Figure 5-25 shows two of such vertices as a byte stream.

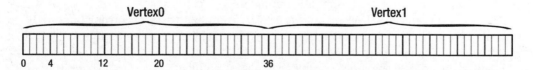

**Figure 5-25.** *Stream containing two MyCustomVertexFormats*

This is the new struct, where you again can identify the three main parts:

```
public struct MyCustomVertexFormat
{
    public Vector3 Position;
    public Vector2 TexCoords;
    public Vector4 Extra;
    public MyCustomVertexFormat(Vector3 Position, Vector2 TexCoords, Vector4 Extra)
    {
        this.Position = Position;
        this.TexCoords = TexCoords;
        this.Extra = Extra;
    }

    public static readonly VertexElement[] VertexElements =
    {
        new VertexElement(0, 0, VertexElementFormat.Vector3, ➥
        VertexElementMethod.Default, VertexElementUsage.Position, ➥
        0),
        new VertexElement(0, sizeof(float)*3, ➥
        VertexElementFormat.Vector2, VertexElementMethod.Default, ➥
        VertexElementUsage.TextureCoordinate, 0),
        new VertexElement(0, sizeof(float)*(3+2), ➥
        VertexElementFormat.Vector4, VertexElementMethod.Default, ➥
        VertexElementUsage.TextureCoordinate, 1),
    };
    public static readonly int SizeInBytes = sizeof(float) * (3 + 2 + 4);
}
```

The top part allows each vertex to store a Position, a Texture coordinate, and an extra Vector4.

Next, you link them to your vertex shader input. You indicate the first Vector3 should be linked to the POSITION0 semantic. Because it is the first data item, it can be found at byte 0 (the second argument).

The second line indicates that the Vector2 containing the Texture coordinate should be linked to the TEXCOORD0 input of the vertex shader. The Position takes up three floats, so the Texture coordinate can be found at position sizeof(float)*3 = 12, which can be verified in Figure 5-25.

The third line links the additional Vector4 to another TEXTURE semantic, because these can be used to pass extra data. Since the TEXTURE0 intrinsic is already used, you link it to the TEXTURE1 intrinsic by specifying 1 as the last argument.

This Vector4 is preceded by Position and Texture coordinate data, occupying three and two floats, respectively, so the extra Vector4 can be found at byte number sizeof(float)*(3+2) = 20, which again is shown in Figure 5-25.

Finally, you indicate one vertex occupies a total of sizeof(float)*(3+2+4) = 36 bytes (three floats for the Position, two for the texture coordinate, and four for the extra Vector4).

## Defining Vertices of Your Custom Format

This code creates the VertexDeclaration and a VertexBuffer containing three vertices of your custom vertex format:

```
myVertexDeclaration = new VertexDeclaration(device, ➡
MyCustomVertexFormat.VertexElements);
MyCustomVertexFormat[] vertices = new MyCustomVertexFormat[3];
int i = 0;

vertices[i++] = new MyCustomVertexFormat(new Vector3(1, 1, -1), ➡
new Vector2(0,1), new Vector4(-1.0f,0.5f,0.3f,0.2f));
vertices[i++] = new MyCustomVertexFormat(new Vector3(3, 5, -1), ➡
new Vector2(0.5f, 0), new Vector4(0.8f, -0.2f, 0.5f, -0.2f));
vertices[i++] = new MyCustomVertexFormat(new Vector3(5, 1, -1), ➡
new Vector2(1, 1), new Vector4(2.0f, 0.6f, -1.0f, 0.4f));

vertBuffer = new VertexBuffer(device, MyCustomVertexFormat.SizeInBytes * ➡
 vertices.Length, ResourceUsage.WriteOnly);
vertBuffer.SetData<MyCustomVertexFormat>(vertices, 0, vertices.Length, ➡
SetDataOptions.None);
```

Each vertex requires a Vector3, Vector2, and Vector4.

## Defining a Vertex Shader Capable of Interfacing with Your Custom Vertex Format

As a result of your efforts, your vertex shader will now receive data for its POSITION0, TEXCOORD0, and TEXCOORD1 semantics. They can be accessed as in the following code:

```
//------- Technique: CustomVertexShader --------
CVVertexToPixel CVVertexShader(float3 inPos: POSITION0, float2 ➡
inTexCoord: TEXCOORD0, float4 inExtra: TEXCOORD1)
{
    CVVertexToPixel Output = (CVVertexToPixel)0;

    float4 origPos = float4(inPos, 1);
    float4x4 preViewProjection = mul(xView, xProjection);
    float4x4 preWorldViewProjection = mul(xWorld, preViewProjection);
    Output.Position = mul(origPos, preWorldViewProjection);

    Output.Extra = sin(xTime*inExtra.xyz);

    Output.TexCoord = inTexCoord;
    Output.TexCoord.x += sin(xTime)*inExtra.w;
    Output.TexCoord.y -= inExtra.w;

    return Output;
}
```

It doesn't really matter how you use the extra inputs; the important thing is that you have them available in your vertex shader. This sample vertex shader first maps the 3D position to 2D screen coordinates. Then it uses the three first floats of the extra Vector4 as frequency modulators and stores the result in the output structure. Finally, the texture coordinate is shifted, while the last float of the extra Vector4 is used to modulate the strength of the shift.

The following is a sample pixel shader, which uses the shifted texture coordinates to sample the texture and adds the three values in the Extra variable to the final color channels:

```
CVPixelToFrame CVPixelShader(CVVertexToPixel PSIn) : COLOR0
{
    CVPixelToFrame Output = (CVPixelToFrame)0;
    Output.Color = tex2D(TextureSampler, PSIn.TexCoord);
    Output.Color.rgb += PSIn.Extra.rgb;
    return Output;
}
```

### Rendering from Your Vertices

This code sets the effect variables and renders the triangle from your vertices:

```
effect.Parameters["xWorld"].SetValue(Matrix.Identity);
effect.Parameters["xView"].SetValue(fpsCam.ViewMatrix);
effect.Parameters["xProjection"].SetValue(fpsCam.ProjectionMatrix);
effect.Parameters["xTexture"].SetValue(texture);
effect.Parameters["xTime"].SetValue(time);

effect.Begin();
foreach (EffectPass pass in effect.CurrentTechnique.Passes)
{
    pass.Begin();
    device.VertexDeclaration = myVertexDeclaration;
    device.Vertices[0].SetSource(vertBuffer, 0, MyCustomVertexFormat.SizeInBytes);
    device.DrawPrimitives(PrimitiveType.TriangleList, 0, 1);
    pass.End();
}
effect.End();
```

## The Code

*All the code is available for download at www.apress.com.*

You can find the XNA code needed in this recipe in the previous text; the following code is the contents of the HLSL file:

```
float4x4 xWorld;
float4x4 xView;
float4x4 xProjection;
float xTime;
```

```
Texture xTexture;
sampler TextureSampler = sampler_state { texture = <xTexture> ; ➥
magfilter = LINEAR; minfilter = LINEAR; mipfilter=LINEAR; AddressU = ➥
mirror; AddressV = mirror;};


struct CVVertexToPixel
{
    float4 Position : POSITION;
    float2 TexCoord : TEXCOORD0;
    float3 Extra    : TEXCOORD1;
};
struct CVPixelToFrame
{
    float4 Color    : COLOR0;
};

//------- Technique: CustomVertexShader --------
CVVertexToPixel CVVertexShader(float3 inPos: POSITION0, ➥
float2 inTexCoord: TEXCOORD0, float4 inExtra: TEXCOORD1)
{
    CVVertexToPixel Output = (CVVertexToPixel)0;

    float4 origPos = float4(inPos, 1);
    float4x4 preViewProjection = mul(xView, xProjection);
    float4x4 preWorldViewProjection = mul(xWorld, preViewProjection);
    Output.Position = mul(origPos, preWorldViewProjection);

    Output.Extra = sin(xTime*inExtra.xyz);

    Output.TexCoord = inTexCoord;
    Output.TexCoord.x += sin(xTime)*inExtra.w;
    Output.TexCoord.y -= sin(xTime)*inExtra.w;

    return Output;
}

CVPixelToFrame CVPixelShader(CVVertexToPixel PSIn) : COLOR0
{
    CVPixelToFrame Output = (CVPixelToFrame)0;
    Output.Color = tex2D(TextureSampler, PSIn.TexCoord);
    Output.Color.rgb += PSIn.Extra.rgb;
    return Output;
}
```

```
technique CustomVertexShader
{
    pass Pass0
    {
        VertexShader = compile vs_1_1 CWVertexShader();
        PixelShader  = compile ps_2_0 CVPixelShader();
    }
}
```

# 5-13. Work with Bump Mapping: Fixed Normal

## The Problem

One of the main problems of a triangle is that it's flat. If you render a large wall using two huge triangles and cover it with a nice texture, the result will look disappointingly flat.

You can add real height detail to a triangle only by splitting the triangle up into smaller triangles, where you can define the 3D position of each vertex. This would, however, consume too much of the resources of your PC.

## The Solution

Instead of using such a brute-force approach, you can use bump mapping. *Bump mapping* is a technique that gives the viewer the impression of height differences within a large triangle by changing the color of each pixel in the triangle.

If you took a picture of a flat, red, plastic board, all the pixels would have almost exactly the same color. On the other hand, if you took a picture of a rough red surface, such as a red brick, all the pixels would have a different shade of red, giving the viewer the impression the brick has a rough surface.

This is the effect you want to simulate. On a rough surface, all the pixels have a different color because they are lit differently. This is because you can split a brick up into thousands of little surfaces, all with a different direction and thus with a different normal vector, as shown on the left side of Figure 5-26. For each different normal, you get a different lighting condition (see Chapter 6).

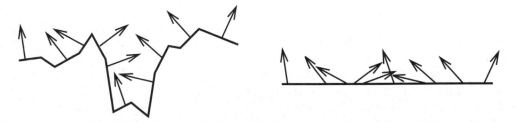

**Figure 5-26.** *A brick has thousands of surfaces, all with a different normal.*

Instead of rendering your bricks using hundreds of triangles as on the left of Figure 5-26, you are going to render them as a surface with just two triangles as on the right of that image. In each pixel of these two triangles, you are going to adjust the default normal a bit. This will cause all the pixels to get a different lighting and thus a different color. Therefore, bump mapping will add a lot of realism if the position of the brick or the light direction changes.

To get the best effects, you don't want to just add random changes to the normals in the pixels, but you want to change it in a correct way, such as the normals indicated on the right side of Figure 5-26. Notice that the normals on the right side of Figure 5-26 are the same as those on the left side. This means that for a certain texture, you should know how much to adjust the normal in each pixel. Usually, the X, Y, and Z coordinates of each deviated normal are saved into the R, G, and B channels of a second image, called the *bump map* (or normal map) of the texture.

So, instead of the brute-force approach of dividing the brick wall into thousands of triangles, you are going to render one quad of two triangles using two textures: one containing the usual image of the bricks containing the usual color for each pixel and another image containing how much the default normal should be deviated in each pixel. You will code a pixel shader that looks up the usual color and the deviated normal for a pixel, use this normal to calculate how much light hits that pixel, and use this value to adjust the brightness of the usual color.

As an introduction to bump mapping, in this recipe you will bump map a flat surface. A flat surface is a simplified case, because it has a constant default normal vector. The more general case of a curved surface is explained in the next recipe.

## How It Works

First you need to define a few triangles describing the flat surface. The following code defines two textured triangles, enough for one big rectangle:

```
private VertexPositionTexture[] InitVertices()
{
    VertexPositionTexture[] vertices = new VertexPositionTexture[6];

    vertices[0] = new VertexPositionTexture(new Vector3(-5, 0, 10), ➡
    new Vector2(0, 2));
    vertices[1] = new VertexPositionTexture(new Vector3(-5, 0, -10), ➡
    new Vector2(0, 0));
    vertices[2] = new VertexPositionTexture(new Vector3(5, 0, 10), ➡
    new Vector2(1, 2));

    vertices[3] = new VertexPositionTexture(new Vector3(-5, 0, -10), ➡
    new Vector2(0, 0));
    vertices[4] = new VertexPositionTexture(new Vector3(5, 0, -10), ➡
    new Vector2(1, 0));
    vertices[5] = new VertexPositionTexture(new Vector3(5, 0, 10), ➡
    new Vector2(1, 2));

    return vertices;
}
```

Because you'll be sampling from textures, next to the usual 3D position you'll also need to specify the texture coordinate (see recipe 5-2). Because all Y coordinates are 0, the two triangles you defined are lying on the floor (in the XZ plane), so you know the default normal vector is pointing upward.

---

■**Note** This is an assumption that is true only for this case; see the next recipe for a general approach.

---

With your vertices defined, you're ready to start coding your .fx file.

## XNA-to-HLSL Variables

As with all 3D effects, you will need to pass in your World, View, and Projection matrices so your vertex shader can transform the 3D positions of your vertices to 2D screen coordinates. To show the effect of bump mapping, you should also be capable of changing the lighting direction.

Furthermore, as mentioned in the introduction to this recipe, you will need to pass two textures to your graphics card: one to sample the usual colors from and a second one to look up how much the default normal should be deviated in each pixel.

```
float4x4 xWorld;
float4x4 xView;
float4x4 xProjection;
float3 xLightDirection;

Texture xTexture;
sampler TextureSampler = sampler_state { texture = <xTexture> ; ➥
magfilter = LINEAR; minfilter = LINEAR; mipfilter=LINEAR; AddressU = ➥
wrap; AddressV = wrap;};
Texture xBumpMap;
sampler BumpMapSampler = sampler_state { texture = <xBumpMap> ; ➥
magfilter = LINEAR; minfilter = LINEAR; mipfilter=LINEAR; AddressU = ➥
wrap; AddressV = wrap;};

struct SBMVertexToPixel
{
    float4 Position : POSITION;
    float2 TexCoord : TEXCOORD0;
};
struct SBMPixelToFrame
{
    float4 Color    : COLOR0;
};
```

The vertex shader will output the 2D screen position of each vertex (as always) together with the texture coordinate. The pixel shader has to calculate the final color.

## Vertex Shader

The vertex shader is very easy, because all it has to do is transform the 3D coordinate to 2D screen space and pass the texture coordinate to the pixel shader:

```
SBMVertexToPixel SBMVertexShader(float4 inPos: POSITION0, float2 ➡
inTexCoord: TEXCOORD0)
{
    SBMVertexToPixel Output = (SBMVertexToPixel)0;

    float4x4 preViewProjection = mul(xView, xProjection);
    float4x4 preWorldViewProjection = mul(xWorld, preViewProjection);
    Output.Position = mul(inPos, preWorldViewProjection);

    Output.TexCoord = inTexCoord;

    return Output;
}
```

As required, the 3D position is transformed by the combination of the World, View, and Projection matrices to obtain the 2D screen coordinate. The texture coordinate is simply routed to the pixel shader.

## Pixel Shader

For each pixel in each triangle, the pixel shader will look up the usual color from the color texture. This time, the pixel shader will also sample the bump map to look up in which direction the default normal should be deviated for that specific pixel.

A normal vector is a 3D vector, defined by three coordinates. For more information on normals, see recipe 5-7. To see why a normal influences the lighting, see recipe 6-1.

For each pixel of the bump map, the three coordinates of the distorted normal are stored in the three color components. However, the three coordinates should be capable of ranging from –1 to 1 (a direction can be along the positive or negative x-, y-, or z-axis), while a color component can be specified only within the [0,1] range (1 indicates full intensity, 0 indicates no intensity). So, you will need to map the value from the [0,1] range into the [–1,1] range, which can, for example, be accomplished by subtracting 0.5 from the value (mapping the value into the [–0.5,0.5] range) and by multiplying the result by 2 (mapping it into the [–1,1] range). This is done during the second and third lines of your pixel shader:

```
SBMPixelToFrame SBMPixelShader(SBMVertexToPixel PSIn) : COLOR0
{
    SBMPixelToFrame Output = (SBMPixelToFrame)0;

    float3 bumpMapColor = tex2D(BumpMapSampler, PSIn.TexCoord).rbg;
    float3 normalFromBumpMap = (bumpMapColor - 0.5f)*2.0f;

    float lightFactor = dot(-normalize(normalFromBumpMap), ➡
    normalize(xLightDirection));
    float4 texColor = tex2D(TextureSampler, PSIn.TexCoord);
```

```
    Output.Color = lightFactor*texColor;

    return Output;
}
```

In a bump map, the three color channels indicate into which direction the default normal in that pixel should be deviated. Pixels where the default normal should not be deviated are bluish (R=0.5, G=0.5, B=1). So, in this specific example of two triangles defined in the XZ plane, such a pixel should get a normal vector pointing upward, in the (0,1,0) direction.

Pixels in the bump map with a color that is different from (R=0.5, G=0.5, B=1) indicate the normal should be deviated from this (0,1,0) direction. In this case, you want the normal to be deviated into the X or Z direction for such pixels. See the next recipe for a general approach.

This is why the pixel shader in this specific example uses the blue color component as the Y coordinate for the resulting normal and the red and green color components as X and Z coordinates for the normal (and is the reason for using the RGB swizzle). As an example, if the color sampled from the bump map equals (0.5,0.5,1), normalFromBumpMap will be (0,1,0), meaning the normal isn't deviated from the default normal (which is Up for both triangles). However, if bumpMapColor = (0.145,0.5,0.855), normalFromBumpMap will be (−0.71,0.71,0), meaning the default normal has been deviated for 45 degrees to the left.

Once you know the normal in each pixel, you normalize the normal (making its length equal 1.0f) as well as the light direction before you take their dot product. As explained in recipe 6-5, this dot product indicates the brightness of the current pixel, so you multiply it with the usual color.

### Technique Definition

Finally, add this technique definition to your .fx file to make it functional:

```
technique SimpleBumpMapping
{
    pass Pass0
    {
        VertexShader = compile vs_2_0 SBMVertexShader();
        PixelShader  = compile ps_2_0 SBMPixelShader();
    }
}
```

# The Code

*All the code is available for download at www.apress.com.*

If you add the three HLSL parts described earlier together, you end up with the complete contents of the .fx file.

This is the XNA code that sets up the technique parameters and actually renders the two triangles:

```
protected override void Draw(GameTime gameTime)
{
    device.Clear(ClearOptions.Target | ClearOptions.DepthBuffer, ➥
    Color.Black, 1, 0);

    //set effect parameters
    effect.CurrentTechnique = effect.Techniques["SimpleBumpMapping"];
    effect.Parameters["xWorld"].SetValue(Matrix.Identity);
    effect.Parameters["xView"].SetValue(fpsCam.ViewMatrix);
    effect.Parameters["xProjection"].SetValue(fpsCam.ProjectionMatrix);
    effect.Parameters["xTexture"].SetValue(myTexture);
    effect.Parameters["xBumpMap"].SetValue(myBumpMap);
    effect.Parameters["xLightDirection"].SetValue(lightDirection);


    //render two triangles
    effect.Begin();
    foreach (EffectPass pass in effect.CurrentTechnique.Passes)
    {
        pass.Begin();
        device.VertexDeclaration = myVertexDeclaration;
        device.DrawUserPrimitives<VertexPositionTexture> ➥
        (PrimitiveType.TriangleList, vertices, 0, 2);
        pass.End();
    }
    effect.End();

    base.Draw(gameTime);
}
```

# 5-14. Add Per-Pixel Detail by Bump Mapping in Tangent Space

## The Problem

Although the previous recipe works well for flat objects where the default normal is constant for all the pixels in all triangles, you'll run into trouble if you want to bump map a curved or cornered surface.

The main problem is that the bump map contains the deviated normal in tangent coordinates, meaning relative to the default normal.

To visualize the problem, let's say you want to render a cylinder, as shown in Figure 5-27. The left side of the figure shows the default normals in the vertices of the cylinder.

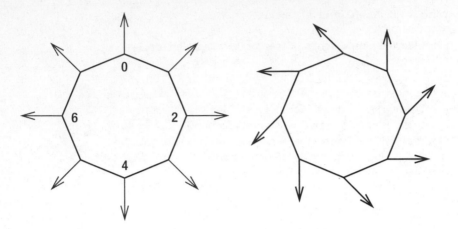

**Figure 5-27.** *Default and bump-mapped normals of a cylinder*

Now imagine you want to bump map this cylinder. As an example, you'll use a bump map that contains the (–1,0,1) normal for all the pixels of the cylinder. This corresponds to a normal deviated for 45 degrees to the left, relative to the default normal.

The correct way to find such a normal would be to stand with your feet on the cylinder at the origin of the default normal, along the default normal, and rotate yourself for 45 degrees to the left. Try to imagine this for the normals of vertices 0, 4, and 6. Your final direction will be different for all the pixels of the cylinder, because it depends on the default normal in that pixel! If you do this for each normal, you'll end up with the normals displayed on the right side of Figure 5-27. These deviated normals are deviated for 45 degrees to the left, *relative to the original normal!*

However, if you want to use this normal to calculate the lighting, you need to find the world space equivalent of this (–1,0,1) normal. This is required, because you must use only two vectors in one calculation if both vectors are defined in the same space, and you'll want to specify the light direction in world space in your XNA application.

## The Solution

The three color components of the bump map contain the coordinates of the normal in tangent space, meaning relative to the default normal. They indicate how much the default normal should be deviated. This local coordinate system is a bit different in each pixel, because it depends on the default normal that can be different for each pixel of a curved surface. This local coordinate system is called *tangent space*.

---

■**Tip**  To get an idea what tangent space looks like, imagine yourself standing on a pixel of the cylinder shown in Figure 5-27, along the default normal. Now imagine that your Up direction (along the default normal) is the z-axis, your Right direction is the x-axis, and your Forward direction is the y-axis.

---

Such a tangent coordinate system for a specific pixel is shown by the three gray arrows in image "a" in Figure 5-28. Most important is to note that the default normal in a pixel is the z-axis of the tangent space (see the previous tip).

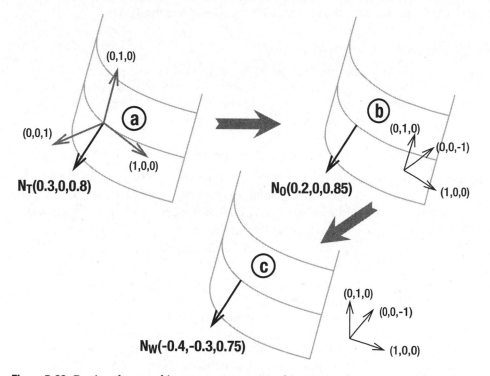

**Figure 5-28.** *Deviated normal in tangent space (a), object space (b), and world space (c)*

The x- and y-axes of the tangent space have to be perpendicular to (make angles of 90 degrees with) this z-axis and to each other. The z-axis is perpendicular to the object (because it is the default normal), while the x- and y-axes have to touch, and not intersect, the object. The x- and y-axes are called the *tangent* and *binormal*.

The three color components you sample from your bump map contain the deviated normal, defined in this tangent space. This is shown as the dark arrow, which would correspond to a normal that has a deviation of X=0.3, Y=0, and Z=0.8 from the default normal. In "a" in Figure 5-28, you see the new normal is deviated a bit toward the x-axis.

In the end, to calculate how much the pixel is lit, you want to take the dot product between this normal that is defined in tangent space and the light direction, which is defined in world (absolute) space in your XNA project. To take a dot product between two vectors, however, both vectors have to be defined in the same space. So, either you transform the light direction from world to tangent space or you transform the deviated normal from tangent to world space. In the first part of this recipe, you will do the latter. The very last paragraph of this recipe deals with the inverse approach.

# How It Works

For each pixel, you will sample the bump map and obtain the deviated normal, relative to the tangent coordinate system. In the end, you want to know this deviated normal in world space coordinates, so you can make the dot product with the direction of the light.

## Tangent Space to World Space Transform

The normal you sampled from the bump map is defined in tangent space. A round tower, which is a cylindrical wall, will serve as an example, as shown in Figure 5-28. For each pixel, the deviated normal first needs to be transformed to object space, which is the space of the tower. This will give you the default normal in object space coordinates.

---

■**Tip**  To get an idea of what the space of the tower looks like, imagine yourself standing with your feet at the origin of the tower, such as at the very center at the inside of the tower. Now, your Up direction (along the tower) is the y-axis, your Right direction is the x-axis, and your Back direction is the z-axis. What you want to find is the deviated normal, specified in your tower's X,Y,Z coordinate system.

---

This transformation is indicated by the arrow going from "a" in Figure 5-28 to "b" in Figure 5-28. In "a" in Figure 5-28, the coordinates of the normal (0.3,0,0.8) are given in the local tangent coordinates, while in the top-right image, the coordinates of the normal (0.2,0,0.85) are defined in object coordinates (verify that with the axes of both systems).

Although this is a meaningful 3D direction, it is entirely possible that you are rendering the tower using a World matrix containing a rotation (for example, to render the Tower of Pisa). In this case, the normal you obtained should get rid of this rotation to obtain the absolute (world) direction of the normal. This is indicated by the arrow going from "b" in Figure 5-28 to "c" in Figure 5-28 (note in this image that the object coordinate system is indeed a rotated version of the world coordinate system). Finally, you obtain the normal vector in world coordinates, ready to be compared with the light direction.

## Defining the Custom Vertex Format

As with any transformation, in order to transform the normal from tangent space to object space, you need to multiply it with the correct transformation matrix. You need to do this in each pixel. To create this matrix, you first need to know the x-, y-, and z-axes of the tangent space (normal, tangent, and binormal) of each vertex. These will probably be different in all vertices, since the default normal and thus z-axis will be different. Since the x- and y-axes have to be perpendicular to the z-axis, the x- and y-axes will also be different in each vertex.

Since the three axes have to be perpendicular to each other, once you know two of them, you can find the last one by taking the cross product of the two you already know. One axis (z) is the default normal, which can be found using the code explained in recipe 5-7. The tangent vector can be supplied by the Model, or you can define it yourself in simple cases such as this cylinder.

**Note** In this case, your vertex shader will calculate the binormal vector by taking a cross product between the normal and tangent vectors. Therefore, your vertices need to store only the normal and tangent vectors. You can also code a custom `Model` processor that calculates the binormal for each vertex and stores it inside the vertices. Simply use the `MeshHelper.CalculateTangentFrames` to do the heavy work for you. As a benefit, your graphics card no longer needs to calculate this vector for each frame.

First you'll need to define a custom vertex format that can store the 3D position, texture coordinate, normal, and tangent data for each vertex. See recipe 5-12 for a detailed description of custom vertex formats.

```
public struct VertPosTexNormTan
{
    public Vector3 Position;
    public Vector2 TexCoords;
    public Vector3 Normal;
    public Vector3 Tangent;
    public VertPosTexNormTan(Vector3 Position, Vector2 TexCoords, ➥
    Vector3 Normal, Vector3 Tangent)

    {
        this.Position = Position;
        this.TexCoords = TexCoords;
        this.Normal = Normal;
        this.Tangent = Tangent;
    }

    public static readonly VertexElement[] VertexElements =
    {
        new VertexElement(0, 0, VertexElementFormat.Vector3, ➥
        VertexElementMethod.Default, VertexElementUsage.Position, 0),
        new VertexElement(0, sizeof(float)*3, ➥
        VertexElementFormat.Vector2, VertexElementMethod.Default, ➥
        VertexElementUsage.TextureCoordinate, 0),
        new VertexElement(0, sizeof(float)*(3+2), ➥
        VertexElementFormat.Vector3, VertexElementMethod.Default, ➥
        VertexElementUsage.Normal, 0),
        new VertexElement(0, sizeof(float)*(3+2+3), ➥
        VertexElementFormat.Vector3, VertexElementMethod.Default, ➥
        VertexElementUsage.Tangent, 0),
    };
    public static readonly int SizeInBytes = sizeof(float) * (3 + 2 + 3 + 3);
}
```

Each vertex needs to store a Vector3 for the Position, a Vector2 for the texture coordinates, and two more Vector3s for the normal and the tangent. This gives a total of 11 floats to be stored and transferred to the graphics card for each vertex. The binormals will be calculated in the vertex shader.

### Defining the Normal and Tangent of Each Vertex

In this example, you will define some triangles to create a tower (a cylindric wall). The normal data will be generated using the code explained in recipe 5-7.

As explained earlier, the tangent direction needs to be perpendicular to the normal and should touch the tower, not intersect. In this case you're defining a vertical tower, so you know the Up direction is nowhere intersecting the tower, yet it is perpendicular to all normals of the tower, making it an ideal tangent direction.

This code generates vertices for a cylinder. For each generated vertex, the 3D position is calculated, and the (0,1,0) Up direction is stored as the tangent direction.

```
private void InitVertices()
{
    List<VertPosTexNormTan> verticesList = new List<VertPosTexNormTan>();

    int detail = 20;


    float radius = 2;
    float height = 8;

    for (int i = 0; i < detail + 1; i++)
    {
        float angle = MathHelper.Pi * 2.0f / (float)detail * (float)i;
        Vector3 baseVector = Vector3.Transform(Vector3.Forward, ➥
        Matrix.CreateRotationY(angle));

        Vector3 posLow = baseVector * radius;
        posLow.Y = -height / 2.0f;

        Vector3 posHigh = posLow;
        posHigh.Y += height;

        Vector2 texCoordLow = new Vector2(angle / (MathHelper.Pi * 2.0f), 1);
        Vector2 texCoordHigh = new Vector2(angle / (MathHelper.Pi * 2.0f), 0);

        verticesList.Add(new VertPosTexNormTan(posLow, ➥
        texCoordLow, Vector3.Zero, new Vector3(0, 1, 0)));
        verticesList.Add(new VertPosTexNormTan(posHigh, ➥
        texCoordHigh, Vector3.Zero, new Vector3(0, 1, 0)));
    }

    vertices = verticesList.ToArray();
}
```

Next, some indices are generated that render the triangles based on the vertices. All of this code is explained in recipe 5-7:

```
vertices = InitVertices();
indices = InitIndices(vertices);
vertices = GenerateNormalsForTriangleList(vertices, indices);
```

With your vertices and indices set up, you're ready to move to your .fx file.

## XNA-to-HLSL Variables

As with all 3D shaders, you'll need to pass the World, View, and Projection matrices. Because bump mapping is useless without light, you can set the direction of the light. Finally, the xTexStretch variable allows you to define how many times the brick texture should be shrunk before it's put on the cylinder.

You'll need a usual texture to sample the color of the bricks from. Next, you'll also need the bump map containing the deviated normals defined in tangent space coordinates for all the pixels.

As always, your vertex shader should transform the 3D position of each vertex to 2D screen coordinates, and the texture coordinate should be passed on to the pixel shader. To allow your pixel shader to transform a normal from tangent space to world space, the vertex shader will calculate a Tangent-to-World matrix, which should also be passed to the pixel shader.

```
float4x4 xWorld;
float4x4 xView;
float4x4 xProjection;
float3 xLightDirection;
float xTexStretch;

Texture xTexture;
sampler TextureSampler = sampler_state { texture = <xTexture> ; ➥
magfilter = LINEAR; minfilter = LINEAR; mipfilter=LINEAR; AddressU = ➥
wrap; AddressV = wrap;};
Texture xBumpMap;
sampler BumpMapSampler = sampler_state { texture = <xBumpMap> ; ➥
magfilter = LINEAR; minfilter = LINEAR; mipfilter=LINEAR; AddressU = ➥
wrap; AddressV = wrap;};

struct BMVertexToPixel
{
    float4 Position : POSITION;
    float2 TexCoord : TEXCOORD0;
    float3x3 TTW    : TEXCOORD1;
};
struct BMPixelToFrame
{
    float4 Color    : COLOR0;
};
```

**■Note** This code passes a 3×3 matrix using a single intrinsic, TEXCOORD1. This will compile, but in the background TEXCOORD2 and TEXCOORD3 are also used, so you cannot use these anymore.

## Vertex Shader

Start with this vertex shader, which does the usual; it transforms the 3D position to 2D screen coordinates and passes the texture coordinate to the pixel shader:

```
BMVertexToPixel BMVertexShader(float4 inPos: POSITION0, ➥
float3 inNormal: NORMAL0, float2 inTexCoord: TEXCOORD0, ➥
float3 inTangent: TANGENT0)
{
    BMVertexToPixel Output = (BMVertexToPixel)0;

    float4x4 preViewProjection = mul(xView, xProjection);
    float4x4 preWorldViewProjection = mul(xWorld, preViewProjection);
    Output.Position = mul(inPos, preWorldViewProjection);


    Output.TexCoord = inTexCoord;

    return Output;
}
```

Next, you need to add some code to your vertex shader that constructs the Tangent-to-World matrix. As explained earlier, this transformation happens in two phases. First you transform the normal coordinates from tangent to object space and next from object to world space.

Start by defining the tangentToObject matrix. To define a transformation matrix, you need to know the basic vectors of the coordinate system, which are the normal, tangent, and bitangent of the tangent space.

Your vertex shader receives the normal and tangent of each vertex. As explained earlier, you can calculate the binormal by making their cross product, because it is the vector perpendicular to the normal and tangent:

```
float3 Binormal = normalize(cross(inTangent,inNormal));
```

With your binormal calculated, you're ready to construct your Tangent-to-Object matrix, because the rows of a transformation matrix are nothing more than three vectors defining the new coordinate system. The vectors of an ideal coordinate system are also normalized, so you take care of this:

```
float3x3 tangentToObject;
tangentToObject[0] = normalize(Binormal);
tangentToObject[1] = normalize(inTangent);
tangentToObject[2] = normalize(inNormal);
```

---

**■Tip** By normalizing the rows of this matrix and because the three row vectors are perpendicular to each other, the inverse of this matrix is the same as the transpose of this matrix. You can find the transpose of a matrix by mirroring the elements over the axis that runs from the top left to the bottom right over the elements, which is much easier to do than calculating the inverse of a matrix.

---

All you should do now is combine the Tangent-to-Object transform with the Object-to-World transform by multiplying their matrices, so you obtain the Tangent-to-World matrix. The Object-to-World matrix is nothing more than the (very common) World matrix (containing, for example, the rotation of your tower), so you end up with this code:

```
float3x3 tangentToWorld = mul(tangentToObject, xWorld);
Output.TTW = tangentToWorld;
```

You pass this matrix on to your pixel shader. Now your pixel shader can easily transform any vector from tangent space to world space by multiplying the vector with this matrix!

## Pixel Shader

With all preparations done in the vertex shader, your pixel shader looks pretty easy:

```
BMPixelToFrame BMPixelShader(BMVertexToPixel PSIn) : COLOR0
{
    BMPixelToFrame Output = (BMPixelToFrame)0;

    float3 bumpColor = tex2D(BumpMapSampler, PSIn.TexCoord*xTexStretch);

    float3 normalT = (bumpColor - 0.5f)*2.0f;
    float3 normalW = mul(normalT, PSIn.TTW);

    float lightFactor = dot(-normalize(normalW), normalize(xLightDirection));
    float4 texColor = tex2D(TextureSampler, PSIn.TexCoord*xTexStretch);

    Output.Color = lightFactor*texColor;

    return Output;
}
```

You start by sampling the bump map at the position corresponding to the texture coordinates of the pixel. This color contains three useful color components, corresponding to the coordinates of the deviated normal, relative-to-tangent space.

As mentioned in the "Pixel Shader" section in the previous recipe, a color component can range only from 0 to 1, while a coordinate of a normal ranges from –1 to 1. So, first subtract 0.5 from the values to bring them into the [–0.5,0.5] range, and then multiply them by 2 to bring them to the [–1,1] range. The result is stored in the normalT variable.

This `normalT` variable contains the deviated normal, defined in tangent space coordinates. A `normalT` value of (0,0,1) indicates that the deviated normal equals the default normal (z-axis in tangent space). A `normalT` value of (0,0.7,0.7), for example, indicates the normal should point 45 degrees between the default normal and the tangent (y-axis in tangent space).

The transformation from tangent space to world space is done by multiplying the `normalT` vector by the Tangent-to-World matrix. The `normalW` value is obtained, containing the normal in world coordinates.

---

**■Note**  You can immediately transform the normal from tangent space to world space, because the Tangent-to-World matrix is the combination of the Tangent-to-Object and Object-to-World matrices.

---

Finally, you know the deviated normal in world space coordinates, so you can make the dot product between this vector and the light direction, which is also given in world space. As usual, and as described in recipe 6-1, this dot product gives you the lighting coefficient and should be multiplied with the color. Since each pixel has a differently deviated normal, each pixel will be lit differently.

## The Code

*All the code is available for download at* www.*apress.com.*

### HLSL Part

Your vertex shader has to construct the Tangent-to-World matrix so your pixel shader can immediately use it:

```
BMVertexToPixel BMVertexShader(float4 inPos: POSITION0, ➥
float3 inNormal: NORMAL0, float2 inTexCoord: TEXCOORD0, ➥
float3 inTangent: TANGENT0)
{
    BMVertexToPixel Output = (BMVertexToPixel)0;

    float4x4 preViewProjection = mul(xView, xProjection);
    float4x4 preWorldViewProjection = mul(xWorld, preViewProjection);
    Output.Position = mul(inPos, preWorldViewProjection);

    Output.TexCoord = inTexCoord;

    float3 Binormal = cross(inTangent,inNormal);

    float3x3 tangentToObject;
    tangentToObject[0] = normalize(Binormal);
    tangentToObject[1] = normalize(inTangent);
    tangentToObject[2] = normalize(inNormal);
```

```
    float3x3 tangentToWorld = mul(tangentToObject, xWorld);
    Output.TTW = tangentToWorld;

    return Output;
}
```

The vertex shader samples the bump map and maps the color into the [–1,1] range to obtain the normal defined in tangent space. By multiplying this vector by the Tangent-to-World matrix, the normal defined in world space is obtained, which can be dotted with the light direction (see recipe 6-7):

```
BMPixelToFrame BMPixelShader(BMVertexToPixel PSIn) : COLOR0
{
    BMPixelToFrame Output = (BMPixelToFrame)0;

    float3 bumpColor = tex2D(BumpMapSampler, PSIn.TexCoord*xTexStretch);

    float3 normalT = (bumpColor - 0.5f)*2.0f;
    float3 normalW = mul(normalT, PSIn.TTW);


    float lightFactor = dot(-normalize(normalW), normalize(xLightDirection));
    float4 texColor = tex2D(TextureSampler, PSIn.TexCoord*xTexStretch);

    Output.Color = lightFactor*texColor;

    return Output;
}
```

## XNA Part

Next, to know the usual 3D position, texture coordinate, and normal, your XNA project needs to provide the tangent for each vertex. This is a vector, perpendicular to the normal. A method that generates such vertices is presented earlier.

Finally, you need to set the effect parameters and render the triangles, for example, using this code:

```
effect.CurrentTechnique = effect.Techniques["BumpMapping"];
effect.Parameters["xWorld"].SetValue(Matrix.Identity);
effect.Parameters["xView"].SetValue(fpsCam.ViewMatrix);
effect.Parameters["xProjection"].SetValue(fpsCam.ProjectionMatrix);
effect.Parameters["xTexture"].SetValue(myTexture);
effect.Parameters["xBumpMap"].SetValue(myBumpMap);
effect.Parameters["xLightDirection"].SetValue(lightDirection);
effect.Parameters["xTexStretch"].SetValue(4.0f);
```

```
effect.Begin();
foreach (EffectPass pass in effect.CurrentTechnique.Passes)
{
    pass.Begin();
    device.VertexDeclaration = myVertexDeclaration;
    device.DrawUserIndexedPrimitives<VertPosTexNormTan> ➥
    (PrimitiveType.TriangleList, vertices, 0, vertices.Length, ➥
    indices, 0, indices.Length/3);
    pass.End();
}
effect.End();
```

## The Inverse Approach

The previous code shows you how to construct the tangentToWorld matrix so each pixel can transform its normal vector from tangent space to world space. This is required before it can be dotted with the light direction, which is also defined in world space.

You can also do things the other way around: you can transform your light direction from world space to tangent space and dot it with the normal in tangent space. This becomes extra interesting because the light direction is the same for each pixel, which makes it possible to transform the light direction in the vertex shader and send the result to the pixel shader. This way, your pixel shader can immediately perform the dot product and no longer has to calculate any kind of transformation!

---

**Note** Using this approach, you need to transform the light vector only three times for each triangle, instead of transforming the normal for each pixel of the triangle.

---

Instead of passing the tangentToWorld matrix to your pixel shader, you will pass the light direction, transformed to tangent space, to your pixel shader:

```
struct BMVertexToPixel
{
    float4 Position : POSITION;
    float2 TexCoord : TEXCOORD0;
    float3 LightDirT: TEXCOORD1;
};
```

In your vertex shader, you already calculated the tangentToWorld matrix. This time, however, you want to transform the light direction from world to tangent space, so you want the inverse of the tangentToWorld matrix.

Calculating the inverse of a matrix is a very complex operation. Luckily, the tangentToWorld matrix was constructed from three perpendicular, normalized vectors (the binormal, tangent, and normal). Usually, you pass the vector as the first argument and the matrix as the second argument to the mul intrinsic:

```
float3 vectorW = mul(vectorT, tangentToWorld);
```

In this special case of three perpendicular normalized vectors, you can transform a vector by the inverse of a matrix by swapping their order in the multiply operation:

```
float3 vectorT = mul(tangentToWorld, vectorW);
```

---

■**Note** This is because the inverse of a matrix constructed from three normalized and perpendicular vectors equals the transpose of the matrix.

---

This is exactly what you want to do for your light direction: you want to transform it from world space to tangent space:

```
Output.LightDirT = mul(tangentToWorld, xLightDirection);
```

You calculate the light direction, expressed in tangent space, and send it to your pixel shader. Since the normal you sample from your bump map and your light direction are both in the same space, you can immediately calculate their dot product in your pixel shader:

```
float3 bumpColor = tex2D(BumpMapSampler, PSIn.TexCoord*xTexStretch);
float3 normalT = (bumpColor - 0.5f)*2.0f;

float lightFactor = dot(-normalize(normalT), normalize(PSIn.LightDirT));
```

# 5-15. Add an Ocean to Your 3D World

## The Problem

You want to add an ocean to your 3D world. You could calculate the 3D positions of all your waves on your CPU, but this would consume a huge amount of resources, and the amount of data you send over to your graphics card each frame would be unacceptable.

## The Solution

In your XNA application, you will simply create a flat grid consisting of triangles. This comes down to creating a terrain, as explained in recipe 5-8, only this time the grid must be completely flat. You will send this to your graphics card once. When it comes to rendering this grid, your vertex shader will add waves to the grid, while your pixel shader will add reflections. Your CPU only has to issue the Draw command, leaving the CPU available for more important work.

Your vertex shader will receive the vertices of the grid and change their heights so the flat grid is reshaped into a wavy ocean. You can find the heights using a sine wave. A single sine wave would result in an ocean that looks too ideal, because each wave of the ocean would look identical.

Luckily, all operations done on the GPU are done four times in parallel, so calculating one sine or four sines takes the same time. Your vertex shader will calculate up to four sines and sum them together, as shown in Figure 5-29. When you set the length, speed, and height of each wave individually, this will result in an ocean in which each wave is unique.

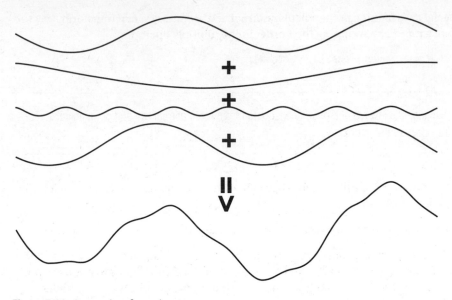

**Figure 5-29.** *Summing four sines*

An ocean will look realistic only when it reflects the environment. In your pixel shader, you will sample the reflective color from the skybox (see recipe 2-8). However, these reflections would again be too perfect, resulting in a glass-like ocean. Therefore, in every pixel, you will bump map (see recipe 5-14) the surface of your ocean, adding little per-pixel calculated ripples to the large waves of your ocean.

Finally, you will adjust the resulting color using the Fresnel term, so your pixel shader interpolates between a deep blue color and the reflective color, depending on the viewing angle.

## How It Works

In your XNA project, you need to import and render a skybox, as explained in recipe 2-8. Next, you need to generate the vertices and indices for a flat grid, which is a simplified version of the terrain generation code presented in recipe 5-8. Use this code to generate your vertices:

```
private VertexPositionTexture[] CreateWaterVertices()
{
    VertexPositionTexture[] waterVertices = new ➥
    VertexPositionTexture[waterWidth * waterHeight];

    int i = 0;
    for (int z = 0; z < waterHeight; z++)
    {
        for (int x = 0; x < waterWidth; x++)
        {
            Vector3 position = new Vector3(x, 0, -z);
            Vector2 texCoord = new Vector2((float)x / 30.0f, (float)z / 30.0f);
```

```
            waterVertices[i++] = new VertexPositionTexture(position, texCoord);
        }
    }

    return waterVertices;
}
```

The grid is flat, because all Y coordinates equal 0. You're storing only the 3D position and texture coordinate inside each vertex. Create your indices using the method described in recipe 5-8.

---

■**Tip** Since you won't be using the Y height coordinates in your shaders, you could construct a custom vertex format that stores Vector2s instead of Vector3s. As a result, each vertex would need to store one less float and as such occupy 4 bytes less memory.

---

With your vertices and indices defined, you're ready to move on to your HLSL effect file.

## XNA-to-HLSL Variables

You'll want to make your ocean as flexible as possible, so expect a lot of values you need to set from within your XNA project.

Because you're dealing with 3D positions that need to be transformed to 2D screen coordinates, you'll need the World, View, and Projection matrices.

Next, you'll want full control over your four waves. Each wave has four controllable parameters: its height, length, speed, and direction.

Because you'll want your vertex shader to update the waves each frame, it needs to know the current time; to add reflection to the water, you'll need to know the 3D position of the camera. Finally, you'll add fine ripples by bump mapping the water surface, so you'll need a bump map, together with two variables allowing you to set the intensity of the bump mapping and the size of the ripples:

```
float4x4 xWorld;
float4x4 xView;
float4x4 xProjection;

float4 xWaveSpeeds;
float4 xWaveHeights;
float4 xWaveLengths;
float2 xWaveDir0;
float2 xWaveDir1;
float2 xWaveDir2;
float2 xWaveDir3;
```

```
float3 xCameraPos;
float xBumpStrength;
float xTexStretch;
float xTime;
```

You'll need a skybox to sample reflective colors from, as well as a bump map:

```
Texture xCubeMap;
samplerCUBE CubeMapSampler = sampler_state { texture = <xCubeMap> ; ➥
magfilter = LINEAR; minfilter = LINEAR; mipfilter=LINEAR; AddressU = ➥
mirror; AddressV = mirror;}};
Texture xBumpMap;
sampler BumpMapSampler = sampler_state { texture = <xBumpMap> ; ➥
magfilter = LINEAR; minfilter = LINEAR; mipfilter=LINEAR; AddressU = ➥
mirror; AddressV = mirror;}};
```

## Output Structures

To look up the reflective color, your pixel shader will need the 3D world position of the current pixel. The Tangent-to-World matrix needs to be constructed by your vertex shader to allow the pixel shader to do some bump mapping.

The pixel shader needs to calculate only the color of each pixel.

```
struct OWVertexToPixel
{
    float4 Position : POSITION;
    float2 TexCoord : TEXCOORD0;
    float3 Pos3D    : TEXCOORD1;
    float3x3 TTW    : TEXCOORD2;
};

struct OWPixelToFrame
{
    float4 Color    : COLOR0;
};
```

## Vertex Shader: Sines

The most important task of your vertex shader is to adjust the height of each vertex of your grid. As explained earlier, you do this by summing four sines.

A sine is a mathematical function that requires one argument. When the argument is increased, the resulting value will follow a wave between –1 and 1.

As an argument to your sine, you will use the position of the vertex in the grid, relative to the direction of the wave. You can do this by taking the dot product between the X,Z position of the vertex and the direction of the wave. This dot product value will be the same for all vertices that are on the same line perpendicular to the wave's direction. If they have the same argument, their sine will be the same, so their height will be the same. This results in your wave lining up nicely in the right direction.

```
OWVertexToPixel OWVertexShader(float4 inPos: POSITION0, float2 ➥
inTexCoord: TEXCOORD0)
{
    OWVertexToPixel Output = (OWVertexToPixel)0;

    float4 dotProducts;
    dotProducts.x = dot(xWaveDir0, inPos.xz);
    dotProducts.y = dot(xWaveDir1, inPos.xz);
    dotProducts.z = dot(xWaveDir2, inPos.xz);
    dotProducts.w = dot(xWaveDir3, inPos.xz);
}
```

Because this shader allows you to sum four sines, you'll need to take four dot products between the X,Z position of the vertex and the direction of the wave. Before using these dot products as an argument to your sines, you will want to divide them by the xWaveLengths variable, allowing you to adjust the lengths of the waves.

Finally, you want your waves to move, so you'll add the current time to the argument. You multiply the current time by the xWaveSpeeds variable, allowing you to define the influence of time on each of your waves, making some waves move slower or faster than others. This is the code you get:

```
float4 arguments = dotProducts/xWaveLengths+xTime*xWaveSpeeds;
float4 heights = xWaveHeights*sin(arguments);
```

The results of the sines are multiplied by the xWaveHeights variable, so you can scale each of the four sines separately.

Remember this code is executed four times in parallel, giving you immediately the current height of the four sines at the current vertex and current time.

Now that you have calculated your sines, add them all together and use them as the height (Y) coordinate for your vertex:

```
float4 final3DPos = inPos;
final3DPos.y += heights.x;
final3DPos.y += heights.y;
final3DPos.y += heights.z;
final3DPos.y += heights.w;

float4x4 preViewProjection = mul(xView, xProjection);
float4x4 preWorldViewProjection = mul(xWorld, preViewProjection);
Output.Position = mul(final3DPos, preWorldViewProjection);

float4 final3DPosW = mul(final3DPos, xWorld);
Output.Pos3D = final3DPosW;
```

This effectively elevates the 3D position of your vertex to the correct height. Once you know the final 3D position of your vertex, you're ready to transform it to its 2D screen position as usual.

In this effect, your pixel shader will need to know the 3D position as well, so you pass the 3D world position to the pixel shader (because the `Output.Position` is not accessible in the pixel shader).

## Pixel Shader: Simplest

With your vertex shader altering the 3D position of each vertex, this simple pixel shader assigns the same color to each pixel and renders them to the screen:

```
OWPixelToFrame OWPixelShader(OWVertexToPixel PSIn) : COLOR0
{
    OWPixelToFrame Output = (OWPixelToFrame)0;

    float4 waterColor = float4(0,0.1,0.3,1);
    Output.Color = waterColor;

    return Output;
}
```

## Technique Definition

Adding the technique definition makes your effect usable as it is. If you update the `xTime` variable each frame, your waves will be updated by the vertex shader:

```
technique OceanWater
{
    pass Pass0
    {
        VertexShader = compile vs_2_0 OWVertexShader();
        PixelShader  = compile ps_2_0 OWPixelShader();
    }
}
```

## Vertex Shader: Normal Calculation

Any kind of lighting calculations in your effect will require the normal in each vertex. In your XNA project, however, you didn't add any normal information to your vertices. A normal vector should be perpendicular to the surface, and with your vertex shader continuously changing the surface, it is also up to the vertex shader to calculate the normals.

You know the normal on a flat surface will be pointing (0,1,0) upward. With your waves going through the surface, you need to know how much you should deviate this (0,1,0) vector.

You can find the amount of deviation at any point of a function (such as a sine) by taking its derivative. It sounds difficult, but luckily the derivative of a sine is simply a cosine. If this gets too abstract, have a look at Figure 5-30. The full curve indicates your sine (wave). You see that the dotted line gives a very good (perfect, actually) indication of how much the normal should be deviated in any point of the wave.

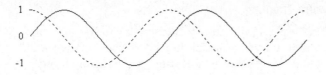

**Figure 5-30.** *A sine (full curve) and its cosine (dotted curve)*

For example, at the very top or bottom of your wave (where the water is flat), the cosine reaches 0, indicating the (0,1,0) vector shouldn't be deviated. At the middle of the slope of your wave, the cosine indicates maximum deviation.

This means that next to taking the sine, you'll also need to take the derivative of your heights function. When you take a look at the earlier heights function, you see that the sine is multiplied with xWaveHeights, which means you'll have to do the same with the derivative function. The derivative of a sine is the cosine, while you also need to divide by xWaveLengths, since dotProducts (the horizontal axis in Figure 5-30) is divided by xWaveLengths in the earlier arguments definition.

```
float4 derivatives = xWaveHeights*cos(arguments)/xWaveLengths;
```

This actually makes sense, because the higher your waves are, the steeper they are, and the more you should deviate your normal. Furthermore, the more you stretch your wave, the less you need to deviate your normal from the (0,1,0) direction.

---

**Note** Both the sine and cosine are multiplied by xWaveHeights. This means that if you set the height of a wave to 0, it will no longer have an impact on the heights of the vertices or the deviation of the normal.

---

Now that you know your mathematical derivatives, sum them together to know how much you should deviate the normal from the (0,1,0) direction in the current vertex. The wave displayed in Figure 5-30 is 2D, so the cosine indicates how much the normal should be deviated forward or backward. Your waves are in 3D, so in the previous sentence you need to replace *forward* with *the direction of the wave*:

```
float2 deviations = 0;
deviations += derivatives.x*xWaveDir0;
deviations += derivatives.y*xWaveDir1;
deviations += derivatives.z*xWaveDir2;
deviations += derivatives.w*xWaveDir3;

float3 Normal = float3(-deviations.x, 1, -deviations.y);
```

Vertices with almost 0 deviation will obtain (0,1,0) as normal, while vertices on slopes of high, short waves will have a normal that is pointing mostly into the direction of this wave.

### Vertex Shader: Tangent-to-World Matrix Creation

When you use the normal generated in the previous section to add lighting to your ocean, it will be shaded just nicely. However, your waves will be looking a bit dull, because they don't have the fine detail of real water. To add this fine detail, you'll bump map the normal vector in each pixel of your ocean water.

Before you can do any bump mapping in your pixel shader, you need to pass it the correct Tangent-to-World matrix. As explained in recipe 5-14, the rows of this matrix are the normal, binormal, and tangent vectors. Now that you already know the normal vector, go on and define the tangent and binormal vectors as well:

```
float3 Binormal = float3(1, deviations.x, 0);
float3 Tangent = float3(0, deviations.y, 1);
```

The three vectors should be perpendicular to each other. Because you have deviated the normal from the (0,1,0) vector, you should also deviate the binormal from the (1,0,0) vector and the tangent from the (0,0,1) vector, by pulling them up or down.

Once you know the three base vectors of your tangent space, it's easy to define the Tangent-to-World matrix, as explained in recipe 5-14:

```
float3x3 tangentToObject;
tangentToObject[0] = normalize(Binormal);
tangentToObject[1] = normalize(Tangent);
tangentToObject[2] = normalize(Normal);

float3x3 tangentToWorld = mul(tangentToObject, xWorld);
Output.TTW = tangentToWorld;

Output.TexCoord = inTexCoord+xTime/50.0f*float2(-1,0);

return Output;
```

You pass the Tangent-to-World matrix to the pixel shader, as well as the texture coordinate that is required to sample at the right position from the bump map.

### Pixel Shader: Bump Mapping

In each pixel, you will deviate the normal to add the illusion of small ripples on the water. If you used one bump map for your whole ocean, you would easily see the pattern of your bump map in the final result. Therefore, in each pixel you will sample the bump map at three different coordinates and average the result. Remember that a color is always defined within the [0,1] region, so you subtract 0.5 from each color to bring them to the [–0.5,0.5] region. Bringing them to the [–1,1] region (the range of XYZ coordinates for a normal) will be done in the next step.

```
float3 bumpColor1 = tex2D(BumpMapSampler, xTexStretch*PSIn.TexCoord)-0.5f;
float3 bumpColor2 = tex2D(BumpMapSampler, xTexStretch*1.8*PSIn.TexCoord.yx)-0.5f;
float3 bumpColor3 = tex2D(BumpMapSampler, xTexStretch*3.1*PSIn.TexCoord)-0.5f;

float3 normalT = bumpColor1 + bumpColor2 + bumpColor3;
```

The three texture coordinates are different, because they are multiplied by a different factor. The XY coordinates of the second texture coordinate have even been changed. In the end, all three deviations are summed together.

This direction should be normalized, but before doing so, you have the opportunity to scale the bump-mapping effect. In a bump map, the blue color component corresponds to the default normal direction, while the red and green components indicate the amount of deviation into the binormal or tangent direction. So if you increase/decrease the red and blue colors, you increase/decrease the deviation and thus the bump-mapping effect!

```
normalT.rg *= xBumpStrength;
normalT = normalize(normalT);
float3 normalW = mul(normalT, PSIn.TTW);
```

The obtained direction is normalized and transformed into world space. You end up with the normal defined in world space, allowing you to compare it to other directions defined in world space.

## Pixel Shader: Reflections

Now that you know the normal vector, defined in world coordinates, for each pixel, you could add correct lighting to your water. However, to make things a bit more realistic, you're going to add reflection to the water first. Because the reflective color will be sampled from the skybox, you'll need a direction to sample the skybox from (see recipe 2-8). You can find this direction by mirroring the eye vector, which is the vector coming from the camera going toward the pixel, over the normal vector, as shown in Figure 5-31.

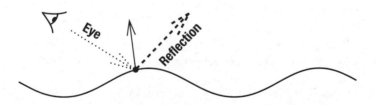

**Figure 5-31.** *Mirroring the eye vector around the normal vector yields the reflection vector*

You can find the eye vector by subtracting the origin point from the target point:

```
float3 eyeVector = normalize(PSIn.Pos3D - xCameraPos);
```

Since both the eye vector and the normal vector are defined in world space, you can perform operations on them. HLSL comes with the reflect intrinsic method, which calculates the reflection vector shown in Figure 5-31:

```
float3 reflection = reflect(eyeVector, normalW);
```

If you sample the skybox texture from this direction, you get the color that is reflected by the current pixel (see recipe 2-8 for more information on the texCUBE intrinsic):

```
float4 reflectiveColor = texCUBE(CubeMapSampler, reflection);
```

## Pixel Shader: Fresnel Term

If you simply assigned this reflective color to each pixel, the reflectivity of your ocean would be maximal everywhere and would look like a wavy mirror. To solve this, you will adjust the reflectivity of the pixels depending of the viewing angle. If you're looking flat over the water, the reflectivity should be high. If you are, however, looking straight into the ocean, the water should have a deep blue color.

A good indicator is the dot product between the eye vector and the normal. If you're look-ing straight into the water, the angle between both vectors is 0 and the dot product is maximal (1 in the case of normalized vectors). If you're looking flat over the water, the angle between the two vectors is 90 degrees, and the dot product is 0. The dot product between the eye and the normal vector is called the *Fresnel term*.

A high Fresnel term (close to 1) indicates minimal reflection, while pixels with a low Fresnel term should behave almost like a mirror. An ocean never behaves like a perfect mirror, though, so you scale your Fresnel term from the [0,1] region to the [0.5,1] region to scale down the reflectivity:

```
float fresnelTerm = dot(-eyeVector, normalW);
fresnelTerm = fresnelTerm/2.0f+0.5f;
```

■**Note** The minus sign is required, because both vectors have opposite directions. The normal points upward, while the eye vector goes downward. This would result otherwise in a negative `fresnelTerm` value.

## Pixel Shader: Specular Reflections

Now that you already know the reflective color and how much to blend this with a deep blue color, you're almost there. You can improve the final result by adding some specular highlights to your water.

As explained in recipe 6-4, this usually depends on the direction of the incoming light. In this case, however, better results are obtained by finding the spots on your ocean that reflect light sources in your cube map. These usually correspond to bright white spots present in the skybox.

To find bright reflective spots, sum the three color components of the reflective color together so bright spots will have a value close to 3. Divide this value by 3 to bring the value into the [0,1] region.

```
float sunlight = reflectiveColor.r;
sunlight += reflectiveColor.g;
sunlight += reflectiveColor.b;
sunlight /= 3.0f;
float specular = pow(sunlight,30);
```

By taking this value to the 30th power, you filter away all but the brightest pixels. Only `sunlight` values greater than 0.975 result in a `specular` value greater than 0.5!

## Pixel Shader: Putting It All Together

Finally, you have all the ingredients available to determine the final color. This code puts them all together:

```
float4 waterColor = float4(0,0.2,0.4,1);
Output.Color = waterColor*fresnelTerm + reflectiveColor*(1-fresnelTerm) + specular;
```

The relation between the deep blue ocean color and the reflective color is given by the Fresnel term. For almost all the pixels, the combination between these two colors makes up the final color of the pixel. For a pixel with an extremely bright reflective color, the specular value will be significantly larger than 0. This will make the final color a lot brighter, giving very bright specular highlights on the spots of the water corresponding to the sun in the environment.

# The Code

*All the code is available for download at www.apress.com.*

## XNA Part

In your XNA project, you have full control over your waves. You can set the speed, height, and length of up to four waves individually. If you want to remove a wave, simply set its height to 0.

This code sets all parameters of your effect and renders the triangles of your ocean:

```
Vector4 waveSpeeds = new Vector4(1, 2, 0.5f, 1.5f);
Vector4 waveHeights = new Vector4(0.3f, 0.4f, 0.2f, 0.3f);
Vector4 waveLengths = new Vector4(10, 5, 15, 7);

Vector2[] waveDirs = new Vector2[4];
waveDirs[0] = new Vector2(-1, 0);
waveDirs[1] = new Vector2(-1, 0.5f);
waveDirs[2] = new Vector2(-1, 0.7f);
waveDirs[3] = new Vector2(-1, -0.5f);

for (int i = 0; i < 4; i++)
    waveDirs[i].Normalize();


effect.CurrentTechnique = effect.Techniques["OceanWater"];
effect.Parameters["xWorld"].SetValue(Matrix.Identity);
effect.Parameters["xView"].SetValue(fpsCam.ViewMatrix);
effect.Parameters["xBumpMap"].SetValue(waterBumps);
effect.Parameters["xProjection"].SetValue(fpsCam.ProjectionMatrix);
effect.Parameters["xBumpStrength"].SetValue(0.5f);
```

```
effect.Parameters["xCubeMap"].SetValue(skyboxTexture);
effect.Parameters["xTexStretch"].SetValue(4.0f);
effect.Parameters["xCameraPos"].SetValue(fpsCam.Position);
effect.Parameters["xTime"].SetValue(time);

effect.Parameters["xWaveSpeeds"].SetValue(waveFreqs);
effect.Parameters["xWaveHeights"].SetValue(waveHeights);
effect.Parameters["xWaveLengths"].SetValue(waveLengths);
effect.Parameters["xWaveDir0"].SetValue(waveDirs[0]);
effect.Parameters["xWaveDir1"].SetValue(waveDirs[1]);
effect.Parameters["xWaveDir2"].SetValue(waveDirs[2]);
effect.Parameters["xWaveDir3"].SetValue(waveDirs[3]);

effect.Begin();
foreach (EffectPass pass in effect.CurrentTechnique.Passes)
{
    pass.Begin();

    device.Vertices[0].SetSource(waterVertexBuffer, 0, ➡
    VertexPositionTexture.SizeInBytes);
    device.Indices = waterIndexBuffer;
    device.VertexDeclaration = myVertexDeclaration;
    device.DrawIndexedPrimitives(PrimitiveType.TriangleStrip, 0, 0, ➡
    waterWidth * waterHeight, 0, waterWidth * 2 * (waterHeight - 1) - 2);

    pass.End();
}
effect.End();
```

■**Note**  The configuration parameters of your waves need to be set only if you want to change the weather conditions. Other parameters, such as the time, View matrix, and camera position, need to be updated every frame or when the camera position changes.

## HLSL Part

You can find the XNA-to-HLSL variables, texture, and output structure declarations as a whole at the beginning of this recipe.

The following code is the vertex shader, which continuously changes the height of each vertex and calculates the Tangent-to-World matrix:

```
OWVertexToPixel OWVertexShader(float4 inPos: POSITION0, float2 ➡
inTexCoord: TEXCOORD0)
{
    OWVertexToPixel Output = (OWVertexToPixel)0;
```

```
float4 dotProducts;
dotProducts.x = dot(xWaveDir0, inPos.xz);
dotProducts.y = dot(xWaveDir1, inPos.xz);
dotProducts.z = dot(xWaveDir2, inPos.xz);
dotProducts.w = dot(xWaveDir3, inPos.xz);

float4 arguments = dotProducts/xWaveLengths+xTime*xWaveSpeeds;
float4 heights = xWaveHeights*sin(arguments);

float4 final3DPos = inPos;
final3DPos.y += heights.x;
final3DPos.y += heights.y;
final3DPos.y += heights.z;
final3DPos.y += heights.w;

float4x4 preViewProjection = mul(xView, xProjection);
float4x4 preWorldViewProjection = mul(xWorld, preViewProjection);
Output.Position = mul(final3DPos, preWorldViewProjection);

float4 final3DPosW = mul(final3DPos, xWorld);
Output.Pos3D = final3DPosW;

float4 derivatives = xWaveHeights*cos(arguments)/xWaveLengths;
float2 deviations = 0;
deviations += derivatives.x*xWaveDir0;
deviations += derivatives.y*xWaveDir1;
deviations += derivatives.z*xWaveDir2;
deviations += derivatives.w*xWaveDir3;

float3 Normal = float3(-deviations.x, 1, -deviations.y);
float3 Binormal = float3(1, deviations.x, 0);
float3 Tangent = float3(0, deviations.y, 1);

float3x3 tangentToObject;
tangentToObject[0] = normalize(Binormal);
tangentToObject[1] = normalize(Tangent);
tangentToObject[2] = normalize(Normal);


float3x3 tangentToWorld = mul(tangentToObject, xWorld);
Output.TTW = tangentToWorld;

Output.TexCoord = inTexCoord+xTime/50.0f*float2(-1,0);

return Output;
}
```

Your pixel shader blends a dull deep blue water color together with a reflective color. The blending depends on the viewing angle, expressed by the Fresnel term. The specular component adds highlights to spots on the water that correspond to light sources in the environmental cube map.

```
OWPixelToFrame OWPixelShader(OWVertexToPixel PSIn) : COLOR0
{
    OWPixelToFrame Output = (OWPixelToFrame)0;

    float3 bumpColor1 = tex2D(BumpMapSampler, xTexStretch*PSIn.TexCoord)-0.5f;
    float3 bumpColor2 = tex2D(BumpMapSampler, ➥
    xTexStretch*1.8*PSIn.TexCoord.yx)-0.5f;
    float3 bumpColor3 = tex2D(BumpMapSampler, xTexStretch*3.1*PSIn.TexCoord)-0.5f;

    float3 normalT = bumpColor1 + bumpColor2 + bumpColor3;

    normalT.rg *= xBumpStrength;
    normalT = normalize(normalT);
    float3 normalW = mul(normalT, PSIn.TTW);

    float3 eyeVector = normalize(PSIn.Pos3D - xCameraPos);
    float3 reflection = reflect(eyeVector, normalW);
    float4 reflectiveColor = texCUBE(CubeMapSampler, reflection);

    float fresnelTerm = dot(-eyeVector, normalW);
    fresnelTerm = fresnelTerm/2.0f+0.5f;

    float sunlight = reflectiveColor.r;
    sunlight += reflectiveColor.g;
    sunlight += reflectiveColor.b;
    sunlight /= 3.0f;
    float specular = pow(sunlight,30);

    float4 waterColor = float4(0,0.2,0.4,1);
    Output.Color = waterColor*fresnelTerm + ➥
    reflectiveColor*(1-fresnelTerm) + specular;

    return Output;
}
```

# 5-16. Apply Catmull-Rom Interpolation in 3D to Generate Additional Vertices

## The Problem

Given a sequence of points in 3D space, you want to construct a nice, smooth curve that goes exactly through these points. The black curve in Figure 5-32 shows such a line, while the gray curve shows what you would get using simple linear interpolation, as described in recipe 5-9.

**Figure 5-32.** *Catmull-Rom spline crossing five points*

This can be quite useful in many cases. As an example, you can use it to generate a racing track, as explained in recipe 5-17. Also, whenever the camera zooms in very closely on a Model or terrain, you can use Catmull-Rom interpolation to generate extra vertices so you can make your Model or terrain as smooth as you want!

## The Solution

If you want to generate the Catmull-Rom spline between two base points, you also need to know the two adjacent base points. In the example of Figure 5-32, when you want to generate the part of the curve between base points 1 and 2, you need to know the coordinates of base points 0, 1, 2, and 3.

The XNA Framework already comes with 1D Catmull-Rom functionality. You can use the MathHelper.CatmullRom method to pass it any four base points, and it will calculate for you any point on the curve between the second and third points. You must also pass a fifth value, between 0 and 1, indicating which point between the second and third points you want.

In this recipe, you'll extend this functionality to 3D and create a sample method that uses this to generate a spline between multiple base points.

## How It Works

XNA provides 1D Catmull-Rom interpolation between single values. Because a Vector3 is nothing more than a combination of three single values, you can obtain Catmull-Rom interpolation by calling the 1D XNA method on the X, Y, and Z components of your Vector3s. The following method is the 3D extension of the default XNA method. Instead of four values, it accepts four Vector3s.

```
private Vector3 CR3D(Vector3 v1, Vector3 v2, Vector3 v3, Vector3 v4, float amount)
{
    Vector3 result = new Vector3();

    result.X = MathHelper.CatmullRom(v1.X, v2.X, v3.X, v4.X, amount);
    result.Y = MathHelper.CatmullRom(v1.Y, v2.Y, v3.Y, v4.Y, amount);
    result.Z = MathHelper.CatmullRom(v1.Z, v2.Z, v3.Z, v4.Z, amount);

    return result;
}
```

This method will return a Vector3, called result, on the spline between v2 and v3. The amount variable allows you to specify the distance between v2, the result, and v3, where 0 will return v2, and 1 will return v3.

### Using the CR3D Method to Calculate the Spline

Now that you have a method capable of doing 3D Catmull-Rom interpolation, let's use it to generate multiple points of a spline.

Given the four base points v1, v2, v3, and v4 in 3D space, the following method returns a list of 20 points on the spline between v2 and v3, with the first point in the returned list being v2.

```
private List<Vector3> InterpolateCR(Vector3 v1, Vector3 v2, Vector3 v3, Vector3 v4)
{
    List<Vector3> list = new List<Vector3>();
    int detail = 20;
    for (int i = 0; i < detail; i++)
    {
        Vector3 newPoint = CR3D(v1, v2, v3, v4, (float)i / (float)detail);
        list.Add(newPoint);
    }
    return list;
}
```

Increase/decrease the detail value if you want to add/reduce the number of points calculated between v2 and v3 (or better, make it an additional argument of the method).

---

■**Note** The last point of the list will be the last point on the spline from v2 to v3 not being v3 itself. This is because in the last call to the CR3D method, you pass in 19/20, which is not equal to 1. You can always add v3 manually, for example, by adding this line before returning: list.Add(v3);.

---

### Joining Multiple Parts of the Spline Together

The previous code generates a spline between the two middle points of four points. For bonus points, the following code shows how you can extend the spline:

```
points.Add(new Vector3(0,0,0));
points.Add(new Vector3(2,2,0));
points.Add(new Vector3(4,0,0));
points.Add(new Vector3(6,6,0));
points.Add(new Vector3(8,2,0));
points.Add(new Vector3(10, 0, 0));

List<Vector3> crList1 = InterpolateCR(points[0], points[1], points[2], points[3]);
List<Vector3> crList2 = InterpolateCR(points[1], points[2], points[3], points[4]);
List<Vector3> crList3 = InterpolateCR(points[2], points[3], points[4], ➥
points[5]);

straightVertices = XNAUtils.LinesFromVector3List(points, Color.Red);
crVertices1 = XNAUtils.LinesFromVector3List(crList1, Color.Green);
crVertices2 = XNAUtils.LinesFromVector3List(crList2, Color.Blue);
crVertices3 = XNAUtils.LinesFromVector3List(crList3, Color.Yellow);
```

First, you define a list of seven points in 3D space. Next, you use the first four points to generate extra points between points[1] and points[2]. You shift one point and get the extra points between points[2] and points[3]. Finally, you retrieve the extra points between points[3] and points[4].

This means you end up with many extra points, all positioned on a spline starting at points[1], going through points[2] and points[3], and ending in points[4] (take a look at Figure 5-32 to get a better idea).

Because you'll want to render these to have a look, you create vertices from all three generated parts of the spline. You first turn the seven base points into vertices so you can render the lines as a comparison. You can do this using this simple method:

```
public static VertexPositionColor[] LinesFromVector3List(List<Vector3> ➥
pointList, Color color)
{
    myVertexDeclaration = new VertexDeclaration(device, ➥
    VertexPositionColor.VertexElements);

    VertexPositionColor[] vertices = new VertexPositionColor[pointList.Count];

    int i = 0;
    foreach (Vector3 p in pointList)
        vertices[i++] = new VertexPositionColor(p, color);

    return vertices;
}
```

This simply turns each Vector3 from a List into a vertex and stores it together with a Color of your choice in an array.

You can render lines between all of these vertices as shown in recipe 5-1:

```
basicEffect.World = Matrix.Identity;
basicEffect.View = fpsCam.ViewMatrix;
basicEffect.Projection = fpsCam.ProjectionMatrix;
basicEffect.VertexColorEnabled = true;
basicEffect.TextureEnabled = false;

basicEffect.Begin();
foreach (EffectPass pass in basicEffect.CurrentTechnique.Passes)
{
    pass.Begin();
    device.VertexDeclaration = myVertexDeclaration;
    device.DrawUserPrimitives<VertexPositionColor> ➡
    (PrimitiveType.LineStrip, straightVertices, 0, ➡
    straightVertices.Length - 1);
    device.DrawUserPrimitives<VertexPositionColor> ➡
    (PrimitiveType.LineStrip, crVertices1, 0, crVertices1.Length - 1);
    device.DrawUserPrimitives<VertexPositionColor> ➡
    (PrimitiveType.LineStrip, crVertices2, 0, crVertices2.Length - 1);
    device.DrawUserPrimitives<VertexPositionColor> ➡
    (PrimitiveType.LineStrip, crVertices3, 0, crVertices3.Length - 1);
    pass.End();
}
basicEffect.End();
```

## The Code

*All the code is available for download at* www.apress.com.

This recipe introduced two methods. The first one is the 3D extension of the Catmull-Rom interpolation that comes with the XNA Framework:

```
private Vector3 CR3D(Vector3 v1, Vector3 v2, Vector3 v3, Vector3 v4, float amount)
{
    Vector3 result = new Vector3();

    result.X = MathHelper.CatmullRom(v1.X, v2.X, v3.X, v4.X, amount);
    result.Y = MathHelper.CatmullRom(v1.Y, v2.Y, v3.Y, v4.Y, amount);
    result.Z = MathHelper.CatmullRom(v1.Z, v2.Z, v3.Z, v4.Z, amount);

    return result;
}
```

The second method is capable of calculating extra points on the spline going through four base points:

```
private List<Vector3> InterpolateCR(Vector3 v1, Vector3 v2, Vector3 v3, Vector3 v4)
{
    List<Vector3> list = new List<Vector3>();
    int detail = 20;
    for (int i = 0; i < detail; i++)
    {
        Vector3 newPoint = CR3D(v1, v2, v3, v4, (float)i / (float)detail);
        list.Add(newPoint);
    }
    list.Add(v3);
    return list;
}
```

# 5-17. Create the Vertices for a Racing Track

## The Problem

Given a list of base points in 3D space, you want to create a racing track that goes through all of these points. You want to create the vertices, calculate the normals, and put a texture over the track automatically.

## The Solution

You can create a racing track from a list of 3D points in a few steps, as shown in Figure 5-33. You start by using the 3D Catmull-Rom interpolation discussed in recipe 5-16 to generate as many extra points as you want that are on a spline between your predefined points. This first step is shown by the arrow going from "a" in Figure 5-33 to "b" in Figure 5-33.

You cannot define triangles based on this single base spline. For each point of your spline, you will calculate the direction perpendicular to the spline and add points at both sides of your spline. This is shown in "c" in Figure 5-33.

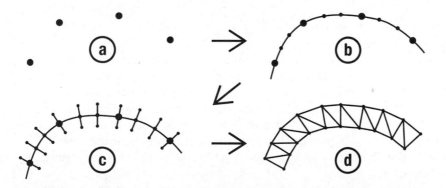

**Figure 5-33.** *Generating vertices for a racing track*

Finally, you will create a TriangleList from these newly calculated points by turning them into a vertex, as shown in "d" in Figure 5-33.

# How It Works

Obviously, you need to start by defining some 3D points you want your track to follow. This list, for example, defines a track in the shape of an 8:

```
List<Vector3> trackPoints = new List<Vector3>();
trackPoints.Add(new Vector3(2, 0, 4));
trackPoints.Add(new Vector3(0, 0, 0));
trackPoints.Add(new Vector3(-2, 0, -4));
trackPoints.Add(new Vector3(2, 0, -4));
trackPoints.Add(new Vector3(0, 1, 0));
trackPoints.Add(new Vector3(-2, 0, 4));
```

Note the seventh point (the crossing point) is one unit higher than the others, so you don't have to put traffic lights on your racing track.

## Calculating the Extra Points Between the Base Points

As a first step toward your track, you will use 3D Catmull-Rom interpolation to calculate a lot of extra points between your base points, as shown in "b" in Figure 5-33. The InterpolateCR method created in recipe 5-16 will be useful here, because it is capable of calculating extra points between any two base points.

However, to create extra points between two base points, you also need to provide the two neighboring base points. For example, if you want to calculate extra points between base points 1 and 2 in Figure 5-34, you will need to pass points 0, 1, 2, and 3 to the InterpolateCR method.

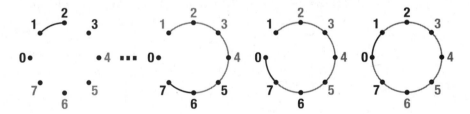

**Figure 5-34.** *End-begin connection using Catmull-Rom*

In general, if you want to calculate extra points between base points i and i+1, you need to provide points i–1, i, i+1, and i+2. This causes a problem at the end of your track, as shown in Figure 5-34. This shows as an example a track of eight base points. You can construct the sections between [1,2], [2,3], [3,4], [4,5], and [5,6] without any problem. However, when you want to calculate the extra points between [6,7], then you need to pass base points 5, 6, 7, and 8. Because your list contains only base points 0 to 7, you have a problem here. Even worse, to create the final two sections between points 7, 0, and 1, you'll even need base points 9 and 10, which obviously don't exist.

Luckily, you know the end of the track should be connected to its beginning, so you know base point 8 is the same as base point 0. The same way, point 9 equals point 1, and point 10 equals point 2. The means you can solve the problem by adding base points 0, 1, and 2 to the end of your list. This should be done at the beginning of the GenerateTrackPoints method, which will create a list containing all the extra points of your whole track:

```
private List<Vector3> GenerateTrackPoints(List<Vector3> basePoints)
{
    basePoints.Add(basePoints[0]);
    basePoints.Add(basePoints[1]);
    basePoints.Add(basePoints[2]);

    List<Vector3> allPoints = new List<Vector3>();

    for (int i = 1; i < basePoints.Count-2; i++)
    {
        List<Vector3> part = InterpolateCR(basePoints[i - 1], ➥
        basePoints[i], basePoints[i + 1], basePoints[i + 2]);
        allPoints.AddRange(part);
    }
    allPoints.Add(allPoints[0]);

    return allPoints;
}
```

After you've copied the first three base points to the end of the base point list, you create a new, empty list that will contain all the center points of your track, corresponding to "b" in Figure 5-33.

The for loop will jump from section to section, create the extra points for such a section using the InterpolateCR method, and add all the points together in the allPoints list.

For each section, the for loop calls the InterpolateCR method and passes basePoints i–1, i, i+1, and i+2, with i starting at 1. This means that the first section created will be section [1,2], as shown at the left of Figure 5-34. The InterpolateCR method will return basePoint 1, together with 19 extra points between basePoints 1 and 2. These 20 points are added to the allPoints list.

The last section that will be added is section [8,9], which is the same as section [0,1].

---

■**Note**  You can adjust the number of extra points calculated by the InterpolateCR method by adjusting the value of the detail variable inside that method.

---

The for loop will continue to loop until all the extra points of all sections have been added to the allPoints list.

At this point, you know all center points of your track, corresponding to "b" in Figure 5-33.

## Calculating the Outer Points

Moving on, for each point you now want to define a new point on each side of the track, as shown in "c" in Figure 5-33, so you can connect them to define your triangles.

To do this, you first need to calculate the side direction in each point. The side direction is the direction that is perpendicular to the direction into which the cars should be driving and perpendicular to the normal direction of your track. For now, let's say the (0,1,0) Up vector is the normal direction at each point in your track.

As always, if you know two directions, you can make their cross product to obtain the direction perpendicular to both directions. In this case, the two directions are the (0,1,0) Up direction and the driving direction, which is the direction from the current point to the next. You can find this direction by subtracting the current point from the next.

```
Vector3 carDir = basePoints[i + 1] - basePoints[i];
Vector3 sideDir = Vector3.Cross(new Vector3(0, 1, 0), carDir);
sideDir.Normalize();

Vector3 outerPoint = basePoints[i] + sideDir * halfTrackWidth;
Vector3 innerPoint = basePoints[i] - sideDir * halfTrackWidth;
```

Since the length of the output vector of a cross product depends on the angle between the two input vectors, you normalize the output vector. This keeps the direction but makes sure the length is exactly 1. Otherwise, the width of the road would have depended on the angle between both input vectors.

Once you've found the side direction, you multiply this with a track width of your choice and add/subtract it from the current point. At this moment, you've calculated the side points of "c" in Figure 5-33.

## Creating the Vertices

Before you can create vertices from these points, you need to provide their normal and texture coordinate. For now, you'll take the (0,1,0) Up vector as the normal direction.

The texture coordinate is a bit harder to find. If you just increased the Y texture coordinate with a constant amount for each point, your texture would look shrunken in certain places where you have defined the base points close to each other. This is because your InterpolateCR will have added exactly twenty points in all cases, whether you've defined two base points very close or very far from each other.

To solve this, you'll keep track of the total distance covered in a distance variable so that longer parts increase the Y texture coordinate more than smaller parts:

```
VertexPositionNormalTexture vertex;
vertex = new VertexPositionNormalTexture(innerPoint, new ➡
Vector3(0, 1, 0), new Vector2(0, distance / textureLength));
verticesList.Add(vertex);
vertex = new VertexPositionNormalTexture(outerPoint, new ➡
Vector3(0, 1, 0), new Vector2(1, distance / textureLength));
verticesList.Add(vertex);
distance += carDir.Length();
```

Note that the distance value is increased after each point of your track has been processed. The textureLength value allows you to stretch/shrink your track texture to your liking, by indicating how much texture corresponds to one distance unit of the track.

You need to do this for each center point of your track:

```
private VertexPositionNormalTexture[] ➥
GenerateTrackVertices(List<Vector3> basePoints)
{
    float halfTrackWidth = 0.2f;
    float textureLength = 0.5f;

    float distance = 0;
    List<VertexPositionNormalTexture> verticesList = new ➥
    List<VertexPositionNormalTexture>();

    for (int i = 1; i < basePoints.Count-1; i++)
    {
        Vector3 carDir = basePoints[i + 1] - basePoints[i];
        Vector3 sideDir = Vector3.Cross(new Vector3(0, 1, 0), carDir);
        sideDir.Normalize();

        Vector3 outerPoint = basePoints[i] + sideDir * halfTrackWidth;
        Vector3 innerPoint = basePoints[i] - sideDir * halfTrackWidth;

        VertexPositionNormalTexture vertex;
        vertex = new VertexPositionNormalTexture(innerPoint, new ➥
        Vector3(0, 1, 0), new Vector2(0, distance / ➥
        textureLength));
        verticesList.Add(vertex);
        vertex = new VertexPositionNormalTexture(outerPoint, new ➥
        Vector3(0, 1, 0), new Vector2(1, distance / ➥
        textureLength));
        verticesList.Add(vertex);
        distance += carDir.Length();
    }

    VertexPositionNormalTexture extraVert = verticesList[0];
    extraVert.TextureCoordinate.Y = distance / textureLength;
    verticesList.Add(extraVert);

    extraVert = verticesList[1];
    extraVert.TextureCoordinate.Y = distance / textureLength;
    verticesList.Add(extraVert);

    return verticesList.ToArray();
}
```

After the for loop, the verticesList contains two vertices for each center point of your track. However, when you render triangles from this list of vertices, there will still be a small gap between the last center point and the first center point. To bridge this gap, you need to copy the side points of the first two center points to the end of your list. However, since the Y texture coordinate of the first two vertices equals 0, you need to adjust this to the current texture coordinate value. Otherwise, the last two triangles would have to span their Y texture coordinate from the last value all the way back to 0, resulting in a lot of texture smashed onto two tiny triangles.

Finally, you convert the List to an Array and return it to the calling code.

## Rendering the Track

With your base points defined and the code ready to be used, add these few lines to convert your base points into a large array of vertices:

```
List<Vector3> extendedTrackPoints = GenerateTrackPoints(basePoints);
trackVertices = GenerateTrackVertices(extendedTrackPoints);
```

With your vertices defined, you're all set to render some triangles to the screen:

```
basicEffect.World = Matrix.Identity;
basicEffect.View = fpsCam.ViewMatrix;
basicEffect.Projection = fpsCam.ProjectionMatrix;

basicEffect.Texture = road;
basicEffect.TextureEnabled = true;
basicEffect.VertexColorEnabled = false;

basicEffect.Begin();
foreach (EffectPass pass in basicEffect.CurrentTechnique.Passes)
{
    pass.Begin();
    device.VertexDeclaration = myVertexDeclaration;
    device.DrawUserPrimitives<VertexPositionNormalTexture> ➥
    (PrimitiveType.TriangleStrip, trackVertices, 0, ➥
    trackVertices.Length - 2);
    pass.End();
}
basicEffect.End();
```

See recipe 6-1 on rendering a TriangleList and recipe 6-2 on rendering textured triangles.

## Bonus Points: Banking

The previous code generates a track that's completely flat. This is because it starts from the idea that the normal vector in each point of the track is the (0,1,0) Up vector. Although this will give a valid track, you'll have a tough time keeping your car on the track in some sharp corners. Don't even think about adding loops to your track.

To make the track more realistic, you'll want to bank your track to prevent your car from sliding out of its corners.

The previous code used the (0,1,0) Up vector as the normal vector to calculate the side vector. This time, you're going to use a more appropriate normal vector. It's quite impossible to calculate this normal to take banking into account. The solution to this is to remember the last normal vector and adjust this for each point in your track.

Using this approach, you need to pick a starting value for the normal. If you make sure your track starts out flat, you can simply use the (0,1,0) Up vector as the starting normal, so define this line before your for loop:

```
Vector3 currentNormal = Vector3.Up;
```

For each point of the track, you should adjust this vector to take the curving of the track into account. The curving can be expressed by the centrifugal direction: it's the direction you need to pull the car so it isn't flying out of the corners of your track, and it's shown in Figure 5-35.

**Figure 5-35.** *Finding the centrifugal direction*

You can find this direction by taking two cross products. First, you need to take the cross product between the direction the car was going to, to reach the current point (lastCarDir), and the direction the car should go to, to reach the next point (carDir). Both directions are indicated in the left part of Figure 5-35. The resulting vector is perpendicular to both and thus sticks out of the paper, making it pretty hard to draw on the image. Next, you take the cross product between this vector and the carDir. This is the centriDir vector and will always point toward the inner side of the curve of the track.

The right side of Figure 5-35 shows a more complex 3D situation.

This is the coded version of the last few paragraphs:

```
Vector3 carDir = trackPoints[i + 1] - trackPoints[i];
carDir.Normalize();
Vector3 lastCarDir = trackPoints[i] - trackPoints[i - 1];
lastCarDir.Normalize();

Vector3 perpDir = Vector3.Cross(carDir, lastCarDir);
Vector3 centriDir = Vector3.Cross(carDir, perpDir);
```

Because the centriDir direction is the inner direction of the curve, the track should be banked perpendicularly to this vector.

To take this into account, for each point of your track you will add this vector to your normal vector. This will result in your side vector slowly becoming perpendicular to the centriDir vector.

However, during a long turn, this will become too dominant, so you need to add some kind of resetting factor. For this resetting factor, you can use the Up vector, which will cause the normal to reset to the Up vector at the end of a turn:

```
currentNormal = currentNormal + centriDir * banking + Vector3.Up/banking;
currentNormal.Normalize();
```

The higher the value of the banking variable, the more the corners in your track will be banked.

From here on, you can use the code from earlier. Just keep in mind that you should use the currentNormal instead of the (0,1,0) Up vector:

```
Vector3 sideDir = Vector3.Cross(currentNormal, carDir);
sideDir.Normalize();
currentNormal = Vector3.Cross(carDir, sideDir);
```

When using this code, your track should be banked in the corners. Even more, this code allows loops in your track!

## The Code

*All the code is available for download at www.apress.com.*

The GenerateTrackPoints method will accept your short list of base points and will extend it to add detail to your track:

```
private List<Vector3> GenerateTrackPoints(List<Vector3> basePoints)
{
    basePoints.Add(basePoints[0]);
    basePoints.Add(basePoints[1]);
    basePoints.Add(basePoints[2]);

    List<Vector3> allPoints = new List<Vector3>();

    for (int i = 1; i < basePoints.Count-2; i++)
    {
        List<Vector3> part = InterpolateCR(basePoints[i - 1], ➥
        basePoints[i], basePoints[i + 1], basePoints[i + 2]);
        allPoints.AddRange(part);
    }

    return allPoints;
}
```

Based on this extended list, the GenerateTrackVertices method creates an array of vertices with which you can render a banked racing track:

```
private VertexPositionNormalTexture[] ➡
GenerateTrackVertices(List<Vector3> trackPoints)
{
    float halfTrackWidth = 0.2f;
    float textureLength = 0.5f;
    float banking = 2.0f;


    float distance = 0;
    List<VertexPositionNormalTexture> verticesList = new ➡
    List<VertexPositionNormalTexture>();
    Vector3 currentNormal = Vector3.Up;

    for (int i = 1; i < trackPoints.Count-1; i++)
    {
        Vector3 carDir = trackPoints[i + 1] - trackPoints[i];
        carDir.Normalize();
        Vector3 lastCarDir = trackPoints[i] - trackPoints[i - 1];
        lastCarDir.Normalize();

        Vector3 perpDir = Vector3.Cross(carDir, lastCarDir);
        Vector3 centriDir = Vector3.Cross(carDir, perpDir);

        currentNormal = currentNormal + Vector3.Up/banking + centriDir * banking;
        currentNormal.Normalize();

        Vector3 sideDir = Vector3.Cross(currentNormal, carDir);
        sideDir.Normalize();
        currentNormal = Vector3.Cross(carDir, sideDir);

        Vector3 outerPoint = trackPoints[i] + sideDir * halfTrackWidth;
        Vector3 innerPoint = trackPoints[i] - sideDir * halfTrackWidth;

        distance += carDir.Length();
        VertexPositionNormalTexture vertex;
        vertex = new VertexPositionNormalTexture(innerPoint, ➡
        currentNormal, new Vector2(0, distance / textureLength));
        verticesList.Add(vertex);
        vertex = new VertexPositionNormalTexture(outerPoint, ➡
        currentNormal, new Vector2(1, distance / textureLength));
        verticesList.Add(vertex);
    }

    VertexPositionNormalTexture extraVert = verticesList[0];
    extraVert.TextureCoordinate.Y = distance / textureLength;
    verticesList.Add(extraVert);
```

```
    extraVert = verticesList[1];
    extraVert.TextureCoordinate.Y = distance / textureLength;
    verticesList.Add(extraVert);

    return verticesList.ToArray();
}
```

Having both methods, it's pretty easy to create a track from just a list of 3D points:

```
List<Vector3> basePoints = new List<Vector3>();
basePoints.Add(new Vector3(2, 0, 4));
basePoints.Add(new Vector3(0, 0, 0));
basePoints.Add(new Vector3(-2, 0, -4));
basePoints.Add(new Vector3(2, 0, -4));
basePoints.Add(new Vector3(0, 1, 0));
basePoints.Add(new Vector3(-2, 0, 4));

List<Vector3> extendedTrackPoints = GenerateTrackPoints(basePoints);
trackVertices = GenerateTrackVertices(extendedTrackPoints);
```

# CHAPTER 6
■ ■ ■

# Adding Light to Your Scene in XNA 3.0

**L**ighting a scene sounds very easy: set the positions of the objects in your 3D world, define the positions of your lights, and—bingo!—you expect your 3D scene to be lit correctly. Although it seems trivial to have your graphics card do this for you, it definitely is not.

For each surface of your objects, the graphics card needs to calculate the amount of lighting that is received by the surface. This amount is based on the angle between the direction of the light and the surface of the triangle. Luckily, the XNA Framework comes with the BasicEffect, which is capable of performing all these calculations for you. The first part of this chapter shows you how you can use the BasicEffect to lighten up your scene.

However, as its name implies, the BasicEffect can be used only for some basic lighting effects. What if you want to have point lights in your scene, such as candles? Or what if you want to have your scene lit by many lights? And why don't your objects cast any shadows?

To answer these questions, you'll have to code your own effects in HLSL. The second part of this chapter starts by showing you how you can create HLSL effects with the same functionality as BasicEffect.

This chapter doesn't stop where the BasicEffect stops, however. You'll learn how to implement additional functionality, such as support for point lights and spotlights. Even more, the final recipes introduce you to the world of deferred rendering, allowing you to light your scene by a large number of lights simultaneously. To top it off, you'll learn how you can combine the shadow mapping technique with deferred rendering so all your objects cast shadows.

Specifically, the recipes in this chapter cover the following:

- Learning the basics about lighting in XNA 3.0, including what is required for correct lighting and why (recipes 6-1 and 6-2).

- Using the BasicEffect to its full potential, making it calculate lighting for each pixel of your screen, and adding specular highlights to reflective surfaces (recipes 6-3 and 6-4).

- Coding your own HLSL effect when the functionality of the BasicEffect is not enough for you. You'll start by implementing the basic functionality of the BasicEffect (recipes 6-5, 6-7, and 6-9).

- Implementing extra functionality, such as support for point lights and spotlights (recipes 6-6 and 6-8).

- Making your scene really come alive by using multiple lights. Since the basic approaches are not scalable enough, you'll jump into deferred rendering to add lighting in screen space (recipe 6-10).

- Adding shadows to your scene using the shadow mapping technique. To make the chapter complete, you'll implement this using the deferred rendering approach, allowing you to have multiple lights casting shadows in your 3D world (recipe 6-11).

# 6-1. Define Normals and Use the BasicEffect

## The Problem

Without correct lighting, your scene will look a lot less realistic. In some cases, the 3D effect will be completely gone when objects are not lit correctly.

As an example, consider a sphere having one solid color. Without any lighting, all pixels of the sphere will have the same color, making the result on your screen look like a flat disc. When correctly lit, the part of the sphere facing the light will have a brighter color than other parts, making the sphere appear as a real 3D object.

## The Solution

In computer graphics, all 3D objects are made up of triangles. You want each of these triangles to be lit correctly corresponding to the incoming light. Figure 6-1 shows a single directional light going from left to right and its impact on six differently positioned quads, each consisting of two triangles.

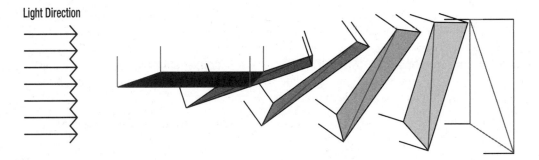

Light Direction

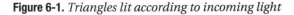

**Figure 6-1.** *Triangles lit according to incoming light*

Simply defining the position of the light source and the position of your objects is not enough for your graphics card to add correct lighting to an object, though. For each triangle of your 3D object, you will need to add some information, allowing your graphics card to calculate the amount of light hitting the surface.

You can do this by specifying the normal vector in each vertex of your object, which are the spikes at the corners of the triangles shown in Figure 6-1. Once you've specified the correct normal in each vertex, the BasicEffect can render your object with correct lighting.

# How It Works

In Figure 6-1, several squares (each consisting of two triangles) are drawn, and their colors represent the amount of incoming light. The more the square is perpendicular to the direction of the light, the more light it receives. The last square is completely perpendicular to the direction of the light so should be fully lit. The first square, however, is positioned along the direction of the light and should therefore receive no light at all.

## Definition of the Normal

How is the graphics card supposed to know how much light the triangle receives? In each corner of each triangle (called a *vertex*; see recipe 5-1), you'll define the direction perpendicular to the triangle. This direction is called the *normal*. This normal direction has been indicated in each vertex of Figure 6-1 as a spike. Because there is only one direction perpendicular to a surface, all vertices of the same quad have the same normal direction.

This normal direction allows your graphics card to calculate how much light hits the triangle. As explained in detail in recipe 6-5, you do this by projecting the normal on the direction of the light, as shown in Figure 6-2. The direction of the light is shown as the long black arrow at the bottom of the image going from left to right. The rotated black bars in Figure 6-2 represent the quads of Figure 6-1. The projections of the normal of each quad on the light direction are shown as the thick black blocks on the light direction. The bigger the black block, the more your triangle should be lit.

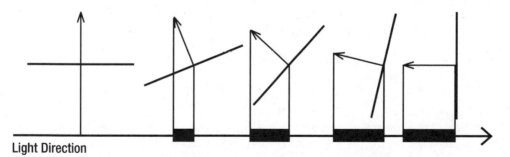

Light Direction

**Figure 6-2.** *Projecting the normal on the light direction*

The normal of the triangle on the left is perpendicular to the direction of the light, so the projection is 0, and the triangle will not be lit. The triangle on the right side has a normal parallel to the light direction, so its projection will be maximal, and the plane will be lit at full intensity.

Given the direction of the light and the normal in a vertex, your graphics card can easily calculate the length of the projection (the thick black block). This is how the graphics card calculates the correct lighting.

## Applying Shading to Your Scene

For each pixel, the graphics card will calculate the amount of lighting that should be applied to that pixel, as described earlier. Next, the graphics card multiplies this amount of lighting by the original color of that pixel.

## Adding Normal Data to Your Vertices

The previous paragraph explains that, next to the 3D position and color, each vertex should also store its normal direction.

XNA comes with one predefined vertex format that allows you to save a normal in each vertex: the VertexPositionNormalTexture struct. This format allows you to save the 3D position, normal direction, and texture coordinate for each vertex. See recipe 5-2 on textured triangles and recipe 5-13 to learn how you can define your own vertex format.

The following method creates an array to hold six such vertices, which define two triangles that create a quad. This quad is lying on the floor, because all Y coordinates of the vertices are 0. Therefore, the normal stored in each vertex is the (0,1,0) Up direction, because this is the direction perpendicular to the quad. The vertex format also expects you to add texture coordinates so the graphics card knows where to sample the colors from an image (see recipe 5-2).

```
private void InitVertices()
{
    vertices = new VertexPositionNormalTexture[6];
    int i = 0;

    vertices[i++] = new VertexPositionNormalTexture(new Vector3(-1, ➥
    0, 1), new Vector3(0, 1, 0), new Vector2(1,1));
    vertices[i++] = new VertexPositionNormalTexture(new Vector3(-1, ➥
    0, -1), new Vector3(0, 1, 0), new Vector2(0,1));
    vertices[i++] = new VertexPositionNormalTexture(new Vector3(1, ➥
    0, -1), new Vector3(0, 1, 0), new Vector2(0,0));

    vertices[i++] = new VertexPositionNormalTexture(new Vector3(1, ➥
    0, -1), new Vector3(0, 1, 0), new Vector2(0,0));
    vertices[i++] = new VertexPositionNormalTexture(new Vector3(1, ➥
    0, 1), new Vector3(0, 1, 0), new Vector2(1,0));
    vertices[i++] = new VertexPositionNormalTexture(new Vector3(-1, ➥
    0, 1), new Vector3(0, 1, 0), new Vector2(1,1));

    myVertexDeclaration = new VertexDeclaration(device, ➥
    VertexPositionNormalTexture.VertexElements);
}
```

The last line makes sure the VertexDeclaration (see recipe 5-1) is created only once, because this will not need to be changed.

---

■**Tip** In this case of a triangle lying flat on the ground, it's easy to calculate its normal. Read recipe 5-7 to learn how you can automatically calculate the normals for a more complex object.

---

## Positive and Negative Normals

A triangle has actually two perpendicular directions. If the triangle is lying on the floor as in the previous code, you could define the normal as pointing upward or downward. So, which one should you use? This is quite important, because choosing the wrong one will result in incorrect lighting and usually in no lighting at all.

As a rule, you need to select the normal that is pointing outward of the object the triangle is part of.

Usually, one face of the triangle can be considered as part of the "inside" of the 3D object it is a part of, while the other face will be part of the "outside" of the object. In such a case, you want to select the normal pointing outward of the object.

## Setting the BasicEffect Parameters

With your vertices defined, you're ready to render your triangles. The second part of this chapter explains how you can code your own HLSL effects, but in the first recipes you'll simply use the BasicEffect. The BasicEffect is a predefined effect that can be used to render stuff using basic lighting effects. Make sure you have one BasicEffect variable that you recycle each frame, because it is too costly to create a new BasicEffect object each frame. Add this variable to the top of your class:

```
BasicEffect basicEffect;
```

And instantiate it in your LoadContent method:

```
basicEffect = new BasicEffect(device, null);
```

The following settings will render your 3D scene lit from one directional light, like the sun:

```
basicEffect.World = Matrix.Identity;
basicEffect.View = fpsCam.ViewMatrix;
basicEffect.Projection = fpsCam.ProjectionMatrix;
basicEffect.Texture = myTexture;
basicEffect.TextureEnabled = true;

basicEffect.LightingEnabled = true;
basicEffect.AmbientLightColor = new Vector3(0.1f, 0.1f, 0.1f);
basicEffect.PreferPerPixelLighting = true;

basicEffect.DirectionalLight0.Direction = new Vector3(1, -1, 0);
basicEffect.DirectionalLight0.DiffuseColor = Color.White.ToVector3();
basicEffect.DirectionalLight0.Enabled = true;
basicEffect.DirectionalLight1.Enabled = false;
basicEffect.DirectionalLight2.Enabled = false;
```

The upper part sets the World, View, and Projection matrices, which are required to transform your 3D scene to your 2D screen. See recipes 2-1 and 4-2 for more information on them. Because you have stored texture coordinates inside each vertex, you can pass a texture to your graphics card and enable texturing so your triangles will get the colors from the image. See recipe 5-2 for more information on textures.

Next, you configure the general lighting settings by first enabling lighting and defining an ambient color. This is the amount of light your objects are always lit with, no matter their orientation relative to your light source(s). You specify a very dark shade of gray, so even in the absence of light, your objects will be shown very faintly.

If your graphics card can handle per-pixel lighting, you enable this. See recipe 6-3 on per-pixel lighting.

Finally, you define your light sources. Using the BasicEffect, you can render your scene being lit from three light sources at once. To do so, you need to set the direction of the light, as well as the light color. Last but not least, you should enable the lights you want to use. In this simple example, you're using only one light.

With your BasicEffect configured, you're ready to render your triangles using the BasicEffect:

```
basicEffect.Begin();
foreach (EffectPass pass in basicEffect.CurrentTechnique.Passes)
{
    pass.Begin();
    device.VertexDeclaration = myVertexDeclaration;
    DrawUserPrimitives<VertexPositionNormalTexture> ➥
    (PrimitiveType.TriangleList, vertices, 0, 2);
    pass.End();
}
basicEffect.End();
```

**■Note** If you turn lighting off by setting basicEffect.LightingEnabled to false, your scene will be rendered at full intensity. As explained in the "Applying Shading to Your Scene" section, the graphics card wants to multiply the original color of each pixel with the amount of lighting in that pixel. If you turn off lighting, the graphics card will simply render the original color of each pixel. This actually corresponds to a lighting factor of 1, meaning full intensity.

### Using World Matrices

Before rendering your triangles, you can set a World matrix on the effect. This allows you to move your triangles to another position in your 3D world or rotate and/or scale them before they are being rendered to the scene (see recipe 4-2). Well-constructed effects (such as the BasicEffect) also apply this transformation to the normal data inside each vertex, if required. For example, if the square in the previous code is rotated, the normals are automatically rotated as well.

The following code shows such an example.

## Normalize Your Normals

---

**Note** Before you read this section, you need to know the difference between a *normal* and the infinitive *to normalize*. As discussed earlier, a *normal* is the direction perpendicular to a triangle. *To normalize* means to make a vector of unity length. When you normalize a vector, you reduce (or expand) it so its length becomes exactly 1.

---

The amount of light a vertex receives should be defined only by the angle between the light and its normal. However, this amount as calculated by the graphics card also depends on the length of the normal and on the length of the light direction. Therefore, you need to make sure both the normals and the light directions you define have a length of exactly 1, which can be done by normalizing them.

When they both have unity length, the amount of lighting will depend only on the angle between them, which is what you want.

## The Code

*All the code is available for download at* www.apress.com.

As a first step toward the correct lighting of your 3D scene, you should provide each vertex with normal data:

```
private void InitVertices()
{
    vertices = new VertexPositionNormalTexture[6];
    int i = 0;

    vertices[i++] = new VertexPositionNormalTexture(new Vector3(-1, ➥
    0, 1), new Vector3(0, 1, 0), new Vector2(1,1));
    vertices[i++] = new VertexPositionNormalTexture(new Vector3(-1, ➥
    0, -1), new Vector3(0, 1, 0), new Vector2(0,1));
    vertices[i++] = new VertexPositionNormalTexture(new Vector3(1, ➥
    0, -1), new Vector3(0, 1, 0), new Vector2(0,0));

    vertices[i++] = new VertexPositionNormalTexture(new Vector3(1, ➥
    0, -1), new Vector3(0, 1, 0), new Vector2(0,0));
    vertices[i++] = new VertexPositionNormalTexture(new Vector3(1, ➥
    0, 1), new Vector3(0, 1, 0), new Vector2(1,0));
    vertices[i++] = new VertexPositionNormalTexture(new Vector3(-1, ➥
    0, 1), new Vector3(0, 1, 0), new Vector2(1,1));

    myVertexDeclaration = new VertexDeclaration(device, ➥
    VertexPositionNormalTexture.VertexElements);
}
```

Before you can render any triangles using the BasicEffect, you should set some of its parameters to define your lighting environment:

```
basicEffect.View = fpsCam.ViewMatrix;
basicEffect.Projection = fpsCam.ProjectionMatrix;
basicEffect.Texture = myTexture;
basicEffect.TextureEnabled = true;

basicEffect.LightingEnabled = true;
basicEffect.DirectionalLight0.Direction = new Vector3(1, 0, 0);
basicEffect.DirectionalLight0.DiffuseColor = Color.White.ToVector3();
basicEffect.DirectionalLight0.Enabled = true;
```

Finally, you can render your triangles. The following code renders the same two triangles nine times, each time with a different World matrix. This World matrix first rotates the triangles and then moves the triangles four units over the rotated x-axis (see recipe 4-2 for the order of matrix multiplying).

```
for (int i = 0; i < 9; i++)
{
    basicEffect.World = Matrix.CreateTranslation(4, 0, 0) * ➥
    Matrix.CreateRotationZ((float)i * MathHelper.PiOver2 / 8.0f);
    basicEffect.Begin();
    foreach (EffectPass pass in basicEffect.CurrentTechnique.Passes)
    {
        pass.Begin();
        device.VertexDeclaration = myVertexDeclaration;
        device.DrawUserPrimitives<VertexPositionNormalTexture> ➥
        (PrimitiveType.TriangleList, vertices, 0, 2);
        pass.End();
    }
    basicEffect.End();
}
```

See recipe 5-1 on rendering triangles.

# 6-2. Share Normals Between Vertices

## The Problem

In the previous recipe, you learned how to make sure each triangle gets lit correctly by supplying normal data in each of its vertices.

However, blindly applying this approach to all triangles of an object will not give the best results. If you give each vertex of a triangle the same normal direction, each vertex of a triangle will be shaded the same, and thus all pixels inside the triangle will get the same shading.

If two neighboring triangles (that are not in the same plane) were shaded like this, all the pixels of one triangle would get the same shading, and all the pixels of the other triangle would get a different shading. This would make it easy to see the border between them, because both triangles get a different final color.

You'd get a much better result if the colors inside the triangles changed continuously from one triangle to the other. To achieve this, the shading must also change continuously from one triangle to the other.

## The Solution

The shading is calculated by your graphics card for the three vertices (corners) of a triangle, because they contain the normal. From there, the shading is interpolated over all pixels inside the triangle. If all normals of the three vertices of a triangle are the same, all pixels inside the triangle will get the same shading. If they are different, the three corners will get different shading, and the pixels inside the triangle will get shaded so the shading changes smoothly between the corners.

Imagine two neighboring triangles, sharing one edge, defined from six vertices. This case is shown in the left part of Figure 6-3. To make sure the color changes continuously from one triangle to another, you need to make sure the colors on both borders are identical. You can achieve this only when the two shared vertices have the same normal and thus the same shading. In the left part of Figure 6-3, this comes down to vertices 1 and 4 having the same normal and vertices 2 and 3 having the same normal.

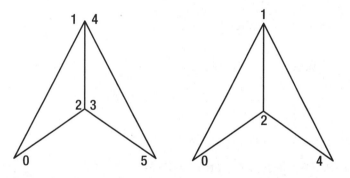

**Figure 6-3.** *Two triangles sharing one edge*

## How It Works

In this recipe, you'll define the two triangles using two approaches. First, you'll render the two triangles so all vertices of the same triangle have the same normal, which will result in equal shading for all pixels inside one triangle. Next, you'll make sure the normals in the shared vertices are the same so you'll get smooth shading across the border of the triangle.

### Each Triangle Its Normal

This approach comes down to finding the direction perpendicular to the triangle and storing this direction in each of its vertices, as done in recipe 6-1.

The following code defines the six vertices shown on the left side of Figure 6-3. All three vertices of each triangle have the same normal direction, perpendicular to the triangle. The left triangle is positioned vertically, so its normal points to the left. The second triangle is positioned horizontally, so its vertices point up.

```
private void InitVertices()
{
    vertices = new VertexPositionNormalTexture[6];

    vertices[0] = new VertexPositionNormalTexture(new Vector3(0, -1, ➥
    0), new Vector3(-1, 0, 0), new Vector2(0,1));
    vertices[1] = new VertexPositionNormalTexture(new Vector3(0, 0, ➥
    -1), new Vector3(-1, 0, 0), new Vector2(0.5f, 0));
    vertices[2] = new VertexPositionNormalTexture(new Vector3(0, 0, ➥
    0), new Vector3(-1, 0, 0), new Vector2(0.5f, 1));

    vertices[3] = new VertexPositionNormalTexture(new Vector3(0, 0, ➥
    0), new Vector3(0, 1, 0), new Vector2(0.5f,1));
    vertices[4] = new VertexPositionNormalTexture(new Vector3(0, 0, ➥
    -1), new Vector3(0, 1, 0), new Vector2(0.5f,1));
    vertices[5] = new VertexPositionNormalTexture(new Vector3(1, 0, ➥
    0), new Vector3(0, 1, 0), new Vector2(1,1));

    myVertexDeclaration = new VertexDeclaration(device, ➥
    VertexPositionNormalTexture.VertexElements);
}
```

Next, define a light that is shining mostly to the right but also a bit down. Make sure you normalize the direction so its length becomes exactly 1:

```
Vector3 lightDirection = new Vector3(10, -2, 0);
lightDirection.Normalize();
basicEffect.DirectionalLight0.Direction = lightDirection;
```

Next, render both triangles using the code from the previous chapter:

```
basicEffect.Begin();
foreach (EffectPass pass in basicEffect.CurrentTechnique.Passes)
{
    pass.Begin();
    device.VertexDeclaration = myVertexDeclaration;
    device.DrawUserPrimitives<VertexPositionNormalTexture> ➥
    (PrimitiveType.TriangleList, vertices, 0, 2);
    pass.End();
}
basicEffect.End();
```

Read the section "Normalize Your Normals" in recipe 6-1 to understand why you need to normalize the light direction.

You should see two triangles, both of which have a solid color, as shown on the left side of Figure 6-4. Because of this, you can easily see the border between them, which is definitely not what you want with larger objects.

**Figure 6-4.** *Separate vertex shading (left), shared vertex shading (right)*

## Shared Normals

This time, you're going to give both vertices 1 and 4, as well as vertices 2 and 3, the same normal direction. One question that comes up is which direction you should pick.

To obtain the smoothest effect, you'll simply take the average of the usual normals. You can do this with the following code:

```
private void InitVertices()
{
    vertices = new VertexPositionNormalTexture[6];

    Vector3 normal1 = new Vector3(-1, 0, 0);
    Vector3 normal2 = new Vector3(0, 1, 0);
    Vector3 sharedNormal = normal1 + normal2;
    sharedNormal.Normalize();

    vertices[0] = new VertexPositionNormalTexture(new Vector3(0, -1,
    0), normal1, new Vector2(0,1));
    vertices[1] = new VertexPositionNormalTexture(new Vector3(0, 0,
    -1), sharedNormal, new Vector2(0.5f, 0));
    vertices[2] = new VertexPositionNormalTexture(new Vector3(0, 0,
    0), sharedNormal, new Vector2(0.5f, 1));

    vertices[3] = new VertexPositionNormalTexture(new Vector3(0, 0,
    0), sharedNormal, new Vector2(0.5f,1));
    vertices[4] = new VertexPositionNormalTexture(new Vector3(0, 0,
    -1), sharedNormal, new Vector2(0.5f,1));
    vertices[5] = new VertexPositionNormalTexture(new Vector3(1, 0,
    0), normal2, new Vector2(1,1));

    myVertexDeclaration = new VertexDeclaration(device,
    VertexPositionNormalTexture.VertexElements);
}
```

First you sum the two normals of the two triangles. Make sure you normalize the result so the length becomes 1 again (see the section "Normalize Your Normals" in recipe 6-1). The resulting direction will be pointing exactly in the middle between Left and Up.

Next, you define the six vertices. The two outer vertices are not shared, so they get their old normal. The shared vertices, however, all get the same normal.

Now, when you render the two triangles, the shading inside the triangles will smoothly change from the outer vertex to the shared edge, as shown in the right part of Figure 6-4. This makes it hard to find the edge between the two triangles, so the user will not see that the object consists of separate triangles.

**Tip** Recipe 5-7 describes how you can calculate the shared normals for larger objects automatically.

You can also use this approach when using indices (see recipe 5-3).

## The Code

*All the code is available for download at www.apress.com.*

You can find the code used to define the triangles earlier in this recipe. This is the code used to render them:

```
basicEffect.World = Matrix.Identity;
basicEffect.View = fpsCam.ViewMatrix;
basicEffect.Projection = fpsCam.ProjectionMatrix;
basicEffect.Texture = blueTexture;
basicEffect.TextureEnabled = true;

basicEffect.LightingEnabled = true;
Vector3 lightDirection = new Vector3(10, -2, 0);
lightDirection.Normalize();
basicEffect.DirectionalLight0.Direction = lightDirection;
basicEffect.DirectionalLight0.DiffuseColor = Color.White.ToVector3();
basicEffect.DirectionalLight0.Enabled = true;

basicEffect.Begin();
foreach (EffectPass pass in basicEffect.CurrentTechnique.Passes)
{
    pass.Begin();
    device.VertexDeclaration = myVertexDeclaration;
    device.DrawUserPrimitives<VertexPositionNormalTexture> ➥
    (PrimitiveType.TriangleList, vertices, 0, 2);
    pass.End();
}
basicEffect.End();
```

---

**■Note**  This example uses a texture with just one solid color in it (blue), so you can be sure all color gradients in the final result are caused by lighting.

---

# 6-3. Add Higher Detail to Your Lighting: Per-Pixel Lighting

## The Problem

In the previous two recipes, the amount of shading was calculated in each vertex, and this shading value was interpolated over all the pixels of the triangle. Therefore, it is called *per-vertex lighting* (or *Gouraud shading*).

In some cases, this does not give the best result. Especially when using large triangles and/or sharp edges, this can give some undesired results.

As an example of this, consider three sides of a cube, as shown on the left side of Figure 6-5. The right side of the image indicates how the shared normal directions should be defined. In this example, the direction of the light is indicated by the four arrows at the top of the right part.

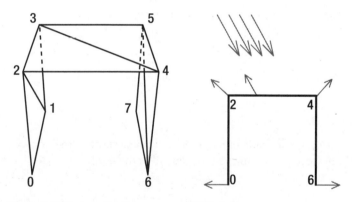

**Figure 6-5.** *Vertex shader vs. per-pixel lighting*

Focus on the roof of the cube, corresponding to the line between vertices 2 and 4 at the right part of Figure 6-5. Using per-vertex lighting, the shading is calculated in vertices 2 and 4. At vertex 4, not a lot of light is received because the normal in vertex 4 is almost perpendicular to the direction of the light. Say it is 20 percent lit. Vertex 2 receives more light, because its normal direction is almost the same as the light direction; let's say it is 80 percent lit. As in per-vertex shading, this shading is interpolated over the pixels of the triangle, and all the pixels between these two vertices receive an amount that is an interpolation between 80 percent and 20 percent. This way, none of the pixels can be 100 percent lit.

However, somewhere between vertices 2 and 4 is a pixel in which the normal is exactly along the direction of the light! This normal is indicated in the right part of Figure 6-5. Clearly, this pixel should be 100 percent lit, while using per-vertex lighting the pixels can receive a lighting only between 80 percent and 20 percent.

## The Solution

Per-vertex lighting calculates the shading exactly only in the vertices and then interpolates the shading over all the pixels between the vertices.

Using per-pixel lighting, you interpolate the normal over all the pixels, allowing you to calculate the exact shading in each pixel.

## How It Works

Using the BasicEffect, it is easy to use per-pixel lighting. When setting your BasicEffect parameters, simply add this line:

```
basicEffect.PreferPerPixelLighting = true;
```

---

■**Note**  For the per-pixel shader to work, you need to have at least a Shader 2.0–compatible graphics card. You can easily check for this basic requirement by evaluating this line:

```
(GraphicsDevice.GraphicsDeviceCapabilities.MaxPixelShaderProfile >= ➡
ShaderProfile.PS_2_0)
```

---

## The Code

*All the code is available for download at* www.apress.com.

This code sets up the vertices shown on the left side of Figure 6-5. Because some of the normals are longer than unity length, make sure you normalize them all in the end:

```
private void InitVertices()
{
    vertices = new VertexPositionNormalTexture[8];

    vertices[0] = new VertexPositionNormalTexture(new Vector3(0, -1, ➡
    0), new Vector3(-1, 0, 0), new Vector2(0, 1));
    vertices[1] = new VertexPositionNormalTexture(new Vector3(0, -1, ➡
    -1), new Vector3(-1, 0, 0), new Vector2(0, 0));

    vertices[2] = new VertexPositionNormalTexture(new Vector3(0, 0, ➡
    0), new Vector3(-1, 1, 0), new Vector2(0.33f, 1));
    vertices[3] = new VertexPositionNormalTexture(new Vector3(0, 0, ➡
    -1), new Vector3(-1, 1, 0), new Vector2(0.33f, 0));
```

```
vertices[4] = new VertexPositionNormalTexture(new Vector3(1, 0, ➥
0), new Vector3(1, 1, 0), new Vector2(0.66f, 1));
vertices[5] = new VertexPositionNormalTexture(new Vector3(1, 0, ➥
-1), new Vector3(1, 1, 0), new Vector2(0.66f, 0));

vertices[6] = new VertexPositionNormalTexture(new Vector3(1, -1, ➥
0), new Vector3(1, 0, 0), new Vector2(1, 1));
vertices[7] = new VertexPositionNormalTexture(new Vector3(1, -1, ➥
-1), new Vector3(1, 0, 0), new Vector2(1, 0));


for (int i = 0; i < vertices.Length; i++)
    vertices[i].Normal.Normalize();

myVertexDeclaration = new VertexDeclaration(device, ➥
VertexPositionNormalTexture.VertexElements);
}
```

Read the section "Normalize Your Normals" in recipe 6-1 to understand why you need the last for loop.

■**Note**  Because XNA does not provide a vertex structure that takes a 3D position, a color, and a normal, this recipe uses a solid blue texture to make sure the base color of each pixel is the same. This way, all variations in color you see are caused only by lighting.

After you've done this, you can render your triangles using per-pixel lighting:

```
basicEffect.World = Matrix.Identity;
basicEffect.View = fpsCam.ViewMatrix;
basicEffect.Projection = fpsCam.ProjectionMatrix;
basicEffect.Texture = blueTexture;
basicEffect.TextureEnabled = true;

basicEffect.LightingEnabled = true;
Vector3 lightDirection = new Vector3(3, -10, 0);
lightDirection.Normalize();
basicEffect.DirectionalLight0.Direction = lightDirection;
basicEffect.DirectionalLight0.DiffuseColor = Color.White.ToVector3();
basicEffect.DirectionalLight0.Enabled = true;
basicEffect.PreferPerPixelLighting = true;
```

```
basicEffect.Begin();
foreach (EffectPass pass in basicEffect.CurrentTechnique.Passes)
{
    pass.Begin();
    device.VertexDeclaration = myVertexDeclaration;
    device.DrawUserPrimitives<VertexPositionNormalTexture> ➥
    (PrimitiveType.TriangleStrip, vertices, 0, 6);
    pass.End();
}
basicEffect.End();
```

# 6-4. Add Specular Highlights to Reflective Surfaces

## The Problem

Even with per-pixel shading enabled, some metallic or shiny objects you render will still look a bit dull. In real life, when looking at a reflective surface such as metal, glass, or some plastic, you will see the area where the light source reflected is very bright. Such an area is indicated by the circle in Figure 6-6. These bright spots are called *specular highlights*.

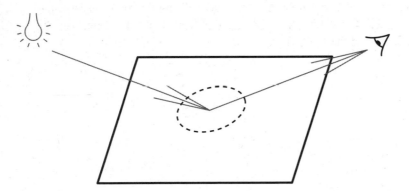

**Figure 6-6.** *Specular highlight*

## The Solution

As with per-pixel lighting, you can enable specular highlights simply by telling the BasicEffect to create them.

---

■**Note** Specular highlights should be added only to reflective materials. Don't add them to soft materials such as clothes or a grass texture, or at least make their impact very weak.

---

## How It Works

You can enable specular highlights with extreme ease using the BasicEffect. For each light, you can specify the specular color. Next, you can set the specular power on the BasicEffect. This power allows you to specify the width of your highlights. The higher the power, the narrower your specular highlights will be. See recipe 6-8 for more details on this.

```
basicEffect.LightingEnabled = true;
basicEffect.DirectionalLight0.Direction = lightDirection;
basicEffect.DirectionalLight0.DiffuseColor = Color.White.ToVector3();
basicEffect.DirectionalLight0.Enabled = true;
basicEffect.PreferPerPixelLighting = true;
basicEffect.DirectionalLight0.SpecularColor = Color.White.ToVector3();
basicEffect.SpecularPower = 32;
```

---

**■Note**  When using specular lighting, you'll always want to use per-pixel lighting because specular highlights typically are small, nonlinear spots. Therefore, they should not be interpolated but rather be calculated separately for each pixel.

---

## The Code

*All the code is available for download at www.apress.com.*

This code defines vertices to render a single quad. It should be called at program startup, and since it uses the reference to the device, it should be called at the end of the LoadContent method.

```
private void InitVertices()
{
    vertices = new VertexPositionNormalTexture[4];

    vertices[0] = new VertexPositionNormalTexture(new Vector3(0, 0, ➥
    0), new Vector3(0, 1, 0), new Vector2(0, 1));
    vertices[1] = new VertexPositionNormalTexture(new Vector3(0, 0, ➥
    -10), new Vector3(0, 1, 0), new Vector2(0, 0));

    vertices[2] = new VertexPositionNormalTexture(new Vector3(10, 0, ➥
    0), new Vector3(0, 1, 0), new Vector2(1, 1));
    vertices[3] = new VertexPositionNormalTexture(new Vector3(10, 0, ➥
    -10), new Vector3(0, 1, 0), new Vector2(1, 0));

    myVertexDeclaration = new VertexDeclaration(device, ➥
    VertexPositionNormalTexture.VertexElements);
}
```

In your `Draw` method, add this code to set up your `BasicEffect` to add specular highlights to your quad:

```
basicEffect.World = Matrix.Identity;
basicEffect.View = fpsCam.ViewMatrix;
basicEffect.Projection = fpsCam.ProjectionMatrix;
basicEffect.Texture = blueTexture;
basicEffect.TextureEnabled = true;

Vector3 lightDirection = new Vector3(0, -3, -10);
lightDirection.Normalize();
basicEffect.LightingEnabled = true;
basicEffect.DirectionalLight0.Direction = lightDirection;
basicEffect.DirectionalLight0.DiffuseColor = Color.White.ToVector3();
basicEffect.DirectionalLight0.Enabled = true;
basicEffect.PreferPerPixelLighting = true;
basicEffect.DirectionalLight0.SpecularColor = Color.White.ToVector3();
basicEffect.SpecularPower = 32;


basicEffect.Begin();
foreach (EffectPass pass in basicEffect.CurrentTechnique.Passes)
{
    pass.Begin();
    device.VertexDeclaration = myVertexDeclaration;
    device.DrawUserPrimitives<VertexPositionNormalTexture> ➥
    (PrimitiveType.TriangleStrip, vertices, 0, 2);
    pass.End();
}
basicEffect.End();
```

# 6-5. Add HLSL Vertex Shading

## The Problem

The `BasicEffect` will render your scene just fine using the lighting you configured. However, if you want to define some fancy effects yourself, the first thing your effects will have to implement correctly is lighting.

In this recipe, you'll learn how to write a basic HLSL effect that performs per-vertex shading.

## The Solution

Pass the 3D position and normal of each vertex to your effect on the graphics card. The vertex shader on your graphics card needs to do two things for each vertex.

First, as always when rendering a 3D world, it should transform the 3D position of each vertex to the corresponding 2D screen coordinate by using the World, View, and Projection matrices.

Second, and specific to vertex lighting, for each vertex it should calculate the amount of light the vertex receives by taking the dot product between the light direction and the normal of that vertex.

## How It Works

---

**■Tip** The HLSL code should be placed in a separate file, ending in .fx. If you're not sure about where to put the code in this file, refer to "The Code" section later in this recipe, which lists the entire contents of the .fx file created during this recipe.

---

First you need to define your vertices in your XNA project. Quite obviously, you need to store the 3D position in each vertex. To allow you to calculate correct lighting in your vertex shader, you also need to provide the normal for each vertex. Read recipe 6-1 to learn why.

You can use the same XNA code in recipe 6-1, which creates six vertices containing a 3D position and a normal (they also contain a texture coordinate, which you won't use here).

Create a new .fx file in your XNA project, and add the following code. It contains the HLSL variables you'll be able to change from within your XNA application.

```
float4x4 xWorld;
float4x4 xView;
float4x4 xProjection;
float xAmbient;
float3 xLightDirection;
```

As always when transforming a 3D coordinate to a 2D screen position, you'll need a View matrix and a Projection matrix (see recipe 2-1). Because you'll also want to be able to move your 3D object in your scene, you'll also need a World matrix (see recipe 4-2). Because this recipe deals with lighting, you want to be able to define the direction of your light. The ambient light value allows you to set the minimum level of lighting; this way, even if an object is not directly lit by a light source, it will still be faintly visible.

Before diving into the vertex shader and pixel shader, you should first define their output structures. First, the output of the vertex shader (and thus the input of the pixel shader) must always contain the 2D screen coordinate of each vertex. Second, your vertex shader will also calculate the amount of lighting in each vertex.

Between the vertex and pixel shader, these values will be interpolated so each pixel gets its interpolated value.

The pixel shader should calculate only the final color of each pixel.

```
struct VSVertexToPixel
{
    float4 Position : POSITION;
    float LightingFactor   : TEXCOORD0;
};
struct VSPixelToFrame
{
    float4 Color    : COLOR0;
};
```

### Vertex Shader

Your vertex shader will (as always) combine the World, View, and Projection matrices into one matrix, which you'll use to transform each 3D vertex into a 2D screen coordinate.

Given the global light direction and the normal direction in a vertex, you want your vertex shader to calculate the amount of shading, according to Figure 6-7. The smaller the angle between the light and normal, the greater the lighting should be. The larger this angle, the less the lighting should be.

You can obtain this value by taking the dot product between both directions. A dot product returns a single value between 0 and 1 (if the lengths of both vectors equal 1).

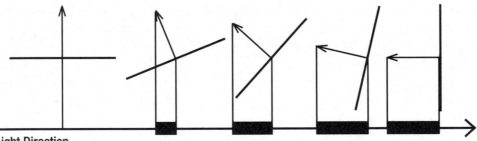

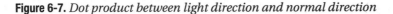

**Light Direction**

**Figure 6-7.** *Dot product between light direction and normal direction*

However, you should negate one of these directions before taking their dot product, because otherwise these directions are the opposite. For example, on the right of Figure 6-7 you see that the normal and light directions have the opposite direction, which would result in a negative dot product.

```
VSVertexToPixel VSVertexShader(float4 inPos: POSITION0, float3 inNormal: NORMAL0)
{
    VSVertexToPixel Output = (VSVertexToPixel)0;

    float4x4 preViewProjection = mul(xView, xProjection);
    float4x4 preWorldViewProjection = mul(xWorld, preViewProjection);
    Output.Position = mul(inPos, preWorldViewProjection);
```

```
    float3 normal = normalize(inNormal);
    Output.LightFactor = dot(rotNormal, -xLightDirection);

    return Output;
}
```

The result of a dot product is a single value, based on the angle between both vectors and the length of both vectors. In almost all cases, you'll want your lighting to be based only on the angle between your normal and light directions. This means you need to make sure all your normals (and light directions) in your whole 3D world have the same length; otherwise, vertices with longer normals will be more lit.

You can do this by making sure the length of all normals is exactly 1, which you do by normalizing the normal.

---

■**Note** The word *normalizing* does not have anything to do with normals; it simply means making the length of a vector exactly 1. See the note in recipe 6-1.

---

### Ensuring Correct Lighting When Using World Matrices

The previous code will work just fine if you set the World matrix of your object to the Identity matrix, meaning the object should be rendered around the (0,0,0) 3D origin (see recipe 5-2).

In most cases, however, you'll want to set another World matrix, allowing you to move, rotate, and scale your object in the 3D world.

As you can see in Figure 6-1, if you rotate your object, you want your normals to be rotated with them. This means all normals should also be transformed by the rotation inside the World matrix.

Any scaling operation contained in the World matrix does not have that much impact on the lighting calculations. You normalize your normals in your vertex shader anyway, making sure the length of the resulting vector becomes exactly 1 (of unity length).

However, if your World matrix contains a translation, you're in trouble. This is because a normal is a vector of maximal length 1. As an example, if you transform such a normal with a matrix containing a translation (movement) larger than two units, then all normals will be pointing into that direction.

This is shown in Figure 6-8, where an object is rendered using a World matrix containing a translation of a few units to the right. As a result, the positions of the vertices (and thus the object) will be moved to the right. The normals, however, when transformed with the World matrix, will now all point to the right while they should have stayed the same! So before you transform your normals with the World matrix, you need to strip away the translation part from the World matrix.

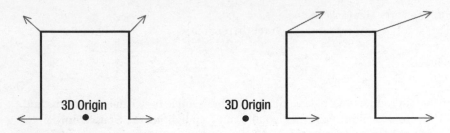

**Figure 6-8.** *Normals affected by translation in the World matrix*

A matrix is a table containing 4×4 numbers. You need to transform the normals only with the rotation contained in the World matrix, but not with the translation inside the World matrix. You can do this by stripping out the rotation part of the matrix, which is stored in the upper-left 3×3 numbers of the matrix. By simply casting your 4×4 World matrix to a 3×3 matrix, you have extracted only the rotational information, which is just what you need! Use this matrix to rotate your normal, as shown in this code:

```
float3 normal = normalize(inNormal);

float3x3 rotMatrix = (float3x3)xWorld;
float3 rotNormal = mul(normal, rotMatrix);

Output.LightFactor = dot(rotNormal, -xLightDirection);
```

### Pixel Shader

First, the three vertices of a triangle are processed by the vertex shader, and their lighting values are calculated. Then, for each pixel in the triangle that needs to be rendered, this lighting value is interpolated between the three vertices. This interpolated lighting value reaches the pixel shader.

In this simple case, you'll give your object a blue color as the base color. To add shading to this triangle, multiply the base color by the sum of the LightFactor (calculated in the vertex shader earlier) and ambient light (set by your XNA application through the xAmbient variable). The ambient factor makes sure no objects will be totally black, while the LightFactor causes the lighting to correspond to the direction of the light:

```
VSPixelToFrame VSPixelShader(VSVertexToPixel PSIn) : COLOR0
{
    VSPixelToFrame Output = (VSPixelToFrame)0;

    float4 baseColor = float4(0,0,1,1);
    Output.Color = baseColor*(PSIn.LightFactor+xAmbient);
    return Output;
}
```

## Technique Definition

Finally, define your technique and which vertex and pixel shaders it should use:

```
technique VertexShading
{
    pass Pass0
    {
        VertexShader = compile vs_2_0 VSVertexShader();
        PixelShader  = compile ps_2_0 VSPixelShader();
    }
}
```

## XNA Code

In your XNA project, import the HLSL file and store it in an `Effect` variable, just like you did for a texture in recipe 3-1. In my example, I called my HLSL file `vertexshading.fx`:

```
effect = content.Load<Effect>("vertexshading");
```

When it comes to drawing your object, you first need to set the parameters of your effect and then render your object, which is quite identical to using the `BasicEffect`:

```
effect.CurrentTechnique = effect.Techniques["VertexShading"];
effect.Parameters["xWorld"].SetValue(Matrix.Identity);
effect.Parameters["xView"].SetValue(fpsCam.ViewMatrix);
effect.Parameters["xProjection"].SetValue(fpsCam.ProjectionMatrix);
effect.Parameters["xLightDirection"].SetValue(new Vector3(1, 0, 0));

effect.Begin();
foreach (EffectPass pass in effect.CurrentTechnique.Passes)
{
    pass.Begin();
    device.VertexDeclaration = myVertexDeclaration;
    device.DrawUserPrimitives<VertexPositionNormalTexture> ➥
    (PrimitiveType.TriangleList, vertices, 0, 2);
    pass.End();
}
effect.End();
```

## The Code

*All the code is available for download at www.apress.com.*

This XNA code renders multiple instances of your object. Because different World matrices are used, the objects will be rendered to different locations in your 3D scene.

The final result is the same as in recipe 6-1, only this time obtained through your own HLSL effect:

```
effect.CurrentTechnique = effect.Techniques["VertexShading"];
effect.Parameters["xView"].SetValue(fpsCam.ViewMatrix);
effect.Parameters["xProjection"].SetValue(fpsCam.ProjectionMatrix);
effect.Parameters["xLightDirection"].SetValue(new Vector3(1, 0, 0));
effect.Parameters["xAmbient"].SetValue(0.0f);

for (int i = 0; i < 9; i++)
{
    Matrix world = Matrix.CreateTranslation(4, 0, 0) * ➥
    Matrix.CreateRotationZ((float)i * MathHelper.PiOver2 / 8.0f);
    effect.Parameters["xWorld"].SetValue(world);
    effect.Begin();
    foreach (EffectPass pass in effect.CurrentTechnique.Passes)
    {
        pass.Begin();
        device.VertexDeclaration = myVertexDeclaration;
        device.DrawUserPrimitives<VertexPositionNormalTexture> ➥
        (PrimitiveType.TriangleList, vertices, 0, 2);
        pass.End();
    }
    effect.End();
}
```

The following code shows the entire contents of your .fx file:

```
float4x4 xWorld;
float4x4 xView;
float4x4 xProjection;
float xAmbient;
float3 xLightDirection;

struct VSVertexToPixel
{
    float4 Position : POSITION;
    float LightFactor    : TEXCOORD0;
};
struct VSPixelToFrame
{
    float4 Color    : COLOR0;
};


//------- Technique: VertexShading --------
VSVertexToPixel VSVertexShader(float4 inPos: POSITION0, float3 inNormal: NORMAL0)
{
    VSVertexToPixel Output = (VSVertexToPixel)0;
```

```
    float4x4 preViewProjection = mul(xView, xProjection);
    float4x4 preWorldViewProjection = mul(xWorld, preViewProjection);
    Output.Position = mul(inPos, preWorldViewProjection);

    float3 normal = normalize(inNormal);

    float3x3 rotMatrix = (float3x3)xWorld;
    float3 rotNormal = mul(normal, rotMatrix);

    Output.LightFactor = dot(rotNormal, -xLightDirection);

    return Output;
}

VSPixelToFrame VSPixelShader(VSVertexToPixel PSIn) : COLOR0
{
    VSPixelToFrame Output = (VSPixelToFrame)0;

    float4 baseColor = float4(0,0,1,1);
    Output.Color = baseColor*(PSIn.LightFactor+xAmbient);

    return Output;
}

technique VertexShading
{
    pass Pass0
    {
        VertexShader = compile vs_2_0 VSVertexShader();
        PixelShader  = compile ps_2_0 VSPixelShader();
    }
}
```

# 6-6. Define a Point Light Using HLSL

## The Problem

Until now, you've been using directional lights to light your scene, which can be useful to add sunlight to your 3D world. Often, you'll also need light coming from a single point, such as from a flashlight or an explosion. Such a light source is called a *point light*.

## The Solution

Pass the 3D location of the point light from your XNA project to your XNA effect. For each vertex, you can calculate the direction from the light source toward the vertex and use this light direction. Once you know the light direction, you can continue as before.

## How It Works

In your .fx file, replace the xLightDirection parameter with this line, allowing you to pass the 3D location of the light source from your XNA project to your HLSL effect:

```
float3 xLightPosition;
```

Next, for each vertex, you'll calculate the direction from the light going toward the vertex. As always, the direction from A to B is found by subtracting A from B. Keep in mind you need the final 3D position of the vertex for this, meaning the original 3D position transformed with the World matrix:

```
float3 final3DPosition = mul(inPos, xWorld);
float3 lightDirection = final3DPosition - xLightPosition;
lightDirection = normalize(lightDirection);

Output.LightFactor = dot(rotNormal, -lightDirection);
```

Because the direction between the light source and vertex will probably be a lot larger than 1, you need to make sure its length becomes unity by normalizing it. Once you know this light direction, you're ready to proceed as in the previous recipe.

When you run this code, in each vertex you will calculate the direction from the light source to that vertex, so this direction will be different for each vertex.

### Distance Attenuation

To make things a bit more realistic, you may want to decrease the influence of a point light as the distance between the light source and the vertex becomes larger. To do this, find this distance by calling the length intrinsic on the lightDirection before you normalize it. Next, divide the LightFactor by this distance; this will cause the intensity of the light to decrease as the distance between the light source and the vertex grows:

```
float3 final3DPosition = mul(inPos, xWorld);
float3 lightDirection = final3DPosition - xLightPosition;
float distance = length(lightDirection);
lightDirection = normalize(lightDirection);

Output.LightFactor = dot(rotNormal, -lightDirection);
Output.LightFactor /= distance;
```

## The Code

*All the code is available for download at www.apress.com.*

In your XNA project, you can position your light source anywhere you want:

```
effect.CurrentTechnique = effect.Techniques["VertexShading"];
effect.Parameters["xView"].SetValue(fpsCam.ViewMatrix);
effect.Parameters["xProjection"].SetValue(fpsCam.ProjectionMatrix);
effect.Parameters["xLightPosition"].SetValue(new Vector3(1, 5, 0));
effect.Parameters["xAmbient"].SetValue(0.0f);
```

This is your complete vertex shader:

```
VSVertexToPixel VSVertexShader(float4 inPos: POSITION0, float3 inNormal: NORMAL0)
{
    VSVertexToPixel Output = (VSVertexToPixel)0;

    float4x4 preViewProjection = mul(xView, xProjection);
    float4x4 preWorldViewProjection = mul(xWorld, preViewProjection);
    Output.Position = mul(inPos, preWorldViewProjection);

    float3 normal = normalize(inNormal);

    float3x3 rotMatrix = (float3x3)xWorld;
    float3 rotNormal = mul(normal, rotMatrix);

    float3 final3DPosition = mul(inPos, xWorld);
    float3 lightDirection = final3DPosition - xLightPosition;
    lightDirection = normalize(lightDirection);

    Output.LightFactor = dot(rotNormal, -lightDirection);

    return Output;
}
```

# 6-7. Add HLSL Per-Pixel Lighting

## The Problem

As shown in recipe 6-3, the best lighting results are obtained using per-pixel lighting, especially for curvy surfaces made out of large triangles. You want to add per-pixel lighting to your own effects.

## The Solution

In the previous two recipes, you calculated the shading value in each vertex. The shading values of the three vertices of a triangle were linearly interpolated to obtain the shading value for each pixel.

In the case of per-pixel lighting, you want to interpolate the normal of the three vertices to obtain the normal in each pixel so that in each pixel you can calculate the lighting factor based on the correct normal. However, as with interpolated shading, you will get faulty results when interpolating the normal from vertex to vertex. This is shown on the left side of Figure 6-9. The flat line indicates a triangle, of which the vertices contain the normal. When you interpolate these two normals over the pixels in the triangle, the interpolated normal will always follow the dotted line. In the center of the triangle, although the interpolated normal will have the correct direction, it will be smaller than the exact normal in that pixel, which is shown in the image.

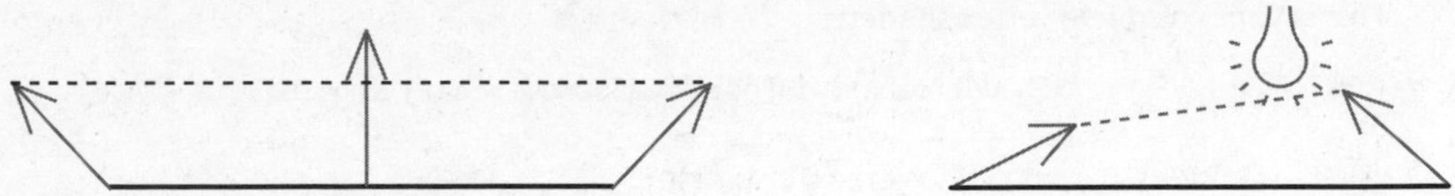

**Figure 6-9.** *Case where the linear interpolation from vertex to pixel shader fails*

The solution is in receiving this interpolated normal in the pixel shader. Because its direction is correct, you can normalize it to make the resulting normal of unity length. Because this scaling factor is different for each pixel, you need to do this in the pixel shader.

---

**■Note** To see why you want to make the length of your normal equal 1, read the "Normalize Your Normals" section in recipe 6-1. Smaller normals will lead to smaller lighting intensities, while you want the lighting intensity to depend only on the angle between the normal and the incoming light.

---

The direction of the light has an identical problem, as shown in the right part of Figure 6-9. The length of the interpolated light direction will follow the dotted curve, which will lead to vectors that are shorter than they should be. Again, you can solve this by normalizing the interpolated light direction in the pixel shader.

## How It Works

As with all recipes in this chapter, your XNA project must interact with your graphics card to render triangles from some vertices that contain at least the 3D position and normal.

You want to design your effect so your XNA code can set the World, View, and Projection matrices, as well as the 3D position of the point light and ambient light in your scene:

```
float4x4 xWorld;
float4x4 xView;
float4x4 xProjection;
float3 xLightPosition;
float xAmbient;


struct PPSVertexToPixel
{
    float4 Position         : POSITION;
    float3 Normal           : TEXCOORD0;
    float3 LightDirection   : TEXCOORD1;
};
struct PPSPixelToFrame
{
    float4 Color            : COLOR0;
};
```

As explained earlier, your vertex shader will output the normal, which will be interpolated over all pixels of the triangle as well as the direction of the light going from your point light to the vertex. The pixel shader has to calculate only the final color of each pixel.

---

■**Note**  In the simpler case of a directional light, the direction of the light will be an XNA-to-HLSL variable, which is constant for all vertices and pixels. Therefore, the vertex shader will not need to calculate this.

---

## Vertex Shader

The vertex shader receives the normal from the vertex, rotates it with the rotation contained in the World matrix (see recipe 6-5), and passes it on to the pixel shader. It also calculates the light direction by subtracting the position of the point light from the position of the vertex (see recipe 6-5). You take into account that the final 3D position of the vertex depends on the current World matrix.

```
PPSVertexToPixel PPSVertexShader(float4 inPos: POSITION0, float3 inNormal: NORMAL0)
{
    PPSVertexToPixel Output = (PPSVertexToPixel)0;

    float4x4 preViewProjection = mul(xView, xProjection);
    float4x4 preWorldViewProjection = mul(xWorld, preViewProjection);
    Output.Position = mul(inPos, preWorldViewProjection);

    float3 final3DPos = mul(inPos, xWorld);
    Output.LightDirection = final3DPos - xLightPosition;

    float3x3 rotMatrix = (float3x3)xWorld;
    float3 rotNormal = mul(inNormal, rotMatrix);
    Output.Normal = rotNormal;

    return Output;
}
```

## Pixel Shader

The normal and light directions are interpolated between the three vertices over all pixels of the triangle. As explained earlier, this can give errors because the lengths of the interpolated vectors can be smaller than they should be. You can solve this by making sure their lengths equal exactly 1 by normalizing them.

Once both directions have been normalized, you take their dot product to find the lighting factor:

```
PPSPixelToFrame PPSPixelShader(PPSVertexToPixel PSIn) : COLOR0
{
    PPSPixelToFrame Output = (PPSPixelToFrame)0;

    float4 baseColor = float4(0,0,1,1);

    float3 normal = normalize(PSIn.Normal);
    float3 lightDirection = normalize(PSIn.LightDirection);
    float lightFactor = dot(normal, -lightDirection);

    Output.Color = baseColor*(lightFactor+xAmbient);

    return Output;
}
```

### Technique Definition

This technique requires a Shader 2.0–compatible graphics card (see the note in recipe 6-3 on how to check for this):

```
technique PerPixelShading
{
    pass Pass0
    {
        VertexShader = compile vs_2_0 PPSVertexShader();
        PixelShader  = compile ps_2_0 PPSPixelShader();
    }
}
```

## The Code

*All the code is available for download at www.apress.com.*

All the HLSL code of your .fx file was already presented fully ordered in this recipe, so the only other code you need is the XNA code that renders your triangles using this technique:

```
effect.CurrentTechnique = effect.Techniques["PerPixelShading"];
effect.Parameters["xWorld"].SetValue(Matrix.Identity);
effect.Parameters["xView"].SetValue(fpsCam.ViewMatrix);
effect.Parameters["xProjection"].SetValue(fpsCam.ProjectionMatrix);
effect.Parameters["xAmbient"].SetValue(0.0f);
effect.Parameters["xLightPosition"].SetValue(new Vector3(6.0f, 1.0f, -5.0f));

effect.Begin();
foreach (EffectPass pass in effect.CurrentTechnique.Passes)
```

```
{
    pass.Begin();
    device.VertexDeclaration = myVertexDeclaration;
    device.DrawUserPrimitives<VertexPositionNormalTexture> ➥
    (PrimitiveType.TriangleStrip, vertices, 0, 6);
    pass.End();
}
effect.End();
```

Make sure you try different positions for your light source to see the effect. The sample code moves the light back and forth over your quads.

# 6-8. Define a Spotlight Using HLSL

## The Problem

A point light as defined in the previous recipe shines light from one point toward all directions. You want to define a spotlight, which behaves exactly like a point light, except that it shines a cone of light, as shown in Figure 6-10.

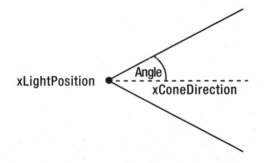

**Figure 6-10.** *Variables that define a spotlight*

## The Solution

In your pixel shader, determine whether the current pixel is in the lighting cone. You can do this by taking the dot product between the direction of the light and the direction of the cone.

## How It Works

Start from the code of the previous recipe. Because a spotlight is more customizable than a point light, you'll add these additional XNA-to-HLSL variables to your .fx file:

```
float xLightStrength;
float3 xConeDirection;
float xConeAngle;
float xConeDecay;
```

The first variable will allow you to increase/decrease the strength of your light. This is also useful for any other type of light and will be necessary when you have multiple lights in your scene (see recipe 6-10). Next, you can specify the center direction of the cone of the spotlight, as well as the width of the cone. Finally, you can indicate how much the lighting intensity should decrease toward the edges of the cone.

Other than that, you need to extend your pixel shader only a bit. In general, you will do the same as with a per-pixel point light (see recipe 6-7), but you will add a check to verify the pixel is in the cone of the light:

```
SLPixelToFrame SLPixelShader(SLVertexToPixel PSIn) : COLOR0
{
    SLPixelToFrame Output = (SLPixelToFrame)0;

    float4 baseColor = float4(0,0,1,1);

    float3 normal = normalize(PSIn.Normal);
    float3 lightDirection = normalize(PSIn.LightDirection);

    float coneDot = dot(lightDirection, normalize(xConeDirection));

    float shading = 0;
    if (coneDot > xConeAngle)
    {
        float coneAttenuation = pow(coneDot, xConeDecay);
        shading = dot(normal, -lightDirection);
        shading *= xLightStrength;
        shading *= coneAttenuation;
    }

    Output.Color = baseColor*(shading+xAmbient);

    return Output;
}
```

Once you've normalized the normal and light direction, you should detect whether the current pixel is in the cone of light. To do this, you want to check the angle between two directions:

- The direction between the current pixel and the light source

- The center direction of the cone

The first direction is the lightDirection, while the second is specified in the xConeDirection variable. Only if this angle is below a certain threshold, the pixel should be lit.

A fast way to check for this is by taking the dot product between both directions. A value close to 1 means a very small angle between both directions, while smaller values indicate larger angles.

To determine whether the angle is not too large, you check whether the dot product is not smaller than a threshold value, stored in xConeAngle. If the pixel is inside the cone, you calculate the lighting factor, called shading. To weaken the lighting effect close to the borders of the cone, you take the coneDot value to the power specified in xConeDecay. As a result, the coneDot value that equals or is smaller than 1 will become smaller for pixels that are far off the center direction of the cone (see the right image in Figure 6-11).

Pixels that are outside the cone will get a shading value of 0, so the light will have no impact on those pixels.

## The Code

*All the code is available for download at www.apress.com.*

Your complete pixel shader was already listed.

In the Draw method of your XNA code, activate this effect, set its parameters, and render your scene:

```
effect.CurrentTechnique = effect.Techniques["SpotLight"];
effect.Parameters["xWorld"].SetValue(Matrix.Identity);
effect.Parameters["xView"].SetValue(fpsCam.ViewMatrix);
          effect.Parameters["xProjection"].SetValue(fpsCam.ProjectionMatrix);
effect.Parameters["xAmbient"].SetValue(0.2f);
effect.Parameters["xLightPosition"].SetValue(new ➥
Vector3(5.0f, 2.0f, -15.0f+variation));
effect.Parameters["xConeDirection"].SetValue(new Vector3(0,-1,0));
effect.Parameters["xConeAngle"].SetValue(0.5f);
effect.Parameters["xConeDecay"].SetValue(2.0f);
effect.Parameters["xLightStrength"].SetValue(0.7f);

effect.Begin();
foreach (EffectPass pass in effect.CurrentTechnique.Passes)
{
    pass.Begin();
    device.VertexDeclaration = myVertexDeclaration;
    device.DrawUserPrimitives<VertexPositionNormalTexture>~VVV
    (PrimitiveType.TriangleStrip, vertices, 0, 6);
    pass.End();
}
effect.End();
```

# 6-9. Add HLSL Specular Highlights

## The Problem

You want to add specular highlights to your 3D scene rendered with your custom HLSL effect. Specular highlights are areas of high illumination surrounding the reflection of a light source, as shown in Figure 6-11.

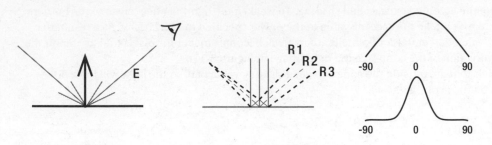

**Figure 6-11.** *Detecting pixels with light direction close to eye vector*

## The Solution

The following discussion will help you determine which pixels should have a specular light component.

The left side of Figure 6-11 shows a light beam, L, coming from a light source hitting a pixel of a triangle. Also in the left image the eye vector is shown, which is the direction going from the camera toward the pixel. If the reflection of L is almost the same as E, the pixel should have a specular light component.

You can find the reflection of L by mirroring L over the normal in that pixel. This mirrored direction is almost the same as the eye direction if the angle between them is small. You can check the angle between these two vectors by taking their dot product (as done in recipe 6-8).

If the angle is 0, meaning both directions are the same and you should add a specular component to your lighting, the dot product will be 1. If both directions are different from each other, the dot product will be smaller.

---

**Note**  A dot product between two vectors A and B is nothing more than (length of A)*(length of B)*(cosine of angle between them). If both A and B are normalized, this even reduces to (cosine of angle between them). If the angle between A and B is 0, the cosine will be 1. If both vectors are perpendicular to each other, the angle will be 90 degrees, and the cosine will be 0. This is shown in the top-right image of Figure 6-11. If both vectors are each other's opposite, the angle of 180 degrees will result in a cosine of –1.

---

This dot product will be positive for all light vectors of which the reflection is less than 90 degrees off the eye vector, as you can see on the top-right side of Figure 6-11. You cannot immediately use this value to base your specular highlights on, because this would add a specular component to all reflection vectors within 90 degrees of the eye vector. You want to narrow this down to reflection vectors within 10 degrees or less.

You can obtain this by taking the result of the dot product to a high power. Taking this dot product to the 12th power, for example, will produce a value larger than 0 only for vectors that are 10 degrees off, which is also shown on the bottom-right side of Figure 6-11.

This will result in a single value for each pixel, indicating the strength of the specular component in that pixel.

## How It Works

As always, you'll want to be able to set World, View, and Projection matrices to transform your 3D positions to 2D screen coordinates. Because this recipe is written for a point light, you need to be able to specify its position. To calculate the eye vector, you need to know the position of the camera. You should be able to set the specular power to control the size of the specular highlights. Because the total amount of lighting could become larger than 1, you should be able to scale down the lighting strength to avoid oversaturation.

---

■**Note**  In most cases, you'll want to scale down the strength of your light sources. Having more than one light would otherwise cause most pixels to be saturated in light, wasting the lighting effect.

---

```
float4x4 xWorld;
float4x4 xView;
float4x4 xProjection;
float3 xLightPosition;
float3 xCameraPos;
float xAmbient;
float xSpecularPower;
float xLightStrength;

struct SLVertexToPixel
{
    float4 Position      : POSITION;
    float3 Normal        : TEXCOORD0;
    float3 LightDirection : TEXCOORD1;
    float3 EyeDirection  : TEXCOORD2;
};
struct SLPixelToFrame
{
    float4 Color         : COLOR0;
};
```

The vertex shader will also calculate the EyeDirection and have it interpolated toward all pixels. The pixel shader still has to output only the color of each pixel.

### Vertex Shader

The vertex shader is not that different from the previous recipe. The only new point of interest is that the eye vector is calculated in the vertex shader. A vector going from one point to another is found by subtracting the source from the target.

```
SLVertexToPixel SLVertexShader(float4 inPos: POSITION0, float3 inNormal: NORMAL0)
{
    SLVertexToPixel Output = (SLVertexToPixel)0;

    float4x4 preViewProjection = mul(xView, xProjection);
    float4x4 preWorldViewProjection = mul(xWorld, preViewProjection);
    Output.Position = mul(inPos, preWorldViewProjection);

    float3 final3DPos = mul(inPos, xWorld);
    Output.LightDirection = final3DPos - xLightPosition;
    Output.EyeDirection = final3DPos - xCameraPos;

    float3x3 rotMatrix = (float3x3)xWorld;
    float3 rotNormal = mul(inNormal, rotMatrix);
    Output.Normal = rotNormal;

    return Output;
}
```

### Pixel Shader

The pixel shader is more interesting. Again, the base color is fixed to blue, so you don't have to waste your attention there. As a good practice, you normalize each direction you receive in your pixel shader, because its length may not be exactly 1 (see recipe 6-3).

As before, you calculate the usual lighting. You multiply it with the xLightStrength to scale it down a bit (assuming xLightStrength is smaller than 1).

```
SLPixelToFrame SLPixelShader(SLVertexToPixel PSIn) : COLOR0
{
    SLPixelToFrame Output = (SLPixelToFrame)0;

    float4 baseColor = float4(0,0,1,1);

    float3 normal = normalize(PSIn.Normal);
    float3 lightDirection = normalize(PSIn.LightDirection);
    float shading = dot(normal, -lightDirection);
    shading *= xLightStrength;

    float3 reflection = -reflect(lightDirection, normal);
    float3 eyeDirection = normalize(PSIn.EyeDirection);
    float specular = dot(reflection, eyeDirection);
    specular = pow(specular, xSpecularPower);
    specular *= xLightStrength;

    Output.Color = baseColor*(shading+xAmbient)+specular;

    return Output;
}
```

Next, you mirror the light direction over the normal using the reflect intrinsic. Because the light direction is shining toward the pixel, its reflection will go toward the eye. This is the opposite direction of the eye vector, so you negate it.

The specular value is found by taking the dot product between the eye vector and the negated reflected light direction. Taking this value to a high power makes sure the value is significantly larger than 0 only for those pixels where both vectors differ less than 10 degrees or so. Again, this value is attenuated by multiplying it by the xLightStrength value.

Finally, the ambient, shading, and specular lighting components are combined to obtain the final color for the pixel.

---

**■Note** The specular component adds white to the final color. If your light has a different color, you should multiply the specular value with the color of your light.

---

## Technique Definition

Here's the technique definition:

```
technique SpecularLighting
{
    pass Pass0
    {
        VertexShader = compile vs_2_0 SLVertexShader();
        PixelShader  = compile ps_2_0 SLPixelShader();
    }
}
```

# The Code

*All the code is available for download at www.apress.com.*

Because all HLSL was already shown fully ordered, I will list only the XNA code needed to render some triangles using this effect:

```
effect.CurrentTechnique = effect.Techniques["SpecularLighting"];
effect.Parameters["xWorld"].SetValue(Matrix.Identity);
effect.Parameters["xView"].SetValue(fpsCam.ViewMatrix);
effect.Parameters["xProjection"].SetValue(fpsCam.ProjectionMatrix);
effect.Parameters["xAmbient"].SetValue(0.0f);
effect.Parameters["xLightStrength"].SetValue(0.5f);
effect.Parameters["xLightPosition"].SetValue(new Vector3(5.0f, 2.0f, -15.0f));
effect.Parameters["xCameraPos"].SetValue(fpsCam.Position);
effect.Parameters["xSpecularPower"].SetValue(128.0f);
```

```
effect.Begin();
foreach (EffectPass pass in effect.CurrentTechnique.Passes)
{
    pass.Begin();
    device.VertexDeclaration = myVertexDeclaration;
    device.DrawUserPrimitives<VertexPositionNormalTexture> ➥
    (PrimitiveType.TriangleStrip, vertices, 0, 6);
    pass.End();
}
effect.End();
```

# 6-10. Add Multiple Lights to Your Scene Using Deferred Shading

## The Problem

You want to light your 3D scene from multiple lights simultaneously.

One approach would be to render your 3D world for each light and to blend in the influence of each light. This would, however, require your scene to be completely re-rendered for each light you wanted to add. This approach is not scalable, because your frame rate would be divided by the number of lights in your scene.

## The Solution

In this recipe, you'll take a radically different approach at rendering your scene than described anywhere else in this book. You will render your 3D screen into a 2D texture only once. Next, you will calculate the lighting of all your lights *for each pixel of this texture*. This means you'll be doing per-pixel processing on your 2D texture, which offers the benefit of having to render your 3D scene only once.

But doing lighting calculations requires the original 3D position of each pixel, right? Correct. Read on to see how you can do this. The whole process will be done in three steps, as shown in Figure 6-12.

*In the first step*, you will render your entire 3D scene into a texture (see recipe 3-8)—not into one texture but into three textures at a time. These are the three textures you want:

- You'll render the base color of each pixel into the first texture (top left in Figure 6-12).

- You'll convert the normals in each pixel to a color and store this color in the second texture (top middle in Figure 6-12).

- You'll store the depth of each pixel (the distance between the camera and that pixel) in the third texture (top right in Figure 6-12).

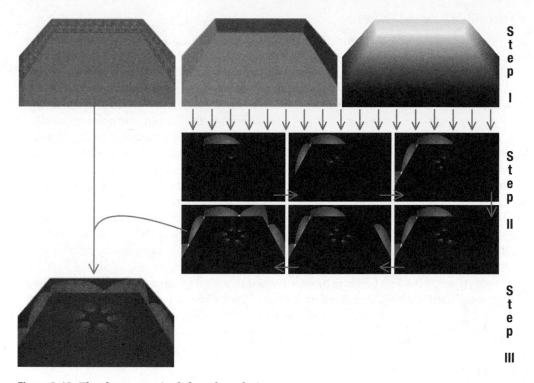

**Figure 6-12.** *The three steps in deferred rendering*

As discussed, this whole operation happens only once, using one pass of a single effect. As a result, this operation takes the same effort as rendering your scene the usual way without lighting calculations (or less, because the effect is very simple).

Now take your time to understand the following lines. For each pixel of your screen, you have stored the depth in a texture. For each pixel, you also know its 2D screen coordinate, because it's the same as its texture coordinate. This means that some way or another, for each pixel of your screen you should be able to re-create the original 3D position. Furthermore, you have stored the 3D normal of each pixel. If you can re-create the 3D position and the normal in a pixel, you are able to calculate the lighting contribution to that pixel for any light!

So, this is what you'll do. After you've generated your three textures, *during the second step* you will activate a new, clean render target. For each pixel of this new target, you'll re-create its original 3D position and retrieve its 3D normal. This allows you to calculate the lighting contribution of the first light in each pixel. You end up with a shading map containing the lighting contribution of your first light.

Repeat this for each of your lights, and add their lighting contributions together onto the shading map. Finally, you have a shading map containing the contributions for all lights. This process is shown for six lights in step II of Figure 6-12.

*In a third and final step*, you'll combine the color map (created in the first step) with the shading map (created in the second step). This is shown as step III in Figure 6-12.

### The Benefit of Deferred Rendering

If you simply rendered your 3D world for each light and combined the results, you would have to transform your 3D world to screen space once for each light in your scene.

Such an operation puts a heavy load both on your vertex shaders and on your pixel shaders. Your vertex shader will have to transform the 3D position of each vertex into a 2D screen coordinate. Furthermore, your pixel shaders will have to calculate many more pixels than there are pixels in your screen. For example, if an object A in the background gets rendered first, your graphics card will calculate the pixel colors using the pixel shader. If an object B is rendered later that is in front of object A, the graphics card will again need to calculate the correct color for these pixels. So, the graphics card has calculated some pixels more than once.

In short, for each light, your vertex shaders need to do a lot of work, and your pixel shaders need to process many more pixels than there are pixels in your screen.

Using deferred rendering, you will perform this operation only once, during the first step. After this, you will do some per-pixel processing on the textures for each light. For each step like this, you will process each pixel exactly once. The final step of combining the color and shading map involves another per-pixel processing step.

In short, your 3D scene needs to be transformed to screen space only once. For each light, your graphics card will need to process each pixel of your screen exactly one time. Your vertex shader will have to do a lot less, and when using multiple lights, your pixel shader will also have to process a lot fewer pixels when using deferred rendering.

## How It Works

Deferred rendering happens in three steps, which you can find explained next.

### Preparation

For each of the three steps, I've created a separate HLSL file. Create these three files (Deferred1Scene.fx, Deferred2Lights.fx, and Deferred3Final.fx), and add their variables to your XNA code:

```
Effect effect1Scene;
Effect effect2Lights;
Effect effect3Final;
```

Don't forget to bind them to the files in your LoadContent method:

```
effect1Scene = Content.Load<Effect>("Deferred1Scene");
effect2Lights = Content.Load<Effect>("Deferred2Lights");
effect3Final = Content.Load<Effect>("Deferred3Final");
```

Make sure you load any geometry required to render your scene in the LoadContent method. In this example, I'll render a simple room from a vertex array, which is initialized in the InitSceneVertices method:

```
InitSceneVertices();
InitFullscreenVertices();
```

The last line calls a method that initializes a second vertex array, defining two large triangles to cover the entire screen. They will be used in the second and third steps, where you need to render the full-screen textures using your own pixel shaders, allowing you to process the full-screen textures on a per-pixel basis. The InitFullScreenVertices method is taken from recipe 2-12.

Next, to keep your code clean, you'll define a RenderScene method, which receives an effect and renders the whole screen using this effect. This simple example renders only three textured walls and a floor from a vertex array. If you want to have Models in your scene, make sure you also render them with this effect:

```
private void RenderScene(Effect effect)
{
    //Render room
    effect.Parameters["xWorld"].SetValue(Matrix.Identity);
    effect.Parameters["xTexture"].SetValue(wallTexture);
    effect.Begin();
    foreach (EffectPass pass in effect.CurrentTechnique.Passes)
    {
        pass.Begin();
        device.VertexDeclaration = wallVertexDeclaration;
        device.DrawUserPrimitives<VertexPositionNormalTexture> ➥
        (PrimitiveType.TriangleStrip, wallVertices, 0, 14);
        pass.End();
    }
    effect.End();
}
```

## Step 1: Rendering Your 3D Scene into Three Textures

In this first step, you'll render your scene into three textures. These textures should contain the base color, 3D normal, and depth for each pixel of the screen. The depth is the distance between the camera and the object to which the pixel belongs.

This will be done using one pixel shader. Instead of rendering to a single render target (see recipe 3-8), your pixel shader will render to three targets at once.

### XNA Code

Start by defining these targets in your XNA code:

```
RenderTarget2D colorTarget;
RenderTarget2D normalTarget;
RenderTarget2D depthTarget;
```

And initialize them in the LoadContent method:

```
PresentationParameters pp = device.PresentationParameters;
int width = pp.BackBufferWidth;
int height = pp.BackBufferHeight;
colorTarget = new RenderTarget2D(device, width, height, 1, SurfaceFormat.Color);
normalTarget = new RenderTarget2D(device, width, height, 1, SurfaceFormat.Color);
depthTarget = new RenderTarget2D(device, width, height, 1, SurfaceFormat.Single);
```

Because the normal has three components, you'll save it as a Color. The depth is a single float value. When your pixel shader writes to multiple render targets simultaneously, their formats must have the same size. Each component of a Color uses 8 bits (256 possible values), so a Color uses 32 bits. A float also uses 32 bits, so this is OK.

With the render targets set up, you're ready to begin rendering. This method performs the complete first step and should be called as the first line from your Draw method:

```
private void RenderSceneTo3RenderTargets()
{
    //bind render targets to outputs of pixel shaders
    device.SetRenderTarget(0, colorTarget);
    device.SetRenderTarget(1, normalTarget);
    device.SetRenderTarget(2, depthTarget);

    //clear all render targets
    device.Clear(ClearOptions.Target | ClearOptions.DepthBuffer, Color.Black, 1, 0);

    //render the scene using custom effect writing to all targets simultaneously
    effect1Scene.CurrentTechnique = effect1Scene.Techniques["MultipleTargets"];
    effect1Scene.Parameters["xView"].SetValue(fpsCam.ViewMatrix);
    effect1Scene.Parameters["xProjection"].SetValue(fpsCam.ProjectionMatrix);
    RenderScene(effect1Scene);

    //deactivate render targets to resolve them
    device.SetRenderTarget(0, null);
    device.SetRenderTarget(1, null);
    device.SetRenderTarget(2, null);

    //copy contents of render targets into texture
    colorMap = colorTarget.GetTexture();
    normalMap = normalTarget.GetTexture();
    depthMap = depthTarget.GetTexture();
}
```

First, you activate the three render targets by binding them to the COLOR0, COLOR1, and COLOR2 output semantics of the pixel shaders. Then, you make sure you clear their contents to black and (more important) set their z-buffer to 1 (see recipe 2-1).

With everything initialized, you're ready to render your scene. Activate the MultipleTargets technique, which you'll define in a minute. Set the World, View, and Projection matrices (the World matrix should be set in the RenderScene method, because this will be different for each object of your scene). Render your scene using the `MultipleTargets` technique by passing this to the `RenderScene` method.

Once the `RenderScene` method has completed, the three render targets will contain the color, normal, and depth value for each pixel of your screen. Before you can save their contents into a texture, you need to deactivate them (see recipe 3-8).

**HLSL Code**

You still have to define the `MultipleTargets` technique, which should render the scene to three targets at once. Start by defining the XNA-to-HLSL variables:

```
float4x4 xWorld;
float4x4 xView;
float4x4 xProjection;

Texture xTexture;
sampler TextureSampler = sampler_state { texture = <xTexture> ; ➡
magfilter = LINEAR; minfilter = LINEAR; mipfilter=LINEAR; ➡
AddressU = wrap; AddressV = wrap;};
```

As always when transforming 3D positions to 2D screen coordinates, you need to specify the World, View, and Projection matrices. Since the walls and floor of the room are textured, you need a texture from which to sample the colors of your pixels. These colors will be saved to the first render target.

Next in line are the output structures of your vertex and pixel shaders:

```
struct VertexToPixel
{
    float4 Position         : POSITION;
    float3 Normal           : TEXCOORD0;
    float4 ScreenPos        : TEXCOORD1;
    float2 TexCoords        : TEXCOORD2;
};
struct PixelToFrame
{
    float4 Color            : COLOR0;
    float4 Normal           : COLOR1;
    float4 Depth            : COLOR2;
};
```

Next to the required `Position` semantic, your vertex shader needs to pass the normal to the pixel shader so it can store this in the second render target. Moreover, because the pixel shader needs to save the depth into the third render target, you need to pass the screen coordinates to the pixel shader. Its X and Y components contain the screen coordinate of the current pixel, while the Z component contains the depth, being the distance from the camera to the object to which the pixel belongs. Finally, the pixel shader needs the texture coordinate so it can sample its color from the texture at the correct position.

The output structure of the pixel shader is quite important. Unlike anywhere else in this book, your pixel shader will generate more than one output. Instead of writing only to the COLOR0 semantic, your pixel shader will also write to the COLOR1 and COLOR2 semantics. Needless to say, each of these outputs corresponds to your three render targets.

Let's move on and discuss the easy vertex shader:

```
VertexToPixel MyVertexShader(float4 inPos: POSITION0, ➥
float3 inNormal: NORMAL0, float2 inTexCoords: TEXCOORD0)
{
    VertexToPixel Output = (VertexToPixel)0;

    float4x4 preViewProjection = mul(xView, xProjection);
    float4x4 preWorldViewProjection = mul(xWorld, preViewProjection);
    Output.Position = mul(inPos, preWorldViewProjection);

    float3x3 rotMatrix = (float3x3)xWorld;
    float3 rotNormal = mul(inNormal, rotMatrix);
    Output.Normal = rotNormal;

    Output.ScreenPos = Output.Position;
    Output.TexCoords = inTexCoords;

    return Output;
}
```

This is very basic stuff. The 3D position is transformed to 2D screen coordinates. The normal is rotated by the rotational part of the World matrix (see recipe 6-5). The texture coordinates are immediately routed to the output. Finally, the 2D screen coordinates are copied into the ScreenPos variable, since the mandatory Position variable is not accessible from within the pixel shader.

It's now time for your pixel shader:

```
PixelToFrame MyPixelShader(VertexToPixel PSIn)
{
    PixelToFrame Output = (PixelToFrame)0;

    Output.Color.rgb = tex2D(TextureSampler, PSIn.TexCoords);
    Output.Normal.xyz = PSIn.Normal/2.0f+0.5f;

    Output.Depth = PSIn.ScreenPos.z/PSIn.ScreenPos.w;

    return Output;
}
```

That was quite easy. The color is sampled from the texture (in my case, the brick texture of the walls) and stored in the first render target. Next are the normals. Since each component of a 3D normal is defined in the [–1,1] range, you need to bring it into the [0,1] range so it can be stored as a color component. You can do this by dividing it by 2 and adding 0.5f to the value.

Finally, you need to save the depth value in the third render target. This depth is stored in the Z component of the ScreenPos variable. Since ScreenPos is the result of a 4×4 matrix multiplication, it is a 4×1 homogenous vector. Before you can use any of the first three components, you need to divide them by the fourth, which is done in the last line of your pixel shader.

Last but not least, here's the technique definition:

```
technique MultipleTargets
{
    pass Pass0
    {
        VertexShader = compile vs_2_0 MyVertexShader();
        PixelShader  = compile ps_2_0 MyPixelShader();
    }
}
```

**Summary of Step 1**

At the end of step 1, you have generated and stored three textures: the first containing the base color, the second containing the normal, and the last one containing the distance for each pixel of your screen.

## Step 2: Generating the Shading Map

Now that you know the color, normal, and depth of each pixel, you can perform the lighting calculations. To do this, you will instruct the graphics card to render two triangles that cover the whole screen. This allows you to create a pixel shader that is called exactly once for each pixel on the screen. In this pixel shader, you will calculate the lighting contribution for one light for a certain pixel.

This process will be repeated for each light in your scene. These repetitions correspond to the six images in step II in Figure 6-12, because that example contains six lights.

This example shows how you can calculate the influence of a spotlight.

**Note** If you want to add a different light, you'll need to adjust the lighting calculation. This is only a small part of the pixel shader; the interesting part remains the same.

**HLSL Code**

In short, this effect will sample the depth of each pixel from the depth map to reconstruct the original 3D position of that pixel. Once you know the 3D position, you can perform your lighting calculations.

To re-create the 3D position, you'll need the inverse ViewProjection matrix, as well as the depth map. Furthermore, you'll need the normal map and some variables that configure your spotlight (see recipe 6-8):

```
float4x4 xViewProjectionInv;

float xLightStrength;
float3 xLightPosition;
float3 xConeDirection;
float xConeAngle;
float xConeDecay;

Texture xNormalMap;
sampler NormalMapSampler = sampler_state { texture = <xNormalMap> ; ➡
magfilter = LINEAR; minfilter = LINEAR; mipfilter=LINEAR; AddressU = mirror; ➡
AddressV = mirror;};
Texture xDepthMap;
sampler DepthMapSampler = sampler_state { texture = <xDepthMap> ; ➡
magfilter = LINEAR; minfilter = LINEAR; mipfilter=LINEAR; AddressU = mirror; ➡
AddressV = mirror;};
```

Next are the output structures for your vertex and pixel shader. Your vertex shader has to generate the obligatory 2D screen coordinate. The texture coordinate is required so each pixel can sample the normal and depth maps at the correct location.

This time, the pixel shader has to generate only one output value: the lighting contribution of the current light to the current pixel.

```
struct VertexToPixel
{
    float4 Position        : POSITION;
    float2 TexCoord        : TEXCOORD0;
};

struct PixelToFrame
{
    float4 Color           : COLOR0;
};
```

Since the six vertices defined in the InitFullscreenVertices method are already defined in screen space coordinates (between the [(−1,−1),(1,1)] range), your vertex shader should simply route the position and texture coordinate to the output:

```
VertexToPixel MyVertexShader(float4 inPos: POSITION0, float2 texCoord: TEXCOORD0)
{
    VertexToPixel Output = (VertexToPixel)0;

    Output.Position = inPos;
    Output.TexCoord = texCoord;

    return Output;
}
```

The pixel shader is where all the cool stuff happens. Start by sampling the normal and depth from the corresponding maps:

```
PixelToFrame MyPixelShader(VertexToPixel PSIn) : COLOR0
{
    PixelToFrame Output = (PixelToFrame)0;

    float3 normal = tex2D(NormalMapSampler, PSIn.TexCoord).rgb;
    normal = normal*2.0f-1.0f;
    normal = normalize(normal);

    float depth = tex2D(DepthMapSampler, PSIn.TexCoord);
}
```

The depth can immediately be sampled from the depth map. The normal has to be remapped from the [0,1] range to the [–1,–1] range, which is the opposite operation as you did in step 1.

The next step is to reconstruct the original 3D position of the pixel. To find this, you'll first need the screen position of the current pixel. The texture coordinate of the current pixel is ideal for this, albeit that it needs to be mapped from the [0,1] texture coordinate range to the [–1,1] screen coordinate range. Since things would otherwise be too easy, the Y screen coordinate needs to be negated:

```
float4 screenPos;
screenPos.x = PSIn.TexCoord.x*2.0f-1.0f;
screenPos.y = -(PSIn.TexCoord.y*2.0f-1.0f);
```

However, the screen position has a third component: it is the distance between the camera and the pixel. This is why you had to generate the second render target. Since you know the depth, you know this third component:

```
screenPos.z = depth;
screenPos.w = 1.0f;
```

The fourth component is required, because you'll multiply this vector with a 4×4 matrix next. You can reshape a Vector3 into a homogeneous Vector4 by setting the fourth component to 1.

At this point, you have the screen coordinate of the pixel, but you want to have the original 3D position. Remember that you can transform a 3D position to a 2D screen coordinate by multiplying the 3D position with the ViewProjection matrix (see recipe 2-1). So, how can you do the opposite—transform a 2D screen position into a 3D position? It's simple; you multiply it with the inverse of this ViewProjection matrix:

```
float4 worldPos = mul(screenPos, xViewProjectionInv);
worldPos /= worldPos.w;
```

This inverse of the ViewProjection matrix will need to be calculated and set by your XNA code, which is very easy to do later.

As the result of a vector multiplication with a 4×4 matrix that returns a homogenous vector, you need to divide the first three components by the fourth before you can use them.

Finally! At this point, you know the 3D position of the pixel. You also know the 3D normal in this pixel. Together, they allow you to perform any kind of lighting calculation. The remainder of the pixel shader calculates the lighting influence of a spotlight and is taken straight from recipe 6-8. This is your complete pixel shader:

```
PixelToFrame MyPixelShader(VertexToPixel PSIn) : COLOR0
{
    PixelToFrame Output = (PixelToFrame)0;

    float3 normal = tex2D(NormalMapSampler, PSIn.TexCoord).rgb;
    normal = normal*2.0f-1.0f;
    normal = normalize(normal);

    float depth = tex2D(DepthMapSampler, PSIn.TexCoord).r;

    float4 screenPos;
    screenPos.x = PSIn.TexCoord.x*2.0f-1.0f;
    screenPos.y = -(PSIn.TexCoord.y*2.0f-1.0f);
    screenPos.z = depth;
    screenPos.w = 1.0f;

    float4 worldPos = mul(screenPos, xViewProjectionInv);
    worldPos /= worldPos.w;

    float3 lightDirection = normalize(worldPos - xLightPosition);
    float coneDot = dot(lightDirection, normalize(xConeDirection));
    bool coneCondition = coneDot >= xConeAngle;

    float shading = 0;
    if (coneCondition)
    {
        float coneAttenuation = pow(coneDot, xConeDecay);

        shading = dot(normal, -lightDirection);
        shading *= xLightStrength;
        shading *= coneAttenuation;
    }

    Output.Color.rgb = shading;

    return Output;
}
```

And here's your technique definition:

```
technique DeferredSpotLight
{
    pass Pass0
    {
        VertexShader = compile vs_2_0 MyVertexShader();
        PixelShader  = compile ps_2_0 MyPixelShader();
    }
}
```

You have created an effect that starts from a depth map, a normal map, and a spotlight and creates a shading map containing the influence of the spotlight on the part of your scene that is visible to your camera.

### XNA Code

In your XNA code, you will call this effect for each of the lights present in your scene. To manage your lights, create this struct, which can hold all the details about one spotlight:

```
public struct SpotLight
{
    public Vector3 Position;
    public float Strength;
    public Vector3 Direction;
    public float ConeAngle;
    public float ConeDecay;
}
```

Add an array of these objects to your project:

```
SpotLight[] spotLights;
```

And initialize it so it can store some lights:

```
spotLights = new SpotLight[NumberOfLights];
```

Now it's entirely up to you to define each of the spotlights. Even more, you can change their settings in the Update method so they will move around your scene!

Next, you will create a method that accepts a SpotLight object. The method will render the lighting contributions of this spotlight onto the render target:

```
private void AddLight(SpotLight spotLight)
{
    effect2Lights.CurrentTechnique = effect2Lights.Techniques["DeferredSpotLight"];
    effect2Lights.Parameters["xNormalMap"].SetValue(normalMap);
    effect2Lights.Parameters["xDepthMap"].SetValue(depthMap);
```

```
effect2Lights.Parameters["xLightPosition"].SetValue(spotLight.Position);
effect2Lights.Parameters["xLightStrength"].SetValue(spotLight.Strength);
effect2Lights.Parameters["xConeDirection"].SetValue(spotLight.Direction);
effect2Lights.Parameters["xConeAngle"].SetValue(spotLight.ConeAngle);
effect2Lights.Parameters["xConeDecay"].SetValue(spotLight.ConeDecay);

Matrix viewProjInv = Matrix.Invert(fpsCam.ViewMatrix * fpsCam.ProjectionMatrix);
effect2Lights.Parameters["xViewProjectionInv"].SetValue(viewProjInv);

effect2Lights.Begin();
foreach (EffectPass pass in effect2Lights.CurrentTechnique.Passes)
{
    pass.Begin();
    device.VertexDeclaration = fsVertexDeclaration;
    device.DrawUserPrimitives<VertexPositionTexture> ➥
    (PrimitiveType.TriangleStrip, fsVertices, 0, 2);
    pass.End();
}
effect2Lights.End();
}
```

You first activate the HLSL technique you just defined. Next, you pass in the normal map and the depth map, which were generated in step 1. The following lines pass the settings for the spotlight. The last variable that is being set is the inverted ViewProjection matrix, which can be constructed easily using the Matrix.Invert method.

Once all the variables have been set, you issue your graphics card to render the two triangles that span the whole screen. As a result, for each pixel of your screen, your graphics card will calculate the lighting contribution of the current spotlight.

The AddLight method renders the lighting contributions of a single light. You will call this method for each of your spotlights and add all their lighting contributions together! You can do this by using additive alpha blending. With additive alpha blending, each lighting contribution is added to the same render target:

```
private Texture2D GenerateShadingMap()
{
    device.SetRenderTarget(0, shadingTarget);
    device.Clear(ClearOptions.Target | ClearOptions.DepthBuffer, Color.Black, 1, 0);

    device.RenderState.AlphaBlendEnable = true;
    device.RenderState.SourceBlend = Blend.One;
    device.RenderState.DestinationBlend = Blend.One;

    for (int i = 0; i < NumberOfLights; i++)
        AddLight(spotLights[i]);
```

```
    device.RenderState.AlphaBlendEnable = false;

    device.SetRenderTarget(0, null);
    return shadingTarget.GetTexture();
}
```

The GenerateShadingMap method first activates a new render target, called shadingTarget. As always, it is first cleared, so the previous contents are discarded. Next, you enable additive alpha blending and add all the lighting contributions of all your lights to the render target. Turn off alpha blending so you don't screw up any future renderings. Finally, the content of the render target is saved to a texture, and this texture is returned to the calling code.

This method should be called as the second line from within your Draw method:

```
shadingMap = GenerateShadingMap();
```

Both the shadingTarget and shadingMap variables still have to be added to your project:

```
RenderTarget2D shadingTarget;
Texture2D shadingMap;
```

Initialize the render target in the LoadContent method:

```
shadingTarget = new RenderTarget2D(device, width, height, 1, SurfaceFormat.Color);
```

Because this render target needs to contain the lighting contribution for each pixel of the screen, the render target needs to have the same dimensions as your screen.

### Summary of Step 2

At this point, you have a shading map containing for each pixel of your screen how much that pixel should be lit.

## Step 3: Combining the Color Map and the Shading Map

The last step is an easy one. The base color of each pixel was stored in the colorMap in step 1. The amount of lighting for each pixel was stored in the shadingMap in step 2. In step 3, you'll simply multiply both to obtain the final color.

### HLSL Code

Your effect should receive both the colorMap and shadingMap textures. To light up parts of the scene that are not covered by any of your spotlights, you'll want to add a little ambient lighting:

```
float xAmbient;

Texture xColorMap;
sampler ColorMapSampler = sampler_state { texture = <xColorMap> ; ➥
magfilter = LINEAR; minfilter = LINEAR; mipfilter=LINEAR; AddressU = mirror; ➥
AddressV = mirror;};
```

```
Texture xShadingMap;
sampler ShadingMapSampler = sampler_state { texture = <xShadingMap> ; ➥
magfilter = LINEAR; minfilter = LINEAR; mipfilter=LINEAR; AddressU = mirror; ➥
AddressV = mirror;};
```

The output structures of the vertex shader and pixel shader, as well as the vertex shader itself, are completely identical to the previous recipe. This is because the vertex shader will receive six vertices defining two triangles that span the whole screen.

```
struct VertexToPixel
{
    float4 Position        : POSITION;
    float2 TexCoord        : TEXCOORD0;
};

struct PixelToFrame
{
    float4 Color           : COLOR0;
};

//------- Technique: CombineColorAndShading --------
VertexToPixel MyVertexShader(float4 inPos: POSITION0, float2 texCoord: TEXCOORD0)
{
    VertexToPixel Output = (VertexToPixel)0;
    Output.Position = inPos;
    Output.TexCoord = texCoord;
    return Output;
}
```

As promised, the pixel shader is very easy:

```
PixelToFrame MyPixelShader(VertexToPixel PSIn) : COLOR0
{
    PixelToFrame Output = (PixelToFrame)0;

    float4 color = tex2D(ColorMapSampler, PSIn.TexCoord);
    float shading = tex2D(ShadingMapSampler, PSIn.TexCoord);

    Output.Color = color*(xAmbient + shading);

    return Output;
}
```

You sample the color and the shading value. Add some ambient lighting and multiply them together. The final color is passed to the render target.

Here's the technique definition:

```
technique CombineColorAndShading
{
    pass Pass0
    {
        VertexShader = compile vs_2_0 MyVertexShader();
        PixelShader  = compile ps_2_0 MyPixelShader();
    }
}
```

### XNA Code

This effect needs to be called by your XNA code at the end of the Draw method. The CombineColorAndShading method listed next first selects the technique, passes the color and shading maps, and sets the ambient lighting value. Finally, the two triangles spanning the whole screen are rendered using the technique you just defined:

```
private void CombineColorAndShading()
{
    effect3Final.CurrentTechnique = ⇒
    effect3Final.Techniques["CombineColorAndShading"];
    effect3Final.Parameters["xColorMap"].SetValue(colorMap);
    effect3Final.Parameters["xShadingMap"].SetValue(shadingMap);
    effect3Final.Parameters["xAmbient"].SetValue(0.3f);

    effect3Final.Begin();
    foreach (EffectPass pass in effect3Final.CurrentTechnique.Passes)
    {
        pass.Begin();
        device.VertexDeclaration = fsVertexDeclaration;
        device.DrawUserPrimitives<VertexPositionTexture> ⇒
        (PrimitiveType.TriangleStrip, fsVertices, 0, 2);
        pass.End();
    }
    effect3Final.End();
}
```

These two triangles need to be rendered to the screen, instead of to a custom render target.

### Summary of Step 3

For each pixel of your screen, you have combined the base color and the light intensity.

## The Code

*All the code is available for download at www.apress.com.*

All effect files were listed completely earlier in the recipe. The same holds for the main methods related to deferred shading. Since you've split up your code into methods, your Draw method stays pretty clean:

```
protected override void Draw(GameTime gameTime)
{
    //render color, normal and depth into 3 render targets
    RenderSceneTo3RenderTargets();

    //Add lighting contribution of each light onto shadingMap
    shadingMap = GenerateShadingMap();

    //Combine base color map and shading map
    CombineColorAndShading();

    base.Draw(gameTime);
}
```

## Performance Tip

For each light, your pixel shader will calculate the lighting influence for all the pixels of your screen. To reduce the number of pixels that need to be processed in step 2, instead of rendering your whole screen, you could render only the part of the screen that might be influenced by the light. You can do this by adjusting the coordinates of the two triangles that would otherwise span the whole screen.

# 6-11. Add Shadowing Capability to Your Deferred Shading Engine

## The Problem

Although you've mastered the basics of lighting in real-time computer graphics, you should have noticed that your objects don't cast shadows. This is because your pixel shader calculates the lighting in a pixel based on the angle between the light direction and the normal. Until now, your pixel shaders didn't take into account any objects between the light and the pixel.

The shadow mapping technique explained in the third series of tutorials on my site (www.riemers.net) generates valid shadowing for a single light, but you want to implement it in the deferred rendering approach.

## The Solution

An excellent technique for adding shadows to your scene is the shadow mapping technique. I've discussed this technique in detail on my site (www.riemers.net).

In short, for each pixel the shadow mapping technique compares the real distance between that pixel and the light against the distance as seen by the light. If the real distance is larger than the distance seen by the light, there must be an object between the pixel and the light, so the pixel should not be lit.

To allow this comparison, the scene should first be rendered as seen by the light, so for each pixel its distance to the light can be saved into a texture.

If you want to implement the deferred rendering version of the shadow mapping technique, you will first need to generate a depth map for each of your lights. Once you've done this, the shadow mapping comparison should be applied in step 2 of deferred rendering.

## How It Works

This recipe will build entirely on the previous recipe, so make sure you start from that code.

Step 1 of the previous recipe will remain unchanged, because you still need the color, normal, and depth values for all pixels of your screen.

### Generating the Shadow Maps

#### XNA Code

Before you can determine the lighting contribution of one of your lights in step 2, however, you will need to generate the shadow map for that light. This shadow map contains the distance between the scene and the light. You will need to add a render target as well as two texture variables: one to store the distances and one black image you'll use to reset the other one:

```
RenderTarget2D shadowTarget;
Texture2D shadowMap;
Texture2D blackImage;
```

Initialize the render target and the black image in your LoadContent method:

```
shadowTarget = new RenderTarget2D(device, width, height, 1, SurfaceFormat.Single);
blackImage = new Texture2D(device, width, height, 1, ➡
TextureUsage.None, SurfaceFormat.Color);
```

Next, go to your GenerateShadingMap method. This method was used to blend the lighting contributions of all lights together into one texture using alpha blending. This can no longer be done, because you'll need to generate a new shadow map between two blending operations. Otherwise, this would result in the shadow map being blended into the shading map.

Instead of alpha blending, you'll save the shading map after each light has added its lighting contribution. To begin with, erase the shading map by using the black image:

```
private Texture2D GenerateShadingMap()
{
    shadingMap = blackImage;

    for (int i = 0; i < NumberOfLights; i++)
    {
        RenderShadowMap(spotLights[i]);
        AddLight(spotLights[i]);
    }

    return shadingTarget.GetTexture();
}
```

For each light, first the RenderShadowMap method is called, which will store the shadow map for that light in the shadowMap variable. Based on this shadow map, the light will add its lighting contributions to the shading map.

The shadow map should contain the distances as seen by the light. Therefore, for each light you should define View and Projection matrices. Extend your SpotLight struct so it can store these:

```
public struct SpotLight
{
    public Vector3 Position;
    public float Strength;
    public Vector3 Direction;
    public float ConeAngle;
    public float ConeDecay;
    public Matrix ViewMatrix;
    public Matrix ProjectionMatrix;
}
```

For a spotlight, it's fairly easy to define these:

```
spotLights[i].ViewMatrix = Matrix.CreateLookAt(lightPosition, ➥
lightPosition + lightDirection,lightUp);
float viewAngle = (float)Math.Acos(spotLights[i].ConeAngle);
spotLights[i].ProjectionMatrix = ➥
Matrix.CreatePerspectiveFieldOfView(coneAngle * 2.0f, 1.0f, 0.5f, 1000.0f);
```

The viewAngle is based on the cone of the spotlight. This way, the area of the render target is optimally used.

The RenderShadowMap method will pass these matrices to the ShadowMap effect that you'll define in a minute. After this, the scene is rendered as seen by the light, and the distance is stored in the shadowMap texture.

```
private void RenderShadowMap(SpotLight spotLight)
{
    device.SetRenderTarget(0, shadowTarget);

    effectShadowMap.CurrentTechnique = effectShadowMap.Techniques["ShadowMap"];
    effectShadowMap.Parameters["xView"].SetValue(spotLight.ViewMatrix);
    effectShadowMap.Parameters["xProjection"].SetValue(spotLight.ProjectionMatrix);
    RenderScene(effectShadowMap);

    device.SetRenderTarget(0, null);
    shadowMap = shadowTarget.GetTexture();
}
```

### HLSL Code

The HLSL code is fairly easy. Since the 3D scene needs to be transformed to 2D screen coordinates, your effect should accept the World, View, and Projection matrices. To be compatible with the RenderScene method that wants to set a texture, your effect will also support the xTexture variable, although it will not use it.

```
float4x4 xWorld;
float4x4 xView;
float4x4 xProjection;
Texture xTexture;

struct VertexToPixel
{
    float4 Position        : POSITION;
    float4 ScreenPos       : TEXCOORD1;
};
struct PixelToFrame
{
    float4 Color           : COLOR0;
};
```

The vertex shader needs to calculate the 2D screen coordinate. This screen coordinate also contains the depth you want your pixel shader to output. Since the POSITION semantic cannot be accessed from within the pixel shader, you copy it into the ScreenPos variable.

The vertex shader is very easy, because all it does is transform the 3D coordinates to 2D screen coordinates:

```
VertexToPixel MyVertexShader(float4 inPos: POSITION0, float3 inNormal: NORMAL0)
{
    VertexToPixel Output = (VertexToPixel)0;
```

```
    float4x4 preViewProjection = mul(xView, xProjection);
    float4x4 preWorldViewProjection = mul(xWorld, preViewProjection);
    Output.Position = mul(inPos, preWorldViewProjection);

    Output.ScreenPos = Output.Position;

    return Output;
}
```

Your pixel shader receives the screen coordinate. Because this is a homogeneous vector, you first need to divide the first three components by the fourth before you can use them. The pixel shader generates the depth as output.

```
PixelToFrame MyPixelShader(VertexToPixel PSIn) : COLOR0
{
    PixelToFrame Output = (PixelToFrame)0;

    Output.Color.r = PSIn.ScreenPos.z/PSIn.ScreenPos.w;

    return Output;
}
```

The technique definition makes your .fx file complete:

```
technique ShadowMap
{
    pass Pass0
    {
        VertexShader = compile vs_2_0 MyVertexShader();
        PixelShader  = compile ps_2_0 MyPixelShader();
    }
}
```

## Adding the Shadow Mapping Constraint to Your Lighting Calculations

### XNA Code

After the shadow map has been rendered for a light, the AddLight method is called. This method starts by activating the shadingTarget and the DeferredSpotLight technique. Both this method and this technique largely resemble those of the previous recipe, except for some small changes. At the end of each light, the current content of the shadingTarget is saved into the shadingMap texture. This allows it to be fed to the next light, through the xPreviousShadingMapContents variable. You also pass in the shadow map.

```
private void AddLight(SpotLight spotLight)
{
    device.SetRenderTarget(0, shadingTarget);
```

```
effect2Lights.CurrentTechnique = effect2Lights.Techniques["DeferredSpotLight"];
effect2Lights.Parameters["xPreviousShadingContents"].SetValue(shadingMap);
effect2Lights.Parameters["xNormalMap"].SetValue(normalMap);
effect2Lights.Parameters["xDepthMap"].SetValue(depthMap);
effect2Lights.Parameters["xShadowMap"].SetValue(shadowMap);

effect2Lights.Parameters["xLightPosition"].SetValue(spotLight.Position);
effect2Lights.Parameters["xLightStrength"].SetValue(spotLight.Strength);
effect2Lights.Parameters["xConeDirection"].SetValue(spotLight.Direction);
effect2Lights.Parameters["xConeAngle"].SetValue(spotLight.ConeAngle);
effect2Lights.Parameters["xConeDecay"].SetValue(spotLight.ConeDecay);

Matrix viewProjInv = Matrix.Invert(fpsCam.ViewMatrix * fpsCam.ProjectionMatrix);
effect2Lights.Parameters["xViewProjectionInv"].SetValue(viewProjInv);
effect2Lights.Parameters["xLightViewProjection"].SetValue( ➥
spotLight.ViewMatrix * spotLight.ProjectionMatrix);

effect2Lights.Begin();
foreach (EffectPass pass in effect2Lights.CurrentTechnique.Passes)
{
    pass.Begin();
    device.VertexDeclaration = fsVertexDeclaration;
    device.DrawUserPrimitives<VertexPositionTexture> ➥
    (PrimitiveType.TriangleStrip, fsVertices, 0, 2);
    pass.End();
}
effect2Lights.End();

device.SetRenderTarget(0, null);
shadingMap = shadingTarget.GetTexture();
}
```

### HLSL Code

Make sure your effect can accept both new textures:

```
Texture xShadowMap;
sampler ShadowMapSampler = sampler_state { texture = <xShadowMap> ; ➥
magfilter = LINEAR; minfilter = LINEAR; mipfilter=LINEAR; AddressU = mirror; ➥
AddressV = mirror;};
Texture xPreviousShadingContents;
sampler PreviousSampler = sampler_state { texture = <xPreviousShadingContents> ; ➥
magfilter = LINEAR; minfilter = LINEAR; mipfilter=LINEAR; AddressU = mirror; ➥
AddressV = mirror;};
```

The only changes you need to make are in the pixel shader. Start from the line where you've calculated the original 3D position of the pixel. You want to find the real distance between this point and the light, as well as the distance stored in the shadow map of the light. If the distance stored in the shadow map is smaller than the real distance, there is another object between the light and the pixel. This means the pixel shouldn't be lit by the current light.

To find the real distance, transform the 3D position by the ViewProjection matrix of the light. After dividing the result by its homogenous component, the distance will be readily available in its Z component:

```
//find screen position as seen by the light
float4 lightScreenPos = mul(worldPos, xLightViewProjection);
lightScreenPos /= lightScreenPos.w;
```

Next, you want to find the distance stored in the shadow map. First you need to find where to sample the shadow map. Bring the lightScreenPos components from the [–1,1] screen position range into the [0,1] texture coordinate range as done in the previous recipe:

```
//find sample position in shadow map
float2 lightSamplePos;
lightSamplePos.x = lightScreenPos.x/2.0f+0.5f;
lightSamplePos.y = (-lightScreenPos.y/2.0f+0.5f);
```

Now you can sample the depth stored in the shadow map. Check whether this distance is smaller than the real distance, which would indicate the pixel should not be lit by the current light:

```
//determine shadowing criteria
float realDistanceToLight = lightScreenPos.z;
float distanceStoredInDepthMap = tex2D(ShadowMapSampler, lightSamplePos);
bool shadowCondition = ➡
distanceStoredInDepthMap <= realDistanceToLight - 1.0f/100.0f;
```

Finally, decide whether the pixel should be lit based on both the shadowCondition and the coneCondition. The resulting shading value should be added to the value already present in the shadingMap, which is done in the last line of the pixel shader.

This is your complete pixel shader:

```
PixelToFrame MyPixelShader(VertexToPixel PSIn) : COLOR0
{
    PixelToFrame Output = (PixelToFrame)0;

    //sample normal from normal map
    float3 normal = tex2D(NormalMapSampler, PSIn.TexCoord).rgb;
    normal = normal*2.0f-1.0f;
    normal = normalize(normal);

    //sample depth from depth map
    float depth = tex2D(DepthMapSampler, PSIn.TexCoord).r;
```

```
//create screen position
float4 screenPos;
screenPos.x = PSIn.TexCoord.x*2.0f-1.0f;
screenPos.y = -(PSIn.TexCoord.y*2.0f-1.0f);
screenPos.z = depth;
screenPos.w = 1.0f;

//transform to 3D position
float4 worldPos = mul(screenPos, xViewProjectionInv);
worldPos /= worldPos.w;

//find screen position as seen by the light
float4 lightScreenPos = mul(worldPos, xLightViewProjection);
lightScreenPos /= lightScreenPos.w;

//find sample position in shadow map
float2 lightSamplePos;
lightSamplePos.x = lightScreenPos.x/2.0f+0.5f;
lightSamplePos.y = (-lightScreenPos.y/2.0f+0.5f);

//determine shadowing criteria
float realDistanceToLight = lightScreenPos.z;
float distanceStoredInDepthMap = tex2D(ShadowMapSampler, lightSamplePos);
bool shadowCondition = ➡
distanceStoredInDepthMap <= realDistanceToLight - 1.0f/100.0f;

//determine cone criteria
float3 lightDirection = normalize(worldPos - xLightPosition);
float coneDot = dot(lightDirection, normalize(xConeDirection));
bool coneCondition = coneDot >= xConeAngle;


//calculate shading
float shading = 0;
if (coneCondition && !shadowCondition)
{
    float coneAttenuation = pow(coneDot, xConeDecay);
    shading = dot(normal, -lightDirection);
    shading *= xLightStrength;
    shading *= coneAttenuation;
}
```

```
    float4 previous = tex2D(PreviousSampler, PSIn.TexCoord);
    Output.Color = previous + shading;

    return Output;
}
```

## The Code

*All the code is available for download at www.apress.com.*

This recipe uses the same code as recipe 6-10, except for the GenerateShadingMap, RenderShadowMap, and AddLight methods. These methods were already listed.

# CHAPTER 7

■■■

# Adding Sounds to Your XNA 3.0 Project

**E**ven the game with the best game play won't feel like a lot of fun if it doesn't have any sounds. If you add a suitable sound to your visual effects together with a background score, your game will immediately feel a lot more finished.

This short chapter shows you how easy it is to add sounds to your XNA project and to manage them.

Specifically, the recipes in this chapter cover the following:

- Playing a sound effect, MP3 file, or WMV file straight from within XNA (recipes 7-1 and 7-2)

- Creating an XAct project to load sound files into your XNA project (recipe 7-3)

- Looping sounds to add a background score to your game (recipe 7-4)

- Making your 3D world really come alive by adding 3D sound positioning to your game (recipe 7-5)

## 7-1. Play and Control Simple .wav Sound Files

### The Problem

You want a fast way to play a sound effect in your game.

### The Solution

Since XNA 3.0, you can load and play sound files straight from XNA, without having to load them using XAct. While this way of doing things removes some of the advanced functionality of XAct, it makes playing a sound effect extremely easy.

### How It Works

Start by adding the sound effect file to your project. This is done the same way as adding an image to your project, as explained in recipe 3-1. The easiest way to do this is by dragging your .wav file onto the Content folder in your Solution Explorer.

Now that your .wav file has been added to your project, declare a SoundEffect variable at the top of your code, which will be linked to the sound effect file later on:

```
SoundEffect myEffect;
```

In the LoadContent method, add this line of code to load a .wav file using the XNA content pipeline:

```
myEffect = Content.Load<SoundEffect>("effect");
```

Now, whenever you want to play this sound effect, use this line of code:

```
myEffect.Play();
```

## SoundEffect.Play() Overloads

The SoundEffect.Play() method has two more overloads, which give you some more control over how the sound is played. The most complex overload accepts four arguments:

- The first argument allows you to set the volume of the SoundEffect as a value between 0.0f and 1.0f. A value 1.0f corresponds to the volume currently set in SoundEffect.MasterVolume, which is by itself a value between 0.0f and 1.0f, where 1.0f corresponds to the general system volume (which can be set through the speaker icon in the Windows system tray).

- The second argument allows you to control the pitch (speed) at which the sound effect is played. You can specify a value between –1.0f and 1.0f, where a negative number results in a slowdown and a positive number in a speedup; 0 indicates normal playback. Note that this can be used to make different versions of a single sound: a shotgun and a pistol could use the same sound effect, played at a different pitch.

- You can set the balance through the third agument as a value between –1.0f and 1.0f. Specifying –1.0f will cause the sound to be played solely through the left speaker, while a positive value will indicate that the right speaker has a larger amplitude than the left speaker.

- The last argument allows you to specify whether the sound should be looped. See the following section for how you can prevent such a sound from looping indefinitely.

## Controlling the Sound Effect

While the code shown previously is all you need to play a sound effect, XNA provides the SoundEffectInstance class, which you can use to pause or stop the effect, change its volume, and more. Start by adding such a variable to the top of your code:

```
SoundEffectInstance myEffectInstance;
```

The SoundEffect object is automatically converted into a SoundEffectInstance object for you the moment you call its Play method:

```
myEffectInstance = myEffect.Play();
```

Now that you have access to this `SoundEffectInstance` object, you can use it to change its pitch and volume or to check whether it has stopped:

```
if (myEffectInstance != null)
{
    myEffectInstance.Volume *= 0.9f;
    if (myEffectInstance.State == SoundState.Stopped)
    {
        myEffectInstance.Dispose();
        myEffectInstance = null;
    }
}
```

This code will continually decrease the volume of the effect and will remove the reference to the object when it has stopped playing.

---

■**Note**  The Zune can play up to 16 `SoundEffectInstances` simultaneously, while there is no hard limit of the total number of `SoundEffectInstances` loaded. The Xbox 360 can play 300 `SoundEffectInstances` simultaneously but can only have 300 loaded at the same time. On the PC, these constraints do not exist. On another note, at the time of this writing, there is a bug in the `SoundEffectInstance.Play` method, which can be circumvented by using the `SoundEffectInstance.Resume` method.

---

# 7-2. Play MP3 or WMA Sound Files

## The Problem

You want to play an MP3 or a WMV audio file from within your XNA game.

## The Solution

XNA can load MP3 and WMV audio files into a `Song` object using the default content pipeline. Once loaded, the `Song` object can be played using the static `MediaPlayer` class.

## How It Works

Start by adding the MP3 or WMV file to your XNA project. This is done the same way as adding an image to your project, as explained in recipe 3-1. The easiest way to do this is by dragging your MP3 or WMV file onto the Content folder in your Solution Explorer.

As with images, you need a code object that links to the sound file. For MP3 and WMV files, you need a `Song` object. Add this object to the top of your code:

```
Song mySong;
```

Link the sound file to this object as usual, using the content pipeline in the LoadContent method:

```
mySong = Content.Load<Song>("sample");
```

You're ready to play the file, using this simple command:

```
MediaPlayer.Play(mySong);
```

The MediaPlayer is a static class, which can play only one sound at a time. This makes it ideal for playing background scores, but you will need the approach explained in recipe 7-1 to play other sound effects in your game.

Both the Song object and MediaPlayer class have some useful properties, such as the total length of a song and the position of the MediaPlayer in the current song:

```
TimeSpan toGo = mySong.Duration - MediaPlayer.PlayPosition;
string myText = "Time remaining for current song: " + toGo.ToString();
```

# 7-3. Play Simple .wav Sound Files Through XAct

## The Problem

You want to load a sound effect through XAct and play it in your game.

---

■**Note**  The Zune does not support the XAct tool; therefore, refer to recipes 7-1 and 7-2 to learn how to play sounds on the Zune.

---

## The Solution

By using XAct, a free tool that comes with XNA Game Studio 3.0, you can create an XAct project that contains all the sound files you're going to use in your game. You can use XAct to visually add/manipulate effects. You can import this XAct project into your XNA project, after which you can immediately play the sounds stored in your XAct project using a single line of code.

## How It Works

First, make sure you have opened an XNA project and saved it somewhere on your disk. To keep things organized, you should create a new folder to store all your audio stuff. In the Solution Explorer of your XNA project, find the Content entry, and right-click it. Select Add ➤ New Folder, and name your folder Audio, for example.

Now, open XAct by clicking the Start menu and then clicking Programs ➤ Microsoft XNA Game Studio 3.0 ➤ Tools ➤ Microsoft Cross-Platform Audio Creation Tool (XAct).

When you start XAct, the first thing you need to do is start a new project by selecting File ➤ New Project. Give your project a fancy name, and navigate to the Content\Audio map of your XNA project to save it there.

You will be presented with a new, empty project. In the tree structure on the left, find Wave Banks, which contains the *waves*, which are the audio files. Right-click Wave Banks, and select New Wave Bank. Next, create a new sound bank by right-clicking Sound Banks and selecting New Sound Bank. A *sound bank* contains *sounds*, which are objects that can actually be played in your XNA project. A sound points to a wave and can optionally add some kind of effect to the wave.

You now should see two panes on the right part of your window. Click the Wave Bank pane. You should see its properties in the bottom-left corner of the XAct window. Find the Name property, and change it from Wave Bank to myWaveBank. Next, click the Sound Bank pane, and change its Name property to mySoundBank. These are the names by which they will be accessible from within your XNA project.

You can use your wave bank to store all your .wav files, so right-click somewhere in its pane, and select Insert Wave File(s). Browse to the .wav file on your disk that you want to play in your game, and hit Open. You should see it has been added to your wave bank. It's shown in red, because you haven't yet made a sound in your sound bank that uses the wave.

---

■**Tip** The location of the file will be stored relative to your XAct project. This can cause trouble if you're changing the location of either your sound file or your XAct project, so you should first copy the audio files to the Content\Audio map before importing them into your wave bank.

---

A wave is a reference to the sound file on your disk, no matter what format the file is in. A sound uses a wave and allows you to add some kind of effect to it, such as manipulating the volume or pitch. From one wave you can make multiple sounds. However, the programmer uses a *cue* to access the sounds. So from each sound, you need to make a cue before you can access it from your XNA code. One cue can contain multiple sounds, so a single line of code can play multiple sounds after each other.

So, before you can play a wave from your wave bank in your game, you need to make a sound and a cue that uses this wave. You can do this easily by selecting your wave and dragging it into the cue area of the Sound Bank pane, as shown in Figure 7-1.

---

■**Caution** Make sure you drag the sound(s) immediately into the cue list at the bottom of the Sound Bank pane, not to the sound list at the top of the Sound Bank pane.

---

The wave and sound banks are separate entities so that you can make multiple sounds from a single wave. This way, you can add different effects to the different sounds relating to the same wave.

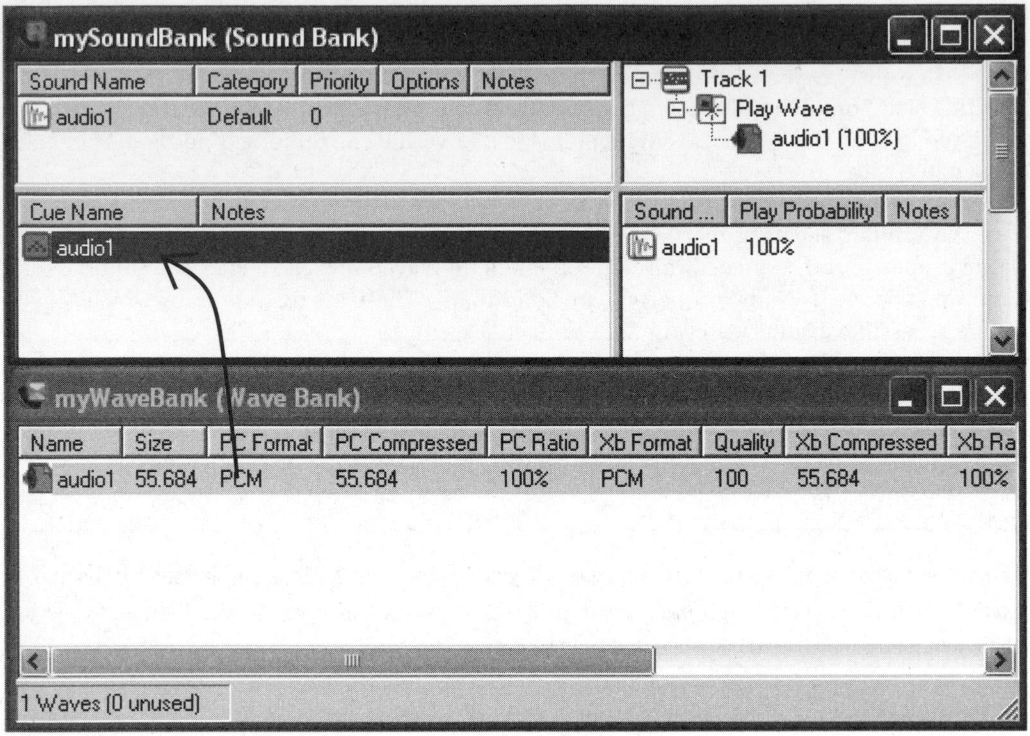

**Figure 7-1.** *Dragging your wave to the cue area*

That's it for the XAct tool; make sure you save your project by selecting File ➤ Save Project. Go to your XNA project, and import this file into your XNA project like you would import an image or object file. You can do this by dragging the .xap file onto the Content\Audio entry in the Solution Explorer of XNA Game Studio 3.0 or by going to your Solution Explorer, right-clicking the Audio entry, and selecting Add ➤ Existing Item.

Right now, the myXactProject.xap file should be listed in the Solution Explorer of your XNA Game Studio 3.0 application.

Whenever you compile your project, the XAct project will be read and converted into binary files, which will be written to the output folder of your project. For each .xap XAct project file you add to your XNA project, the XNA content pipeline will create an .xgs XNA game sound binary file (having the same name as the XAct project), an .xwb binary file for each wave bank in your XAct project, and an .xsb binary file for each sound bank in your XAct project.

In your XNA project, you need to link each of these three files to a variable. So, first declare them at the top of your code:

```
AudioEngine audioEngine;
WaveBank waveBank;
SoundBank soundBank;
```

Then link them to the binary files (which will be created/updated whenever you compile your project), for example, in the Initialize method:

```
audioEngine = new AudioEngine("Content/Audio/MyXACTproject.xgs");
waveBank = new WaveBank(audioEngine, "Content/Audio/myWaveBank.xwb");
soundBank = new SoundBank(audioEngine, "Content/Audio/mySoundBank.xsb");
```

The soundBank variable will contain all the playable cues. However, when you instantiate a new SoundBank, you need to pass it an AudioEngine, so you need to initialize this first. Whenever you play a cue from your soundBank, it will look up the wave from the WaveBank associated with its AudioEngine, so you also need the second line.

---

■**Note**   The myWaveBank and mySoundBank names were assigned by you in the XAct tool earlier in this recipe.

---

Now, whenever you want to simply play a sound, all you have to do is call the PlayCue method of the soundBank variable and pass it the name of the cue you want to play!

```
soundBank.PlayCue("audio1");
```

To make sure all the cues are removed from memory when they have finished, make sure you call the Update method of your audioEngine each frame:

```
audioEngine.Update();
```

---

■**Caution**   Whenever you make changes to your XAct project and save it to file, you cannot simply run the .exe of your XNA project and expect it to apply the changes you made in your XAct project. You first need to recompile (which is done each time you hit F5) your XNA project so the content pipeline creates new binary files from your XAct project.

---

## The Code

All the code is available for download from www.apress.com.

You need three global variables through which you can play all sound cues contained in your XAct project:

```
AudioEngine audioEngine;
WaveBank waveBank;
SoundBank soundBank;
```

Initialize them somewhere during the startup of your project:

```
protected override void Initialize()
{
    audioEngine = new AudioEngine("myXactProject.xgs");
    waveBank = new WaveBank(audioEngine, "myWaveBank.xwb");
    soundBank = new SoundBank(audioEngine, "mySoundBank.xsb");
    base.Initialize();
}
```

Play sounds using the soundBank.PlayCue method, such as after a key press, as shown in the following code. Make sure you call the audioEngine.Update method each frame:

```
protected override void Update(GameTime gameTime)
{
    if (GamePad.GetState(PlayerIndex.One).Buttons.Back == ButtonState.Pressed)
        this.Exit();

    KeyboardState keybState = Keyboard.GetState();
    if (keybState.IsKeyDown(Keys.Space))
        soundBank.PlayCue("audio1");

    audioEngine.Update();

    base.Update(gameTime);
}
```

Now when you run this code, the sound will be played each time you press the spacebar.

# 7-4. Loop Sounds

## The Problem

You want to loop sounds to play background music or to play a continuing sound, such as the noise of a car engine.

---

■**Note**  Because the Zune doesn't support XAct, you'll want to use the third overload of the SoundEffect.Play() method to loop your sound, as explained in the corresponding section in recipe 7-1.

---

## The Solution

Using the XAct audio tool, it's extremely easy to indicate that a sound should loop continuously. You'll want to create and keep track of a Cue object in your XNA code, because you'll need to be able to pause or stop the sound from playing.

You can also programmatically detect when a sound has finished playing, which is useful if you want to switch background music. You do this by checking the IsStopped member of the Cue.

# How It Works

### Looping a Sound Indefinitely

You can easily make a sound loop by setting its LoopEvent property to Infinite in the XAct audio tool. To do this, open your XAct project, and select the sound you want to loop in your sound bank. Once you've selected the sound, the Play Wave entry should be visible in the upper-right corner of the Sound Bank pane. Click the Play Wave node, as shown in Figure 7-2.

After clicking the Play Wave node, its properties should be visible in the Properties box in the bottom-left corner of your XAct window. Find the LoopEvent property, and set it to Infinite. Make sure you save your XAct project.

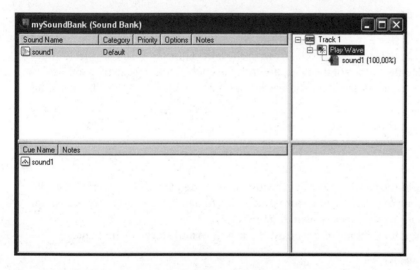

**Figure 7-2.** *The Play Wave node becomes visible after selecting the sound.*

Now when you recompile your XNA project and play the cue using the code from the previous recipe, it will loop indefinitely. Because you'll want some kind of control that allows you to stop the cue, you need to create a Cue object to store a reference to the cue:

```
Cue cue1;
```

Fill this object by calling the GetCue method on your soundBank variable. On this Cue object, you can call the Play method to start the cue:

```
cue1 = soundBank.GetCue("audio1");
cue1.Play();
```

This should start playing the cue indefinitely, as you defined in the XAct audio tool. Only this time, you have a reference to the cue, which you can use to pause, resume, or stop the cue:

```
cue1.Pause();
cue1.Resume();
cue1.Stop(AudioStopOptions.Immediate);
```

**Caution** After you've stopped a cue from playing, you cannot simply call Play on the cue again. You first need to load it again from the soundBank by calling its GetCue method.

### Checking Whether a Sound Has Finished Playing/Changing Background Music

You can check whether a sound cue has finished playing by checking its IsStopped property:

```
if (currentCue.IsStopped)
    //do something
```

If you want your XNA program to cycle through a few background sounds, you should create an array to hold the names of the cues, and not the cues themselves, which are useless once they have been played. You will need these additional variables to create a background looping system:

```
string[] bgCueNames;
Cue currentCue;
int currentCueNr = 0;
```

The array will hold the names of the background cues to be played. The currentCue will store the cue that is playing so you can check whether it's finished, and the currentCueNr variable is needed so your program can activate the next cue.

This is the method that initializes the array of cue names and starts the first cue:

```
private void InitSounds()
{
    audioEngine = new AudioEngine("Content/Audio/MyXACTproject.xgs");
    waveBank = new WaveBank(audioEngine, "Content/Audio/myWaveBank.xwb");
    soundBank = new SoundBank(audioEngine, "Content/Audio/mySoundBank.xsb");

    bgCueNames = new string[5];
    bgCueNames[0] = "bgAudio1";
    bgCueNames[1] = "bgAudio2";
    bgCueNames[2] = "bgAudio3";
    bgCueNames[3] = "bgAudio4";
    bgCueNames[4] = "bgAudio5";

    PlayBGCue(0);
}
```

For this to work, you'll first have to create an XAct project, as shown in recipe 7-1, containing the five cues. The PlayBGCue method that actually starts a cue is easy:

```
private void PlayBGCue(int cueNr)
{
    currentCue = soundBank.GetCue(bgCueNames[cueNr]);
    currentCue.Play();
}
```

It stores a reference to the cue currently playing in the currentCue variable, so you can check its IsPlayed property in an UpdateSounds method that you can call from your main Update method:

```
private void UpdateSounds()
{
    if (currentCue.IsStopped)
    {
        if (++currentCueNr == bgCueNames.Length)
            currentCueNr = 0;

        PlayBGCue(currentCueNr);
    }

    audioEngine.Update();
}
```

If the current cue has finished playing, you increment the currentCueNr, while setting it back to 0 if it has become larger than the number of playable cues, 5 in this case. Finally, you call the PlayBGCue, so the next sound starts playing.

---

**Note** The ++ before the currentCueNr indicates you want the value of currentCueNr to be incremented *before* the whole line gets evaluated. If you wrote currentCueNr++, the condition will be false if the currentCueNr is 4, and after that, the value is incremented to 5, which will give an OutOfRange exception at the GetCue method. By writing ++currentCueNr, if the currentCueNr is 4, the value is first incremented to 5, so the condition will be true, and the value will be reset to 0.

---

By putting the Update call on the audioEngine in this method, all you have to call in the Update method is this UpdateSounds method.

## The Code

*All the code is available for download from www.apress.com.*

Since you can find all the code for the looping background playlist earlier in the chapter, the following code starts a looping sound as defined in the first part of this recipe by pressing the spacebar and ends it by pressing the Enter key:

```
protected override void Update(GameTime gameTime)
{
    GamePadState gamePadState = GamePad.GetState(PlayerIndex.One);
    if (gamePadState.Buttons.Back == ButtonState.Pressed)
        this.Exit();

    KeyboardState keyState = Keyboard.GetState();


    if (keyState.IsKeyDown(Keys.Space) || (gamePadState.Buttons.B == ➥
    ButtonState.Pressed))
    {
        if ((cue1 == null) || (cue1.IsStopped))
        {
            cue1 = soundBank.GetCue("audio1");
            cue1.Play();
        }
    }
    if (keyState.IsKeyDown(Keys.Enter) || (gamePadState.Buttons.A == ➥
    ButtonState.Pressed))
        if (cue1 != null)
            cue1.Stop(AudioStopOptions.Immediate);

    audioEngine.Update();

    base.Update(gameTime);
}
```

The first time the spacebar is pressed, the cue1 variable will be null. When the user presses the Enter key, the cue is stopped. When the user presses the spacebar again, the cue is restarted.

Once again, note that you need to re-create the cue1 variable (by calling the GetCue method) after the cue has been stopped.

# 7-5. Play Sounds from a 3D Location Relative to the Camera: 3D Sound

## The Problem

To add some more realism to your 3D game, you want to be able to give each of your sounds a location in 3D space. This way, an explosion to the right of your camera will be played mainly on the right speaker, so the user gets the impression the explosion is really on his right side. Even if the explosion is not in sight of the camera, the user will be able to know something happened on his right side.

---

**■Note**  Since the Zune doesn't support the XAct tool and the `Apply3D()` method used in the following solution only accepts `Cue` objects, 3D sounds are only supported on the PC and Xbox 360.

---

## The Solution

XNA has made all of this easy. For each sound, you have to set the 3D location of the camera
and the location of the sound origin using the `Apply3D` method of the `Cue` object of the sound.
Note that every time the camera or the sound source moves, you need to update your `Cue` by
calling this method.

## How It Works

If you want to set the 3D position of a sound source, you first need to create an `AudioEmitter`
object for the sound source and an `AudioListener` object for your camera. When you pass both
to the `Apply3D` method of the `Cue`, XNA will calculate how the sound is distributed over the
speakers (or headphones) connected to your system.

This method creates both objects:

```
private void UpdateSoundPosition(Cue cue, Vector3 sourcePos, Vector3 camPos, ➥
Vector3 camForward, Vector3 camUp)
{
    AudioEmitter emitter = new AudioEmitter();
    emitter.Position = sourcePos;

    AudioListener listener = new AudioListener();
    listener.Position = camPos;
    listener.Forward = camForward;
    listener.Up = camUp;

    cue.Apply3D(listener, emitter);
}
```

For the emitter (your audio source), you need to set only the position. For the listener
(your camera), however, you also need to set the Forward and Up vectors, because when the
camera is rotated over 180 degrees, left and right are switched.

When you have created and filled both objects, you can pass them to the `Apply3D` method
of the `Cue`. This needs to be done whenever either the sound source or your camera moves.

You need to call this `Apply3D` method *before* you call the `Play` method on the cue for the
first time. Therefore, make sure you don't call `Play` on your `Cue` yet:

```
protected override void Initialize()
{
    fpsCam = new QuakeCamera(GraphicsDevice.Viewport, new Vector3(0,0,5) , 0, 0);

    audioEngine = new AudioEngine("Content/Audio/MyXACTproject.xgs");
    waveBank = new WaveBank(audioEngine, "Content/Audio/myWaveBank.xwb");
    soundBank = new SoundBank(audioEngine, "Content/Audio/mySoundBank.xsb");

    cue1 = soundBank.GetCue("audio1");

    base.Initialize();
}
```

In your Update method, whenever you update the position of your camera or the position of the audio source, you should call the UpdateSoundPosition method:

```
protected override void Update(GameTime gameTime)
{
    GamePadState gamePadState = GamePad.GetState(PlayerIndex.One);
    if (gamePadState.Buttons.Back == ButtonState.Pressed)
        this.Exit();

    MouseState mouseState = Mouse.GetState();
    KeyboardState keyState = Keyboard.GetState();

    fpsCam.Update(mouseState, keyState, gamePadState);

    float time = (float)gameTime.TotalGameTime.TotalMilliseconds/1000.0f;
    Vector3 startingPos = new Vector3(0, 0, -10);
    Matrix rotMatrix = Matrix.CreateRotationY(time);
    modelPos = Vector3.Transform(startingPos, rotMatrix);

    UpdateSoundPosition(cue1, modelPos, fpsCam.Position, ➥
    fpsCam.Forward, fpsCam.UpVector);

    if (cue1.IsPrepared)
        cue1.Play();

    audioEngine.Update();

    base.Update(gameTime);
}
```

The upper half of this method checks for user input and passes this input to your 3D camera, as explained in recipe 2-3. The middle block of code updates the position of your audio source. With your camera and source updated, you should call the UpdateSoundPosition method, so your cue1 object is informed about the latest positions. If your cue1 wasn't playing already, you start it now.

---

■**Caution**  The 3D effect is obtained by controlling the volume of the left and right speakers separately. This means that any stereo information in the sound will get lost: first the sound is converted to mono, and then the left and right volumes are set corresponding to the 3D location of the object.

---

## The Code

*All the code is available for download from www.apress.com.*

All the `Initialize`, `UpdateSoundPosition`, and `Update` methods were already listed earlier.

## Extra Information

The XAct audio tool allows you to graphically add some very nice 3D audio effects to your cues, such as distance attenuation and Doppler shift. Because this is done graphically, this can be demonstrated far better in a movie than in a book. The `http://creators.xna.com` website contains some very nice movies on adding 3D audio effects to your cues.

# CHAPTER 8

■ ■ ■

# Networking in XNA 3.0

The XNA 3.0 Framework contains networking capabilities, allowing you to play your game on multiple PCs, Zunes, and Xbox 360 consoles. Once again, the XNA team has made sure the same code can be used to connect multiple Zunes, PCs, and/or Xbox 360 consoles to a session over the network.

This chapter shows and explains how you can set up a networking session and how you can connect to an existing session. Next, you will learn how you can send data to and receive it from other players over the network. You'll also learn how you can use the lobby functionality that comes with XNA.

Specifically, the recipes in this chapter cover the following:

- Letting your user select or create an account before you access any network features (recipe 8-1)

- Creating a network session or searching for existing sessions (recipes 8-2 and 8-3)

- Learning how you can send and receive data over the network once you are connected to a session (recipe 8-4)

- Implementing asynchronous network operations so you can keep the user informed about any progress made so far (recipe 8-5)

- Adding rich presence information to the player, which can be seen by other users (recipe 8-6)

- Using the basic lobby functionality that comes with XNA (recipe 8-7)

## 8-1. Sign In for Networking Services

### The Problem

Before you can connect with other players, you first need to sign in with an account or create a new one. This can be an offline account if all players are connected to the same network or an online Live account if you want to connect through the Internet.

Signing in is required before you can access any of the networking functionality in XNA. It also allows other players to see your name, as well as some additional details you might have provided.

---

■**Note** This is not required for the Zune. An XNA game on the Zune starts with a `SignedInPlayer` having the name you assigned to your Zune device.

---

## The Solution

Signing in with your account is extremely easy. All you need to do is call the `Guide.ShowSignIn` method, which will allow the user to select an existing account or create a new one.

## How It Works

Before you can use any of the networking functionality of XNA, you should add the `GamerServicesComponent` to your `Game`.

### Adding the GamerServicesComponent

This `GameComponent` (see recipe 1-7) makes sure the entire networking engine is updated at regular intervals in the background. As with any `GameComponent`, it should be loaded from within your `Game` constructor:

```
public Game1()
{
    graphics = new GraphicsDeviceManager(this);
    Content.RootDirectory = "Content";

    Components.Add(new GamerServicesComponent(this));
}
```

### Displaying the Sign In Interface

This sample program will switch between two states you will define: `SignIn` and `SignedIn`. As long as the program is in the `SignIn` state, the Sign In interface will be shown to the user until an account is selected or created. Once a valid account has been selected, the program will move on to the `SignedIn` state.

Start by declaring these two states:

```
public enum GameState {SignIn, SignedIn}
```

Then declare a variable that holds the current state:

```
GameState currentGameState = GameState.SignIn;
```

This will cause your program to start in the `SignIn` state. During the update cycle of your program, you will check which state your program is in. If this is the `SignIn` state, you want to let the user select an account. However, since the player can select an account to automatically sign in, it is possible that an account is signed in already the moment you start the `GamerServicesComponent`. Therefore, you'll first want to check whether there is an account currently signed in:

```
if (Gamer.SignedInGamers.Count < 1)
{
    Guide.ShowSignIn(1, false);
    log.Add("Opened User SignIn Interface");
}
else
{
    currentGameState = GameState.SignedIn;
    log.Add(Gamer.SignedInGamers[0].Gamertag + " logged in - proceed to SignedIn");
}
```

If no account has been logged in, you activate the Sign In interface, allowing the user to select or create an account. Once an account has been selected, Gamer.SignedInGamers.Count will no longer be 0. During the next update phase, the current state will be set to SignedIn, and a message containing the name of the player is added to a log.

**Note** The contents of this log will be printed to the screen in the Draw method. See recipe 3-5 for more information about writing text to the screen.

The Guide.ShowSignIn method takes two parameters. The first one indicates how many players should be asked to sign in. On an Xbox 360 console, up to four players can sign in at the same time, while this is limited to only one on a Windows-based machine. The second argument specifies whether only online Live accounts are allowed to sign in, which is useful if you want to use the Live servers for matchmaking.

**Note** Keep in mind that the user can cancel the Guide interface, which results in no account being selected.

Because you cannot open the Guide interface twice at the same moment, you should check whether the Guide is currently closed before you call the Guide.ShowSignIn method. You can do this by checking the IsActive property of your Game, which will be true only if the window of your game is active, if it is not minimized, and if the Guide is not shown.

## The Code

*All the code is available for download from www.apress.com.*

The entire Update method is shown next. The IsActive property is checked, after which the Guide.SignIn method is called if no account has been signed in yet. Once a valid account has been signed in, the state changes to SignedIn.

```
protected override void Update(GameTime gameTime)
{
    if (GamePad.GetState(PlayerIndex.One).Buttons.Back == ButtonState.Pressed)
        this.Exit();

    if (this.IsActive)
    {
        switch (currentGameState)
        {
            case GameState.SignIn:
            {
                if (Gamer.SignedInGamers.Count < 1)
                {
                    Guide.ShowSignIn(1, false);
                    log.Add("Opened User SignIn Interface");
                }
                else
                {
                    currentGameState = GameState.SignedIn;
log.Add(Gamer.SignedInGamers[0].Gamertag + " logged in - proceed to SignedIn");
                }
            }
            break;
            case GameState.SignedIn:
            {
            }
            break;
        }
    }

    base.Update(gameTime);
}
```

# 8-2. Create a Network Session

## The Problem

You want to create a networking session so other Xbox 360 consoles, Zunes, or PCs can find and join your session.

## The Solution

One machine first needs to start a networking session, which you can do easily using the NetworkSession.Create method. The machine that created the session will be the host of the session.

After the session has been created, all machines connected to the session, including the host, should listen for any events raised by the session, such as players joining or leaving the session.

## How It Works

You will need to include the `Microsoft.XNA.Framework.Net` namespace from this recipe on to the end of this chapter. This is done by adding the following line to the `using` block at the very top of your code file:

```
using Microsoft.Xna.Framework.Net;
```

In this recipe, your program will cycle through three self-defined states. As in the previous recipe, you'll start in the `SignIn` state where the user is asked to select an account. The `SignedIn` state of the previous recipe is replaced by the `CreateSession` state, where you'll create a new network session and listen for its events. Eventually, you end up in the `InSession` state.

Start by defining these states:

```
public enum GameState { SignIn, CreateSession, InSession}
```

The `SignIn` state has already been discussed in the previous recipe. Let's start coding the `CreateSession` state.

### Creating a Network Session

During this state, you will create a new network session. Start by adding this variable to your code:

```
NetworkSession networkSession;
```

You can create a new network session and store it in the variable you just defined using the `NetworkSession.Create` method, as shown here:

```
networkSession = NetworkSession.Create(NetworkSessionType.SystemLink, 4, 8);
```

This line will cause the machine to host a new session to which other players can connect. As you can see, this method expects three arguments.

The first argument specifies the type of session that should be created. A session of the `NetworkSessionType.Local` type should be created if all players are connected to the same machine. For example, four players can have their own controllers attached to the same Xbox 360 console.

If one or more players are on different machines, which are connected to the same network, you should create a session of the `NetworkSessionType.SystemLink` type. The `NetworkSessionType.PlayerMatch` type works the same way as the `SystemLink` type, but it will allow users to connect to sessions over the Internet, making use of the Live servers. At this moment, however, in order to use these servers, you need to buy a Live Gold membership for all participating Xbox 360 consoles.

---

■**Note**  Since the Zune can create network connections only to other Zunes, you can use only the
`NetworkSessionType.Local` and `NetworkSessionType.SystemLink` session types for the Zune.

---

The second argument specifies whether multiple players connected to the same machine
can join the network. If not, you should specify that there can be only one player for each
machine. If you want, for example, to start a local session, you should allow more than one
player to connect through the same machine.

---

■**Note**  A local player is a user playing on the machine on which the code is running. For now, XNA 3.0
supports only one local player on each Windows-based machine and Zune, while up to four players can be
connected to one Xbox 360 console. Each of these four players is considered local only by the other three
players connected to the same machine.

---

The last argument specifies the maximum number of players that can connect to the session. Since you're dealing with multiplayer games, this number should be at least 2, while it
should be equal to or less than the upper limit, which is 31 for the PC and Xbox 360 and 8 for
Zune devices.

The `NetworkSession.Create` method has an overload that accepts two more arguments.
The first specifies the number of player slots that should be kept available for friends. This
way, only players you've marked as friends will be able to join the session. The last argument
allows you to tag your session with a `NetworkSessionProperties` object so others can find it
more easily. See recipe 8-3 for an example of this.

---

■**Note**  If the machine is not connected to any network at all, the `NetworkSession.Create` method will
throw an error, so you will want to encapsulate it inside a `try-catch` structure.

---

Now that you're hosting a new session, you can set some of its properties. An important
property defines what should happen if the host quits the session. You can specify that XNA
should automatically elect one of the clients/peers to become the new host by setting the
`AllowHostMigration` property to `true`:

```
networkSession.AllowHostMigration = true;
networkSession.AllowJoinInProgress = false;
```

As you can see, you can also specify whether clients are allowed to join the session once
the game has started.

---

**■Note** Special care should be taken with host migration. If any game data was stored exclusively on the old host when it quits the session, it is impossible to have this data transferred automatically to the new host. You'll want to have the crucial game data copied to at least two machines so that if the host quits, you can copy this data to the new host.

---

Since XNA 3.0, local network sessions will no longer end the moment a local player leaves the game. Instead, the session will continue as long as there is at least one player connected to the session.

## Hooking to the Session Events

Now that your machine is hosting a network session, it would be nice to know when other people have joined the session. You can do this by hooking a self-defined method to the GamerJoined event of the network session. Whenever a player joins the session, the session will automatically raise this GamerJoined event. As a result, all methods hooked to the event will be called.

This line will cause the self-defined GamerJoinedEventHandler method to be hooked to the GamerJoined event:

```
networkSession.GamerJoined += GamerJoinedEventHandler;
```

In the GamerJoinedEventHandler method, you can put all code that should be executed whenever a new player joins the session. This following simple example will cause a line of text containing the name of the player to be printed to the screen:

```
void GamerJoinedEventHandler(object sender, GamerJoinedEventArgs e)
{
    log.Add(e.Gamer.Gamertag + " joined the current session");
}
```

As with all event-handling methods, this method will receive the object that raised the event (in this case, the network session), as well as a second argument containing specific information that comes with this type of event. In this case, the GamerJoinedEventArgs contains the Gamer object corresponding to the player who just joined the session.

The network session can raise other events that you might want to listen for. These include the GamerLeft event and the GameStarted and GameEnded events that indicate when the session switches from lobby to game mode (see recipe 8-7), as well as the SessionEnded and HostChanged events.

The SessionEnded event is fired when the host quits the session while AllowHostMigration was set to false or when the host calls the Dispose method on the network session. The HostChanged event is fired when the host quits the session while AllowHostMigration was set to true.

The following code will listen for the GamerJoined, GamerLeft, and HostChanged events fired by the network session and will print a corresponding line to the screen:

```
void HookSessionEvents()
{
    log.Add("Listening for session events");
    networkSession.GamerJoined += GamerJoinedEventHandler;
    networkSession.GamerLeft += GamerLeftEventHandler;
    networkSession.HostChanged += HostChangedEventHandler;
}

void GamerJoinedEventHandler(object sender, GamerJoinedEventArgs e)
{
    log.Add(e.Gamer.Gamertag + " joined the current session");
}

void GamerLeftEventHandler(object sender, GamerLeftEventArgs e)
{
    log.Add(e.Gamer.Gamertag + " left the current session");
}

void HostChangedEventHandler(object sender, HostChangedEventArgs e)
{
    log.Add("Host migration detected");

    NetworkSession eventRaisingSession = (NetworkSession)sender;
    if (eventRaisingSession.IsHost)
        log.Add("This machine has become the new Host!");
}
```

In the case of a host migration, the sender object (which you know is a network session) is first cast to a NetworkSession object so you can query its properties. Among them is the IsHost property, which you can use to detect whether this machine has become the new host of the session.

Make sure you call the HookSessionEvents method immediately after you've created your session. This is what the CreateSession state in the Update method should look like:

```
case GameState.CreateSession:
{
    networkSession = NetworkSession.Create(NetworkSessionType.SystemLink, 4, 8);
    networkSession.AllowHostMigration = true;
    networkSession.AllowJoinInProgress = false;
    log.Add("New session created");

    HookSessionEvents();
    currentGameState = GameState.InSession;
}
```

The session is created, the AllowHostMigration and AllowJoinInProgress values are set, and the program is listening for any events raised by the session.

## Updating the Network Session

Once you are connected to a session, you should update it at regular intervals. An obvious spot to do this is during the update cycle of your game. For now, this is the only thing that's being done during the InSession state:

```
case GameState.InSession:
{
    networkSession.Update();
}
break;
```

# The Code

*All the code is available for download from www.apress.com.*

Here, you can find the resulting Update method. The program will start in the SignIn state, after which a session will be created in the CreateSession state. The program ends in the InSession state.

```
protected override void Update(GameTime gameTime)
{
    if (GamePad.GetState(PlayerIndex.One).Buttons.Back == ButtonState.Pressed)
        this.Exit();

    if (this.IsActive)
    {
        switch (currentGameState)
        {
            case GameState.SignIn:
            {
                if (Gamer.SignedInGamers.Count < 1)
                {
                    Guide.ShowSignIn(1, false);
                    log.Add("Opened User SignIn Interface");
                }

                else
                {
                    currentGameState = GameState.CreateSession;
log.Add(Gamer.SignedInGamers[0].Gamertag + " logged in - proceed to CreateSession");
                }
            }
            break;
            case GameState.CreateSession:
```

```
            {
                networkSession = ➥
NetworkSession.Create(NetworkSessionType.SystemLink, ➥
                4, 8);
                networkSession.AllowHostMigration = true;
                networkSession.AllowJoinInProgress = false;
                log.Add("New session created");

                HookSessionEvents();
                currentGameState = GameState.InSession;
            }
            break;
            case GameState.InSession:
            {
                networkSession.Update();
            }
            break;
        }
    }

    base.Update(gameTime);
}
```

# 8-3. Join a Network Session

## The Problem

You want to search your machine, the network, or the Live servers for active sessions of your game. You want to select one session from the list of detected sessions and join it.

## The Solution

You can search for active sessions using the NetworkSessions.Find method. This will return an AvailableNetworkSessionCollection object containing all the active sessions. You can join one of them using the NetworkSession.Join method, specifying the session to join as the argument.

As always when connecting to a session and as described in the previous recipe, make sure you listen for any events raised by the session.

## How It Works

In this recipe, you'll add and define the SearchSession state to the states defined in the previous recipes:

```
public enum GameState { SignIn, SearchSession, CreateSession, InSession}
```

Once again, the program starts in the SignIn state, allowing the user to select an account. Next, instead of immediately creating a new network session, you will first try to find and join an existing session and move to the InSession state. If no active sessions are found, you will move to the CreateSession state, which is explained in the previous recipe.

## Searching for Active Sessions

You can search for all active sessions using the NetworkSession.Find method. This method expects three arguments, which allow you to filter the results. The method will return only the active sessions of the same type as the first argument and only with the same number of allowed players on one machine as the second argument. You can find an example of the last argument at the end of this recipe.

```
AvailableNetworkSessionCollection activeSessions = ➥
NetworkSession.Find(NetworkSessionType.SystemLink, 4, null);
```

---

■**Note** As with the NetworkSession.Create method, the NetworkSession.Find method will throw an error if the machine is not connected to any network. Therefore, you'll want to encapsulate it inside a try-catch structure.

---

All sessions that have been detected and fulfill the three filter arguments are stored inside an AvailableNetworkSessionsCollection. If no sessions can be found, this collection will be empty.

## Joining an Active Session

If at least one session has been detected, you can join it using the NetworkSession.Join method:

```
AvailableNetworkSession networkToJoin = activeSessions[0];
networkSession = NetworkSession.Join(networkToJoin);
```

This will connect your program to the session specified as the argument. In this example, you'll join the first session of the activeSessions. Before doing this, you might want to check whether there is at least one open player slot, which is indicated by the networkToJoin.OpenPublicPlayerSlots.

---

■**Note** An AvailableNetworkSession contains a lot of useful information, such as the QualityOfService property that is useful for determining how fast the connection is between your machine and the session host.

---

The final SearchSession state might look like this:

```
case GameState.SearchSession:
{
    AvailableNetworkSessionCollection activeSessions = ➥
    NetworkSession.Find(NetworkSessionType.SystemLink, 4, null);
    if (activeSessions.Count == 0)
    {
        currentGameState = GameState.CreateSession;
        log.Add("No active sessions found - proceed to CreateSession");
    }
    else
    {
        AvailableNetworkSession networkToJoin = activeSessions[0];
        networkSession = NetworkSession.Join(networkToJoin);

        string myString = "Joined session hosted by " + networkToJoin.HostGamertag;
        myString += " with " + networkToJoin.CurrentGamerCount.ToString() + ➥
        " players";
        myString += " and " + ➥
        networkToJoin.OpenPublicGamerSlots.ToString() + ➥
        " open player slots.";
        log.Add(myString);

        HookSessionEvents();
        currentGameState = GameState.InSession;
    }
}
break;
```

You start by finding all active network sessions that fulfill the three filter arguments: a connection of the type SystemLink, a max localGamers parameter of 4, and a NetworkSessionProperties parameter of null. If no sessions can be detected, you move to the CreateSession state to create your own session, as explained in the previous recipe. If at least one active session can be found, you join the first session that was found. A more advanced example would print all available sessions to the screen and allow the user to select one.

Finally, you print some properties of the session you joined to the screen, such as the name of the hosting player, the number of players who have already joined the session, and the number of open player slots.

Last but not least, you start listening for any events raised by the session (see recipe 8-2) before moving to the InSession state.

### Using the NetworkSessionProperties to Filter the Detected Sessions

When you search for active sessions using the NetworkSession.Find method, you can specify three arguments so the method will return only those sessions that have been created using the same three arguments.

As mentioned earlier, the first two arguments allow you to specify the type of sessions to search for, as well as the maximum number of local players allowed in the sessions.

However, if your game has become quite popular, the Find method will still return a huge number of active sessions. Therefore, when you create a session, it might be useful to specify a NetworkSessionProperties object, which can contain up to eight integer values. It's entirely up to you to choose what these eight integers stand for. For example, you might let the first integer indicate the difficulty settings of the game, the second the number of bots, and the third the map that will be played on. Here, we've used null, because we haven't set this object yet.

When other players search for active sessions, they will be able to search for games that are, for example, played on a specific map.

### Creating a Session with NetworkSessionProperties

To specify the NetworkSessionProperties, you should use the second overload of the NetworkSession.Create method, which accepts two more arguments. This allows you to pass in your properties as the last argument.

After you've created a new NetworkSessionProperties object, it's entirely up to you to specify up to eight integer values. In the following example, only two values are being set. After this, pass the properties as the last argument to the NetworkSession.Create method, and you're ready to go:

```
NetworkSessionProperties createProperties = new NetworkSessionProperties();
createProperties[0] = 3;
createProperties[1] = 4096;

networkSession = NetworkSession.Create(NetworkSessionType.SystemLink, ➥
4, 8, 0, createProperties);
```

### Searching for Sessions with Specific NetworkSessionProperties

You can do the same thing to search for sessions with specific properties. Simply create the NetworkSessionProperties object, specify the properties that you're looking for, and pass it to the NetworkSession.Find method:

```
NetworkSessionProperties findProperties = new NetworkSessionProperties();
findProperties[1] = 4096;

AvailableNetworkSessionCollection activeSessions = ➥
NetworkSession.Find(NetworkSessionType.SystemLink, 4, findProperties);
```

In this example, only one property, instead of two, was specified. The Find method will return all available methods that have 4096 as the second property, no matter what the other seven are.

## The Code

*All the code is available for download from www.apress.com.*

The Update method shown next handles the basics of session management.

When the program starts, the user is requested to sign in with an account. Next, the program will search for active sessions, and if at least one is found, the session is joined.

If no active sessions can be found, the program will create its own session. Either way, you will be connected to a session, so the program should listen for any events raised by the session. You'll end in the InSession state, which will update the sessions at regular intervals.

This allows the same code to be run on multiple machines. If they are connected to the same network, the first machine should create the session, while the others should detect and join it automatically.

```
protected override void Update(GameTime gameTime)
{
    if (GamePad.GetState(PlayerIndex.One).Buttons.Back == ButtonState.Pressed)
        this.Exit();

    if (this.IsActive)
    {
        switch (currentGameState)
        {
            case GameState.SignIn:
            {
                if (Gamer.SignedInGamers.Count < 1)
                {
                    Guide.ShowSignIn(1, false);
                    log.Add("Opened User SignIn Interface");
                }
                else
                {
                    currentGameState = GameState.SearchSession;
log.Add(Gamer.SignedInGamers[0].Gamertag + " logged in - proceed to SearchSession");
                }
            }
            break;
            case GameState.SearchSession:
            {
                NetworkSessionProperties findProperties = new ➥
                NetworkSessionProperties();
                findProperties[0] = 3;
                findProperties[1] = 4096;

                AvailableNetworkSessionCollection activeSessions = ➥
NetworkSession.Find(NetworkSessionType.SystemLink, ➥
                4, findProperties);
                if (activeSessions.Count == 0)
                {
                    currentGameState = GameState.CreateSession;
log.Add("No active sessions found - proceed to CreateSession");
                }
```

```
                else
                {
AvailableNetworkSession networkToJoin = activeSessions[0];
networkSession = NetworkSession.Join(networkToJoin);

string myString = "Joined session hosted by " + networkToJoin.HostGamertag;
myString += " with " + networkToJoin.CurrentGamerCount.ToString() + " players";
myString += " and " + ➥
networkToJoin.OpenPublicGamerSlots.ToString() + ➥
" open player slots.";
                    log.Add(myString);

                    HookSessionEvents();
                    currentGameState = GameState.InSession;
                }
            }
            break;
            case GameState.CreateSession:
            {
                NetworkSessionProperties createProperties = new ➥
                NetworkSessionProperties();
                createProperties[0] = 3;
                createProperties[1] = 4096;

                networkSession = ➥
                NetworkSession.Create(NetworkSessionType.SystemLink, ➥
                4, 8, 0, createProperties);
                networkSession.AllowHostMigration = true;
                networkSession.AllowJoinInProgress = false;
                log.Add("New session created");

                HookSessionEvents();
                currentGameState = GameState.InSession;
            }
            break;
            case GameState.InSession:
            {
                networkSession.Update();
            }
            break;
        }
    }

    base.Update(gameTime);
}
```

# 8-4. Send/Receive Data Over the Network

## The Problem

Creating and joining a network session is one thing, but what good is a network session if you're not sending and receiving any data?

## The Solution

When the player is connected to the session, you can store all the data you want to send in a `PacketWriter` stream. Once this has been done, you can send this `PacketWriter` to all players in the session using the `LocalNetworkPlayer.SendData` method.

Before receiving any data for a player on the local machine, you should check whether the `LocalNetworkGamer.IsDataAvailable` flag is set to `true`, which indicates data has been received and is ready to be processed.

As long as this flag is `true`, you should call the `LocalNetworkGamer.ReceiveData` method, returning a `PacketReader` containing all the data another player has sent to the local player.

## How It Works

This recipe builds on the results of the previous recipe, which allowed multiple machines on the same network to connect to each other through a session. The program ends in the `InSession` state, which simply calls the `Update` method of the session.

Here, you will make the `InSession` state actually do something, so your player will send some data to all other players in the session. As an example, you'll send the number of minutes and seconds that the program has been running.

Next, you'll listen for any data available to your player. If there is data available, you will receive the two numbers and put them into a string, which you'll print to the screen.

To send and receive data, you'll need one `PacketWriter` object and one `PacketReader` object, so add these two variables to your code:

```
PacketWriter writer = new PacketWriter();
PacketReader reader = new PacketReader();
```

There's no reason to have more than one `PacketWriter` object and one `PacketReader` object in your project.

### Sending Data to Other Players in the Session

You should first store all the data you want to send to other players in the `PacketWriter`. You can do this by passing your data as the argument to its `Write` method:

```
writer.Write(gameTime.TotalGameTime.Minutes);
writer.Write(gameTime.TotalGameTime.Seconds);
```

After you've stored all your data in the `PacketWriter`, you can send it over to all the other players using the `SendData` method of your local player:

```
LocalNetworkGamer localGamer = networkSession.LocalGamers[0];
localGamer.SendData(writer, SendDataOptions.None);
```

The SendDataOptions argument will be explained at the end of this recipe. Quite important, the SendData method has an overload that allows you to send data to a specific player only, instead of to all players connected to the session.

That's all you need to do to have your data sent to the other players connected to the session!

## Receiving Data from Other Players in the Session

Basically, to receive data from another player, you do the inverse: you call the ReceiveData method of your local player, which will return you a PacketReader containing all data sent by another player. Call one of the PacketReader.Read methods to obtain your data from the PacketReader:

```
NetworkGamer sender;
localGamer.ReceiveData(reader, out sender);

string playerName = sender.Gamertag;
int minutes = reader.ReadInt32();
int seconds = reader.ReadInt32();
```

The ReceiveData method will store the data inside the PacketReader stream. As a bonus, the player who sent you the data will be stored in the second argument. This way you know who the data is coming from.

When you read the data from your PacketReader, you need to make sure you do it in the same order as you stored it. Also, because the PacketReader simply contains a stream of bytes, you need to say which objects you want to be constructed from the bytes. For example, an integer requires fewer bytes than a matrix, so at some point, you'll need to tell the PacketReader which kind of objects you want to be restored.

The minutes and seconds you sent over in this example are integers, so you want to reconstruct two integers from the stream of bytes. Have a look at the different Read methods of the PacketReader, and note which objects are supported. If you send over a Matrix, you'll want to use the ReadMatrix method to reconstruct it from the byte stream. Use the ReadSingle method to reconstruct the float, the ReadDouble method to read a double, and the ReadInt16 method to read a short. Since a regular int uses 32 bits (4 bytes), you use the ReadInt32() method in the preceding code.

## LocalGamer.IsDataAvailable

If multiple players are sending you data, chances are you'll have multiple byte streams waiting to be read by your code. This can also happen if another player is calling SendData more frequently than you're calling ReceiveData.

In these cases, you can query the localGamer.IsDataAvailable property, because this will stay true as long as there is a byte stream waiting for your local gamer.

As long as data is available to your player, the following code will receive a new PacketReader and read the GamerTag property of the player who sent the data. Next, the number of minutes and seconds that player's program has been running is read from the PacketReader.

```
while (localGamer.IsDataAvailable)
{
    NetworkGamer sender;
    localGamer.ReceiveData(reader, out sender);

    string gamerTime = "";
    gamerTime += sender.Gamertag + ": ";
    gamerTime += reader.ReadInt32() + "m ";
    gamerTime += reader.ReadInt32() + "s";
    gamerTimes[sender.Gamertag] = gamerTime;
}
```

To let this example actually do something, the data is parsed into one string, called gamerTime, which is stored inside a Dictionary. A Dictionary is the default generic .NET lookup table, which you can create by adding this variable to your code:

```
Dictionary<string, string> gamerTimes = new Dictionary<string, string>();
```

The previous code will create one entry in the Dictionary for each player who has sent data to you. Each time new data is received from a player, that player's entry in the Dictionary is updated. You can print the strings inside the Dictionary to the screen in the Draw method.

Whenever a player leaves the session, you'll want to remove the corresponding entry from the Dictionary. An excellent way to do this is by capturing and responding to the GamerLeft event:

```
void GamerLeftEventHandler(object sender, GamerLeftEventArgs e)
{
    log.Add(e.Gamer.Gamertag + " left the current session");
    gamerTimes.Remove(e.Gamer.Gamertag);
}
```

## SendDataOptions

When you send data to other players in the session, you expect all your messages to arrive at the receiver in the same order as you sent them. Because of the structure of the Internet, your messages might arrive in a different order than how you sent them. Even worse, some of your messages may not arrive at all!

Luckily, you can specify two important factors for each packet you send. Before you can decide on them, you should know what they are, what their benefits are, and, quite important, what their drawbacks are:

- *Order of arrival*: Should the data packets be received in the same order as they were sent?

- *Reliability*: Is the data you're sending absolutely crucial, or can game play survive in case some packets are lost?

These two questions have yes/no answers, giving you four possible combinations. The `LocalNetworkGamer.SendData` accepts a `SendDataOptions` flag as a second argument, which allows you to specify one of these four combinations (it also accepts a fifth flag, `SendDataOptions.Chat`, which is discussed later in this recipe):

- `SendDataOptions.None`: Specifies the data packets you're sending are not crucial and the order in which they are received doesn't really matter.

- `SendDataOptions.InOrder`: Specifies the data packets you're sending have to be received in the same order that you sent them but still it's no big deal if one or more data packets are lost.

- `SendDataOptions.Reliable`: Specifies the opposite of `SendDatOptions.InOrder`. Use this if your data is crucial, meaning all the data you send has to reach the receiver. However, it doesn't really matter whether the data packets are received in a different order from how you sent them.

- `SendDataOptions.ReliableInOrder`: Indicates all the data has to reach the receiver and arrive in the same order that you sent it.

Well, that's easy; I'll pick the last one! Unfortunately, some of these options come with a drawback, explained here:

- `SendDataOptions.None`: There's no speed penalty; data is simply wished good luck and sent over.

- `SendDataOptions.InOrder`: Before they are sent, all packets are assigned a sequence number. The receiver checks these numbers, and if a packet A is received after a newer packet B is received, packet A is simply discarded. This is an easy check and takes almost no time, but some of your data might be thrown away although it actually succeeded in reaching the destination.

- `SendDataOptions.Reliable`: In this case, the receiver checks to see which packets are missing. When packet C seems to be missing from the packet stream ABDE, the receiver kindly requests the sender to resend packet C. In the meantime, packets D and E are accessible to your XNA code.

- `SendDataOptions.ReliableInOrder`: Use this only when your data requires it. When the receiver detects packet C is missing from the stream ABDE, it asks the sender to resend package C. This time, subsequent packets D and E are not passed on to XNA by the receiver until packet C has been successfully received. This can cause severe lag, because all subsequent packets are stalled and stored in memory until packet C has been resent and received.

As a general rule of thumb, it is safe to use `SendDataOptions.InOrder` for most game data, while `SendDataOption.ReliableInOrder` should be used as little as possible.

## SendDataOptions.Chat

Before you start sending data over the Net, you need to keep one thing in mind: person-to-person chat messages sent over the Internet must not be encrypted, as it is prohibited by law.

Since this encryption is, by default, done for all data you send using the localGamer.SendData method, you should use SendDataOptions.Chat to indicate XNA must not encrypt such chat messages. If you want, this can be used in conjunction with the other SendDataOptions, like this:

```
localGamer.SendData(writer, SendDataOptions.Chat | SendDataOptions.Reliable);
```

Note that you can send encrypted and unencrypted messages mixed together. One thing to keep in mind is that if you do so, ordered chat data will only be ordered relative to the chat data and not to the encrypted data. As an example, let's have a look at the case where you first send a chat message, followed by a data message, chat message, and data message, as shown on the left side of Figure 8-1.

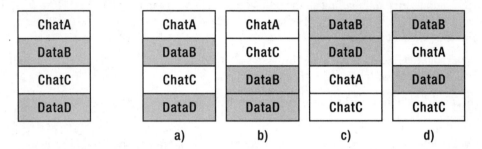

a)   b)   c)   d)

**Figure 8-1.** *Sending four packets in order (left) and the three possible ways of receiving them*

The right part of Figure 8-1 shows the four possible ways of how the data might arrive at the receiver. In case a, the packets have arrived in exactly the same order they were sent in. In cases b and c, the order of the packets has changed. The important thing to note, however, is that in both cases the first chat packet A is received before the second chat packet C, and that the first data packet B is received before the second data packet D.

Since both data and chat packets can be sent during the same frame, you need to make sure you don't mix them up at the receiving side. One possible way to do this is to add a small preamble to your packets before sending them, indicating whether they are data or chat packets. This is shown in the following code, where the D denotes a data packet and the C a chat packet:

```
writer.Write("D");
writer.Write(gameTime.TotalGameTime.Minutes);
writer.Write(gameTime.TotalGameTime.Seconds);

LocalNetworkGamer localGamer = networkSession.LocalGamers[0];
localGamer.SendData(writer, SendDataOptions.ReliableInOrder);

writer.Write("C");
writer.Write("This is a chat message from " + localGamer.Gamertag);
localGamer.SendData(writer, SendDataOptions.Chat|SendDataOptions.ReliableInOrder);
```

On the receiving side, simply check whether the packet is a D or C packet, and handle the packet accordingly:

```
while (localGamer.IsDataAvailable)
{
    NetworkGamer sender;
    localGamer.ReceiveData(reader, out sender);

    string messageType = reader.ReadString();
    if (messageType == "D")
    {
        string gamerTime = "";
        gamerTime += sender.Gamertag + ": ";
        gamerTime += reader.ReadInt32() + "m ";
        gamerTime += reader.ReadInt32() + "s";

        gamerTimes[sender.Gamertag] = gamerTime;
    }
    else if (messageType == "C")
    {
        lastChatMessage[sender.Gamertag] = reader.ReadString();
    }
}
```

## Multiple Local Players

If multiple players are connected on the same machine, you'll want to iterate through them to send and receive their data.

Sending their data to all players is quite straightforward:

```
//send data from all local players to all other players in session
foreach (LocalNetworkGamer localGamer in networkSession.LocalGamers)
{
    writer.Write(gameTime.TotalGameTime.Minutes);
    writer.Write(gameTime.TotalGameTime.Seconds);
    localGamer.SendData(writer, SendDataOptions.ReliableInOrder);
}
```

Keep in mind that you can use an overload of the SendData method to send data to only one specific player.

Receiving data for all your local players playing on the same machine isn't that difficult either. Just make sure you loop your code until the IsDataAvailable flag of all your local players is set to false:

```
foreach (LocalNetworkGamer localGamer in networkSession.LocalGamers)
{
    while (localGamer.IsDataAvailable)
    {
        NetworkGamer sender;
        localGamer.ReceiveData(reader, out sender);
```

```
            string gamerTime = localGamer.Gamertag + " received from ";
            gamerTime += sender.Gamertag + ": ";
            gamerTime += reader.ReadInt32() + "m ";
            gamerTime += reader.ReadInt32() + "s";
            gamerTimes[sender.Gamertag] = gamerTime;
        }
    }
```

## The Code

*All the code is available for download from www.apress.com.*

The following is the Update method, including the extended InSession state. In this state, all players on your machine will send data to all other players in the session. Next, they will receive all data that was sent to them.

If you run this program on multiple consoles, the consoles will automatically connect to the session created by the first machine. Next, they will start sending timing data to each other and print any data they received to their screen in the Draw method.

```
protected override void Update(GameTime gameTime)
{
    if (GamePad.GetState(PlayerIndex.One).Buttons.Back == ButtonState.Pressed)
        this.Exit();

    if (this.IsActive)
    {
        switch (currentGameState)
        {

            case GameState.SignIn:
            {
                if (Gamer.SignedInGamers.Count < 1)
                {
                    Guide.ShowSignIn(1, false);
                    log.Add("Opened User SignIn Interface");
                }
                else
                {
                    currentGameState = GameState.SearchSession;
                    log.Add(Gamer.SignedInGamers[0].Gamertag + " logged in - proceed to SearchSession");
                }
            }
            break;
            case GameState.SearchSession:
```

```
            {
                AvailableNetworkSessionCollection activeSessions = ➥
                NetworkSession.Find(NetworkSessionType.SystemLink, ➥
                4, null);
                if (activeSessions.Count == 0)
                {
                    currentGameState = GameState.CreateSession;
log.Add("No active sessions found - proceed to CreateSession");
                }
                else
                {
AvailableNetworkSession networkToJoin = activeSessions[0];
networkSession = NetworkSession.Join(networkToJoin);

string myString = "Joined session hosted by " + networkToJoin.HostGamertag;
myString += " with " + networkToJoin.CurrentGamerCount.ToString() + " players";
myString += " and " + ➥
networkToJoin.OpenPublicGamerSlots.ToString() + ➥
" open player slots.";
                    log.Add(myString);

                    HookSessionEvents();
                    currentGameState = GameState.InSession;
                }
            }
            break;
            case GameState.CreateSession:
            {
                networkSession = ➥
NetworkSession.Create(NetworkSessionType.SystemLink, ➥
                4, 8);
                networkSession.AllowHostMigration = true;
                networkSession.AllowJoinInProgress = false;
                log.Add("New session created");

                HookSessionEvents();
                currentGameState = GameState.InSession;
            }
            break;
            case GameState.InSession:
            {
                //send data from all local players to all other players in session
                foreach (LocalNetworkGamer localGamer in networkSession.LocalGamers)
```

```
        {
            writer.Write(gameTime.TotalGameTime.Minutes);
            writer.Write(gameTime.TotalGameTime.Seconds);
            localGamer.SendData(writer, SendDataOptions.ReliableInOrder);
        }

        //receive data from all other players in session
        foreach (LocalNetworkGamer localGamer in networkSession.LocalGamers)
        {
            while (localGamer.IsDataAvailable)
            {
                NetworkGamer sender;
                localGamer.ReceiveData(reader, out sender);

                string gamerTime = localGamer.Gamertag + " received from ";
                gamerTime += sender.Gamertag + ": ";
                gamerTime += reader.ReadInt32() + "m ";
                gamerTime += reader.ReadInt32() + "s";
                gamerTimes[sender.Gamertag] = gamerTime;
            }
        }

        networkSession.Update();
    }
    break;
    }
}
```

# 8-5. Search for Networking Sessions Asynchronously

## The Problem

Some networking operations, such as downloading a player profile or searching for available sessions, can take a lot of time. Using the easiest set of methods as shown in the previous recipes, these operations will cause your program to stall until the operation has been completed, while you will want to keep the user informed about the progress!

## The Solution

XNA provides an asynchronous alternative for almost all networking methods that require some time to complete. The asynchronous counterpart of the NetworkSession.Find method, for example, is the NetworkSession.BeginFind method.

At the beginning of an asynchronous operation, XNA will launch a second thread on which the operation is performed, allowing it to run in parallel with your main program. As an advantage, your main program will only initiate the asynchronous operation and continue immediately. This allows you to provide the user with any information you like while the asynchronous operation is running in the second thread.

Once the asynchronous operation has completed, the result will be passed to a method that you have to specify. This allows you to process the results gathered by the asynchronous operation.

# How It Works

This recipe will explain how to use the NetworkSession.BeginFind method. All other asynchronous operations in XNA follow the same principles.

This recipe is the asynchronous version of recipe 8-3. In that recipe, your program started in the SignIn state and went through the SearchSession, CreateSession, and InSession states. In this recipe, you'll add the Searching state, which allows you to provide the user with information while the operation is running in the background:

```
public enum GameState { SignIn, SearchSession, Searching, CreateSession, InSession}
```

### Starting the Asynchronous Operation

The SearchSession state becomes very easy, because all it has to do is initiate the asynchronous operation:

```
case GameState.SearchSession:
{
    NetworkSession.BeginFind(NetworkSessionType.SystemLink, 2, null, ➡
    EndAsynchSearch, null);
    log.Add("ASynch search started - proceed to Searching");
    log.Add("Searching");
    currentGameState = GameState.Searching;
}
break;
```

The NetworkSession.BeginFind method will cause a second thread to be created in the background. This thread will perform the search in parallel with your main program. As a benefit, you program doesn't wait at the NetworkSession.BeginFind line as it did with the NetworkSession.Find method. Instead, it immediately continues to the Searching state.

The NetworkSession.BeginFind method requires five arguments. The first three are the same as for the NetworkSession.Find method, as described in recipe 8-3.

To understand the fourth argument, I'll now discuss what happens when the search in the background finishes. The second thread will call one of your methods and pass it the results. This means you have to specify which method should be called, which can be done using the fourth parameter. In this example, you instruct the second thread to call the EndAsynchSearch method when it finishes, which you can find next.

The last argument allows you to identify the asynchronous operation, which can be useful in case you have multiple asynchronous operations running at the same time. See recipe 1-9 for an example of this argument.

## In the Meantime . . .

While the search is running in the background, you're free to do whatever you want in the Searching state. In this simple example, each time the Update method is called, a dot will be added to the last line that's being printed to the screen:

```
case GameState.Searching:
{
    log[log.Count - 1] += ".";
}
break;
```

## NetworkSessions.EndFind

When the second thread that's running in the background has finished its asynchronous search, it will call the method you specified as the fourth argument in the NetworkSession.BeginFind method. In the previous code, I specified the EndAsynchSearch method, which you can find here. It looks complicated, but the main part is taken from the SearchSession state of the previous recipe. Most asynchronous callback methods expect an IAsyncResult object, which can contain useful values set by the initializing method (BeginFind). See recipe 1-9 for an example where this IAsyncResult object is being queried.

```
private void EndAsynchSearch(IAsyncResult result)
{
    AvailableNetworkSessionCollection activeSessions = ➥
    NetworkSession.EndFind(result);
    if (activeSessions.Count == 0)
    {
        currentGameState = GameState.CreateSession;
        log.Add("No active sessions found - proceed to CreateSession");
    }
    else
    {
        AvailableNetworkSession sessionToJoin = activeSessions[0];
        networkSession = NetworkSession.Join(sessionToJoin);

        string myString = "Joined session hosted by " + sessionToJoin.HostGamertag;
        myString += " with " + sessionToJoin.CurrentGamerCount.ToString() + ➥
        " players";
        myString += " and " + ➥
        sessionToJoin.OpenPublicGamerSlots.ToString() + ➥
        " open player slots.";
        log.Add(myString);

        HookSessionEvents();
        currentGameState = GameState.InSession;
    }
}
```

The method receives the results from the asynchronous operation as the argument.

For each method that begins an asynchronous operation, you can find a method that is capable of processing its results. In this case of the NetworkSession.BeginFind method, you can pass the results to the NetworkSession.EndFind method, which will process the results into an AvailableNetworkSessionCollection object. From here on, things remain identical to the previous recipe.

## The Code

*All the code is available for download from www.apress.com.*

Here, you can find the main switch block inside the Update method. This code will cause the program to move from the SignIn state to the SearchSession and Searching states. However, it will be the EndAsynchSearch method, which you can find earlier, that decides whether to move to the CreateSession or InSession state.

```
switch (currentGameState)
{
    case GameState.SignIn:
    {
        if (Gamer.SignedInGamers.Count < 1)
        {
            Guide.ShowSignIn(1, false);
            log.Add("Opened User SignIn Interface");
        }
        else
        {
            currentGameState = GameState.SearchSession;
            log.Add(Gamer.SignedInGamers[0].Gamertag + ➥
            " logged in - proceed to SearchSession");
        }
    }
    break;
    case GameState.SearchSession:
    {
        NetworkSession.BeginFind(NetworkSessionType.SystemLink, ➥
        2, null, EndAsynchSearch, null);
        log.Add("ASynch search started - proceed to Searching");
        log.Add("Searching");
        currentGameState = GameState.Searching;
    }
    break;
    case GameState.Searching:
    {
        log[log.Count - 1] += ".";
    }
    break;
    case GameState.CreateSession:
```

```
        {
            networkSession = NetworkSession.Create(NetworkSessionType.SystemLink, ➥
            4, 8);
            networkSession.AllowHostMigration = true;
            networkSession.AllowJoinInProgress = false;
            log.Add("New session created");

            HookSessionEvents();
            currentGameState = GameState.InSession;
        }
        break;
        case GameState.InSession:
        {
            networkSession.Update();
        }
        break;
    }
}
```

# 8-6. Add Rich Presence Information

## The Problem

You want to set the rich presence information for the player, which is shown to other Xbox
Live players when they view the player through the Xbox Guide or on www.xbox.com.

## The Solution

Most games add rich presence information to the player, so other people can see which game
they're playing and what they're currently doing in that game. You can set this information in
the Gamer.SignedInGamers[0].Presence property.

## How It Works

As with all networking functionality in XNA, before you can set the rich presence information
of a player, you first need to make sure your player has been signed in to Xbox Live.

There are 60 PresenceModes that you can choose from, which are very easy to set on a
player that has been signed in:

Gamer.SignedInGamers[0].Presence.PresenceMode = GamerPresenceMode.AtMenu;

All PresenceModes are listed in Table 8-1.

**Table 8-1.** *The 60 PresenceModes*

| PresenceModes | | | |
| --- | --- | --- | --- |
| ArcadeMode | ExplorationMode | OnlineCoOp | StoryMode |
| AtMenu | FoundSecret | OnlineVersus | StuckOnAHardBit |
| BattlingBoss | FreePlay | Outnumbered | SurvivalMode |
| CampaignMode | GameOver | Paused | TimeAttack |
| ChallengeMode | InCombat | PlayingMinigame | TryingForRecord |
| ConfiguringSettings | InGameStore | PlayingWithFriends | TutorialMode |
| CoOpLevel | Level | PracticeMode | VersusComputer |
| CoOpStage | LocalCoOp | PuzzleMode | VersusScore |
| CornflowerBlue | LocalVersus | ScenarioMode | WaitingForPlayers |
| CustomizingPlayer | LookingForGames | Score | WaitingInLobby |
| DifficultyEasy | Losing | ScoreIsTied | WastingTime |
| DifficultyExtreme | Multiplayer | SettingUpMatch | WatchingCredits |
| DifficultyHard | NearlyFinished | SinglePlayer | WatchingCutscene |
| DifficultyMedium | None | Stage | Winning |
| EditingLevel | OnARoll | StartingGame | WonTheGame |

For some modes (Stage, Level, Score, CoOpStage, CoOpLevel, VersusScore), you can also set a value that indicates a player's stage or level or current score. This can be done, as in the following example, where you indicate the player is currently on level 15:

```
Gamer.SignedInGamers[0].Presence.PresenceMode = GamerPresenceMode.Level;
Gamer.SignedInGamers[0].Presence.PresenceValue = 15;
```

# 8-7. Move from the Lobby to the Actual Game

## The Problem

After creating a session, you want to give all your players the time to gather, chat, and allow them to signal that they're ready for the game to begin.

## The Solution

XNA comes with basic built-in lobby functionality in the shape of the sessions' state and the IsReady property of a player.

A session will start in the Lobby state. Only the host can call the NetworkSession.StartGame method, which will move the session into the Playing state. The host can base this decision on the status of the IsReady flags of all players.

## How It Works

When the session has been created, the SessionState property of the session will have the Lobby value. While in this state, you should allow all players in the session to signal they're ready, which they can do by setting their IsReady flag to true. Here, we do this by allowing the player to press the R button on the controller to indicate readiness. This value can be read by all other players in the session:

```
case GameState.InSession:
{
    switch (networkSession.SessionState)
    {

        case NetworkSessionState.Lobby:
        {
            if (keybState != lastKeybState)
            {
                if (keybState.IsKeyDown(Keys.R))
                {
                    LocalNetworkGamer localGamer = networkSession.LocalGamers[0];
                    localGamer.IsReady = !localGamer.IsReady;
                }
            }
        }
        break;
        case NetworkSessionState.Playing:
        {
        }
        break;
    }

    networkSession.Update();
}
```

The host should detect whether all players have set their IsReady flags to true. The easiest way to do this is by checking the NetworkSession.IsEveryoneReady value, which indicates exactly this. If everyone is ready, the host can call the NetworkSession.StartGame method, which will move the state of the session from Lobby to Playing:

```
case NetworkSessionState.Lobby:
{
    if (keybState != lastKeybState)
    {
        if (keybState.IsKeyDown(Keys.R))
        {
            LocalNetworkGamer localGamer = networkSession.LocalGamers[0];
            localGamer.IsReady = !localGamer.IsReady;
        }
    }
}
```

```
        if (networkSession.IsHost)
        {
            if (networkSession.AllGamers.Count > 1)
            {
                if (networkSession.IsEveryoneReady)
                {
                    networkSession.StartGame();
                    log.Add("All players ready -- start the game!");
                }
            }
        }
    }
break;
```

When the state changes to Playing, the session raises its GameStarted event, which all players can listen for. This allows them to render the game screen and start sending and receiving game data.

The host should call the NetworkSession.EndGame method when the host decides the game has ended. This will reset the IsReady properties of all players to false and return to the Lobby state. In the following code, this is done when the player presses the E button:

```
case NetworkSessionState.Playing:
{
    if (networkSession.IsHost)
    {
        if (keybState != lastKeybState)
        {
            if (keybState.IsKeyDown(Keys.E))
            {
                networkSession.EndGame();
            }
        }
    }
}
break;
```

This will raise the GameEnded event of the session, which all players might want to listen for so they can, for example, render the lobby graphics.

## The Code

*All the code is available for download from www.apress.com.*

This InSession state contains the most basic code that allows multiple players to signal their IsReady flags and allows the host to move from the Lobby state to the Playing state and back:

```
case GameState.InSession:
{
    switch (networkSession.SessionState)
    {
        case NetworkSessionState.Lobby:
        {
            if (keybState != lastKeybState)
            {
                if (keybState.IsKeyDown(Keys.R))
                {
                    LocalNetworkGamer localGamer = networkSession.LocalGamers[0];
                    localGamer.IsReady = !localGamer.IsReady;
                }
            }

            if (networkSession.IsHost)
            {
                if (networkSession.AllGamers.Count > 1)
                {
                    if (networkSession.IsEveryoneReady)
                    {
                        networkSession.StartGame();
                        log.Add("All players ready -- start the game!");
                    }
                }
            }
        }
        break;
        case NetworkSessionState.Playing:
        {
            if (networkSession.IsHost)
            {
                if (keybState != lastKeybState)
                {
                    if (keybState.IsKeyDown(Keys.E))
                    {
                        networkSession.EndGame();
                    }
                }
            }
        }
        break;
    }

    networkSession.Update();
}
break;
```

# Index

# You Need the Companion eBook

**Your purchase of this book entitles you to buy the companion PDF-version eBook for only $10. Take the weightless companion with you anywhere.**

We believe this Apress title will prove so indispensable that you'll want to carry it with you everywhere, which is why we are offering the companion eBook (in PDF format) for $10 to customers who purchase this book now. Convenient and fully searchable, the PDF version of any content-rich, page-heavy Apress book makes a valuable addition to your programming library. You can easily find and copy code—or perform examples by quickly toggling between instructions and the application. Even simultaneously tackling a donut, diet soda, and complex code becomes simplified with hands-free eBooks!

Once you purchase your book, getting the $10 companion eBook is simple:

❶ Visit **www.apress.com/promo/tendollars/**.

❷ Complete a basic registration form to receive a randomly generated question about this title.

❸ Answer the question correctly in 60 seconds, and you will receive a promotional code to redeem for the $10.00 eBook.

THE EXPERT'S VOICE™

2855 TELEGRAPH AVENUE | SUITE 600 | BERKELEY, CA 94705

**Offer valid through 9/09.**